About the Authors

Professor Michael Rutter completed his basic medical education at the University of Birmingham, qualifying in 1955. After taking residencies in internal medicine, neurology and paediatrics, he proceeded to the Maudsley Hospital, London, for training in general psychiatry and then child psychiatry. He spent the 1961–2 year on a research Fellowship studying child development at the Department of Paediatrics, Albert Einstein College of Medicine, New York, returning then to work in the Medical Research Council Social Psychiatry Research Unit. In 1965 he took an academic position at the University of London's Institute of Psychiatry where he has remained ever since, becoming Professor and Head of the Department of Child and Adolescent Psychiatry in 1973. During the academic year 1979–80 he was a Fellow at the Center for Advanced Study in the Behavioral Sciences, Stanford, California. His research interests include stress resistance in children, psycho-social development in an ecological context, schools as social institutions, reading difficulties, interviewing skills, neuropsychiatry, infantile autism and psychiatric epidemiology. His publications include some fifteen books and over 130 scientific papers. Professor Rutter also continues a busy clinical practice seeing children and adolescents. Penguin have also published his books *Helping Troubled Children* and *Maternal Deprivation Reassessed*.

Henri Giller gained his Ph.D. from the University of Cambridge in 1982 and he also holds the degrees of LL.B. (1974) and LL.M. (1975) from the University of London. From 1974 to 1975 he was part-time lecturer in law at the Polytechnic of North London and for the following four years he was first research student, then research associate at the Institute of Criminology, Cambridge. During 1979–80 he was a research fellow at Wolfson College, Cambridge, and research associate at the Institute of Psychiatry in London. Since 1980 he has been lecturer in law at the University of Keele. Dr Giller has been involved in many research projects concerning the problems of youth and crime and is at present working on a comparative analysis of Anglo-American juvenile justice and an examination of the work of police juvenile liaison departments. He has published, with A. M. Morris, *Justice for Children* (1980), *Care and Discretion* (1981) and they also edited *Providing Justice for Children* (1982). He has also contributed to many collections of readings and numerous leading journals in this field.

Juvenile Delinquency
Trends and Perspectives

Michael Rutter and
Henri Giller

The Guilford Press
New York   London

Published in the USA in 1984 by
The Guilford Press
A Division of Guilford Publications, Inc.
200 Park Avenue South
New York, NY 10003

Copyright © Michael Rutter and Henri Giller, 1983

All rights reserved.

No part of this publication may be reproduced, stored in a retrieval system, or transmitted, in any form or by any means, electronic, mechanical, photocopying, recording, or otherwise, without the prior permission of the copyright owner.

Printed in the United States of America

Library of Congress Cataloging in Publication Data

Rutter, Michael.
  Juvenile delinquency.

  Bibliography: p.
  Includes indexes.
  1. Juvenile delinquency. I. Giller, Henri. II. Title. HV9069.R93
1984   364.3'6   84-496 ISBN 0-89862-632-3

Contents

Preface and Acknowledgements	13

1 Concepts, Measures and Processes — 15
Outline of processing — 16
  The offence — 16
  Police recording of offence — 18
  Identification of suspect — 19
  Decision on how to deal with suspect — 20
  Sentencing decisions — 22
  Implications of findings on processing — 24
Self-report studies — 26
  Frequency of delinquent activities — 27
  Differences between delinquents and
    non-delinquents — 27
  One-time offenders — 29
  Possible biases in findings on offenders — 29
  Bias in self-report studies — 31
Victim surveys and observation methods — 31
The behavioural characteristics of offenders — 33
Sub-classification of delinquency and conduct disorders — 37
  Seriousness of delinquency — 38
  Socialized and unsocialized patterns — 39
  Aggression and stealing — 41
  Conduct disorders with and without emotional
    disturbance — 42
  Personality dimensions — 43
  Clinical approaches — 44
Conclusions — 45

2 Developmental Trends, Continuities and Discontinuities — 47
Age trends — 47
Moral development — 53

Continuity and course of antisocial behaviour	54
Implications for views on personality development	61
Conclusions	62

3 Historical Trends — 65

Official statistics	66
Cautioning and other changes in police practice	72
Changes in legislation and recording of offences	80
Clear-up rate	84
Willingness to report	84
Conclusions on crime trends in official statistics	88
Self-report, victimization and other data on crime trends	89
Inter-generational comparisons	89
Vandalism	90
Self-report delinquency data	93
Victimization surveys	94
Overall conclusions on crime trends in the U.K.	94
International comparisons	95
Historical trends in other aspects of adolescent behaviour	98
Educational standards	98
'Generation gap'	99
Sexuality and marriage	99
Psychiatric disorder and related problems	100
Changes in society and the family	101
Opportunities for crime	101
War and its after-effects	104
Immigration	104
Unemployment	105
Divorce	106
Working mothers	108
Changing patterns of family building	109
Changing roles and expectations of women	110
Kinship and community support patterns	111
Television	112
Hospital admissions	112
Industrialization and urbanization	113
Environmental lead	113
Improved physical health	114
Standards of living	115

	Civil strife and conflict	116
	Conclusions on possible reasons for the increase in crime	118
4	**Sex, Social Class and Race**	**120**
	Sex differences	120
	Variations in sex ratio	123
	Sex differences in aggressivity, hyperactivity, and dishonesty	125
	Sex differences in response to family discord	127
	Possible 'intrinsic' factors	129
	Recidivism	131
	Conclusions on sex differences in delinquency	132
	Social class	132
	Strength of the social class association	133
	Meaning of the association	137
	Is delinquency 'normal' in some social groups?	139
	Does the meaning and significance of delinquency vary by social group?	140
	Social group influences in delinquent activities	141
	Civil strife	145
	Race	148
	Historical background	148
	Immigration	152
	Crime and delinquency among blacks in the U.S.A.	153
	Crime and delinquency among blacks and Asians in the U.K.	155
	Conclusions	161
5	**Causes and Correlates – Individual Characteristics**	**163**
	I.Q. and scholastic attainment	163
	Strength of I.Q.–delinquency association	163
	Meaning of associations	165
	Body build, physical illness and disability	168
	Body build	168
	Physical disabilities	169
	Physiological characteristics, avoidance learning and stimulus seeking	171
	Physiological characteristics	171
	Avoidance learning	172

8   Contents

	Stimulus seeking	173
	Delinquency and hyperactivity	173
	Personality characteristics	175
	Genetic factors	176
	Conclusions	179

6   Causes and Correlates – Psycho-social Factors   **180**
  Family influences   180
    Dimensions of family functioning   181
    Association with delinquency or with conviction   186
    Cause, correlate or consequence   188
    Which environmental mechanism?   190
  Films and television   191
  Labelling   196
  School factors   199
  Area influences   202
    Urban–rural differences   202
    Intra-urban differences   204
    Ecological correlations and explanations   206
  Physical environment and situational effects   210
  Social change   215
  Conclusions   219

7   Protective Factors   **221**
  Delinquent outcomes in youths from a low-risk background   222
  The outcome of non-delinquent boys from a high-risk
       background   223
  Characteristics of the social group   225
    Chosen change of peer group   226
    School: composition of pupil body   226
    Parental supervision   228
    School drop-out   228
    Moving away   229
  Employment   231
  Marriage   232
  Change of circumstances   235
  One good relationship   236
  Compensatory 'good' experiences   237
  Coping mechanisms   239

Interactive effects		240
Conclusions		241

8 Theories and Explanations — **242**
Concepts and issues — 242
Anomie/strain theories — 245
Sub-cultural approaches — 247
Differential association — 248
Social control theories — 250
Social learning theories — 252
A microsocial approach to coercive family processes — 253
Psycho-analytic theories — 256
Biological theories — 257
Situational perspectives — 260
Limited rationality or 'choice' theories — 261
Labelling perspectives on 'secondary deviance' — 263
Reactive conceptions of deviance and the 'new criminology' — 264
Conclusions — 265

9 Prevention and Intervention — **267**
Issues in evaluation — 268
  Has the planned intervention actually taken place? — 268
  What was the nature of the intervention? — 270
  Sampling and matching — 271
  Outcome measures — 274
Behavioural approaches — 276
  Institutional applications — 277
  Behavioural methods applied to individuals in the community — 280
  Family interventions — 281
  Overview on behavioural approaches — 283
Counselling and psychotherapy — 284
Individual differences in response to counselling/psychotherapy — 285
Varieties of institutional care — 288
  Therapeutic versus correctional regimes — 288
  Variations between institutions of ostensibly similar type — 289

10   *Contents*

Custodial and non-custodial approaches	292
Incapacitation	293
Non-custodial penal measures	295
Attendance centres	295
Suspended sentences and adjournment	296
Cautioning	297
Probation	298
Community programmes and diversionary policies	299
School projects	299
Community programmes	300
Intensive community-based treatments	302
Diversionary policies	303
Deterrence	304
Laboratory experiments	305
Field experiments	305
Time-series analyses	306
Cross-sectional studies	307
Conclusions on deterrence	309
Policing	310
'Physical' crime prevention measures	313
Target hardening	313
Target removal	315
Removing the means to crime	315
Reducing the pay-off	316
Environmental management	317
Conclusions on 'physical' crime prevention	317
Overall conclusions on prevention and intervention	317

10   Implications for Research, Policy and Practice   **320**

Research and policy	320
Prevention	323
Measures affecting individual predisposition	325
Ecological interventions	329
Current circumstances	331
Situations and opportunities	332
Conclusions on prevention	335
Treatment and correction of offenders	336
Response to first and minor offenders	337
Response to subsequent or more serious offences	339
Removal from home and institutional placements	347

Conclusions on treatment and correction 350
Research needs 352
   Historical trends 352
   Intervention and prevention 353
   Policing and processing 355
   Individual differences 356
   Environmental influences 358
   Continuities between childhood and adult life 361
Conclusions on research needs 361

References 363
Author Index 417
Subject Index 429

Preface and Acknowledgements

We have sought to assess what was known on the topic of juvenile delinquency with respect to its origins, causation, course, remediation and outcome; and in so doing to derive implications on research strategies that are likely to be fruitful in the future, and on policies and practices that might be effective. The topic has been considered in the context of contemporary society, but also we have paid attention to historical trends in delinquent activities, with particular reference to the query as to whether there has been an increase in crime during recent years. Where relevant and possible we have attempted to draw parallels between delinquency and other aspects of adolescent behaviour and problems.

The field of juvenile delinquency is an immense one and, if our task was to be at all manageable, it was essential that certain limits be set. Accordingly, we restricted the scope of our review in four main respects. Firstly, as research up to the mid-60s has been well reviewed previously (as, for example, by West, 1967, and Wootton, 1959), we have focused mainly on more recent work. Nevertheless, we have tried to indicate something of the nature of the continuities and discontinuities with earlier concepts and findings. Secondly, we have paid most attention to the commoner varieties of delinquent activities and, in particular, we have not considered sex offences or drug abuse. Also, we have not given special consideration to the problem of non-attendance at school. Thirdly, we have not dealt with the extensive literature on the justice system as such. Of course, there are aspects which had to be taken into account in considering the meaning of delinquent behaviour and, obviously, in deriving implications for policy and practice it was necessary to discuss these in the context of judicial practices. However, in that task we have taken empirical research findings (rather than socio-political views or a philosophical stance) as our starting point. Fourthly, we have based our discussion mainly on research undertaken in Britain and North America. But, in order to determine how far it was justifiable to derive general principles about delinquent behaviour, we made a more limited survey of the world literature in English-speaking journals and books.

This book is based on a report to the (British) Home Office and

Department of Health and Social Security, and we are grateful to both for the financial support which enabled the review to be undertaken and for helpful comments on our findings and conclusions. The views expressed here, however, are entirely our own and are not intended to represent Departmental policy.

Finally, we are deeply indebted to the many people who have aided us in our task. They are too numerous to name individually but we would like to give particular thanks to colleagues at the Cambridge Institute of Criminology, at the Home Office Research Unit and at the Center for Advanced Study in the Behavioral Sciences, Stanford, California (where M.R. was a Fellow for much of the time while the book was being written). We much appreciate their guidance in drawing our attention to relevant research, in showing us errors in our thinking and generally in clarifying our thoughts. Needless to say, however, none of them is responsible for our conclusions or interpretations.

MICHAEL RUTTER
HENRI GILLER

1
Concepts, Measures and Processes

In this book we review empirical research findings on various aspects of juvenile delinquency, of the characteristics of young offenders, and of the results of different forms of judicial and therapeutic interventions designed to prevent or control delinquent activities. At first sight there seems to be no difficulty in defining the subject matter of our review, in that there would be general acceptance of the opinion that 'A crime is an act that is capable of being followed by criminal proceedings' (Williams, 1955). Of course, that definition does recognize, through its use of the phrase 'capable of being followed by', that not all offences result in prosecution and conviction. As a consequence it is obvious that official statistics are likely to underestimate the 'true' extent of crime, simply because not every offender is caught. That circumstance alone means that we must examine the use of official statistics rather carefully in order to determine what biases they may introduce. This step is an essential one, in that most research into delinquency uses official statistics as its main measure of delinquent activities. However, as we shall see, the true state of affairs is much more complicated than the straightforward matter of who gets caught.

It is now well documented that the criminal justice system constitutes a multi-stage, multi-faceted process involving a sequence of interactions between the community, the offender and social control agents (see, for example, Feldman, 1977; Wheeler, 1967). The acknowledgement that all stages of the production of criminal statistics provide examples of the social construction of meaning has become a criminological truism (see Bottomley, 1973).

The point at issue, therefore, is not whether we should trust the statistics which are generated, but rather to what use we put our scepticism. In this connection, criminologists have directed their attention to the question of what the statistics on the level of recorded crime can tell us about the nature of unrecorded crime – what has come to be called 'the dark figure' (Walker, 1971). Biderman and Reiss (1967) have cogently argued that two distinct lines of inquiry have emerged on this issue: the so-called 'realist' and 'institutionalist' approaches. The 'realist' approach assumes that an objective crime 'reality' exists and, therefore, that measures (such as self-report and victimization studies) should be developed in order to provide a more valid picture of that reality. In contrast, the 'institutionalist' approach has concentrated on the activities of the agencies which handle crime reports and on the process by which crime rates are *created*. Here, the assumption is that there is no 'reality' in the sense of individual behaviour that is independent of the processing procedure. Rather, the reality lies in the interactions that constitute social control operations (see, for example, Box, 1971; Kitsuse and Cicourel, 1963; Erikson, 1966; Wilson, 1968a and b). The concepts and issues involved in these two contrasting approaches emerge most easily through a consideration of the process by which an individual 'act' gets translated into an official 'statistic' (see Feldman, 1977; Wilson, 1968a and b; Rumbaut and Bittner, 1979; Clarke and Hough, 1980).

Outline of processing

The offence

The process starts with the legal definition of the behaviours which may give rise to court proceedings. This definition has varied over time, and, of course, it also varies from place to place. Obviously, the definition involves decisions on which acts are to be regarded as criminal. As Walker (1980) notes, the principles which underlie such decisions are both complex and controversial. For example, several laws seem to be designed primarily to compel people to act in *their own* best interests, rather than because *society* needs to be protected. The laws on under-age drinking of alcoholic beverages constitute a case in point. It is striking that countries vary greatly on the age when drinking is permissible, and even within the United States the law varies from state to state. In considering the question of whether crime is increasing or decreasing (see Chapter 3), we need to be aware that new laws can alter levels of crime overnight by introducing new offences or removing old ones from the statute. The same applies to changes in the law concerning the age of criminal responsibility, which is now 10 years in the U.K., but which was 8 before 1964. Similarly, the size of the child population at risk of being brought to court may be changed as a result of non-criminal legislation. For example, the raising of the school-leaving age in the U.K. to 16 years in 1973 meant that, for the first time, 15 year olds could be brought to court on the grounds of school non-attendance. Even inflation can alter criminal statistics! For example, the offence of criminal damage refers to cases in which the damage exceeds a cost of £20. At one time such a figure would serve to restrict the offence to quite major damage, but massive inflation in recent years has meant that it no longer does so.

Finally, there are a variety of ill-defined grounds, involving no crime as such, on which young people can be brought to court. These may involve the charge that they were behaving in a way that suggested that they *might* later commit an offence (being a suspected person loitering with intent to commit an arrestable offence*), or they may involve the rather vague grounds of being 'beyond control' of their parents or 'in moral danger'. It is obvious that even at the point of defining what constitutes an offence there are very wide grounds of discretion (if not to say ambiguity).

The next two points in the process are the recognition that a delinquent act has been committed, followed by the decision to act on that recognition by notifying the police. On the first point, there are certain types of offence (such as exceeding the speed limit, or taking prohibited drugs, or fraud) which may escape observation and so be known only to the offender. However, that is not the case with most offences. But empirical findings emphasize the huge variations that exist with the second point. For example, Sturman's (1978) survey of vandalism, in which householders, shopkeepers, and the head teachers of schools were interviewed, showed that the number of incidents of vandalism far exceeded those known to the police. The survey of Post Office records (on telephone kiosk vandalism) and of local authority records gave the same picture. It is apparent that police records greatly underestimate the extent of vandalism, except perhaps for the most costly incidents.

Victim surveys show that the same applies to assaults, robberies, burglaries and theft (see, for example, Skogan, 1977; Hindelang, 1976 and 1978; Sparks *et al.*, 1977). For example, Sparks *et al.* (1977) found that only about a tenth of offences reported by victims appeared in police records; similarly, in the United States, some 82 per cent of cases of larceny are *not* reported to the police, and even 32 per cent of auto theft and 60 per cent of assaults are not notified. On the other hand, the same data indicate that most of the unreported crimes are relatively minor. There are some serious crimes that go unreported, but the proportion is much less. Various reasons for not reporting are given by victims, but opinions that 'it wasn't worth the effort' or 'it was unimportant' predominate.

In this connection it is important to note that in the great majority of cases, the initiative in whether or not to make a crime known to the authorities lies

---

* This offence was abolished in the U.K. in October 1981 by Section 8 of the Criminal Attempts Act.

with individuals other than the police (see, for example, Reiss, 1971; Coleman and Bottomley, 1976; Bottomley and Coleman, 1980; McCabe and Sutcliffe, 1978; Mawby, 1979). The general finding is that only about one in six crimes are discovered by the police themselves. On the other hand, police activities may influence crime reporting by the general public. For example, Schnelle *et al.* (1975) found that the experimental introduction of a police walking patrol in two areas in the U.S.A. resulted in a substantial increase in reported crime (although it made no difference to the number of arrests). Also, of course, there are some offences (most notably the 'suspected person' offence) which are almost entirely a matter of police discretion, and differences in police practice over time or between areas may make a substantial difference to the delinquency statistics for that offence (see, for example, Wilson, 1968).

There is even more scope for discretion in the notification of truancy, being 'beyond control', or being 'in moral danger'. A very large number of children in secondary school truant (see, for example, Hersov and Berg, 1980), but only a tiny proportion of them are brought to court for non-attendance. In many cases schools take no action, and in others they take actions which involve no judicial intervention.

Not much evidence is available on the possible biases involved in the decisions on whether to notify the police and press prosecution. However, there are indicators that they exist. For example, Cameron (1964) found that store detectives not only tended to follow adolescents and blacks rather than white adults, but also, among those apprehended, blacks were more likely to be prosecuted. Similarly, Robin (1970) reported that employing firms brought charges against only one-third of executives apprehended for a delinquent act, compared with two-thirds of cleaners.

Police recording of offence

The fact that a supposed crime is reported to the police does not mean that it is recorded as such. Police are expected to investigate the reports that they receive, and their recording of the incident will reflect the results of their inquiries. Some reports are written off as 'no-crimes' in that it transpires that indeed no crime has been committed (for example, the owner finds the bicycle that he thought had been stolen). But also, many are written off because the victim did not wish to prosecute, or because the incident formed part of a complicated domestic situation, or because of police discretion in deciding the most appropriate action in the circumstances. A variety of studies in both the U.K. and the U.S.A. have shown that this kind of 'writing off' occurs in a significant minority (rates vary from 1 per cent to nearly half) of reported 'crimes' (see, for example, Lambert, 1970; Black, 1970; Skolnick, 1966; Bottomley and Coleman, 1980; McCabe and Sutcliffe, 1978; Sparks *et al.*, 1977). Black's (1970) study of police practice in two American cities indicated that the police showed a strong tendency to follow the wishes of the complainant on whether formal or informal action should be taken. Sometimes they chose to follow an informal procedure when the complainant asked for formal action; this tendency was more marked in the case of minor offences. Also, however, they were more likely to make an official report when the complainant was very deferential than when he was antagonistic or merely civil. But from the concern of how to interpret official statistics, the more important feature of these findings is the considerable variation between police forces in the proportion of reported incidents written off as 'no-crimes'. For example, McCabe and Sutcliffe (1978) noted a rate of less than 2 per cent in Salford but 6 per cent in Oxford; other figures have shown variations between police forces in England and Wales which extend from less than 1 per cent to more than 8 per cent (see Bottomley and Coleman, 1980).

Identification of suspect

A further stage in the process involves the identification of a suspect for the recorded crime. This is generally thought of in terms of the detective work of the police department, and sometimes there is the implicit assumption that the 'clear-up' rate for crimes can be used as a measure of police efficiency. However, studies of the detection process (see, for example, Greenwood *et al.*, 1977; Bottomley and Coleman, 1980) show that this would be a mistaken assumption for the most part. In about a quarter of all incidents a ready-made suspect is available at the outset (most commonly because of identification by the victim or complainant). Of the remainder, a high proportion are cleared up because someone charged with another offence asks for other delinquent acts 'to be taken into account' by the court. Only in a minority of cases does 'detective work' by the police force (at least as ordinarily thought of) lead *directly* to clear-up. Of course for certain crimes, especially the more serious ones, such detective work is crucial, but the conclusion must be that for crimes considered as a whole the police have relatively little scope for increasing the clear-up rate. Not surprisingly, therefore, the clear-up rate has altered very little over the years (Home Office, 1980). However, for obvious reasons, the clear-up rate does vary greatly according to the type of offence, being lowest for burglary and robbery, and generally high for violence against the person.

Decision on how to deal with suspect

Given that a suspect has been identified, the police then have considerable discretion as to whether to take no formal action (perhaps just to admonish and release, or perhaps to ensure that the parents or some 'therapeutic' service are already dealing with the matter), to give an 'official' caution, or to take the suspect to court. Studies in the United States have shown that informal responses are more likely in the case of first offenders or minor crimes. One study (Piliavin and Briar, 1964) of 66 police–juvenile encounters showed that informal actions were more likely when the youth acted in a cooperative and respectful manner, but this finding failed to take into account either the seriousness of the offence or whether it was a first offence, and the Black and Reiss (1970) study of 281 encounters did not find this effect. Sullivan and Siegel (1972) undertook a pilot study to assess the items utilized by police officers in coming to a decision on whether to release a suspect with a warning, bring him to the station and then release, or arrest. Twenty-four police officers were presented with a single case history of a 14 year old apprehended as drunk and disorderly, and then asked to rank twenty-four items of information in terms of their importance in coming to a decision on processing. The type of offence was most important, and age next so. However, the attitude of the offender was often crucial in coming to a final decision. The findings are very severely limited in terms of their reliance on a single case history of a very minor delinquent act. While the results provide no basis for generalization and, in particular, do not justify inferences that the attitude of offenders is an important factor in decision-making with more serious offences, the methodology is a potentially useful one. The evidence from other studies (see Hepburn, 1978; Liska and Tausig, 1979; Thornberry, 1979) is somewhat variable, but generally it points to the conclusion that police disposition is most strongly influenced by the seriousness of the offence and whether or not the suspect is a first offender; after these have been taken into account, race, and possibly socio-economic status, make a lesser contribution to the decision.

Disposition practices have also been shown to vary between police forces. For example, Wilson (1968) compared a western and an eastern city in the United States. Juveniles in the western city were more likely to be processed, and of those who were processed more were arrested or cited. Wilson suggests that the differences arose because the western city's police force constituted a centralized, highly organized, professional department; whereas the police force in the eastern city was highly decentralized, with a more community-based, fraternal, non-professional ethos.

The most thorough analysis of this matter in the U.K. is provided by Landau's (1981) study of 1,603 police decisions on juveniles in London. The results showed that charges were most likely to be brought immediately (rather than referring the case to the juvenile bureau) if the juvenile was male, black, had previous convictions or referrals, was involved in a crime of violence, or was above the age of 14. Multivariate analyses showed that previous criminal record and type of offence played the major role in police decisions. But, even after these variables were taken into account, older juveniles were more likely to be charged, and black youths were also more likely than white youths to be taken to court for crimes of violence, burglary and 'public disorder and other offences'. In addition, decisions varied according to where the crimes were committed. Crimes of violence and of public disorder were dealt with more harshly in the socially disadvantaged inner city areas, but, conversely, burglary was more likely to lead to an immediate charge in the more prosperous outer suburbs where most homes were privately owned.

An earlier London study (Bennett, 1979; Farrington and Bennett, 1981) of some 900 juvenile first offenders in one London police division also showed that seriousness of offence and age were the two factors most strongly associated with disposition. There was a slight tendency for a higher proportion of middle-class offenders to be cautioned for more serious offences, but this trend ceased to be significant when other variables were taken into account (Farrington and Bennett, 1981). No effect of race on disposition was found. A more detailed study of 47 cases suggested that an unfavourable attitude by the juvenile when interviewed was associated with an increased likelihood of being taken to court rather than cautioned; those from a manual background were also more likely to be taken to court. An analysis of juvenile bureaux records in Bristol and Wiltshire (Priestley *et al.*, 1977) indicated that age, previous convictions, school status, number and value of offences were the variables most strongly associated with decisions on whether to prosecute. Social and 'welfare' items did not appear relevant, but the analysis of these variables was necessarily limited by reliance on official documents. In May's (1975) Aberdeen study there was no association between social class and disposition. National figures (Home Office, 1980), like all the more local studies, confirm that younger children are more likely to be cautioned, and girls most so. The figures also show considerable variation between areas in the use of cautions even when type of offence is held constant. Thus, the cautioning rate for violence against the person ranged from 10 per cent to 50 per cent, and for burglary from 16 per cent to 59 per cent.

Clearly, the research findings are agreed in showing that the decisions on how to deal with suspects are most strongly influenced by the seriousness of the offence, whether the youth has a previous record, and age. The findings on other variables are both weaker and less consistent but it seems that, to some extent, disposition may be influenced by the youth's demeanour, race and social background.

Sentencing decisions

Finally, once an offender has appeared in court and been found guilty, decisions have to be taken on sentencing. As with police decisions on how to deal with suspects, the magistrates have very considerable discretionary powers, not only on the sentence to be given but also on how they come to their decision and on the weight they attach to features of the offence, of the offender and of his home circumstances. An almost inevitable consequence of this discretion is extensive variation between magistrates' courts in their sentencing practices with both juveniles (Grünhut, 1956; Parker *et al.*, 1981) and adults (Tarling, 1979). Several rather different research strategies have been used to investigate the factors associated with this variation.

Naturally, the seriousness of the offence, the person's previous record, and age influence sentencing decisions (Priestley *et al.*, 1977). But these are not the only matters to be taken into account. Traditionally, juvenile courts have been expected to deal with offenders in terms of social welfare concerns and the needs of the offender, as well as factors involving the offence (Parsloe, 1978). Accordingly, the first issue is whether sentencing discrepancies are explicable in terms of variations between courts in the types of offenders dealt with, and by differences in local circumstances and resources. It has been found that this is part of the explanation, but only part. Grünhut (1956), for example, found that some four-fifths of juveniles lived in areas where the sentencing practices approximated the general pattern, but there were some courts with practices which were markedly out of line even when all due allowance had been made for differences in intake and other relevant factors. Tarling (1979) found the same with magistrates' courts dealing with adults.

Mott's (1977) study of decision-making in one juvenile court showed that magistrates attached most weight to the home background of the offender and next most weight to the seriousness of the offence. A follow-up showed that the boys with adverse family circumstances had a higher re-conviction rate than those without (55 per cent *v.* 29 per cent over the subsequent five years), suggesting that it was appropriate to take family features into account. However, the association was of only moderate strength, and Mott argued that greater weight should be given to other factors.

Other investigations have compared courts in order to determine whether decisions were influenced by the magistrates' attitudes towards crime or by the ways in which courts were organized. Hogarth's (1971) investigation of Canadian courts indicated that magistrates' personal characteristics and attitudes may influence sentencing decisions, but other research has shown that individual views are of rather minor importance in determining variations between courts in sentencing practice (see, for example, Hood, 1972). To a considerable extent this is a consequence of the ways courts operate – with several magistrates attached to each court and with magistrates being guided in their decisions by court clerks, by sentencing guide-lines, and by the chairman of the bench of magistrates. It has been found that individual courts tend to remain fairly consistent over time in their sentencing practices in spite of changing rotas of magistrates (Tarling, 1979). This suggests the importance of influences in the organization and tradition of individual courts. Moreover, interviews with court personnel have shown that they are concerned to maintain consistency within their own practice, but are largely unaware of patterns of sentencing in neighbouring courts and tend to regard such knowledge as irrelevant to their own decisions (Tarling, 1979).

A further approach to the factors involved in decision-making has been provided by studies of the contribution of social inquiry reports. Unlike the situation in adult courts (Hine and McWilliams, 1981; Thorpe, 1979), it seems that such reports tend to increase rather than decrease intervention. Thus, some half of the juveniles who receive a care order (which means residential care in most instances) do so on only their first or second court appearance, and for the majority the order is made on the basis of a recommendation by a social worker (Giller and Morris, 1981). Thorpe and his colleagues (1980) sought to investigate the use of care orders through a study of 112 young offenders subject to care in one authority. Researchers and senior care staff rated the case files on the need for care according to three criteria: (i) whether the child constituted a danger to himself or the community; (ii) whether his home could provide adequate care and control; and (iii) the presence of specific medical, educational, vocational or psychiatric needs. On this basis, it was decided that 87 per cent of care orders had been 'inappropriately' made! The finding certainly raises the possibility that care orders are being made far too readily on inadequate grounds, but it is important to note the very considerable limitations of the study. Firstly, only the records of offenders subject to care were scrutinized. Accordingly, it could be the case that a similar study of those not in care would show that many of them should be in care but were not. Secondly, the reliability and validity of the researchers' judgements are unknown, and it should not necessarily be assumed that they were superior to those of the social workers involved in making the recommendations. Thirdly, the operational criteria used may not have been the most appropriate. Thus, the two examples given of home circumstances requiring a care order were 'no home in the community' and 'persistent parental hostility'. It is obvious that there may be completely inadequate parental care and control without either of these features. Fourthly, the case files may not include all the detailed information on family functioning which constituted the basis of the social worker's recommendations. The investigation by Thorpe et al. (1980) raises important questions and constitutes a valuable first step into the study of social inquiry reports, but their conclusions cannot be accepted as proven.

Implications of findings on processing

This brief survey of the results of empirical inquiries into the factors associated with decisions on processing serves to emphasize the very indirect link between acts of delinquency and official statistics on delinquency. The findings point to the need for study of the process itself and of the ways in which variations occur. The issue tends to be raised in terms of the possibility of bias in police or judicial actions. However, as we have seen, part of the variation results from differences in the delinquent activities themselves. The seriousness of the offence and the presence of previous convictions constitute the two most important factors associated with processing decisions to take official actions of one sort or another. It is also apparent that the commonly held assumption that variations in processing are primarily a function of police decisions is wrong. Rather, some of the major variations are due to differences in the actions of the *general public* in recognizing and reporting offences. On the other hand, the police do have considerable discretion with respect to the identification of certain offences and to actions at some stages of the processing with all offences. It seems that, in practice, this discretion is utilized mainly with minor offences. However, there are unexplained variations in processing between areas, and to some extent between responses to different types of suspects within areas. Inevitably, the police have to decide how to distribute their time and attention and this means that there may be a particular focus on what is thought to be a problem area (Gill, 1977;

Armstrong and Wilson, 1973), a problem group (Cohen, 1972), or a problem crime (Parker, 1974). So far, the studies of the development of police and judicial concepts of what are 'problems' and of the operation of these concepts have tended to be small-scale and partisan (considering the process from the viewpoint of the adolescents rather than of the police or of both groups), but the observations made suggest that people do develop stereotypes of which sorts of individuals are 'delinquent types' and that these stereotypes may influence the course of processing (see, for example, Cicourel, 1976). There is a need to investigate further the reasons for these variations in processing and the implications that follow from their existence.

The further question which stems from studies of processing is whether routine statistics or research findings based on convictions or convicted offenders provide any sort of valid picture of the extent of juvenile crime or the characteristics of juvenile delinquents. Obviously it would be quite unwarranted to take official statistics as a measure of the true absolute level of delinquent acts in the community. The somewhat different questions of whether official statistics provide a valid index of *changes* in delinquency rates over time are considered in Chapter 3. Here we simply note that the questions are different. It would be possible for official statistics to be quite useless as an absolute measure of delinquency but nevertheless still constitute a satisfactory *index*, provided that the ratio between the 'real' rate and the 'official' rate remained constant.

Of course, that argument assumes that it is, in some sense, meaningful to talk about a 'real' rate. That would be disputed by those who take a labelling perspective or a reactive conception and by those who espouse the 'new criminology' (see Plummer, 1979, and Gibbs and Erickson, 1975, for reviews of these approaches). While these three approaches differ from each other in important ways, to a greater or lesser extent they are similar in focusing on (i) the fact that a delinquent act has no intrinsic properties – it is delinquent just because society has deemed it so; (ii) the fact that there are major variations in the process by which an act becomes translated into the object of some judicial intervention – some individuals who are known to have stolen come before the courts, whereas others who have behaved in a similar fashion do not; (iii) the fact that the subsequent course of behaviour of individuals is likely to be influenced by whether and how they enter the judicial system – the notion that 'labelling' increases the likelihood that a person will act in accord with the label of delinquent or deviant is one example of this kind; and (iv) the view that delinquency can only be considered within the context of social control – the new criminology's claim that delinquency constitutes a socio-political response by an oppressed group, and that criminal laws are used to control those who are exploited, takes the position furthest.

There can be no doubt that these newer sociological developments in the study of deviance have added an important dimension to criminology. The empirical findings discussed above demonstrate that there are important questions to be asked about why and how variations in the sequence of processing arise. However, these new perspectives largely, or entirely, ignore the possibility that society's response to deviant behaviour might have something to do with an individual's behaviour *prior* to that response. Put in a somewhat over-simplified form, their argument assumes that everyone commits delinquent acts and that the difference between those who commit many and frequently and those who commit few and rarely has little to do with qualities of the individual. In order to examine that possibility in greater detail we need to consider the results of self-report studies.

Self-report studies

The very substantial literature on self-report delinquency studies undertaken in the United States and the United Kingdom has been well summarized in several recent papers (see Hood and Sparks, 1970; Farrington, 1973; Hindelang *et al.*, 1979; Elliott and Ageton, 1980). As the main results of all the major studies are in generally good agreement, the findings can be briefly summarized and illustrated here.

The usual procedure has been to prepare a standard list of specified delinquent activities. Each item on the list is then presented to the youth (usually on a card), the youth being asked to respond by indicating whether he has undertaken the specified activity and, if he has done so, with what frequency and whether it resulted in police action. In most cases, anonymity as well as confidentiality is assured. Only a few investigators have systematically assessed the reliability and validity of the answers, but the results from the studies that have done so are reassuring. Thus, the re-test reliability over prolonged periods of time is quite high; the answers agree well with other independent reports; and scores on self-report measures provide a good prediction of later court appearances (see Gold, 1966; Erickson, 1972; Farrington, 1973; Osborn and West, 1978; Shapland, 1978). Clark and Tifft (1966) compared two administrations of the test, one with and without the use of a 'lie detector'. The lie detector findings suggested that 92 per cent of replies were honest (although not too much should be made of this observation in view of the poor validity of the lie detectors – see Lykken, 1981). Also,

Kulik *et al.* (1968) found that anonymity made little difference to boys' responses. Moreover, West and Farrington (1977) showed that the boys' accounts of their criminal convictions agreed well with official records.

Frequency of delinquent activities

The findings are entirely consistent in showing that the great majority of young people have committed delinquent acts at some time. West and Farrington (1973) found that 90 per cent of boys in one area of inner London admitted, at the age of either 14–15 or 16–17, deliberately travelling without a ticket or paying the wrong fare; 82 per cent breaking the windows of empty houses; and 65 per cent buying cheap, or accepting as a present, something known or suspected of being stolen. Similarly, Gladstone (1978), in a survey of vandalism among 11–15 year olds in a northern city, found that 65 per cent had written on walls in the street; 48 per cent had broken the glass in a street lamp; and 28 per cent had broken a car radio aerial. Broadly comparable figures apply to isolated examples of theft, as shown in Belson's (1978) survey, which found that 70 per cent had stolen from a shop and 35 per cent from family or relations. Willcock (1974) found that almost no youths (2.6 per cent) admitted no offences at all, that the mean number of offence types per person was 5.6, and that 40 per cent admitted between four and six types. The findings clearly justify the conclusion that criminal conduct of one kind or another is 'widespread and occurs on a major scale' (Belson, 1975).

Self-report studies have also shown that only a tiny minority of delinquent acts lead to a court appearance, although this proportion varies markedly by type of offence. West and Farrington (1977) calculated that of the youths buying cheap, only 1.5 per cent had been convicted for it; stealing from slot machines (5.4 per cent) and shoplifting (8.3 per cent) were also associated with a low rate of conviction. On the other hand, the risk was rather greater for 'taking and driving away' (38.3 per cent) and very substantial (61.9 per cent) for breaking and entering.

Differences between delinquents and non-delinquents

However, it would be quite wrong to assume from these figures that official delinquents do not differ from the general population in any important way. To begin with, most of the percentages quoted above refer to relatively minor, and often isolated, delinquent acts; the proportion admitting frequent major acts has been much lower in all surveys. Thus, breaking into a big store, garage, warehouse or pavilion was admitted to by only 10 per cent of boys in West and Farrington's (1973) study; using any kind of weapon in a fight by 22 per cent; getting into a house or flat to steal things by 9 per cent; and attacking a policeman who was trying to arrest someone else by 6 per cent. Also, it has been found that the amount of delinquent activities by youths who had been convicted of some offence far exceeds that of those who had had no contact with the police; in Shapland's (1978) study a mean score of 20 compared with 9. West and Farrington (1973) found that 54 per cent of recidivists had a score of 21 or more compared with only 10 per cent of those without any police record, and conversely, whereas a third of those without a record had scores of less than 12 without any serious offences, this was so for *no* recidivist. Overall the self-report delinquency score correlated 0.54 with official delinquency, a correlation closely similar to that (0.51) obtained by Erickson and Empey (1963) in an American study a decade earlier. It is apparent that there is a quite strong association between self-reported delinquent acts and official convictions, such that the youths who have appeared in court tend to be those with more serious and extensive delinquent activities.

Another way of looking at the same issue is to ask whether the non-convicted youths with a high self-reported delinquency score had an increased risk of later convictions. West and Farrington's (1973) findings showed that they did. Of the 80 youths with high self-report scores, 41 had official records by the age of 17. Of the 39 who did not, a further 19 had police contacts as juveniles or an adult conviction a few years later. Thus, *three-quarters* of the youths with a high self-report delinquency score at 14–16 had been officially processed in one way or another by the age of 21 (West and Farrington, 1973).

A further check is provided by an examination of the factors associated with high self-report delinquency scores. West and Farrington (1973) found that the behaviours associated with official delinquency were also those associated with high self-report scores. These included 'daring' and 'troublesomeness' as rated by teachers at 8 and 10 years, and by classmates at 10; as well as measures of antisocial attitudes and way of life as reported by the youths themselves. Similarly, poor parental supervision, parental criminality and other adverse family characteristics were associated with both self-reported delinquency and official delinquency. Gladstone (1978) showed the same with respect to self-reported vandalism. Lax parenting and negative experiences at school were both associated with an increased risk of high involvement in vandalism – especially if combined with an association with a 'tough' group of peers. Only 6 per cent of boys with none of these features were highly involved in vandalism, compared with 19–25 per cent of those with one of these features; 36–53 per cent of those with two; and 60 per cent of those with three.

We may conclude that there are immense differences between boys who have a high rate of self-reported delinquent activities and those who have a low rate. The view that everyone is somewhat delinquent and that there are no meaningful differences between those who are slightly so and those who are markedly so can be firmly rejected.

One-time offenders

The view that official delinquents do not differ from non-delinquents can be equally firmly rejected. To the contrary, they differ in a host of different features. But it is not sufficient to leave the matter there. First, there is the further question of whether these differences apply as much to one-time offenders as they do to recidivists. The findings show that they do not. Erickson and Empey (1963) found that, like official non-delinquents, most one-time offenders had committed only rather minor delinquent acts. Similarly, West and Farrington (1973) found that boys with a police contact only (i.e. an official caution or some form of informal action not resulting in a criminal record) differed only slightly from non-delinquents in terms of both personal characteristics and family background; one-time offenders differed rather more; but major differences were found only with recidivists. Whatever measure is used, police contact boys and one-time offenders show only slight to moderate differences from non-delinquents. However, the same findings show that there is no threshold or cut-off. These 'mild' delinquents show the *same* features as recidivists, it is just that they show them to only a slight extent.

Possible biases in findings on offenders

A second question concerns the possibility of bias in findings on offenders. We have seen already that the self-report findings indicate that, on the whole, 'official' delinquents are those youths who are most seriously delinquent. To that extent, the use of findings based on convicted offenders are likely to be valid. But the overlap between self-report findings and convictions (or cautions) is far from complete. Accordingly, we need to ask whether the findings with respect to young people with high delinquency on self-report measures but no convictions, and on those with convictions but relatively low self-report scores, suggest bias.

Farrington (1979) provides data on both groups from the Cambridge Study of Delinquent Development. Broadly speaking, the first group differed from those non-delinquent on both self-reports and official records in much the same way as did official delinquents with high self-report scores, but the differences were much less marked. Thus, the high self-report boys without delinquent records were twice as likely to be reported as daring (44 per cent *v.* 20 per cent), one and a half times as likely to have a low verbal score (39 per cent *v.* 25 per cent) or be rated as dishonest (28 per cent *v.* 18 per cent), and somewhat more likely to be rated as troublesome (21 per cent *v.* 15 per cent). These findings, together with the evidence that many of them subsequently acquired criminal records, suggest that these boys were generally similar to official delinquents but that they were somewhat less extreme. On the other hand, the differences between them and non-delinquents were somewhat less in the case of family characteristics, and it may be that the presence of a less adverse family background played some part in preventing (or delaying) the taking of official action.

The findings on the boys with official records but relatively low self-report scores provide no indication that they were a weakly antisocial group which should not have been processed. Indeed, in their behavioural features they were *more* characteristic of delinquents than were the group with high self-report scores but no official records. Thus, they were *more* likely to be rated as troublesome at school (42 per cent *v.* 21 per cent), as daring (51 per cent *v.* 44 per cent), and as dishonest (43 per cent *v.* 28 per cent), and equally likely to have a low verbal score (37 per cent *v.* 39 per cent). The family characteristics showed little evidence of bias against socially disadvantaged people, in that these two groups were closely comparable in terms of slum housing, and included *fewer* of low social class (9 per cent *v.* 21 per cent), although somewhat more with a low family income (20 per cent *v.* 15 per cent) or with a large family size (28 per cent *v.* 18 per cent). On the other hand, the convicted boys did come from a more deviant background in some respects; more of their fathers had an erratic job record (17 per cent *v.* 5 per cent) and more parents were rated as uncooperative when the boys were aged 8 (23 per cent *v.* 10 per cent). Accordingly, it may well be that to some extent a boy's family background is taken into account in deciding whether or not to take official action over his delinquent activities.

Putting these findings together, it may be inferred that it does *not* seem that the processing of boys committing delinquent acts introduces any *major* biasing effects* on the characteristics of offenders. Thus, for most purposes,

* This conclusion applies to boys coming before the courts for the general run of delinquent activities. It does not necessarily apply to those brought to court on a 'suspected person' charge (see Chapter 4), or to those appearing as 'beyond control' or 'in moral danger'. These vague categories allow much greater room for discretion, and systematic evidence is lacking on how such discretion is exercised.

the study of boys with official records constitutes a near enough approximation to the study of boys whose behaviour is much more seriously delinquent than that of the general population. But there are *some* biases in processing. As these are most likely to occur with mildly delinquent acts, and as young people receiving cautions or making just one court appearance tend to be only mildly delinquent, there is much to be said for a focus on *recidivist* delinquency if the aim is to identify characteristics of any sort which are associated with delinquent *behaviour* and which are not merely an artefact of processing decisions.

Bias in self-report studies

Up to this point, our discussion has involved the implicit assumption that self-report studies provide the best valid estimate of delinquent activities. We noted that the empirical findings were generally reassuring on the reliability and validity of self-report measures. However, there are some serious problems in the use of self-report studies – problems, moreover, which provide important limitations in their use for studying the correlates of delinquency.

The most important of these are: (i) many of the self-report scales are heavily weighted in terms of quite minor delinquent activities and omit some of the more serious criminal acts (see Elliott and Ageton, 1980); (ii) some of the studies are based on such small numbers that the sample could not be expected to include many serious delinquents (for example, 51 boys in the Shapland, 1978, study); (iii) the non-response rate in many studies has been quite high, so that major distortions could arise from missing data (for example 27 per cent non-response in the Elliott and Ageton, 1980, study); and (iv) as with other types of data (see Cox *et al.*, 1977), those individuals for whom self-reports are not obtained tend to be heavily weighted in terms of youths already delinquent or with characteristics associated with an increased risk of delinquency. Hirschi and Selvin's (1967) data illustrate the last point. Of the boys with a police record and a low grade in English a mere 38 per cent completed the questionnaire, compared with 79 per cent of boys without a record and with a high grade in English. The pattern clearly opens the way to serious biases as a result of the absence of data on a high proportion of boys known to be delinquent.

Victim surveys and observation methods

Just as self-report studies are designed to assess the 'true' proportion of youths engaged in delinquent activities, so victim surveys are designed to ascertain the true prevalence of delinquent *acts*. The usual procedure is to interview people from the general population in order to obtain systematic information regarding their experience, during a specified period of time, of being the victim of delinquent acts (see Hindelang, 1976). For example, in the American National Crime Panel Studies, householders are asked to give details of all incidents during the previous six months in which they were a victim of a crime of rape, robbery, assault or personal larceny. Similarly, business people are asked about robbery and burglary victimizations during the same period.

As already noted, victim surveys have all shown that there is a great deal of minor crime, and some major crime, which is not reported to the police. However, the results of these investigations are also useful in showing something of the *pattern* of crime, as well as its extent. American data show that, in general, the young, the black and the poor are those most likely to be the victims of crime (see Empey, 1978). The one major exception to this overall trend concerns victims of household crimes such as burglary, where (for obvious reasons) rates of victimization increase in accord with levels of income. The survey by Sparks *et al.* (1977) in Britain also showed that males reported a slightly higher incidence of victimization than did females, but this difference reached statistical significance only when crimes of violence, assaults, robberies and thefts from the person were combined. Non-white respondents were more likely to report incidents of victimization for offences against the person and, to a lesser extent, for property offences other than burglary. But, as Sparks *et al.* point out, caution is needed in the interpretation of these findings in view of the evidence of respondent bias with respect to both social class and ethnic background. It appeared that white respondents and those with a higher family income were more likely to report threats and attempts – especially with regard to violent offences. Black respondents and poorer people were more likely to dismiss these as not worthy of mention, reporting only crimes involving a greater level of actual violence. It may be inferred that the tendency for crimes to affect black people and those of lower status disproportionately is probably greater than the figures indicate.

The figures based on violent crimes known to the police in London provide a similar picture (Stevens and Willis, 1979). In 1975, black and Asian people made up 7.9 per cent of the population, but they constituted 13.5 per cent of the victims of all crimes of violence, and 17 per cent of those resulting in serious injury or a fatality. Victim reports on their attacker also showed that the majority of attacks (80 per cent of those causing a fatal or serious injury and 62 per cent of those causing slight or no injury) occurred *within* racial groups – a finding in keeping with those on all such crimes in both the U.K. and the U.S.A., whether or not reported to the police (see Bottoms and Wiles, 1975; Sparks *et al.*, 1977).

While these findings seem to be well substantiated, it should be noted that victim surveys involve important methodological problems (see, for example, Levine, 1976 and 1978; Singer, 1978). They are heavily reliant on the accuracy of people's memories and it is uncertain how far there is under-reporting or over-reporting of the amount or seriousness of crimes; there is also difficulty in determining how far events scattered in time are telescoped into the period for report. Also, especially with some crimes (such as vandalism – see Sturman, 1978), there is a problem in knowing whether the same incident is being reported by several different people or indeed whether it is being duplicated in the reports of a single informant because the damage has been left unrepaired. One means of attempting to check the validity of victim reports has been to use a 'reverse record check' – that is to interview, on a double-blind basis, a victim selected from police files as having been the subject of a crime (Hindelang, 1978). These have shown that whereas the great majority of burglary victims (88 per cent) and robbery victims (80 per cent) report the crime selected from survey files, the proportion was lower for rape (67 per cent) and much lower (47 per cent) for assault. The rate of recall was especially low when the offender was related to the victim. It is apparent that these figures suggest that biases in victim reporting may be quite important in the case of assault.

Observation data provide much the same picture as victim surveys in showing that most crimes tend to be concentrated in less affluent areas. For example, the surveys by Mawby (1977a) and Mayhew *et al.* (1980) of telephone kiosk vandalism showed that it was most prevalent in the most disadvantaged council housing estates (as assessed, for example, by social class, or proportion of unemployed or single-parent families, or population turnover), and least prevalent in areas of private or owner-occupied accommodation.

As official statistics, too (see Chapter 6), show that crime tends to be concentrated in less affluent areas, we may conclude that the victims of many (but not all) types of crime tend to be disadvantaged members of society.

The behavioural characteristics of offenders

Before discussing the correlates of delinquency (see Chapters 4–6), we need to ask how far delinquent activities occur as an isolated feature and how far they form part of a broader pattern of behavioural deviance. In short, are delinquents different from the rest of the population only in terms of the frequency with which they have engaged in criminal activities, or are there other more general features of their patterns of emotions, behaviour and relationships which characterize them as different?

Empirical research findings from a variety of different studies utilizing a range of behavioural measures are agreed in showing that both occur. That is to say, there are some delinquents who are distinctive solely in terms of their having committed delinquent acts but, as a whole, delinquents tend to differ from non-delinquents in many ways other than illegal acts. This was evident, for example, in May's (1975) analysis of the teacher questionnaire findings on juvenile delinquents in Aberdeen. Not unexpectedly, delinquents were more likely than non-delinquents to be rated as showing antisocial behaviour (truancy, destructiveness, fighting, disobedience, lying, stealing and bullying). However, it was striking that they were also more likely to have exhibited relationship difficulties (irritable, solitary and not much liked), attentional and activity level problems (over-active, fidgety, twitches and poor concentration), unhappiness or misery, and a mixed bag of other difficulties including nail-biting and frequent complaints of aches and pains. In addition, they were more than twice as likely to be enuretic (although this last difference failed to reach statistical significance as a result of small numbers). These features were most marked in the case of recidivists, but most of them also differentiated one-time offenders and those given police warnings. A fifth of delinquents had a total score on the questionnaire in the deviant range (a rate twice that in the population as a whole), but nearly as many (18 per cent) had a zero score on the scale.

Similarly, West and Farrington (1973), in their longitudinal study of London boys, found that peer ratings (at age 10) of dishonesty, troublesomeness, daring and (to a lesser extent) unpopularity were all associated with delinquency – as were teacher ratings of troublesomeness and self-ratings of aggression. More detailed interview data from the youths themselves at the age of 18 showed that delinquents were less conforming and less socially constrained in all aspects of their lives than non-delinquents. More were heavy drinkers (at least twenty pints of beer per week), got involved in fights when drinking, smoked heavily, were sexually promiscuous, gambled heavily, had discordant relationships with their parents, were in debt, had erratic work histories, sustained injuries, started fights, used a weapon to injure someone, and expressed anti-authority attitudes.

These differences apply particularly to recidivists who show a wide range of social and interpersonal problems which persist into adult life. This is shown, for example, by Osborn and West's (1980) comparison (in the same longitudinal study) of persisting recidivists, temporary recidivists (i.e. those with at least two convictions but who had no convictions after their nineteenth birthday – up to the time of assessment at 24), and non-delinquents. The persisting recidivists were much more likely to have had at least eight weeks' unemployment during the previous two years (59 per cent *v.* 9 per cent in the temporary recidivist group and 11 per cent in the non-delinquents); to have unpaid debts (55 per cent *v.* 5 per cent and 4 per cent); to have been involved in fights (59 per cent *v.* 23 per cent and 11 per cent); to be heavy drinkers (over £20 weekly on alcohol: 32 per cent *v.* 18 per cent and 0 per cent); and to be separated from their children for reasons other than illness (36 per cent *v.* 9 per cent and 4 per cent). For example, 6 of the 22 persistent recidivists had left their children following marital rows.

Other studies have produced generally similar findings. In Britain, the National Survey findings (Mulligan *et al.*, 1963) showed that teachers' reports rated future delinquents significantly higher than non-delinquents on 'aggressive maladjustment'; Stott (1960) found that maladjustment, as assessed on the Bristol Guides, differentiated boys on probation from controls; and Ouston (1983) found that teachers' ratings of deviance in pupils' behaviour, emotions and relationships at the age of 10 were associated with later delinquency, especially in girls. Similarly, in the United States, teacher ratings of various kinds have consistently been shown to be associated with later delinquency (Conger and Miller, 1966; Hathaway and Monachesi, 1963; Khleif, 1964; Kvaraceus, 1960; Reckless and Dinitz, 1967). Jessor and Jessor (1977), in their American longitudinal study, found life-style differences between delinquents and non-delinquents which were generally similar to those identified by West and Farrington – marijuana use, high alcohol consumption, precocious sexual activity, low commitment to scholastic achievement, and anti-establishment attitudes.

It is clear that, although some offenders are otherwise unexceptional in their behaviour, delinquents as a group tend to be distinctive in a wide range of behaviours that differentiate them from non-delinquents. The basic question, however, is what interpretation to place on these findings. Certainly, the possibility that this is simply the usual pattern of behaviour for working-class boys can be ruled out. As West and Farrington (1973 and 1977) showed, these behavioural features differentiate delinquents and non-delinquents even within a working-class group, and the differences are maintained even after controlling for social class variables. Indeed, the differences were maintained even after matching on much more detailed and discriminating measures of family background (for example, income, parental criminality, family size, and degree of parental supervision).

But these findings do not rule out the possibility that the behavioural and attitudinal features characterize a chosen life style which is 'normal' for a *smaller* subgroup or subculture. Indeed some of the measures clearly do reflect a life style rather than any aspect of behavioural 'disorder' or 'impairment'. On the other hand, some of the results do not seem compatible with that interpretation. It is difficult to see, for example, how severely discordant intra-familial relationships, misery and unhappiness, bed-wetting, or attentional deficits could be accepted as part of a chosen life style.

The same picture emerges from epidemiological studies of 'conduct disorders' in the general population. This is a psychiatric category rather than a legal one, but refers to a group of antisocial behaviours which overlaps substantially with delinquency. In the Isle of Wight survey of 10–12 year old children (Rutter, Tizard and Whitmore, 1970), the term was used to refer to disorders involving abnormalities of behaviour, emotions and relationships that were sufficiently marked and sufficiently prolonged to be causing persistent suffering and/or social impairment, and in which the predominant pattern was of behaviour giving rise to social disapproval. The diagnosis was based on detailed information from the child himself and from his parents, together with more limited data from teachers. About 3 per cent of 10–12 year olds were regarded as having a conduct disorder ($5\frac{1}{2}$ per cent of boys and $1\frac{1}{2}$ per cent of girls). The key finding for the present discussion was that on all measures the children with conduct disorders also showed a much increased rate of misery and unhappiness, of relationship difficulties, of attentional deficits and of bed-wetting.

Clinic studies show much the same, and particularly highlight the very great overlap between conduct disorders and over-activity or attentional deficits (Sandberg *et al.*, 1978; Stewart *et al.*, 1980 and 1981), an overlap which is equally evident oon general population surveys (Sandberg *et al.*, 1980). Of course, it has to be emphasized that the concept of 'conduct diisorder' is far from synonymous with delinquency. In particular, the former concept specifies that social impairment must be present. Because of this, necessarily it identifies only a subgroup of delinquents. Nevertheless, taken in conjunction with the studies of delinquents (discussed above), the findings indicate that a significant proportion of delinquents (especially recidivist delinquents) do show a variety of immmportant problems in other spheres of their functioning – particularly in attention, in mood, and in relationships. Follow-up studies into adult life, of both clinic and non-clinic children, show that antisocial behaviour in childhood is followed by a substantially increased risk, not only of adult criminality, but also of marital problems and breakdown; of difficulties in parenting; of a poor job record and unemployment; of financial dependency; of social isolation; of alcohol problems; and of mental disorder (Robins, 1966, 1978 and 1979).

It is evident that significantly more delinquent than non-delinquent children show this broader range of social, emotional and behavioural problems. But many delinquents, especially one-time offenders or those committing minor delinquencies, do *not* show any other difficulties of note. The observation raises the question of whether or not it is possible to make meaningful subdivisions within the overall group of delinquents.

Sub-classification of delinquency and conduct disorders

The consistent observation that delinquent youths are a rather varied group and that some patterns of delinquency, but not others, overlap with aggression, poor peer relationships, hyperactivity, attentional deficits and emotional disturbance suggests that there is a need to categorize different types of delinquency or conduct disorder. On the whole, clinicians tend to be agreed that the group is heterogeneous; disagreements concern *how* and on what basis it should be subdivided.

Nevertheless, it is not self-evident that the heterogeneity gives rise to useful replicable sub-categories. West and Farrington (1977), in their detailed longitudinal study of London boys, noted that delinquents differed from non-delinquents in a wide range of life-style characteristics of which 'aggressiveness, irregular work habits, immoderation in the pursuit of immediate pleasure, and lack of conventional social restraints are the most prominent'. They argue that '... the findings vindicate the concept of the delinquent character' (p. 160) and Farrington *et al.* (1982) went on to claim that 'convicted juveniles and young adults were a relatively homogeneous group of thieves'.

Robins and her colleagues (Robins, 1978; Robins and Ratcliff, 1980a) have attempted to test the validity of the concept of a single syndrome of antisocial behaviours by utilizing data from three long-term longitudinal studies of very different populations. They suggest that the single syndrome hypothesis is supported by four well replicated findings: (i) that each *separate* type of childhood deviance is independently correlated with the *overall* level of adult deviance; (ii) that each separate type of adult deviance is predicted by the overall level of childhood deviance; (iii) that the overall level of deviant behaviour in childhood is a better predictor of adult deviance than any one particular child behaviour; and (iv) that these relationships do not depend on the continuation of the *same* behaviour from childhood into adulthood. Indeed, as many other studies have shown (for example,

Wolfgang *et al.*, 1972; Thornberry and Figlio, 1978; McClintock, 1963; Mott, 1973; Soothill and Pope, 1973; West and Farrington, 1973 and 1977), most offenders (with the partial exception of minor sex offenders) commit quite a varied range of offences with little evidence of specialization. It may be concluded that, as a group, delinquents of all types have many features in common and that little is to be gained by subdividing juvenile delinquency according to (legal definitions of) types of offences. On the other hand, not only are there many disturbances of conduct which do not involve delinquent acts as such, but also it may be that the group should be subdivided on characteristics other than type of offence.

Seriousness of delinquency

Certainly it is apparent that there are meaningful and important differences according to the 'severity' of the delinquency as measured in various ways. As already noted, all studies have shown that the degree of recidivism is associated with many other features in the youth's behaviour as well as with the strength of associations with psycho-social variables linked with delinquency (see, for example, Erickson and Empey, 1963; May, 1975; Ouston, 1983; West and Farrington, 1973 and 1977). Individuals receiving a caution or with just one conviction differ from the general population to a much lesser extent than do recidivists. On the other hand, this seems to be a matter of degree rather than a categorical distinction, in that single offenders differ from non-delinquents *in the same way* as do serious recidivists, even though the differences are not as great.

Similarly, it has been shown that the *range* of delinquent activities, as assessed by the number of different items on a self-report measure, results in meaningful distinctions (see West and Farrington, 1973). Following Sellin and Wolfgang's (1964) pioneering work, there have been attempts to measure the seriousness of crimes according to the type of offences (see Walker, 1978; Sparks *et al.*, 1977; Rossi *et al.*, 1974; Wadsworth, 1979). It has been found that people agree moderately well in their ranking of the seriousness of different crimes – with seriously violent offences rated worst, and offences such as truancy, drunkenness, and minor shoplifting all being rated much more lightly. However, offences involving violence tended to be rated somewhat more seriously by males and by persons of high social status (Walker, 1978), and consensus seems to be greater among the better educated (Rossi *et al.*, 1974). Wadsworth (1979) showed that a rating of the social acceptability of crimes as judged by degree of victim involvement and personal space violation had differentiating value in so far as the factors associated with delinquency tended to be most strongly associated with the most serious delinquency.

Measures of the range, frequency and seriousness of offences have all been found to provide useful ways of grading the severity of delinquent activities; the different measures overlap greatly, but possibly the best differentiation may be obtained by a combination of the three different facets of seriousness.

Socialized and unsocialized patterns

On the basis of their factor analytic study of clinic records many years ago, Hewitt and Jenkins (1946) suggested the importance of distinguishing between 'unsocialized aggression' and 'socialized delinquency'. More recent statistical studies of symptom correlations both by Jenkins and his co-workers (Jenkins, 1973) and by others (see Quay, 1979) have often, but far from always (Field, 1967) come up with similar groupings. Unsocialized aggression is generally held to involve unpopularity, teasing, quarrelsomeness and other reflections of poor peer relationships, but lying, malicious mischief and fire-setting may also be associated. Thus, the syndrome or behavioural dimension seems to consist of the combination of socially disapproved behaviour, social maladjustment and disturbed interpersonal relationships. In contrast, socialized delinquency is said to refer to a form of delinquency with stealing, truancy, staying out late at night, running away from home, and gang activities but with adequate peer relationships.

The main justification for the distinction between the two hypothesized types of conduct disturbance comes from the evidence showing that they differ in terms of family background and of outcome. Thus, Hewitt and Jenkins (1946) found that unsocialized aggression was associated with broken homes, family hostility and maternal rejection; and socialized delinquency with social disadvantage, parental neglect and delinquent associates. As both the child behaviours and the family variables were noted by the same clinician, the associations could be just an artefact of the bias or preconceptions of the workers who rated the records. Nevertheless, the findings were broadly replicated by Lewis (1954) in an independent study of a rather different sample (children taken into the care of the local authority) – although once again the child and family ratings were made by the same person. Hetherington et al. (1971) used measures of parent–child interaction based on a modification of the Revealed Differences Test to compare 'neurotic delinquents' and 'socialized delinquents' (as determined by the Quay and Peterson personality questionnaire). Their measures were not directly comparable with those used in the earlier studies but the findings were somewhat similar in showing greater parental harmony, paternal dominance and permissiveness in the socialized group, but conflict, maternal dominance and restrictiveness in the unsocialized group. The only outcome research utilizing this sub-classification is that by Henn *et al.* (1980), whose twelve-year follow-up study of institutionalized delinquents indicated that the socialized group had a significantly better prognosis in terms of adult convictions and imprisonment.

These results, even though based on a rather small number of investigations, provide some justification for Jenkins's differentiation of conduct disorders on the basis of presence or absence of personal relationships and loyalties. However, other research shows that many questions remain on the validity of the subdivision. In the first place, socialized delinquency is sometimes equated with delinquency which is a culturally accepted form of behaviour in certain socially disadvantaged high-delinquency areas (such as that described by Mays, 1954, in the Liverpool dock area, or by Willmott, 1966, in the East End of London). However, this parallel appears to be unjustified, not only because areas of social disadvantage tend also to be areas of increased family pathology, but also because delinquents from a socially deprived background have been found just as likely as others to show personal maladjustment and poor peer relationships (Stott, 1960 and 1966; Conger and Miller, 1966; West and Farrington, 1973), and just as likely to become sociopaths in adult life with a high rate of both social and psychiatric pathology (Robins, 1966 and 1978).

A second problem is that by no means all factor analytic studies show that socially disapproved behaviours fall into these two patterns (see Achenbach and Edelbrock, 1978; Quay, 1979). Moreover, even those investigations which agree on the factors do not necessarily agree on the specific behaviours which constitute the factors. Thus, stealing from home was a feature of unsocialized disorders in one study (Jenkins and Boyer, 1967), but of socialized disorders in another (Kobayashi *et al.*, 1967). It has been a general finding that many delinquents do not fit either category and many have elements of both clusters of behaviours. Accordingly, it has been found necessary to make the differentiation on just one or two key features rather than on the overall pattern of antisocial behaviour. Nevertheless, when this has been done by giving precedence to the presence/absence of enduring peer relationships (Henn *et al.*, 1980; Rutter *et al.*, 1970), the differentiation has been shown to have good inter-rater reliability.

However, the need to do this (together with the observation that the quality of peer relationships varies in continuous fashion) raises the further question of whether the differentiation really refers to distinct syndromes or, rather, whether it concerns variables present to a greater or lesser degree in all children. It is relevant that other research (Roff *et al.*, 1972; Sundby and Kreyberg, 1968) has shown that the quality of peer relationships predicts outcome in both delinquent and non-delinquent groups. Perhaps what matters is the degree of personality disturbance rather than the type of conduct disorder. There is little doubt that the extreme patterns of socialized and unsocialized disorders differ sharply. The unresolved key questions are: (i) does the difference refer to *syndromes* or to personality (or other) dimensions? and (ii) which of the various different features of the patterns constitutes the crucial distinction? In the latter connection, we have to consider the possible importance of the differentiation between aggression and stealing.

Aggression and stealing

Many retrospective and prospective studies have shown that aggressive antisocial behaviour in young children is associated with the later development of delinquency (Farrington, 1978; Robins, 1966; West and Farrington, 1973; Wolfgang *et al.*, 1972; Wadsworth, 1979), and there can be no doubt that there is a substantial and meaningful overlap between aggression and delinquency. Moreover, this association is not just a reflection of the link between aggression and violent crime, as the Cambridge Study in Delinquent Development (Farrington, 1978) showed that boys who were aggressive at the age of 8 or 10 had an increased risk of non-violent crime as well as of violent crime (although, not unexpectedly, the association was greater with the latter). However, this could reflect the overlap between stealing and aggression in earlier childhood (before the youngsters could be 'officially' delinquent), and it is important to ask what happens in the later development of children who are aggressive but who do not steal, and vice versa. The only data of this kind are provided by Moore *et al.* (1979), in a small study of children referred for treatment to the Oregon Social Learning Project, the children being compared with a group of normal children. It was found that only 13 per cent of the children with aggression in the home (but no stealing) became delinquent by the time of follow-up at the age of 14–20, a rate no greater than that (15 per cent) in controls of the same age, but well below that (56 per cent) of children who stole (but without a court record when first referred). Aggressive and non-aggressive thieves had similar risks of court appearances.

The implication is that stealing and aggression are frequently associated, but that this association is evident from at least middle childhood and that aggression *on its own* at the age of 8–10 may not carry any increased risk of delinquency. At the moment the idea may be regarded as no more than suggestive, not only because the findings come from a single unreplicated study based on quite a small sample, but also because the sample was a special one in terms of receiving very intensive treatment and in terms of the aggression being mainly or only evident in the family. It is quite unclear whether the same findings would apply to children showing aggression with peers or with adults outside the home as well as in the family. Nevertheless, it is noteworthy that in Wolff's (1971) cross-sectional correlational study of the behaviour of children referred to a psychiatric clinic, the cluster of aggressive, over-active behaviours showed no link with the cluster of delinquent behaviours (lying, stealing, wandering). Similarly, in the Isle of Wight general population epidemiological study of children aged 10 and 11 (Rutter, Tizard and Whitmore, 1970), there was a substantial subgroup with non-delinquent conduct disorders. However, what is unknown in both studies is whether those aggressive children who were non-delinquent in middle childhood began to steal later.

Further evidence suggesting the utility of differentiating between stealing and 'pure' aggression comes from Patterson's (1981a and 1982) studies of clinic children which suggest they differ in parental characteristics (as assessed by M.M.P.I. (Minnesota Multiphasic Personality Inventory) profiles), in family patterns (the parents of thieves tend to show a distant, uninvolved pattern of interaction in contrast to the more actively hostile punitive environment of the families of aggressive children), and in response to an intensive behaviourally oriented family treatment programme (the thieves were more likely to relapse). However, so far the findings are based on rather small numbers and must therefore be regarded as tentative rather than firm.

In short, there are slender pointers to the possibility that aggressive disorders, at least those confined within the family, may constitute a syndrome or dimension of behaviour which is relatively separate from stealing and related delinquent activities.

Conduct disorders with and without emotional disturbance

It is relatively common for children and adolescents with delinquent behaviour, and especially those with more widespread conduct disorders, to show emotional disturbance, particularly as evidenced by depressive mood (Rutter, Tizard and Whitmore, 1970). It might be thought that the presence or absence of emotional disturbance would constitute an important differentiating feature within the broad group of young people engaged in delinquent activities. However, what little evidence there is suggests that it does not to any decisive extent. The epidemiological features of 'pure' and 'mixed' conduct disorders in the Isle of Wight inquiry were fairly similar at 10–11 years (Rutter, Tizard and Whitmore, 1970), although at 14–15 years the mixed conditions were somewhat intermediate in pattern between emotional and conduct disorders (Graham and Rutter, 1973). Their overall course between the two age periods was also somewhat intermediate, in that 75 per cent of the children with conduct disorders at 10–11 years still had a socially handicapping psychiatric problem at 14–15; the comparable figures were 58 per cent and 46 per cent respectively for those with mixed and with emotional disorders. The pattern of changing symptomatology between middle childhood and adolescence, however, showed a good deal of shift from conduct disorders to mixed disorders or vice versa, but very little shift from emotional disorders to mixed disorders and none to conduct disorders (Graham and Rutter, 1973). In that study, outcome was assessed in terms of psychiatric state, but a somewhat comparable comparison was made with respect to the continuation of delinquency in the small pilot follow-up study by Power *et al.* (1972). The presence of 'psychiatric disorder or serious emotional disturbance' was found to have no predictive power regarding re-conviction during the next three years for boys assessed at the time of their first court appearance. The evidence is both slender and inconclusive, with the differentiation according to the presence or absence of emotional disturbance being made in very few investigations. Nevertheless, such evidence as there is does not suggest that it is likely to prove to be of crucial importance.

Personality dimensions

Attempts to subdivide delinquents according to personality dimensions derive from a variety of rather different theoretical perspectives. The best established categorization is that based on the presence or absence of 'psychopathy' (Hare, 1970; Hare and Schalling, 1978). However, the concept of psychopathy has proved elusive and difficult to define as well as to measure (Lewis, 1974; Hodgins, 1979), and there is no agreement on definition. Most of the research on this concept has been undertaken with incarcerated male adult criminals, so that the applicability of the findings to criminals outside prison, let alone to juvenile delinquents, remains quite uncertain. Nevertheless, it has been found that psychopaths differ from non-psychopathic criminals on a variety of psycho-physiological indices, although there is some inconsistency on the specific autonomic features found, so that there is limited agreement on the theoretical inferences to be drawn. Probably the best replicated finding, stemming from Lykken's (1957) pioneering research, is that psychopaths show reduced anxiety and are impaired in their passive avoidance learning in relation to punishment (Hodgins, 1979). As discussed in Chapter 5, there is some very limited empirical evidence that this differentiation may have some limited validity in juveniles. The possibility that physiological measures may be used to differentiate subgroups of delinquents who differ in personality features is certainly worth exploring further but so far the concept of psychopathy has not led to any very satisfactory sub-categorization within the broad group of delinquencies.

A quite different approach to personality assessment comes from the I-level or Development of Interpersonal Maturity theory, which proposes that individuals can be meaningfully described in terms of seven successive levels of interpersonal maturity (Sullivan, Grant and Grant, 1957; Warren, 1977). It has been most widely employed in the California Community Treatment Project, which has sought to determine whether 'passive conformist', 'power-oriented' and 'neurotic' delinquents differ in their responses to treatment (Palmer, 1974; Warren, 1977). The data are reported in ways which are often difficult to follow (the project findings are discussed more fully in Chapter 9), but it appears that neurotic delinquents respond better in an intensive community programme than in the more traditional discipline-oriented programme; whereas the reverse is true of the power-oriented delinquents. Matching of delinquent with therapist style was said to be particularly crucial in the former group (Palmer, 1973). The findings are provocative, especially in terms of their implications for methods of intervention, but there are problems in the construct validity of the I-level classification (Austin, 1975) and the empirical findings need independent replication before much can be built on them. Nevertheless, there is some other research (such as that by Craft, 1966, showing that immature psychopaths responded better to a paternalistic regime than to a more psychotherapeutically oriented approach) which suggests the possible utility of using personality assessments as a means of subdividing conduct disorders. However, the approach has still to be adequately tested, and presumably it suffers from the limitation that it would be less easy to apply to younger children.

Clinical approaches

Finally, there are the more clinically oriented approaches to classification. Scott (1965) proposed a four-fold aetiology-based subdivision: (i) well-trained to the wrong standards; (ii) reparative and avoidance patterns; (iii) untrained; and (iv) repetitive maladaptive delinquency. Rich (1956), on the other hand, suggested a motivational subdivision of types of stealing: (a) 'marauding' offences with others, that is stealing without planning when the opportunity presented; (b) 'proving' offences, such as stealing cars to demonstrate one's manhood; (c) 'comforting' offences, often from parents, either as a substitute for loss of love or as an expression of resentment regarding wounded feelings; and (d) 'secondary' offences with a clear idea of what can be stolen and with precautions against detection. Both classifications emphasize the variety of delinquent patterns, especially in relation to those young people referred to psychiatric clinics. While the categories appear to correspond to some of the types of conduct disturbance seen at clinics, their validity and utility remain untested.

The empirical research findings suggest that the quality of peer relationships, the 'maturity' of personality, the presence of 'psychopathic' characteristics, the severity and persistence of delinquent activities, and the distinction between 'pure' aggression and stealing may all constitute useful means of differentiation. However, not only have these different approaches not been adequately tested (and, even less, compared with one another) but it remains quite uncertain whether a categorical or a dimensional approach would be more applicable.

Conclusions

There continues to be controversy over the concepts and measures of delinquency, and especially over the question as to whether it is justifiable at all to consider offenders as a meaningful group of individuals, or delinquencies as a valid group of behaviours. The controversy stems in part from ideological issues, but also in part from the empirical findings on the complexity and apparent arbitrariness of the processing of offenders. Only a tiny proportion of delinquent acts result in prosecution, and at all stages of the process, from the definition of certain sorts of behaviours as 'delinquent', to the notification of the police that a delinquent act has been committed, to the taking of a suspect to court, there is a wide range of discretion available as to which course in the process to pursue. In part this discretion lies with members of the general public, or with non-police officials (for example, those in schools or stores), but in part it lies with the police and the courts. Many strong claims have been made that the whole process is seriously biased to the disadvantage of the poor and the black. Empirical findings suggest that these biases have often been overstated – many of the variations in processing have been shown to be strongly linked with the seriousness and persistence of the delinquent activities. Nevertheless, troubling variations in processing remain, and further investigations are needed into their origin, meaning and implications. It might also be questioned whether it is wise to retain offences (such as the recently removed 'suspected person' offence) which are very vague and open to wide variations in interpretation and operation.

However, while there are indeed potential (and actual) biases in processing, the research evidence strongly suggests that there are real and important differences between delinquents and non-delinquents. Although, certainly, great caution is needed in the utilization of official statistics, it would be unwarranted to abandon them. The greatest problems lie in the findings based on cautions, minor delinquent activities and one-time offenders. Currently, many young people are processed for quite trivial offences, and these individuals differ little from the rest of the, non-delinquent, population. On the other hand, recidivist delinquents tend to show a much broader range of features which differentiate them from non-delinquents. In part these features represent an antisocial life style but, at least in some delinquents, they also involve personal problems and social impairments. In their case, the delinquency constitutes part of a broader pattern of difficulties. But there does not seem to be any threshold or cut-off which differentiates this more extreme group. Rather, they seem to constitute the end of a continuum.

Many attempts have been made to subdivide delinquents in ways which would provide a more useful organization of the heterogeneity. Some of these have involved dimensional approaches and others a categorical system. There are sufficient useful leads from the findings so far to make this an area of research worth pursuing – but so far there is no means of subclassification that has been adequately validated.

2
Developmental Trends, Continuities and Discontinuities

As noted in the previous chapter, delinquency is often associated with other forms of 'troublesome' behaviour and, in some cases, with a more widespread disturbance of conduct. Hence, in considering developmental trends, continuities and discontinuities, it will be necessary to broaden the discussion to include these associated behavioural features. This broadening does not involve any presupposition that all delinquency constitutes part of a general disorder of conduct (for, manifestly, it does not), nor does it require an assumption that the developmental course will be the same for delinquency as for these other associated behaviours. Rather, we need to examine the empirical findings in order to ask how far there are behavioural precursors of delinquency which may be identified in early or middle childhood before delinquent acts first occur and before the first court appearance. Similarly, we need to question whether other forms of behavioural deviance continue even after overt delinquent activities cease.

Age trends

It is often considered that disorders in pre-school children show a rather undifferentiated pattern, so that the diagnostic categories used with older children are inapplicable. Thus, neither the British Waltham Forest general population epidemiological study of 3 year olds by Richman and her colleagues (1982) nor the American Martha's Vineyard study of the same age group (Earls, 1980) attempted any classification of the psychiatric problems which were studied. On the other hand, factor analytic and statistical clustering studies of both clinic and non-clinic pre-school children have shown much the same differentiation of emotional and conduct disorders as that found in older children (Behar and Stringfield, 1974; Kohn, 1977; Wolkind and Everitt, 1974). While the most frequent problems among 3 year olds in the general population concern enuresis, eating and sleeping difficulties (Richman et al., 1982; Earls, 1980), the commonest reason for psychiatric referral at that age is unmanageable behaviour (Bentovim, 1973; Wolff, 1961).

The findings on age trends in conduct disturbances are somewhat contradictory and difficult to interpret because studies vary in their samples and measures. Most of the epidemiological or longitudinal studies rely on reports from parents or from teachers, and these are likely to be strongly influenced both by their perceptions and concepts of the behaviour in question, and also by their implicit or explicit use of some kind of norm. For example, in the Buckinghamshire inquiry (Shepherd *et al.*, 1971) the measure of 'destructiveness' relied on a parental rating of whether the child was 'very destructive' or 'about as destructive as most children of the same age'. Age trends will be much influenced by what behaviours parents regard as 'destructive' and by their notions of how 'most children' of that age behave. It would be quite possible for there to be major changes in children's actual behaviour without it being reflected in changes in the ratings; conversely, children's behaviour could remain the same but the ratings show a change simply because parents' concepts of what is normal have altered with the child growing older. It is only very detailed interviewing or direct observation studies which can reduce the impact of these distortions (although they cannot entirely eliminate them). A further difficulty comes from the possibility that there may be changes in the central tendency for certain behaviours, but little or no alteration in the frequency of the same behaviour in its extreme form (or, of course, vice versa). Thus it could be that children, as a whole, show a marked tendency to be more negativistic and oppositional at about the age of 2–4, but that extreme negativism as an 'abnormal' behaviour shows no great age trend. With these caveats in mind we may now turn to the empirical findings.

So far as temper outbursts are concerned, the best developmental data are still provided by Goodenough's (1931) classical study of 2–7 year old children, which involved a combination of detailed daily reports from parents and direct observations. She found that anger outbursts reached their peak frequency for normal children during the second year. After the age of 2 years there was a progressive shortening of the more violent initial stage of angry behaviour, but also a lengthening of such after-effects as sulking, whining or brooding. During all the pre-school years after the first, over half of the outbursts arose from some conflict with parental authority – not surprisingly the content of the conflict tended to change with age, from issues over toileting and prohibited activities in the second year, to refusal to put away toys and clashes over clothing in the fifth year.

Other studies (Levy and Tulchin, 1923 and 1925; Macfarlane *et al.*, 1954), too, have suggested that 'negativism' is most prevalent during the pre-school years.

Disagreements with playmates were infrequent causes of tempers in the first three years in the Goodenough (1931) study, but accounted for a fifth of outbursts during the fourth and fifth years. Dawe (1934) found that younger nursery school children started more quarrels but the older ones were more likely to become physically aggressive; Appel (1942) also showed that among 2 year olds quarrels tended to centre around disputes over possessions, whereas in older children aggression arose over disputes concerning joint play. It is apparent, of course, that these age trends reflect changing patterns of emotional expression and alterations in children's peer relationships at least as much as they reflect developmental shifts in 'conduct disturbance'.

For trends during the school years we have to rely on either questionnaire (Shepherd et al., 1971) or interview (Macfarlane et al., 1954) data rather than observations. However, the evidence is fairly consistent in showing that tantrums are at a peak about the age of 3 and diminish steadily thereafter. Thus, in the Buckinghamshire study (Shepherd et al., 1971), weekly tantrums were reported for 10 per cent of 5 year olds but only 2 per cent of 15 year olds. On the other hand, in the Waltham Forest general population follow-up study of both normal and problem groups from 3 years to 8 years there was no change in the prevalence of 'tempers' between these two ages. However, this negative finding is as likely to mean that parents' perceptions of what is an 'abnormal' temper outburst have altered in relation to real changes in the children's behaviour, as that the frequency of tantrums failed to alter between 3 and 8 years. That is, the likelihood is that the true frequency of tantrums goes down with age but the parental tolerance of tantrums decreases in parallel.

Similar data may be used to examine age trends in other forms of socially disapproved behaviour. These show that, in the population as a whole, destructiveness and lying also tend to diminish after the pre-school years, although age trends for the extremes are less consistent (Macfarlane et al., 1954; Shepherd et al., 1971; Rutter and Yule, 1981). Rutter and Yule (1981) used the same teacher questionnaire with children aged 5, 9, 11 and 14 on the Isle of Wight (the 9 and 14 year old data refer to the same children studied at different stages in their school career). Between 5 and 9 years there was a substantial drop in the rates of destructiveness and bullying and stealing – the drop being greater for girls than boys. Between 9 and 14 years there was little further change. It seems highly probable that the meaning of these behaviours at 5 years (when tearing books, taking toys apart and taking other people's belongings more often seem to be extensions of normal childish activities rather than deliberately delinquent acts) is not the same as that in later childhood. Similarly, although empirical data are lacking, it would probably be found that scribbling and painting on wallpaper is at a peak during the pre-school years and falls thereafter. The rise in graffiti between 11 and 13 years (but slight drop between 13 and 15 years), evident on self-report data from Mortimore's (1978) study of London schoolchildren, almost certainly refers to a different type of behaviour in spite of the fact that phenomenologically both concern 'writing on walls'.

All data (self-report, teacher report and administrative statistics) are agreed in showing a marked increase in truanting, absconding and other forms of unjustified absence during the period of secondary schooling (Rutter and Yule, 1981; Mortimore, 1978; Rutter, 1979a). This generally reaches a peak during the final year of compulsory schooling.

The data on age trends during the school years discussed so far all refer to relatively specific behaviours of one type or another. Many forms of childish socially disapproved behaviour (such as tantrums or destructiveness) tend to diminish as children grow older; whereas others (such as truancy) increase. In order to complete the picture we need to consider more global measures of conduct disturbance. Very few findings on age trends with such measures are available. However, Kohn (1977), in his longitudinal study of 400 children in six New York day centres, included data for scores of a teacher questionnaire factor made up (at its negative end) of items concerned with anger, rebelliousness, cruelty and disruptiveness. Boys showed an increase in this form of disturbance between first and second grade, and girls a more gradual increase from first to third grade. In both sexes there was a fall between third and fourth grades (greater in girls than boys). The author interpreted the initial increase in disturbance on entering school as a response to the stresses of that environment. Data on changes between 10 and 14 years are provided by the Isle of Wight study, which showed that conduct disorders were of roughly similar frequency at both ages (Rutter, 1979a). Although comparisons across studies are hazardous in view of differing methodologies, the rate at 8 years in the Waltham Forest study (Richman *et al.*, 1982) appeared much the same. Similarly, mothers' questionnaire data from the Manhattan study of 6 to 18 year olds indicated that over the school years conflict with parents, fighting and delinquency all remained at about the same level, or increased slightly in frequency (Gersten *et al.*, 1976). Satisfactory data for comparison with the pre-school period are not available.

Longitudinal studies using criminal statistics, such as those by the Gluecks (1940), the McCords (1959), Wolfgang *et al.* (1972) and Robins (1966), show that patterns of delinquent activities in the same individuals tend to change as they get older (see Cline, 1980; West, 1982). In particular, theft and other property offences decline in frequency during the transition to adulthood, whereas violent crime increases during late adolescence to reach a peak in the early twenties, and both drunkenness and drug offences only become a common problem during early adult life.

Self-report data from the children themselves also show some age trends in the form of antisocial behaviour. For example, Shapland (1978), in a study from a town in the British Midlands, found that 24 per cent of 11–12 year olds said that they had stolen school property compared with 63 per cent of the *same* boys when re-interviewed at 13–14; similar trends were apparent for stealing from juke boxes or telephone kiosks, for truanting and for smashing or slashing public property. Farrington's (1973, 1981b) prospective study of London boys showed that the peak age for shoplifting was before 14 but that most offences reached a peak during the 15–18 period. Drug use and violence showed a particularly great increase during middle and later adolescence.

Thus, it is apparent that to some extent the patterns of antisocial behaviour change with increasing age. The self-report data also suggest a substantial increase during adolescence in the amount and range of delinquent *activities* (Shapland, 1978), although there is probably less change then in the number of *individuals* engaging in antisocial behaviour. Good data are lacking on just when stealing and other delinquent activities begin. Of course official statistics show that delinquency reaches a peak during the middle or late teens (Rutter, 1979a), with many individuals not receiving their first conviction until well into adolescence or even early adult life (Farrington, 1979; Cline, 1980). But this simply reflects the fact that, by law, young children cannot be convicted, that the police are less likely to prosecute young first offenders and that it may take some time for delinquent activities to be detected. Certainly, both self-report data and behavioural ratings from teachers and others make clear that most delinquent individuals already show some form of antisocial behaviour during middle childhood or pre-adolescence (Robins, 1978; Farrington, 1979; Cline, 1980). Little is known about delinquent activities or their precursors during the early primary school years.

The data already discussed suggested that, at least between 10 and 15 years, and probably between 8 and 15 years, it is likely that there is little change in the overall proportion of children showing disturbances of conduct, although patterns of behaviour and the administrative recognition of delinquent activities change during these years.

But, while rates of conduct disturbance may not change much during middle childhood and adolescence, both criminal statistics (Cline, 1980) and self-report data (Knight, Osborn and West, 1977) show that delinquent acts, as well as convictions, tend to diminish during early adult life to a substantial extent. Interestingly, the reduction in delinquent activities as young people enter adult life which is seen in official criminal statistics probably *under*estimates the change. Several studies have suggested that although the rate at which crimes are committed *decreases* with age, the chances of being caught and punished may increase* (Boland and Wilson, 1978). It seems that a juvenile is about twice as likely to get away with a robbery as an adult. Accordingly, it is probable that the real drop in delinquent activities between the mid-teens and the late twenties is even greater than appears.

Not only is it relatively uncommon for individuals to become seriously criminal for the first time in adult life (Robins, 1978) – although they may not necessarily have had convictions as juveniles (Farrington, 1979) – but also, many men who were recidivist delinquents during their adolescence give up their criminal activities during their twenties (Osborn and West, 1980). The Cambridge Study in Delinquent Development utilized detailed interview data to determine whether the lack of adult criminal convictions in this group was accompanied by changes in non-detected delinquent activities and by alterations in the men's general life style (Osborn and West, 1980). Juvenile recidivists with no convictions between the ages of 19 and 24 ('temporary recidivists') were compared with those who sustained convictions during that age period ('persisting recidivists'). The latter group were markedly different from non-delinquents in a wide range of life-style measures (they were more likely to have very heavy expenditure on tobacco and alcohol, more likely to have been in fights, and more likely to be providing grossly unsatisfactory care for their children). In contrast, with the exception of heavy smoking, most of the temporary recidivists were closely similar to the non-delinquents. It appeared that the giving up of criminal activities *was* associated with a real giving up of antisocial behaviour and with a change to a non-deviant life style.

It should be added that the persistence of delinquent activities is associated with their age of onset. Several studies have shown that the younger the age at first onset, the greater the number of re-arrests and the greater the likelihood of adult recidivism (see Sellin, 1958; Hamparian *et al.*, 1978; Sinclair and Clarke, 1981; West, 1982). In the Cambridge study, for example, 61 per cent of men first found guilty of offences before their fourteenth birthday were re-convicted between 19 and 25 years, compared with only 36

---

* Although, as Zimring (1979) points out, there are potential biases in the data which give rise to this conclusion.

per cent of those first convicted between the ages of 17 and 19. Persistence into adult life was also a function of the extent to which delinquent acts were or were not part of a generally antisocial life style as assessed at 18 years (using eleven characteristics such as high self-reported aggression, heavy gambling, an unstable job record and involvement in antisocial groups). Of the delinquents with a score of 5 or more on the antisocial life-style scale, 64 per cent had subsequent convictions as compared with 34 per cent for those with a score of 4 or less. This was *not* just a reflection of the number of previous convictions, as the antisocial life-style score predicted continuing recidivism even after that had been taken into account (Osborn and West, 1978). For example, of the men with two convictions by their nineteenth birthday and a high score, 68 per cent were re-convicted by the age of 23 compared with 30 per cent of those with two convictions but low scores. A familial record of criminality (in fathers or brothers) also predicted continuing recidivism in adult life, but other family variables were rather weaker predictors.

These findings are in keeping with earlier results based on convicted offenders (for example, Mannheim and Wilkins, 1955; Davies, 1969; Simon, 1971). These have shown that recidivism is most likely when there has been a court appearance at an early age; when the offender is a member of a delinquent group; when there are poor family relationships, a lack of firm consistent discipline, and a lack of family cohesion; when there are strikingly abnormal personality features; and when (in older boys) there is a poor work record and persistent heavy drinking.

Moral development

Because most delinquency takes the form of some kind of dishonest act, it might be thought that age trends in delinquent behaviour should reflect developmental changes in morality. However, the link between the two is quite tenuous. At about the age of 2, infants first show signs of becoming aware of adult standards, of recognizing that they can cause events that result in adult disapproval, and of being upset by that disapproval (Kagan, 1981). This sense of self-awareness may be said to constitute the beginning of morality; a beginning that seems to be a function of biological maturation in a social setting rather than of any particular pattern of upbringing. Of course, thereafter, the *specific* internal standards acquired by children will be influenced by their experiences inside and outside the family. Nevertheless, neither the subsequent course of moral development nor the factors that influence it are well established (Graham, 1980). Probably, helpful or altruistic behaviour increases in early childhood, at least up to the age of 8 or 9 (Bryan and London, 1970), but there do not appear to be any very consistent age trends in either honesty or resistance to temptation, although there is a progression with age in the kinds of reasons children give for moral behaviour (see Kohlberg, 1976). Young children's moral judgements tend to be based on matters of reward and punishment; in middle childhood there is a growing awareness of general rules and social conventions regarding behaviour, and at maturity there is said to be a morality of self-determined individual principles of conscience which may transcend such laws.

Clearly, there is likely to be some sort of connection between moral reasoning and different forms of moral behaviour, but research findings show that the connections are somewhat indirect and inconsistent (Blasi, 1980; Lickona, 1976; Jurkovic, 1980; Kupfersmid and Wonderly, 1980). Certainly some individuals are generally more honest than others, but people's tendency to behave honestly or resist temptations varies considerably according to situations and circumstances. Moreover, there are rather weak associations between how people behave and the maturity of their moral judgements. Probably there is a slight tendency for delinquents to use rather immature styles of moral reasoning, but as a group they are quite heterogeneous morally and, at least as studied up to now, knowledge on the course of moral development has shed little light either on the development of delinquent behaviour or on its continuation or cessation.

Continuity and course of antisocial behaviour

Given that the *rates* of conduct disturbance do not change greatly during the secondary school years (although they do in adult life), the next question is to what extent is this a function of continuities in antisocial behaviour at an *individual* level. In other words, are the rates made up of the same individuals at each age, or, rather, do a large number of children show conduct disturbances at some point in their development but with these rarely persisting for long? While the answer depends to some extent on how conduct disturbances are assessed, the weight of evidence certainly suggests a very substantial degree of continuity at least during the school years.

Of course, as self-report data show, the *majority* of boys commit some form of delinquent act at some stage in their development so that, in itself, this can scarcely be regarded as abnormal. On the other hand, most of these acts are of a fairly trivial nature and more serious delinquencies are decidedly less common. Thus, Shapland (1978) found that 96 per cent of boys admitted, at the age of either 11 or 14, that they had trespassed somewhere they were not supposed to go: 80 per cent had gone into a bar when under age; but only about half that many had stolen from large stores; and a mere 8 per cent had broken into a shop, store or garage. The figures from other studies (for example, Belson, 1975; Gold, 1970; Farrington, 1973) show a generally similar pattern, and it is clear that, even on self-report data, serious or frequent delinquency is a minority phenomenon. In this connection, it is relevant to note that minor delinquencies follow a pattern which, in some respects, is rather different from serious or persisting delinquency (Hindelang, Hirschi and Weis, 1979). For example, there is a lesser sex difference with minor offences and also a weaker association with social class.

Nevertheless, although serious or frequent delinquent activities are shown by only a relatively small proportion of boys (and an even lower proportion of girls), quite a substantial minority of young people (especially in the large cities) appear in the courts and are found guilty of some offence. For example, West and Farrington (1973 and 1977), in a general population study of working-class London boys, found that some 30 per cent had acquired a criminal record by the age of 21; Ouston (1983) found a rate of 29 per cent for boys and 6 per cent for girls by the age of 17 in another inner London sample; Havighurst *et al.* (1962) found that 39 per cent of boys and 8 per cent of girls in a mid-western U.S. city had some contact with the police during adolescence, and in a longitudinal study by Wolfgang *et al.* (1972) of Philadelphia boys the delinquency rate was about 35 per cent. The figures from other studies are in the same general range (Farrington, 1979). On the other hand, in each of these studies about half of these delinquents have only one conviction before adult life and only about half go on to have an adult crime record (West and Farrington, 1977; Farrington, 1979).

Very few data are available on the continuities in disturbances of conduct in early childhood. Minde and Minde (1977), in a nine-month follow-up of children registered for junior kindergarten in Toronto, found a high persistence for temper tantrums (91 per cent) and for difficulties in management (73 per cent) in the small group of children with general behavioural deviance when first seen, but rather lower persistence for the same behaviours among controls (36 per cent and 32 per cent respectively). These same behaviours showed an association with aggressivity–hostility at school – an association which stood out in contrast to the generally very low level of concordance between parent and teacher ratings.*

Richman *et al.* (1982), using similar measures, provide data on continuities

---

* Low correlations between parent and teacher ratings have also been found in older age groups of children (Rutter et al., 1970; Shepherd et al., 1971).

between 3 and 8 years in the Waltham Forest epidemiological/ longitudinal study. Of the children with clinically significant disorders at the age of 3, 62 per cent still showed disorders at 8 compared with a rate of 22 per cent with disorder in the control group. In that the disorders were not classified according to type at 3, it is not possible to determine persistence separately for disturbances of conduct. However, it was found that the factors associated with persistence included male sex (73 per cent persistence *v.* 48 per cent for girls); difficulties in management at 4 years (81 per cent *v.* 49 per cent for those without that behaviour); and high activity level at 4 years (87 per cent *v.* 45 per cent). Also, conduct disorders in boys at 8 years were those most likely to be associated with prior behavioural difficulties at 3 years. Putting the findings together, it is evident that most of the boys with extreme restlessness and/or marked difficulties in management at 3 or 4 were showing conduct disorders at 8. The same degree of persistence was not found for girls, with the consequence that tantrums and difficulties in management showed a male preponderance at 8 which had not been evident at 3.

The findings are paralleled by those from the Fels longitudinal study (Kagan and Moss, 1962), which showed that, in the sample as a whole (as distinct from a problem group), aggressiveness and 'behavioural disorganization' (meaning destructive acts, rages and tantrums) in the preschool years showed greater persistence into the middle childhood years for boys than for girls.

Further data on continuities in conduct disturbance in middle childhood come from Kohn's (1977) longitudinal study of New York day-care children. Pooled scores for grades 1 and 2 on the anger-defiance (conduct disturbance) factor correlated 0.60 with pooled scores on the same factor for grades 3 and 4. Even after partialling out the effects of both demographic variables and other aspects of behaviour, the correlation was still highly significant ($p < 0.001$) and of moderate size (0.36).

Olweus (1979) has reviewed the limited evidence on the temporal stability in early childhood of aggressivity in males, which indicates uncorrected correlations of 0.48 to 0.72 over periods of 6 to 18 months for both direct observation data and teacher ratings. However, apart from the studies discussed above, no data are available on the strength of the links between the pre-school years and middle or later childhood.

Much more is known regarding the continuities in disturbance of conduct in older children. In his review, Olweus (1979) concludes that the correlation (corrected for attenuation) between two measures of aggression separated by time ranges from about 0.75 when the time interval is 1 year to about 0.4

when the time interval is 21 years. Of course, the use of correction factors is open to objection and may give rise to artificially high correlations; nevertheless, however assessed, it is clear that there is a substantial degree of consistency over time.

This conclusion, although well substantiated by the empirical findings, runs counter to commonly held views, and it is necessary to consider some of the main reasons why aggressivity has sometimes appeared to show low longitudinal consistency. Olweus (1980a) points out that some of the low correlations over time are a consequence of low reliability; but, in addition, some of the measures refer to highly specific behaviours as measured over a very brief span of time in just one restricted environment. Such limited measures provide an inadequate basis for the measurement of any postulated general style of behaviour. Although cross-situational consistency is greater than sometimes claimed, nevertheless, of course, individuals do behave in somewhat different ways in different circumstances. Moreover, they may show aggression in a variety of different specific behaviours. If the intention is to assess a general characteristic of behaviour, it is necessary to sample behaviour in several different ways or on several occasions (Epstein, 1979). *Composite* measures of this kind show quite substantial consistencies over time. This conclusion is by no means confined to aggression; it is a general feature of the measurement of behaviour. Thus, single sub-tests in any broad-range test of intelligence (such as the Wechsler scales) show rather low longitudinal consistency (because they are relatively unreliable and because they tap specific as well as general attributes) – in contrast to the much greater consistency of I.Q. scores based on whole tests.

The same issue of consistency may be examined in a different way by determining the extent to which a varied range of measures of troublesome, difficult or socially disapproved behaviours in elementary school relate to delinquency as shown in adolescence. Studies of this kind (Conger and Miller, 1966; Farrington, 1978; Havighurst *et al.*, 1962; Ouston, 1983; Robins, 1978; West and Farrington, 1973 and 1977; Wolfgang *et al.*, 1972) show substantial continuities. For example, West and Farrington (1973), using a combination of teacher ratings at 8 and 10 years and peer ratings at 10 years, found that of the most troublesome children 27 per cent became recidivist delinquents, in marked contrast to the rate of 0.7 per cent among the least troublesome children. Expressed in reverse fashion, it is apparent that 68 per cent of recidivists had been in the most troublesome group at primary school compared with 12 per cent of non-delinquents.

However, this behavioural continuity is much greater with recidivism than with children who receive only one conviction. Thus, in the same West and

Farrington (1973) study, only 34 per cent of one-time delinquents were in the most troublesome category at the age of 8–10. Similarly, Ouston (1983) found that whereas 45 per cent of boys with at least three convictions had shown deviant behaviour on teachers' ratings at the age of 10 (compared with 22 per cent of non-delinquents), this was so for only 23 per cent of those with just one or two court appearances.

Interestingly, in contrast to the findings on conduct disturbance at the preschool period, delinquency in girls was much more strongly associated with prior behavioural deviance than was the case with boys (Rutter et al., 1979). Of the girls with low scores on the teachers' questionnaire at the age of 10, only 4 per cent became delinquent compared with 21 per cent among those with conduct-type deviance. Apparently, many boys *without* general problems of conduct disturbance become one-time delinquents (although far fewer become recidivist), whereas this is less often the case with girls. In girls even a single conviction often tends to have been preceded by previous indications of troublesome, difficult or disturbed behaviour.

The course and outcome of children's conduct disturbances has been demonstrated in several longitudinal and follow-up studies with highly consistent findings (see Robins, 1979; Farrington, 1979; Cline, 1980). As already noted, about half the youths who receive a conviction as juveniles do not appear in court again, and even among those with several convictions a substantial proportion cease offending in early adult life. To that extent, the long-term outcome for delinquency must be regarded as fairly good in that their criminal 'career' comes to an end. Moreover, as Osborn and West (1980) showed, at least in their study, this was usually associated with the taking up of a generally normal pattern of social activities and personal relationships. However, this optimistic conclusion must have several caveats. Not only is the Osborn and West follow-up the only one with detailed data on social functioning, but it extends only to the age of 24. Earlier data from their own study showed that a parent's criminal record in the distant past was still associated with a substantially increased risk of delinquency in the sons (Osborn and West, 1979). This may well be because criminality is associated with unemployment, dependence on welfare (Knight and West, 1977) and poor supervision (West and Farrington, 1973) – features which may continue after criminal activities cease. Of course, whether this implies genetic transmission, or the effects of labelling, or the continuation of some form of non-criminal personal deviance in the ex-delinquent parent which affects the upbringing of the children, remains quite uncertain. Be that as it may, it is clear that in many cases delinquency proves to be a transient phenomenon with few identifiable sequelae at least in early adult life.

However, to a considerable extent these transient delinquents have appeared different from recidivist delinquents (and more similar to non-delinquents) from the outset. Quite apart from the measures of troublesome behaviour already discussed, one-time delinquents are less deviant than recidivists in their family background and characteristics, in their educational accomplishments, in the extent and nature of their self-reported antisocial activities, and in their social life patterns (West and Farrington, 1973 and 1977). It would be quite misleading to consider these one-time delinquents as unexceptionable apart from the delinquent act(s) which led to their conviction, in that they did differ significantly from non-delinquents in a host of ways. Nevertheless, the differences were much less than those found with recidivists. Expressed another way, it is evident that the greater the weighting of personal or family factors associated with delinquency the greater the likelihood that the delinquency will continue (Osborn and West, 1978).

These findings help to explain why the outcome for delinquency (as assessed from follow-up studies of children or adolescents appearing before the courts) appears rather better than the outcome either for conduct disorders in young people referred to psychiatric clinics or for those whose conduct disturbance is defined in terms of deviance on multiple indicators. Not only are these latter groups more likely to show a pervasive disturbance of personality functioning and more likely to come from a seriously disturbed family, but also the follow-ups have usually been based on a much wider range of social indicators than just the presence or absence of reconvictions. Research findings have been consistent in showing that clinic-referred children with conduct disorders are more likely than children with emotional disorders (and much more likely than those without disorder) to show persisting psychiatric and social impairment.

This has been apparent in follow-up studies from childhood to adolescence, as in the Isle of Wight inquiries (Graham and Rutter, 1973), and in the comparable follow-up from 10–14 in inner London (Rutter, 1977c). It has been similarly shown in the follow-up studies from adolescence to early adult life (Masterson, 1958 and 1967; Annesley, 1961; Warren, 1965); and also in the long-term follow-ups from childhood to adulthood (Morris *et al.*, 1956; Michael *et al.*, 1957; Michael, 1957; Mellsop, 1972; Robins, 1966). It is clear that the prognosis for conduct disorders is generally worse than that for emotional disorders regardless of the age of ascertainment (in spite of the suggestion to the contrary by Gersten *et al.*, 1976). Moreover, the same studies also show that the disorders tend to run true to form in that adult antisocial personality disorders have almost always been preceded by conduct disturbances in childhood (Robins, 1978). Emotional disorder in childhood or adolescence rarely leads on to sociopathy or antisocial behaviour in adult life. On the other hand, the reverse is not true. Conduct disorders tend to be followed by a wide range of emotional, social, and relationship problems in addition to antisocial behaviour – hence the use of the term 'sociopathy' (Robins, 1966 and 1978). As a consequence, conduct disorders may sometimes be followed by emotional disorders, at least for a time (Graham and Rutter, 1973). Of course, too, many youngsters with conduct disturbances also grow up to be reasonably well-functioning adults – none of the follow-up studies of antisocial children have shown rates of adult sociopathy in excess of 50 per cent or so.

Comparable follow-ups of high-risk groups in the general population (Robins, 1978) have given rise to very closely comparable findings, so that it is clear that the conclusions are not restricted to clinic samples. Rather they apply to any group of boys showing a wide variety of frequent antisocial activities. Robins has summarized the findings as follows:

(1) adult antisocial behavior virtually *requires* childhood antisocial behavior;
(2) most antisocial children do *not* become antisocial adults;
(3) the variety of antisocial behavior in childhood is a better predictor of adult antisocial behavior than is any particular behavior;
(4) adult antisocial behavior is better predicted by childhood *behavior* than by family background or social class of rearing;
(5) social class makes little contribution to the prediction of serious adult antisocial behavior. [Emphasis added.]

These conclusions appear reasonably well supported so far as serious and persisting adult antisocial behaviour *as a whole* is concerned. However, the West and Farrington (1977) longitudinal study of London boys showed that a minority of adult criminals were free of significant conduct disturbance during childhood – as judged both by their own contemporaneous self-reports and by teaching ratings as well as by court records. Hence, it seems that criminal behaviour *can* begin for the first time in adult life. Moreover, when it does it is particularly associated with a family background of low social status and parental criminality, but *not* so much with the measures of poor parental behaviour and poor supervision associated with delinquency that begins in childhood and persists into adult life. Thus, although certainly there are substantial links between socially disapproved behaviour in childhood and similar behaviour in adult life, there are also important discontinuities.

The question remains, however, on how far the links that do exist extend over time and, in particular, how far conduct disturbances in very early childhood lead on to adult antisocial behaviour. Although it is clear that the longer the duration of time the less strong the links, almost no data on children with disorders are available to link infancy with adulthood. The nearest approach is the Fels longitudinal study, which looked at the long-term predictive power of 'behavioural disorganization' in the pre-school years (Kagan and Moss, 1962). Very low correlations with adolescent and adult ratings were found, but the findings apply to ratings in a basically normal sample and it cannot necessarily be assumed that the same would apply to a much more deviant clinic sample (although, of course, they might well do).

The scope and value of different forms of therapeutic intervention are discussed in detail in Chapter 9. Here it is necessary only to touch on the question of whether there are effective treatments and, if there are, whether they modify any of the conclusions above on course and outcome. Earlier reviews have generally concluded that all forms of intervention have proved ineffective, but recent work suggests that this may be unduly negative. Nevertheless, it remains true that no form of treatment or of penal response has had sufficient effect to alter the general pattern of findings on course and continuity outlined above.

Implications for views on personality development

That raises, perhaps, the implications of the findings for general conclusions on continuities and discontinuities in personality development. Does the relative consistency in behavioural functioning, as evident with respect to disorders of conduct, together with the evidence on the very limited impact of therapeutic interventions, imply that personality characteristics are established early in development and are very difficult to alter thereafter? There are many reasons why this would be a totally inappropriate conclusion. In the first place, the continuities found are of only moderate strength, so that there is plenty of room for change at all stages of development. Secondly, it is helpful to differentiate between 'continuity', meaning that a person shows the same *behaviour* across different time periods, and 'stability', meaning that an individual retains the same *position* over time relative to others on a behavioural dimension – to use Emmerich's (1964, 1968) terminology. The implication is that, relatively speaking, a person may continue to be more antisocial than his peers but that in absolute terms his overall level of antisocial activity may nevertheless fall. Indeed, this is what the changes in early adult life reflect for many individuals.

Thirdly, it is necessary to differentiate between stability in behaviour over *time* and consistency over *space*. As Mischel (1979) puts it: 'No one seriously questions that lives have continuity and that we perceive ourselves and others as relatively stable individuals who have substantial identity and stability over time, even when our specific actions change across situations. But although ... [this] is not in dispute, there is serious disagreement about the nature, degree and meaning of the cross-situational breadth of behaviors ...'. In fact, there is some evidence regarding the importance of situational influences in affecting the *overall level* of antisocial behaviour in that context (see Rutter, 1979a), although such influences may not greatly alter the relative ranking of individuals with respect to antisocial behaviour across the contexts. Thus, the finding of situation effects does not invalidate the notion of personality traits (Eysenck and Eysenck, 1980). However, it may also be that individual predispositions help determine how people respond to different situations (Epstein, 1979). Not only may there be person–situation interactions, but also some individuals may be much less influenced than others by situations. In this connection, it may be relevant that the greatest situational effects have usually been found with non-deviant samples rather than with the persistently antisocial individuals considered here.

Finally, it is important to recognize that, at least in part, the lack of lasting effects of the various forms of intervention is due to the presence, rather than the absence, of situational effects. As Clarke and Cornish (1978) and O'Donnell (1977) point out, it is not that residential treatments are without an impact on current behaviour. To the contrary, institutional environments appear to have a marked influence on current behaviour; it is just that the benefits do not persist when the young people return home to a totally different environment which maintains its delinquency-producing characteristics. They suggest that the implication is that efforts might be better directed towards changing the home environment rather than attempting to alter individual characteristics. How far that is either practicable or useful remains to be determined. Nevertheless, the suggestion does underline the fact that we really do not know how far the continuities over time in antisocial behaviour are mainly a function of the importance of individual personality features, and how far a function of the effects of a relatively unchanging noxious environment.

Conclusions

During the pre-school years, the taking of other people's possessions, temper tantrums, angry outbursts, lying, tearing books and breaking toys are all quite common. These socially disapproved behaviours become progressively less frequent from the age of 4 or 5 onwards, although there may be a temporary increase on starting school. It is observations of this kind which have led some theorists (see Chapter 8) to argue that children start antisocial and *learn* later to be prosocial. However, although it is apparent that some recidivist delinquents were already showing over-active disruptive behaviour in the pre-school years, we know rather little about the continuities and discontinuities between these normal childish 'antisocial' activities and later delinquency. There are some links in extreme groups, but we lack good evidence on the generality or strength of the associations over time.

There seems to be little change between 8 or 10 years and 15 years in the overall proportion of children showing some form of antisocial behaviour. However, during adolescence there is a substantial increase in the amount and range of delinquent activities – as well as a change in pattern (with truanting, serious vandalism, and stealing from juke boxes or telephone kiosks becoming more common). Other crimes, especially violent crime, increase during late adolescence. But although the amount of delinquent *activities* increases, it is likely that there is a much smaller increase in the number of *individuals* engaging in antisocial behaviour.

Then during early adult life, as assessed from both self-reports and official statistics, there is a marked fall in criminal behaviour – with many juvenile offenders ceasing to be delinquent. While a few individuals turn to crime for the first time in adult life, this is not a common occurrence (and is far less frequent than the giving up of crime), so that the effect is a striking reduction in the rate of delinquent activities during the early and middle twenties.

Against this background of a marked drop in the rate of crime in early adult life, there is additional evidence showing substantial continuities in antisocial behaviour at an *individual* level. That is to say, although delinquent activities constitute a 'passing phase' in many boys, in others it poses a most persistent problem. Moreover, the individuals who are most delinquent or aggressive or antisocial at one age tend also to be those most delinquent/ aggressive/antisocial at later ages. This persistence over time tends to be most marked in those who started their delinquent activities unusually early, and in those whose delinquent acts form part of a broader pattern of social and interpersonal difficulties.

During the last ten years or so there has been much dispute in psychology over the respective merits of 'trait' and 'situational' approaches to personality development. But recently there has been a considerable rapprochement between these views, as it has become apparent that they deal with different, but complementary, aspects of behavioural functioning. Situational influences are indeed important in affecting the overall level of antisocial behaviour in any particular context, but such influences may not greatly alter the relative ranking of individuals with respect to antisocial behaviour across contexts. Thus, a particular child may be consistently more likely than his peers to engage in delinquent activities (the importance of 'traits'), but whether in fact he engages in such activities will depend to a considerable extent on the situation he finds himself in (the importance of 'situations'). Also, however, it is apparent that some of the continuities over time in individual behaviour are due to a lack of change in the environment as well as to characteristics of the individual.

Official statistics

But the official statistics do suggest that there has been a very substantial increase in crime during the last half century or so since the First World War, with a particularly sharp rise between the mid-50s and mid-60s (Radzinowicz and King, 1977). Six main periods can be discerned (McClintock and Avison, 1968; Home Office, 1978). From 1900 until the beginning of the First World War the crime rate remained fairly stable; during the next fifteen years it rose about 5 per cent per annum; it then fluctuated but remained roughly stable until 1954; over the next ten years crime increased at the record rate of about 10 per cent per annum; during the next decade or so crime continued to increase but at a more variable and, in general, somewhat slower rate, with a levelling off or possibly even a fall in the last few years. It appears that the increase in recidivism has been greater than that for first offences, and McClintock and Avison (1968) estimated that, allowing for population changes, convictions had trebled whereas crime had increased nine-fold.

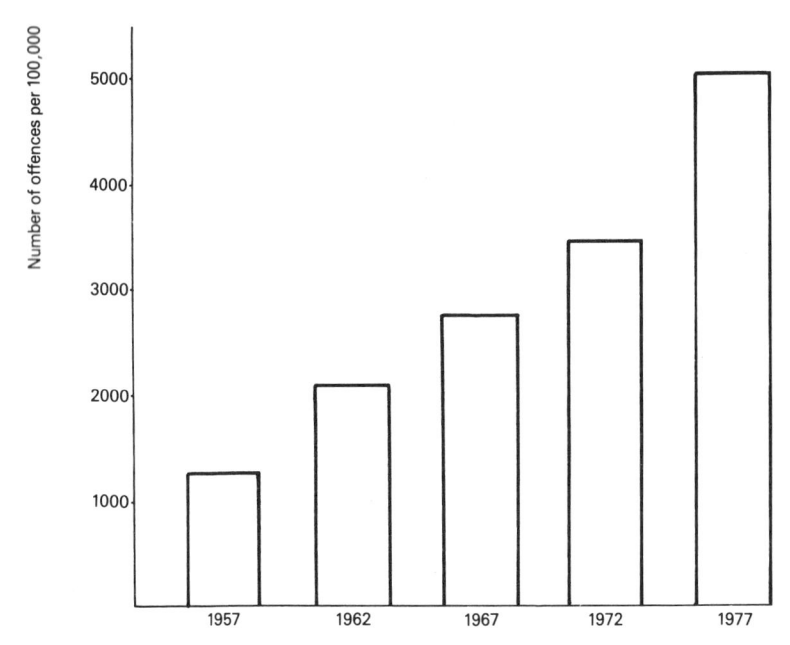

Figure 1.   *Indictable offences per 100,000 population (1957–77) (from Table 2.2, Home Office, 1980)*

3
Historical Trends

A concern over 'crime waves' and rising levels of juvenile delinquency is far from a new phenomenon (see, for example, Gibbs, 1974; Pearson, 1975; Springhall, 1977). West (1967) quotes a report on the English scene published in 1818:

> The lamentable depravity which, for the last few years, has shown itself so conspicuously among the young of both sexes, in the Metropolis and its environs, occasioned the formation of a Society for investigating the causes of the increase of Juvenile Delinquency.

Comparisons with previous centuries are problematic but, as Pearson (1975) points out, it is quite likely that there have been times in the past when violence and lawlessness have been at least as great a problem as they are supposed to be now. He draws attention to 'Engels's fiery Manchester', 'the foggy streets and rookeries of Dickens's London' and 'Edwardian England when "scuttlers" and "ikes" roamed the streets, much in the same way that the "mugger" haunts the "inner city" today'. Indeed, there is good empirical evidence that, at least in some respects, the situation today is *better* than it was in days gone by. For example, offences of drunkenness fell by half between 1911 and 1975 (Donnan and Haskey, 1977), and the proportion of the population incarcerated in prison during the last half of the nineteenth century was considerably higher than it is today (West, 1967). Crime statistics, too, suggest that violent assaults were at a peak in the eighteenth century, and that most forms of crime showed a decline during the mid-nineteenth century (Gurr *et al.*, 1977). Indeed, the detailed historical analyses by Gurr and his colleagues showed that there was a consistent trend in most Western societies for crime rates to fall steadily and markedly over the 100 years from the early nineteenth century to just after the First World War. There is no reason to suppose that crime now is generally more prevalent than in earlier centuries. To the contrary, the overall picture suggests that theft and violence were more of a problem 150 years ago than they are today.

During the years since the Second World War, crimes of violence against the person have shown a particularly marked increase, although the rise began during the mid-1930s.

The total population figures for the period 1957 to 1977 are summarized in Figure 1, which shows a 290 per cent increase over those two decades. The official crime statistics (Home Office, 1980) show that the increases have been apparent in all parts of Britain. However, the pattern can be seen more readily if the figures are given separately for several major urban/metropolitan centres and for some police forces in parts of the country which are largely made up of small towns and rural areas (see Table 1). It is clear that the increase in crime rates between 1921 and 1971 was a universal phenomenon. At all times the rates of crime in the big cities has exceeded that

Table 1 Indictable crimes known to the police per 1,000 population for selected years and police forces (Data provided by Home Office)

Police Force	1921	1931	1938	1953	1971
Metropolitan Police	2.3	3.2	11.0	11.9	43.1
Birmingham	1.6	3.4	6.2	11.7	48.6
Liverpool and Bootle	12.4	14.1	16.1	22.4	73.9
Manchester and Salford	2.8	4.2	6.2	21.0	84.0
Sheffield and Rotherham	3.0	6.7	6.6	9.0	33.9
Devon and Cornwall	1.7	3.5	5.6	10.2	26.0
Lincolnshire	2.3	3.6	6.0	9.5	33.9
Suffolk	1.4	1.7	2.9	8.8	21.2
North Wales	2.1	2.2	3.1	7.0	31.8
Cumbria	2.2	2.2	3.0	6.6	26.7

Notes:
1. Definitions of indictable crimes have changed over time.
2. Area boundaries may have changed slightly over time.

in rural areas, but the large proportional increase has occurred in all parts of the country.

Nevertheless, there are curious and unexplained differences in the extent and timing of the change in crime rate in different police forces, with resulting alterations in the rankings. For example, in 1921 the crime rate in Liverpool/ Bootle (12.4 per 1,000) was several times that in Manchester/Salford (2.8), but as a result of massive increases in the latter area between 1938 and 1953 (6.2 to 21.0) and between 1953 and 1971 (21.0 to 84.0), the rate in Manchester/Salford in 1971 exceeded that in Liverpool/Bootle (84.0 compared with 73.9). Similarly, the rise in crime rate in most areas between 1938 and 1953 did not apply in London to any significant extent (an increase from 11.0 to 11.9 only). In all areas the increase in crime rate tended to be greatest between 1953 and 1971.

Throughout this century, the great bulk of crime has always involved stealing of one kind or another (Home Office, 1980). While simple theft is still the commonest variety of stealing, there have been some interesting changes in distribution since the Second World War. Most especially, there has been a disproportionate increase in shoplifting (which has increased from 3 per cent of the total in 1945 to 14 per cent in 1978), taking of motor cycles (from 1 per cent to 22 per cent), and in thefts from motor vehicles (8 per cent to 20 per cent). Thefts of pedal cycles have declined over the same period (15 per cent to 7 per cent).

Crimes of violence comprise less than 4 per cent of recorded crime (Home Office, 1980), but this class of offence has shown one of the greatest increases throughout the post-war period – from 4,746 in 1945 to 94,960 in 1979. Within this offence category, however, there have been major changes in the pattern of recorded offences. In 1945, 28 per cent of violent crimes against the person were of the most serious nature (such as homicide or serious wounding). By 1975, the proportion had dropped to 9 per cent and by 1979 it was a mere 6 per cent. The main factor leading to this redistribution seems to have been a massive increase in non-serious wounding. However, the fall in the *proportion* of most serious violence was not associated with a fall in the *absolute* amount. To the contrary, serious violence has also increased substantially since the Second World War; it is just that the rate of increase has not been anything like as great as that for more petty violence.

As we discuss in more detail below, this general pattern of rising crime rates over the last two or three decades has been a pervasive phenomenon in most Western societies, with broadly comparable changes occurring in both Europe and the United States (see, for example, Bronfenbrenner, 1976; Gurr, 1979; Zimring, 1978 and 1979).

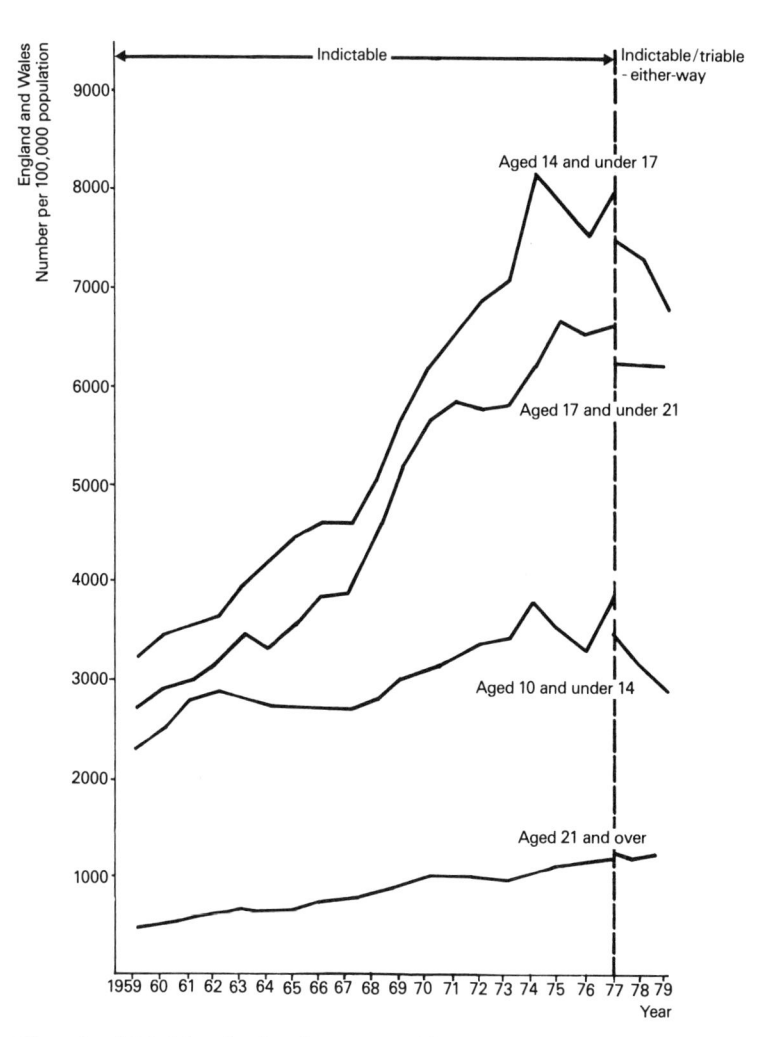

Figure 2. *Males[1] found guilty of, or cautioned for, indictable/triable-either-way offences[2] per 100,000 population in the age group by age (Home Office, 1980)*

1. Other offenders, i.e. companies, public bodies etc., are included with males aged 21 and over because separate figures are not available before 1976.
2. Adjusted for changes in legislation.

70 Juvenile Delinquency

These figures given so far apply to the population as a whole, and it is necessary now to consider how far the trends apply also to children and adolescents. In fact, it is clear that the trends are at least as evident for juveniles as they are for adults, as illustrated in Figures 2 and 3. Thus, the number of offenders per 100,000 population rose from 3,224 in 1959 to 7,995 in 1977 for males aged 14–17, an increase of 148 per cent, compared to a rise of 136 per cent for males aged 21 and over. The comparable figures for females showed a rise of 379 per cent for those aged 14–17 and 281 per cent for those aged 21 and over. The same data emphasize that there has been little change in the crime rates for boys since the mid-70s. For example, the rate of offenders per 100,000 population of 14–17 year olds was 8,191 in 1974 and 7,858 in 1978. For females, however, rates have continued to rise, albeit at a slower rate. The comparable figures for 1974 and 1978 were 1,490 and 1,617.

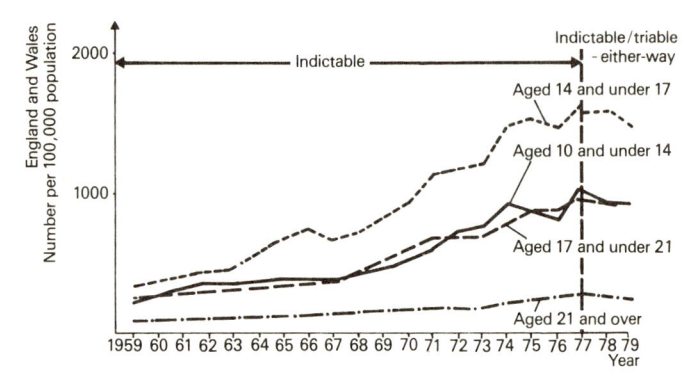

Figure 3. *Females found guilty of, or cautioned for, indictable/triable-either-way offences*[1] *per 100,000 population in the age group by age* (*Home Office, 1980*)

1. Adjusted for changes in legislation.

The result of this greater and more prolonged rise in female delinquency has led to a major alteration in the male–female ratio for delinquency in 14 to 17 year olds (see Figure 4). In 1957 the ratio was 10.79 to 1, but by 1977 it had fallen to 4.97 to 1 – more than a halving of the male crime preponderance. This disproportionate increase in female delinquency is also evident in U.S. figures (see Steffensmeier, 1978).

Table 2 provides a breakdown of the crime trends between 1950 and 1978 for 14 to 17 year olds according to type of offence. As in adults, much the

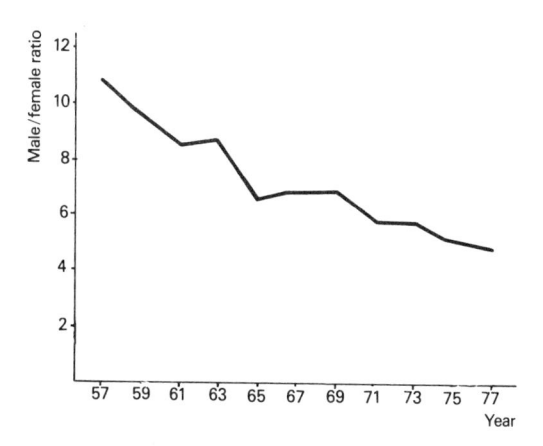

Figure 4. *Sex ratio for indictable offence rates in 14–17 year olds (Data from Home Office, 1978)*

Table 2 14–16 year old males found guilty 1950–78, by type of offence (Data provided by Home Office)

Offence	1950	1955	1960	1965	1970	1978	% Increase 1950–78
Larcency	10,073	9,434	15,290	21,587	26,706	37,946[1]	+276%[2]
Breaking & entering	4,219	3,550	7,789	10,800	16,164	21,320	+405%
Robbery	83	69	140	238	516	681	+720%
Violence against the person	190	334	1,238	1,714	2,512	4,738	+2,394%
Fraud/False pretences	42	74	134	189	389	846	+1,914%
Receiving/Handling stolen goods	560	515	1,206	2,037	2,911	—[3]	+420%[4]

1. Includes receiving/handling stolen goods.
2. Probably an over-estimate because it includes receiving/handling stolen goods.
3. No separate listing, included with larceny.
4. Based on 1970 figures – hence probably an under-estimate.

greatest increase is seen with offences involving violence against the person – the largest proportional increase for this offence occurring between 1955 and 1960. Larcency showed the least increase, but even so between 1950 and 1970 the number of offences more than doubled, and again the greatest proportional change occurred in the late 1950s.

Cautioning and other changes in police practice

As discussed in the previous chapter, many factors and happenings intervene between the committing of a delinquent act and conviction in a juvenile court. As only a very small proportion of delinquent acts result in conviction, we need to consider the possibility that the rise in crime rate has been a result of variations in these other factors rather than of any change either in the amount of delinquent activities or in the number of individuals engaging in such activities.

One of the most striking changes in practice in recent years has been the massive increase in the use of police cautioning (Home Office, 1980). White Papers (Home Office, 1965, 1968) during the 1960s encouraged the use of cautioning by the police, and the 1969 Children and Young Persons Act gave statutory recognition to this procedure as a means of diverting children from the courts. Most police forces set up juvenile bureaux to make the decision whether or not to refer particular children to the juvenile court. The bureaux are not regarded as a specialist department and little formal training is given to the officers running them. However, a special selection of volunteers is made, and qualities of understanding juvenile problems are looked for (see Oliver, 1973 and 1978, for a description of the Metropolitan Police bureaux).

The usual procedure, once it has been established that the child has committed an offence, is for the bureau staff to collect information about the child from their own records, from social services, from the school, and from other relevant agencies, and usually there is a visit to the child's home. On the basis of this information, the chief inspector in the bureau decides on the most appropriate course of action for that child – to take no further action, to caution, or to prosecute. There are four criteria for a caution: (i) the available evidence must be sufficient to sustain a successful prosecution; (ii) the juvenile must admit the offence and that he knew it was wrong; (iii) the parent must consent to the use of cautioning; and (iv) the victim of the crime must consent to leave the matter to the police. The caution is usually administered in a formal way to bring home the gravity of the occasion. In most areas that is usually the end of the matter, but sometimes the police undertake follow-up supervision and offer guidance and advice. They

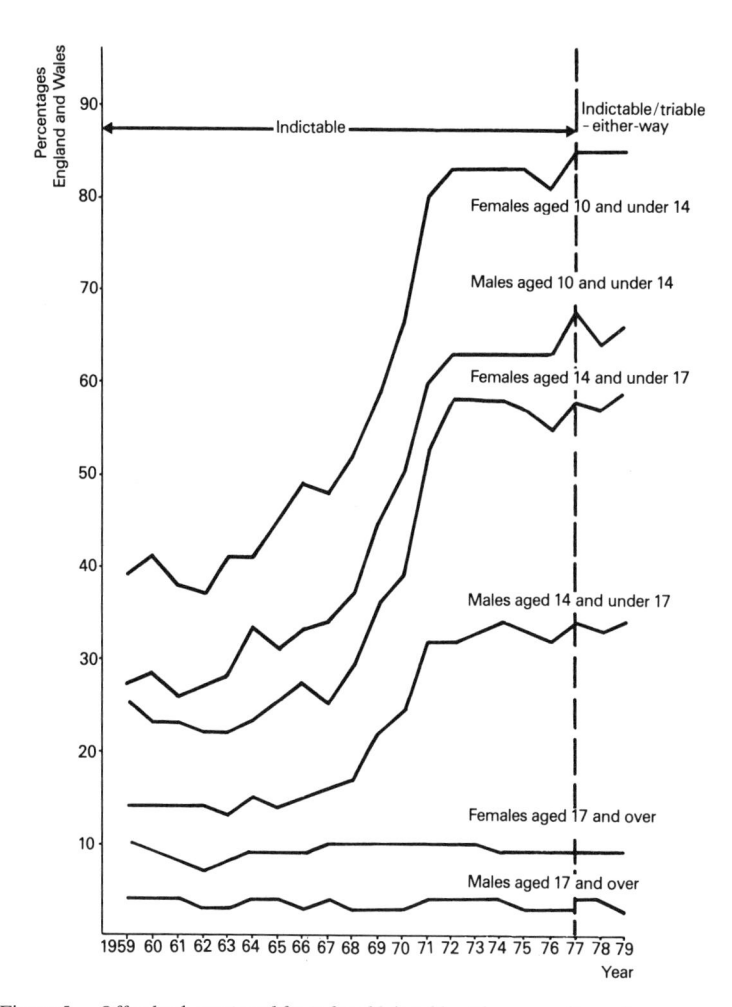

Figure 5. *Offenders[1] cautioned for indictable/triable-either-way offences[2] as a percentage of offenders found guilty or cautioned, by age (Home Office, 1980)*

1. Other offenders, i.e. companies, public bodies etc., are included with males aged 17 and over because separate figures are not available before 1976.
2. Adjusted for changes in legislation.

may also refer the child to the social service department on a voluntary basis.

In 1959, 26 per cent of male offenders aged 10 and under 14 were cautioned for indictable offences; by 1978 this had risen to 64 per cent (see Figure 5). For girls of the same age the increase over the same time period was from 39 per cent to 84 per cent. Similar increases occurred in the 14–17 age group; but in all years, younger children were more likely to receive cautions, and within any age group girls more so than boys.

This increase in cautioning has been associated with alterations in the pattern of convictions which differ by age group (see Figures 6(a) and (b), and 7(a) and (b)). In boys under the age of 14, the marked increase in the use of cautions has been accompanied by a *decrease* in the number convicted. The implication is that young people who would have appeared in court before were now being cautioned and hence were being 'diverted' from the courts. However, two other changes occurred at the same time. Firstly, there was a reduction in the number of non-indictable offences – largely as a result of changes in legislation (see below) – and secondly, when cautions and convictions for both non-indictable and indictable offences are summated, it is clear that the overall effect was an increase in processing for 10 to 14 year olds – from 39,329 in 1955 to 61,069 in 1978. The question arises as to whether 'diversion' was accompanied by a 'widening of the net', so that juveniles who might previously have been dealt with by an informal warning or a no further action decision were now being given an official caution (Ditchfield, 1976; Farrington and Bennett, 1981).

This issue is further highlighted by the findings for the 14–17 age group, which show that the increase in cautions in that age group was accompanied by a lesser (but still very considerable) increase in convictions. Non-indictable offences diminished slightly, but the net effect was a massive total increase – from 37,019 to 119,339. If corrections are introduced for the changes in legislation and if the figures are applied to the general population base, it may be calculated that the proportional increase between 1964 and 1978 in boys aged 14–16 who were convicted was +50 per cent, and for girls in the same age group it was +60 per cent (Farrington and Bennett, 1981). For both boys and girls in the younger age group of 10–13 there were small net decreases (-30 per cent and -27 per cent respectively).

The links between these various changes are difficult to identify in national figures because police practices vary across the country and because the changes took place at differing times in different areas. Nevertheless, Ditchfield (1976) noted two features which suggested a net-widening effect: (i) those areas of the country with the greatest number of cautions were also the areas with the largest increase in known offenders; and (ii) some areas with

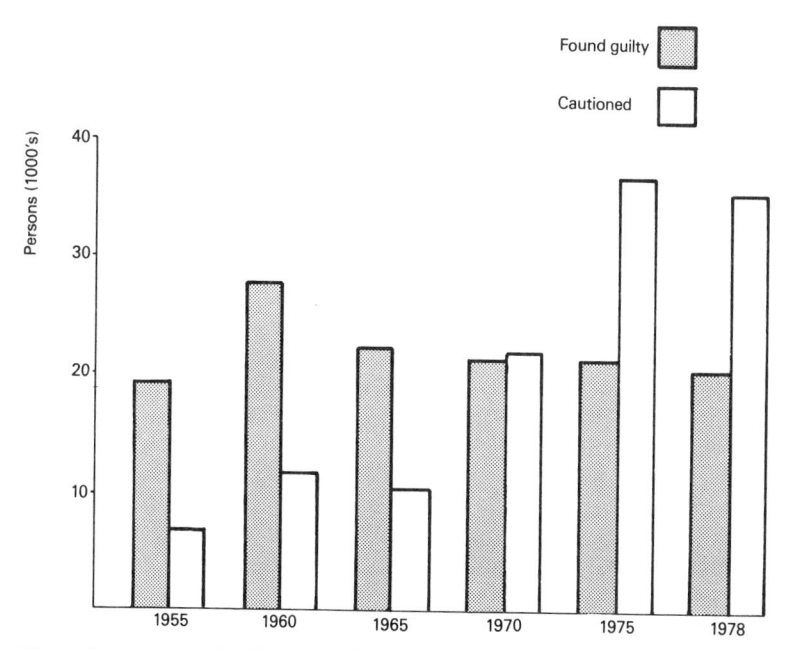

Figure 6(a). *Boys under 14 years – indictable offences (Data from Home Office)*

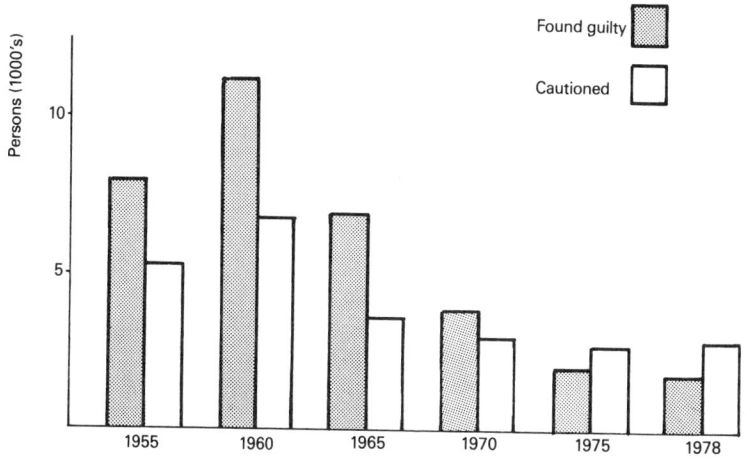

Figure 6(b). *Boys under 14 years – non-indictable offences (Data from Home Office)*

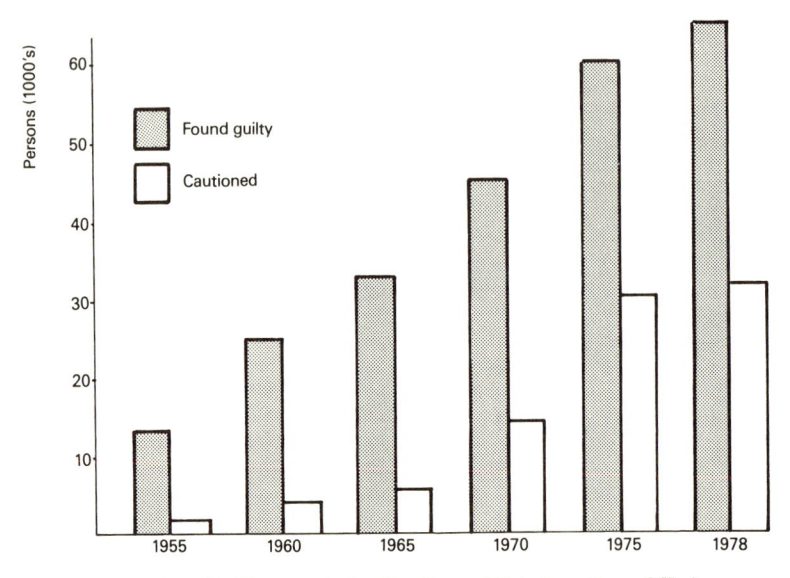

Figure 7(a). *Boys 14–17 years – indictable offences* (*Data from Home Office*)

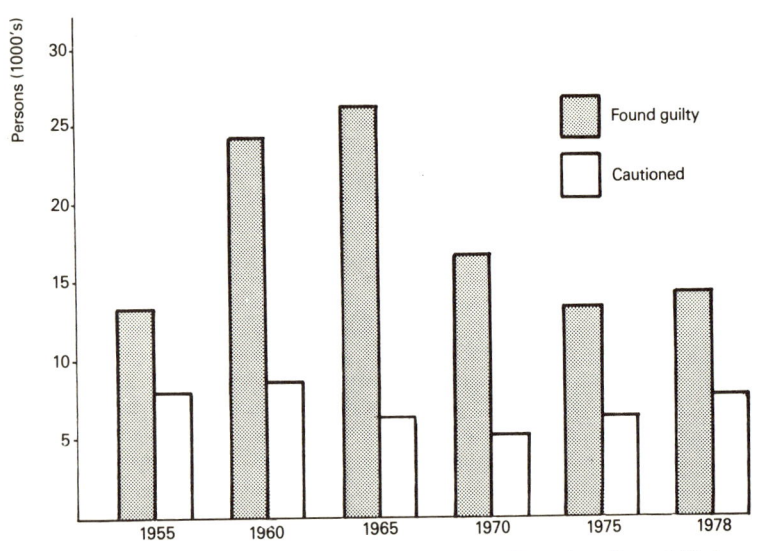

Figure 7(b). *Boys 14–17 years – non-indictable offences* (*Data from Home Office*)

increasing rates of cautioning also showed large increases in the ratio of juveniles to adults in the offender population – increases which could not be accounted for by alterations in the age structure of the population. This latter point is pertinent because it suggests that factors relevant to the increase in the processing of juveniles did not apply to adults.

Farrington and Bennett's (1981) analysis of the data from the Metropolitan Police District (London) helps to pinpoint further the possible effects of the increase in cautioning because, in this Force, cautioning was introduced in 1968 and was in operation in every division by 1970. The findings showed that the arrest rate for 10–13 years olds almost doubled (an increase of 85 per cent after correction for the introduction of the Theft Act in 1969) between 1968 and 1970 – a far greater increase than that in either the preceding or the succeeding two years. There was also a lesser increase (+44 per cent) in arrests for 14–16 year olds. Farrington and Bennett (1981) argue convincingly that the size of the increase in arrests over such a short period of time strongly suggests that there had been a substantial widening of the net, that is that the police were now arresting young people whom previously they would have dealt with informally.*

The conclusion from these analyses is that part of the apparent rise in crime during the late 1960s is likely to have been due to a widening of the range of delinquent activities which were considered serious enough for official processing. However, the rise in the crime rate during the 1950s and early 1960s (which was even greater) cannot be attributed to cautioning, as it was less used at that time.

An extremely conservative estimate (i.e. a considerable under-estimate) of the rate of crime increase corrected for this net-widening effect can be obtained by disregarding all cautions and restricting crime figures to official findings of guilt only. A further correction can be introduced by restricting the analysis to first offenders only. In this way the figures apply to true increases in the number of *offenders*, rather than in the number of *offences* (which could increase as a result of an increase in recidivism rather than of delinquent individuals). These data are shown in Table 3.

The table is based on the Home Office statistics for 1965 analysed by McClintock and Avison (1968), and from the 1977 statistics analysed by Farrington (1981a). The figures are obtained by cumulating the percentage of persons first convicted in a given year together with the percentages for

* It appears that most juvenile bureaux actively encourage schools and shopkeepers to report children to them, rather than deal informally with the children themselves, and in the former juvenile liaison schemes which preceded the bureaux it seemed that some of the children dealt with would probably not have been taken to court hitherto (Taylor, 1971).

Table 3 Proportion of population with convictions in England and Wales in 1965 and 1977

	Percentage convicted for first time		Accumulated % persons convicted	
	1965[1]	1977[2]	1965	1977
Males				
age 10–12	1.02	0.66	3.06	1.98
13–14	2.13	1.99	7.33	5.96
15–16	1.75	2.87	10.82	11.70
17–18	1.61	2.96	14.04	17.62
19–20	1.34	2.07	16.71	21.76
Females				
age 10–16	0.29	0.30	2.03	2.10
17–20	0.24	0.64	2.98	4.66

1. Figures derived from McClintock and Avison (1968), Table IV.3, p. 302.
2. Figures from Farrington (1981a), based on Home Office (1977 and 1978).

earlier age groups in previous years (for example, for those aged 17 in 1980, aged 16 in 1979, 15 in 1978 and so forth). The procedure, of course, relies on the accuracy of information on whether any particular offence has been committed by a 'first offender'. Doubts have been expressed on this point, in that delays in reporting and other difficulties may mean that some individuals appear as first offenders in more than one age group (Walker, 1971), and for this reason, until the recent data used in these analyses, the Home Office discontinued publishing the information. However, there is no reason to suppose that any inaccuracies in the figures will have differed between 1965 and 1977, and the comparison may be taken as a fair rough estimate.

The results show that, in the 10–14 age group, the risk of conviction was lower in 1977 than in 1965 – a result expected on the basis of the exclusion of cautions. But for the older age groups it was substantially greater, and the net effect was that the cumulative figure was greater in 1977 from 15 onwards. In 1965 it was estimated that 16.7 per cent of males would have received a conviction by the age of 20, whereas in 1977 it was 21.8 per cent – an increase of 30 per cent. The comparable figures for females were 3 per cent in 1965 and 4.7 per cent in 1977 – an increase of 56 per cent.

The implication is that the net-widening effect does not adequately account for the increase in crime rate, although undoubtedly it played a major part in the rise during the late 60s and early 70s. Yet another means of examining the matter, however, is provided by the figures on first offenders

Table 4 Increase in juvenile recidivists between 1955 and 1963

Age Group	1955	1959	1962	% Increase 1955–62
8–14	3,244	4,388	5,356	65%
14–17	4,062	6,501	8,924	120%
17–21	4,653	8,792	12,447	168%

(From Table 8.1, p. 224, in McClintock and Avison, 1968)

and recidivists. McClintock and Avison (1968) showed that there had been a major increase in recidivists between 1955 and 1962 (see Table 4). A comparison with the figures for first offenders showed that the increase in recidivists for 8–13 year olds and for 14–16 year olds was slightly greater than that for first offenders (77 per cent v. 52 per cent and 132 per cent v. 128 per cent respectively – see Table 6.21, p. 181, McClintock and Avison, 1968). The Home Office figures for first offenders and recidivists in 1978 (see Table 10.2, p. 184; Home Office, 1979) show that the proportion of recidivists had risen substantially since 1954–5. In 1954–5 the proportion of recidivists among convicted 14–16 year olds was 35 per cent; in 1962 the figure was the same; but by 1977 it had risen to 52 per cent (for 15–16 year olds). The same rise had occurred in the 17–20 age group, from 43 per cent in 1966 to 44 per cent in 1962 to 64 per cent in 1977. Evidently, the rise in crime rate has been greater for recidivists than for first offenders – a finding which runs counter to that which would be expected on the basis of a net-widening effect (as this would have its most immediate impact on the numbers of first offenders, although it could well have some secondary impact on the numbers of recidivists*).

Adequate data do not exist to enable a more direct analysis of possible changes in police practice. However, there is reasonable circumstantial evidence to suggest that changes have occurred. Perhaps the two strongest sets of evidence are: (i) the increase in arrest rate associated with the increase in use of cautioning (as discussed above); and (ii) the *reduction* in the proportion of violent crimes resulting in serious injury (see above). The point here is that if there had been a general increase in violent offences this should affect all levels of seriousness of violence to approximately the same degree. Accordingly, the finding that much the largest rise was with minor violence

---

* Two studies (Gawn, Mott and Tarling, 1977; Farrington and Bennett, 1981) have shown that the recidivism rate is less for juveniles who have been cautioned than for those taken to court. In part, at least, this is likely to be a consequence of cautioning being used for less serious delinquents, but the implication is still that the greatest effect of the use of cautioning is likely to be on the number of first offenders rather than on the number of recidivists.

suggests that the threshold had been lowered so that lesser acts of violence which would have been disregarded hitherto are now being drawn into the net. Taken together, these findings* suggest that a significant proportion of the increase in crime during the late 60s to early 70s, and some of the earlier increase, was due to a net-widening effect. On the other hand, the evidence just discussed also suggests that there was a rise in crime rate above and beyond any such effect. The matter can be examined more closely, however, by considering changes in very serious offences which are unlikely to have been affected by any changes in police practice. The findings on that point are discussed below when considering possible reporting biases.

Changes in legislation and recording of offences

We have already noted the existence of several pieces of legislation which are likely to have had an effect on crime statistics. The Theft Act 1968 reclassified the previously non-indictable offence of taking and driving away a motor vehicle into the indictable offence of unauthorized taking, while the Criminal Damage Act 1971 reclassified many previously non-indictable offences of malicious damage into the indictable offence of criminal damage. Both served artificially to inflate rates of indictable crime by about 21 per cent (see Farrington and Bennett, 1981). However, as already shown, it is possible to correct the figures for the result of this change in legislation, and the corrected figures have continued to show increases in crime rate. The Criminal Law Act 1977 also redefined certain offences in ways that served to broaden them (as these changes mainly apply to adults and are too recent to affect statistics on crime trends we shall not consider them further here). Another important change (but one resulting from Home Office instructions rather than legislation) was the alteration in 1950 of police practice in the classification of offences (Walker, 1971). Prior to 1950, returns were based on the offence of which the offender was ultimately found guilty. After that date, the instruction was that the offence should be recorded in terms of the one originally thought to have been committed, and not the one on which the offender was convicted. Because it is not uncommon for people to be convicted for a somewhat lesser offence, the effect was an artefactual inflation of

---

* A third piece of evidence that is sometimes used in this connection is the much greater use of 'suspected person' arrests for black people than for whites (see Chapter 4). While this does suggest that police may be using their powers of discretion to utilize this charge more readily with young blacks, the absolute level of usage is very low and there has been no consistent increase in its usage between 1976 and 1979 – 3,501 in 1976, 3,447 in 1977, 3,791 in 1978 and a slight drop again in 1979 (Central Statistical Office, 1980).

more serious offences (from non-indictable to indictable and, within indictable, to more serious categories). McClintock *et al.* (1963) estimated that this change alone would have increased crimes of violence in London by about 7.5 per cent; and together with other minor reforms it is likely that the illusory increase due to changes in recording practice was about 13.5 per cent.

Two pieces of legislation were designed to have the reverse effect – that is to say, they sought to reduce the number of children subject to official processing. The first, the raising of the minimum age of criminal responsibility from 8 to 10 in 1964, did indeed have that effect. The second, the Children and Young Persons Act 1969, proved to be more controversial. Underlying the proposals was the belief that delinquency was often a normal part of growing up and that criminal proceedings were inappropriate in the case of trivial delinquent activities. Serious delinquency, on the other hand, was regarded as evidence of the child's need for help and guidance. In these cases, the delinquency was thought to be the result of family inadequacies or breakdown. Protecting society from delinquency and aiding the delinquent child's development were seen as essentially complementary. The role of the juvenile court was to enable the child to receive the help or treatment required – the exact form of the intervention being left to the discretion of those with specialist skills. Although the formal composition and constitution of the juvenile court were left virtually unchanged by the Act, its jurisdiction was altered radically. Children under the age of 14 were no longer to be referred to court solely on the grounds that they had committed offences – rather, 'care and protection' proceedings should be brought on the basis of the child's needs. Criminal proceedings could still be brought for adolescents between the ages of 14 and 17, but only after mandatory consultation between police and social services, and with the expectation that most children in this age group, too, would be dealt with under 'care and protection' proceedings.

The general aims of the Act were to reduce the number of children appearing before the juvenile court, and to make the commission of an offence no longer a sufficient ground for intervention. The juvenile court was to become not only a welfare-providing agency, but also an agency of last resort; referral to the juvenile court was to take place only where a voluntary and informal agreement could not be reached between social workers, the child and his parents.

Integral to these proposals was the creation of an enlarged and more significant role for local authority social workers, with considerable power placed in their hands to vary and implement the dispositions made by the courts. Magistrates were no longer to make detailed decisions about the kind of treatment appropriate for the child. Social workers, within the limits of the particular order, were to determine this. Attendance centres and detention centres were to be replaced by a new form of treatment, 'intermediate treatment', to be designed and shaped by social services (see Chapter 9).

While the changes planned in the 1969 Act were radical, they have not been implemented to any meaningful extent. The juvenile courts function very much as before. Criminal proceedings for offenders under 14 have not been prohibited, nor have they been restricted in the case of offenders between the ages of 14 and 17. Similarly, the minimum age qualification for a Borstal sentence has not been increased from 15 to 17, and detention centres and attendance centres have not been phased out. Even the sections of the Act which were implemented have had minimal impact. Care proceedings on the commission of an offence are now possible, but between 1971 (the year the Act was partially implemented) and 1978 the number actually decreased. The traditional 'punitive' disposals, which were to have been abolished, have been used increasingly by juvenile courts. The 'intermediate treatment' schemes, designed to keep children out of institutions, have not been fully developed, and the use of supervision in the community has been only slightly greater than probation before the Act. In all, the distribution of measures used by the juvenile court indicates that there has been little change in the direction intended.

Between 1968 and 1978 (Home Office, 1979) there was little alteration in the pattern of sentences for 10–13 year olds, but for 14–16 year old males the proportion given attendance centre orders rose from 7 to 11 per cent, detention centre orders from 4 to 9 per cent, and Borstal training from 2 to 3 per cent. Conversely, probation/supervision orders came to be used less frequently (a drop from 24 per cent to 14 per cent). Examination of sentencing patterns over longer periods of time shows that these trends cannot be attributed entirely to the new legislation, in that they were already evident from 1964 onwards. However, the Act clearly failed in its intention to reduce the use of punitive measures.

Since 1971 there has been a parallel increase in the number of 'secure' places within the 'community home' system (in what were previously called 'approved schools'). It seems that, compared with earlier times, children are now placed more readily in these secure facilities, and by no means all these children present particularly severe problems (Cawson and Martell, 1979; Millham et al., 1978).

Similarly, the policy of community care endorsed by the 1969 Act has not been implemented in the ways intended. It is relatively frequent for care orders to be made in the case of children for whom informal community support measures have not been tried. Both Cawson (1978) and Thorpe (1977) found that some two-fifths of care orders (for children who committed offences) were made on the children's first court appearance, often for offences which did not appear serious. Also, it was observed that residential placements were made before alternative measures had been tried. Recent evidence indicates the continuing growth of this phenomenon (see Giller and Morris, 1981).

The 1969 Act took away from magistrates the power to decide the placement of a child made subject to a care order; instead, this discretion was vested in social service departments. Because some children on care orders are placed at home, there has been an increasing feeling among magistrates, police and justice clerks that the system is falling into disrepute (see Berlins and Wansall, 1974; Morris and Giller, 1979; Giller and Morris, 1976). It has been said that such children:

deride the powerlessness of the courts to deal with them, commit further offences after having been placed in the care of the local authority, and are led to think they can break the law with impunity. (House of Commons Expenditure Committee, 1975, ii:463)

In the words of the Magistrates Association:

The lack of other measures forces courts to send youngsters to detention centres and Borstals who might not otherwise go. (House of Commons Expenditure Committee, 1975, 135)

Or, again, the Department of Health and Social Security (1972) has stated:

If the court commits a child to care ... the presumption *must be* that there are strong reasons for the view that the child's needs cannot be met, at any rate at that stage, in his own home. [Emphasis added]

But alternative views have been expressed, for example, by the British Association of Social Workers in their evidence to the House of Commons Expenditure Committee:

Lack of resources is the central problem. A 'residential' care order would not help as the court making the order would not also be able to produce the facility. (House of Commons Expenditure Committee, 1975, ii:221).

In Chapters 9 and 10, we return to these issues in considering policies on prevention and intervention. With respect to possible effects on secular crime trends, however, it is clear that there have been no identifiable consequences of the 1969 Act. In the first place, very little of the Act has been implemented and, contrary to its principles, the main observable change has been an *increase* in the use of punitive or restrictive measures. This has been accompanied by a reduction in the power of magistrates with respect to the choice of placement on a care order, but the combination of these two rather different features makes it impossible to disentangle which is likely to have led to what. Secondly, the crime statistics show that the main increase in delinquency occurred during the late 50s and 60s, before the 1969 Act. The rise levelled out during the 70s, and in recent years there has even been a slight fall. Thus, if there was any significant effect on rates of crime (which seems quite doubtful), it is as likely to have been a decrease as an increase.

Clear-up rate

Over the years the police clear-up rate (that is, the proportion of recorded offences for which a person has been arrested, summoned or cautioned) has always differed considerably from one offence group to another. Whereas some four-fifths of crimes involving violence against the person are cleared up, this happens with only about a third of burglaries or cases of criminal damage. This difference is likely to be due to the greater ease of detection of some offences, greater police attention to others, and also to the fact that there are some offences for which reporting is directly associated with the discovery of the offender. However, the clear-up rate for each type of offence has altered very little over the years and, if anything, the trend has been for a slightly reducing clear-up rate in recent years for some offences (see Figure 8). For example, the clear-up rate for criminal damage was 38 per cent in 1969 but 30 per cent in 1979; and for robbery it dropped from 40 per cent in 1969 to 31 per cent in 1979 (Home Office, 1980). Some of this drop may be explicable in terms of changes in the offence (rising inflation has meant that criminal damage, which is restricted to a value of £20 or greater, has come to involve more minor offences), but whatever the reason, it is clear that the rise in crime can *not* be due to any rise in clear-up rate as there has been none.

Willingness to report

As discussed in Chapter 1, only a minority of crimes are reported to the police by the general public. Moreover, there is evidence to indicate that communities differ somewhat in their willingness to report crimes (Conklin, 1971). It is obvious, therefore, that there is enormous scope for alterations in reporting to lead to entirely artefactual changes in the crime rate. Eck and

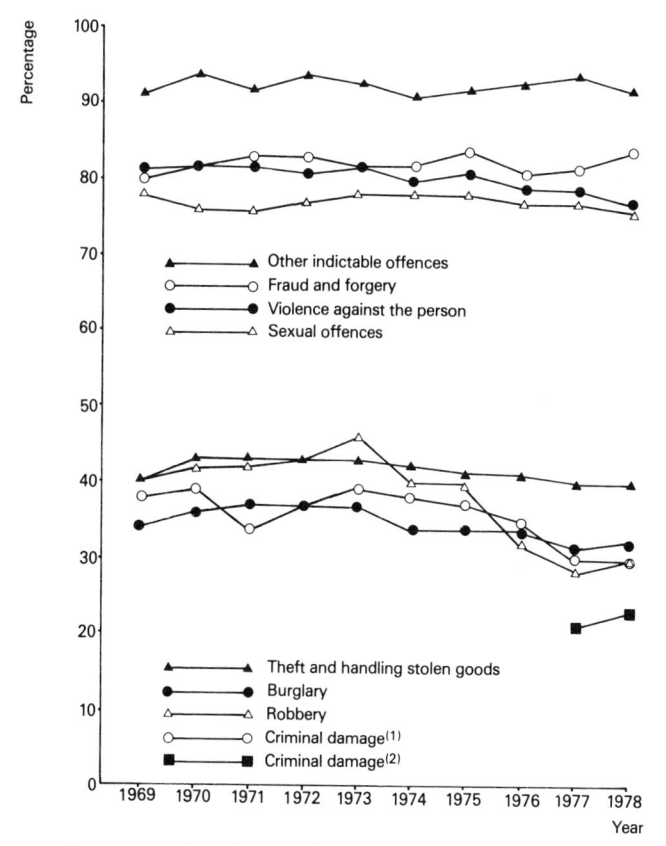

Figure 8. *Clear-up rates for indictable offences recorded by the police by offence group* (*Home Office, 1980*)

1. Excluding 'other criminal damage' of value £20 and under.
2. Including all criminal damage (estimated).

Riccio (1979) showed the potential for this effect in their analysis of the victimization data in the United States for the years 1973, 1974 and 1975. According to the National Crime Survey, victimization rose from 36,925,000 to 40,483,000 between 1973 and 1975 – an increase of 9.6 per cent. But, over the same period of time, the proportion reported to the police also rose from 34.4 per cent to 37.0 per cent, resulting in a rise of 17.6 per cent. A rise of a mere 2.5 per cent in reporting was associated with an artefactual doubling of the increase in crime as it would be reflected in official statistics! The data refer to the amount of crime that people *said* they reported to the police, rather than to the amount they actually reported, which could be different. Nevertheless, the general point remains – relatively small increases in the proportions of crime reported, *if combined with some real increase in crime*, could result in rather larger increases in crime as shown in official statistics. While it is possible for an effect of this kind to have occurred, we lack data on whether *in fact* this has happened. Unfortunately, no victimization data are available prior to the mid-1960s and hence we have no means of knowing whether the proportions of crimes reported in the era of the greatest crime increase were substantially different from those now. Indeed, we have no truly comparable data prior to 1973. The 1966 American victimization survey (Ennis, 1967) does not suggest that the reporting rate was lower then than it is now – if anything, the reverse – but the data are not truly comparable with the 1973–5 surveys.

The British data, derived from the General Household Surveys of 1972, 1973, 1979 and 1980, refer only to burglary and theft in a building, but these, too, do not suggest any major change in the level of reporting over this period. However, the data are weak and somewhat contradictory. The most direct measure of reporting comes from the answers given by victims of burglary to the question, 'Was this incident reported to the police?' In 1972, 76 per cent of burglaries were said to have been reported, and in 1979, 75 per cent (O.P.C.S., 1981) – i.e. no change. An alternative approach is provided by the calculation of the ratio of estimated offences committed (as provided by the Household Survey data) to the number of offences recorded by the police (from Home Office Statistics). The ratios for the years 1972, 1973, 1979 and 1980 were 1.99 (± 0.24), 2.00 (± 0.24), 1.80 (± 0.22), and 1.62 (± 0.20) respectively (Home Office, 1981a). The Home Office conclude that these figures mean a drop from 2 to 1 in 1972/3 to 1.7 to 1 in 1979/80, but the differences over time become statistically significant only when the 1980 data are included and pooled with 1979. In view of the uncertainties of ratios based on estimates, together with the rather different findings from the answers to the direct question on reporting, this seems to be a rather shaky inference. Moreover, the ratio data refer to *police recording* and not to public reporting of crimes. Also, of course, they apply to possible changes during the mid-1970s when official statistics indicate only a minor increase in crime, and not to the 1950s and 1960s when the greatest rise occurred.

Nevertheless, it is possible to obtain an impression of whether changes in reporting *are likely* to constitute an explanation both by calculating how big a change would be required to account for the trends over time in crime rates, and by looking at trends for crimes where the reporting factor is unlikely to be important.

The first step can be taken simply by calculating the proportional increase in crime rates over a given time period. McClintock and Avison (1968) show that the crime rate per 100,000 population in 1901 was 249 compared with 2,374 in 1965. If we assume a reporting rate of, say, 35 per cent in 1965 this would mean that the 'true' rates for that year should be 6,783, once unreported crimes are included. If the true crime rate in 1901 had been exactly the same, the reporting rate for that year would have had to have been 3.7 per cent (i.e. 249 crimes reported out of a total of 6,783). That is a quite implausible figure.

The second step can be taken by looking at changes in very serious crimes for which reporting is likely to have been high at all times. Table 5 gives the figures for murder, attempts to murder and felonious wounding for the years 1930 to 1963 (Home Office, 1964). All three offences showed substantial increases over this time period, although there was no increase in the murder rate between 1940 and 1955. Much the largest increase occurred with felonious wounding, which could have been due to a tendency to include less serious woundings in this category, but this is less likely to have happened with attempted murder and could not have happened with murder, in which there was an increase in spite of legislation in 1957 to *remove* some cases of homicide from the murder classification.

Table 6 provides figures for more recent years for homicide involving the killing of someone not known to the victim,* in which the rate doubled

Table 5 Some violent offences 1930–63, England and Wales (From Home Office, 1964)

	1930–34	1935–9	1940–44	1945–9	1950–54	1955–9	1960–63
Felonious wounding	176	286	304	577	1,022	1,395	1,873
Attempts to murder	79	76	97	179	154	169	203
Murder (of persons 1 yr +)	103	107	138	141	130	138†	143†

* This figure excludes homicide due to terrorism, as the recent increase in terrorism may be associated with factors which have little to do with the general run of delinquent activities.

† As a result of the Homicide Act 1957, these figures are under-estimates in that some cases previously classified as murder were excluded by the Act.

88 Juvenile Delinquency

Table 6 Some violent offences 1969–78, England and Wales (From Home Office, 1979)

	1969–70	1971–2	1973–4	1975–6	1977–8	% Increase 1969–70 to 1977–8
Homicide stranger (non-terrorist)	42	69	66	87	82	95%
Acts endangering life (firearms)	165	196	237	262	235	42%
Other acts (firearms)	602	951	1,397	2,055	2,372	294%

between 1969 and 1978 (Home Office, 1979), and rose substantially again in 1979 (Home Office, 1980). Similarly, crimes of violence against the person involving the use of firearms, in which life was endangered, showed a 42 per cent increase, and other acts of violence involving firearms showed an even greater increase (294 per cent). Again, the biggest increase was seen with the less serious crimes, in which there was a possibility that there had been a tendency to alter the threshold for inclusion. Possibly this is suggested by the fact that the increase was greatest in the case of air weapons (a rise from 591 in 1969 to 3,671 in 1977), but even the use of pistols more than doubled (233 to 566) so that it is unlikely that a change in threshold constitutes a sufficient explanation. The increases over the years have been very substantial even with offences in which reporting biases or classification biases are unlikely to have played a part.

Of course, these figures apply to adults rather than juveniles (separate figures for juveniles are not available with this degree of breakdown on type of offence), but it seems probable that the same pattern would apply.

Conclusions on crime trends in official statistics

This review of factors which could have influenced the rise in crime figures as shown in official statistics shows that it is virtually certain that much of the apparent rise in the number of offenders has been illusory. Firstly, the increase has been greater in the case of recidivists than of first offenders – indicating that the increase in *acts* of delinquency has been greater than that in the number of *people* committing such acts. Secondly, a small part of the increase is known to be due to changes in the classification of offences which followed both new legislation and alterations in police recording practice. Thirdly, there is strong circumstantial evidence that there has been a tendency to widen the net in a way which means that some individuals are now being brought into the official process for acts which would have been dealt with informally in a previous era (and so not been included in the statistics). Fourthly, it is possible (although quite uncertain) that there may be an increasing tendency for members of the general public to report to the police offences which they would have not reported hitherto.

Nevertheless, as we have discussed, there are sound reasons for assuming that, even when all of these factors have been generously taken into account, a real rise remains. The evidence of a true increase in crime is strongest in the case of the more serious offences involving personal violence. The main reason for this difference by type of offence is simply that it is easier with crimes of serious violence to rule out artefactual influences of various kinds. It would be unsafe to infer that, in actuality, the increase in violence has been greater than that in different forms of stealing – there is no reliable evidence to decide on this point one way or the other. The evidence for a real rise in crime rate is also greater for the 1950s and 1960s time period than it is for the 1970s decade. It seems rather dubious whether there has been any significant increase since the mid-70s and the appearance is of a levelling off, or even slight fall, in the overall crime rate in recent years.*

These tentative conclusions are based entirely on official statistics and, before coming to any more firm overall conclusion, we need to turn to evidence from other sources.

Self-report, victimization and other data on crime trends

Inter-generational comparisons

The data on crime trends derived from official statistics which we have discussed so far have referred to the findings for the population as a whole. An alternative strategy is provided by the results of specific research projects in which there are data on rates of crime in fathers and sons at the same age (see Rutter, 1979a). Two projects, one American (Robins *et al.*, 1975) and one British (West and Farrington, 1977), have published data of this kind. Robins *et al.* (1975), in a study of crime in two generations, reported a similar rate of juvenile delinquency in the fathers to that in the sons (31 per cent in both), and in the mothers to that in the daughters (14–16 per cent). West and

---

* This conclusion applies to the overall rate in the population as a whole. As discussed in Chapter 4, it is possible that there may well have been an increase during the 1970s in crime among black teenagers in the U.K. Moreover, some serious crimes, especially homicide, seem to be still increasing.

Farrington (1977) do not present their data in the same form, but their figures show that by the age of 15 the delinquency rate in the sons (13.1 per cent) was little different from that in their fathers (11.5 per cent). Both sets of figures seem out of keeping with the marked increase in delinquency over time shown by the criminal statistics. However, there are several reasons why these two-generation studies might be expected to show a different picture. Firstly, both concern high-risk populations and it may be that the main rise in crime has affected what in previous generations have been low-risk groups.* Secondly, not only are the samples special in various respects and hence not representative of the general population, but, more particularly, the two generations are special in *different* respects. One generation was chosen because it met various risk criteria, but the other generation was chosen because it consisted of the fathers (or sons) of the first sample. As a result the two generations are likely to differ from the general population in different ways. Thirdly, in the Robins study the sons are atypical in a further respect in that they are predominantly first-born. Fourthly, as both studies mainly concern just one boy per family the figures will be an under-estimate of the total population prevalence (because delinquency is commoner in boys from large families and instead of counting *all* the boys in each large family only one was included). We may conclude that two-generation family studies do not provide a good test of historical trends.

Vandalism

Over recent years there has been much concern over vandalism (not only in Western countries but also in Eastern Europe), and there has been a general impression that the problem is increasing (see, for example, Home Office Standing Committee on Crime Prevention, 1975; Stone and Taylor, 1977; Central Policy Review Staff, 1978). At first sight this seems to be demonstrated by the fact that of all offences recorded as known to the police, criminal damage has shown by far the greatest increase in recent years – from 17,000 offences in 1969 to 124,000 in 1977. However, these statistics refer only to cases where the damage exceeded a cost of £20. It is obvious that the severe inflation in recent years would be enough in itself to account for much of the rise. Also, it is relevant that there is an exceptionally low rate of reporting to the police (see Clarke, 1978), particularly of the most common but less expensive types of vandalism (such as breaking of windows on

---

* The observation that in the U.S.A. the rise in crime has been greater for suburban and rural areas than for the inner city (see Zimring, 1978) is in keeping with that suggestion.

housing estates, or damage to street lights, or slashing of seats on buses). Accordingly, changes over time in the number of cases of criminal damage may well reflect alterations in public sensitivity and awareness of the problem, and hence their tendency to report cases. It is evident that the available statistics are very patchy and inadequate and quite unsuitable for the accurate assessment of historical trends with respect to vandalism as a whole. In addition, it must be said that technically there is no such offence as 'vandalism'. It is generally taken to mean wilful damage to public or private property and amenities, but of course this covers a most disparate set of activities, ranging through the smashing up of abandoned cars or old prams on rubbish dumps, the breaking of windows in unoccupied houses, football excursion train hooliganism, the desecration of school lavatories, political graffiti, and damage as a by-product of theft. Rather than attempt any overall measurement of vandalism, a better appraisal may be obtained by focusing on certain specific areas of damage (some of these are reviewed in Rutter, 1979a).

Thus, the Post Office in the U.K. keeps records of vandalism to public telephone booths. Figure 9 gives the figures for the 1970–78 period in terms of the number of cases of damage per number of kiosks. Several things are evident from the graphs. Firstly, it is clear that the tendency for vandalism to increase was not only halted but was reversed during the early 1970s. This is likely to have been a result of the extensive strengthening programme with respect to the equipment (see Chapter 9). Secondly, in the country as a whole,

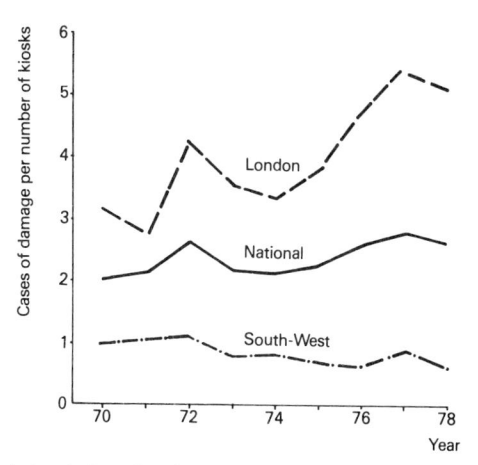

Figure 9. *Trends in telephone booth vandalism (Data from Post Office Telecommunications, 1979)*

92 *Juvenile Delinquency*

although vandalism has slightly increased in recent years, there is no indication of any marked change. Thirdly, however, it is evident that not only do the levels of vandalism vary greatly between different parts of the country, but so also do the historical trends. In 1970 the vandalism rate in the southwest was below half the national average; apart from an increase in 1977-8 it has progressively fallen over the last six years, and the rate is now less than quarter of the national average. In sharp contrast, the London rates have always been high and although, as in the rest of the country, vandalism decreased in the mid-70s, the rate has risen again during the last four years to reach a level twice the national average. We may conclude not only that preventive measures have probably had an effect in reducing vandalism but also that this effect has been far from uniform throughout the country. In the metropolis things have got worse to some extent, whereas in rural areas this has not been the case.

The British Transport Police annual reports provide information on damage to railway stock and property. Summary offences (which are mainly ticket frauds and railway bye-law prosecutions for trespass, minor forms of stone-throwing, and the like) as a whole have remained at a pretty constant level over the last eighteen years, but the number of juveniles who were prosecuted was halved between 1960 and 1969. During the last ten years there have been both increases and decreases but the overall level is slightly below that of a decade ago. The number of indictable offences per year among juveniles, on the other hand, rose slightly in the early 60s, then fell again to remain fairly steady until a very sharp rise in the early 70s, followed by a further fall back to the level of the early 60s. The indictable offences include quite a mixed bag of offences under various Acts, but many deal with behaviours which clearly involve wilful damage of a kind which might properly be regarded as vandalism. Again, it seems that various preventive actions (see Chapter 9) are likely to have been effective in reducing the problem.

Damage to school property is another area where it should be possible to obtain data on historical trends. However, apart from arson (where apparently the number of major fires showed an increase from 12 in 1965 to 90 in 1976 – Stone and Taylor, 1977), no very satisfactory figures are available. It is clear that schools and authorities vary greatly in what they consider worth reporting, that there is no common standard for measurement, and that most statistics are kept in the form of costs of repair. A recent Home Office project in Manchester (Gladstone, 1980) illustrates how inflation may cause those figures to distort historical trends. Between 1969 and 1977 the cost of repairing damage identified as vandalism in schools more than quadrupled, from about £42,000 to £179,000. However, over that same period building costs also rose considerably, and when costs were adjusted for inflation it became apparent that there had been little change over the eight years. On the other hand, as both these data and others (Stone and Taylor, 1977) show, any single figure for trends is bound to be misleading in view of the huge variations between schools in rates of vandalism (see also Rutter *et al.*, 1979). Some schools show a picture of steady improvement over the years whereas in others there is evidence of a steadily worsening problem.

Self-report delinquency data

No self-report data showing trends over time are available for the U.K., but one such study from the United States has been published (Gold and Reimer, 1975). The sources of data derive from the first and second National Surveys of Youth in 1967 and 1972. The first survey involved the interviewing of 847 boys and girls aged 13–16 years, and the second 661 in the same age range. The main finding was that there was a marked increase (nine- or ten-fold) in the use of illicit drugs, mainly marijuana, by both sexes between 1967 and 1972, and that in girls (but not boys) the frequency of drinking (alcohol) doubled. It was striking that the increase in the use of drugs was also accompanied by an increase in the tendency to perceive this as a normal adolescent activity. Excluding drugs, there was little overall change in the frequency or seriousness of delinquent activities between 1967 and 1972. There was a slight decrease in white males but not in blacks (who reported more assaults and more carrying of concealed weapons in 1972). Girls showed little change over the five years. Some information was also obtained on parent–child relationships. These data indicated that the amount of autonomy that parents permitted their sons increased significantly from 1967 to 1972, and that parent–son relationships became significantly less close.

The data suggest that there was little change in the extent of delinquent activities among 13–16 year olds in the United States over the five-year time span studied. However, there must be serious reservations about the validity of the finding because (i) there was a high non-response rate, such that only 71 per cent of subjects were interviewed; (ii) the measure used was heavily weighed towards minor delinquencies; (iii) the sample size for some sub-groups was too small for the study of serious delinquencies (for example, only 53 black males in 1967 and 33 in 1972); and (iv) only one teenager per household in the age groups was interviewed (thus reducing the effect of large

94 *Juvenile Delinquency*

families, a pertinent consideration as delinquency is more frequent in youths from large families).

Victimization surveys

As with self-reports, data on historical trends from victimization surveys are available mainly from the United States. As noted above, these showed a moderate increase in crime between 1973 and 1974 (from 36,925,000 to 39,694,000 – a rise of 7.5 per cent) and a smaller increase (2 per cent) in the following year (Eck and Riccio, 1979). The increases for violent crime in the two years were not as great, but the pattern was the same (a 3 per cent rise between 1973 and 1974 and a 0.9 per cent rise between 1974 and 1975). As noted in Chapter 1, there are some concerns over the validity of victimization data, so that it would not be justifiable to place much weight on these rather small changes. However, certainly the findings are consistent with a picture of slight continuing increase in crime during the 1970s in the United States.

The only British victimization data providing evidence on historical trends are those derived from the General Household Surveys in 1972, 1973 and 1979 (Home Office, 1981a; O.P.C.S., 1981). In each of these years, householders were asked the same questions: 'During the last twelve months, has anyone got into your house/flat, etc. without your permission and stolen or attempted to steal anything?' Analysis of the figures showed that the level of offences of domestic burglary and theft had not changed over the seven years between 1972 and 1979 – the rate of burglaries being 29 per 1,000 households in both 1972 and 1979 (O.P.C.S., 1981). Although these rates are higher than those based on serious offences recorded by the police, the same trend (or, rather, lack of trend) over time is evident in both (the police figures showing a rate of 1.5 recorded offences per 1,000 households in 1972 and 1.6 in 1979).

Overall conclusions on crime trends in the U.K.

It is evident that these other sources of data on crime trends are not much help in coming to a decision on how far crime among juveniles in the U.K. has been increasing since the Second World War. The self-report data are available only for the U.S.A., and the data from the U.K. on vandalism show a rather mixed picture. Nevertheless, all the findings are reasonably consistent in suggesting that probably there has been only a small increase in crime during the 1970s. Data other than official statistics are not available for the 1950s–1960s period, when it appeared that the largest increase occurred. We conclude that it is likely that there was a substantial true increase in crime during these years, although nothing like as great as that suggested by the official crime statistics, and that the upward trend continued to a lesser extent during the early 70s and then levelled off.

International comparisons

The overall pattern of historical trends in crime in the United Kingdom appears closely similar to that found in most other industrialized societies. Detailed comparisons are difficult in view of variations in the age at which children attain criminal responsibility, in the definitions of crime, in its reporting, and in the police and judicial systems which have been established to deal with juvenile delinquency. However, the very fact that the trends do appear so generally similar provides strong circumstantial evidence that the trends in any one country are unlikely to be due solely to alterations in police or court practice.

Zimring (1979) has provided a detailed analysis of trends in American youth violence, concluding that the dramatic increase in youth violence during the 1960s was followed by a period of greater stability during the 1970s. The arrest rates for homicide by youths aged 13–20 almost doubled (from 7.6 per 100,000 to 14.0) between 1960 and 1970, but there was only a 4 per cent increase during the next five years and a fall of 8 per cent between 1975 and 1977. The pattern for robbery was somewhat similar, with a rise from 118 per 100,000 in 1960 to 205 in 1970 (+74 per cent), a smaller further rise to 254 in 1975 (+24 per cent) and then a fall to 210 in 1977 (−17 per cent). Aggravated assault, on the other hand, was the exception in showing a continuing increase in the early 70s, although, once again, a slight fall between 1975 and 1977. The statistics on all offences show that the growth in violent crime has been greater than that for property offences – although, as in other countries, property offences outnumber violent crimes by 10 to 1 (U.S. Department of Justice, 1980). For crime as a whole the increase during the 70s (+39 per cent) was much less than that during the 60s (+144 per cent). The American statistics also showed that black youths were more heavily involved in violent crime than in property offences (a black/white ratio of 7.2:1 for homicide and 8.6:1 for robbery but only 3.9:1 for burglary and 3.0:1 for auto theft).

The Canadian statistics show a huge increase in reported crime between 1901 and 1965 – a twenty-five-fold increase overall, but most of this is accounted for by traffic offences. Juvenile convictions fell during the late 20s and 30s, rose to a peak between 1941–5, fell again after the war, but rose steadily once more from the trough of 273 per 100,000 in 1951–5 to 370 five years later and 481 in 1961–5 (Giffen, 1976). For all offences the overall rates in Canada are well below those in the United States.

European data have been analysed by Gurr *et al.* (1977; Gurr, 1979). The reported rates of crime vary greatly between countries, partly as a result of national differences in criminal justice systems, but the evidence suggests that the comparisons of *trends* in different countries is probably reasonably valid. All the Scandinavian countries showed a rising rate of known crimes against persons during the 1960s, although the increase was much less than that observed in the U.K. and U.S.A.

The German-speaking countries in Europe have shown less marked increases during the post-war years in overall crime rates. Nevertheless, between 1952 and 1972, offences by those in the 14–18 age group in Germany nearly doubled. While the rate for adults fell between 1963 and 1970, offences by juveniles aged 14–18 increased some 60 per cent and by those aged under 14 by 48 per cent. In Switzerland, too, the number of convictions for children between 14 and 18 rose steadily between 1960 and 1971. By 1975, however, convictions in this age group had fallen sharply, largely due to a raising of the age of criminal responsibility to 15.

In Australia there was an increase in crime during the 1960s. Formal police–juvenile contacts rose in one region by 268 per cent between 1960 and 1975, but it appears that, in part, this reflected a greater tendency for the police formally to warn children, rather than an increase in delinquent activities as such (Challinger, 1977). Kraus (1977) found that there had not been the rapid increase in property offences by juveniles as seen in the U.K. and U.S.A., but there was an upward trend in the rates of assault and malicious damage by juveniles, in line with an almost world-wide phenomenon of increasing violence not motivated by gain.

Understandably, the crime statistics in developing countries are both less systematic and less readily comparable than those in industrialized societies. It appears that violent crimes are more frequent than in developed nations, but theft and fraud are less common (United Nations, 1977). Even so the statistics suggest that, as in other parts of the world, rates of juvenile offences have been rising steadily over recent decades (Clinard and Abbott, 1973).

The one country that appears to be strikingly out of line with Europe and America, in both levels and trends of crime, is Japan. Despite unparalleled industrial growth and urban concentration, crime fell from 1.6 million penal code offences in 1948 (excluding traffic violations) to 1.2 million in 1973; a rate generally well below that in other comparable countries (see Clifford, 1976; also Japan Ministry of Justice, 1980). In most European and American cities rates of homicide and of rape doubled during the 1960s, whereas the rates in Tokyo and Osaka rose only slightly during the same period. Overall rates of theft in Japan have been falling since 1960, and although crimes against persons increased six-fold between 1945 and 1960, they have been falling rapidly and steadily since then (Gurr, 1979). The pattern for juveniles is somewhat different, in that there was a sharp increase during 1945–9 during the period of general post-war difficulties, a substantial decrease during the early 1950s, but then a rise to a peak in 1964. Since then, the rates have fallen in older juveniles but risen in younger age groups. Rates of theft have risen, but violent crimes did not become more frequent during the 1960s when rates were rising throughout most of the rest of the world. Most recently, however, juvenile involvement in violent crime has shown signs of increasing. Interestingly, the proportion of delinquent juveniles from broken or poor families has been gradually declining, although crime rates have continued to be higher among those migrating to the cities and living without their families.

Although rates of crime among women have remained fairly steady between 1946 and 1972 (1.3 per 1,000 to 1.1), the *ratio* of male to female offenders has halved (from 14:1 to 7:1), so paralleling the changes in the U.S.A. and the U.K. So far as other social indices are concerned, it is perhaps noteworthy that, unlike most other countries, Japan has had a fairly stable divorce rate; but also, at a time when suicide rates in young adults have tended to be falling in some countries, they have risen in Japan (from 22.1 for males aged 20–39 after the Second World War to 40.9 in 1954, and from 16.8 to 23.7 for females in the same age group).

Obviously, an understanding of *why* the pattern of trends in crime in Japan (especially for adults) has been so different from those in the rest of the world would be extremely helpful in increasing our appreciation of the factors that control delinquency rates. However, it is not easy to discern just what lessons should be learned. Some possibilities may be ruled out. For example, industrialization and urbanization are frequently seen as predisposing to crime (see, for example, Clinard and Abbott, 1973, with respect to trends in developing countries). But Japan has experienced *greater* urban and industrial growth than countries in Europe and North America during this period. Some suggestions put forward by Clifford (1976), in his review of the issue, include the structure, discipline and conformity expected in Japanese culture; the lesser conflicts between labour and capital and between social classes (in spite of clear hierarchies in Japanese society); the great restraint exhibited by Japanese police and their greater involvement in the community (but combined with great efficiency and vigorous law enforcement); and greater public participation in crime control. We lack data to show whether these (or other) explanations have validity, but the question remains an important one relevant to those in all societies.

Historical trends in other aspects of adolescent behaviour

Just as there may be useful lessons to be learned from international comparisons, so, too, it may be informative to compare historical trends in juvenile delinquency with trends in other aspects of adolescent behaviour. There is an all too common assumption that the answers to rising rates of crime necessarily lie in improved police efficiency or more effective judicial interventions. An examination of the possibility that the change in delinquent activities may be part of a broader pattern of change in adolescent behaviour may serve as a corrective. As these historical trends have recently been reviewed in some detail by one of us (Rutter, 1979a), only the main findings will be summarized here.

Educational standards

The question of whether educational standards are rising or falling would seem to be quite straightforward, but in fact the issues have proved to be both conceptually complex and methodologically difficult. Nevertheless, there is some empirical evidence on a few of the key indices. In the U.K., it seems that reading standards increased up to the mid-60s, but thereafter they levelled off and may actually have fallen slightly (Start and Wells, 1972). National examination results in 'O' levels at 16 and 'A' levels at 18 have shown a considerable overall improvement since the Second World War, but something of a levelling off over the last decade (see Rutter, 1979a). However, the statistics are not presented in a form which enables one to determine the reason for the increased number of exam passes. These could have occurred as a result of either (i) the opening up of educational opportunities to a broader segment of the population, or, alternatively, (ii) better examination performance by children of any given level of ability. National figures on school attendance are not available, but local statistics suggest that during the last decade or so absenteeism rates in secondary schools have been rising (this does not seem to have occurred in primary schools).

Copperman (1978) has summarized the findings on trends regarding educational attainment in the U.S.A. The statistics indicate that from the beginning of this century until the mid-50s academic achievements rose steadily. This improvement was reflected both in falling rates of illiteracy and in rising rates of college entry. From the mid-50s to the early 60s scholastic attainments increased sharply, but then the pattern changed. The academic skills of younger children have continued to increase, albeit at a slower rate. In sharp contrast, there is an increasing body of evidence that the reading, writing and computing skills of secondary schoolchildren have deteriorated. Exact parallels between the U.S. and the U.K. are not possible because standards are measured in different ways in the two countries, and because in both the evidence is rather fragmentary and incomplete. Nevertheless, it seems reasonably clear that during the period from the mid-50s to the mid-60s, when crime rates were worsening, educational attainments were improving. After that, the patterns in the two countries may differ. Although in both countries there has been concern over a possible levelling off or falling in standards, the evidence suggests that this mainly applies at secondary level in the United States, whereas in Britain there is no clear age trend.

'Generation gap'

The supposed 'generation gap', the estrangement of young people from their parents, constitutes part of the myth of adolescence. However, empirical findings indicate that it is at most a half-truth (Rutter, 1979a). Of course, parent–child relationships do change during the teenage years, and young people come to develop important ties with their peer group, but the notion that this usually means a weakening of family relationships or an alienation from parents has proved to be wrong; while this happens in some cases it is far from the rule. A further development of that myth is that the 'generation gap' has been widening. As already noted, Gold and Reimer (1975) did observe a slight reduction between 1967 and 1972 in the closeness of parent–adolescent relationships in the U.S.A., but other studies have all produced contrary findings (Hill and Aldous, 1969; Jennings and Niemi, 1975; Bell, 1971; Reiss, 1976). The balance of evidence suggests that there has *not* been any appreciable widening of the 'generation gap'.

Sexuality and marriage

Many studies have shown that there have been marked changes over recent years in the sexual attitudes and behaviour of teenagers (see, for example, Yankelovich, 1974; Sorenson, 1973; Schofield, 1965 and 1973; Farrell and Kellaher, 1978; Court, 1976; Leete, 1979; Pearce and Farid, 1977). Sexual activity begins at an earlier age; premarital sexual relationships have become more frequent; and the number of teenage pregnancies has risen greatly. The trend towards increasing popularity of marriage has been halted and fewer teenagers now are marrying, although probably more are living together and having children outside marriage. The rate of illegitimate births to single teenage girls has remained quite high, in spite of a greater utilization of birth control and a marked increase in the number of abortions. To some extent these changes represent a change in attitudes and in life style, but to an important extent also they represent a lack of family planning among young people, and especially among young working-class boys.

Psychiatric disorder and related problems

No satisfactory data are available on trends in overall rates of psychiatric disorder in young people; psychiatric clinic attendance and hospital admission rates have risen in the U.K., but this is at least as likely to be due to an expansion of facilities as to any increase in true prevalence of disorder (Court, 1976). On the other hand, it seems clear that rates of suicide have been *increasing* in the 15–19 age group (doubling over the last twenty years in adolescent girls). This rise is particularly striking as it occurs against a background of *falling* rates in other age groups (Adelstein and Mardon, 1975). The patterns in the United States (Murphy and Wetzel, 1980) and Canada (Hellon and Solomon, 1980) have been broadly similar; in both countries there has been a significant rise in suicide rates among young people, with a less consistent pattern in older age groups.

Although completed suicides have been rising in frequency among young people, their absolute rates in this age group are very low compared with those in older age groups. Attempted suicide, in contrast, is at its peak in late adolescence and early adult life. Scottish data (Kreitman, 1977) indicate that, like completed suicide, attempted suicide rates have risen very greatly during the late 60s and 70s, especially in girls.

Accurate data on historical trends with respect to the prevalence of anorexia nervosa are lacking, but clinic studies have been consistent in indicating a very considerable increase over recent decades (Duddle, 1973; Kendell *et al.*, 1973; Theander, 1970). There must be uncertainty as to how far the rise in incidence in these three series is due merely to better identification of cases, but the consistency and extent of the rise suggest that probably the disorder is becoming more frequent.

There are many difficulties involved in the accurate assessment of the prevalence of problem drinking and of alcoholism. Nevertheless, all the various indices agree in the picture they provide of changes over time (Donnan and Haskey, 1977). From the early years of this century until the mid-1940s or 1950s there was a steady fall in alcohol problems in the U.K. There was then an upturn, but the rates in 1975 were still well below those in 1911. But during the decade between 1965 and 1975 alcoholism seemed to increase markedly, with the increase particularly noticeable in young people. The same trend has been apparent in the U.S.A. (Kelley, 1974).

There is extensive evidence that drug use among adolescents in both the U.K. and the U.S.A. has become very much more widespread than in previous generations (see Rutter, 1979a). In the U.K. the greatest rise occurred during the early 1960s, although the rise had begun in the 1940s (Bewley, 1975). However, dependence on opiates has remained at a very low level compared with that in the U.S.A. Surveys in the United States showed that drug use of all types increased between the mid-60s and mid-70s (U.S. National Commission on Marijuana and Drug Abuse, 1973), and drug dependence among young people continues to be a substantial problem.

Altogether the evidence regarding suicide, attempted suicide, anorexia nervosa, alcoholism and drug dependence all suggest that psychiatric problems among adolescents in the U.K. and U.S.A. may be increasing. These increases parallel those which apply to juvenile delinquency, especially recidivist delinquency. Of course, it remains quite uncertain whether these historical trends all have the same explanation. But, clearly, there is the possibility that at least part of the increase in recidivist delinquency may be associated with a general rise in adolescent problems, rather than with anything directly due to crime control as such. At present, means are not available to test that possibility.

Changes in society and the family

If we are to achieve any understanding of some of the possible explanations for this rise in adolescent problems generally, and of delinquency in particular, we need to consider some of the other changes that have been taking place in society and in the family. Many of these were reviewed by Rutter (1979a), and only the main findings of that review are summarized here. However, there are some additional factors which also need to be considered.

Opportunities for crime

The first major change which requires emphasis is the substantial expansion in opportunities for crime. The most obvious of these, of course, is the huge

102 Juvenile Delinquency

increase in the number of motor vehicles. At the beginning of this century cars were a rare curiosity, whereas now the majority of households in the U.K. own one (Central Statistical Office, 1980). The relevance of this is indicated by the fact that auto-crime (meaning the unauthorized taking of vehicles, vehicle theft and the theft of property from vehicles) accounts for about a quarter of recorded known indictable crime (see Mayhew *et al.*, 1976). Even this figure does not include deaths from dangerous driving (nor, of course, the huge volume of traffic offences). In Sweden the number of automobile thefts quadrupled between 1950 and 1957, but the number of vehicles on the road rose by almost the same amount, so that the number of thefts per registered vehicle rose only 29 per cent over the same period (Christiansen, 1960). Hence, it seems reasonable to infer that at least part of the explanation for the rise in auto-crime is just that there were more cars available to steal. But that cannot be the whole explanation. For example, auto-crime in London rose by over 80 per cent between 1970 and 1974, at a time when the number of available vehicles (i.e. those without steering locks – see Chapter 9) *fell* by over a half.

The massive expansion of self-service stores since the Second World War has also been important in making shoplifting easier to carry out. In 1950 there were less than 500 self-service grocery shops in England; ten years later there were 6,500 – a thirteen-fold increase (Walsh, 1978). This is likely to have played a part in the increase in shoplifting, in that shoplifting is much more frequent in self-service stores than in those with a counter service. In Walsh's (1978) Exeter survey no self-service store was without a case of shoplifting in the previous year, whereas 32 per cent of counter-service shops had had no case. It appears that shoplifting is discouraged by the presence of shop assistants who are there to serve customers (Walsh, 1978). Of course, too, there has been a considerable proliferation during this century of automatic meters of one kind or another – including telephone kiosks (which at one time were a particularly vulnerable target for theft).

It is significant that auto offences, shoplifting and larcenies from automatic meters are three offences for which there has been a particularly great increase over the years, so that they now constitute a much greater proportion of total thefts than they did in the past* (McClintock and Avison, 1968). Crucial questions in relation to this observation are whether crime has been merely *displaced* from one type of theft to another, whether the increase in these particular offences simply added to the crime total without affecting

---

* This is no longer so in the case of thefts from automatic meters, which between 1969 and 1979 showed a substantial *drop* – from 53,000 to 21,000 (Home Office, 1980) – a drop which is probably related to 'target hardening' measures (see Chapter 9).

the rate of other offences, whether the expansion of specific crime opportunities had a more general delinquency-amplification effect so that other crimes rose in parallel, or whether increased crime opportunities made it more likely that previously non-delinquent individuals would become involved in crime. It is not possible to provide a clear decision between these alternatives, in that the increase in crime opportunities occurred at the same time as a multitude of other changes, making it impossible to differentiate the effects of each. However, with the possible exception of shoplifting in adult life (which is one of the very few crimes with a tendency towards a female preponderance in adults and where it is relatively common for there to be no other type of offence – Gibbens and Prince, 1962), the first alternative seems unlikely. It is also made less plausible by the finding that other crimes rose at the same time as auto offences, shoplifting and larcenies from automatic meters – although their rise was less marked, certainly there was no compensatory drop. There was no adequate means of deciding between the other alternatives.

In addition to these specific expansions in crime opportunities there have been changes with a more general effect. For example, it may well be that the tremendous movement away from private houses to large impersonal tower block estates has made homes more vulnerable to both vandalism and theft, as a result of the reduction in natural surveillance (see also Chapter 6). Vandalism is most likely to occur in the unsupervised public and semi-public areas of public housing estates (see Wilson, 1978). In the U.K. vandalism has been found to be less on housing estates with resident caretakers (Department of the Environment, 1977), and in North America it has been shown that apartment blocks with doormen are less vulnerable to burglary (see Waller and Okihiro, 1978). At least in part, it is likely that crime has increased not so much because people have become more criminal, but rather because it has been easier to commit crimes and there have been greater opportunities for delinquent activities.

Another factor which may be pertinent in this connection is the rise in the proportion of women going out to work (see below). Its relevance lies in the fact that the extent to which a dwelling is left vacant (as it will be if both parents have jobs outside the home) has been shown to be strongly associated with the risk of burglary (Reppetto, 1974; Waller and Okihiro, 1978).

The matter of opportunity may also be of some relevance regarding the consistent finding that crime rates are higher in the cities than in small towns (see Chapter 6). It may well be that cities increase predisposition to crime in some way, but still it was a striking observation, in West and Farrington's (1973) longitudinal study of London boys, that the delinquent youths who moved out of London in late adolescence or early adult life were more likely to give up crime than those who remained in the metropolis (West, 1982 – this finding is discussed in more detail in Chapter 7).

A further change which might be mentioned under the heading of increased opportunities is the much greater availability of drugs. In parallel with increases in the misuse of drugs of dependence, drug offences have also risen in frequency (much more so in the U.S.A., however, where the laws on drugs are quite different). Whether the rise in the use of drugs among young people in the U.K. has had any appreciable effect on overall crime rates seems doubtful. Offences connected with drugs make up a tiny proportion of juvenile offences, and studies of patients attending drug clinics, as well as studies of offenders, indicate that in most cases delinquent activities *preceded* the taking of drugs (see Connell, 1977).

War and its after-effects

Some years ago, Wilkins (1960) suggested that children born during the Second World War were an unusually delinquent generation. His conclusions were challenged at the time (Walters, 1963), and subsequent figures (Rose, 1968) have shown that the suggestion was wrong – crime rates continued to rise among those born after the war. However, it has also been argued (on the basis of comparing trends in combatant and non-combatant nations) that the experience of war may reduce inhibitions against violence and so play a part in the rise in violent crimes (see Archer and Gartner, 1976; discussed further in Chapter 6). While it is possible that war, and the social upheaval that often accompanies it, has effects on rates of juvenile delinquency, time series comparisons do not suggest marked direct effects. Crime rates did not increase to any marked extent after the First World War, and the greatest rise after the Second World War began nearly a decade after the war came to an end.

Immigration

International migration on a substantial scale was common to all western European countries during the 1950s and 1960s (Little, 1978), at a time when crime rates were showing their most dramatic rise. In the U.K. the pattern also changed to a significant extent, in that there was a particularly large influx of Asians and of black people from the New Commonwealth. Although the major influx of people from other cultures, and from an ethnic background which differed from that of the majority of people in the U.K.

at the time, has been blamed for all manner of problems (including the rise in delinquency), the empirical findings do not suggest a very direct link with the increase in crime.

Firstly, studies of crime rates among immigrants themselves during the 1950s and 1960s (at the peak of the crime 'wave') showed that they were responsible for very little crime and, indeed, probably had a crime rate somewhat below that of the indigenous population (Lambert, 1970). As discussed more fully in Chapter 4, that still applies to Asians, although it is likely that the crime rate among young blacks (mainly from a West Indian background) has shown a recent rise.

Secondly, current figures (at least in London) do not now show any significant association between crime rates for areas and the proportion of people from ethnic minorities living in those areas (Stevens and Willis, 1979). On the other hand, earlier studies (Lambert, 1970) had shown that there was a tendency for black immigrants to live in areas where much crime was committed, although they were not themselves responsible for most of the crimes. The most likely explanation of the earlier finding was that patterns of racial discrimination in housing, together with local authority housing policies (which placed much weight on duration of residence in allocating council housing), forced many immigrant families to live in disadvantaged areas which tended to house a disproportionate number of criminals.

Thirdly, and most crucial of all, the rise in crime in the U.K. has applied to a roughly similar extent in areas with a relatively high proportion of immigrants (such as London and Birmingham) and areas (such as the West Country, Cumbria and North Wales) with a negligible immigrant population (see Table 1, p. 67). Taken together, these three findings strongly suggest that immigration has had little, if anything, to do with historical trends in crime rates.

Of course, it is possible that racial discrimination and hostility experienced by immigrants have played a part in the apparent recent rise in crime among young blacks, and it could be that the tensions and resentments associated with particularly rapid rises in the proportion of immigrants (or ethnic minorities) in some areas may add to the social problems there. Both issues are important in their own right, but it seems implausible that they have played any substantial role in relation to the general rise in crime rates.

Unemployment

Throughout the world, unemployment rates have risen very greatly over the last decade (Central Statistical Office, 1978). Between 1971 and 1977, the rates in France increased from 2.8 per cent to 5.2 per cent and in the U.K. from 3.9 per cent to 6.9 per cent. Since 1977, unemployment figures have continued to rise in Britain. During the 1970s unemployment rates in the U.S.A. doubled, to reach 7 per cent. Moreover, the increase in unemployment has disproportionately affected young people so that the numbers of young men out of work in the 18–20 age group went up from 14,000 to 75,000 between 1966 and 1978, and for the under-18s from 11,000 to 67,000 (Diamond, 1978). The duration of unemployment has also gone up most markedly in the 'school-leaver' age group. It is tempting to link this appalling worsening in the employment situation with the rise in crime – on the grounds that (i) undoubtedly unemployment is a demoralizing experience; (ii) unemployed youths are more likely than those in work to be hanging about the streets in areas which present opportunities for crime; (iii) criminals are more likely than non-delinquents to be unemployed (see, for example, Wootton, 1959; Bottoms and McClintock, 1973; West, 1982); and (iv) there is some suggestion that young men are more prone to commit offences during periods of unemployment than at other times (East et al., 1942).

Nevertheless, tempting though it is, the link between overall levels of unemployment and overall levels of juvenile delinquency is a tenuous one, at best. Some years ago in the United States, Glaser and Rice (1959) found positive correlations between unemployment rates and rates of *adult* property crime, but there was no such association for juveniles. Indeed, if anything, the reverse seemed to apply, with *less* delinquency during periods of high unemployment. Research since then (see Chapter 6) has produced rather contradictory and inconclusive findings, and it is apparent that the most marked recent rise in delinquency in the U.K. (mid-50s to mid-60s) *preceded* the major rise in unemployment. While it would be foolhardy to suppose that the massive increase in unemployment during the 1970s has been (or will be) without effects on rates of crime, it is evident that alterations in levels of unemployment over this century do *not* account for the major changes in crime rate.

Divorce

The divorce rate in Britain has been going up steadily since 1857, but there was a large rise after the Second World War and a further surge in 1972 following the Divorce Law Reform Act (Leete, 1976). The divorce rate per 1,000 population rose from 25.4 in 1961, to 74.4 in 1971, leapt up to 119.0 in 1972, and has continued to rise more slowly up to a rate of 129.1 in 1977

(Office of Population Censuses and Surveys, 1979). The number of children involved in divorce has risen even further, because the increased divorce rate has been especially marked in marriages with dependent children (Leete, 1976). Divorce trends in other industrialized nations have been broadly similar, although the absolute levels vary from country to country. One consequence of the rising divorce rates, as well as of the high illegitimacy ratio, has been the increasingly large number of children being brought up in single-parent households (see Leete, 1978a and b; Bronfenbrenner, 1976). The socio-economic disadvantages suffered by one-parent families are very considerable (see Finer, 1974; also Rutter and Madge, 1976), and children reared in such circumstances show increased problems in educational attainment, behaviour and social adjustment (Finer, 1974; Ferri, 1976). Juvenile delinquency is associated with family discord and disharmony (see Chapter 6), and it might be supposed that the rising divorce rate reflects increased marital conflict and hence might be associated with an increase in youngsters predisposed to delinquent activities.

Indeed, it is possible that this is occurring but it has proved to be remarkably difficult to determine whether or not it is so. The first question is what the increase in divorce rate means, and what changes in family life it reflects. There are no satisfactory data upon which to base any judgement of whether marital disharmony and discord are becoming more or less common, or even whether overt marital breakdown is increasing in frequency. Clearly, in times past when divorce was less easily obtained, many marriage breakdowns resulted in desertions or separations rather than divorce, although in other cases parents may have continued to live together in a state of tension and disharmony. Data are lacking on historical trends regarding informal separations, and even less is known on possible changes in the level of harmony in married couples remaining together. Not surprisingly, opinions differ on the question of whether more marriages are breaking down or whether it is just that more broken marriages are ending in divorce (Chester, 1972; McGregor, 1967; Thornes and Collard, 1979). As far as we can judge, both are occurring, but there is no way of coming to an accurate assessment of either trend.

As a consequence, we cannot determine whether it is likely that the increase in divorce has played any part in the rise in crime rate. It is true that divorce rates were rising at about the same time as the increase in delinquency, but far more than a rough temporal coincidence is required to test a causal hypothesis. At an individual level, marital discord and breakdown are associated with an increased risk of delinquency and of conduct disorders more generally (see Douglas *et al.*, 1968; Gibson, 1969; Gregory, 1965;

Rutter, 1971; West and Farrington, 1973). But also, the delinquency risk for boys in *un*broken quarrelsome-neglecting homes seems to be greater than for those in broken homes (McCord and McCord, 1959; Power *et al.*, 1974). Accordingly, it could be suggested that an increase in the use of divorce could be a good thing if it meant that fewer children were spending prolonged periods in quarrelsome hostile homes. On the other hand, recent research has clearly indicated that divorce does *not* necessarily bring marital conflict to an end (Hetherington *et al.*, 1978, 1979a and b; Wallerstein and Kelly, 1980). Bitterness between divorcing parents sometimes escalates rather than diminishes following separation, and the usual pattern is for children's problems to increase during the year after divorce, although by two years they have again reduced in most cases. Moreover, parental remarriage may have either adverse or beneficial effects on children's behaviour and adjustment (Murchison, 1974; Biller, 1974; Pilling and Pringle, 1978). Accordingly, it is not obvious whether, overall, an increasing divorce rate would be *expected* to increase or decrease crime rates, and next to nothing is known on which effect (if any) it has *actually* had. *If* families have become discordant and hostile, then this *might* serve to increase the likelihood of delinquent activities, but not only is it uncertain whether in fact this has happened, but also it is likely that the impact would be considerably modified by whether divorce made the solutions to family disharmony better or worse.

Working mothers

In both the U.K. and the U.S.A. there has been a steady increase since the Second World War in the proportion of working mothers. In 1948 only a quarter of women in the U.S.A. with school-age children were in the labour force, whereas in 1974 half were (Bronfenbrenner, 1976). In the U.K. the number of married women in the labour force rose from 2.7 million in 1951 to 6.7 million in 1976 (Central Statistical Office, 1978). The main change has been the increasing tendency for women with dependent children to go out to work. Not surprisingly, the number of pre-school children in group day care of one type or another has also risen greatly.

It is not obvious whether this change would be expected to have any impact on delinquency. Maternal employment as such shows no consistent association with delinquency (see, for example, Douglas *et al.*, 1968; Wadsworth, 1979; West and Farrington, 1973) or with any measure of child disturbance (Pilling and Pringle, 1978); and the research findings suggest that most children in good quality day care develop normally (see Rutter,

1981b). An increase in mothers going out to work might actually have benefits if it protected mothers from some of the emotional stresses associated with unrelieved child-rearing (see Brown and Harris, 1978a). On the other hand, it could have serious disadvantages if the quality of day care was poor. No good evidence is available on whether the conditions in day care are getting better or worse (although it is likely that they may be improving in at least some respects), nor on whether going out to work has, on balance, made things easier or more difficult for the mothers of young children. For all these reasons, it seems implausible that changes in maternal employment have had any substantial effect on rates of delinquency, although it could not necessarily be assumed that there have been no effects on the conditions of child-rearing.

Changing patterns of family building

The annual fertility rate for women aged 15–44 was 114.9 per 1,000 women in 1901; there was a brief temporary sharp rise just after the First World War, but otherwise there was a steady fall until the mid-1930s, when it reached a low of 59. The fertility rate then rose slightly over the next twenty years to reach 71.6 in 1951; there was then a progressive rise to a peak of 93.0 in 1964; and since then a steady fall once more to a trough of 58.8 in 1977, followed by a minimal rise to 60.7 in 1978 and a slightly larger one to 64.0 in 1979 (Central Statistical Office, 1972 and 1980; Court, 1976; Office of Population Censuses and Surveys, 1979). This marked fall in fertility rate over the last fifteen years has been apparent in almost all major European countries and has been even more marked in the U.S.A. Not surprisingly, this recent fall in birth rate has been accompanied by a progressive reduction in the number of children per family, so that the average number of births per woman now stands at less than two.

Alongside this change in family size, there has been a very marked fall in the number of births conceived premaritally in the U.K. – a fall of a third between 1966 and 1975 (Thompson, 1976), and an increasing tendency to delay child-bearing for several years after marriage (Central Statistical Office, 1978; Court, 1976; Leete, 1979). In view of the known association between large family size and delinquency (see Chapter 6), and the hazards experienced by children born to teenage mothers (see Shaffer *et al.*, 1978), it might be expected that these changes would be associated with a *reduction* in the risks of delinquency. However, no clear effect of that kind has been observed. It could be suggested that delinquency rates rose most sharply during the 'baby boom' of the 50s and early 60s, but against the suggestion that this involved any kind of causal link is the continuing rise in delinquency during the late 60s when birth rates were falling, and the observation that delinquency rates after the First World War were much lower than they are now, in spite of the average family size being much greater.

However, it would be naïve to expect any very direct association between changes in family size and changes in delinquency rates, both because at an individual level the links may be indirect and because other changes in family building have been occurring at the same time. For example, illegitimacy ratios have been rising in both the U.K. and the U.S.A. (Bronfenbrenner, 1976; Pearce and Farid, 1977), but this has been paralleled by many more single mothers electing to keep their illegitimate children rather than having them adopted (Central Statistical Office, 1978; Leete, 1978a and b). In the past, illegitimate children have shown increased rates of educational and behavioural problems (Crellin *et al.*, 1971), but it may be that illegitimacy now has a different meaning in changed social circumstances and altering attitudes to marriage. Once more, it is not self-evident what effects on delinquency would be expected and certainly it is not known whether there have been any effects in actuality.

Changing roles and expectations of women

Since the Second World War there have been major changes in the roles and expectations of women. The already mentioned increase in mothers going out to work is one reflection of this trend towards greater emancipation. The rising proportion of girls continuing in further education in the U.K. (Central Statistical Office, 1972 and 1978) is another. In both the U.S.A. and the U.K., studies have shown an increasing acceptance of premarital sexual relationships (see, for example, Bell, 1971; Farrell and Kellaher, 1978; Reiss, 1976; Sorenson, 1973; Yankelovich, 1974), accompanied by changing views on personal freedom and by an emphasis on sharing and openness. There has been a marked rise in the proportion of young people using effective methods of contraception and, especially, a shift from methods controlled by the male (the sheath or withdrawal) to those controlled by the female, such as the 'pill' (Cartwright, 1976; Central Statistical Office, 1977). Abortions and female sterilizations (again, representing the female's control of child-bearing), too, have increased very greatly (Central Statistical Office, 1972; Deschamps and Valantin, 1978; Dryfoos, 1978; Office of Population Censuses and Surveys, 1979; Reiss, 1976).

There have been attempts to argue that the increasing female criminality is a consequence of women's increasing emancipation or the effects of the women's liberation movement (Adler, 1977). However, as Smart (1979) pointed out, it would be difficult on that basis to account for the increasing percentage of women offenders in the 1935–46 decade, when there was not a similar increase during the 1946–55 decade. On the other hand, as Austin (1981) notes, while the recent proportional increase in female theft is no greater than that between 1935–46, the recent increase in violent crime among women is substantially greater than that during earlier periods. The effect, or lack of it, of changing roles of women on the steady trend for females to be increasingly involved in crime has been much discussed recently, without any adequate resolution of the issue (see, for example, Adler, 1977; Giordano, 1978; Heidensohn, 1968; Jensen and Eve, 1976; Smart, 1979; Steffensmeier, 1978). Of course, too, it remains a matter of debate just how far female emancipation has progressed. There have always been very substantial and widespread sex differentials in wages and salaries, with women's earnings far below those of men in both Britain and the United States (see Rutter and Madge, 1976; Suter and Miller, 1973). Up to now, there has been only a quite limited narrowing of the gap.

Kinship and community support patterns

Bronfenbrenner (1979) has eloquently argued the need to take an ecological view of human development, by which he means that the individual interactions (between parent and child or between two peers) will inevitably be influenced by the social context within which they occur, and by the more extended set of relationships of which each dyad forms one part. Within this general framework of concepts, concerns have been expressed that there have been historical trends towards a reduction of kinship and community ties, of parent–child interaction, of parental involvement in the activities of their adolescent offspring, and of children's involvement in the care of dependent younger children.*

These ideas have considerable potential importance, but it is not at all certain whether there has been any appreciable weakening of family ties (see Quinton, 1980), let alone whether such postulated changes have had any impact on delinquent activities. While undoubtedly in the U.K. there has been a substantial reduction since 1961 in the number of young married couples living with their parents (Central Statistical Office, 1978), studies of the general population show that most families with dependent children are

---

* See also Whiting and Whiting (1975) for cross-cultural anthropological evidence on the possible importance of this last item.

still in close contact with grandparents. As for community ties and relationships, again we lack systematic data on whether these have altered and, if they have, what effects have followed. The matter is an important one and warrants more detailed study than it has received up to now (see also Chapter 6).

Television

As part of the pattern of increasing prosperity, there has been a huge increase in the number of people with television sets – as shown, for example, by the increase in TV licences from 2 million in 1951 to 17 million in 1978 (Central Statistical Office, 1972 and 1978). Moreover, among those with TV sets, the weekly hours of viewing have gone up steadily. Concerns have been expressed about its inhibiting effect on family conversation. Maccoby (1951) found that most families had no conversation while the television was on, and that the TV set tended to dominate and determine family life while it was in operation. As Bronfenbrenner (1976) put it: 'The primary damage of the television screen lies not so much in the behaviour it produces as the behaviour it prevents – the talks, the games, the family festivities, and arguments through which much of the child's learning takes place and his character is formed.' The suggestion sounds plausible, but we lack evidence on whether family activities have truly diminished as a result of television.

A further concern (discussed more fully in Chapter 6) is that the increasing portrayal of violence on the television screen may have increased the likelihood of violent behaviour by the adolescents who view the programmes. As we argue later, the evidence suggests that some effect of this kind may operate, but the effect is probably of only quite modest strength – a possible minor contributory factor, but not one likely to account for any major trends in rates of delinquency.

Hospital admissions

Although there have been major improvements in the health of children (which might be expected to be associated with a reduced need for hospital admission), Douglas (1975) found that first-born children of mothers aged 23 years or less in the 1964–73 generation were twice as likely to have been admitted to hospital during the pre-school years as those in the earlier 1946–50 generation. Moreover, although admissions today tend to be for shorter periods, children now are nearly *three* times as likely to have *multiple* admissions to hospital. In that both Douglas (1975) and Quinton and Rutter

(1976) found that repeated hospital admissions are associated with an increased risk of later behavioural disorder (Douglas also showed that this was accompanied by an increased rate of delinquency), it might be suggested that the increase in hospital admissions could here play a small part in the rise in crime rate. This is possible, but the strength of the association suggests that, at most, it is unlikely to have made more than an extremely minor contribution. Nevertheless, the increase in hospital admissions does constitute a cause for some concern.

Industrialization and urbanization

It tends to be assumed that industrialization and urbanization are necessarily and causally associated with a rise in crime (see Chapter 6 for a more detailed discussion of the evidence on the empirical associations found). However, it is highly questionable how far these trends are in fact causally linked (see, for example, Christiansen's 1960 analyses for Sweden and Denmark), and urbanization could not account for the recent rise in crime in the U.K., both because the rise has been apparent in urban and rural areas (see above) and because urbanization in the U.K. has increased very little since the 1930s. Of course, the rapid urbanization which has taken place throughout the world during the last 150 years has constituted one of the most striking and dramatic changes in recent times (Davis, 1973; Basham, 1978). Furthermore, it is a change which has brought with it many psycho-social problems, especially in developing countries (Clinard and Abbott, 1973). It would be foolish to suppose that it has had no effect on patterns of delinquency, but the fact remains that it cannot be held responsible for the post-war rise in crime in Britain.

Environmental lead

Bryce-Smith and Waldron (1974) have argued that sub-clinical poisoning by environmental lead may be responsible for a significant part of crime and delinquency. The evidence up to 1979 on the associations between raised lead levels and impaired cognitive/behavioural functioning was systematically reviewed by Rutter (1980a), with the conclusion that: 'persistently raised blood lead levels in the range above 40 μg/100 ml may cause slight cognitive impairment (a reduction of one to five points on average) and less certainly may increase the risk of behavioural difficulties'. Since then further evidence has become available suggesting that the risks probably also apply to lead levels well below 40 μg/100 ml (Rutter and Russell Jones, 1983). In that lead is a neuro-toxin without known benefits, these findings provide a sufficient indication for the recommendation that immediate steps should be taken to reduce greatly the level of lead in the environment (Department of Health and Social Security, 1980). But, even so, there are *no* grounds for the suggestion that lead might be responsible for rising crime rates. Firstly, the effects of lead which have been demonstrated concern cognitive and attentional deficits. So far, no associations with crime or delinquency have been shown (the matter has not been examined in any of the published studies). Secondly, although practically important, the associations found between lead levels and behaviour are far too weak to account for any major change in crime rate. Thirdly, such weak evidence as is available suggests that it is unlikely that environmental lead levels have increased enough during the period of rising crime rates to account for the rise.

Improved physical health

Most of the changes discussed so far referred to factors which might conceivably be associated with an increase in delinquency, provided various assumptions were met. However, the last two concern changes which, if they had any impact on delinquency, might be expected to reduce it. Throughout this century, the health and development of children has progressively improved (see Court, 1976). For example, children aged 10–14 have gained some 2–3 centimetres in height each decade. Conditions such as rickets and tuberculosis have become quite rare in the U.K., general standards of nutrition have much improved, and the life expectancy of children has greatly increased. In parallel with children's improving nutritional status in the Western world, there has been a definite trend towards accelerated maturation in height and weight in both boys and girls during the last 100 years (Tanner, 1970) – although it seems that this trend may now have halted.

In that there are only rather weak links between physical health and delinquency (see Chapter 5), no particular effect on delinquent behaviour should be expected to follow these gains. It should be added that the increasingly advanced physical maturation has happened to coincide with a progressive extension of education to later and later ages. This coincidence suggests the possibility of an increasing potential clash between the necessity for physically mature children to remain economically dependent on their parents, and their ability and need to be psychologically *in*dependent. It is not known how far this has in fact occurred, nor whether it has led to increasing family tensions in later adolescence, nor (if it has) whether this has had any effect on delinquent behaviour. However, the point of mentioning this possibility is that it is *possible* that improvements in physical health may have been associated with some minor psychological disadvantages.

Standards of living

The next change to mention is the major reduction in poverty and in poor living conditions which has taken place since the turn of the century (see Rutter and Madge, 1976; Rutter, 1979a; Diamond, 1978). For example, in 1911 about one-third of households in the U.K. were overcrowded to the extent of having more than one person per room, but by 1961 this proportion had fallen to 11 per cent and by 1977 to 3.2 per cent (Hole and Pountney, 1971; Central Statistical Office, 1978). Similarly, the Royal Commission figures in the U.K. (Diamond, 1978) showed that the true purchasing power of those in the bottom three deciles of income had increased by about 25 per cent between 1961 and 1974, although with a slight decline in 1975–6. It is clear from all the evidence that there has been a very marked and widespread improvement in living conditions over this century. In so far as delinquency is generally thought to be associated with poverty and social disadvantage, one might have expected this increased affluence to have been accompanied by a reduction in delinquency. Obviously, it has not been so. At first sight, this would seem to provide a strong indication that, in fact, poverty does *not* predispose to delinquency.

However, while that could be the case, there are several reasons why it would be an unjustified inference. Firstly, the total population figures misrepresent the circumstances of children (see Rutter, 1979a) – far more of whom suffer poor living conditions than the overall figures suggest. Secondly, although the general level of prosperity has risen greatly during this century, the *distribution* of incomes has changed little (Diamond, 1978) – so that it may be that the proportion of people feeling poor (because their income is more than a certain amount below the average) has not altered. Thirdly, it is likely that people's expectations of what they need have risen over the years. As patterns of expenditure change and as new commodities become available, the living standards of earlier times no longer apply (Townsend, 1979). While it is not self-evident that 'relative' measures of poverty are always to be preferred to 'absolute' indices (Madge, 1980), it could well be that it is marked *inequalities* in income or a lack of access to valued activities, rather than any overall income level, that predispose to crime (Braithwaite, 1979). The few data relevant to the hypothesis that changes over time in income distribution are associated with changes in crime rate are inconsistent and inconclusive (Danziger and Wheeler, 1975; Krohn, 1976), suggesting that this is not likely to be an important factor. However, more information is required before any firm conclusions are warranted. Fourthly, it may be that people's feelings of security and prosperity are related as much to their power to control their own destiny as to their absolute level of income. In that connection, the existence of the 'poverty trap' (the situation by which, over a substantial range of earnings, people cannot increase their income, because any increase in wages is entirely offset by the loss of benefits) has served to make things worse rather than better. The only possible conclusion is that we have remarkably little understanding of the psychological consequences of variations in prosperity and poverty. So far as delinquency is concerned, it appears unlikely that the *absolute* level of income is the crucial feature, but that does not necessarily mean that economic factors are of no importance. The issue needs to be re-examined in a more discriminating fashion.

Civil strife and conflict

Finally, we need to consider the possibility that changes in the level of crime are a consequence of socio-political factors, and in particular of the extent of civil strife and conflict. Two separate issues are involved here: (i) whether times of strife tend also to be periods with high levels of crime; and (ii) if they are, what socio-political forces govern strife and conflict. The most systematic analyses of the evidence on the first point were undertaken by Gurr, Grabosky and Hula (1977) in their study of historical trends in crime and conflict in London, Stockholm, Sydney and Calcutta during the last 200 years or so. As they point out, there are at least four rather different reasons why one might find a general relationship between high crime and civil conflict. Firstly, both might be rooted in social tensions; secondly, prolonged group conflict could increase the breakdown of moral order; thirdly, élites faced with real or threatened resistance may respond by intensifying efforts at social control with increased policing, prosecuting, and punishment; and fourthly, periods of strife are likely to present greater opportunities for crime. It was found that, in the four cities studied, sharp increases in crime (so-called 'crime waves') more often than not coincided with periods of civil strife (as evidenced by public order offences, labour conflict, strikes, civil disobedience, ethnic conflict, and terrorist activity). For example, this was apparent in London in 1956–72 and, of course, in the United States during the same time period. Altogether, 19 of the 29 (66 per cent) substantial increases in violent crime in the four cities coincided with serious internal conflict, and Gurr and his colleagues concluded that there were significant links between strife and crime. On the other hand, there have been periods of sharply rising crime rates without significant civil strife (for example, London in the 1820s), and also times of great strife without rising crime (for example, the period of the Stockholm riots in the 1840s and the strike-ridden years of the 1920s and early 1930s). Furthermore, the timing has sometimes suggested that the increases in crime preceded the strife rather than the other way round – for example, this seems to have been the case in Sweden after the Second World War. There is the impression of some sort of connection between civil strife and rising crime (quantification of the association is difficult both because of the problems in measuring strife and because of uncertainties over time relationships – as well, of course, as a result of the difficulties in assessing changes in crime rates), but equally there is a lack of good explanations for the many important periods when changes in strife were not accompanied by changes in crime, or vice versa.

The second question on the possible ways in which socio-political forces influence strife and/or crime has proved equally difficult to answer. Once again, comparisons across countries and over time have been used to tackle the issues. Group conflict theories all assume that strife arises from competition between groups for valued conditions and positions – with the use of power and control crucial (Gurr *et al.*, 1977; McDonald, 1976). The problem here is how to derive testable hypotheses from this general notion and how to develop meaningful and appropriate measures of changes in levels of competition, power and control. Gurr *et al.* (1977) looked for possible associations between various measures of changes in police activity (including size of the police force) and changes in crime rate over the last two centuries, in the four cities they studied, and found no consistent effect. Economic conditions, too, have shown an inconsistent relationship with crime. In the nineteenth century both theft and assault increased during periods of economic slump and declined when conditions improved again, but economic changes in either direction have had little connection with crime in the twentieth century. McDonald (1976) used a variety of indices to look at possible socio-political influences on crime – with respect to both international and British crime figures over recent years (and to a more limited extent over the first half of this century). It was concluded that official crime rates were *not* higher in societies with widespread poverty and illiteracy, nor were they higher in societies with heterogeneous populations, low rates of voting and limited democracy. In England and Wales high crime rates in recent years have been related to economic prosperity and greater expenditure on the welfare state and, to a lesser extent, to expenditure on the

118 *Juvenile Delinquency*

police force. However, as evident in both McDonald's data and that presented by Gurr *et al.*, even these links prove inconsistent if analyses are extended to other nations or other time periods. McDonald (1976) concluded that 'predictions from conflict theory ... were not well borne out' (p. 288); and Gurr *et al.* (1977) summarize the state of the art with the statement: '... there is little empirical basis for confidence about the contemporary efforts of policies informed by humanitarian faith in equalization of opportunity and rehabilitation, or by conservative reliance on strict authority and firm punishment' (p. 767). Nevertheless, it seems that some policies of public order can increase strife. Gurr *et al.* use the example of Calcutta to argue that the mix of inconsistent repression and lack of reform is usually fatal. They suggest that '... The fundamental precondition for public order is congruence between the cultural values of the ordinary members of society and the operating codes of order and opportunity maintained by political élites' (p. 767). In the long term, effective crime control probably relies on a degree of public consensus on goals and values. However, it is less clear just what steps are needed to bring that about, and it is obvious that changes in crime rate occur for many reasons other than variations in the extent of that consensus.

Conclusions on possible reasons for the increase in crime

Although there are many social changes associated with the rise in delinquency, considerable doubt remains on which (if any) are responsible for the changes in crime. It seems reasonably clear that an increase in opportunities for crime has played some part, but it is uncertain how much general effect this has had on crime. There are several factors commonly thought to have been associated with the rise of crime in the U.K., for which the empirical evidence suggests that this belief is mistaken. Factors in this category include immigration, unemployment, the increase in the proportion of working mothers, industrialization and urbanization, and environmental lead pollution. There are some factors, such as rising levels of divorce, the effects of television, and more frequent hospital admission, which may have played some minor role (the circumstances associated with divorce perhaps more so), but none of these seems likely to have had a sufficient impact to make a great deal of difference. There are others, such as weakened family ties and reduced family interaction, which might have had some impact if they had occurred, but there is doubt on whether they have done so. Clearly, there have been some changes in the roles and expectations of women, but we do not know whether these have had any effect on crime. Finally, there are certain changes in society, such as increased affluence, better living conditions, improved physical health, and a reduced size of the average family, which might have been expected to have had benefits, but where no such benefits are identifiable. The reasons for changes in the crime rate remain largely unknown, and research into the matter (although methodologically difficult to undertake) might be rewarding.

4
Sex, Social Class and Race

Delinquent activities are common in all segments of the population. However, before considering the various individual and psycho-social factors associated with crime, we discuss in this chapter some of the ways in which delinquent activities vary according to the broad demographic variables of sex, social class and race.

Sex differences

Criminal statistics in all countries have consistently shown that more males than females appear before the courts for delinquent activities (Wootton, 1959). For example, the British National Survey (Douglas *et al.*, 1966; Wadsworth, 1979) found that 18 per cent of males, but only 2.5 per cent of females, had been convicted or officially cautioned before their twenty-first birthday; Farrington (1981a and b) used the British Home Office (1978) figures to calculate that 12 per cent of males compared with 2 per cent of females are convicted by the age of 17; Jonsson's (1967) figures for Stockholm showed that 9 per cent of boys and 1 per cent of girls had an official delinquency record by the age of 14; Christiansen and Jensen (1972) found a similar ratio in Denmark; and various American studies (see Farrington, 1979) have shown much the same. Examination of the types of offences committed also indicates that girls are especially less likely to be involved in crimes involving damage to property or injury to other persons (Wadsworth, 1979; Home Office, 1980; McClintock and Avison, 1968).

The question arises, of course, as to whether these highly consistent sex differences in official crime and delinquency statistics reflect *real* differences in delinquent behaviour, or rather whether they result from biases in police or court practice. Perhaps there is a chivalrous reluctance to prosecute females, or perhaps there is a greater tendency to deal with delinquent activities in girls by means of non-judicial interventions (such as by psychiatric referral or social work procedures). These possibilities can be tested in several different ways.

To begin with, an analysis of official statistics is informative. These show that: (i) the sex difference applies equally (indeed especially) to very serious crimes such as homicide, robbery or aggravated assault, where there is likely to be less police discretion (Zimring, 1979); (ii) girls are more likely than boys to be brought before the court for non-criminal matters such as being in 'moral danger' or 'beyond control' (Campbell, 1981; Caplan *et al.*, 1980; Davies, 1976; Home Office, 1978); and (iii) girls are more likely than boys to be cautioned rather than brought to court (Home Office, 1979), but girls brought to court tend to have committed lesser offences (Cockburn and Maclay, 1965; May, 1977; Wadsworth, 1979) and, especially, are more likely to be placed in some form of institutional care for lesser offences (Chesney-Lind, 1979; Cockburn and Maclay, 1965; Cowie *et al.*, 1968; Ganzer and Sarason, 1973; Kratcoski, 1974; May, 1977). It is evident that, in many respects, girls tend to be treated *more*, rather than less, harshly by the courts and, hence, that it is unlikely that the male preponderance in delinquency is an artefact of police or court leniency towards females.

Self-report delinquency data provide another means of examining the same question. Like official statistics, they tend to show that more boys than girls are involved in delinquent activities, but the sex ratio in most studies has been substantially less than that evident in court figures (Cernkovich and Giordano, 1979; Gold, 1970; Hindelang, 1971; Jensen and Eve, 1976; Kratcoski and Kratcoski, 1975). The results would seem to suggest both that there is a 'real' difference between boys and girls in the extent and frequency of delinquent activities but that the size of the difference is less than the official statistics suggest. However, it may well be that self-report data underestimate the size of the sex difference in seriously delinquent activities because the questionnaires tend to include many very minor acts which, on their own, would be rather unlikely to result in prosecution. Hindelang *et al.* (1979), in reviewing a variety of self-report studies, observed that although the sex ratio for minor theft tended to be in the 1.5 to 2.5 to 1 range, that for assault and major theft tended to be about 3.5, and for strong-arm theft (i.e. with violence) it averaged 4.5 across studies. Similarly, Gold (1970), Elliott and Voss (1974), Dentler and Monroe (1961), and Hindelang (1973) all found that the sex ratio for more serious or more frequent delinquency was several times that for minor or occasional delinquent acts.

The same issue may be examined by means of total population epidemiological studies utilizing data from parents and teachers as well as from the young people themselves. Usually, such studies have been concerned to assess the prevalence of conduct disturbances as more globally defined, rather than delinquent activities as such. This means that they would include disorders involving such items as aggression, destructive behaviour, and fire-setting in the home, which might not constitute 'official' delinquency. Equally, however, the concept of conduct disorder includes the notion of social impairment, so that isolated delinquent acts without any other evidence of disturbed behaviour would not be included.

With one exception (Leslie, 1974), such epidemiological studies have been consistent in showing a male preponderance for disturbances of conduct in all age groups from at least age 5 to adulthood (Rutter, Tizard and Whitmore, 1970; Rutter *et al.*, 1975a, 1976a; Werry and Quay, 1971; Graham and Rutter, 1973; Shepherd *et al.*, 1971; Remschmidt *et al.*, 1977; Lavik, 1977; Kastrup, 1977). We may conclude that boys are indeed more prone to show disorders of conduct of both a delinquent and a non-delinquent variety. However, it should be added that in most of these studies, as in the self-report data, the sex ratio has been somewhat lower than that in the official statistics.

The possibility that delinquent activities in girls are more likely to be dealt with by means of psychiatric or social work referral than by prosecution can be examined by looking at psychiatric clinic data. It does seem that the courts are more likely to refer delinquent girls for clinical assessment (Caplan *et al.*, 1980), and girls are more likely than boys to be placed in the care of the local authority on moral, rather than delinquency, grounds, there being little sex difference in 'care' proceedings on the grounds of being 'beyond control' (Home Office, 1978). However, even if these various different grounds are summated there is still a marked male preponderance. If delinquent girls were being diverted from the courts to psychiatric clinics, it would be expected that girls would be preponderant among young people attending clinics and diagnosed as having a conduct disorder. However, clinic data are consistent in showing that this is not the case; to the contrary, there is a marked excess of boys among the clinic clientele with that diagnosis (see Rutter, Tizard and Whitmore, 1970; Rutter, Shaffer and Shepherd, 1975). It is evident that a diversion explanation for the sex imbalance in the delinquency figures cannot be sustained.

Yet another explanation is that boys and girls are equally likely to exhibit psycho-social problems in response to internal or external stressors but that, whereas boys respond with delinquency, girls respond with emotional disorder or mental illness (Smart, 1977). It is conceivable that this might explain the crime figures for adults, in that depression and neurosis are very much commoner in women than in men (Weissman and Klerman, 1977), but that suggestion cannot be supported for juveniles. The point is that epidemiological studies have been consistent in showing either an equal sex ratio for emotional disorders in childhood or, at most, a marginally greater prevalence in girls (see Rutter, Tizard and Whitmore, 1970). Even if all forms of disorder are summated there is still a male preponderance.

However the evidence is looked at, the conclusion is the same. There is a true preponderance of both delinquent activities and conduct disorders in males. While this sex difference is at its greatest with official statistics, it is evident also in epidemiological data based on self-reports, parental data and reports from teachers. There are undoubted differences in the ways in which boys and girls are dealt with by 'authorities' and official agencies of various kinds, but these cannot account for the sex difference in delinquent activities.

Variations in sex ratio

The conclusion that the sex difference is valid does not necessarily mean that it is a result of intrinsic biological qualities. Hence, before coming to a consideration of possible explanations for the sex difference, we need to pay attention to the circumstances in which the sex ratio has been found to vary.

Rather few data are available for the pre-school period, but such data as there are show less consistent sex differences in disturbances of conduct (obviously, delinquency as such cannot be studied at that age). Richman *et al.* (1982) found no sex differences at 3 years in difficulties in management – although there was a male preponderance at 4 years (Richman, 1977), and even at 3 years hyperactivity was more common in boys (Richman *et al.*, 1982). Whether disturbances of conduct in reality do not show a sex difference until 4 or 5 years remains uncertain, both because of the paucity of data and because of the difficulty in categorizing types of disorder in very young children.

Cultural factors provide a second source of variations in the sex ratio in delinquent activities. Both clinic (Nicol, 1971) and general population studies (Rutter *et al.*, 1974) have shown that conduct disorders show a lower sex ratio in children from a West Indian background. Delinquency data for juveniles in London also show that there is a somewhat reduced sex ratio in those from a West Indian background – but a much increased sex ratio in those from Asian and Cypriot families, where female crime is exceedingly uncommon (Ouston, 1983). In the United States, too, both self-report data (Cernkovich and Giordano, 1979; Berger and Simon, 1974) and criminal statistics (Forslund, 1970; Green, 1970) show a tendency for the sex ratio to be lower among blacks than among whites for the more serious crimes, and perhaps especially for those involving personal violence.

Secular trends reflect a third source of variation in sex ratio. During the last few decades, delinquency and crime statistics have shown a progressive narrowing of the difference in rates between the sexes (Adler, 1977; Rutter, 1979a; Steffensmeier, 1978, 1980). In Britain, the United States and many other countries, female crime has been rising at a higher rate than male crime, with the result that the sex ratio for delinquency has been falling. There is still a very great male preponderance, but nevertheless the change in sex ratio has been considerable – a drop from 11:1 in 1957 to 5:1 in 1977 in the United Kingdom (Home Office, 1978).

The possible reasons for the change in sex ratio for crime and delinquency have been much discussed in recent years, without any adequate resolution of the issue. It has been argued that the increasing female criminality is a consequence of women's growing emancipation or the effects of the women's liberation movement. However, as noted in the previous chapter, it is difficult on that basis to account for the observation that the increasing involvement of women in theft was as great in the 1936–45 decade as in the 1955–75 period, but did not increase during the 1946–55 decade (Austin, 1981; Smart, 1979). It is only for violent offences that the main increase applies to the 1965–75 decade.

The finding that in Japan the rate of female crime did *not* rise between 1946 and 1972 (Clifford, 1976) can be used either to support the emancipation argument (on the grounds that women are less emancipated in Japan than in the U.K. or the U.S.A.) or to reject it (on the grounds that the *change* in the position of women in Japanese society has altered greatly since the Second World War, even if it has proceeded less far than in most Western societies). Others have suggested that to a considerable extent the rise in female crime may be due to the ever-increasing spread of self-service stores which tend to make it easier to shoplift, shoplifting being one of the few crimes which are relatively more frequent in women (Steffensmeier, 1978). But that does not explain the fact that violent crimes by women have risen to an even greater extent than the various forms of theft (Home Office, 1978). In the U.K., a further possible factor is the effect of the rise in the proportion of adolescents from West Indian families during the 1960s and 70s (Little, 1978). This is relevant because, as noted above, disruptive and antisocial behaviour is relatively more frequent in black girls than white girls. However, the proportion of West Indian youngsters in most parts of the country remains too low for it to be plausible that the change in ethnic composition of English youth could have had much effect on the statistics – especially as the rise in female delinquency preceded the main influx of West Indian families (Rutter, 1979a).

It is not possible entirely to rule out the possibility that the change in sex ratio of offenders has been due to changes in police practices or in judicial responses to female offenders, but it seems most unlikely that this could constitute a sufficient explanation. Rather, the rise in delinquency among adolescent girls and young women during recent years seems to be a 'real' phenomenon. But its cause has yet to be determined, and none of the hypotheses put forward so far appear particularly plausible.

We may conclude, therefore, not only that the higher frequency of conduct disturbances in males is an almost universal phenomenon (at least after the infancy period), but also that the *extent* of the sex difference varies considerably across cultures and time. There have been a variety of suggestions on possible reasons for both sets of findings, but without any resolution of the controversies on this topic, for which theoretical speculations far outstrip the empirical data (see Eme, 1979, for an informative review of possible explanations for sex differences in childhood psychopathology).

Sex differences in aggressivity, hyperactivity, and dishonesty

In seeking to account for the sex differences in crime and delinquency, it is appropriate to turn first to the evidence on sex differences in those behavioural features which might be related to delinquency. As the empirical evidence on these matters has been extensively reviewed by Maccoby and Jacklin (1974, 1980a and b), only the main conclusions will be given here. Although their review of research findings has come under recent attack (Tieger, 1980), their reply (Maccoby and Jacklin, 1980b) deals adequately with the points which are crucial for the issues considered here.

Observational studies are generally consistent in showing that males are more aggressive in their interactions with peers, and in indicating that this sex difference is evident at least as early as the pre-school years and continues through subsequent phases of development. The greater aggression of boys is shown both verbally and physically but is most marked in interactions with other boys.

Research findings strongly suggest that, to an important extent, the greater aggressivity of boys has a biological basis. The main evidence is: (i) the sex difference is apparent from early childhood; (ii) although cross-cultural data are rather meagre, it seems that the sex difference applies across the cultures studied; (iii) the sex difference applies similarly to sub-human primates; (iv) pre-natal androgens have an organizing function in early development which influences the degree of aggressivity shown at a later age; and (v) alterations in circulatory testosterone levels in adult life have an effect on aggressivity.

The last finding, of course, is of little relevance to sex differences in aggression in pre-pubertal children (when there is little difference between boys and girls in male hormone levels), but it emphasizes the potential role of later biological influences. The findings on the correlates of variations in testosterone level *within* males are much less consistent, but two recent studies suggest that there may be some association with aggressivity and disinhibition, although not with delinquency as such (Olweus et al., 1980; Daitzman and Zuckerman, 1980).

In arguing that there is good evidence for a biologically determined sex difference in aggressivity, it should also be emphasized that: (i) there are major individual differences among both boys and girls; (ii) the two sexes overlap in aggressivity; (iii) aggression is also much influenced by social-learning and situational factors; and (iv) just as testosterone influences aggression, so also the expression of aggression influences hormone levels.

Aggressivity undoubtedly constitutes the behaviour with the best established and most marked sex difference that is biologically determined in part. However, there is somewhat less consistent evidence that high activity levels are also more characteristic of boys than girls; and that females are more likely to show nurturant responses to young children and to respond empathically to someone else's distress (see also Hoffman, 1977).

Less is known about sex differences in honesty and morality, but various experimental studies, in which children (who did not realize that they could be observed) were given the opportunity to cheat, have shown no consistent sex difference in cheating, although there has been a tendency for girls to be more liable to confess and to express moral attitudes (see Maccoby, 1966). Interestingly, the one 'real life' experimental study, in which adults were given an opportunity to steal in a situation in which they were unaware that they could be observed, also showed rather minor sex differences (Milgram and Shotland, 1973), although the numbers were far too small for this to be a reliable finding. However, there is a rather inconsistent association between moral maturity, cheating in an experimental situation, and delinquent activities (see Kupfersmid and Wonderly, 1980).

It would be wrong to regard delinquency as mainly a matter of dishonesty. While it is certainly the case that most delinquent acts involve theft, and hence a form of dishonesty, also most involve risk-taking, aggression or predatory behaviour of one kind or another. The behaviours most closely associated with delinquency involve aggressivity and hyperactivity, rather than dishonesty, and it is these behaviours which show the most consistent sex difference. It remains possible that temperamental factors play a part in

Sex differences in response to family discord

One of the early observations from British epidemiological studies (Rutter, 1970) was the apparently greater vulnerability of boys to family stress and discord. It was found that whereas antisocial problems in boys were much more common when there was severe marital discord, this was not the case for girls except to a minor extent. The same sex difference was evident when total deviance was considered, so it was clear that the finding was not an artefact of sex differences in diagnosis. This finding has now been replicated to a greater or lesser extent in further epidemiological studies in the U.K. (Wolkind and Rutter, 1973; Rutter *et al.*, 1975a; Whitehead, 1979) and, more importantly, in several American studies using quite different sets of measures for both marital discord and conduct disturbances (Emery and O'Leary, 1982; Porter and O'Leary, 1980; Hetherington *et al.*, 1978 and 1979a and b; Block *et al.*, 1981). Porter and O'Leary (1980), in a study of school-age clinic children, found that marital adjustment (as assessed on the Short Marital Adjustment Test) and overt marital hostility (as indexed by maternal report on the O'Leary–Porter scale) were both significantly correlated with problem behaviours in boys (assessed using the Quay and Peterson checklist), but not in girls. A similar later study by Emery and O'Leary (1982), using the same measures, confirmed the sex difference in response to marital discord. Block and her colleagues (1981), in a non-clinic longitudinal study of children aged 3–7, found that an index of parental disagreement on child-rearing was significantly related to a range of behavioural measures in the children – but with the associations significantly stronger for boys than for girls. Hetherington *et al.* (1978, 1979a and b) used a combination of observation, diary, questionnaire and interview methods in their study of children in intact and divorcing families. They showed that the impact of marital discord was more pervasive and more enduring for boys than for girls. Moreover, Cadoret and Cain (1980), in a study of adoptees separated at birth from their biological parents, found that an adverse family environment (as shown by psychiatric disorder or divorce in the adoptive family) was more strongly predictive of antisocial behaviour in boys than in girls. The only strikingly negative finding is that from the epidemiological longitudinal study by Richman *et al.* (1982) of 3–8 year olds in London. Family discord and stresses of various kinds were associated with disorder in *both* boys and girls, with associations somewhat stronger for girls than for boys. These findings apply to overall disorder, rather than to disturbances of conduct, but even so they disagree with those from other investigations. It remains unclear whether the failure to find a greater male vulnerability in this study represents a real age difference (such that the susceptibility in boys develops after the school-age period) or whether it is a function of differences in samples or measures. However, with this one exception (and the reduced sex difference in Whitehead's 1979 study of 7 year olds) it appears that boys are more likely than girls to develop disturbances (especially of conduct) when exposed to family discord and disharmony. Whether girls are truly more resilient or whether they show the psychological scars in other ways, which perhaps may not become overt until they are older, cannot be determined from these data.

Various possible explanations have been tentatively suggested for these findings. For example, Rutter (1970) pointed to the *lack* of evidence for relevant sex differences in variables such as attachment, suggestibility, identification, conditionability and physiologic responses to stress which might be invoked as explanations. On the other hand, there was the possible parallel with the well-documented greater male vulnerability to a wide range of physical stresses, which raised the possibility of a similar constitutionally determined male susceptibility to psychological stresses. Whitehead (1979) suggested that, at least with respect to divorce, the difference may be due to the children usually remaining with the mother (so that boys are more likely to lack a positive role model). This may well be a relevant factor with respect to children's responses to divorce, but it cannot account for the sex difference in response to discord in intact families. On the other hand, Hetherington *et al.* (1978, 1979a and b) found that warring parents were more likely to argue and quarrel in front of their sons than their daughters. Accordingly, at least in part, the sex difference could be a consequence of differences between boys and girls in the extent of their *exposure* to discord. Eme (1979) points to the human and animal evidence (Quadagno *et al.*, 1977; Reinisch and Karow, 1977) that pre-natal androgens influence aggressivity, and suggests that this may affect the predisposition to antisocial disorders. Eme also noted that there are sex differences in some temperamental features which are linked with later behavioural disorders.

Block *et al.* (1981) put forward three other possible explanations. Firstly, the salience of the two parents may differ for boys and girls; for girls the lesser salience of the father – as suggested by Lamb (1976) – may attenuate the effects of parental disagreement. Secondly, it could be (as suggested by Gunnar-Vongnechten, 1978) that being able to control their environment is more important for boys than for girls – and hence that the capricious environment of a discordant family is more disturbing for boys. Thirdly, they suggest that the process of socialization has different implications for the two sexes – with the need to control aggressivity being greater for boys than for girls.

Emery and O'Leary (1982), in their empirical investigation, explored the possibility that boys and girls in discordant families would differ in their perceptions of parental discord or in their feelings of being accepted and loved, but neither hypothesis received support. Instead, Emery and O'Leary favoured some form of differential modelling explanation for the sex differences.

Yet a further possibility is that parents and teachers respond differently to disruptive behaviour in boys than they do to similar behaviour in girls. There are a variety of pointers suggesting that to some extent this is the case (see review by Maccoby and Jacklin, 1974). However, it also appears that the true picture is a more complex two-way interaction in which the final outcome (for both parents and children) is likely to be shaped by the fact that boys and girls respond differently in a host of different ways. Quite apart from the reactions to discord which have already been discussed, there is evidence, for example, that a responsive supportive parenting style is associated with high academic achievement in boys but low achievement in girls (for example, Claeys and DeBoek, 1976), and that whereas social competence in girls is associated with a challenging abrasive parenting style, in boys it is associated with parental warmth (Baumrind, 1981). Similarly, most recently, Martin, Maccoby and Jacklin (1981) have replicated their own earlier finding that boys and girls responded in opposite ways to maternal intrusiveness. The evidence so far is too fragmentary for firm conclusions on the precise nature of the sex differences in parent–child interaction, and even less on the reasons for the differences, or on their role (if any) in the determination of sex differences in disturbances of conduct. Nevertheless, what is clear is that there are important questions here which require an answer, and that further research should prove fruitful.

Possible 'intrinsic' factors

Given that, for whatever reason, disturbances of conduct in girls seem *less* often to have arisen as a result of family discord, disharmony and stress, it is necessary to ask whether such disturbances in girls are *more* likely to have a genetic basis. The evidence on this point is both scanty and inconclusive, but the few relevant genetic data have been considered by Cloninger *et al.* (1978). They note that, in the St Louis study, female probands with an antisocial personality disorder (A.S.P.) had more male and female relatives with A.S.P. than did male probands with the same condition. The same pattern was found for crime in Danish twins. Cloninger *et al.* (1978) conclude that '... both criminal and antisocial women are more deviant than criminal and antisocial men in terms of the genotypic and other transmisable influences that contribute to the liability to develop these disorders'. However, they are careful to point out that these data apply to adult criminality, which probably differs from juvenile delinquency in having a greater genetic component.

Various studies of delinquent girls and women in institutional settings (see, for example, Cowie *et al.*, 1968; Goodman *et al.*, 1976) have noted rather high rates of psychiatric disorder – rates which were higher than in other samples of male delinquents. For example, Goodman *et al.* (1976), in their eight-year follow-up study of Borstal girls, found that about a fifth had been admitted to a psychiatric hospital at some time. But as these comparisons were not based on either matched samples or identical measures, there must be considerable doubt on the validity of the findings on sex differences. Moreover, institutional samples are inappropriate for the study of this issue, in view of the impossibility of differentiating factors associated with delinquency from factors associated with institutional placement. However, the tendency for girls to receive institutional placements for less serious offences than boys (May, 1977) would seem to *decrease* the likelihood of finding greater deviance in girls (because a wider range of girls are being institutionalized) – making the institutional findings more, rather than less, striking.

Rather than speculate further, what are needed are good data on comparable non-institutionalized samples of male and female offenders. Few studies of this kind have been undertaken, but recent data are provided by May (1977) from his total population study of Aberdeen children and adolescents; by Wadsworth (1979) from the British National Survey; by Ouston (1983) from a study of inner London teenagers; by Caplan *et al.* (1980) on a Canadian sample of delinquents referred for clinical assessment; by Offord (1982) in a study of Canadian boys and girls placed on probation; and by Simons *et al.* (1980) using self-report data from an American survey of adolescents. All studies are in agreement in showing many similarities between delinquent boys and girls both in their patterns of behaviour and in their family background. This was evident, also, in Davies's (1976) study of girls appearing before one particular juvenile court in London (although she had no direct comparison with a male sample). We may conclude that there is a very considerable degree of communality between delinquent boys and girls.

But some differences were found in these studies, although they did not always reach statistical significance. Both May and Ouston found that delinquency in girls was more strongly associated with lower intelligence or lower academic attainment than it was in boys (but this was not so in Wadsworth's data). May (1977) found that delinquency in girls was more strongly associated with attendance at a high-delinquency school, but in Ouston's sample the reverse was found (Rutter *et al.*, 1979). Ouston found that delinquency in girls was more strongly associated with low social status and possibly with behavioural deviance as assessed on a teacher questionnaire, but this was not so in Caplan's study of a more selected sample, although in Wadsworth's data delinquency in girls did tend to show a slightly stronger association with low social status than was found for boys. Both Caplan *et al.* and Wadsworth found that female delinquency was rather more likely to be associated with family disruption and separation experiences than was the case with male delinquency. This was even more strongly apparent in Offord's (1982) study. With girls, break-up of the home and changes in parent-figure (as by admission into foster care) were especially strongly associated with delinquency; whereas in boys, deviant family patterns in *intact* homes were more important.

It is all too obvious that the data are both too few and too contradictory for firm conclusions. There are some weak indications that female delinquency may be somewhat more likely to be associated with greater deviance in other forms of behaviour or in family difficulties (and perhaps especially with removal from home), but the findings are not consistent. The matter warrants further study.

Recidivism

Even less is known on the course of delinquent activities in girls. However, Wadsworth (1979) found that girls tended to commit lesser offences and were less likely to become recidivist. Unfortunately, the published analyses do not show whether the lower proportion of recidivists among the girls was a function of their generally less serious crimes. The follow-up by Goodman *et al.* (1976) of Borstal girls may be roughly compared with Gibbens and Prince's (1965) somewhat similar follow-up of Borstal boys; the results do not suggest any major difference in outcome. However, the social data (obtained on two-thirds of the group) in the Goodman *et al.* follow-up emphasized the need to look at outcome in terms which are broader than just presence or absence of re-conviction. For example, of the 59 girls who had children, 27 had one or more adopted, fostered, placed in care or looked after solely by grandparents. This was particularly a feature of the tiny group of persistent offenders who also showed a high degree of personal difficulties (5 of the 9 had been psychiatric in-patients during the follow-up).

Conclusions on sex differences in delinquency

It is clear that surprisingly little is known on delinquency in girls. Of course, to a considerable extent the relative research neglect of female delinquency is a consequence of the fact that it is a much less frequent phenomenon than male crime. But it warrants a much greater research investment than it has received up to now, both because an understanding of why girls are less prone to delinquency might give insights into the genesis of delinquent behaviour generally, and because an explanation of why there has been an increase in female crime since the Second World War might provide leads on the factors which determine changes in overall delinquency rates.

Social class

There has long been a widespread assumption that juvenile delinquency and adult crime are both very much more frequent in those of low social status. Moreover, this presumed strong association between delinquency and social class constitutes the basis for most of the leading sociological theories of crime. However, as Hirschi (1969) pointed out in his review of the empirical evidence on this point, most research data contradict these sociological assumptions. Tittle *et al.* (1978), in their re-examination of social class findings from a wide variety (largely American) of self-report and official delinquency studies, concluded that the data '... show only a slight negative association between class and criminality'. They go on to argue: '... numerous theories developed on the assumption of class differences appear to be based on false premises. It is now time, therefore, to shift away from class-based theories to those emphasizing more generic processes.' In contrast, Braithwaite (1981), reviewing the same field, has argued that most studies have found *some* link between class and delinquency, even if the link has been less strong than once thought. In view of the important theoretical implications which stem from the presence or absence of social class associations, we need to consider the evidence in some detail. Several rather different issues are involved.

Strength of the social class association

The first question concerns the strength of the delinquency–social class association. In discussing the findings on this matter, there are five subquestions which require attention. As Hirschi (1969) and Tittle *et al.* (1978) based most of their review on investigations in the United States, there is the query whether the very weak social class correlation evident in American data applies similarly to the U.K. Tittle *et al.* (1978) also concluded that the data showed a secular trend for official statistics studies, with social class associations evident in reports prior to 1950, but diminishing progressively thereafter. Do British figures confirm this trend? A further point in the Tittle *et al.* (1978) review is that social class associations have sometimes been apparent in official statistics but almost never has this been found in self-report studies. Do British data confirm this observation and, if confirmed, does the difference reflect biases in self-report data or biases in police or judicial practice? A further question is whether the social class association, in so far as there is one, applies merely to trivial or serious offences? Finally, are the findings influenced by which measure of social class is employed?

Recent British data on unselected samples of offenders are provided by the British National Survey (Wadsworth, 1979), the Aberdeen survey (May, 1975), the inner London study of young people attending twelve secondary schools (Rutter *et al.*, 1979; Ouston, 1983) and, on a socially more restricted sample, the West and Farrington (1973) longitudinal study of London boys. All studies show some association between social status variables and delinquency. Thus, in the National Survey (Wadsworth, 1979), whereas 22 per cent of boys from 'lower-manual' families were delinquent, only 4 per cent of boys from 'upper-middle' families had been convicted. The Aberdeen figures (May, 1975) showed that some 6 per cent of boys from a non-manual background made a juvenile court appearance, compared with 17 per cent of those whose father held a skilled manual job and 27 per cent of those whose father held an unskilled or semi-skilled job. Ouston's (1983) London data showed much the same, the social class difference in delinquency rates being somewhat greater for boys (a range extending from 17 per cent in non-manual to 35 per cent in unskilled or semi-skilled manual) than for girls (1.6 per cent to 7.5 per cent). We may conclude that recent British data which utilize official statistics do show some association between social class and delinquency, although they also indicate that delinquency occurs in *all* social groups and is far from restricted to low social status individuals.

British self-report data, too, have generally shown some association between social class and delinquency (for example, Belson, 1968; McDonald,

1969; Farrington, 1979), although the association has been much weaker than in official statistics data. For example, Belson (1968) found that 15 per cent of boys from professional or managerial homes reported stealing compared with 25 per cent of those from an unskilled manual background. McDonald (1969) found no social class difference for serious theft or for breaking and entering, but truancy (32 per cent in upper-middle-class boys v. 49 per cent in lower-working-class boys), the carrying of weapons (16 per cent v. 24 per cent), and various other offences showed some social class trend.

Parent and teacher report data for conduct disorders (rather than for delinquency as such), too, whether based on interviews or questionnaires, have shown rather weak and inconsistent associations between deviant behaviour of all kinds and social class (see Rutter, Tizard and Whitmore, 1970; Shepherd *et al.*, 1971; Rutter *et al.*, 1975a; Graham and Rutter, 1973). In many investigations no social class association was found, but others showed a tendency for disturbances of conduct to be rather more frequent in young people from families in which the father held a semi-skilled or unskilled job.

The disparity between official statistics and self-report data needs discussion (see below), but on either set of data there seems to be *some* social class correlation in Britain in contrast to what has been claimed to be a negligible one in the present-day United States. Our consideration of the extent to which this is a real difference between the two countries is better postponed until after we have discussed the various other methodological considerations.

The question of secular trends in British data can be examined by reconsidering the findings in terms of the year in which the boys reached their seventeenth birthday. For Wadsworth's sample this was 1963, for May's it was 1968–71, and for Ouston's it was 1977. As all showed a roughly comparable social class association, we can dismiss any major change over this period of time (the 1960s and 70s). Nevertheless, it is true that earlier studies (for example, Mannheim *et al.*, 1957; Morris, 1957) tended to show rather stronger social class associations, and it may be that as the crime rate has risen the social class differentials have narrowed somewhat, with the main change occurring prior to the mid-50s. However, it should be noted that one study, based on data in the early 60s of a randomly selected sample of young people appearing in London juvenile courts (Palmai *et al.*, 1967) showed no social class differential for delinquency. Moreover, Little and Ntsekhe (1959), studying another London sample a few years earlier, had also shown a social class distribution which was not greatly different from that in the general population. The social class association even then was a somewhat inconsistent one, with stronger associations evident both before and after that period.

The next point concerns the apparent disparity between official statistics and self-report data, with the social class association rather weaker in the latter. One problem with this comparison is that the two do not necessarily tap the same domain of behaviour. As both Hindelang *et al.* (1979) and Elliott and Ageton (1980) note in their reviews of this topic, many self-report questionnaires are largely made up of quite trivial behaviours (such as cutting classes, drinking when below age, or setting off fireworks in the street), which would be unlikely to result in prosecution in most cases. If official and self-report delinquency are to be compared it is necessary to use self-report data which refer to somewhat more serious offences. When this is done, much of the discrepancy between them disappears. As West and Farrington (1973) noted, self-reported delinquents have family background features which are generally comparable to those found with official offenders. Moreover, Elliott and Ageton's (1980) self-report data for American youth *did* show a social class differential for serious crimes against persons (with a non-significant trend also for those against property).

Rather than pursue that matter further, we need to consider whether there are social class biases in the detection or processing of delinquents. Early studies suggested that there was a distinct tendency for the lower-class boy to be more likely to be picked up by the police and sent to the juvenile court (see Hardt and Bodine, 1965). More recent data confirm that there is some tendency of this kind. For example, Belson (1968) found that boys in the top social group who admitted to a lot of stealing were much less likely to have been caught by the police. However, this was not particularly apparent in the West and Farrington study; indeed, the group of official delinquents who *denied* delinquency on self-report were especially likely to be from relatively more favoured social groups (Farrington, 1979)! Bennett (1979), in a London study, found that, compared with working-class youths, middle-class offenders were slightly more likely to be cautioned rather than sent to court – but this social class differential applied only to minor offences. There are too few data for any firm conclusions on the matter, but it may be accepted that probably there is some social class differentiation in the detection and processing of delinquents, which accounts in part for differences in delinquency rates.

The possible importance of the seriousness of offences in social class differentials has been examined in both British (Wadsworth, 1979) and American (Elliott and Ageton, 1980) studies, with similar conclusions. Using official delinquency data for youths in the National Survey, Wadsworth found that the social class difference did not apply to very minor offences and was most striking with serious offences against property or persons. May (1975), in Scotland, found that boys from a lower social class background were more likely to be recidivist and had more offences recorded even at first court appearance. Theft was the predominant offence in all social groups but, relatively speaking, vandalism, fraud and motoring offences were somewhat more frequent in middle-class boys. Similarly, using self-report data, Elliott and Ageton (1980) found no social class differential for status offences, hard drug use, or public disorder, but there was a differential for predatory crimes against property (a mean of 7 in the middle-class group compared with 14 in the lower-class) and against persons (a mean of 3 versus 12). While further data on this point are needed, it seems that the main social class effect is seen with serious offences and especially with crimes of violence.

The final question regarding the strength of social class associations asks whether the way in which social status is measured influences the findings. Two main findings emerge from this consideration. Firstly, the difference in delinquency rate applies mainly to the extremes of the social class distribution, with little variation in the middle of the range. For example, in the British National Survey both the 'lower-middle' and the 'upper-manual' groups had delinquency rates of 12 per cent. In the Elliott and Ageton (1980) study, too, the biggest differential was between lower-class youths and the rest (i.e. 'working' and 'middle'). The second point is that parental occupation or education, as measures of social status, show a generally weaker association with delinquency than do measures of poverty, unemployment or reliance on welfare. For example, Hirschi (1969), using self-report data from a Californian high-school sample, found no consistent association with either parental occupation or education. But boys whose fathers had been unemployed and on welfare had a rate of recidivism twice that in the rest of the population. Also, in their predominantly working-class London sample, West and Farrington (1973; Farrington, 1979) found only a weak association with social class but a somewhat stronger one with family income. These observations raise the important question of the meaning of the social status differential, but before turning to that issue we need to summarize the main findings so far.

The evidence suggests that there is a modest (but not strong) association between low social status and delinquency, but that this association applies mainly at the extremes of the social scale, that it is due in part to social class differentials in detection and prosecution, and that, in so far as it applies to real differences in delinquent activities, the association is largely confined to the more serious delinquencies. Moreover, even that association is more strongly evident with measures of parental unemployment or reliance on welfare than with indices of parental occupation or education.

We now need to return to the question of whether or not there are real differences between the U.S.A. and the U.K. in social class differentials for delinquency. No entirely satisfactory answer is possible on the basis of published data. On the one hand, the overall pattern of findings seems generally comparable in the two countries – so that the conclusions in the previous paragraph probably apply to both. On the other hand, at least some of the data do suggest that the social class–delinquency associations may be slightly greater in Britain. There are no strong grounds for supposing that this *should* be the case. Although, certainly, the social milieu is not the same in the two countries, social mobility is approximately the same (Rutter and Madge, 1976). Perhaps the two most obvious differences are the much higher proportion of young people receiving higher education in the United States (see Rutter, 1979a) and the different racial situation (see below). While real differences cannot be completely ruled out, at least part of the explanation is likely to lie in differences in measurement. Firstly, the Elliott and Ageton (1980) findings suggest that there *is* a social class differential for more serious crimes in the U.S.A., and that the previous negative findings may have been due to a focus on minor delinquencies. Secondly, the measurement of social status in the United States may be less discriminating, because of the large proportion of the population who receive higher education and because there are less well standardized social class measures for the population as a whole.

Meaning of the association

The next question, given that there is some trend to explain, is what does it mean? Perhaps the key findings here are that (i) measures of parental unemployment or reliance on welfare show a stronger association with delinquency than do occupation or education; and (ii) social status measures overlap greatly with measures of parental behaviour or family relationships which relate to delinquency in *all* social groups. The key issue is whether the association with delinquency applies to low social status *per se*, or rather to low social status only when it is accompanied by parental deviance or inadequacy of some kind. The crucial point here is that people may be in a low social status occupation for a host of reasons, most of which have nothing to do with their qualities as a parent, but in some cases the low social status does reflect personal problems of one kind or another. For example,

Robins *et al.* (1962) showed that individuals who were antisocial as children were more likely than other children to end up in low social status occupations both because the antisocial behaviour in childhood interfered with educational achievement and because such behaviour in adult life led to poor job performance. They concluded that '... The disproportionate incidence of antisocial children in the lower classes apparently can be partially explained by their high rate of antisocial fathers, whose own deviance has determined their low social status.' Similarly, more recently, Rutter, Quinton and Liddle (1982) have shown that children reared in institutions, compared with family-reared children of similar social background, were more likely to be in low social status occupations in their mid-20s – their low status being associated with a variety of personal problems such as difficulties in personal relationships, psychiatric disorder and criminality. West (1982), too, has shown that criminal fathers tend to be often unemployed and on welfare. The question, then, is whether low social status is associated with delinquency when low status is not accompanied by these other problems.

No very good answer is available, in that very few studies have had the necessary data on family and parental features other than occupation and education. But it seems that when it has been possible to investigate the matter, the social class correlations either disappear or weaken once the appropriate other family variables have been taken into account. Thus, Farrington (1979) found that the association between social class and delinquency was lost when parental supervision was taken into account. In the same study (West and Farrington, 1973), parental criminality maintained a significant association with delinquency in the sons after controlling for family income, but the reverse applied in only one of three comparisons. Family income ceased to have any association with delinquency after controlling for the child's level of intelligence.

The data are too few for firm conclusions, but the indications are that most of the modest association between social class and delinquency is probably due to the parental and family problems sometimes associated with low social status rather than to low social status *per se*. The distinction is an important one for an understanding of the origins of delinquent behaviour, and the matter should be subjected to more rigorous investigation.

However, in addition, it is necessary to ask whether the social class associations are mediated environmentally or genetically. Curiously, there is only one study which has tackled that question. Mednick *et al.* (1983), in an investigation of adoptees, compared the extent to which crime was associated with the social class of the biological parents (who did not participate in rearing) and the association between crime and the adoptive parents' social class. Interestingly, it was found that both had statistically significant effects of approximately equal strength – indicating that there were both genetic and environmental effects.

Is delinquency 'normal' in some social groups?

A further question with respect to social class is whether delinquency is ever a 'normal' sub-cultural phenomenon. Mays (1954) examined patterns of delinquency in an underprivileged part of Liverpool with a high crime rate. A detailed (but largely non-quantitative) study was made of a sample of 80 adolescent boys in regular attendance at a youth club – two-fifths had official delinquent records and over three-quarters admitted to behaviours which, if they came to police notice, would be regarded as indictable offences. Mays (1954, 1972) argued that this delinquency was part of an identifiable lower-working-class pattern of behaviour to which the majority of normal healthy, but underdisciplined, boys conformed. Willmott (1966), too, on the basis of an interview study of adolescent boys in the East End of London, argued that much of their petty thieving and 'lifting' from work was a normal pattern of behaviour for their social group and was regarded lightly by most local people.* Downes (1966), similarly, suggested that much working-class delinquency is part of the sub-cultural ethos for that social group.

Two rather different questions arise in connection with these hypotheses. The first is whether any delinquency can be regarded as 'normal' in the dual senses of being a characteristic of the majority of members of some sub-cultural group *and* of being regarded as acceptable forms of behaviour by most people in that group. The answer to that question is a clear-cut 'Yes'. The self-report studies provide abundant evidence that minor delinquent acts are committed on occasion by the majority of individuals, and it is obvious that there are certain kinds of dishonesties or illegal acts which give rise to very little general social disapproval (for example, exceeding the speed limit, under-age drinking, minor tax fiddling). The second question is whether this phenomenon is particularly characteristic of, or confined to, lower-working-class groups. The answer to that question, on the basis of the same data, is an equally clear-cut 'No'. On the contrary, there are many examples of such 'normal' delinquencies in all social groups. Of course, it is true that the *specific* behaviours in this class differ somewhat by social groups – as obviously they must do, if only for reasons of opportunity. For example,

---

* But he noted that within this broad group of minor delinquents there was a rather different, rebellious minority of serious recidivist delinquents whose behaviour arose in a different way.

140 *Juvenile Delinquency*

Belson (1968) found that stealing milk off doorsteps, stealing from a stall or barrow, or taking goods from the docks or a goods yard were much more frequent among working-class boys. But it is not difficult to think of equally striking middle-class equivalents (Wootton, 1959; Cicourel, 1968). The possibility remains that such normal delinquencies, although occurring in all social groups, are more common in low social status populations. But even that does not seem to be the case. As already noted, both the official statistics and self-report data indicate that there are negligible social class differences for *minor* delinquencies.

It should also be asked whether these very common and lightly regarded delinquencies are truly 'normal'. After all, both dental caries and measles are exceedingly frequent, but no one would doubt that they constitute disease states. Statistical frequency on its own provides an uncertain guide to normality. Nevertheless, there are good reasons for supposing that many of these minor delinquencies are indeed 'normal' in most usually accepted senses. Not only are they frequent but, also, most constitute a passing phase without identifiable sequelae. Furthermore, the young people who admit to these minor delinquencies, or even those who are one-time 'official' offenders, seem to differ little from the rest of the population (see, for example, Belson, 1968; West and Farrington, 1973). It cannot be said that the behaviours are desirable, nor should it be supposed that they are without meaning, but they are of rather minor personal and social significance when considered in relation to recidivist delinquency.

Does the meaning and significance of delinquency vary by social group?

An extension of the previous question is provided by the query as to whether delinquency has different correlates in different social groups. The supposition underlying the query is that, if much of lower-working-class delinquency is normal (as already seen, that part of the supposition is not supported in so far as it specifies a difference from middle-class groups), then working-class delinquents should be less likely to show personal psychopathology and less likely to come from deviant backgrounds. Contrary to this view, those studies which have examined the issue, both in Britain (for example, Stott, 1960, 1966) and the United States (for example, Conger and Miller, 1966), have found general maladjustment to be just as common in delinquents from a deprived background as in those from middle-class homes. It could be argued that the measures of maladjustment in these studies were potentially misleading, in that they might merely reflect middle-class values and hence have a different meaning in a working-class culture.

There may be something in this suggestion, but the finding in a high-delinquency working-class area in London that delinquents tend to be *un*popular with their peers (West and Farrington, 1973) runs counter to the 'normal sub-culture' view. American follow-up studies, too, have shown that boys rejected by their peers are those most likely to become delinquent (Roff *et al.*, 1972). The only exception in Roff's study was that in the very lowest socio-economic group, delinquents were both most rejected *and* most liked by their peers – perhaps suggesting a normal sub-culture of delinquency in a proportion of very low status children. However, even within a high delinquency area, the families of recidivist delinquents stand out as different (Jephcott and Carter, 1954), and the family factors which predict recidivist delinquency in middle-class groups predict similarly in working-class groups (see, for example, McCord, 1979; Robins, 1978; West and Farrington, 1973).

Social group influences in delinquent activities

From the evidence considered thus far, it is apparent that the idea that delinquency is largely confined to low social status groups can be firmly rejected, and the further notion that delinquency has different origins when it occurs in working-class boys must also be abandoned. But perhaps the most important contribution of the sociological writers has not been on the specifics of social class *per se*, but rather on the broader view that delinquency must be considered as a form of human social behaviour (rather than a type of personal disorder), and that like any other kind of social behaviour it will be influenced by social and cultural forces as well as by personal and familial factors.

The inter-relationships of neighbourhood, school, work and culture may have implications for the development of delinquency. Studies by Sugarman (1967), Hargreaves (1967) and Corrigan (1979), for example, have drawn attention to the ways in which schools can foster the development of delinquent sub-cultures among lower-stream pupils. Such concerns have been taken up and more widely elaborated by those who have analysed youth cultures and style in their relationship to class, wider culture and ideology. This analysis, usually of a Marxist orientation, has produced a flood of theoretical and ethnographic work which attempts to delineate the meaning of youth sub-cultures for their members and to determine how that meaning relates to and meets a reaction from other cultural groups. The work of the Birmingham Centre for Contemporary Cultural Studies (see Hall *et al.*, 1978; Clarke and Jefferson, 1976; Cohen, 1972), and Murdoch's work at

Leicester University (see Murdoch and McCron, 1976) have been seminal in this field.

Basically, this orientation has sought to reintroduce 'class' as a dimension of sub-cultural theory and to show that sub-cultures may serve as solutions to shared problems and contradictions in adolescent life. Each of these authors has attacked the myth of classlessness surrounding the notion of 'teenager' or 'adolescent', and has argued, instead, for a recognition of 'class' membership as a key element in social experience. Youth, it is said, carry on and develop old (now eroded) traditions of working-class life through their activities. These youth groups with their varying styles are expressions of the still unresolved contradictions in the parent culture.

Class and inter-generational differences, it is suggested, produce 'focal concerns' for the youth sub-culture. These 'focal concerns', from the viewpoint of the youth involved, include not only elements borrowed and adapted from the parent culture (such as territoriality, group-mindedness, notions of masculinity and male dominance), but also elements which the youth themselves use to emphasize their distinctiveness – as in forms of dress, music, language, and styles of social activities. In the wider society, youth is employed as a metaphor for social change – a 'scapegoat' or 'moral panic' concept displacing social anxiety attendant on the breakdown of the classless consensus of the post-war period (Hall *et al.*, 1978).

To some, this approach to working-class youth culture smacks too much of a romantic over-sentimentalization (Woods, 1977), and undoubtedly there has been very little empirical verification of its theoretical elements. Moreover, the work to date has concentrated on the top and bottom of the class structure, with a neglect of the large body of youth in the intermediate status. Nevertheless, this form of analysis has made a contribution to the understanding of young people's behaviour (and hence indirectly to the study of juvenile delinquency). It provides the paradigm within which different levels of analysis, and different epistemological orientations, may come together to produce an adequate explanation of particular youth problems. As Cohen (1972) suggests, an adequate analysis of sub-cultures should exist at three levels: historical, structural and phenomenological.

To date, there have been several examples of this approach, covering the world of 'Mods and Rockers' (see Cohen, 1972), 'Teddy boys' (Jefferson, 1976), 'Skinheads' (Clarke and Jefferson, 1976; Clarke, 1976), 'Glamrock' (Taylor and Wall, 1976), and 'Rastafarians' (Hebdige, 1976). Here we shall take the issue of football hooliganism to illustrate the content of such an analysis.

Such an analysis (largely based on the work of Taylor, 1971; Clarke, 1978, and Marsh *et al.*, 1978) begins by looking at the context within which football hooliganism takes place – both historically and interactionally. Traditionally the game of football involved a complicated relationship between the game and the mass of its supporters, largely from the male working class, and showed cultural values characteristic of both that class and the game itself. These values included an appreciation of toughness, physical dexterity, and the collective effort of the team.

In the post-war period, however, the game of football and the expectations of 'appropriate' behaviour while attending a match are thought to have changed. In an attempt to win back the crowds, in the face of an unprecedented boom of alternative leisure pursuits for the working class, the game re-organized itself in a more businesslike way, seeking to become more spectacular and more professional. But this, in turn, produced new expectancies from the spectator. It is suggested that hooliganism emerged from the ways in which the traditional forms of watching football had to respond to the modifications in the game itself – in part a consequence of the changed relationship. The young fans have taken the traditions of spectatorship, and have extended and modified them. By collectively organizing themselves on the terraces at the 'ends' of the field, they create a parallel physical challenge to that which is being exhibited on the field. Chanting, taking territory, and violence merely extend the contest of the game into the terraces. Violence, therefore, takes place within the context of a problem about the appropriate style of watching football. In addition, the creation and continuance of the stereotype of the 'football hooligan' in the media exacerbates the phenomenon by precipitating the expectation to act in certain ways on these occasions. By simplifying the causes of disruption, stigmatizing those involved, creating a public panic about it and then exerting stricter control, an amplification of the problem ensues (see Hall *et al.*, 1978). Against such a background, therefore, it is said that we must look at the meaning of the activity for its members.

The first point to note is that, despite the widespread concern surrounding 'football hooliganism', very little quantitative information exists on the extent of the phenomenon. What is known is that football crowds tend to be predominantly male, more youthful than elderly, and with a large proportion of people from the lower socio-economic groups. While attendance at football matches has substantially decreased since the period immediately after the war – 41.3 million in 1948–9 compared with 26.2 million in 1976–7 – the younger element in the crowds has grown. Such small-scale studies as there are (see, for example, Trivizas, 1980; Sports Council, S.S.R.C. Report,

1978) suggest that ejection and arrests for disturbances involve only a small proportion of the total crowd, that the majority of the offences are committed by the male working class, and that about two-thirds of offenders have no previous criminal record (although most of those who committed assault *did* have previous convictions).

In a non-quantitative study of hooliganism among the fans of Oxford United and Millwall, Marsh *et al.* (1978) found that violence was only a small part of life on the terraces, and that much of the violence was contained by internal and informal controls which shaped the adhesion of terrace life. Marsh suggests that there is a distinctive career structure for the youths on the terrace to achieve social standing. To begin with, there were the 'Novices', the boys of 9, 10 and 11, 'drawn to the terraces by the prospect of immediate membership of a society which offers excitement, danger and a tribal sense of belonging'. Then, there were the 'Rowdies', boys of 15 and 16 who chanted the loudest, wore the most extreme clothes and ran around a lot. Some of them had specialized roles, for example, that of 'aggro leader' or 'nutter'. Lastly, there were the 'Town Boys', older boys and young men up to the age of 25 who had previously demonstrated their personal worth and character in the Rowdies and who could then rest on their reputations. While this group would still participate in acts of violence if called upon, they were essentially 'graduates' of the terraces, eventually retiring to other parts of the ground to watch the match with wives and girl-friends.

Marsh *et al.* (1978) suggest a clear system of roles, rules and shared meanings throughout their analysis. They argue that the mode of dress, the chanting, the half-hearted attempts to invade the opposite territory and confront others with 'aggro', all conformed to a ritual of behaviour which the various groups shared. Serious physical violence occurred only when the rules were breached. Moreover, such ritual posturing arrays, Marsh suggests, have always been integral to human cultures, apparently serving to ritualize aggression. The study suggests important hypotheses which warrant further investigation, but the findings must be considered as tentative in view of the methodological limitations of the work so far.

This approach to the study of juvenile behaviour differs from most of the other research we cite in its central concern with the *meaning* of behaviour in its social *context*. As a result, it has focused on group activities and on the understanding of individual acts when considered in relation to social group interactions. Undoubtedly, it has been of value in drawing attention to phenomena largely ignored by other investigators. These socio-cultural considerations have potential implications for a wide range of delinquent activities, if only because so much juvenile crime is undertaken jointly with other youths. But the implications are potential rather than actual. As already noted, these hypotheses so far lack an adequate empirical underpinning. But it is at least as important to note what is left unexplained, even if such verification could be obtained. In that only a minority of football spectators engage in 'hooliganism' (however defined), what differentiates those who do from those who do not? How does this form of behaviour in a large crowd relate to delinquent activities undertaken individually or with just a few other individuals (as is the case with most delinquency)? Most writings on crowd behaviour assume that people in crowds are likely to behave differently from the way they would in isolation, and as a result may commit offences that they would not commit in other circumstances. This may well be so but does this apply to more extreme forms of behaviour? Trivizas (1980) observed that whereas 75 per cent of assaults on a constable in circumstances other than a football crowd were by individuals with a previous conviction, this was so for only 60 per cent of such offences at football matches. The suggestion is that fewer offences at football matches were committed by recidivist delinquents or criminals – but equally it could be argued that, as in other circumstances, those committing more serious offences differ from those involved in more minor delinquencies.

Civil strife

Rioting and civil disorder constitute a particular form of crowd violence which gave rise to much concern in the United States in the aftermath of the massive disturbances which occurred in some twenty-three cities during the summer of 1967 (Kerner, 1968). Similar concerns hit the headlines in Britain in 1981 (Scarman, 1981), as a result of the scenes of widespread group violence and disorder in London, Liverpool and the industrial Midlands. The circumstances were not identical in all cases, but the events shared the characteristics of a tumultuous violent crowd which attacked the police with dangerous missiles or other weapons, and of subsequent extensive looting and damage to local shops and property. The communal disturbances generally occurred in socially disadvantaged, slum or ghetto areas; in most cases they involved a strong racial element; and usually they occurred in the context of tense and distrustful police–community relationships. In this book we do not aim to deal with the phenomenon of civil strife. However, it requires some attention both because such disorders involve delinquent acts (with serious assaults on members of the public as well as on police and other officials, widespread breaking into and stealing from commercial and private premises, arson and extensive damage to buildings and vehicles), and because of the suggestion of links between civil strife and more everyday varieties of delinquency (see Chapter 2; also Hall *et al.*, 1978).

Little systematic information is available on the individuals who participated in these riots. However, the Kerner (1968) report suggested that the typical American rioter was a black teenager or young adult, a drop-out from school, and either unemployed or working in a menial job. However, in these respects he did not differ strikingly from the majority of his neighbours who did not participate in the violence or looting. It is not known what proportion of the rioters had been involved in other delinquent activities, nor is it known whether they shared the background characteristics of ordinary delinquents.

The inquiries which followed both the American and the British series of outbreaks of civil disorder came to broadly similar conclusions (Kerner, 1968; Scarman, 1981). Firstly, the disturbances constituted spontaneous crowd reactions which arose against a background of communal tension and resentment, precipitated by incidents many of which involved police actions perceived as unwarranted harassment. Actions by militants sometimes fuelled the flames of unrest but did not start the uprising. Secondly, the disorders arose in inner city areas with major social problems in terms of poor housing, inadequate education and high unemployment which disproportionately affected ethnic minority groups. Thirdly, a major cause of the outbreaks of communal violence was the widespread feeling of hostility towards and distrust of the police in the area. Fourthly, the breakdown of police–community relationships was associated with instances of racial prejudice, and with the harassment of both guilty and innocent alike which comes from 'hard' policing methods involving the frequent use of 'stop and search' tactics to control crime.

These conclusions stem from a detailed consideration of the circumstances surrounding the riots rather than from empirical studies to determine the causes of civil strife. Indeed, there is remarkably little research that is directly relevant to these issues. While it is clear that the disturbances affected inner city areas with serious social disadvantage, it is equally apparent that poverty, lack of education and unemployment cannot be regarded as sufficient causes. Historical analyses do not show a consistent association between any of these social indices and rates of crime, and it is obvious that there have been prolonged periods of socio-economic privation without civil strife (see Chapter 6). The question is why the disturbances occurred *when* they did and *where* they did, in that there have been other times and places with similarly bad social conditions but no rioting.

The answer provided by the inquiries is that there was an interaction between the frustrations and resentments associated with discrimination and disadvantage on the one hand, and abrasive police practices which eroded community support on the other. Certainly it is evident that the rioting areas were indeed ones with poor police–community relations, and there can be little doubt that this played an important part in the genesis of the disturbances. However, there are few systematic data on the role of different patterns of policing in generating such tensions, and it remains uncertain how far the hostile relations stemmed from police practices *per se* and how far from the socio-political context within which they occurred. Nevertheless, it is clear that effective policing relies heavily on good police–community relations and on community support for police activities. Accordingly, patterns of policing that create tensions or distancing between the police and community agencies or groups; that are felt to be discriminatory because they rely on some form of group membership (such as a black skin or living in a particular area) as identification of likely delinquents; or that involve intrusive interventions (as with 'stop and search' tactics) which impinge on non-offenders as well as on delinquents, are all liable to have adverse side-effects which seriously detract from their efficacy as crime-prevention measures.

Four main lines of investigation have been followed which have produced findings relevant to these considerations. Firstly, there are the studies of police work, and of the steps involved in crime detection and the apprehension of offenders (Clarke and Hough, 1980; Morris and Heal, 1981). These indicate that police work covers a wide range of activities, only a proportion of which are directly related to the control of crime and some of which concern social assistance of various kinds. It is also apparent, as noted above, that police effectiveness is heavily dependent on community cooperation (see also Chapters 1 and 9 for a further discussion of these findings). Secondly, experimental investigations have attempted to determine whether increases in different types of patrolling have any impact on rates of crime (see Chapter 9). These show that in most circumstances they have little effect. Thirdly, there are time-series analyses of the associations between changes in levels of police manpower and changes in rates of crime (see McDonald, 1976; Gurr *et al.*, 1977). These show generally insignificant and inconsistent relationships. On the whole, it seems that the police force expands as a *consequence* of increasing civil strife (or crime) but that there is no regular *effect* on crime. Fourthly, there have been a few attempts to look at the effects of community policing, in which the aim is to gain the support of the general public in crime prevention rather than to fight crime directly through the activities of the police acting on their own (see Morris and Heal, 1981).

148 *Juvenile Delinquency*

The observations so far are encouraging, but there is a paucity of systematic empirical data on the extent to which different patterns of policing actually influence either community attitudes to the police or community participation in crime prevention. We may conclude that aggressive police tactics are unlikely to reduce crime, and that it is probable (although not proven) that they will worsen the situation through an adverse effect on community support and cooperation.

The phenomena of crowd violence – whether on the football terraces or as a response to 'unpopular' police activities in sensitive areas or at political demonstrations – are important. It cannot be assumed that the individuals involved share the same characteristics as those involved in other forms of violence (nor should it be assumed that necessarily they do not) and, regardless of the characteristics of the individuals, we need to determine why and in what circumstances crowd violence occurs, and when and how it develops riot proportions. The research so far has provided a few useful leads, but no clear answers are yet available.

Race

There needs to be an interest in patterns and rates of delinquency in ethnic minority groups, if only because such groups constitute a substantial proportion of the child and adolescent population in many of the urban centres of the U.K. and the U.S.A. If effective services are to be developed for the total population, we have to ask whether the characteristics and origins of delinquency in any of its major constituent parts are different from those in the population as a whole. It was for these reasons that we considered possible differences according to sex and social class, and here we do the same with race. But before discussing the findings on delinquency as such, it is necessary to sketch in a little of the background.

Historical background

To some extent Britain has always been culturally heterogeneous. However, during the period following the Second World War there were major changes which have altered the population composition quantitatively, if not qualitatively. It is also relevant that in at least two respects the situation in the U.K. differs from that in other European countries. International migration on a substantial scale was common to all Western countries during the 1950s and 60s, and official estimates suggested that migrant workers made up 6 per cent of the working population in the E.E.C. in 1973 (see Little, 1978). But unlike those in most other European countries, many migrants to the U.K. had an automatic right of entry and were settlers rather than guest workers. They also differed from the majority of migrants in the rest of Europe in being easily identifiable by the colour of their skin.

During the 1950s and 60s there was a very substantial increase in immigration to the U.K. from the New Commonwealth – with over half of these of Asian origin and a third from the West Indies (see Little, 1978). Although ethnic minorities still make up a relatively small proportion of the total population, they constitute a rather larger proportion of the child population (some 7 per cent in the country as a whole). This is a consequence of the fact that most immigrants were young adults of an age to have children, accentuated by a tendency of West Indian families to have rather more children than their white counterparts (Rutter *et al.*, 1975b). Furthermore, there is a considerable concentration of black people in relatively few areas, so that places such as Bradford, Birmingham and London have a fifth or more of their school entrants born to women from the New Commonwealth.

Because the marked increase in immigration from the New Commonwealth in the 1950s and 60s was followed by a major restriction on immigration in the 70s (see below), there has been one further change which needs comment. In 1970 about half the children in ethnic minority groups had been born abroad, either coming with their parents or joining them later. That is no longer so today; the great majority of children of black parents were born and brought up in Britain. Whatever difficulties they may experience stem not from immigration but from cultural differences with their parents, from social disadvantage, from differences in upbringing and from racial discrimination.

Probably because of both the rapidity of the growth of immigration during the previous decade and its visibility as a result of skin colour, public fears regarding the supposed effects of immigration grew during the 1960s and 70s (see Little, 1978). The consequence was legislation to severely restrict entry from the New Commonwealth – legislation which in turn led to fears and resentments among immigrant families. The issue of ethnic minorities became emotionally charged. One aspect of this charged atmosphere has been the accusation from some quarters that black people are particularly heavily involved in crime, and the counter-accusation from other quarters that the police unfairly discriminate against blacks – particularly with respect to arrests under Section 4 of the 1824 Vagrancy Act for being a suspected person loitering with intent to commit an arrestable offence – the 'suspected person' or so-called 'sus' arrest* (see Stevens and Willis, 1979; Select Committee, 1976–7). We consider the evidence on both points below.

Studies during the 1960s showed that racial discrimination in the U.K. was widespread in relation to both employment and housing (Daniel, 1968). More recent research has shown that these forms of discrimination have diminished (McIntosh and Smith, 1974), but young black people leaving school still face substantial discrimination in the job market; black school-leavers require four times as many interviews in careers offices to obtain jobs as do white school-leavers of similar educational qualifications, and unemployment among black teenagers is much higher than among their white counterparts (Rutter and Madge, 1976; Little, 1978). In the last few years this situation has greatly worsened in that while unemployment rates in the U.K. have sharply increased, this increase has been disproportionately great among young blacks and Asians (see Stevens and Willis, 1979). The experience of racial hostility and discrimination is something that still makes life difficult for teenagers from ethnic minority backgrounds.

However, it would be seriously misleading to regard all ethnic minority groups as similar. Not only was the background of Asian families quite different from that of West Indian families† prior to their migration to the U.K., but also their experiences after arrival have not been the same. Some of the main features were summarized in Rutter (1979a).

James (1974) described the strong family ties of Sikh families in the U.K. and the constraints on children which stemmed from religious or cultural duties and rituals. Arranged marriages are still common, there are restrictions on the social life of teenagers (especially of girls) and home upbringing for girls tends to be seen as largely a preparation for marriage and motherhood. Children's questioning and explanations are actively encouraged but many children have to be bilingual because Punjabi continues to be spoken at home. On the other hand, Taylor's (1976) study of young Indians and Pakistanis in Newcastle showed that they did better educationally than their white contemporaries and achieved substantial equality in employment. Although these young men from Asian families had experienced racial hostility and had cultural concepts which differed from those of their parents this had not stopped them from making considerable advances on a broad front.

Patterns of upbringing also tend to be somewhat different in families of West Indian or African origin (see Rutter and Madge, 1976). Thus, Holman (1973) found that West African students were much more likely than indigenous or other immigrant groups to make use of private fostering arrangements for pre-school children – arrangements that did not always provide high quality care. It has been found, too, that West Indian

* As already noted, this offence was abolished in the U.K. in October 1981.

† These are by no means the only ethnic minorities in the U.K., but as they constitute the two largest groups we focus most of our discussion on them.

children in the U.K. are frequently discouraged from touching and playing with objects at 1 year (Hood *et al.*, 1970), make less excursions, have less toys and play fewer games with parents than white children of indigenous origin at 3 years (Pollak, 1972), and at 10 years are more disciplined and controlled than their white peers (Rutter *et al.*, 1975b). It is not at all that the West Indian parents are unconcerned but it does appear that they do not always appreciate the developmental importance of play, communication, and parent–child interaction in the early years. More West Indian mothers go out to work when their children are young, and more use private child-minding arrangements which may be of poor quality. Somewhat more mothers lack the support of a husband and West Indian families are two or three times as likely to have at least four or five children. Single parenthood, large family size, and an absence of extended family support (because grandparents often remain in the West Indies) make it more difficult for West Indian families to cope on their own at times of crisis, and perhaps because of this, more children are admitted into the care of the local authority (Fitzherbert, 1967; Yudkin, 1967).

The situation with respect to social disadvantage is somewhat complicated and differs markedly between ethnic minority groups. Asian fathers tend to include a particularly high proportion of self-employed, salesmen, and shopkeepers with considerable entrepreneurial success (Taylor, 1976), whereas West Indian fathers are more likely to be found in unskilled or semi-skilled manual jobs of lower status than those they held prior to immigration (see Rutter and Madge, 1976). All surveys have shown that a higher proportion of black people, compared with the indigenous white population, live in poor quality housing. For all too many, overcrowding, multiple occupancy, and a lack of basic household amenities characterize their homes. On the other hand, faced with grave difficulties in obtaining local authority rented accommodation, West Indian parents have shown considerable drive and initiative in buying their own homes, and home ownership is more common than among native white families (Richmond, 1973; Rutter *et al.*, 1975b). Unfortunately, many of the properties bought have been in poor repair and on short-term leases, so that the ultimate benefits remain rather uncertain.

Asian children who have received all of their education in this country show scholastic attainments which are in general comparable to those of the white indigenous population. However, many studies have shown that this is not the case with children of West Indian origin. They tend to be developmentally disadvantaged at the age of 3 (Pollak, 1972); they show lower vocabulary scores at school entry and infant school (Barnes, 1975); their reading attainments are lower at the age of 10 (Yule *et al.*, 1975); and their disadvantages with respect to literacy are just as great at 15 (Little, 1978). Clearly, the educational difficulties experienced by black adolescents are very considerable. The reasons for this state of affairs, and hence the choice of remedies, remain matters for controversy (see Rutter and Madge, 1976; Rutter, 1979a). However, it should be noted that the difficulties in achieving high attainment are not a matter of lack of educational commitment. Rutter *et al.* (1975b) found that West Indian families were just as likely as others to take their children to the library, to buy books for them and to help with homework. Moreover, both the earlier study by Townsend and Brittan (1972) and the more recent investigations by Gray (1981) have shown that West Indian adolescents are more likely to stay on at school into the sixth form. Gray *et al.* (1980) also found that they had better attendance rates at secondary school. It is evident that black teenagers show a determination to succeed in education despite their relative underachievement.

Following this brief overview of some of the background and circumstances of young people in the U.K. from an Asian or West Indian background, we need to consider some of the findings from research in other countries on associations between delinquency and immigration or ethnic minority status, before turning to the empirical findings from the U.K.

Immigration

As already noted, most young people in the U.K. from an ethnic minority background were born in the U.K. However, equally, most of their parents were immigrants. Patterns of immigration vary greatly from country to country and also over time, so that it would be unwise to assume that there is any generally applicable relationship between immigration and crime. Nevertheless, studies in several different countries have suggested a somewhat predictable pattern (see, for example, Ross, 1937, in the United States, and Shoham *et al.*, 1966, in Israel). It seems that first-generation immigrants tend to display rates of criminality which are well below those of the native population; second-generation immigrants have substantially higher rates, often above those of the population as a whole; and thereafter subsequent generations approximate more closely to the patterns usual for the country.

We shall consider below the evidence on how far this pattern applies to ethnic minorities in the U.K. However, the evidence on which the hypothesis about the change in rates of crime from the first to the third generation of immigrants is based stems largely from findings on *white* immigrants. Accordingly, it may be appropriate to discuss first the findings from the U.S.A. on differences in patterns of delinquency between blacks and whites. Nevertheless, very great caution is needed in making any kind of extrapolation to the situation in the U.K. Of course, there are parallels in that in both countries black people experience various forms of racial discrimination and hostility. West Indian youngsters also share some of the educational disadvantages of American blacks (although Asian teenagers do not). But also there are major differences in their background and circumstances (as evident from the brief description given above) as well as in the social milieu of the two countries. Perhaps the major reason for considering the American evidence is not any kind of mistaken assumption that findings from the U.S.A. can be extended to the U.K., but rather that the research well exemplifies some of the methodological issues that do need to be considered in any investigations of possible differences in delinquency patterns according to ethnic origin.

Crime and delinquency among blacks in the U.S.A.

All studies using official crime statistics have found that crime rates among blacks in the U.S.A. have consistently been well above those for whites. This has been so with the nation-wide Uniform Crime Reports (Kelley, 1977), and also with more detailed studies of local samples, as in the Wolfgang *et al.* (1972) longitudinal study. The same studies have been consistent, too, in finding that the main difference between blacks and whites applies to more serious offences and especially to those involving violence. Thus, as Hindelang *et al.* (1979) point out, the ratio of black to white arrest rates for more serious property offences exceeds that for less serious crimes (3.14 *v.* 1.71); and that for violent crimes is several times that for property offences (9.08 *v.* 3.14). There is a marked tendency for the victims of assaults to be the same race as that of their assailant (Bottoms, 1973; Bottoms and Wiles, 1975; Hindelang, 1976).

In sharp contrast, self-report studies have tended to show negligible differences between the delinquency rates of black and white youths (see Hindelang, 1978; Hirschi, 1969). These largely negative findings have led many commentators to conclude that the race differences in arrests are likely to have risen through police and court processing biases of one kind or another, and have little or no basis in actual behaviour (see, for example, Quinney, 1970; Taylor *et al.*, 1974). However, recent studies have thrown doubt on that conclusion. In the first place, as Hindelang (1978) pointed out, most of the self-report studies have had several important limitations: (i) they are weighted towards the less serious offences and, for this reason, are not comparable with official statistical data; (ii) many have drawn samples from school populations, with the consequence that the black group is likely to have been biased as a result of their higher drop-out rate; (iii) some are based on very small numbers (especially the Gold studies, on which much reliance is placed by many reviewers); (iv) most have a substantial non-response rate likely to introduce bias; and (v) delinquents and delinquency-prone groups are consistently less likely than non-delinquents to complete self-report questionnaires (see Hirschi, 1969, pp. 45–6).

Secondly, the National Youth Survey which was designed to meet these criticisms (Elliott and Ageton, 1980) did show race differences. The sample consisted of 1,726 youths, of whom 259 were black. The self-report instrument allowed separate analyses according to the seriousness and type of offence. The results showed a total self-reported delinquency rate that was greater in blacks than in whites (mean score of 79 $v.$ 46). A more detailed analysis indicated that the differences were greatest with respect to serious offences against persons (aggravated assault and sexual assault), to vandalism, to evading payment offences, and to high-frequency offenders. There were no differences between whites and blacks for theft or for serious crimes against property. All these differences remained after controlling for social class differences between blacks and whites. However, it was notable that there was a race by class interaction for predatory crimes against persons, with a particularly high rate for lower-class black youth (and negligible white–black differences in 'working' and 'middle' classes).

Similar findings were evident in Berger and Simon's (1974) self-report survey of some 3,000 14–18 year olds in Illinois, of whom over 10 per cent were black. Acts of violence were more than twice as common among black males (for example, 43 per cent $v.$ 20 per cent for persons of low social status in intact homes), with an even greater excess among black females (for example, 39 per cent $v.$ 11 per cent for low S.E.S. persons in intact homes). In contrast, there were no consistent black–white differences for theft.

The third reason for concluding that the black–white difference in crime rates shown in official statistics may have some validity is provided by victimization data (Hindelang, 1978; Hindelang *et al.*, 1979). These are based on interviews with a national probability sample, in which analyses are undertaken on the answers to questions about offenders from people reporting that they were subject to robbery, rape or assault *and* were able to report on the offender's characteristics. The findings showed that the identified offenders were black 3 to 5 times as often as expected on the basis of their representation in the general population. By comparison with the Uniform Crime Reports, it was possible to calculate how far the official figures were likely to have been distorted by differential reporting of crimes to the police. This showed that it was unlikely that there had been any significant distortion for either rape or robbery, but that probably there had been such bias for assault, and especially for aggravated assault.

Or course, there are problems in the use of victimization data, not the least of which is the uncertainty about the validity of the victim reports. In addition, the use of *national* data of any kind is open to the bias introduced by the combination of (i) the much higher crime rates in the major cities, and (ii) the much higher proportion of blacks in these same cities. It will be appreciated that, in order to correct for this bias, black–white comparisons need to be examined on a city by city basis (which they were not in the data published by Hindelang, 1978).

Putting these data together, we may conclude that the strong probability is that there is a real difference between blacks and whites in the U.S.A. in crimes involving violence against the person. Almost certainly the difference with respect to theft is very much less, but conclusions are less certain on crimes not involving violence. The findings suggest that the black–white difference is not just a function of social class variations, but the data are inadequate for a more detailed investigation of whether the differences are explicable in terms of family circumstances, living conditions, or area of residence.

A comparison of the different methods of assessment also suggests that, at least with minor crimes involving theft, the official statistics probably greatly exaggerate the extent of black–white differences. This raises the question of possible biases in police or judicial processing which may act to the disadvantage of blacks (see, for example, Piliavin and Briar, 1974; Black and Reiss, 1970; Sullivan and Seigel, 1972; Chambliss and Nagasawa, 1969; Terry, 1965). The evidence on such biases is not very satisfactory, in that many studies do not equate for the seriousness of offences and many of the conclusions about discriminatory handling rely on rather indirect inferences. Nevertheless, at least for minor offences, it does seem that there may well be a tendency for police to be more likely to pursue complaints against blacks. However, it may well be that this occurs not so much as a result of deliberately prejudicial handling but rather as a consequence of selective factors in the whole law enforcement process (Cicourel, 1976).

Crime and delinquency among blacks and Asians in the U.K.

With these various conceptual, substantive and methodological issues in mind, we turn now to findings in the U.K.

Not very much is known about the rates of crime in those areas, mainly docklands, where black settlements have been established for several generations (see Little, 1947; Richmond, 1954; Banton, 1955; Collins, 1957; Bloom, 1969). However, the data suggest that the rates of juvenile and adult crime have been generally similar to those in the rest of the population. These findings indicate that the increase in delinquency supposed to be characteristic of second-generation immigrants is not inevitable. But, of course, they apply to an era when the employment situation was much better than it is now and when 'race' was not the emotive issue that it tends to be today.

McClintock's (1963) study of crimes of violence was one of the first to provide relevant data on the more recent situation. If his data are compared with the 1961 census figures (see Bottoms, 1967), it is apparent that Commonwealth immigrants (as adults) were considerably more likely to be involved in domestic disputes. When these are discounted, there was still a probable slight excess of other crimes of violence (about 1.5 times expectation). However, inevitably the comparison was a very approximate one in view of uncertainties about the census data on immigrant groups and the inability to make the necessary age adjustments.

One of the most systematic early studies was conducted by Lambert (1970) in Birmingham, in which he made a detailed study of one sector of the city over a four-month period. The main general conclusion from his data was that first-generation immigrants – both Asian and West Indian, adults and children – were *no more* delinquent than the indigenous white population, and in some respects were *more law-abiding*. But three other findings are also relevant to the issues under consideration. Firstly, although not themselves responsible for the crimes, black immigrants tended to live in high crime areas (as a result of their difficulties in finding appropriate housing). This association with areas of delinquent activities would be likely to create a misleading impression in the public image that the black immigrants were themselves delinquent, which for the most part they were not. Secondly, compared with the native white population, black immigrants were more likely to be involved in personal disputes, involving violence. Many of these types of crime seemed to result from tensions between landlords and tenants, or from the strain of poor housing conditions. Thirdly, black immigrants seemed more likely to be involved in drug and motoring offences. Asians, but not West Indians, received many convictions for failing to tax, insure and licence their vehicles. Belson's (1968) self-report study refers to much the same era. He found that black boys had slightly lower rates of theft than white boys, but the finding applies to a questionnaire which was weighted towards very minor delinquencies.

Rather limited data are available on juvenile delinquent activities among children from immigrant families during the 1960s. However, several surveys using teacher questionnaires suggested that they were likely to show rates of difficult behaviour at school that were above those found in non-immigrant children (Schools Council, 1970; Bagley, 1972; Rutter *et al.*, 1974). The higher rate applied to restlessness, poor concentration and socially disapproved conduct of various kinds. The only study to use more detailed interview assessments (Rutter *et al.*, 1974) confirmed that the West Indian children's behaviour at school did tend to be more disruptive than that of other children, but the difference was substantially less than that on the questionnaire. The findings also showed that these difficulties were not evident at home and, at school too, were not accompanied by either emotional disturbances or difficulties in getting along with other children. It appeared that many of these conduct disturbances may have been immediately reactive to difficulties at school, perhaps in part due to the children's relatively high rate of educational retardation (Yule *et al.*, 1975) and in part to the tendency for them to attend schools with characteristics known to be associated with high rates of problem behaviour (Rutter *et al.*, 1975b).

However, it was also found that, as in white children, these behavioural problems were associated with factors such as family disruption, being admitted into care, and disturbed parent–child relationships (Rutter *et al.*, 1975b). The one striking difference was found in sex-linked diagnostic patterns. As in clinic studies (Graham and Meadows, 1967; Nicol, 1971), conduct disorders were especially common in West Indian girls – in contrast to their relative infrequency in white girls.

While the data are inadequate for any firm conclusions, the general picture of the situation up to about 1970 was a reasonably consistent one. Overall, children and adults in black or Asian immigrant families had rates of delinquency and crime which were comparable to, or rather below, those of the native white population. But adults in these families did show an increased tendency to become involved in personal disputes involving some form of (usually minor) violence. While the young people in immigrant families were no more delinquent than their peers, those of West Indian origin tended to be somewhat more disruptive at school. In spite of the unexceptionable rate of delinquency, it was also clear that West Indian children tended to have a higher rate of features which are known to be associated with an increased risk of delinquency (see later chapters). These included an increased rate of low educational attainment, of large family size, of family disruption, and of admission into care (see Rutter and Madge, 1976).

During the 1970s, indications that the situation might be changing began to appear. Whereas Lambert (1970) had found that West Indians and Asians were *under*-represented at 'approved schools' (for delinquent youths), new data of a less systematic kind began to suggest that West Indians were coming to be *over*-represented (Pearce, 1974). The unemployment rate among West Indian boys in the teenage years after leaving school rose markedly, and it seemed that many unemployed youngsters were getting into trouble with the police (Community Relations Commission, 1974). In some areas relations between the police and the young black community became strained, so that minor difficulties seemed to escalate in a way that precipitated police action (Banton, 1973). It appeared that boisterous defiant behaviour in response to police authority, in part culturally determined and in part a reaction to colour prejudice, sometimes made West Indians more liable to arrest at times of crowd disturbance. Some of these youth–police tensions seemed to arise from misunderstandings and differences in expectations on both sides.

Several writers have also suggested that second- and third-generation West Indian youths have developed a distinctive sub-culture which may facilitate the development of a deviant life style (Hall *et al.*, 1978; Frith, 1978; Pryce, 1979; Brake, 1980). Its most extreme expression is said to take the form of 'colonizing' certain streets or neighbourhoods, with distinctive roles and styles which emphasize black pride (for example, Rastafarianism), with crime part of the value system. Seen in this light, the role of the police is said to be one not only of enforcing the law, but also of confronting a culture that they do not understand (Dodd, 1978). Some have extended this analysis to suggest that black crime and its policing signify fundamental class schisms (Hall *et al.*, 1978), and many accusations have been made that the police discriminate against blacks (see Cain, 1973; Humphrey, 1972; Moore, 1975; Institute of Race Relations, 1979).

These writings emphasize that there are likely to be sub-cultural factors which need to be taken into account in coming to an understanding of possible changes in patterns of delinquent activities among black teenagers and in patterns of community–police relations. However, it has to be said that empirical data are lacking on the extent to which black youths are actually involved in distinctive sub-cultures. It should be added that such evidence as there is suggests that many black teenagers appear to be committed to education (as indicated by their high rate of staying on at school after the age of 16; Gray, 1981) and by their actively seeking work (Commission for Racial Equality, 1978). It would be a mistake to assume that the undoubted police–black community tensions necessarily mean that the black community as a whole rejects society's norms. Empirical research is needed to determine just how far there are distinctive West Indian youth sub-cultures, how many and which young people are part of such social groups, the factors which lead to the development of sub-cultures, and the implications for delinquent activities and their control. Such research has yet to be undertaken.

With those considerations as background, we turn now to the empirical evidence on the current situation. Batta *et al.* (1975) studied the delinquency patterns for Asians, half-Asians, and other juveniles aged 10–16 in a northern town during 1970–72. The delinquency data came from official statistics and the base figures for the population at risk from the Education Department records. The results showed that the mean crime rate for Asians (both Indian and Pakistani) was less than half that for the rest of the population, but the rate for the small group of half-Asians was about double expectation. A more recent re-appraisal of statistics in the same town (Mawby *et al.*, 1979) showed that in 1974–6 Asian juveniles continued to have an offender rate well below that of the rest of the population.

The most systematic recent study is that by Stevens and Willis (1979), who made a detailed study of arrests in London in 1975. Their results showed that Asian crime rates were substantially lower than white rates, except for a slight excess of assaults in all age groups over 15 years. Taken in conjunction with the Batta *et al.* (1975) study and the findings from earlier investigations, it is clear that the Asian community is a generally law-abiding one.

In sharp contrast, the rate of arrests for blacks (largely West Indian but including those from Africa) was very much higher than that for the white population of the same age and sex, with the differences apparent in both juveniles and adults. The largest excess was seen with robbery (a rate of 160 per 100,000 compared with an expected rate of 22), with other violent theft (60 *v.* 6) and with assault (466 *v.* 85). With other indictable arrests, there was only a two-fold difference.

It was not possible to determine directly how far the higher crime rate in blacks was explicable in terms of those psycho-social factors known to predispose to delinquency. However, an indirect assessment was made by utilizing census data on such characteristics as housing tenure and overcrowding for each area (the 22 police districts), and then correlating these with the arrest rate for each area. Three main findings emerged from this rather complex set of regression analyses: (i) the social factors that correlated with white arrest rates were not always the same as those that correlated with black or Asian arrest rates (for example, unemployment predicted only white rates): (ii) taken together, the social factors accounted for much of the variance between police divisions in arrest rates (35 per cent to 70 per cent according to type of crime); and (iii) inclusion of an 'ethnic factor' significantly increased the proportion of the variance accounted for in the regression. Considerable caution is needed in the interpretation of these findings because they refer to area correlations and variance and not to individuals. However, it may tentatively be inferred that part, but probably not the whole, of the excess arrest rate for blacks is likely to be due to psycho-social disadvantage. On the other hand, Ouston (1983), in a study of delinquency among juveniles in inner London, found that the higher rate of crime among black youths *was* wholly accounted for in terms of the combination of their lower social class and lower levels of intelligence/scholastic attainment compared with those in the indigenous white population.

The next question concerned the explanation of that proportion of such variance as may not be due to social disadvantage. Stevens and Willis (1979) note the many different ways in which the higher arrest rate in blacks might come about. Other data (Sparks *et al.*, 1977) suggest that only a minority of crimes are reported to the police – leaving open possible distortions as a result of race biases in reporting. Distortion could also arise at the stage when offences are officially recorded, or when detection of suspects occurs (i.e. there could be a higher 'clear-up' rate for crimes by black persons), or in the arrest of suspects (if there were a greater tendency to arrest blacks mistakenly). Stevens and Willis note that the very extreme excess of arrest for 'other violent theft' (mostly snatching handbags without causing injury) and for 'sus' (i.e. as a person loitering with intent to commit a crime), where the rates were 14 to 15 times expectation, suggests that such processing biases may play a part. But they emphasize, too, that calculations show that there would have to be a very large element of processing discrimination to account for the whole of the black–white difference in arrest rate.

Further data are provided from police reports on victims' accounts of their assailants. These showed that the 'coloured' rate (presumably this would include both Asians and blacks) was 8 times expectation. Of course, it could be that when victims are uncertain of the identity of their attacker they may be more likely to say that he is coloured than white. But it seems unlikely that this provides a complete explanation, in that the excess of 'coloured' assailants still applied when the victim was black. As in the United States, the majority of attacks are intra-racial. This was particularly so in the case of attacks involving serious injury. Cases in which there was a 'coloured' attacker but a white victim were especially likely to involve no injury (50 per cent cases *v.* 21–22 per cent for intra-racial or white on coloured crimes), and rarely involved serious or fatal injuries (4 per cent *v.* 10–13 per cent for the other groups).

In three respects, the findings of these various studies are quite clear-cut. Firstly, the delinquency rate for Asians has been equal to or lower than that for the white population at all times when it has been studied. Secondly, in sharp contrast to the situation in the 1950s and 1960s, the arrest rate for blacks is now substantially above that for whites, especially for violent crimes (although the degree of 'violence' involved is often minimal). Thirdly, most violent crimes occur between two people who are of the *same* skin colour.

Beyond these three reasonably well established findings there is much greater uncertainty. The victim data, taken in conjunction with the arrest findings, suggest that very probably there is a real excess of violent crimes committed by blacks. However, the excess indicated in the victim data is less than that shown by the arrest figures, and there must be doubt about how great an excess exists. There is even more doubt on how far the excess applies to other crimes.

No firm conclusions are possible on how far there have been distortions in processing. However, the disparity between the arrest data for violent crimes and the victim data, taken in conjunction with the high no-injury rate in cases with a white victim and 'coloured' assailant, and the extremely high rate of black 'sus' arrests, suggests that distortions are likely to have occurred at some stage. It should be emphasized that these need not necessarily involve deliberate discrimination of any kind; they could just as well have arisen as a consequence of differential reporting of crimes, of differential patrolling of areas with a large black population, and of an increased liability to 'sus' arrests, arising from the high unemployment rate in young blacks causing them to be on the streets during the day.

Finally, it is evident that very little is known on the origins of delinquent activities within black groups. There is, of course, every reason to suppose that the major factors associated with crime in white people apply also to black people. One of the features of criminological research in different cultures is the relative consistency with which the same associations appear (Friday, 1980). But we know next to nothing of why crime rates should be lower in Asian youths and higher in West Indian youths, or why the excess of crime in young blacks tends to involve violence against persons (in the U.S.A. and apparently in Britain, too), or why disorders of conduct seem to be relatively more frequent in black girls, or whether socio-cultural or socio-political (as well as individual) factors play an important role in the genesis of delinquent activities among young blacks. All these issues need to be investigated.

Conclusions

As Barbara Wootton (1959) pointed out some years ago, the one variable most strongly and consistently associated with delinquency is male sex. Yet we have very little understanding of why this should be so. Research in recent years has provided some useful leads to follow, and it is to be hoped that these will be pursued systematically. The apparent, but disputed, links between low social status and crime remain a matter of controversy. We conclude that in all probability a true association exists, but it is of moderate strength only and it is likely that, to a large extent, it is a consequence of the problems that may accompany low status, rather than low social status *per se*. However, that suggestion constitutes just an hypothesis and research is needed to explore the possibility. In recent years, more attention has been paid to social group phenomena which may involve delinquent activities. These are of potential importance but, so far, most of the theoretical notions on this topic lack adequate empirical verification. Finally, there are many important questions that need to be answered on racial issues. Doubts remain on the true facts regarding delinquent behaviour in ethnic minorities, but it seems clear that the situation has changed over the last decade or so and, whatever the origins of the change, the present state of affairs is rightly giving cause for concern. There are crucial issues involved which are open to research and which should be investigated.

5
Causes and Correlates – Individual Characteristics

During recent years it has become unfashionable to study juvenile delinquency in terms of individual characteristics. One of the main reasons has been the repeated demonstration in self-report studies (see Chapter 1) that most young people have committed delinquent acts at some time. It has seemed inappropriate, therefore, to examine the possibility that delinquency might be due to some kind of personal 'abnormality' when the phenomenon of delinquency is so exceedingly common. But, as already pointed out, although it is true that isolated minor delinquent acts may be undertaken by almost anybody, only a small minority engage in repeated and persistent delinquency. It is quite possible that this subgroup might be associated with particular personal features. Even with the broader delinquent group as a whole, of course, it could be that an individual's characteristics on some personality or other dimension might be associated with a greater or lesser predisposition to commit delinquent acts. The very limited evidence on both these possibilities is examined in this chapter. We start with the best established of the associations.

I.Q. and scholastic attainment

Strength of I.Q.–delinquency association

Although largely ignored by criminology theorists, there is now a very substantial body of empirical research that shows a consistent association between lower I.Q. and an increased risk of delinquency (see Hirschi and Hindelang, 1977, for a good review of both the findings and the conceptual issues). This association applies to self-report data, to teacher ratings of disruptive behaviour, to convictions, and to clinical assessments of conduct disturbance. Also, it has been evident in both British and American studies. For example, in their longitudinal study of London boys, West and Farrington (1973) found that 20 per cent of those with an I.Q. of 90 or below became recidivist compared with 9 per cent of those with a score of 91–98, 5 per cent of those with an I.Q. of 99–109, and only 2 per cent of those with an I.Q.

of 110+. The findings for educational attainment were similar but, in both cases, the association with one-time delinquency was very much weaker. Moreover, the association still held after controlling for family size and family income. On the other hand, it disappeared after controlling for troublesome behaviour. This finding suggests that lower I.Q. was associated with troublesome behaviour as shown at 8 and 10 years, and that the link with delinquency was solely due to this prior association rather than to any direct effect on delinquency *per se*.

May's (1975) data from his total population survey of Aberdeen children are also consistent with this suggestion. He found that primary school truancy was significantly associated with a variety of other disturbances of conduct and that, in turn, both were associated with an increased risk of delinquency. I.Q. (as assessed on a group test at 9–10 years) was negatively correlated with both truancy and delinquency. However, it was striking that the association between I.Q. and delinquency was much stronger among good attenders than among truants. Unfortunately, May does not indicate the extent to which I.Q. correlates with delinquency after the effects of *total* behavioural deviance (rather than just truancy) are partialled out. However, as in the West and Farrington (1973) study, it is evident that, at least in part, the association between I.Q. and delinquency is due, to its earlier association with troublesome behaviour in the classroom.

American data do not deal directly with this issue but they confirm that the I.Q.–delinquency correlation is *not* just a reflection of race or social status. Thus, in Hirschi's Californian study (Hirschi, 1969; Hirschi and Hindelang, 1977), not only was the correlation between I.Q. and delinquency stronger than that between social status and delinquency, but I.Q. continued to show a significant correlation with delinquency even after taking into account the effects of race and social status. Other research findings are congruent with these and, as Hirschi and Hindelang (1977) conclude, I.Q. seems to have an association with official delinquency which is as strong as that between either social class or race and crime.

Self-report data point to a similar conclusion. For example, Bachman *et al.* (1978), in their American longitudinal study, showed consistent associations between educational attainment and self-reports of both aggression and serious delinquency. These associations were as strong at seventh to ninth grade as they were later, indicating that the link was already well established fairly early in schooling and did not increase in strength later. Similarly, West and Farrington (1973, 1977) found that self-reported delinquents tended to score relatively low on tests of verbal and non-verbal intelligence and on tests of educational attainment. Once again, associations were evident early in schooling. Hirschi (Hirschi, 1969; Hirschi and Hindelang, 1977) also showed an association between I.Q. and self-reported delinquency in both white and black youths.

The links between both I.Q. and educational attainment on the one hand, and non-delinquent disturbances of conduct on the other, was shown in the Isle of Wight survey of 10 year olds (Rutter, Tizard and Whitmore, 1970), the London survey of the same age group (Rutter *et al.*, 1975a; Sturge, 1982), Clark's (1970) Scottish survey, and the Inner London Educational Authority surveys (Varlaam, 1974), as well as in a variety of earlier studies. The Isle of Wight study showed, moreover, that the associations between I.Q. or reading and deviant behaviour were maintained even after controlling for family size and social class. On the whole, the associations were stronger with reading than with I.Q., and this was especially the case with the overall designation of conduct disorder in boys (based on information from parents, teachers and the children themselves).

Meaning of associations

The links, then, are well established, but what do the associations mean? The various possible alternatives have been explored by several different investigators, with results which are both inconsistent and inconclusive. However, two possibilities can be ruled out – at least as major explanations. Firstly, there is the suggestion that the association simply reflects the ability of the bright delinquent to avoid detection or prosecution (for example, Doleschal and Klapmuts, 1973). This is contradicted both by the associations with self-reported delinquency (see above) and by the finding that the I.Q.–conviction association disappears once the I.Q.–troublesome behaviour association has been taken into account (West and Farrington, 1973). Secondly, there is the possibility that delinquency or disturbances of conduct cause poor intellectual performance, educational failure and school dropout. Clearly, delinquency cannot be held responsible for the low I.Q. scores, as the low scores antedate the delinquency. It is more difficult to test the possibility that disturbances of conduct so interfere with learning that they lower cognitive performance and scholastic attainment. However, several findings cast doubts on the hypothesis. Richman *et al.* (1982) showed that I.Q.–behavioural disturbance associations were already present as early as 3 years and did not increase over the next five years. Moreover, persistence of psychiatric problems (there was no separate analysis with respect to conduct disturbance) between 3 and 8 years was not accompanied by any intellectual deterioration, and cognitive scores in the general population showed no significant correlation with behavioural measures taken during testing. Rutter *et al.* (1976b) also showed that changes in psychiatric disorder were unassociated with changes in cognitive performance.

Of the possibilities which remain, there are two main contenders, each of which has some support in some populations. There is the hypothesis that educational failure leads to low self-esteem, emotional disturbance and antagonism to school, which may contribute to the development of disturbances of conduct and of delinquent activities (Schonell, 1961; Mangus, 1950; Cohen, 1956; Rutter *et al.*, 1970). There are three different types of evidence which support this suggestion. Firstly, there is the comparison of children who show *both* reading difficulties and antisocial behaviour with those showing 'pure' reading difficulties and 'pure' conduct disturbances. Both Rutter *et al.* (1970) on the Isle of Wight and Varlaam (1974) in London found that the combined group was most like the 'pure' reading difficulties group and rather dissimillar to the 'pure' conduct disturbance group. Because, in the combination group, conduct disturbances were linked with the characteristics associated with reading difficulties rather than with those associated with antisocial behaviour, it was argued that the findings suggested that in these cases antisocial disorder may have arisen, in part, as a result of educational failure. On the other hand, Sturge's (1982) findings, using the same research strategy, were only partially supportive of the hypothesis.

The second type of evidence comes from the very few investigations showing that improving academic performance through behaviour modification or other procedures may markedly reduce discipline problems in the classroom (Ayllon and Roberts, 1974; Gates and Bond, 1936).

Thirdly, there is the observation that delinquency rates fall after leaving school (Phillips and Kelly, 1979). The possible importance of educational failure in predisposing to delinquency is most strikingly shown in Elliott and Voss's (1974) longitudinal study of American high-school students. Those pupils who subsequently dropped out of school showed markedly higher delinquency scores on a self-reporting questionnaire (and markedly higher police contact rates) than those who completed their full time at high school – confirming the association between educational failure and delinquency. However, in terms of the mechanisms involved, the striking finding was that the delinquent activities of the drop-outs markedly diminished *after* they left school. Furthermore, the timing of the reduction in delinquent activities coincided with the period of leaving school rather than with age (as shown by comparing the timing in groups who dropped out early or late in their schooling). Elliott and Voss conclude that it is the combination of educational failure and the school's response to that failure which predispose to delinquency. Poor educational attainment (or low intellectual level) is much less important in the genesis of delinquency in the different circumstances of the work place. This interaction view is also supported by Robins and Hill's (1966) finding that educational failure is not characteristic of individuals whose delinquency begins in adult life. On the other hand, West and Farrington (1977) found that low I.Q. was almost as frequent among men first convicted in early adult life as among those convicted as juveniles.

There are also two sorts of contrary evidence against the 'educational failure causes conduct disturbance' hypothesis. Firstly, the finding that I.Q. and behavioural disturbance are already associated as early as the age of 3 or 4 (Richman *et al.*, 1982) is inconsistent with the hypothesis. Secondly, the one study to examine the sequential relationship of conduct disorders and reading difficulties (McMichael, 1979) showed that disturbances of conduct frequently preceded reading difficulties, and even at school entry were already associated with poor performance on reading readiness tests. At least within the 5–7 age group studied, there was nothing to suggest that reading difficulties *caused* antisocial behaviour. However, as McMichael (1979) points out, that does not necessarily mean that this does not occur in older children. We may conclude that educational failure *may* increase the likelihood of conduct disturbances in *some* older children, but clearly this mechanism fails to account for the overall association.

Another possibility is that both cognitive deficits and conduct disturbance to some extent share a common etiology – either in terms of socio-familial variables or temperamental characteristics. This explanation is favoured by Offord *et al.* (1978) on the grounds that, in their study of boys on probation in Ottawa, delinquents did not differ significantly from their sibs in terms of either I.Q. or scholastic failure. On the other hand, although the difference fell short of significance, it was notable that whereas 51 per cent of the delinquents showed poor school performance only 33 per cent of their brothers did so. Also, the delinquents whose antisocial behaviour followed poor school performance differed from the 'primary' delinquents (without scholastic difficulties) in showing more symptoms of a *non*-antisocial type – which might be thought to suggest the possible role of emotional disturbance resulting from educational failure. Richman *et al.* (1982) also favour a common etiology hypothesis on the basis of the presence of an I.Q.–behaviour correlation as early as the age of 3. Of course, these data apply to a broader range of disorders than conduct disturbances and in many cases (as shown by their own data) conduct disturbances do not arise until later in childhood. Nevertheless, a common etiology is certainly suggested for those whose disorders are already apparent at the age of 3.

This raises the further question of what sort of etiology might be relevant. Offord *et al.* (1978) place weight on family factors, but three different sorts of findings are inconsistent with this suggestion. Firstly, in their own study, they identify no family variables which differentiate children with either delinquency or school failure from those without both problems (of course, that is a consequence of their within-family design, but by the same token it raises questions about their other negative findings on sib–sib comparisons on which they base their argument). Secondly, Richman *et al.* (1982) found that whereas cognitive and behavioural measures at 3 or 4 years were associated with persistence of disorders to 8 years, family measures were not. Thirdly, West and Farrington (1973) found that I.Q. still correlated with delinquency even after controlling for family variables. Similarly, Noblit (1976), in an American study of high-school students, found that grade point average (a measure of educational attainment) was associated with delinquency even within social class groups and after controlling for delinquent associates. Of course, that is not to suggest that family variables are not important in the genesis of conduct disturbance and reading difficulties. On the contrary, there is good evidence that they are important. Nevertheless, it does seem that family variables may not account for the *association* between the two conditions. None of these studies has utilized measures of temperament, so the possibility that temperament constitutes the crucial common etiological variable remains open.

It is all too apparent that no single explanation for the I.Q.–conduct disturbance association can be maintained. Possibly the major link may be found to lie in the temperamental features which predispose to both educational failure and antisocial behaviour. However, the main evidence on this suggestion comes from ruling out other explanations rather than from any data in direct support. In addition, it is probable that in some cases educational failure may increase the predisposition to conduct disturbance. Family factors also may play a subsidiary role.

Body build, physical illness and disability

Body build

For many centuries there have been widely held stereotypes concerning the personality attributes associated with different physiques and builds, but modern interest in the topic was stimulated by Sheldon's (Sheldon *et al.*,

1940) classification of physique according to three components: mesomorphy (chunky and muscular), endomorphy (fat and rounded), and ectomorphy (long and lean). In spite of early claims of strong links between body build and personality, empirical findings have generally shown rather low correlations between physical and psychological attributes (see Rees, 1973, for an extensive review). That applies also to associations between physique and delinquency.

In their classic study of institutionalized delinquents in the U.S.A., the Gluecks (Glueck and Glueck, 1956) found that, compared with non-delinquents, delinquent boys were twice as likely to have a mesomorphic build. Comparable findings have been reported in several English studies of institutionalized delinquents (Gibbens, 1963; Epps and Parnell, 1952). However, the validity of these associations as reflections of any type of causal connection between body build and delinquency remains extremely doubtful in view of the inappropriate choice of control groups in most studies and the restriction to *institutionalized* delinquents. In so far as there is any link with body build, it is as likely to be with incarceration as with delinquent behaviour (it is not implausible that the tougher, athletic-looking delinquents are more liable to be 'put away' than fragile-looking, skinny ones).

Be that as it may, Wadsworth (1979), in the British National Survey of the total population, found that delinquents (and especially more serious delinquents) tended to reach puberty *later* than non-delinquents, and to be somewhat smaller and lighter. No somatotyping was undertaken, but these results are the opposite of those expected for mesomorphs (who tend to reach puberty somewhat earlier than average). However, it was found that the associations between delinquency on the one hand and height, weight and puberty on the other were greatly reduced or disappeared once relevant social factors had been taken into account. Similarly, West and Farrington (1973) found no association between delinquency and either height–weight ratio or strength of grip (measured by dynamometer) in their general population study of working-class London boys. From these results it seems unlikely that physique plays any substantial role in the origins of delinquent behaviour.

Physical disabilities

Most (but not all) early investigations showed that physical ailments and defects were somewhat more frequent among delinquents than non-delinquents (see West, 1967). Stott (1966) found that ill-health was associated with delinquency and, within a delinquent group, with maladjustment as measured on the Bristol Social Adjustment Guide; on this basis he postulated that both stemmed from biologically determined 'multiple congenital impairments'. In the British National Survey, Wadsworth (1979) found that delinquents were more likely than non-delinquents to have been admitted to hospital during the first five years of life. An earlier report on the same study by Douglas (1975) showed that this risk applied only to multiple admissions or single admissions lasting longer than a week. In the West and Farrington (1973) study of working-class London boys, those found to be more clumsy were also more prone to become delinquent, but clumsiness was associated with I.Q. and the association between clumsiness and delinquency disappeared when I.Q. was taken into account.

More recently, Lewis and Shanok (1977) compared the medical records (only in the one major general hospital serving the area) of 109 randomly selected delinquents with a sample of 10 per cent non-delinquents with similar demographic characteristics and matched for age, sex and race, finding that delinquents had more accidents and injuries and more hospital attendances. A comparison within the delinquent group showed that this excess (and particularly that of accidents or injuries in the first four years) was mainly found in those with criminal fathers (Lewis *et al.*, 1979a). A parallel comparison (Lewis *et al.*, 1979b) between incarcerated and non-incarcerated delinquents showed that the former had experienced more head and face injuries and more physical abuse; they had also experienced more perinatal difficulties (although, as in other studies, this variable did not differentiate delinquents from non-delinquents).

It is clear from these findings that the slight excess of physical illness, accidents and disability among delinquents is associated with parental problems and with adverse childhood experiences (as evident in both physical abuse and the stresses of recurrent hospitalization). Although both Stott (1966) and Lewis *et al.* (1979a and b) have been inclined to place weight on biological impairment, sometimes involving brain damage, as one of the causal factors of delinquency, not only is the evidence of neural dysfunction inferential but also the physical features are so strongly associated with psycho-social deviance and disadvantage that it is not possible from published data to determine which mechanisms might be operative. However, as noted above, no consistent associations have been found between complications of pregnancy or delivery and delinquency (Pasamanick and Knobloch, 1966; West and Farrington, 1973). Brain damage has been shown to increase the risk of psychiatric disorder and educational retardation quite substantially (see Rutter, 1981f) and, because of that, it probably also increases the risk of delinquency (although there is no *specific* association with delinquency). Accordingly it may play an important causal role in a few individual cases, but brain damage (however assessed) is present in only a tiny minority of delinquents and it is likely that it is of negligible importance in the genesis of delinquent behaviour in the population as a whole.

Physiological characteristics, avoidance learning and stimulus seeking

Physiological characteristics

Several studies have shown associations between antisocial behaviour and autonomic reactivity. Thus, Wadsworth (1976) found that delinquent boys in the British National Survey had had lower pulse rates at the age of 11 than non-delinquent boys; this tendency was most marked in those committing violent or sexual offences. Similarly Davies and Maliphant (1971a) found lower base heart rates among '*refractory*' adolescents at a boarding school (defined in terms of teacher nominations) compared with controls; the '*refractory*' boys also showed a lesser increase in pulse rate following a noxious stimulus than did controls, and had a higher Pd ('psychopathy') score on the Minnesota Multiphasic Personality Inventory (Davies and Maliphant, 1971b). West and Farrington (1977) found that delinquents were less likely than non-delinquents to have a *fast* pulse rate when measured at the end of an interview (perhaps reflecting a lesser response to stress), but the proportion of slow pulse rates did not differentiate the groups. Borkovec (1970) compared 'psychopathic', 'neurotic' and 'normal' institutionalized delinquents (the categories being defined in terms of scores on the Quay and Peterson Behaviour Problem checklist). He found that, as measured by skin conductance, the 'psychopathic' delinquents showed lower initial reactivity to a moderate intensity auditory tone. Similarly, Siddle *et al.* (1973 and 1976) found that the most antisocial boys in an institutionalized delinquent group tended to be those with a lower skin conductance reactivity and with a longer recovery time.

So far the autonomic responsivity of delinquents has been studied with too limited a range of measures for any firm general conclusions to be possible. But the findings point to a responsivity which is reduced compared with that in normal boys. The within-group comparisons suggest that this characteristic may be most likely to be found with the more seriously antisocial boys or with those with 'psychopathic' personality traits. There is an obvious parallel with the results of studies with 'psychopathic' adults who have tended to show small sluggish skin conductance responses to noxious stimuli

(Hare, 1970; Hare and Schalling, 1978). The implication is that when delinquency is accompanied by 'psychopathic' features (meaning, broadly, a combination of a failure to sustain close personal relationships, a lack of empathy or feeling for other people, impulsiveness, a lack of guilt at a failure to learn from social experiences), it may be associated with diminished autonomic reactivity. However, as noted in Chapter 1, the concept of 'psychopathy' has proved elusive and difficult to define as well as to measure, and there is some inconsistency in the specific psycho-physiological characteristics which have been found (Hare, 1970; Hare and Schalling, 1978; Hodgins, 1979).

Moreover, although the psycho-physiological findings for delinquent children show parallels with those for 'psychopathic' adults, they show the same parallels with those for 'hyperkinetic' children. Although the results are somewhat inconsistent, there has been a general tendency for them to be slower to respond to stimulation and to show smaller autonomic responses (Hastings and Barkley, 1978). The links between 'hyperactivity', delinquency and 'psychopathy' remain quite uncertain, but it is clear that they overlap to an important extent (see below). With respect to the interpretation of findings in all three groups, it should not necessarily be assumed that the autonomic characteristics are constitutional in origin, although they may be. The findings are provocative, potentially important, and worth following through with further research, but so far the ideas on autonomic reactivity can only be considered as hypotheses with some preliminary empirical support.

Avoidance learning

These autonomic features have usually been associated with the notion, deriving from Lykken's pioneering research (1957), that 'psychopaths' show reduced anxiety and impaired passive avoidance learning following punishment. This view has received substantial empirical support in adults (see Hare, 1970; Trasler, 1973; Hare and Schalling, 1978; Hodgins, 1979), although one study found that 'psychopaths' could learn to avoid when their anxiety was aroused by having to pay financially for their failures (Schmauk, 1970). The matter has been little studied in children or adolescents, but Davies and Maliphant (1974), in their study of 'refractory' 11–16 year olds, examined avoidance learning by administering brief electric shocks for errors (and giving money or sweets for correct responses) in a task which required subjects to over-compensate for the effect of a particular visual illusion. In each experiment, 'refractory' boys made more errors and received more shocks, and were especially more likely to make a further error after receiving a shock. The study had important limitations in experimental design, but the findings are consistent with the hypothesis of impaired passive avoidance learning. The matter warrants further study.

Stimulus seeking

Some years ago Quay (1965; 1977a) proposed that 'psychopaths' were motivated by an abnormally great need for stimulation. Several studies with children and adolescents have attempted to test this hypothesis in relation to rather broader concepts of conduct disorder. Orris (1969) found that, within a group of delinquents, those high on the 'conduct disorder' dimension were more likely to show poor performance on a vigilance task requiring continuous attention than those with high scores on either 'anxiety-withdrawal' or 'socialized aggression'. He also noted that the conduct disorder boys were more likely to engage in boredom-relieving activities such as singing and talking to themselves. More recently, Whitehill *et al.* (1976) compared 8 'refractory' and 8 'tractable and sensitive' 9–13 year old boys from a treatment centre for disturbed children with 7 controls from a nearby school. The task involved watching 103 slides representing various views of the concrete façades of a modern building, the subject being able to control the speed of presentation. The 'refractory' boys spent significantly less time viewing the slides and showed a greater tendency to accelerate the speed of presentation. A second study (DeMyer-Gapin and Scott, 1977) of the first two groups of children compared their response to novel slides with that to the same boringly repetitive slides of a concrete building. Both groups looked longer at the novel slides, but the 'refractory' boys habituated more quickly (that is, their looking time fell more quickly). Four of the 'refractory' boys, but none of the 'tractable' ones, grew restless, fidgety and talkative during the procedures. The results of both studies were interpreted in terms of 'stimulation-seeking', but it could equally be argued that the findings merely confirm that 'refractory' boys tend to be restless, inattentive, and easily bored by externally imposed tasks.

Delinquency and hyperactivity

Nevertheless, the observations of inattentiveness among antisocial boys emphasize the need to draw comparisons with the 'hyperkinetic' syndrome. The validity of this diagnosis as representing a nosologically distinct entity has been questioned by many reviewers (for example, Ross and Ross, 1976;

Loney, 1980; Rie and Rie, 1980; Ferguson and Rapoport, 1983; Rutter, 1982a). But it is generally held to imply a disorder with an onset before the age of 3 in which the two cardinal features are developmentally inappropriate inattention and impulsivity (American Psychiatric Association, 1980). The links with delinquency are indicated by four well-substantiated findings.

Firstly, there is a huge overlap between hyperactivity and attentional deficits on the one hand, and disturbances of conduct on the other (Cantwell, 1980). Factor analytic studies show that the two forms of behaviour are often included in the same factor, and even when they appear in different factors, the two factors tend to intercorrelate highly (Achenbach and Edelbrock, 1978; Quay, 1979). As shown by both general population (Sandberg, Wieselberg and Shaffer, 1980) and clinic studies (Sandberg, Rutter and Taylor, 1978; Stewart *et al.*, 1981), most children with disorders of conduct are also hyperactive, and vice versa. Furthermore, the correlates of hyperactivity and the correlates of conduct disorder tend to be closely similar (Sandberg, Rutter and Taylor, 1978). Little is known on whether hyperactive delinquents differ from other delinquents, but a study by Offord *et al.* (1979) of boys on probation in Canada suggested that those who were definitely hyperactive tended to be more antisocial; also they showed worse school performance and, on average, had a lower birthweight.

Secondly, long-term follow-ups of hyperactive children referred to clinics in early or middle childhood show that they have an increased risk of later delinquency (Weiss, 1983), and retrospective accounts of delinquent boys suggest that they showed early temperamental features of a kind often associated with hyperactivity (Olweus, 1980b).

Thirdly, family history studies show associations between hyperactivity, delinquency, alcoholism and sociopathy (Cantwell, 1974; Morrison and Stewart, 1973; Stewart *et al.*, 1980).

Fourthly, the attentional deficits thought to be characteristic of delinquents are closely similar to those associated with hyperactivity. The research on the latter group is extensive and has been well reviewed by Douglas and Peters (1979). They conclude that hyperactive children are not particularly distractable but that they may perform better in stimulating environments (and hence may be said to be 'stimulus-seeking'), that they do not show any abnormalities in selective attention, but that they *do* show an important impairment in vigilance and sustained attention.

It is all too clear that there are major problems in drawing together these varied findings using many different measures on differently defined (but overlapping) groups. Nevertheless, there are good pointers to the probability that a subgroup of delinquents are characterized by diminished autonomic reactivity, impaired passive avoidance learning, stimulus seeking and impaired vigilance and sustained attention. It is not known how far these four features are associated with each other, it is not clear what proportion of delinquents show these characteristics, and it remains uncertain whether, within delinquent populations, the characteristics are associated with degree or persistence of antisocial behaviour. But it does appear that further research to resolve these issues would be worthwhile.

Personality characteristics

There has long been an interest in the possibility that criminality is systematically associated with particular personality dimensions, and (quite apart from the psycho-physiological and attentional measures just considered which could be regarded as facets of personality) there has been a host of empirical studies, utilizing a variety of tests, which have sought to examine the issue both in the United States (Schuessler and Cressey, 1950; Waldo and Dinitz, 1967; Tennenbaum, 1977) and in Britain (Eysenck, 1977; Powell, 1977; Farrington et al., 1982). The majority of investigations have indeed shown differences between delinquent and non-delinquent groups, but there are numerous problems in the interpretation of these differences. In the first place many of the studies concerned incarcerated individuals (so that it remains uncertain how far the findings reflect incarceration rather than delinquency), and many have utilized control samples which were inadequately matched on key variables. Secondly, too, some of the findings seem largely tautological either because the item content of the personality questionnaires explicitly refers to criminal behaviour or because they deal with other forms of conduct disturbance. For example, the 'P' ('psychoticism') scale items on the Eysenck scale (Eysenck and Eysenck, 1973), which are most strongly associated with antisocial behaviour, include 'yes' responses to questions such as 'Are you in more trouble at school than most children?' or 'Would you take drugs which may have strange or dangerous effects?' (Allsop and Feldman, 1976; Farrington et al., 1982). Such items are relevant to the question (already discussed) of how far delinquency is associated with wider manifestations of conduct disturbance, but it is less obvious that the 'P' dimension contributes to hypotheses regarding the role of personality characteristics in the genesis of such conduct disturbance. Thirdly, particularly so far as children are concerned, it is dubious whether the questionnaires really assess enduring personality dimensions. Few data are available on continuities over time, but those that exist suggest fairly low consistency. For example, the correlation between 16 years and 26 years for 'neuroticism' on the Eysenck scale was 0.32 in the British National Survey (Douglas and Mann, 1979), and Bronson (1967) reported similar figures from the Berkeley Guidance Study for Q sort measures of expressive *v.* reserved and controlled *v.* explosive.

Probably Eysenck's measures of 'neuroticism' (N) and 'extraversion' (E), which have been utilized in a few studies of non-incarcerated children and adolescents, involve the least tautologies. In the Cambridge study of London boys, Farrington *et al.* (1982) found that neither N nor E was associated with juvenile delinquency (although there was a non-significant tendency for the neurotic extravert quadrant to be associated with a slightly increased risk of delinquency – 24.8 per cent *v.* 18.9 per cent), but N and the NE quadrant were significantly associated with *adult* criminality (for both N and NE a rate of $21\frac{1}{2}$ per cent *v.* 11 per cent). Forrest (1977) similarly found no association between N and juvenile delinquency, although he did find a link with *low* E (i.e. the reverse of that postulated by Eysenck). There are a larger number of studies relating N and E to self-report measures of antisocial behaviour (see Powell, 1977 and Farrington *et al.*, 1982 for reviews). The findings are somewhat inconsistent, but the commonest pattern is for N and E to be associated with self-reports of antisocial behaviour in older, but not younger, boys and girls. However, the correlations have been generally quite low (much lower than those for the 'P' dimension on the same scale) and several investigations have produced contrary findings. The findings for adults (mainly with respect to prisoners) are wholly inconsistent with respect to E, but show a consistent tendency for high N to be associated with criminality.

There are difficulties in drawing conclusions from these findings, both because the self-report data are open to the serious objection that the associations may merely reflect a rating bias which applies to both the personality questionnaires and to the delinquency questionnaires, and because the high N may reflect a *response* to incarceration rather than a predisposition to delinquency. Moreover, the correlations are in any case not high enough to have much predictive power. Nevertheless, the indications are that probably there is some real (but rather minor) tendency for high N to be associated with a somewhat increased risk of delinquency in older adolescents and young adults, but not in younger children.

Genetic factors

Possible genetic factors in the production of antisocial disorders have been considered both in terms of chromosome anomalies (Shaffer *et al.*, 1980; Witkin *et al.*, 1976) and polygenic influences (Crowe, 1978; Christiansen,

1977a and b). With respect to the former (although there are some negative findings reported), it appears that both a long arm on the Y chromosome (Kahn *et al.*, 1969; Christensen and Nielsen, 1974; Nielsen and Nordland, 1975) and an extra Y chromosome (see review by Zellweger and Simpson, 1977) probably carry a slightly increased risk of behavioural problems, including those which involve conduct disturbance. However, not only is the association with psychopathology rather non-specific, but also the increased risk is only modest (i.e. many individuals with a long arm on the Y or an XYY are behaviourally unexceptionable) and the vast majority of individuals with conduct disturbance show no form of chromosomal anomaly.

The evidence on possible polygenic influences for juvenile delinquency is rather limited, but it is consistent in suggesting that genetic factors probably play a rather minor role in juvenile delinquency *considered as a whole* (Shields, 1977). Thus, twin studies have shown similarly high concordance rates in both monozygotic and dizygotic pairs (Rosanoff *et al.*, 1941; Hayashi, 1967; Shields, 1977), and studies of adoptees have found no association between criminality in the biological parent (who did not rear the children) and maladaptive behaviour in the adopted children (Bohman, 1970 and 1978; Bohman and Sigvardsson, 1978; Cadoret *et al.*, 1975).

On the other hand, the weight of evidence does suggest the probable importance of polygenic influence in persistent antisocial disorders in adults, most cases of which will have begun in childhood.

Twin studies generally show somewhat greater concordance within MZ than DZ pairs (Christiansen, 1977a and b). Many of the earlier studies are open to serious objections on the grounds of possibly biased sampling, but the two most recent studies, based on Scandinavian twin registers (Christiansen, 1977b; Dalgaard and Kringlen, 1976), have also shown MZ–DZ differences in concordance – 35 per cent *v.* 13 per cent and 26 per cent *v.* 15 per cent respectively. The findings for females are much sparser, but the concordance rates are similar (Cloninger *et al.*, 1978). The Dalgaard and Kringlen (1976) study nevertheless concluded that '. . . hereditary factors are of no significant importance in the etiology of common crime', so that some discussion of their findings is needed.

Their reasons for the negative conclusion were two-fold: firstly, that the MZ–DZ difference was much less with a broader definition of crime which included motor vehicle law offences and treason during the Second World War; and secondly, that the concordance difference virtually disappeared when similarities in environment were taken into account. The first ground seems without substance, in that such a wide definition of crime is quite different from that usually employed. Moreover, even with the 'narrow' definition, 'violation of vagrancy law' constituted the second commonest type of crime, so that the figures scarcely apply to serious crime. Most puzzling of all is their surprisingly low rate of crime. Out of some 6,000 male twins in same-sexed pairs (the figure is an estimate because Dalgaard and Kringlen do not give the figures separately for males in same-sex pairs), there were only 165 with a criminal record (2.8 per cent) even using the broad definition – a rate far below that in Christiansen's comparable study in Norway. Their findings on the effects of similarity in environment, although employed to negate a genetic hypothesis (on the grounds that the MZ–DZ difference was only 23 per cent v. 21 per cent when there was strong closeness of environment), could equally well be used to support it (on the grounds that the MZ–DZ difference was much strengthened when there was not strong closeness of the environment – 40 per cent v. 12 per cent). However, in view of the other reservations noted above and the very small numbers, both arguments must be regarded as inconclusive. It is necessary to turn to other kinds of data.

These are provided by the adoptee studies (Crowe, 1978), which are consistent in showing that *adult* criminality and 'psychopathy' are associated with the same conditions in the *biological* parents but not in the *adopting* parents (Hutchings and Mednick, 1974; Crowe, 1974; Schulsinger, 1972). Cadoret and Cain (1980) have shown similarly that antisocial behaviour and alcoholism in the biological parents predict adolescent antisocial behaviour in adopted children separated at birth from their biological parents. The findings point strongly to a genetic influence. However, Bohman's (1978) study of Swedish adoptees indicated that in large part the genetic predisposition applied to alcoholism (which in turn made crime more likely) rather than to crime *per se*. The initial findings suggested that this might constitute the whole explanation, but more recent analyses (Bohman *et al.*, 1983) have shown that there is some genetic effect even in the absence of alcohol abuse. Thus, there was an excess of crime in the adopted sons of biological criminal fathers who were non-alcoholic as compared with that in the sons of non-criminal non-alcoholic fathers (8.9 per cent v. 4.9 per cent). As in Cadoret and Cain's (1980) study, the genetic effect with respect to criminality was stronger in women than in men. The rate of petty criminality in the biological parents of criminal women was more than double that of their male counterparts (50 per cent v. 21 per cent – Bohman *et al.*, 1983).

We may conclude that the weight of evidence suggests that although polygenic influences are of only minor importance in the broad spectrum of juvenile delinquency (in which some half of offenders come before the courts on just one occasion), nevertheless genetic factors probably play a significant (although not preponderant) role in antisocial personality disorders which continue into adult life. This is also suggested by the data from non-adopted groups, which show that the strongest association is between recidivism in the father and recidivism persisting into adult life in the sons. In the Cambridge study (Osborn and West, 1979), 40 per cent of the sons of recidivist fathers were also recidivist, and 24 per cent were very persistent recidivists, compared with 13 per cent and 4 per cent respectively for the sons of non-criminal fathers. In sharp contrast, there was little association between paternal recidivism and transient delinquency in the sons (a rate of 14.5 per cent *v.* 11.4 per cent for the sons of non-convicted fathers). Of course, these data cannot distinguish between genetic and environmental effects but, taken in conjunction with the twin and adoptee data (which can), the evidence suggests that the genetic influence largely applies to recidivism persisting into adult life. Of course, the question of just *what* is inherited remains unanswered. It is unlikely to be criminality as such; rather it may be supposed that the hereditary influence probably involves some aspect of personality functioning which predisposes to criminality (although just what that might be remains a matter for conjecture).

Conclusions

The findings on individual characteristics as possible predisposing factors in the genesis of delinquent behaviour are somewhat inconclusive. Much of the difficulty stems from the combination of rather weak measures and a tendency to study delinquents as a total group without differentiating between those individuals committing isolated delinquent acts and those in whom the delinquency constitutes a part of a broader antisocial personality disorder which persists into adult life. The evidence suggests that it is likely that individual features will be of no more than minor importance in the former group but may well be of greater significance in the latter. Probably the best leads apply to cognitive and educational retardation, hyperactivity and attentional deficits, autonomic reactivity, stimulus seeking and passive avoidance learning. However, temperamental variables also warrant study. While it remains unclear how often and by what mechanism these features predispose to delinquency, there are pointers indicating that they may well be of some importance in the subgroup of more serious, widespread and persistent antisocial disorders. That possibility warrants more systematic study than it has received up to now.

6
Causes and Correlates – Psycho-social Factors

Numerous studies over the last half-century or so have shown that delinquency tends to be much more frequent in young people coming from particular kinds of family or social backgrounds. The evidence that these associations between psycho-social factors and delinquency exist is well known and the main facts are not in dispute. Consequently, we have not thought it necessary to discuss the findings on these broad associations in any detail. Those interested in pursuing the matter further can refer to the various key studies and overall review papers we cite. But although the main facts are not a matter of controversy, their interpretation is. Accordingly, in this chapter we pay most attention to the meaning of the statistical associations and to the various different interpretations which may be put on them.

Family influences

A variety of studies have examined family variables by comparing institutionalized delinquents and controls, but these are open to the objection that any differences found may be a function of the judicial decision to commit the delinquent to an institution rather than anything to do with the development of delinquent activities as such. Accordingly, for the most part, attention will be confined to studies of general population samples in which the family measures *ante*dated the boy's conviction. The results of such studies are in good agreement in showing that the most important variables associated with both juvenile delinquency and adult criminality include parental criminality; poor parental supervision; cruel, passive or neglecting attitudes; erratic or harsh discipline; marital conflict; and large family size (see Bahr, 1979; McCord and McCord, 1959; McCord, 1979; Wadsworth, 1979; West and Farrington, 1973, 1977; Wilson, 1980). Much the same family variables are associated with non-delinquent disturbances of conduct (see reviews by Hetherington and Martin, 1979; Hinde, 1980; Rutter, 1977a and b).

The validity and wide applicability of these associations has been shown by the repeated finding that the family variables associated with conduct disorders and delinquency have been generally similar in different social and ethnic groups, and in countries with rather different cultures and systems of social control (see, for example, Rohner, 1975; Friday, 1980; Werner, 1979). These family measures, usually based on interview data, concern rather broad aspects of family functioning, and observational studies of sequences of family interaction in the home have attempted to go further in delineating the actual processes of maladaptive interaction which are associated with disturbances of conduct (see Patterson, 1981b, 1982). It has been found that the parents of problem children differ from the parents of normals in being more punitive (Patterson, 1982; Snyder, 1977), in issuing more commands (Delfini et al., 1976; Forehand et al., 1975; Lobitz and Johnson, 1975a), in being more likely to provide attention and positive consequences following *deviant* behaviour (Snyder, 1977), possibly in being less likely to perceive deviant behaviour (Bogaard, 1976; Reid and Patterson, 1976), in being more likely to be involved in prolonged sequences of coercive negative interchanges with their children (Patterson 1981a, 1982), in giving more vague commands (Forehand et al., 1975) and in being less effective in stopping their children's deviant behaviour (Patterson, 1981a, 1982).

The causal nature of at least some of these family characteristics is shown by four different types of evidence. Firstly, parents of normal children were able to make their children behave more badly by issuing more commands (Lobitz and Johnson, 1975b). Secondly, the study of sequences of family interaction showed that hostile or coercive parent (or sib) actions were associated with an increased likelihood that the child's hostile or aggressive behaviour would continue (Patterson, 1977). Thirdly, behavioural interventions which focus on altering these patterns of coercive interchanges have proved successful in reducing the children's social aggression (Patterson, 1982). However, so far it has not been determined within the treated groups whether the degree of change in parental behaviour is correlated with the degree of change in the children's conduct disturbance. Fourthly, the family variables which are associated with delinquency are also predictive of recidivism *within* a delinquent group (see Chapter 2).

Dimensions of family functioning

The family variables associated with juvenile delinquency, whether based on interview, observation or rating scale measures, have been conceptualized in somewhat different ways by different investigators. These differences in concept reflect differences in causal theories and hypotheses, and it will be necessary to consider the relative standing of these theories later in this volume (see Chapter 8), but in the meanwhile we can summarize some of the main types of family characteristics which require explanation in any theoretical formulation. These may be discussed under six main headings: (i) characteristics of the parents; (ii) intra-familial discord; (iii) weak relationships with parents; (iv) ineffective supervision and regulation of the children's behaviour and activities; (v) socio-economic disadvantage; and (vi) family size.

Of the parental characteristics associated with delinquency, criminality is the most striking and most consistent. Thus, in Jonsson's (1967) Swedish study, 17 per cent of the fathers of delinquent boys were recidivist compared with 4.5 per cent of the fathers of non-delinquents. Expressed the other way round, West and Farrington (1973; Farrington *et al.*, 1975), in their prospective general population study, found that 39 per cent of boys with criminal fathers acquired delinquency records compared with 16 per cent of those with non-criminal fathers. The findings from other studies (for example, Robins and Lewis, 1966; Robins *et al.*, 1975) are closely similar. Two further features require mention: (a) the association between parental criminality and delinquency in the offspring is strongest when the parental crime record is both recidivist and extends into the time period during which the children are being reared (Osborn and West, 1979; Robins *et al.*, 1975); and (b) it is not only parental *criminality* which is associated with delinquency in the offspring – the association applies also to persistent social difficulties (excessive drinking, poor work record and frequent unemployment, reliance on social welfare) and to serious abnormalities of parental personality (for example, West and Farrington, 1973; Robins and Lewis, 1966). Moreover, parental criminality is often associated with these other psycho-social features (see, for example, Knight and West, 1977).

Several possible explanations need to be considered for the association between parental criminality and delinquency in the offspring. Probably in part it represents a genetic factor, but this is unlikely to constitute the sole explanation in that the evidence suggests a relatively weak hereditary influence for juvenile delinquency as a whole (although a rather stronger one for recidivist delinquency which persists into adult life – see the preceding chapter). It could be a consequence of greater police surveillance of criminal families, so that the sons are more likely to be caught and convicted. Again, there is some evidence that this occurs (West and Farrington, 1973; West, 1982), but it cannot be the whole story in that there is a strong link with self-reported delinquency even after controlling for convictions (Farrington, 1979). It is unlikely to be a consequence of any *direct* inculcation of delinquent behaviour in that parents rarely engage in delinquent activities with their children, and it is unlikely to be solely a direct copying or imitation of parental crime in that many criminal parents ceased offending when the children were very young or even before they were born (see West, 1982). On the other hand, it may well be that criminal parents provide a model of aggression and antisocial attitudes, if not of criminal activities as such. Also, as already noted, parental criminality is associated with poor supervision, family discord, unemployment, reliance on welfare and a host of other family factors which may be as important in the genesis of delinquency as the criminality *per se*.

The intra-familial discord associated with delinquency has been evident in a variety of different ways, including frequent and prolonged quarrelling; temporary separations of the parents as a result of discord; divorce or permanent separation of the parents; expressed hostility and negative feelings between family members; rejecting attitudes towards the children; frequent shouting at and punishment of the children; and a marked tendency for minor specific disagreements between two family members to escalate into prolonged and unproductive hostile interchanges which come to involve everyone else in the vicinity (see references cited above). While it is not clear from these observations just which aspects of these features are crucial, it is evident that the discord is associated with a negative and unpleasant family atmosphere, disruptions and separations of the family, and ineffective methods of dealing with family problems and disputes.

Weak relationships with parents have been reflected in items such as a lack of joint family leisure activities (Gold, 1963; West and Farrington, 1973); lack of intimate communication between parent and child (Hirschi, 1969); lack of affectional identification with parents (Hirschi, 1969); parental reports of a difficulty 'getting through' to their children and of their children tending to withdraw from the family by going off to their room, or staying out of the house, or just not doing things with the family (Rutter *et al.*, 1976a); a lack of parental warmth or affection (McCord and McCord, 1959; Rutter, 1971; West and Farrington, 1973), and parental reports that they do not identify with the role of parent and are not attached to their children (Patterson, 1982). It is apparent that many of these measures are inferential (and some are clearly weak); it is also evident that it is quite difficult to separate the notion of weak relationships from the closely associated notions of discord and poor supervision of the children. However, to some extent this may be done by comparing what happens to children reared continuously in institutions from infancy onwards. Usually long-stay children's homes are not particularly quarrelsome places, but they are characterized by frequent changes in house-parents and by weaker family ties. The recent finding (Rutter, Quinton and Liddle, 1983) that, at least in girls, an institutional upbringing is associated with a much increased risk of psycho-social problems, suggests that weak relationships may be important in their own right. However, so far it is not known whether this applies to boys as well as to girls, nor whether it is specifically linked with delinquency. Consequently, there must be some continuing uncertainty on the extent to which weak parent–child relationships predispose to delinquency if the family atmosphere is free of discord and disharmony and if supervision is adequate.

Much of the early literature on delinquency, and indeed on child development more generally, was largely concerned with discipline in terms of either the methods used or the severity of punishment. More recent research suggests that these may not be the most important aspects. Rather, attention has come to be focused on the extent of supervision, on the clarity of parental expectations, and on the efficiency of disciplinary methods. Thus Wilson (1980) found that, of all the family variables she examined, weak parental supervision was the one most strongly associated with delinquency. Weak supervision was assessed in terms of items such as no rules about the child saying where he is going or about when he has to return home, the child being allowed to roam the streets, the mother not knowing where the child was, and the child having many independent activities. Similarly, Patterson (1982) summarizes his findings on the family features associated with delinquency as being subsumed under four main headings: (i) lack of 'house rules' (so that there is neither any predictable family routine for meals or chores nor any clear expectations on what the children may and may not do); (ii) lack of parental monitoring of the child's behaviour (so that they do not know what he is doing or how he is feeling and tend not to respond to deviant behaviour because they have not themselves seen it); (iii) lack of effective contingencies (so that parents are inconsistent in their response to unacceptable behaviour – they shout and nag but do not follow through, and do not respond with an adequate differentiation between praise for prosocial activities and punishment for antisocial); and (iv) a lack of techniques for dealing with family crises or problems (so that conflicts lead to tension and dispute but do not end in resolutions). As Patterson explicitly recognizes, so far there is only rather weak empirical evidence supporting the view that these constitute the four key aspects of parental supervision and of family functioning generally. Nevertheless, the pointers certainly suggest that an *awareness* of children's behaviour, together with the details of how discipline is managed (i.e. the *process*, rather than which global method) and its *efficiency* (i.e. whether, regardless of methods, it is successful in changing the child's behaviour in the desired direction and in leading to conflict resolution and harmony), are the aspects likely to prove important.

The fifth dimension concerns various aspects of socio-economic disadvantage such as poverty, overcrowding and poor housing, as shown in numerous studies (see references cited above). The interpretation of the association is much complicated by the fact that serious socio-economic disadvantage tends in turn to be rather closely associated with the other family dimensions already discussed. These other variables (parental criminality, poor supervision, etc.) are still associated with delinquency even within socially disadvantaged groups (see, for example, West and Farrington, 1973; Wilson, 1974; Wilson and Herbert, 1978). Accordingly, it seems likely that, at least in part, poverty and poor living conditions predispose to delinquency, not through any direct effects on the child, but rather because serious socio-economic disadvantage has an adverse effect on the *parents*, such that parental disorders and difficulties are more likely to develop and that good parenting is impeded. In this way, there may be a chain of adversities which starts with socio-economic disadvantage and which leads to the child only through the parents. Of course, it is also the case that criminal or psychopathic parents are more likely to *experience* poverty and poor living conditions because of their frequent periods of unemployment and their difficulties in managing their affairs adequately (see Rutter and Madge, 1976). In so far as that is the case, the socio-economic factors might have no *direct* connection with delinquency. The question of whether poverty and poor housing also have a direct impact on the children which predisposes to delinquency remains unresolved.

The sixth dimension, large family size, remains somewhat of an enigma. To begin with, it is partially confounded with birth order and spacing effects. West and Farrington (1973) found no association between ordinal position once family size had been taken into account. The *low* rate of delinquency in only children seems to be due mainly to their being in a one-child family rather than to their being first-born. However, Wadsworth (1979) suggested that the crucial feature may be the duration of time during which the child experiences relatively exclusive maternal attention (i.e. without the rival needs of siblings near in age or of very young children in the family). While his data are consistent with that hypothesis, unfortunately they were not expressed in a form which allowed any adequate test of this suggestion in competition with alternative possibilities. Both these investigators found that family size was associated most strongly with delinquency in socially disadvantaged sections of the population (as assessed by either income or occupational status), with at most a weak connection with delinquency in middle-class families. This suggests that it may not be family size *per se* which is crucial, but rather the disadvantages which tend to accompany large family size in poorer sections of the community. However, Offord's (1982) data suggest that it may be some form of male '*contagion*' or potentiation of delinquent behaviour that is important. He found that delinquency was associated with the number of *brothers* in the family, but not with the number of sisters. When one boy in a family is delinquent it is more likely that others in the family will be affected also (Robins *et al.*, 1975). An alternative possibility is provided by the rather stronger links between large family size and educational backwardness. It could be that family size is associated with delinquency largely because it has a prior association with low verbal intelligence and poor reading skills which then, in turn, predispose to delinquency (see the preceding chapter). The mechanisms underlying the link between large family size and delinquency remain rather obscure.

Association with delinquency or with conviction

In spite of a general consensus on the empirical findings concerning the association between family variables and delinquency, there is continuing disagreement on their meaning. Several rather different issues need to be considered. To begin with, there is the question of how far they represent anything more than a methodological artefact. Thus, Farrington (1979) has argued that 'most aspects of a stressful family environment produce convictions rather than delinquent behaviour'. He bases this argument on the Cambridge study findings which show that: (i) most family variables are associated with *both* self-reported delinquency and official convictions; and (ii) most of the associations with conviction remain significant after statistically partialling out the effects of self-reported delinquency; but (iii) many of the associations with self-reported delinquency cease to be significant after partialling out the effects of conviction. He infers that this means that the associations with self-reported delinquency are, therefore, no more than secondary consequences of the more basic association between family influences and conviction. The empirical analyses undertaken by Farrington (1979) are both important and illuminating, but a review of the total body of empirical evidence indicates that the conclusions he draws rest on a very shaky base and are probably wrong. Firstly, as he himself points out, some family features (namely parental criminality and poor supervision) *were* significantly associated with self-reported delinquency even after partialling out the effects of conviction. Of course, in itself, this is not inconsistent with Farrington's argument. But it should be noted that these exceptions refer to two of the best-established family correlates of delinquency. The family variables that Farrington considers are *not* associated with delinquent behaviour as such, refer either to value-laden ratings of uncertain validity (i.e. poor parental child-rearing behaviour) or to variables (i.e. erratic paternal job record, low family income, or large family size) which are unlikely, of themselves, to cause delinquency directly.

Secondly, family variables showed much the strongest association with the *combination* of self-reported delinquency and conviction. If the family variables were causally linked only with conviction, there should be no familial differences between convicted delinquents who did and who did not report their own delinquencies – but this is not what was found. Indeed, in many instances the family difference associated with conviction was *less* than that associated with self-reported delinquency. For example, there was a 20 per cent difference in the proportion of boys from large families between the convicted delinquents with and without self-reported delinquency, but only a 6 per cent difference within the group of boys without self-reported delinquency between those with and without a conviction. The main reason for the statistical findings which form the basis of Farrington's argument is that there is generally little difference in family background between the non-convicted boys who do and who do not report behaving in delinquent ways. That is important but it is not self-evident that that comparison should be given greater weight than those noted above. It should be added that both Farrington's analyses and the alternative comparisons given here have to assume that the groups which differ on either self-report or conviction do *not* differ on the seriousness of their antisocial activities – an assumption which is almost certain to be wrong in both cases.

Thirdly, it is legitimate to partial out the effects of conviction only when the conviction *preceded* the self-report. The point is that whereas the experience of being publicly labelled as delinquent may increase *later* delinquent activities (Farrington, 1977), it could not possibly increase *previous* delinquent activities. The appropriate analysis, therefore, would have been a contrast between the partial correlations according to whether the conviction preceded or followed the self-report. Unfortunately, this was not done.

Fourthly, Farrington's (1979) conclusions are at variance with the several studies which show substantial associations between family variables and disturbances of conduct or antisocial behaviour within groups of children either below the age at which they could be convicted or whose disorders were unassociated with conviction. Examples of this kind are provided by the Richman *et al.* (1982) study of 3–8 year old London children; the Rutter *et al.* (1975a) study of 10 year old children in London and the Isle of Wight;

the Hetherington et al. (1979a and b) study of divorcing families; and the Quinton et al. (1976) study of children of mentally ill parents. However, Farrington's own data (West and Farrington, 1973) provide, perhaps, an even more interesting case in point. It was found that the various family variables which correlated significantly with delinquency ceased to show significant associations once the effects of 'troublesomeness' had been taken into account. In contrast, 'troublesomeness' continued to relate significantly to later delinquency regardless of which family variables were taken into account. The importance of these findings lies in the two facts that (i) the 'troublesomeness' ratings were made when the boys were aged 8 and 10 *before* they were first convicted, and (ii) the family variables were significantly associated with the boys' troublesome behaviour (West and Farrington, 1973). The implication is that family stresses lead to troublesome and disruptive behaviour which then, in turn, predisposes to delinquency. In short, the family variables seem to be associated with conduct disturbance as a whole rather than with delinquency as such. As Farrington (1979) suggests, the adverse family factors also play a part in the decision to bring the delinquent boys to court, but the evidence indicates that this is in addition to (rather than in place of) its effect in the processes leading to delinquent activities.

Cause, correlate or consequence

The next issue is the meaning of the association between family variables and disturbances of conduct in terms of the implications regarding possible mechanisms. Several alternatives need to be considered. The associations may simply reflect a prior association with some third factor; they may represent genetic influences; they may be a consequence of the disturbing effect of the child's behaviour on family functioning; or they may mean that family stresses or difficulties lead to delinquency through some kind of environmental effect.

The first possibility may be examined by determining both whether the association still holds up after controlling for other variables and whether changes in the one are associated with changes in the other. Of course, the decision on which 'other' variables to control for is crucial. However, it is clear from several studies that the family associations still hold up after taking into account social status and neighbourhood, and indeed that they predict well within populations which are fairly homogeneous in social class characteristics (for example, West and Farrington, 1973, 1977; McCord, 1980; Robins, 1978; Rutter *et al.*, 1975c; Wilson, 1980). It is also evident from the long-term follow-ups that the associations with *adult* antisocial behaviour are mediated through antisocial behaviour in the *child* – that is to say, that early family stresses have long-term effects largely because they lead to forms of disturbance in the child which tend to persist, rather than because there are delayed or 'sleeper' effects (Robins, 1978; West and Farrington, 1973, 1977). The findings that changes for the better in family relationships are associated with a reduced risk of later conduct disturbance (Rutter, 1971), that changes in the patterns of relationship after divorce – either for the better or for the worse – tend to be associated with parallel changes in the children's behaviour (Hetherington *et al.*, 1979a and b; Wallerstein and Kelly, 1980), and that persistent family problems are associated with an increased risk of recidivism even within a group of boys who are already delinquent (Power *et al.*, 1974; Osborn and West, 1978), make it unlikely that the association is merely an artefact of some prior association with a third variable.

The question of whether the mechanism is genetic or environmental is more difficult to answer. The evidence (discussed in Chapter 5) that genetic influences are *not* very powerful in the case of juvenile delinquency (although they are more important with recidivist criminality extending into adult life) makes a purely genetic mechanism unlikely in the case of children. However, the matter may be investigated more directly by comparing the associations with biological and adoptive parental characteristics in early adopted groups. Few data of this kind are available, but the Cadoret and Cain (1980), Hutchings and Mednick (1974) and Crowe (1974) studies of adopted children all show associations between experiential variables and delinquency (psychiatric disorder or divorce in the adoptive family and institutional rearing in the Cadoret and Cain study; criminality in the adoptive parent in the Hutchings and Mednick inquiry; and adverse early life experiences in Crowe's investigation; in addition to the genetic effect shown by the associations with criminality in the biological parent). Interestingly, in the latter two studies this environmental effect was only evident in the group which was genetically vulnerable by virtue of having had a criminal biological parent. The suggestion (which needs replication) is that, in these circumstances, the genetic factor may operate in part by rendering the individual more susceptible to environmental hazards. (It should be noted that this does *not* seem to be the explanation of the genetic mechanism with some other disorders, for example schizophrenia, where family rearing variables seem to have most effect in the *absence* of a genetic predisposition – Rosenthal *et al.*, 1975).

The possibility that some of the association is a result of an influence of the child on the parents rather than the other way round is difficult to test rigorously. Certainly there is evidence that children can and do have effects on parents (Bell and Harper, 1977), and it may well be that the association in part reflects this direction of effect. On the other hand, some of the associations (such as that with parental criminality) cannot operate in that direction and others (for example, large family size) are most unlikely to do so. In other cases, too, there is often evidence that the family discord and difficulties antedated the child's disturbance (Rutter, 1971) but often it is not possible to be sure which way the causal arrows run. The importance of the child's role in parent–child interactions is emphasized by the evidence that parental actions which are effective with normal children are not effective with socially aggressive children (Patterson, 1981a, 1982). It seems likely that the causal influences are bi-directional but that, at least with some of the family variables, the preponderant effect is likely to be from parent to child.

Which environmental mechanism?

While we may reasonably conclude that family influences do indeed have some kind of environmental impact which plays a part in the process by which children develop disturbances of conduct, the precise mechanisms by which they operate remain rather obscure, although it has proved possible to rule some out. Thus, it is now clear that 'broken homes' are associated with delinquency and conduct disturbances because of the discord associated with the break, rather than because of the family break-up *per se* (Rutter, 1971, 1982b). The relevant evidence includes the following: (i) whereas divorce and separation are associated with a much increased risk of delinquency, parental death is not (Douglas *et al.*, 1968; Gibson, 1969; Gregory, 1965); (ii) parental discord is associated with antisocial disorder in the children even when the home is unbroken (Craig and Glick, 1963; McCord and McCord, 1959; Tait and Hodges, 1962; Rutter, 1971; Power *et al.*, 1974; Porter and O'Leary, 1980); (iii) the extent of discord is associated with the likelihood of disorders in the children even in groups in which all the homes are broken (Hetherington *et al.*, 1979a and b; Hess and Camera, 1979; Wallerstein and Kelly, 1980); and (iv) children removed from home into the care of the local authority because of family difficulties or breakdown already showed an excess of disturbed behaviour *before* they were separated from their families (Lambert *et al.*, 1977). On all these grounds it is evident that it is the discord, rather than the separation from the parents, which is crucial. On the other hand, recent studies have made it abundantly clear that the notion that divorce necessarily brings family discord to an end is seriously mistaken (Hetherington *et al.*, 1979a and b; Wallerstein and Kelly, 1980; Hess and Camera, 1979). Not only may discord sometimes continue long after the break-up, but also it is apparent that the adaptations required by the divorce often bring new stresses for the family which may make things worse before they make them better. Furthermore, the conclusion that it is the discord which matters leaves wide open the question of *how* it operates.

Several possibilities have been suggested. Firstly, it could be that it is the efficiency of parental supervision and discipline which matter, and that the discord is important only in so far as it is associated with erratic, deviant and inefficient methods of bringing up children (Wilson, 1974, 1980). Certainly, supervision has proved to be an important variable in nearly all studies which have examined associations with antisocial behaviour, but the close links between the different types of family stress and difficulty make it very difficult to disentangle their separate effects (West and Farrington, 1973). Alternatively, it could be that modelling is important (Bandura, 1969) and that family discord is relevant because it provides the child with a model of aggression, inconsistency, hostility and antisocial behaviour which he then copies. A third alternative is that the discord constitutes the setting for sequences of coercive family interaction in which hostile or coercive behaviours serve to perpetuate aggressive encounters. Patterson's (1977, 1979, 1982) careful and systematic moment-by-moment observational studies in the home strongly suggest that this does indeed occur, although it is not clear just which psychological mechanism these coercive sequences reflect. A fourth alternative is that a child needs loving relationships with his parents in order to develop appropriate social behaviour later (Bowlby, 1969), and that it is the difficulties in social relationships which constitute the basis of antisocial conduct. The ameliorating effect of a good relationship with one parent, even in the presence of general family discord (Rutter, 1971; Rutter, Quinton and Liddle, 1983) is consistent with this suggestion, but the finding is also open to a variety of different interpretations. It is all too obvious that with discord, as with other family variables, we have very little notion of just how it operates. If we are to take the matter further, studies of the effects of change and of planned therapeutic interventions will be necessary, as well as more discriminating correlational studies within an epidemiological framework.

Films and television

The question of the possible impact of films and television on young people's behaviour, with particular reference to the possibility that frequent exposure to scenes of violence might increase the predisposition to violent or delinquent activities, has been subject to several extensive recent reviews of research findings (see especially Stein and Friedrich, 1975; Brody, 1977; Eysenck and Nias, 1980; National Institute of Mental Health, 1982). Reviewers are agreed in the conclusion that 'there is little doubt that violence on film seems able to induce aggressive imitation in young children and a more general state of aggressiveness in both younger and older subjects' (Brody, 1977). There are a plethora of laboratory studies which attest to this conclusion (see Bandura, 1969, in addition to the reviews cited above), and there is no need to consider that body of evidence further here. However, what is less certain is the extent to which this phenomenon occurs in natural surroundings outside the laboratory. Brody (1977) concluded that the evidence suggested that adverse effects were restricted to susceptible groups – especially pre-school children and older children 'whose development has been seriously impaired by the absence of normal socializing influences'. Stein and Friedrich (1975) noted that violent television appears to have its greatest impact on individuals who are already aggressive, but also argued that 'there is some evidence that both aggressive attitudes and aggressive behaviour patterns are built up over time as a function of long-term exposure to high levels of violence'.

The research issues, and hence the problems in drawing conclusions on policy implications, may be highlighted by a brief consideration of the several rather different research strategies which have been employed. Firstly, statistical control techniques have been applied to cross-sectional data – as in Belson's (1978) study of 12–17 year old London boys. He showed that high *exposure* to television violence was significantly correlated with frequent *use* of violence, even after controlling for the various background factors associated with violent behaviour. On this basis, and because the reverse did not hold (i.e. there was no significant association after controlling for background factors associated with TV viewing) he concluded that TV violence, especially when it occurred in the context of close personal relations and was presented as justified, predisposed to violent behaviour through the reduction or breaking down of inhibitions against being violent. While the pattern of correlations certainly suggests that TV *may* have an effect, the evidence is necessarily circumstantial, and the analysis is heavily dependent on the identification of the appropriate background factors which are thought to predispose to TV viewing and to violence.

Secondly, naturalistic longitudinal studies have examined correlations over time. Thus, Lefkowitz *et al.* (1977) showed that boys' preference for violent television correlated 0.21 with their concurrent aggressiveness and

0.31 with their aggressiveness ten years later. Because the reverse did *not* apply, i.e. aggression in third grade did *not* correlate significantly with TV viewing ten years later, it was concluded that television had predisposed to violence rather than the other way round. The authors also suggested that violence has a cumulative effect which shows up more over time than it does when aggression is measured at the same point in time as the viewing. However, this pattern did not apply to girls and it is important to note that cross-lagged panel correlation analyses, such as those of Lefkowitz *et al.*, may be distorted by varying reliabilities in measurement and by changes in the strength of causal relationships over time (Kenny, 1975). Hence, the causal influence remains rather uncertain.

Thirdly, experiments have been undertaken in naturalistic settings in which children have randomly assigned to groups exposed to different types of television or film viewing. For example, Friedrich and Stein (1973) observed aggressive and prosocial behaviour during free play in nursery-school children exposed to aggressive, prosocial and neutral TV programmes during a nine-week summer programme. They found that the children who saw aggressive programmes showed a sharp decline in their tolerance of delay and, among those above average in aggressivity at the outset, an increase in interpersonal aggression. Similarly, Berkowitz, Parke and their colleagues (Berkowitz *et al.*, 1978; Leyens *et al.*, 1975; Parke *et al.*, 1977) studied delinquent boys living in cottages within minimum security institutions. Boys in cottages where highly aggressive films were shown on five consecutive nights were compared with boys in cottages where non-violent commercial films were shown. The results showed that a diet of aggressive films stimulated the boys to increased aggression during the movie week, and to a lesser extent in the following period as well. Some of the influence was clearly imitative in nature. Again there is the inference that viewing violence increased the tendency to behave in violent ways (at least in this predisposed group of delinquents). In both studies only rather short-lived effects were observed,* and 'violence' was defined in rather broad terms.

Fourthly, there is one study (Schramm, Lyle and Parker, 1961) in which there was a comparison between two small communities (in Western Canada), in one of which TV was available and in one of which it was not.

---

* Also, Feshbach and Singer (1971) obtained contrary results in which the group watching violent television was significantly *less* aggressive. However, there were no baseline data, the ratings were not made by external observers, and there were complaints from the boys about the boring nature of the non-violent programmes. It seems likely that the apparent increase in aggression in the non-violent TV group was a consequence of their frustration and resentment at being deprived of their usual television fare.

No differences between the communities in 'aggressive attitudes' were found. Unfortunately, conclusions from this study are limited by the nature of the populations studied (which had little in common with the inner city groups showing high levels of delinquency), by the less violent nature of television programmes in that era, and by the design (which was concerned with the effect of TV as a whole rather than with the effects of violent programmes).

The interpretation of these (and other) data also needs to take into account the evidence on the possible mechanisms which might be involved. To begin with, surveys indicate that aggressive or maladjusted children are more likely to spend a great deal of time watching television (Himmelweit et al., 1958; Schramm et al., 1961) and, on the whole, prefer violent programmes (Stein and Friedrich, 1975). Moreover, one experimental study (in adults) showed that the expression of aggression increased men's tendency to choose violent films to watch (Fenigstein, 1979). It seems likely, therefore, that part of the association between aggression and the watching of violent films or TV programmes is due to the influence of personality characteristics and of behavioural features on the *choice* of viewing. On the other hand, the evidence taken as a whole in conjunction with the experiments in both the laboratory and the natural environment suggests that the causal effect is likely to be bi-directional – such that the prolonged viewing of violent films or TV may have some effect in predisposing boys to behave in violent ways. Various mechanisms have been considered.

There is the possibility of direct imitation. In this connection there are numerous anecdotal accounts of delinquents modelling their behaviour on a particular incident on television, in a film, or on newspaper reports of a particularly dramatic or unusual crime. However, an individual's claim to have copied someone else's action does not show that that was actually what occurred, and the one experimental attempt in adults to induce direct imitation of antisocial acts failed to do so (Milgram and Shotland, 1973). On the other hand, that study was not concerned with children or adolescents, it did not refer to susceptible individuals, and it did not involve physical assault. Moreover, there is evidence from studies of other forms of behaviour that publicity may result in directly imitative acts. Thus, Barraclough et al. (1977) found a statistical association between the newspaper reporting of suicide inquests and suicides in men under 45 the following week. This, taken together with the observation that suicides increase briefly after the publicity given to suicides of famous people, and with other evidence of 'suicide contagion', suggests that newspaper reporting as well as television and films may sometimes give rise to imitative behaviours in other people. But the same evidence also suggests that this effect is seen in only a tiny minority of susceptible individuals. Furthermore, it remains quite uncertain whether publicity increases the *frequency* of any broad class of behaviour such as delinquent activities, or whether it merely influences its timing or particular form. The evidence is inconclusive, but it seems likely that, although direct imitation may occur on occasions, this mechanism is of negligible importance in any overall association between TV violence and delinquent activities.

An alternative mechanism involves emotional arousal which thereby stimulates aggressive impulses. Certainly, there is good evidence that watching violent films does indeed lead to emotional arousal in many people. Moreover, laboratory studies show that in some circumstances this can be associated with an increased tendency to behave in an aggressive fashion. On the other hand, this is a rather immediate and short-lived effect, and it seems implausible that this triggers antisocial or aggressive behaviour in real life, other than quite rarely (Brody, 1977). It should be added that it has also been claimed that watching violent films may actually reduce aggression by means of a 'cathartic' process in which the fantasy expression of aggressive feelings *reduces* tension (Feshbach and Singer, 1971). But the weight of evidence clearly suggests that in most circumstances violent films have a stimulating, rather than cathartic, effect. The original notion of catharsis, in which it was thought that the expression of feelings reduced tension by the discharge of energy, has been discredited.* Whether the fantasy expression of aggression increases or reduces aggressive propensities is likely to depend on how this affects the person's own perceptions and ideas on the justification of aggressive activities (Berkowitz, 1973).

This possibility is linked with a third mechanism – namely, the effect of films or television on social attitudes, stereotypes and standards. The specific suggestion usually made in this connection is that prolonged exposure to violence can in some way 'desensitize' people to violence in such a way that inhibitions against violence are reduced and that violent solutions to personal frustrations or problems come to be regarded as more acceptable and more 'normal'. Undoubtedly, the media can influence people's ideas, beliefs

---

* Brody (1977), in his review, was inclined to the view that there may be something in the notion of catharsis, but in coming to that conclusion he had to substantially redefine the word. The point is that it has been repeatedly found that the mere expression of aggressive feelings has no consistent effect in reducing tension (see, for example, Hokanson *et al*., 1963; Mallick and McCandless, 1966; Kahn, 1966). Aggression to a third person tends not to reduce tension, whereas aggression to the person who has frustrated or angered you does lead to a reduction. Fantasies about aggression certainly can reduce tension but they can also increase it – which outcome results depends very much on the type of fantasy and the manner in which it changes the situation or the person's feelings about it.

and general views about issues, as many studies have shown (Brody, 1977; Stein and Friedrich, 1975). Moreover, the findings suggest that this effect is most pronounced in children. But the evidence mainly concerns short-term effects, and little is known on the extent to which films or television can have an enduring effect on attitudes and on standards of behaviour. It seems unlikely that it could have much effect when it runs counter to other influences, but it is more probable that it might play some role in enhancing family, school or societal influences when they are of a similar kind.

It is apparent that no one study is conclusive and that there are serious limitations to each of the research strategies. Nevertheless, the findings point to the probability that films and television may have *some* impact on attitudes and behaviour. It is likely that the effect on delinquent activities is quite small when considered in relation to other causal factors. However, in children who are already aggressive or liable to behave in delinquent ways, and especially when the influence of the media is consonant with influences in the home, the prolonged viewing of violent programmes may have *some* effect in increasing the predisposition to behave in a violent or antisocial manner. In so far as this is the case, the effect is most likely to operate through the long-term influence of the media in suggesting that such behaviours may be acceptable, or even desirable, rather than through any more immediate or direct effects.

Labelling

The judicial response to delinquency may well have corrective, therapeutic or deterrent intentions, but it also has the effect of providing a public recognition or 'labelling' of someone as a delinquent – a labelling which may influence how the individual views himself and, in turn, how he behaves. Thus, Becker (1963) suggested that 'one of the most crucial steps in the process of building a stable pattern of deviant behaviour is likely to be the experience of being caught and publicly labelled as a deviant'. As part of the Cambridge longitudinal study of working-class boys in London, Farrington (1977) tested the hypothesis that individuals who are convicted (and hence labelled) will increase their delinquent behaviour as a result. Youths with similar self-reported delinquency scores at the age of 14 were compared with respect to their scores at 18, according to whether or not they had received a guilty finding in court. The average score of the boys with a guilty finding increased from 59.5 to 69.3 over the four years, whereas the average score of those not appearing in court fell from 59.4 to 51.3 – a difference which could not be accounted for in terms of difference between the two groups in family background. A further analysis of changes between the ages of 18 and 21 in relation to conviction showed a closely comparable pattern (Farrington *et al.*, 1978). As other (less well controlled) studies have produced similar indications of deviance amplification (Gold, 1970; Gold and Williams, 1969), it may be concluded that convictions may lead to an increase in or an intensification of delinquent behaviour.

On the other hand, it seems that this effect may wear off after a few years. Farrington *et al.* (1978) found that the high delinquency scores of youths first convicted before the age of 14 significantly *decreased* by the age of 21 regardless of whether or not there had been further convictions and regardless of whether the youths had received an institutional sentence. Other research, too, has suggested that the effect may be most marked with first offenders, with even a reversal of effect in recidivists (Klein, 1974).

However, as Walker (1980) has pointed out, the finding that delinquent behaviour may increase following conviction does not necessarily mean that the increase has occurred as a result of labelling, and even if labelling is the operative mechanism, it does not follow that this has its effect through an impact on self-image. Instead of a labelling effect, it could be that the judicial intervention itself increases the chances of delinquency because of the experiences it entails (such as the increased interaction with other delinquents),* because of the resentment engendered,† or because a 'therapeutic' response may take responsibility away from the young person.‡ Alternatively, it is conceivable that the results of court appearance were so trivial that the youth 'learned' that crime 'paid' and that he need not fear the consequences of getting caught.

Of course, that is not to say that stigma does not occur. Indeed, at least so far as employment is concerned, there is good evidence that there is discrimination against adults with a criminal record (Boshier and Johnson, 1974; Buikhuisen and Dijkterhuis, 1971; Schwartz and Skolnick, 1962). But here the effect is direct rather than through any impairment of self-esteem or reinforcement of a self-image of 'being a delinquent'. Actually, the

* This seems to be a possible explanation for the finding in one study (O'Donnell *et al.*, 1979) that a community treatment programme *increased* the chances of non-delinquents becoming delinquent although it had a beneficial effect on those already delinquent.

† This may have occurred in the Army study which showed an association between heavy punishment and higher levels of offending (Hart, 1978).

‡ This constitutes one possible explanation for Berg's (1980a and b) finding, from a well planned random allocation study, that truants dealt with by social work supervision were more likely to remain away from school and more likely to engage in delinquent activities than those dealt with by adjournment, with return to court contingent on whether the child continued truanting.

empirical evidence on the effects of court appearance on self-esteem and self-image are rather inconclusive.

Farrington found that youths first convicted between the ages of 14 and 16 increased in their hostile attitudes to the police following conviction (Farrington, 1977), and that youths first convicted between the ages of 18 and 21 increased in their own expressed aggressiveness (Farrington *et al.*, 1978). This finding is a reasonably solid one because the attitudes were measured in a systematic fashion using a standard questionnaire (asking for agreement or disagreement with statements such as 'the police are always roughing people up' in the case of hostility to the police, and 'anyone who insults me is asking for a fight' in the case of expressed aggressiveness); because the measures were available both before and after conviction; because it was possible to relate the change in attitude to the period in which the conviction occurred; and because it was possible to compare the attitude changes in the convicted group with those in a non-convicted group with similar self-report delinquency scores prior to conviction. No other study has had similarly rigorous controls, although some have data which are relevant to the issues.

Gibbs (1974) compared delinquents and non-delinquents and found that the former saw themselves as being more delinquent than other boys, but they registered reduced self-esteem for only a brief period after their apprehension by the police; Ageton and Elliott (1974), in their longitudinal study of American schoolchildren, found that police contact was followed by an increasing orientation towards delinquency, especially among white youths; Jenson (1972), in a cross-sectional study, found a rather inconsistent association between delinquency and a negative self-concept (again, especially in whites); Fisher (1972) found no change in teacher grading assessments following a child being placed on probation; and Foster *et al.* (1972) found (in a study which lacked controls) that delinquents did not report perceiving any change following court appearance in their interpersonal relationships with family, friends or teachers.

The data from the West and Farrington study clearly show that the first appearance in court tends to be followed by an increase in delinquent activities and by a change in attitudes, but that this process does not seem to be intensified by further subsequent convictions. The mechanisms involved in this type of response remain rather uncertain but, although the evidence is decidedly weak and inconclusive, it does not seem that it is primarily due to a fall in self-esteem.

School factors

Several studies have documented very large differences in delinquency rates between high schools serving much the same areas (Power *et al.*, 1967, 1972; Gath *et al.*, 1977; Reynolds and Murgatroyd, 1977; Reynolds *et al.*, 1976; Rutter *et al.*, 1979), and similar differences between schools have also been found for psychiatric referral rates (Gath *et al.*, 1977), for truancy or absenteeism, and for disruptive behaviour in the classrooms of both primary and secondary schools (Goldman, 1961; Heal, 1978; Pablant and Baxter, 1975; Reynolds and Murgatroyd, 1977; Reynolds *et al.*, 1976, 1980; Rutter *et al.*, 1975c). The authors of all these studies have drawn the implication that school factors may have played a part in influencing pupils' behaviour in ways which affect the overall rates of conduct disturbance. However, before drawing that conclusion it is important to pay attention to possible non-causal interpretations and methodological artefacts (these are discussed in greater detail in Rutter, 1983).

Undoubtedly the most serious potential source of bias is selective intake to the schools – that is, that some schools admit a far higher proportion of behaviourally difficult children and that the differences between schools in delinquency rates are simply a consequence of these differences in intake. Several studies have indeed shown that there *are* major variations between schools in their intakes (Farrington, 1972; Rutter *et al.*, 1979), and in one study of a small number of schools – only four took as many as 40 boys from the sample studied (Farrington, 1972) – most of the school variation was explicable in terms of intake differences. However, in the larger study by Rutter *et al.* (1979), the school variations in extent of disruptive behaviour, in delinquency (for boys but not girls), and in absenteeism were *not* solely due to the intake factors measured. Of course, this type of analysis is necessarily limited by the variables measured at intake, and it will always remain possible that the school variations were a consequence of some intake variable which was not measured. Accordingly, it is essential, in testing the causal hypothesis, not only to show that the school variations were *not* a result of intake factors but also to determine whether they *were* systematically associated with characteristics of the schools. This association was found in the detailed study by Rutter *et al.* (1979) of twelve London secondary schools; measures of the social and organizational characteristics of schools, based on systematic time and event sampled observations in the classroom interviews with teachers and questionnaires from pupils, showed substantial correlations with measures of pupil behaviour. The overall pattern of findings, together with the evidence against other alternative explanations strongly suggested a possible causative influence of schools on children's behaviour in that setting. Nevertheless, in order to test that hypothesis rigorously, intervention studies are needed to determine whether planned change of school practice is followed by the predicted changes in pupil behaviour. Such studies have yet to be undertaken and the causal hypothesis remains unproven, in spite of fairly strong circumstantial evidence in support.

However, assuming for the moment that the statistical associations actually do represent causative influences, it is important to consider both *what* is being affected and also *which* aspects of schooling are relevant in that connection. Firstly, the Rutter *et al.* (1979) findings, in keeping with earlier studies concerned with school variations in scholastic attainment (Jencks *et al.*, 1972), indicated that school influences have a negligible impact on the extent of individual variation and, moreover, that compared with family variables, school factors account for only a small amount of population variance in children's behaviour or scholastic attainment. Nevertheless, school variables did seem to have a considerable impact on the *overall level* of behavioural disturbance or of scholastic attainment. In other words, in all schools children vary greatly in their behavioural and cognitive features, but in some schools there is a general tendency for the pupil group as a whole to be either better behaved or more generally disruptive. It is that general tendency which appears to be shaped by school characteristics.

Secondly, school factors had a considerably greater effect on children's behaviour in the classroom than on delinquent activities outside school. Moreover, the school features that were most important for each were not quite the same. The school processes associated with children's behaviour in the school (as reflected in measures of items such as disruptions in the classroom and extent of graffiti and damage in the school) included styles and skill of classroom management, the models of behaviour provided by teachers, the extent of rewards and encouragement, the giving of responsibility to pupils, the degree of academic emphasis and levels of expectations for the pupils, and the general quality of pupil conditions. On the other hand, although these school processes may have had some impact on delinquency, much the greater effect stemmed from the academic balance in the intake. Even after taking account of children's individual characteristics, it appeared that a child attending a school with a high proportion of intellectually less able children was more likely to become delinquent than a child of similar initial characteristics from a similar background who attended a school with a more even academic balance in the intake. In that academic balance did not have any substantial impact on teacher behaviour (as measured), the inference is that the mechanism involved peer group influences of some kind.

Other studies, too, have emphasized this peer group effect both within and between schools. Hargreaves (1967), for example, in a participant observation study of one school, suggested that the structural organization of the school (in which rigid streaming by general ability was combined with a lack of rewards for lower stream pupils) led to a 'delinquency sub-culture' in the lower streams. Kratcoski and Kratcoski (1977), in a small-scale study of three American high schools, found that the number of self-reported offences was related to the *proportion* of working-class youths in the school (the rate of offences being highest in the one that was preponderantly working-class), but that offence rate was not associated with the social status of the youth *himself*. Indeed, the offence rate for middle-class youths in the preponderantly working-class school was substantially higher than that for working-class youths in the two schools with a roughly 50:50 working–middle social class distribution. There was no difference between the self-reported delinquency rates of working-class and middle-class youths *within* any of the three schools. This study was based on rather small numbers, and the lack of data on other variables means that considerable caution is needed in drawing inferences. Nevertheless, as in the much larger-scale study by Rutter *et al.* (1979), which took into account a much broader range of variables, the findings suggested that the balance of intake to schools may have an important impact on delinquency rates – an effect which probably operates through the peer group 'sub-culture'.

But, as the Rutter *et al.* (1979) study findings suggested, the ethos of a school is by no means entirely shaped by the intake of pupils. The actions taken by staff can do much to create a positive atmosphere which enhances good behaviour and which, indirectly, may help to reduce the rate of delinquency. A school with a disadvantaged intake need not necessarily be a high-delinquency school. Finlayson and Loughran (1976) also showed that factors other than intake mattered, by means of their comparison of two pairs of schools in an industrial city in the north of England. Although the two schools in each pair were matched on the social characteristics of their catchment areas (using factors such as unemployment rates, illegitimacy rates, proportion of children in care and proportion of children deloused), they differed sharply in delinquency rates. The differences in delinquency rate were paralleled by differences in the pupil perceptions of the school – regarding task orientation and emotional tone or satisfaction (both of which were lower in the high-delinquency schools), and rigidity of social control (the teachers at the high-delinquency school were said to be more authoritarian in their use of power). The study findings are limited by the lack of data on the pupils' behaviour and attitudes at the time they entered the school, and by the absence of measures on the school actions which led to these perceived differences in atmosphere and style. Nevertheless, the implication is that the climate of a school* is not predetermined by its intake and that differences in climate or organizational style are associated with differences in delinquency rate.

There are too few data on school influences on delinquency rates for any firm conclusions to be drawn. But the findings suggest that there *is* an influence (its strength remains uncertain), and that both the balance of intake to the school in terms of intellectual ability and social status, and factors concerned with the ethos or social organization of the school, have an impact.

Area influences

Over the last half century, since the pioneering studies by Shaw and MacKay (Shaw, 1929; Shaw and MacKay, 1942) and their colleagues in the Chicago School of Sociology, numerous investigations have shown that delinquency rates vary greatly according to geographical area – with rates tending to be highest in poor overcrowded areas of low social status in industrial cities and lowest in more affluent spacious rural areas (see Baldwin, 1979, for a good review). This oft-times repeated observation has led both to dismissals of the findings as no more than a statement of the obvious (Wootton, 1959), and to attempts to utilize them as a basis for theories of crime and urbanism (see Baldwin and Bottoms, 1976). However, it should be noted that there are two rather different sets of findings that require explanation (namely urban–rural differences and intra-urban differences), which may or may not reflect the same forces.

Urban–rural differences

Crime statistics have shown fairly consistently that delinquency rates are substantially higher in the cities than in small towns, and higher in both of these than in rural areas (McClintock and Avison, 1968; Clinard, 1968). However, these data refer to where the offences were *committed* rather than where the offenders *lived*; moreover, they could reflect differences in police practice or in opportunities for crime rather than any effect related to predispositions to delinquent activities. Accordingly, it is necessary to turn

* No differences were found between delinquent and non-delinquent pupils at the same school in their perception of the school climate. This effectively rules out the possibility that the differences between schools on their perceived climate was simply an artefact of a difference in perception between delinquent and non-delinquent pupils.

to other sources of data in order to determine the validity and meaning of the finding. All of these confirm the reality of the urban–rural difference with respect to both offences and the proportion of individuals with disturbances of conduct (both delinquent and non-delinquent). Thus, victim surveys (Aromaa, 1974; Ennis, 1967) and self-report studies (Christie *et al.*, 1965; Clark and Wenninger, 1962) from both Europe and the United States have shown that delinquent activities are more common in urban areas. Moreover, psychiatric surveys utilizing detailed behavioural data from teachers and parents have also shown marked city–rural differences in rates of conduct disturbance. Thus, a two-fold difference was evident in Lavik's (1977) comparison of Oslo with a rural area in Norway and in the Rutter *et al.* (1975a and c) comparison of London with the Isle of Wight. The differences applied to both children and adolescents but were most marked with the chronic disorders beginning in early or middle childhood (Rutter, 1979a). However, it is important to note that the city–rural difference was by no means confined to disturbances of conduct in young people, as it also applied to emotional disturbances in both young people and their parents (Lavik, 1977; Rutter *et al.*, 1975a and c; Rutter and Quinton, 1977), to reading difficulties (Berger *et al.*, 1975), to adult criminality (Rutter *et al.*, 1975b; Rutter and Quinton, 1977), and to various measures of family discord and adversity (Rutter *et al.*, 1975c; Rutter and Quinton, 1977).

It is clear that these differences are not reporting artefacts in that they are shown by a wide variety of measures and hold up even when the same methods are applied by the same team of investigators in the two areas. However, one further source of bias must also be considered in that it is possible that the differences could just mean that people with psycho-social problems of various kinds tend to move away from rural areas to accumulate in cities. Certainly, there may be a drift of disturbed individuals into poor, slummy city areas (Levy and Rowitz, 1970 and 1971), but drift could not account for the London–Isle of Wight differences in that they held up even after comparisons were confined to those born and bred in the two areas (Rutter *et al.*, 1975c; Rutter and Quinton, 1977). Further evidence showing that drift does *not* account for area differences in crime rates stems from the West and Farrington study of London boys, which showed that delinquency rates fell in those who moved away from London (Osborn, 1980). Accordingly, it seems likely that, in addition to drift, the city environment is in some way associated with factors which predispose to psycho-social disorder.

So far as children and adolescents are concerned, the further question arises as to whether the area effect (whatever its nature and origin) operates directly on them, or rather whether it operates through effects on the family.

So far as the London–Isle of Wight comparison was concerned (Rutter *et al.*, 1975c; Rutter and Quinton, 1977), the higher rate of child disorder in London was almost entirely explicable in terms of the greater frequency of family adversity in the metropolis (as shown by variables such as parental criminality and mental disorder, marital discord and large family size). When the rates of disorder in the two areas were re-compared after controlling for the presence of family adversities, there was no longer any significant difference between London and the Isle of Wight in the prevalence of child psychiatric disorder (either of the emotional or conduct disturbance type). Of course, that only pushes the question back one stage further, to ask why London families were more likely to be disadvantaged and what it was about life in Inner London which predisposed to adult mental disorder, crime and family discord.

A variety of possible explanations have been suggested (see Baldwin and Bottoms, 1976; Quinton, 1980; Rutter, 1981c) without any very satisfactory answers. However, as similar issues apply to the intra-urban differences, those will be discussed together.

Intra-urban differences

Many studies have shown that within cities, the suburbs, and towns there are marked variations between geographical areas in rates of crime and delinquency (Baldwin, 1975; Baldwin and Bottoms, 1976; Morris, 1957). Delinquency rates have been shown to vary between boroughs (Wallis and Maliphant, 1967), between wards in a borough (Edwards, 1973), between enumerations districts within a ward (Gath *et al.*, 1977), and even between streets in a small neighbourhood, so that the high-risk areas may be very small as well as quite large (Jephcott and Carter, 1954). Moreover, the high-delinquency areas are often rather scattered, with no very obvious connection with particular neighbourhoods as they are ordinarily thought of (Baldwin and Bottoms, 1976; Gath *et al.*, 1977). On the other hand, it has also been shown that the area differences in delinquency rates remain rather stable over quite long periods of time (Wallis and Maliphant, 1967; Castle and Gittus, 1957).

In attempting to understand the meaning of this very well-documented phenomenon, it needs to be noted that the area differences are by no means restricted to disturbances of conduct. On the whole, the areas with high rates of juvenile delinquency also have high rates of adult crime, social problems, alcoholism and psychiatric disorder (see, for example, Castle and Gittus, 1957; Gath *et al.*, 1977). Both suicide (Sainsbury, 1955) and parasuicide

(Kreitman, 1977) also tend to be commoner in socially disadvantaged areas, which overlap (but are not synonymous) with the high-delinquency areas. Illegitimate birth, divorce and mental hospital admissions follow much the same pattern.

Again, several possible methodological artefacts need to be considered. The first limitation is that most of the data refer to criminal statistics or hospital attendance figures, so that it is unclear how far the variations reflect differences in social control procedures or clinic referral practices rather than real differences in prevalence. The observation that suicide and parasuicide, as well as illegitimate births and divorce, also show area differences suggests that it is unlikely that the variations are solely a result of administrative practices. Delinquency self-report data from city samples (Clark and Wenninger, 1962; McDonald, 1969) are somewhat inconclusive, but they, too, point to probable real differences in prevalence.

A further possibility is that the differences reflect either the drift of disadvantaged or deviant individuals into less desirable areas or the results of local authority allocation of 'problem families' to particular housing estates. The evidence on both suggestions is decidedly limited, but the questions were investigated by Baldwin and Bottoms (1976) in their ecological study of Sheffield. It was found that the residents who moved into high-delinquency estates were indeed more likely to have a *previous* crime record than those who moved into low-rate estates (19.2 per cent *v.* 7.4 per cent); on the other hand, this difference was largely the result of just one high-rate estate which took over a quarter of residents with prior convictions. Houses in high-rate estates also tended to remain vacant for longer, indicating that they were generally viewed as 'less desirable' by potential tenants. It is likely (for a variety of different reasons – see Baldwin and Bottoms, 1976) that to some extent housing authorities do make selective placements, but this would not be relevant to the area differences with respect to delinquency rates in owner-occupied housing. We lack the data needed to determine the importance of either 'drift' or 'segregation' as determinants of area differences in crime or social problems. Nevertheless, we may tentatively conclude that both processes operate but that even in combination, they probably do not totally account for the area differences. However, it is clear that the possibility requires further study.

The fact that the incoming residents to high-rate estates have been shown to differ from those moving into low-rate estates makes it essential to control for these prior differences when making area comparisons. Unfortunately, that has not been done satisfactorily in any of the area studies. The nearest approach has been to examine area differences in child guidance referral rates

(Gath et al., 1977) or delinquency rates (Reiss and Rhodes, 1961) *within* social class categories. These studies have shown that the area differences are not solely explicable in terms of the social class of the individuals in them, and that, on the whole, the social status of the *area* may be as important as (or more important than) the social status of the *individual*. However, there are too few studies that have examined the matter for there to be much confidence in the conclusion and, of course, social class is not the only, or indeed even the most relevant, variable to take into account. It seems that there may be an area effect which goes beyond individual characteristics and, therefore, that an ecological approach may be justified, but that is about as much as can be said.

Ecological correlations and explanations

In recent years the most frequent statistical approach to area analyses has been to correlate census tract variables with offender rates according to administratively defined geographical units. The results have usually shown that the high-delinquency areas are those with a high proportion of low social status individuals, a low proportion of owner-occupiers, a high proportion of overcrowded homes and various features such as shared accommodation, many single people and many immigrants thought to reflect 'social organization' (for example, Bagley, 1965; Baldwin and Bottoms, 1976; Beasley and Antunes, 1974; Gath et al., 1977; Lander, 1954; Morris, 1957; Wallis and Maliphant, 1967). In these respects, the findings are fairly consistent (although there are some differences in findings between studies). The problem lies in knowing quite what they mean.

Certainly these ecological correlations do *not* mean that these associations apply at an individual level. Robinson (1950) has shown why this is the case in his discussion of the 'ecological fallacy'. Nevertheless, it is important to consider whether any of them might operate through some direct effect on individuals.

The variables of population density and of personal overcrowding are, perhaps, the two most likely contenders in this connection. However, the results of empirical research on both are somewhat contradictory and inconclusive (Choldin, 1978; Baron and Needel, 1980; Freedman, 1979; Gove et al., 1979; Schmidt and Keating, 1979). In general, it seems that personal crowding (as reflected, for example, in person–room ratio) has a somewhat stronger association with psycho-social problems than does overall population density (as reflected, for example, in persons per area). But in both cases the context and social meaning seem crucial, with feelings of lack of personal control over the social environment, unwanted social encounters, lack of safety, lack of privacy and negative evaluations of the residential environment all important. Architectural design may influence people's feelings of being overcrowded without altering the actual level of crowding. Thus, one study showed that people in high-rise dwellings reported seeing more people they did not recognize in the lobby; expressed a lower sense of control, safety and privacy; had less informal social relations with neighbours; and felt more crowded (McCarthy and Saegert, 1978). Another study (Baum and Davis, 1980) showed that students living in a long corridor dormitory reported more crowding and residential social problems than those living in a short corridor or in a long corridor modified so that space was shared between fewer residents (in a way which did not change the degree of crowding).

With respect to possible area influences which operate at the community level, various suggestions have been investigated. Jones (1958) argued that problem estates were characterized by high rates of mobility which created a general sense of instability and lack of effective community norms of behaviour. However, Baldwin and Bottoms (1976) showed that this did not apply in Sheffield, where there was no association between delinquency rates and turnover of dwellings; nor did it apply in the study by Maccoby *et al.* (1968) of Cambridge, Massachusetts. On the basis of his Exeter study findings, Bagley (1965) suggested that the lack of adequate recreational facilities was a feature of high-delinquency areas, but again this could not be confirmed in Sheffield (Baldwin and Bottoms, 1976). Rex and Moore (1967) and Pahl (1970a and b) have drawn attention to the potential importance in terms of constraints and conflicts of different housing classes. Baldwin and Bottoms (1976) provide some limited confirmation of the possible relevance of patterns of housing tenure, in that their area correlations in Sheffield differed somewhat according to type of tenure; however, the meaning of these differences remains rather uncertain.

A major limitation of most area studies stems from their use of administrative definitions of areas and their reliance on census data to define the characteristics of the areas. However, census tracts will rarely coincide with the areas felt to constitute 'neighbourhoods' or 'communities' by the people living in them. But even the concept of neighbourhood involves difficulties, both because it need not coincide with social communities or sub-culture (Clarke, 1976) and because residents vary considerably in their views on the boundaries and characteristics of the neighbourhoods in which they live (Haney and Knowles, 1978; Lee, 1968 and 1973). Community ties tend to increase with length of residence (Kasarda and Janowitz, 1974), but even with long-standing residents identification is often associated more with friendship networks and kinship ties than with geographical boundaries (Gans, 1962).

Even so, a useful alternative strategy which has been rarely employed is to compare high- and low-delinquency neighbourhoods in terms of the social perceptions of the residents in them. Maccoby *et al.* (1968) did this with respect to two areas of Cambridge, Massachusetts, which were similar in socio-economic status but which showed a three-fold difference in delinquency rates and an eight-fold difference in truancy rates. The two areas did not differ in terms of either population mobility or expressed attitudes to delinquency. But more residents in the high-delinquency area reported that they did not like the neighbourhood (26 per cent *v.* 15 per cent), fewer knew more than five neighbours well enough to borrow something (28 per cent *v.* 50 per cent), and fewer felt that they shared the interests and ideas of other people in the area (33 per cent *v.* 59 per cent). The study was based on rather small numbers (just over 100 interviews in each area) and was not very fully reported, but the findings suggest the possible relevance of feelings of social integration. Of course, that leaves unexplained *why* such differences developed, and Quinton's (1980) data from the London–Isle of Wight study suggest that the *availability* of friends and kin is unlikely to constitute the explanation.

The strategy of contrasting high- and low-delinquency areas by means of detailed interviewing of the people living in the areas was also followed by Clinard and Abbott (1973), in their comparison of slum areas in Kampala (Uganda) with high and low crime rates. Both areas had very poor facilities (for example, *none* of the people in the low-delinquency area had water taps in their yards or houses, and only 19 per cent of those in the high-delinquency area had taps), with facilities rather *worse* in the *low-*delinquency area. Property crimes in the high-delinquency area were double and crimes against the person 1.5 times those in the low-delinquency area. People in the two areas did not differ in their view that theft was wrong, but those from the high-crime area had fewer negative attitudes towards fighting, prostitution, wife-beating and illegal beer-brewing. There were no differences between the areas in participation in official organizations (such as unions or city-wide cooperatives) or civic events, in contact with kin, in the presence of friends outside the area, or in willingness to give financial help to others; the high-crime community tended to have slightly higher-status occupations, but fewer owned their own homes. The major differences seemed to apply to the *quality* of relationships; people in the low-crime area perceived a greater firmness and stability in heterosexual relationships, were more likely to participate in local community organizations, visited the homes of a greater range of people, and changed residence less often.

These findings indicate that it is not enough to be concerned with the 'objective' demographic or other features of high-delinquency areas.* We must also ask how an area is *perceived* by people living in and outside it, and how the adverse reputations of some areas were created and maintained over time. In Britain, where much inner city housing is owned by the local authority, public housing department policies may play a part. It is not necessarily that authorities operate a deliberate segregation policy (Baldwin and Bottoms, 1976), but rather that practical considerations mean that 'problem tenants' tend not to be offered houses with high rents or situated in 'high-class' areas, so creating a *de facto* concentration of families with difficulties in particular housing estates. This effect is likely to be accentuated by the cultural changes and stereotypical responses which tend to follow, so serving to create 'problem estates' through the establishment of spirals of delinquency amplification. While systematic quantified investigations to examine the relative effects of different factors have yet to be undertaken, participant observation studies have provided useful data on some of the leads to follow (see, for example, Wilson's 1963 account of difficult housing estates in Bristol; Armstrong and Wilson's 1973 account of the manner in which the Easterhouse area of Glasgow was transformed into a 'problem area', and Gill's 1977 description of the history of a council housing estate in Liverpool).

'Problem tenants' tend to be people with large families, and hence their concentration in one estate means that the area is going to be one with an unusually high concentration of children and adolescents, the age group in which delinquency is at its peak. Systematic studies have shown high correlations between rates of vandalism and child density in housing estates (Mawby, 1977a; Wilson, 1978; Mayhew *et al.*, 1979), so that one effect is likely to be an immediate increase in the most clearly visible signs of delinquency, namely graffiti and the damage resulting from vandalism. The deterioration in the reputation of the area may be accelerated through stereotypes created in the media. The use of police cars and vans to patrol the streets, instead of policemen on the beat (because of concerns about the danger of the area), may increase the distance between police and residents of the area. Because of the reputation of the estate, young people standing at street corners are more likely to be viewed with suspicion by the police and

---

* Baldwin's (1979) review of ecological and areal studies clearly brings out both the tautological nature of some of the ecological statistical analyses and also the grave limitations of the multivariate statistical approach as a means of defining the distinctive characteristics of high-delinquency areas.

therefore identified for questioning in the case of any delinquent activities in the area. Young people in turn are likely to resent what they feel as unreasonable police intrusion without cause, creating a recipe for a spiral of mutual resentment and hostility which may serve to 'legitimize' delinquent or violent activities as a way of 'getting back' at the police who have come to be seen as oppressive. Young people living in an area with a 'problem' reputation may encounter discrimination at school or in getting jobs after leaving school just because it is assumed they, as individuals, are likely to share the characteristics which are stereotypical for the area. It will be appreciated that these suggestions on possible factors in the process by which 'problem areas' are created are just that – suggestions stemming from reports of observations and interviews with people in such areas. Systematic research to test these ideas is needed.

Physical environment and situational effects

Recently there has been an upsurge of interest in the effects of the physical environment in regulating people's behaviour and in possible situational influences on delinquent activities (see Clarke, 1978, 1980). The impetus for this interest did not stem from ecological studies (rather it came from a concern about the possibilities of effective prevention through situational measures – see Clarke and Mayhew, 1981 – and from architectural considerations – see Newman, 1973a and b and 1975), but as Baldwin (1979) noted, it nevertheless carries the potential for increasing our understanding of ecological effects.

The most influential of the reports on architecture was Oscar Newman's (1973a) book, *Defensible Space*, which suggested that physical design features in housing estates could either predispose towards or protect against crime. Using a concept of 'defensible space' (meaning personal territory with a clearly identifiable status and a layout which enables people to know their neighbours and easily spot strangers), he argued that extensive semi-public areas in estates increased vandalism both because the areas were not felt to belong to any particular group of residents (and hence were not looked after or protected by them), and because the nature of their design made surveillance of intruders by the residents difficult. The relevant factors were summarized in terms of four main elements: (i) the creation of perceived zones of territorial influence; (ii) the provision of surveillance opportunities for residents and their agents; (iii) the creation, by physical design, of certain perceptions of a housing project's uniqueness; and (iv) the juxtaposition of the project with 'safe zones' in adjacent areas.

The main quantitative evidence presented by Newman (1973a and b) to support this thesis came from a comparison of vandalism and crime rates on two housing estates of similar size and overall density situated on opposite sides of the same street, together with a more broad-scale analysis of the types and locations of crimes within a large number of New York housing projects. This empirical base for Newman's ideas has been widely criticized on several different grounds, including (i) a lack of adequate attention to the characteristics of the tenants entering the projects; (ii) an inadequate control for household density; (iii) a failure to specify whether the physical design features were supposed to influence the amount of crime committed by its inhabitants, or whether architecture merely influenced the *opportunities* for crime by residents and outsiders alike (see Bottoms, 1974; Hillier, 1973; Mawby, 1977b; Mayhew, 1979). Further data analyses by Newman (1975 and 1976) indicated that the characteristics of the residents (such as the proportion of one-parent families and the number of children) were better predictors of crime and vandalism than were physical design features. Nevertheless, physical design features improved the level of prediction, with the size of the housing project, the number of housing units sharing an entrance to a building, and building height as the most crucial variables.

Newman's ideas have been tested in London by Wilson (1978), who confirmed that most damage did indeed occur in those semi-public areas which were out of general sight, and that vandalism was particularly high in blocks with impersonal entrances used as a through-way to other locations, in large blocks characterized by extensive semi-public space which could not easily be supervised by residents, and in blocks with little or no landscaping of the grounds. The implication of the last finding is that a pleasant environment may make it less likely that people will want to damage it, but, as postulated by Newman, the other findings suggest that public surveillance may reduce opportunities for vandalism. In this connection it should be emphasized that Newman's suggestion is not just that the *amount* of surveillance matters, but rather that physical design features may influence the areas for which residents *feel responsible*. Wilson's data are consonant with that hypothesis but do not provide a rigorous test of it. As in Newman's research, physical design features did not account for the greatest proportion of the variance; rather, child density proved to be the single variable most strongly associated with vandalism.

A further study to test Newman's suggestions, this time in the United States, is that by Brantingham and Brantingham (1975a and b), who analysed burglary rates according to city blocks. They found that blocks on the border of a neighbourhood (defined in terms of its social, economic and architectural homogeneity) had a burglary rate more than twice that for blocks in the interior of a neighbourhood. Moreover, within both border and interior blocks (defined in terms of neighbourhood), rates differed according to whether apartments were interior or border in terms of relatively homogeneous subsets within the block. Brantingham and Brantingham (1975b, p. 280) concluded:

> ... the crucial interactive relationship between the residents of a homogeneous neighbourhood is that of 'mutual awareness' rather than the overt interactive process of 'neighbouring'. Residents of a homogeneous neighbourhood are likely to have implicit perceptions of routine behavioural patterns amongst neighbours whose names might not be known, and on the part of appropriately present non-residents (e.g. milkmen, postmen, police). We would speculate that this sort of perceptual awareness would be strongest on the interior of the neighbourhood and weakest on the borders where perceived neighbours straying from bordering neighbourhoods might be most common and least likely to challenge. Similarly, burglars might well perceive the relative social anonymity available to them in border areas and select targets in border areas rather than interiors.

Waller and Okihiro (1978), in their study of Toronto, also found that victims of burglary were more likely than non-victims to live in a neighbourhood of low social cohesion (62 per cent *v.* 45 per cent); more likely to be in a house with poor surveillability (59 per cent *v.* 36 per cent); more likely to live near subsidized public housing (over half *v.* 12 per cent); more likely to live on the lower floors of the apartment block (76 per cent *v.* 40 per cent); and less likely to be in a block with a doorman (0 per cent *v.* 16 per cent).

These few empirical findings suggest that the notion of 'defensible space' may have *some* validity, although physical design features have less influence on the rate of vandalism on housing estates than the characteristics of the population of tenants. So far there have been relatively few attempts to apply 'defensible space' concepts in practice (see Mayhew, 1979). Such attempts as there have been seem to have had some benefits but, on the whole, the results have been rather disappointing – especially in the apparently rather weak effect of physical design changes on the social interactions and groupings of the tenants. However, the research undertaken up to now has been far from definitive, and the ideas warrant more extended and discriminating testing.

Newman's theorizing on physical design has been directly focused on housing estates, and on the potential importance of architectural features as determinants both of what is felt to be 'private' and also of the semi-public areas which are felt to be a joint responsibility of groups of residents. The main point is that a design which extends the former, and which ensures that the latter are split up according to relatively small groups of residents who will know one another, is likely to reduce vandalism.

These ideas carry no necessary implications for totally public areas, and it is these which are most likely of all to be vandalized. Thus, in the Home Office Manchester survey, there were 19.2 incidents per property for schools, 7.8 for telephone kiosks, 3.4 for shops, but only 0.04 per property for private dwellings (see Sturman, 1978). But, by extension, it is possible that surveillance of public properties could affect the amount of vandalism.

This possibility was examined by Mawby (1977a) and Mayhew et al. (1979) in their studies of telephone kiosks. In a small-scale study of vandalism to 27 telephone kiosks in residential areas of Sheffield, Mawby found that vandalism was greatest in kiosks with heavy usage and high takings. When kiosk use was controlled for, there was a slight tendency for vandalism to be more frequent in kiosks on public roads away from amenities; vandalism was also more common in council housing areas than in areas of privately rented or owner-occupied property. Mayhew et al. (1979), in a much larger-scale study in London, also found that vandalism was more prevalent in kiosks surrounded by local authority housing. Surveillance proved to be important only in so far as there was slightly less vandalism in kiosks overlooked by windows of private dwellings. Pablant and Baxter (1975), similarly, found that vandalism was somewhat less frequent in schools where the property was clearly visible to nearby residents and where the surrounding area was well illuminated. Conversely, high-vandalism schools tended to face railroad tracks, motorways or vacant land. Data were not presented on the extent to which this association might be due to some third variable.

Taken together, the findings suggest that the sheer amount of surveillance by residents of totally public properties may have a marginal effect on the extent of vandalism but, in itself, it is not a major influence – probably because most people do not consider that it is their responsibility to look after totally public buildings such as telephone kiosks. It seems that this situation is rather different from that in housing estates, where physical design features may affect both the possibilities of effective surveillance *and* people's perception of their own responsibilities for semi-public areas.

However, there is also the further issue of the consequences of more or less effective surveillance by employees who *do* have an explicit responsibility for particular areas. Post Office evidence suggests that rented call-boxes in premises such as pubs, shops and launderettes, which are given some supervision by staff, suffer almost no vandalism in comparison with those in kiosks (Mayhew *et al.*, 1979). Likewise, car parks with attendants have lower rates of auto-crime; football hooliganism on trains has been reduced by a variety of means, including permission for the club stewards to travel free of charge, and shoplifting is discouraged by the presence of assistants to serve customers (Walsh, 1978). In a study of bus vandalism (Mayhew *et al.*, 1976), supervision of passengers by the driver and conductor had an important effect on vandalism, this being higher on one-man operated buses and on the rear top deck of all buses. Similarly, in a study of the impact of closed-circuit television in four South London underground stations (Burrows, 1980), the incidence of thefts and robberies declined significantly after it was introduced. This is in keeping with research in the United States (Newman, 1973; Reppetto, 1974) and Canada (Waller and Okihiro, 1978), which has shown that apartment blocks with doormen are less vulnerable to burglary.

Contrary to popular belief, however, increasing the use of the police to deter, detect and apprehend offenders does not seem particularly effective as a general strategy (Kelling *et al.*, 1974; Reppetto, 1974; Clarke and Hough, 1980; Burrows *et al.*, 1979). Obviously the police cannot be everywhere at once and, moreover, much crime takes place in private (Clarke, 1980). More limited efforts through community policing may have more success, if not in reducing crime then at least in improving relations between the police and the public and reducing the fear of crime. A community project in West London organized by N.A.C.R.O., in which the police were involved, reported an improvement in community morale, reduction in the fear of crime, and some decline in vandalism (N.A.C.R.O., 1978). Further research, especially into those forces adopting 'community policing', is needed to provide more definitive information.

The findings from research generally, then, are in agreement in showing the potential importance of situational effects (see Rutter, 1979a; Clarke and Mayhew, 1981). Only a few children are completely honest and well-behaved in all circumstances – the majority will be disruptive or will cheat or steal given the right circumstances. This effect, however, is by no means confined to disturbances of conduct – there are close parallels with alcoholism (Royal College of Psychiatrists, 1979), with drug dependency (De Alarcón, 1972), and with suicide (Adelstein and Mardon, 1975). In each case, there is evidence that availability factors affect behaviour (see Chapter 9).

Nevertheless, many questions remain regarding situational effects. Their strength is not known, and there are few findings on the particular characteristics of the physical environment which increase or decrease the likelihood of disturbances of conduct. It also remains quite unclear how far the effects are a result of particular environments affecting people's *motivation* to behave in disruptive or delinquent ways, and how far they are a consequence of limitations in the *opportunities* to behave in these ways. In addition, we remain ignorant of the extent to which situational factors truly *reduce* crime rather than just *displace* it from one area to another or from one type of activity to another. As noted, there are various pointers to the probable importance of situational effects, and it is evident that their further study would be most worthwhile, but the existing knowledge on the topic is still very limited.

Social change

During this last century there have been immense changes in society, many of which might be expected to have an impact on children and adolescents (see Rutter, 1979a, for a review of these – also Chapter 3). One of the most important challenges to social scientists is to assess the consequences of these massive social changes (see Campbell and Converse, 1972), but it must be said that researchers have had little success in this task so far. Accordingly, all that we can do here is review some of the possible research strategies and speculate on what might emerge if these approaches were extended. The potential importance of the issues is obvious. As we observed in Chapter 3, one of the most striking features of crime statistics in most European and North American countries has been the steady rise in rates of delinquency since the First World War. As this same time period has been marked by equally striking social changes, it is both natural and essential to ask the question whether the two forms of change are in any way linked.

One possible research strategy has been the utilization of international comparisons. The logic of this approach lies in the identification of countries which differ in terms of their experience of some important social change, but which are similar in other respects. Archer and Gartner (1976) used this strategy in their comparisons of combatant and non-combatant nations to determine whether waging war might foster crime and violence, and in particular whether wars might be followed by a rise in homicide rates. The First and Second World Wars, the Vietnam war, and various other more restricted wars were used for this purpose. As they emphasize, there are immense difficulties in ensuring that like is being compared with like. However, the comparisons suggested that combatant nations were more likely than non-combatant nations to experience post-war increases in homicide rates, and that this was especially the case if there were high rates of battle death. Archer and Gartner point out that wars involve many different forms of social change, and they attempt to contrast various alternative hypotheses as to which mechanism might be most important.

Their conclusion is that a legitimation model is the most plausible – that is, that the presence of authorized or sanctioned killing during war makes violence more acceptable, and that this legitimation has a residual effect on the level of homicide in peacetime society afterwards. While their data point in that direction, they cannot be said to be definitive. However, the main point of referring to this study is not the specific conclusion (which in any case refers to adults more than to juveniles), but rather the potential value of this strategy.

It could be used, for example, to study the effects of urbanization and industrialization, which has been one of the most striking and dramatic changes throughout the world over the last couple of centuries (Davis, 1973; Basham, 1978). As already noted, delinquency and crime rates in all countries tend to be substantially higher in the cities than in small towns or rural areas, but is it urbanization and industrialization *per se* which predispose to crime? International comparisons would be informative in this connection because the timing of urbanization has varied considerably, with little change in the U.K. since the 1930s, but huge increases in urbanization in Japan and the U.S.S.R. during the middle years of the twentieth century, and lesser changes in the U.S.A. The comparative figures on secular trends in crime rates in these countries do not suggest any close connection between urbanization and crime. For example, crime in Japan has tended to decrease during a period of unparalleled industrial growth and urban concentration (Clifford, 1976). On the other hand, it has been suggested that the rate of increase in crime in developing countries has tended to be greatest at the times when industrialization and the creation of urban centres are at their peak (Clinard and Abbott, 1973). Of course, in many developing countries these changes have been accompanied by the breakdown of tribal and family ties, massive migration, and the spread of shanty-town slums, so that the situation differs from that in more developed nations. A more systematic set of international comparisons taking these factors into account would be worthwhile.

An alternative research strategy for the study of the effects of social change is the aggregate time series method (see Dooley and Catalano, 1980), in which the *timing* of social or economic changes is linked with the timing of changes in delinquency rates or some other behavioural indicator. Such studies have tended to show parallels between rises and falls in unemployment and rises and falls in suicide rates. But there are many problems in analyses of these sort, not the least of which is the uncertainty of what length of time-lag to use. Is the effect of rising unemployment on suicide or delinquency likely to be immediate, or one year delayed, or five years delayed?

At first sight, the British figures do not suggest any close connection between unemployment and rising crime rates. Unemployment figures were at their peak during the inter-wars period of the Depression, and more recently have risen very sharply once again during the 1970s (Diamond, 1978); but crime rates remained fairly stable during the Depression, with the largest increase during the late 50s and 60s and a slowing down of the increase during the last few years, when unemployment rates have been going up sharply (McClintock and Avison, 1968; Home Office, 1980). Similarly, in the U.S.A., crime rates rose during the middle and late 60s at a time when unemployment rates declined (Phillips *et al.*, 1972). But links have been postulated on the basis of earlier figures (see, for example, Fleisher, 1966),* and it is evident that many other variables would have to be taken into account in any adequate investigation of the matter. Such systematic studies would be informative.

A further development of the time-series approach is provided by the analysis of links between specific forms of social change and specific crimes (see Cohen and Felson, 1979a and b). For example, Cohen and Felson postulated that the increase in the U.S.A. between 1960 and 1971 in the proportion of households unattended during the day should be associated with an increase in daytime, but not nighttime, residential burglary; similarly, it was postulated that the increase in the volume of sales at retail businesses, together with the fall in the number of employees, should be reflected in a greater increase in shoplifting than in thefts from other forms of businesses. The data generally supported their hypothesis that changes in the pattern of routine activities have provided the opportunity for many specific forms of illegal activity to occur.

A third research strategy has been the study of changes in the behaviour or adaptive functioning of individuals following some major social change such as migration or rehousing (see studies cited in Rutter and Madge, 1976). However, few studies have had both before and after data on comparable groups who have and who have not experienced the change. These data are essential for any systematic comparison, in view of the strong likelihood that those individuals who migrate or who are rehoused are far from a random sample of the population. However, as already noted, such information was available in West and Farrington's (1973) longitudinal study of London boys, in which it was found that moving away from London was associated with a significant reduction in both self-reported delinquency

* Although the findings are inconsistent, and have been interpreted by some reviewers as showing no systematic link between the economic conditions of a society and its crime rate (Cohen and Felson, 1979a and b).

and convictions (Osborn, 1980). Those who moved out of London showed a drop between 14 and 21 years in mean rank scores for self-reported delinquency from 54 to 41, there being no such reduction in the group who remained in London and who were matched on self-report at 14. This research strategy could be utilized with great effect for other social changes, and it is to be regretted that so few of the other longitudinal studies have taken advantage of these opportunities (which exist only with longitudinal data).

In all of these strategies it is important to consider the meaning and implications of the particular indices of social change which are used. For example, most cross-sectional studies have shown significant associations between delinquency and poverty or poor housing. But time-series analyses appear sharply to contradict those correlations. Thus, since the turn of the century there has been a very great improvement in housing conditions in Britain as well as a marked reduction in poverty (see, for example, Central Statistical Office, 1978; Diamond, 1978; Rutter and Madge, 1976); but these *improvements* in living conditions have been accompanied by an *increase* in crime rates (see Chapter 3). It would seem from these figures that poverty and poor housing cannot play any role in the causal processes leading to delinquency. But that conclusion assumes that it is the *absolute* levels that matter, and it may be that that is not so. Although the general level of prosperity has risen greatly during this century, the *distribution* of incomes has changed surprisingly little (see Diamond, 1978). If the most relevant issue is how a person fares *relative* to other people, rather than how well off he is in absolute terms, things have not altered much. Also, people's expectations and their expectations of what they 'need' have increased greatly (see Rutter, 1979a). At the turn of the century there were no television sets, cars were a rare curiosity, and automatic washing machines were not yet available. Accordingly, the question of their purchase did not arise. But today most people would regard a television set as a 'necessity', and increasingly cars and washing machines are coming into that category. As a result, people today may *feel* very poor if they lack these amenities whereas this was not so 100 years ago. Increases in real income do not necessarily mean that people perceive themselves as better off. A further possibility is that income and housing conditions have no link with delinquency across the range as a whole, but that there is a relatively high threshold below which socio-economic adversity does predispose to delinquency. In this connection it is relevant that the total population figures for living conditions misrepresent the circumstances of young people, because poverty and overcrowded housing are particularly likely to be experienced during the period of family life when there are dependent children, and that this is especially so for large families (see Rutter and Madge, 1976; Rutter, 1979a). As a result, many children today still experience poverty and poor housing for some period of their life (Wedge and Prosser, 1973).

It is evident, even from this brief discussion of some of the issues, that the investigation of the effects of social change is no easy matter. Nevertheless, with many of the social indices there is a striking disparity between the results of cross-sectional analyses (which tend to show a link with delinquency) and secular change analyses (which tend not to show any consistent link). The apparent paradox has yet to be resolved.

Conclusions

A wide range of psycho-social variables are associated with delinquency; with many of them there is also reasonably good circumstantial evidence that, to some extent, they constitute part of the causal processes for delinquency. The family characteristics most strongly associated with delinquency are: parental criminality, ineffective supervision and discipline, familial discord and disharmony, weak parent–child relationships, large family size, and psycho-social disadvantage. Less is known about the precise mechanisms by which these family variables have their effects, but recent observational studies of interaction in the home offer promise of progress on this question. More research of that type is required.

It is probable that films and television may have some impact on attitudes and behaviour, although the effect on delinquent activities is quite small when considered in relation to other causal factors. Nevertheless, in children who are already aggressive or liable to behave in delinquent ways, and especially when the influence of the media is consonant with influences in the home, the prolonged viewing of violent programmes may have *some* effect in increasing the predisposition to behave in a violent or antisocial manner.

The judicial response to delinquency may well have corrective, therapeutic or deterrent intentions, but it also has the effect of providing a public recognition or 'labelling' of someone as a delinquent – a labelling which may influence how the individual views himself and, in turn, how he behaves. A boy's first appearance in court tends to be followed by an increase in delinquent activities and by a change in attitudes. But this process does not seem to be intensified by further subsequent convictions.

Research findings on school influences are rather limited, but the results suggest that there *is* an influence, although its strength remains unknown. The factors involved in the school influence seem to concern the balance of the pupil intake in terms of intellectual ability and social status (with the effect probably acting through the peer group), and also variables reflecting the school ethos or social organization.

Delinquency rates are substantially higher in the cities than in small towns or rural areas, and, even within cities, areas vary markedly in rates of crime. It is clear that these area differences are not reporting artefacts and are not solely due to the drift of delinquent individuals into poor areas. However, so far, we have a rather limited understanding both of how high-delinquency areas are created and of the mechanisms involved in these broader socio-cultural influences. The topic is one which needs further research investment.

In recent years there has been an increasing interest in the effects of the physical environment in regulating people's behaviour and in possible situational influences on delinquent activities. Much of this interest stems from suggestions that physical design features in housing estates could either predispose towards or protect against crime. Research findings confirm the potential importance of situational effects, but many questions remain on the strength of their effects and on their mode of operation. Again, this is an area where further studies are needed.

During this last century there have been immense changes in society, many of which might be expected to have an impact on children and adolescents. However, the investigation of the effects of social change has proved to be a difficult matter, and our knowledge on this topic remains quite limited.

7
Protective Factors

Many studies have attempted to combine factors which have been found to carry a markedly increased risk of delinquency, in order to determine how accurate a prediction of delinquency could be developed (see Glueck and Glueck, 1950 and 1964; Craig and Glick, 1963; Tait and Hodges, 1971; Farrington, 1979; Robins and Hill, 1966; Wadsworth, 1979; West and Farrington, 1973; West, 1982). There are a variety of technical problems in the development of predictive instruments (see, for example, Voss, 1963; Rose, 1967) which need not concern us here. However, two main findings stand out from all research of this kind. Firstly, many young people from a 'high-risk' background do *not* become delinquent; and secondly, a number of those who lack high-risk features *do* become delinquent. Naturally, the relative proportions vary according to how the predictive factors are used. It is possible to develop a combination of 'severe' high-risk factors such that a majority of youths with these features become delinquent. But if a 'severe' high-risk approach of this kind is followed, it is found that many delinquents are missed (because many have only a 'moderate'-risk background and a few have a low-risk). For example, in Craig and Glick's (1963) application of the Glueck scales, four-fifths of the boys with a very high score became delinquent but such scores picked out only a third of delinquents. If the cut-off was lowered to a level where the majority of delinquents were identified, then over half the 'risk' group did *not* become delinquent.

It should be appreciated that these results do *not* mean that only weak predictors can be found. On the contrary, the associations found have been very strong. For example, referring again to the Craig and Glick study, they found that a mere 5.6 per cent of the 'low-risk' group became delinquent, compared with 19.6 per cent of the 'medium-risk' group and an overwhelming 82.4 per cent of the high-risk group. Rather the problem is one of numbers. Because low scores are so much more frequent than high scores in the general population, there is bound to be a substantial *number* of false negatives and false positives, even though the *proportion* of correct predictions (or 'hits') in the different groups is impressively high. This effect severely limits the practical utility of prediction instruments if the intention is to find a means of picking out the young people who will become delinquent when older. However, it is very debatable whether this would be a useful exercise even if it could be made to produce better predictions.*

But the findings are of considerable interest in their own right in posing two questions, the answers to which could provide a better understanding of the development of delinquent behaviour. Firstly, what are the characteristics and circumstances of the boys from an apparently low-risk background who become delinquent? Secondly, what is different about the non-delinquent boys† from a high-risk background – that is, what factors served to protect them from delinquency?

Delinquent outcomes in youths from a low-risk background

West and Farrington (1973) provided some useful data relevant to the first question in their analysis of the features of the 53 delinquents (including 17 recidivists), in their longitudinal study of some 400 working-class London boys, who did not appear to have the background handicaps associated with delinquency. Several different sorts of explanation seemed to be operating. Firstly, the boys who became delinquent 'against prediction' were a less seriously delinquent group, whose delinquent activities were less markedly different from the general population (they had half as many convictions as the 'correctly predicted' delinquents and were much less likely to have convictions as adults). On the other hand, the 53 did include 17 recidivists, some of whom were seriously and persistently delinquent by any criteria. Secondly, some of the 'non-predicted' delinquent boys did have *some* high-risk factors – it was just that they fell below the particular cut-off point used (the inevitable threshold problem in any attempt to use a categorical system). But this did not account for all the boys, as some were rated as having *no* high-risk features. Thirdly, it was apparent that in some cases this was a consequence of measurement difficulties. In four out of the five cases of recidivist delinquency in boys with no high-risk features, the parents were noted at the time to be unsatisfactory informants and two mothers had totally refused to cooperate. The boys had no risk features simply because information was *lacking*, rather than because information was available to

---

* Also, there are ethical issues if the scales are used to 'label' non-delinquent children as ones liable to become delinquent.

† So far, systematic data of an extensive kind are only available from studies of boys, but the same question could usefully be used with respect to girls. However, it is already clear, from those studies which have included both sexes, that one of the most powerful protective factors in relation to a range of deviant outcomes is being a girl (Rutter, 1979b and 1982b – see also Chapter 4)! But while the sex difference is well established, the reasons for it remain obscure.

indicate the absence of risk features. Information that subsequently came to light suggested that, had all the facts been available at the time, three of the five cases would have been rated high-risk. Nevertheless, a careful review of all information still showed that there were a few boys (these two recidivists and a larger number of one-time offenders) who became delinquent without any identifiable features which might have been expected to predispose to delinquency. This relatively small subgroup remains an enigma, and its existence emphasizes that we remain some considerable way from an adequate understanding of the development of delinquent behaviour.

The outcome of non-delinquent boys from a high-risk background

However, in this chapter we wish to focus on the other 'paradoxical' group – the boys from a high-risk background who do *not* become delinquent. Once more, we need to start with a consideration of methodological issues and, again, the most relevant data are provided by the West and Farrington study (West and Farrington, 1973; West, 1982). The high-risk group was defined in terms of a parent or sibling with a criminal record acquired before the age of 17, plus at least two out of six other adversities (born illegitimate, family on social welfare, been in the care of the local authority, permanently separated before the age of 15 from one or both parents for reasons other than death, slum housing, and from a sibship of at least 5). 54 boys met these criteria, and two-thirds of them (36) had convictions by the age of 22; but 18 did not. These 18 were systematically compared with a control group of 25 non-delinquents, both groups being re-interviewed at the age of 23 or 24.

Two main findings emerged from the comparison. Firstly, many of the supposedly non-delinquent men were not so. Two had acquired convictions during the two years following their identification as non-delinquent but before being interviewed; two more had convictions for minor offences not normally included in the criminal records ('disturbing the peace' and 'drunk and disorderly'); and several others reported offences which had not led to conviction (in fact 40 per cent of the non-delinquent group from a high-risk background did so, compared with only 1 control (3.7 per cent). It is evident that at least some of the 'non-delinquency' was an artefact of imperfect measurement. Nevertheless, this was not so with others who appeared truly non-delinquent in spite of coming from a high-risk background.

But the findings also showed that many of those who were not delinquent *were* socially impaired in other ways, and a number were extreme social isolates. For example, considering the two 'high-risk, non-delinquent' and 'control, non-delinquent' groups as a whole, the former were much more likely to have been unemployed for six weeks or more during the previous two years (53 per cent *v.* 4 per cent), to be living in unsatisfactory conditions (67 per cent *v.* 4 per cent), to have *no* social contacts other than with parents or siblings (29 per cent *v.* 0 per cent), to lack a heterosexual relationship (50 per cent *v.* 20 per cent), and to be of lower intelligence (56 per cent with a score below 90 *v.* 15 per cent). Fewer of the high-risk group (39 per cent *v.* 58 per cent) had married, but of the few who had, 4 out of 7 (compared with 4 out of 15 among controls) had married young – before the age of 21. Also, 3 of the 7 marriages in the high-risk group broke down in comparison with only 2 out of 15 in the control group. Earlier results (West and Farrington, 1973) had also shown that many of the 'high-risk, non-delinquent' group were abnormally nervous, withdrawn and unhappy individuals. Of course, the absolute numbers involved in these comparisons were necessarily rather small, but many of the differences were large and striking. The overall pattern of results was clear-cut in showing that many of the young people from a high-risk background who escaped involvement in delinquent activities were socially handicapped in a variety of other ways. For at least half of them, the outcome could only be classified as poor – they had escaped delinquency only to suffer in other ways.

This finding, together with the oft-repeated observation that recidivist delinquent juveniles and adults frequently show a host of other interpersonal and social problems (see Chapter 1), emphasizes that serious and persisting delinquency is *not* just a matter of activities which happen to be against the law. That may well apply to the very much commoner picture of minor, transient delinquencies, but with many recidivists the delinquency is just one aspect of a much broader range of personal problems. The results just discussed emphasize that, in some cases, youths from a high-risk background may show these other social difficulties without engaging in delinquent activities. The observation serves as a reminder that outcome studies of therapeutic or judicial interventions (see Chapter 9) need to assess more than just the presence or absence of further convictions if misleading pictures of success or failure are to be avoided.

By the same token, these results indicate that the outcome for boys from a *seriously* adverse background is rather worse than has usually been supposed. If a *range* of outcome measures is used, it seems that relatively few escape their background in the sense of achieving social competence, although some show their difficulties in ways other than delinquency. Moreover, although the numbers in the West (1982) study were too small for an adequate test of the suggestion, it appears that it may well have been the very nature of these other social difficulties which protected the boys from delinquency. One consequence of extreme social isolation is that the boys will not have become part of a delinquent social group, with its social pressures to join in delinquent activities.

However, even in West's small group of boys from a very seriously adverse background there were a few who made a success of their lives in spite of appalling experiences. West (1982) cites the example of one boy, born illegitimate, who spent long periods away from home in the care of the social services, whose father deserted the family, and whose mother had multiple social problems and attempted suicide several times. Nevertheless, in spite of leaving school at 15 without taking any exams, he later obtained a good job, made a successful marriage, owned his own (good-quality) home, and was generally hard-working and self-confident (although also described as 'egocentric'). The young man stated: 'I left home when I was 16, but in spirit I left home long before.' There were too few of these 'success stories' in West's group of youths from a very high-risk background for any analysis of what it was that enabled them to overcome adversity and show such resilience. However, the findings indicate that there *are* resilient individuals even in a very high-risk group. Other researches (and other findings from the West and Farrington study) show that resilience and recovery are very much more frequent among young people from a slightly less extreme, but nevertheless seriously adverse, background. In the remainder of this chapter we consider the very limited empirical findings that are available on the factors associated with resilience in the face of adversity. Some of this evidence refers to factors which seem to protect specifically against delinquency, but some of the research has been concerned with conduct disorders and other more broadly defined deviant outcomes. The work is briefly reviewed here because it might provide useful pointers on leads to follow in delinquency research but, of course, it cannot necessarily be assumed that the specific findings generalize to delinquency.

Characteristics of the social group

The bulk of juvenile delinquency consists of delinquent activities undertake in conjunction with peers. It might therefore be supposed that whether or n a young person is part of a delinquent peer group could help determine involvement or lack of involvement in crime. The major difficulty here, course, is the problem of sorting out which is cause and which effect. If you delinquents *choose* to associate with other delinquents because they share interest in breaking the law, any links found between delinquency an delinquent peer group could simply reflect that choice. On the other h it could be argued with equal force that most boys would participate in delinquent activities in the right circumstances, but that whether *in fact* they do so may depend on the lead set or the example given by the friends with whom they associate. Or, at a more basic level and making no assumptions about who leads whom, it could be suggested that whether or not a boy finds himself in circumstances conducive to delinquency will depend on the social group activities in which he engages. Probably the best way to differentiate between these two opposing causal hypotheses is to look at the effects of a *change* in peer group.

Chosen change of peer group

This may be done by looking at voluntary changes in peer group. Knight and West (1975) examined this matter through the use of longitudinal data obtained in the West and Farrington (1973) prospective study of London boys. 27 persistent recidivists were individually matched with 27 temporary recidivists (defined according to the presence or absence of convictions between 17 years and 18–19 years), so that they were comparable as juveniles in terms of both convictions and self-reported delinquency. Interview data, at 18–19 years, indicated that fewer of the temporary recidivists (46 per cent) than the persistent recidivists (83 per cent) were still going around in an exclusively male group of four or more at the age of $17\frac{1}{2}$. Spontaneous comments by the youths suggested that disengagement from the influence of peer groups was an important feature in the abandonment of delinquent habits. The finding is suggestive, but no more than that, because the information on peer groups was retrospective and could well have been influenced by what happened subsequently. A somewhat stronger test is provided by the same comparison in terms of whether delinquency continued *after* the interview at 18–19 years (Osborn and West, 1980). It was found that 95 per cent of the persistent recidivists were still going around in all-male groups at 18–19, whereas this was so for only 62 per cent of the temporary recidivists (West, 1982). Again, the finding is in keeping with the view that the peer group exerts an influence – but the inference is very weak, both because the groups differed in family background characteristics and because it could be that a decision (for other reasons) to give up delinquent activities *led* to the youth leaving the peer group, rather than the other way round.

School: composition of pupil body

A somewhat stronger test is provided by *involuntary* changes in peer group which do not result from a personal choice. The change from primary school to secondary school approximates to that situation – or, at least, it does so in inner London, where children from the same primary school disperse to a large number of secondary schools and, similarly, each secondary school draws from a very large number of feeder primary schools (see Rutter *et al.*, 1979). The test of the differential association hypothesis is provided by the comparison of rates of delinquency (in boys comparable in other respects at the time of secondary transfer) according to whether boys went to schools with a high or low intake of behaviourally deviant pupils. The results of this comparison in the Rutter *et al.* (1979) study of 12 inner London secondary schools showed that delinquency rates were somewhat higher in schools with an intake including a high proportion of behaviourally deviant boys, but the association was much stronger with the characteristics of the intake on intellectual level and ethnic background. The finding that these 'balance of intake' measures were *not* significantly associated with teacher behaviour, or with the characteristics of the school as a social organization, allows the inference that the delinquent outcome was being influenced in some way by the characteristics of the peer group.

However, this is an inference based on circumstantial data, rather than a direct observation. Three limitations need particular emphasis. Firstly, the data available on family characteristics were quite limited and it is possible (although not likely) that the association was in reality due to differences in the family background of boys at 'high-risk' and 'low-risk' schools. Secondly, no measures on peer groups as such were obtained, so that it is not known with whom the delinquent boys *actually* associated (as distinct from being at the same school). Thirdly, the school effect was most marked with respect to the intellectual characteristics of the intake rather than to its behavioural features, so that uncertainty remains on the mechanisms involved. However, perhaps not too much should be made of the weaker associations with the boys' behaviour at 10, as the measure dealt with a wider range of deviant behaviour than that associated with delinquency and was not designed to predict delinquency.

West and Farrington (1973 – see also West, 1982) found much smaller school effects, but other studies (see Chapter 6) have found school differences as substantial as those in the Rutter *et al.* (1979) report. It seems probable from these findings that there *can* be a peer group influence which modifies the likelihood of a boy engaging in delinquent activities. However, more and better empirical data are required in order to investigate these hypothesized effects. In particular, future studies need to include more direct assessment of the peer group itself.

Parental supervision

The relatively strong and consistent associations between parental supervision and delinquency were discussed in Chapter 6. The precise mechanisms involved in the association are not adequately understood – and, in any case, are difficult to disentangle because efficient supervision tends to be associated with a variety of other aspects of 'good' parenting. However, it is worth noting in relation to possible peer group influences that one aspect of effective supervision seems to be the regulation of peer group activities. Thus, Gladstone (1980), in the Home Office study of vandalism in a northern city in England, found that vandalism was least likely when parents were successful in ensuring that the boys did not roam the streets at will and were not involved in a 'tough group'. Of those boys whose parents took a strict attitude to gang involvement and who were successful in restricting it, only 15 per cent were in the high-vandalism group, compared with 64 per cent of those whose parents took a lax attitude and who were associated with a tough group. Similarly, Wilson (1974 and 1980) found, in two separate studies, that parental supervision was the most powerful of all variables in accounting for children's delinquent activities (as measured by either self-report or convictions). Again, supervision was measured primarily in terms of the parents' regulation of peer group activities outside the home.

The data from these studies are cross-sectional, so that it is not possible to reject the possibility that poor supervision was simply the response of a despairing parent who had had to admit lack of control over an already delinquent child. However, closely similar results were obtained in West and Farrington's (1973) longitudinal study, in which the parental measures were obtained *before* the child became delinquent. Although it is true that they were not necessarily obtained before the child became troublesome in his behaviour (indeed in most cases troublesome behaviour *had* begun earlier), it seems likely (but not certain) that the parental supervision had truly influenced the child's behaviour.

School drop-out

Various studies have shown that pupils who drop out of school (Bachman *et al.*, 1978; Elliott and Voss, 1974), like those who truant frequently (Robins and Ratcliff, 1980b), are much more likely to be delinquent than young people who remain at school until completion of their education. However, as noted in Chapter 6, Elliott and Voss (1974) found that dropping out of school was nevertheless associated with a *reduction* in delinquent activities.

They suggested various reasons why this should occur – in terms of the effects of school failure. But their findings also indicated that self-report delinquency scores were lower if the drop-out obtained regular work and, even more so, if he married. Both findings suggest that the change of peer group may have played a part in the process. Bachman *et al.* (1978), in the *Youth in Transition* longitudinal study, did not analyse changes in delinquency levels according to *when* drop-out occurred. But they did report that the drop-out stood out as most different in terms of aggression and delinquency while still at school – differences being less in later years. These and other data (see, for example, McKissack, 1973) suggest that leaving school, if it associated with a move into regular employment, may be accompanied b a reduction in delinquent activities – possibly as a result of the change in peer group.

Moving away

As discussed earlier (see Chapter 6), there are substantial differences between different geographical areas in rates of delinquency. There are many possible explanations of why this should be so, but one concerns the effects of a delinquent peer group. This effect was examined by Buikhuisen and Hoekstra (1974), by taking a group of male offenders coming to the end of a term of imprisonment in a prison for juveniles. The group was subdivided into those who returned to their former address and those who moved to another neighbourhood. The re-conviction rate was significantly less in those who moved (60 per cent) than in those who returned (76 per cent). A more detailed analysis showed that the benefits of moving were greatest in the case of those who moved away from an unstable family and/or an asocial environment. Among those from a more favoured environment it made less difference whether or not they moved away.

A similar analysis was undertaken by West (1982), who showed that delinquents were more likely than non-delinquents to move house, and that recidivists were particularly frequent movers. Hence, as a general rule, changes of address were associated with an *increased* rate of delinquency. However, the reverse applied to those who moved away from inner London. For example, at 14 years only 5.4 per cent of those living outside London had been convicted during the preceding four years, compared with 11.7 per cent of those remaining in London. At 21 years the differential was just as great – 15.7 per cent *v.* 33.1 per cent. This clear and consistent trend held at all ages, and could not be accounted for by any tendency for the non-delinquents to be more likely to move out of London – rather, the reduced rate of convictions appeared to be a consequence rather than a cause of the moves. Nor could the difference be explained in terms of variations in police surveillance. There was a definite reduction in the mean rank* scores on self-reported delinquency among those who moved away from London (54.1 at 14 to 40.6 at 21), there being no such reduction in those who remained in London. However, in contrast to these striking and consistent findings on delinquent activities (whether assessed on self-report or convictions), the move away from London was *not* followed by any changes in many of the antisocial life variables (such as unemployment, aggressive attitudes or excessive drinking). The implication is that the youths had not changed in their basic life styles but that this was less likely to be associated with criminal acts – either because there had been a break-up of delinquent peer group associations or because there were fewer opportunities for crime outside London.

While the empirical evidence remains rather fragmentary and circumstantial, with the conclusions on mechanisms inferential, the consistent impression is that young people's delinquent activities are influenced by the social group in which they find themselves. The observation that this effect applies even when the change of social group was not brought about through the choice of the youth (such as in changes of school and of neighbourhood) provides strong support for the suggestion that the change of social group may *influence*, as well as be associated with, changes in behaviour. However, the analysis of the ways in which one event leads to another in a causal chain is a complicated procedure, full of methodological hazards. Lee Robins (Robins and Tarbleson, 1972; Robins and Wish, 1977; Robins *et al.*, 1979) has been foremost among social scientists in showing how a variety of statistical strategies may be employed to disentangle the succeeding stages in such a developmental process. So far these approaches have been employed largely to study the sequence by which one type of deviant act leads to another, but the same principles apply equally to the study of events or experiences that *disrupt* or change the course of a deviant sequence. This is a style of research that needs to be applied to the questions of possible 'protective' experiences which *reduce* the likelihood of delinquency in young people from a high-risk background. In that connection, the social group warrants special attention in terms of a factor much discussed in theoretical expositions (see Chapter 8) but rather neglected in empirical studies.

---

* Mean rank scores were used in preference to absolute levels in order to take account of age differences in the amount of delinquent activities.

Employment

The full meaning of the consistent associations between unemployment and delinquency is difficult to discern (see Wootton, 1959). On the one hand, unemployment is obviously a part of a delinquent life style. Thus individuals who have been delinquent from childhood, when followed into adult life, are much more likely than non-delinquents to have frequent periods of unemployment (see West and Farrington, 1977; West, 1982). In these cases the unemployment cannot possibly have caused delinquency, in that the delinquency long preceded entry into the workforce. Moreover, in part, the frequent periods of unemployment result from being given the sack, often for unsatisfactory behaviour at work (Davies, 1969). In addition, some of the association reflects the lack of education and lack of work skills of many delinquents. Thus, in the West and Farrington (1977) study, the recidivists were mainly found in those with jobs of the lowest social status. The relevance of this factor is that many low-status occupations (such as labourers on building sites) are particularly liable to involve periods of unemployment (see Rutter and Madge, 1976). Hence, in part, the association between unemployment and delinquency is a reflection of the prior association of both with unskilled labouring work.

But, of course, people in jobs of all levels and types can become unemployed for reasons quite beyond their control. That is especially the case now, in a period of high unemployment when people in all walks of life are experiencing redundancies and unemployment. The question which arises, then, is whether in these circumstances the experience of unemployment puts people at an increased risk of becoming delinquent, and whether the holding of a secure job is in any way protective.

The only really satisfactory way to answer that question would be through longitudinal analyses, in which delinquency measures were available for several points in time for otherwise comparable groups in which one experiences redundancy or involuntary unemployment whereas the other does not. So far as we are aware, such data have never been obtained and published. We recommend that they should be, as the issue of the effects of unemployment is such an important one.

In the meantime, a rather less satisfactory approach is provided by the longitudinal studies which look at the links between unemployment and delinquency – but without differentiating loss of jobs due to general changes in the job market.

As already noted, Elliott and Voss (1974) found that delinquency rates were slightly higher among male high-school drop-outs who were unemployed.

But in females, the reverse applied* – perhaps because the social world of the unemployed man is quite different from (and much more prone to provide opportunities for crime than) that of the housewife. But in that study it was not possible to relate *changes* in employment to changes in delinquent activities.

However, that was attempted in the Bachman *et al.* (1978) longitudinal study of some 2,000 adolescent boys in American high schools, studied in tenth, eleventh and twelfth grades and again one and five years beyond high school. Some subjects were lost during the study, but 74 per cent were still participating at the end of the eight years. Self-report delinquent measures were available for all five assessment occasions. It was found that unemployment and delinquency intercorrelated: those who were unemployed five years after high school were already more delinquent than average in tenth grade, but the differences between the unemployed and the employed tended to increase over time and were fairly substantial at the end of the study. Multivariate analyses controlling for the earlier delinquency measures showed a somewhat reduced relationship between employment and delinquency, but the presence of some association suggested that unemployment constituted an experience which somewhat increased aggression and delinquency. The effect was not a particularly powerful one, and the controls introduced by the multivariate analyses were less rigorous than desirable as a result of the rather low reliability (0.50 to 0.55) of the delinquency measures. Nevertheless, the findings suggest that employment and unemployment may constitute influences on young people's behaviour which serve to protect from or predispose towards delinquency. The matter needs to be studied further.

Marriage

As Knight *et al.* (1977) comment, criminologists have long speculated on the relationships between marriage and delinquency. However, two rather contrasting views have been put forward. On the one hand, *very early* marriage

* This observation needs to be replicated, with better controls for other factors, before much attention is paid to it. However, if confirmed, it would provide an interesting contrast to the situation with respect to adult depression (see Brown and Harris, 1978a), when employment seemed to serve a *protective* function in women with young children. It remains uncertain whether this came about through improved economic circumstances, the alleviation of boredom, an increase in social contacts, an enhanced sense of personal worth, or a variety of other mechanisms. But the observation emphasizes that the effects of employment need to be considered separately according to different outcomes and also according to the woman's circumstances at the time – for instance, whether or not she has young children at home.

may be associated with an *increased* rate of delinquency because the psychosocial adversities which predispose to delinquency also predispose to teenage marriages (see Hurwitz, 1952; Martin and Webster, 1971). On the other hand, it has also been suggested that stable, marriage-oriented relationships provide a strong influence towards conformity and law-abiding behaviour (Downes, 1966).

The Knight *et al.* (1977) analyses from the Cambridge Study of Delinquent Development were concerned with the effects of marriage under the age of 21. They found that youths with a marked antisocial life style (as shown by items such as heavy gambling, an unstable work record, and heavy drinking) were somewhat more likely than others to marry before 21. A more detailed item analysis showed that this association was largely explicable in terms of early extensive sexual experience. Among the men married before they were 21, there were 25 delinquents – these were matched, on an individual basis for age and convictions, with unmarried delinquents. The married men had a delinquency record during the two years following marriage which did not differ from that of the unmarried men during the same time period. It was concluded that marriage had no demonstrable general effect on criminality. Although getting married did not seem to reduce delinquency (as assessed on either self-reports or convictions), it was followed by a reduction in some of the social habits linked with delinquency (such as heavy drinking, prohibited drug use, time away from home), but not those most directly associated with criminality, such as aggressive behaviour, hostility to the police and unemployment. An analysis with the fathers showed that those who married women with a criminal record had a much worse criminal record after marriage than those who married non-delinquent women (an average of 3.9 further convictions versus 0.8), in spite of their premarital delinquent record being closely similar. Exact matching confirmed the reality of the difference.*

Findings from the *Youth in Transition* longitudinal study (Bachman *et al.*, 1978) showed that those who married early to become parents were more likely to have been unusually aggressive beforehand, but that 4–5 years after

* Other evidence suggests that this effect extends to a range of behaviours which have nothing to do with delinquency. That is, people tend to change their attitudes according to those of their associates, and marriage is no exception to this. Thus, for example, Newcomb *et al.* (1967) found that girls changed their attitudes to be in keeping with the prevailing ethos at the school they attended. Subsequently, they tended to choose as marriage partners men whose attitudes were similar to their own recently acquired views. But the few girls who married men whose attitudes differed from the school ethos tended to change their own views. The implication is that whether marriage serves to perpetuate delinquent activities or bring them to a stop will probably depend on *whom* a person marries. The important thing is not likely to be the marriage state *per se*, but rather the character of the social group and style of life associated with a particular marriage.

leaving school the difference in aggressivity had diminished. Single youths tended to increase their use of illicit drugs after leaving high school, but this increase was less marked among married youths. Unfortunately, the data were not analysed according to the timing of marriage. Nevertheless, the general pattern of results is in keeping with the view that youths with an antisocial life style are somewhat more likely than average to marry early, but that the experience of marriage has a longer-term effect in reducing some (but not other) features of their life style. As already noted, Elliott and Voss (1974) found that marriage in men was associated with decreased delinquency but in women with increased crime. Again, the findings were not analysed according to the date of marriage.

It would seem likely from this rather contradictory and inconclusive set of findings that it makes little sense to consider marriage as a unitary variable. Whether marriage increases or decreases delinquent tendencies may well be largely determined by what sort of change (if any) in social group and personal relationships it entails. This is suggested, for example, by Knight *et al.*'s (1977) major difference in outcome according to whether or not the spouse was also delinquent.

The findings from Rutter, Quinton and Liddle's (1983) follow-up of institution-reared women throws some light on these processes. Young people in children's homes (mostly for very prolonged periods) in middle and later childhood were followed up when they were aged 21–27. A comparable group of family-reared individuals from the same socially disadvantaged area of inner London were followed up and studied in the same way. As might be expected, the institution-reared men and women had a rate of criminality, social impairment and psychiatric disorder much above that in the control group. The institution-reared women were much more likely to have married or cohabited for a negative reason (that is, they stated that they married primarily to *get away* from a situation), to have had early and multiple cohabitations/marriages, to have a socially deviant or delinquent spouse, to have children early, and to have made a first cohabitation/marriage which ended in disruption. In these cases, the early marriage often served to perpetuate and intensify the young people's psycho-social problems. The finding parallels that from Quinton and Rutter's (1983a and b) retrospective study of mothers whose children had been taken into care as a result of serious family problems. These mothers were more likely than controls to have come from discordant unhappy homes, but also they were more likely to have made an early marriage in their teens to escape from their plight. Not surprisingly, these marriages made only as an attempted solution to childhood problems frequently proved unsatisfactory, and most failed.

Because the marriages tended to be made to socially deviant individuals from a similarly deprived background, these marriages tended to perpetuate and intensify their disadvantage, often with the additional burden of children born to immature teenagers living in unsatisfactory housing conditions. Whether a later marriage to a non-deviant partner would have a more beneficial effect remains to be seen, but the circumstantial evidence suggests that it may well do so. The effects of marriage need to be re-examined in terms of whether marriage results in an improvement or deterioration in the individual's psycho-social situation, and an increase or decrease in contact with delinquent individuals and/or crime opportunities.

Change of circumstances

The findings on the social group and on marriage both point to the possible importance of a change in social circumstances, with the implication that if a change for the better occurs, it may well bring benefits in terms of a reduction in delinquency. Other evidence is in keeping with that suggestion. For example, Rutter (1971) investigated children, all of whom had been separated from their parents as a result of family discord or family problems. Within this group of children, who had experienced severe early stresses, those who were still in homes characterized by discord and disharmony were compared with those who were now in harmonious happy homes. The results showed that conduct disorders were less frequent when discord had ceased. A change for the better in family circumstances was associated with a marked reduction in the risk of conduct disturbance. This was also shown more directly in the observation that whether or not disorders (not necessarily involving conduct problems) in the children of divorcing parents diminished was related to whether or not divorce improved family relationships (Hetherington, Cox and Cox, 1978; Wallerstein and Kelly, 1980). When the divorce brought harmony, the children's problems tended to improve, but when marital discord and/or parental difficulties continued, the children's disorders, too, tended to persist. This effect was also implied in the finding by Stewart *et al.* (1978) that unsocialized aggressive boys who had been admitted to a psychiatric in-patient unit were more likely to improve if, following discharge, they went to a situation which entailed the *loss* or *absence* of a deviant parent. This applied to 7 of the 14 who improved but to none of the 8 who did not (in 3 cases antisocial or alcoholic fathers had left home, in one case an antisocial mother left as a result of divorce, and 3 were in foster homes). The sample studied was small and the data on follow-up were not independent of the changes in the family (because most reliance was placed on parental reports), but the findings are suggestive, with the effect of loss of a deviant parent an issue worth further explanation. The same point emerged from the follow-up by Tonge *et al.* (1980) of multi-problem families and their adult offspring. It appeared that many of those who had improved in their functioning had benefited from the presence of a steady and supportive partner; and also that marital break-up had sometimes improved circumstances when it resulted in the loss from the home of a severely deviant member.

These findings refer to the effects of a change of circumstances on children already showing some form of conduct disturbance, but the same question arises in a similar way with respect to changes in the home environment at an earlier stage, when the home is characterized by adverse features known to be associated with delinquency. Certainly, there is evidence that major changes in the environment can lead to major effects* in terms of alterations in children's social behaviour (see Clarke and Clarke, 1976; Rutter, 1981a). While it may be supposed that these alterations are likely to carry implications for the risk of later delinquency, the matter has not been investigated specifically.

One good relationship

Most research into the effects of family discord has been solely concerned to determine the adverse sequelae. It has been noted that children vary greatly in their responses but, until recently, little attention has been paid to

* Adoption is the earliest and most radical of social changes in our society. It seems that the rates of delinquency and of conduct disturbance in children adopted in infancy is not much different from that in the general population (Bohman, 1978; Raynor, 1980; Seglow *et al.*, 1972), and rather better than that of children from a similar background who are fostered, reared in an institution or returned to their biological parents (Bohman and Sigvardsson, 1978 and 1980), as well as better than those reared by criminal or alcoholic parents (West and Farrington, 1973; Nylander, 1979; Rydelius, 1981) or raised as illegitimate children (Crellin *et al.*, 1971). Adoption later in childhood may also have important benefits (Tizard, 1977; Triseliotis, 1978 and 1980), although whether it is associated with a reduced rate of delinquency is more doubtful (Triseliotis, 1980). However, none of these studies was primarily designed to determine how far, and in what circumstances, adoption reduces the risk of delinquency for children from a high-risk family background. Such an investigation would be most worthwhile. The most rigorous test of the 'protective' effect of adoption would be provided by a comparison of the outcomes for adopted and non-adopted children of the same parents. That design would be difficult to obtain, but a near-enough approximation could be obtained by matching adopted and non-adopted children on the characteristics of their biological parents and then comparing the outcomes of the two groups in terms of delinquency and other features. Studies of adopted children often *imply* such a comparison, but appropriate matching (or the equivalent statistical controls) is essential if inferences are to be drawn on the supposed benefits of adoption.

the reasons for these individual differences. However, there are a few leads. It has been found that a good relationship with one parent serves to protect children brought up in an otherwise discordant, unhappy home. Children with one good relationship were less likely to develop conduct disorders than other children in similar homes whose relationships with both parents were poor. The few relevant findings from other studies are also consistent with the protective effect of a good relationship with a parental figure (Conway, 1957; Pringle and Bossio, 1960; Pringle and Clifford, 1964; Rutter, Quinton and Liddle, 1983; Wolkind, 1971). However, a recent prospective study of children's behaviour during the two years following parental divorce (Hetherington, Cox and Cox, 1979a and b) has indicated that the relationship must be both a particularly good one and also one with a parent currently living with the child in order for these to be a significant buffering effect. Robins *et al.* (1975) found that black children living in broken homes of low social status were less likely to drop out of school if brought up by grandparents. In these circumstances, the extended family appeared to provide continuity and support in an otherwise unstable situation. Werner and Smith (1981) also found that resilient children in the Kauai longitudinal study tended to have better sources of emotional support both within and outside the family.

Most of these studies have not been concerned with delinquency *per se*, and it would be premature to conclude that one good relationship could serve to protect children from criminality. The importance of the research lies less in the substantive findings (which are quite meagre on this point) than in the indication that it might be fruitful to consider the possible mitigating effect of good experiences and relationships as well as the deleterious effects of bad ones.

Compensatory 'good' experiences

That suggestion raises the questions both of whether good relationships outside the family can have a protective effect similar to that which apparently stems from those within the immediate family (no sound evidence is available on that question), and also whether '*good*' experiences can in any way counterbalance the ill-effects of '*bad*' experiences. Intuitively, it seems not unreasonable to suppose that a balance between pleasant and unpleasant events might be important in determining how people cope with stress (Lazarus *et al.*, 1980). However, there is very little empirical evidence on how far that is in fact the case.

Of course, as discussed in Chapter 6 and, with respect to peer group effects, earlier in this chapter, there is the evidence on the impact of schooling. It seems that some schools are more successful than others in helping children to function well both educationally and behaviourally (see Rutter, 1983), and that children from disadvantaged and discordant homes are less likely to show disruptive behaviour if they attend better-functioning schools. *Perhaps*, to a limited extent, good experiences at school can mitigate stressful experiences within the home (Rutter, 1979b). But that remains an indirect inference which has still to be tested directly.

Even if it proves to be the case, questions will remain on the mechanisms involved. As already noted, some aspect of the peer group appeared to be most important with respect to school differences on rates of delinquency. However, in the case of disruptive behaviour in the classroom other school factors seemed more influential. These included appropriately high expectations, good group management, effective feedback to the children with ample use of praise, the setting of good models of behaviour by the teachers, pleasant working conditions, and giving pupils positions of trust and responsibility (Rutter *et al.*, 1979). If experiences at school are actually protective, several possibilities on mechanisms need to be considered. Firstly, it could be that, to some extent, good experiences in one setting can 'make up for' bad ones in other settings – the notion that it is the *balance* between positive and negative that matters.

Alternatively, it may be that the protection comes through a sense of achievement and high self-esteem. In the Rutter *et al.* (1975a and c) epidemiological study of 10 year old children in inner London, measures were obtained on children's behaviour at school (from a teacher questionnaire), on scholastic attainment (by group test), and on family functioning (by parental interview). The findings showed that the rate of behavioural disorder among children from seriously deprived or disadvantaged homes was considerably less if they had above average attainment than if their attainments were average or below average (Rutter, 1979b). Of course, the results do not necessarily mean that the protective effect is mediated through high self-esteem. It could be simply that intellectually able children are constitutionally more resilient – or that the ways in which children are treated by their teachers varies according to their attainments. Nevertheless, further investigations to determine the importance (or otherwise) of a sense of personal worth could be informative.

Thirdly, it is possible that the key factor concerns the opening up of opportunities. Anecdotal evidence suggests that many people who have made the best ultimate adjustment in spite of seriously adverse experiences are those who managed to avoid becoming pregnant or fathering a child during their teens, who continued longer in education, whose careers took them away from their disadvantaged circumstances, and who married someone from a more favoured background. As Tonge *et al.* (1980) observed in their follow-up of a small group of multi-problem families in Sheffield, the majority of individuals in the second generation who were socially successful had become so at the expense of family contact – in terms of either dropping kin ties or maintaining an emotional distance. The same applied with the young man in the West (1982) study quoted above. So far this process remains little investigated.

Coping mechanisms

In recent years, psycho-social researchers have increasingly come to see the process of *coping* as the key to an understanding of stress reactions (see Murphy and Moriarty, 1976; Coelho *et al.*, 1974; Antonovsky, 1979; Lazarus and Launier, 1978). In this context, coping is usually meant to include both the individual's attempts directly to alter the threatening conditions themselves, and his attempts to change his appraisal of them so that he need not feel threatened. In other words, coping must have the dual function of social problem-solving and a regulation of emotional distress; the means of meeting these objectives may involve either a manipulation of the environment or intra-psychic processes or both. Nearly all the research on coping with stress has been undertaken with adults, and scarcely any has been concerned with delinquent behaviour. Moreover, there are numerous conceptual and methodological problems that are inherent in the study of coping (see Cohen and Lazarus, 1979; Rutter, 1981e). Nevertheless, there is a growing body of research into social problem-solving in childhood (see Urbain and Kendall, 1980; Shure and Spivack, 1978; Spivack *et al.*, 1976). The evidence shows some association between poor problem-solving and conduct disorders in childhood; and evaluation studies have indicated that children and parents can be helped to improve their social problem-solving skills. There is some indication that this may be associated with concomitant benefits in other aspects of behavioural functioning, but evidence is weakest on this point and on the generalization and persistence of any gains obtained. Too little is known as yet for any claims to be made regarding the role of coping mechanisms or of their possible protective effects. But further explanation of the issues seems likely to be useful.

Interactive effects

The last issue* to discuss with regard to protective factors is the question of possible *interactive* effects. This issue arises in several different ways. For example, Rutter *et al.* (1975c), in their epidemiological study of 10 year olds in inner London, identified six family variables (severe marital discord, low social status, overcrowding or large family size, paternal criminality, maternal psychiatric disorder, and admission into the care of the local authority – see Rutter and Quinton, 1977), which were strongly and significantly associated with disorder (mainly conduct disorder) in the child. One very striking finding was that no one of these factors was associated with disorder when it occurred in the absence of all the others – the presence of one adverse factor was associated with a risk no higher than that for children without any adversities. However, when any two stresses occurred together the risk went up *four*-fold. With three and four concurrent stresses the risk went up several times further still. It seemed that there was an *interactive* effect such that the risk which attended several concurrent stressors was much greater than the sum of the effects of the stressors considered individually.†

The fact that, in some circumstances, the presence of one adversity or stressor may *potentiate* the damage caused by another has been noted in a number of different studies. For example, it was found that children from a chronically deprived home background were more likely to be adversely affected by recurrent admission to hospital (Quinton and Rutter, 1976). The same applies to the interaction of biological and social factors. Thus, over a decade ago, Drillien (1964) noticed that the effect of low birthweight on intelligence was most marked in children who also had the added disadvantage of poor social circumstances. Sameroff and Chandler (1975) have emphasized the same *interactive* effect with more recent data. This was also

---

* In terms of variables accounting for individual differences in children's responses to adverse experiences, there is also the major topic of factors in the child. These are not considered in this chapter, in that the focus is on modifiable features. But it should be noted that research has clearly shown the importance of variables such as age, sex, genetic background, and temperament (see Rutter, 1981e).

† This issue was also examined in the National Child Development Study with the claim that the results showed *no* interaction effect (Essen and Wedge, 1980). Unfortunately, the statistical analysis which was employed did not test the notion of interaction as used here. The crucial point is that the demonstration that a variable has a significant main effect is *not* the same as showing that a variable has a significant effect in the absence of all other variables (see Brown and Harris, 1978b, and Rutter, 1979b). It needs to be appreciated that there is more than one type of statistical model for interactions (see Everitt and Smith, 1979).

shown in the follow-up study of Kauai children (Werner *et al.*, 1971; Werner and Smith, 1977).

In these connections there is the important possibility that, in some cases, variables may be largely inert on their own but nevertheless serve as *catalysts* when combined with stressors of some kind – to use a chemical analogy. That is, there may be factors which have little effect in the absence of stressors but which, in their presence, serve to increase or decrease the adverse effects. A number of studies have suggested that something of this kind occurs with the presence of good personal relationships and effective social supports and kinship ties (see Rutter, 1981e). Again, these studies have not been concerned with either children or delinquency, but the mechanisms are ones that could well apply to the processes involved in those cases in which criminality arises in response to personal adversities or stresses of one type or another.

Conclusions

It has been necessary to consider research outside, as well as inside, the field of delinquency in order to examine the possible operation of protective factors – meaning those that *reduce* the risk of delinquency in children from a high-risk background. Nevertheless, even with delinquency, there are pointers to the possible importance of the peer group, of employment and of marriage. Other investigations have suggested the potential value of looking at the effects of changed environmental circumstances, of the mitigating effect of one good relationship, of compensatory good experiences, of coping mechanisms and of interactive effects. Research into these issues has scarcely begun, but the very limited findings so far suggest that the topic of protective factors may turn out to be an important one.

8
Theories and Explanations

For several decades, starting in the 1930s, the study of crime gave rise to a rich body of theorizing. Psychologists sought to explain individual differences in predisposition to crime in terms of both personality factors and family influences; and sociologists sought to relate social group differences in delinquent activities to theories of society and of the social origins of human behaviour. However, during the last fifteen years or so there have been only a few major advances in theories on the causation of delinquency, and interest in the major theories which used to dominate the field has gradually declined (see Gibbs and Erickson, 1975; Elliott, Ageton and Canter, 1979). It is not that they have been disproven, but rather that the *origins* of crime have ceased to be the predominant concern; instead the interest has shifted to *reactions* to deviance, the processing of delinquents, the operation of the law and, especially, to socio-political issues.

Concepts and issues

At the same time as these developments in the sociology of deviance, there has also been a move away from the monolithic grand theories which attempted to account for the entire range of delinquent behaviours in terms of some single unifying causal process. Rather than search for this 'criminologist's stone' (see Walker, 1977), there has come to be a general acceptance of the need for multifactorial explanations (see Hirschi and Selvin, 1967; Elliott *et al.*, 1979; Bahr, 1979; Feldman, 1977; West, 1967; Johnson, 1979). However, this type of modern eclecticism has also been criticized, on the grounds that it is so flexible and complex that it gives rise to no practical implications of any help whatsoever (Wilkins, 1964), and that it serves as a way of avoiding the implications of negative evidence (Matza, 1964). It is said that if crime can be due to A, and/or B, and/or C, *ad infinitum*, then whenever evidence is produced against any one cause, there can always be recourse to one of the others. Actually, as Walker (1977) notes, that is not a fair criticism of eclecticism so long as (i) the eclectic's list of possible causes is a finite one, and (ii) every one of his named possibilities is capable of being falsified empirically. Whether or not a multi-causal theory is *useful* with respect to policy implications is another matter. Up to now they have not been particularly useful, but in part this has been because most of the hypothesized causal processes have been expressed in rather general terms and because there has been a lack of specificity regarding the circumstances in which any particular mechanism is thought to operate (Walker, 1977).

Walker (1977) has gone further still in suggesting that any kind of scientific explanation may be inappropriate for much that we seek to understand in the field of human behaviour. He notes that scientific explanations rely on generalizations taking the form of 'laws' which specify the *mechanisms* involved. It is that specification which gives science its predictive power. But the social sciences have had great difficulty in going beyond 'as if' analogies to precise mechanisms of causation. While not arguing for a complete abandonment of the scientific approach, Walker urges that at least some of its territory should be taken over by what he calls 'narrative explanations'. By these he means accounts of how something *might* have happened, of why something is *not impossible*. His criticisms of scientific explanations have force but, as he recognizes, the 'narrative' alternative means a rejection of the idea that there can ever be a reduction of law-breaking through any intervention designed to affect any stage of the possible causal processes involved. We return later to how far that degree of pessimism is justified.

A further limitation of most criminological theories, as with most theories of development generally (Rutter, 1980b), is that they do not start with the empirical findings which require explanation. They have not been proposed with that purpose primarily in mind; instead they express a view about society and about human behaviour which is then extended to criminality. Accordingly, their main limitation is not that they are completely wrong in what they suggest. On the contrary, many provide convincing partial explanations for some phenomena (although not others). The limitations lie in their failure to deal with (or often even to notice) some of the most striking empirical findings that need to be taken into account. For example, few focus on the markedly higher rate of delinquent activities in males, or the fact that about half of juvenile delinquents never return to court again, or the major diminution in antisocial behaviour in early adult life, or the associations between cognitive performance and disturbances of conduct, or the situational variations in delinquent behaviour, or the marked rise in the crime rate over the last half-century.

These (and other) omissions need to be borne in mind as we review some of the leading theoretical approaches. However, this list of empirical observations highlights another difference – that is, that there are several quite different kinds of causal questions and explanations (see Rutter and Madge, 1976; Rutter, 1979a). For example, psychological theories have mainly focused on the 'who' question – that is, why *this* person is delinquent and *that* person is not. Traditional sociological theories have tended to deal with a somewhat different form of 'who' question – namely, why the *rate* of delinquency in one social group differs from that in another. More recent sociological theories have taken yet another perspective on the 'who' question – that is, why some individuals are treated or *processed* as social deviants whereas others are not. But causal questions need not be concerned with 'who' at all. For example, the fact of situational variations forces one to ask 'when' and 'where' questions, not why is X delinquent rather than Y, but why do X and Y behave in delinquent ways in *these* circumstances but yet not in *those*? Similarly, the changing rates of crime over time pose the 'how many' question – that is, why are delinquent activities more common *now* than they were at some times in the past? It is obvious that the causal mechanisms may be quite different in these varied types of causal questions. It is *not* that one type of question is more important than the others. They are complementary to each other and, if we are to have an adequate understanding of how delinquent activities arise, we shall need to seek answers to them all.

A further point which requires emphasis is that, even with a narrowly expressed version of any one specific type of causal question, it would be futile to expect to find a 'basic' cause. Instead we are forced to consider causal *processes* or causal chains. Suppose, for the sake of illustrating the point, that it could be shown that one cause of delinquency was lack of parental supervision. We would still need to ask why it occurred with this son but not that one, or his sister. Moreover, there would have to be the further question of why the parents failed to provide adequate supervision. Perhaps the answer might lie in their poor living conditions. But then again, one has to ask why were they in poor housing? Perhaps because of a combination of a poor record of employment and the existing governmental housing policy. Are these then the basic causes? Obviously not. At each further stage it will be necessary to ask why that circumstance arose. Moreover, it should not be assumed that the most effective intervention will be that which tackles the most basic cause. Rather, the efficacy will depend on the stage at which interventions are most likely to result in change, as well as the stage at which they can influence most people. Of course, too, it should not be assumed that the factors which cause delinquent activities to *begin* are the same factors which cause them to *continue*. The disparate effects of social factors at different stages in the causal process were well illustrated in the analysis by Robins *et al.* (1977) of stages in the progression to narcotic addiction – the same is likely to apply with other forms of behaviour.

In turning now to a consideration of particular theories of crime, we have not attempted an exhaustive or comprehensive account of current theoretical work.* Not only are there many theories, but also each has several variations. There would be no useful purpose served in trying to cover them all. Instead, we have chosen to comment rather briefly on a dozen or so approaches that illustrate the current schools of thought which underpin much empirical criminological research and which have relevance to discussions of practice and policy.

Anomie/strain theories

Merton (1938 and 1957) has been the most influential 'strain' theorist, with his general explanation of deviant behaviour based on Durkheim's concept of anomie. In essence, the basic premise is that delinquent behaviour is the result of socially induced pressures and, in particular, that it results from the 'strain' caused by the gap, or anomic disjuncture, between cultural goals and the means available for achievement of those goals. Young people in the lower social strata experience frustrations from the lack of opportunity to participate in the rewards of economic success (Merton, 1957), or from the lack of ability to acquire social status and prestige (Cohen, 1956). Merton noted that a person may react to this strain by rejecting the cultural goals or the legitimate means ('ritualism' or 'retreatism'), by using illegitimate means to reach the goals ('innovation'), or by substituting a new set of goals and means ('rebellism'). The two conditions in society thought to create anomie were (i) greater emphasis on certain success goals than on the means to reach them, and (ii) restriction in certain social groups of the legitimate means of achieving success. It is clear that anomie is a class-based theory which assumes that most delinquent behaviour is concentrated in the lower social classes.

Accordingly, the major piece of disconfirming evidence is the inconsistent, and often weak, associations between social class and criminal behaviour (see Chapter 4). In addition, high aspirations in working-class youths have not been found to be related to delinquency (see Hirschi, 1969; Elliott and Voss, 1974; and Short, 1964 for evidence from studies with empirical data

---

* See Feldman, 1977; Glaser, 1979; Kornhauser, 1978; and Trasler, 1973, for fuller descriptions.

on this point). On a more theoretical level, the theory fails to explain why one type of adaptation to strain occurs rather than another (for example, innovation rather than retreatism), or why some individuals under strain conform while others deviate; and it has been criticized for being too general and for its concept of deviance as an outcome rather than a process (see Bahr, 1979). Also, the fact that most delinquent boys eventually become law-abiding adults constitutes a major source of difficulty for strain theories, as the conditions in the model do not change during adolescence or on attainment of adulthood (Hirschi, 1969).

It is evident that, in its original form, anomie is untenable as a general theory of delinquency. However, several variations have been put forward, the two most important of which are Cloward and Ohlin's (1960) attempted integration of Merton's concept of anomie with Sutherland's (1939) theory of differential association, and Cohen's (1956) postulation of the importance of denial of status as a factor in the development of delinquent gangs. The particular contribution of Cloward and Ohlin was their attempt to explain why strain results in one form of deviance rather than another, the suggestion being that the particular adaptation will depend on the availability of illegitimate means and the opportunities for learning deviant roles. These ideas have been tested most systematically by Elliott and Voss (1974), who confirmed the importance of association with delinquent friends (see below) and of the link with educational retardation, but found only very weak relationships with perceived failure to achieve the culturally defined goals or with aspirations or attributions of blame.

Cohen (1956) differed in his emphasis on the importance of the immediate goal of status and respect in the eyes of one's peers rather than the long-term goals of economic success. He suggested that the standards of school are middle-class standards, and that children who cannot achieve in school may react not only against the cultural standards emphasizing academic achievement but also against those which demand a respect for property. This change of norms is often accompanied by ambivalence with the consequence of an exaggerated and disproportionate response – hence the delinquency. Once again, in so far as the denial of status is seen as a characteristic of the working classes, the theory fails to account for middle-class delinquency. Moreover, it is not at all clear from the theory why the delinquent response should mainly take the form of theft (the theory is primarily concerned with destructive behaviour, which constitutes a minority of delinquent acts), or why most of the delinquency should occur outside school when the denial of status is within it. Moreover, it is doubtful whether many delinquents hold overtly oppositional views or feel frustrated (see, for example, Downes, 1966;

Willmott, 1966; Hirschi, 1969; Matza, 1964), and, of course, most delinquency does not take place within organized delinquent gangs (the subject matter of Cohen's theorizing).

The strength of these developments of the anomie theory lies in their emphasis on the known association between educational failure and delinquency, and on their recognition that much juvenile delinquency occurs within the context of the peer group. It seems likely that the theories are wrong in their detailed postulates of the mechanisms involved, and in their emphasis on the social structure of society; also, the original notion of strain has not been empirically supported. On the other hand, it remains possible that concepts of the effects of lack of status (at an individual rather than society level) and of the problems that stem from educational failure may still have some validity.

Sub-cultural approaches

The sub-cultural approach has in common with the anomic theories an assumption that delinquency is concentrated in lower-working-class groups, but it differs in that it postulates neither strains nor frustrations. Rather, it suggests that delinquency is simply 'normal' behaviour for the particular sub-culture and hence that it is learned in the same way as any form of social behaviour (Mays, 1954, 1972; Willmott, 1966; Downes, 1966). The major contribution of this approach has been the recognition that some forms of (at least minor) delinquent behaviour constitute an accepted part of the social activities of adolescents. These vary somewhat according to social group, but clearly there are illegal acts which are not subject to severe social disapproval in the groups in which they are common (for example, scrumping, breaking windows in unoccupied buildings, writing on walls, pinching off the backs of lorries, not paying full fare on public transport, etc.). The self-report studies (see Chapter 1) confirm the high frequency of such acts; also in keeping with the 'normal sub-culture' view is the consistent evidence that in most cases delinquency does not persist after adolescence and that many delinquents, especially minor first-time offenders, do not show any general disturbance of behaviour, emotions or relationships. In these cases, it seems reasonable to consider the development of delinquent activities in the same way as any other form of social behaviour, without the need to postulate that delinquents constitute a different or special group in any sense.

But these conclusions apply to minor delinquent acts in all social groups, and the same self-report studies indicate that these more everyday delinquencies do *not* show any substantial social class differential. Moreover, even within a working-class culture, recidivist delinquents *do* stand out as different from their peers in a host of ways (see Chapter 1). Furthermore, those studies which have examined the matter have found general maladjustment to be as common in delinquents from a deprived background as in those from middle-class homes (Stott, 1960, 1966; Conger and Miller, 1966; West and Farrington, 1973; Roff *et al.*, 1972); and the factors that predict outcome in one social group predict similarly in others (see, for example, Robins, 1978).

The consistent evidence that the *victims* of most crime in high-delinquency socially disadvantaged areas are other poor people (see Empey, 1978), and that slum-dwellers are as condemnatory of most delinquent acts as anyone else (see studies reviewed by Kornhauser, 1978, p. 218) runs completely counter to sub-cultural theory as a general explanation of crime. As Kornhauser (1978) comments: 'The belief that powerless people will endorse in their subcultures actions by which they are grievously injured is unreasonable ... No *group* of people will construct a culture or a subculture that makes their own lives impossible ... That is why the search for subcultures that differ markedly in their orientation to crime is doomed to failure' (p. 218).

While the evidence is more meagre than one would wish, it may be concluded that it is probable that in all social groups there are types of petty theft and vandalism which are so common and so lightly regarded that they may be considered 'normal'. But this phenomenon applies in all strata of society (and not, as usually postulated, just in working-class groups). Also, it is unlikely that a 'normal sub-culture' type of explanation accounts for more than a minority of cases of recidivist delinquency in any social group.

Differential association

Sutherland's (1939) theory of differential association has as its main propositions: (i) criminal behaviour, like any other behaviour, is learned; (ii) learning is determined through the process of association with those who commit crimes; (iii) *differential* association is the specific causal process; (iv) roughly speaking, the changes of criminality are determined by the frequency and consistency of a person's contacts with patterns of criminal behaviour; (v) the nature of these associations are such as to favour violations of the law rather than conformity to it; (vi) individual differences are important only through their influence on differential association; and (vii) cultural conflict is the underlying cause of differential association (Sutherland and Cressey, 1970). As Cressey (1964) pointed out, the major problem lies in defining what sort of associations favour violations of the law.

There are many observations which are consistent with the general notion that mixing with delinquents makes it more likely that you yourself will become delinquent. Most delinquent acts are committed in the company of other children; delinquency is as strongly associated with delinquency in a person's brothers and sisters as with crime in the parents (see, for example, Farrington *et al.*, 1975; Robins *et al.*, 1975); young people living in a high-delinquency area or attending a high-delinquency school are more likely to become delinquent than similar children living in other areas or attending other schools (see Chapter 6); boys who claim delinquents as friends are more likely to admit delinquent behaviour than boys who say their friends are not delinquent (Voss, 1963; Johnson, 1979); the probability of a boy committing a specific delinquent act has been found to be statistically dependent upon the commission of similar acts by other members of his friendship group (Reiss and Rhodes, 1964); and the number of delinquent acts committed by a boy's friends and acquaintances are predictive of his own future convictions (West and Farrington, 1973).

But none of these findings clearly differentiate between a differential association effect and the possibility that it is just that youngsters prone to delinquency seek out like-minded friends (Glueck and Glueck, 1950; Robins and Hill, 1966), or that groups of friends are all subject to some other criminogenic influence. However, the evidence (discussed in Chapter 7) that a *change* of peer group is associated with a *change* in the likelihood of delinquent activities provides strong support for the idea that differential associations do have an effect.

As Bahr (1979) notes, if differential association is to provide a *sufficient* explanation, two further propositions must be met. Firstly, the correlations between family variables (such as parental supervision) and criminality should be negligible once controls for criminal associations have been introduced. Secondly, the correlations between criminal associations and rate of delinquency should be maintained after controlling for family variables (although the correlation might be expected to decrease as the orientation of the family becomes more law-abiding). Both Stanfield (1966) and Jensen (1972) found that parental discipline and supervision continued to show significant associations with delinquency irrespective of peer group contacts – findings contrary to the first proposition. On the other hand, the second proposition has been supported by most studies (see Chapter 7). Liska (1969), using research on attitude formation and change, suggested that the differential association effect is most likely to apply when attitudes are not yet well formed or when social interaction is restricted, but that when neither of these apply the effect is more likely to operate in the opposite direction (i.e. delinquent behaviour determines delinquent associations).

The evidence indicates that differential associations with criminal patterns do influence the development of delinquent activities, but that they interact with family variables, and that family variables also have an independent direct influence of their own.

Social control theories

Whereas differential association theory seeks to explain why some people *do* commit delinquent acts, social control theories start from the opposite position. In social control theory there is the assumption that *everyone* has a predisposition to commit delinquent acts, there is no need for special motivational postulates, and the issue is how people learn *not* to offend (Hirschi, 1969). In contrast to the cultural deviance (i.e. sub-cultural and differential association) theories discussed above, the question is why people violate the rules in which they believe, and *not* why people differ in their beliefs about what is acceptable conduct. It is argued that although there are direct social controls (as through external restriction and punishments), indirect and internalized controls based on affectional identification with parents are the most crucial (Nye, 1958). According to Hirschi (1969), delinquent acts result when an individual's bond to society is weak or broken. The key elements in that bond are provided by *attachment* to other people, *commitment* to an organized society, *involvement* in conventional activities, and *belief* in a common value system.

These ideas were tested by Hirschi (1969) in a questionnaire study of some 4,000 high-school students in California. The results showed that self-reported delinquency was associated with lack of attachment to parents, as assessed by measures of intimacy of communication, affectional identification and closeness of mother's supervision; and that this relationship held across social classes. But it did *not* hold when the father had a history of welfare or unemployment. The results also showed that the presence of delinquent friends was strongly associated with delinquency, irrespective of levels of attachment to parents; that delinquency was associated with poor scholastic performance and with *low* aspirations; that delinquency was more likely to occur when there were *weak* attachments to friends; but also that delinquency was associated with involvement in peer group activities such as riding around in cars, as well as with lack of involvement with homework; and that delinquency was more frequent in boys who expressed a lack of respect for the police and a view that it was all right to get around the law if you could get away with it. While the study has all the limitations of reliance on cross-sectional questionnaire data, with data missing on over a quarter of the sample, it constitutes one of the best thought out attempts to test empirically the contrasting predictions of social control, social strain and cultural deviance theories. The results provide support for all the main social control postulates regarding the importance of attachment, commitment, involvement and belief. The finding that attachment to peers was associated with a *decreased* risk of delinquency was especially striking, but it was not confirmed in Hindelang's (1973) replication, which otherwise gave closely similar findings. The results of other studies, too, have been broadly comparable (see Bahr, 1979). But as Hirschi (1969) noted, the finding that associations with delinquent peers were important, even after controlling for parental attachment, is inconsistent with the theory.

Although not discussed by him in this connection, the consistent finding of the importance of parental criminality (see Chapter 6) is also inconsistent. Hirschi (1969) suggested that the theory must be modified to include some notion of the effect of peer group processes, and possibly the importance of delinquency in contributing to an adolescent's self-esteem (as suggested by the potency of adult-status items such as smoking, drinking, dating and driving a car). Elliott, Ageton and Canter (1979) concurred in this view, noting that one of the major weaknesses of social control theories has been the fact that weak bonds and lack of restraints cannot alone account for the specific form or content of the behaviour which results. It is necessary to add on the concept that delinquent activities have a social meaning which is rewarded in some way by the social groups in which it occurs – and it is within that framework that they propose an integrated model that synthesizes strain, social learning and social control perspectives. Their model is broadly in keeping with the empirical findings, but, as they recognize, its complexity and all-inclusiveness make it difficult to test or falsify. Johnson (1979) has also attempted another eclectic synthesis of sociological theories – again on the basis of a self-report delinquency study. The findings suggest that the key influences are delinquent associates, delinquent values, school experiences and parent–child relationships. The statistical technique of causal path analysis was used to determine how these variables interacted to form a causal process leading to delinquency. The model has the same strengths as that of Elliott *et al.* (1979), but would be equally difficult to test.

Social learning theories

Unlike the theories considered up to this point, social learning theories do not postulate a single mechanism for the origins of delinquent activities. Many include concepts of a biologically influenced individual predisposition and of social reaction, although they differ in the weight attached to these additional notions. Eysenck (1977), for example, lays a great deal of emphasis on genetically determined personality attributes, whereas Feldman (1977) suggests a lesser contribution except in the case of more extreme criminality. What the learning theories have in common is a view that, essentially, delinquent activities are not different in kind from other forms of behaviour, and that learning variables exert a major influence on the acquisition, performance and maintenance of criminal behaviour (see Feldman, 1977, for a good account of this approach to criminality, and Cairns, 1979, for a thoughtful appraisal of social learning approaches to social development as a whole). The hypothesized learning process involves both learning *not* to offend (as a result of training in socially acceptable behaviours, maintained by negative consequences for infractions and positive consequences for rule-keeping); and also learning *to* offend (maintained by intermittent positive consequences for offending). Obviously the central concept here is that behaviour is maintained or inhibited by its consequences. It is also suggested by some theorists (for example, Feldman, 1977) that cognitive processes are relevant in the maintenance or change of behaviour. These may involve, for example, the establishment of a self-reinforcement system for delinquent activities (as with a sense of pride in criminal skills); and the development of a denial or distortion of perceptions of the effects on the victim ('he's a mug anyway' or 'he's covered by insurance' or 'he deserved it') in order to justify the criminal acts and to reduce guilt or distress regarding the victims of offences. Social learning theories also differ from other theories in their concern with situational variables and the factors which determine that delinquent activities occur in these circumstances but not those.

Because learning theory approaches are so broad and complex in their implications, they are difficult to test in their totality. Certainly there is an abundance of evidence that, like any behaviour, both antisocial and pro-social activities are strongly influenced by learning experiences. Hence, the importance of social learning can scarcely be in doubt. Moreover, it has the great merit of tackling the question of situational factors in crime, an issue largely ignored by most other theories. Nevertheless, while the social learning approach has considerable general validity (and practical utility) in terms of its accounting for variations in social performance, it also has important limitations. Thus, it includes so many different concepts that it is virtually impossible to falsify,* it avoids the problem of sex differences, it rather overlooks age changes and developmental factors, and it lacks specificity on just *how* antisocial behaviour is acquired and why there are such marked individual differences in behaviour (Cairns, 1979). Furthermore, there are many unresolved problems – for example, in accounting for the observation that punishment is less effective with antisocial children and may actually *increase* their antisocial behaviours; that *excessive* punishment seems to be a feature of the families of aggressive children but that a lack of discipline is more often a feature of the families of thieves (although some are very punitive); that coercive interchanges tend to be longer in the families of aggressive children; and that antisocial behaviour diminishes so markedly in early adult life (see Patterson, 1976, 1979, 1981a, 1982 – also Chapter 6).

A microsocial approach to coercive family processes

Most of the research into social learning has been in the form of laboratory experiments designed to test the effects of one or other type of learning – modelling, external reinforcement, self-reinforcement, etc. The findings are consistent in confirming the operation of these learning processes. But the application of these results to concepts of the ways in which delinquent behaviour develops in real life is seriously limited by lack of detailed knowledge on what learning *actually* takes place in the families of delinquent youths. As Patterson (1979) put it:

> Given the current commitment to laboratory analogue studies ... it is entirely possible that field studies will show that the findings are irrelevant for many settings ... [it may be that] ... positive reinforcers are simply not dispensed contingent upon children's aggressive behaviors or aggressive behaviors modeled in complex social situations may not be attended to and therefore have little impact ... For final status within a theory, a variable, like a successful debutante, must put in an appearance in the real world of social interaction.

---

* This problem is particularly acute in the case of the notion of 'reinforcement', which, as Bricker and Bricker (1974) point out, is a circular or tautological concept, in that it cannot be defined in terms that are independent of its effects. This means that, for example, if it is found that punishment *increases* delinquent activities in some children, then it has to be assumed that in these cases punishment is reinforcing (or 'rewarding'), regardless of any general views to the contrary. The point is that positive reinforcement is defined in terms of its effect in increasing the likelihood that a behaviour will continue and *not* in terms of its affective or pleasurable quality.

It was in response to this need that over the last decade or so, Patterson and his colleagues at the Oregon Social Learning Center have been engaged in a programme of detailed microsocial analyses of sequences of observed natural family interactions in the home. The result has been what Patterson (1976, 1979, 1981a, 1982) has called a 'performance theory' of coercive family processes. In keeping with other social learning approaches, Patterson's views do not involve a single basic mechanism. But the most important aspects of his approach are the careful moment by moment analysis of how parental discipline *actually* operates in the families of aggressive and delinquent children, and his linking of these molecular analyses with more molar aspects of family functioning. One of the outstanding paradoxes in previous research has been the observation that the parents of aggressive children tend to punish deviant behaviour *more* than the parents of normal children, yet, far from suppressing aggression, this has seemed to encourage it. The findings from the Oregon group suggest that this is because of two separate features of family functioning. The parents of aggressive children provide an inadequate and ineffective set of conditions for the learning of prosocial and the avoidance of antisocial behaviours because: there is a lack of a clear set of household rules; a lack of adequate monitoring of the children's behaviour and activities; a lack of clear labelling of events as deviant or non-deviant; a lack of effective contingencies (with no adequate differentiation between parental responses to desired and to undesired behaviours by the child); a lack of encouragement and warm interest in the child, a lack of effective problem-solving, and a failure to 'follow-through' on discipline. The result is a chaotic and confusing set of messages which provide no unambiguous guidance to the child on how he is expected to behave.

But at the same time this is accompanied by frequent coercive interchanges, frequent punishment and a lack of pleasurable family interactions. The last feature was illustrated by Patterson's (1981a, 1982) observation that the families of antisocial children rarely engaged in prolonged 'how-was-your-day?' type interchanges during which children received *non*-critical parental attention and interest, with a discussion that provided ample opportunities both for explicit 'that's good' statements, and for an exchange of information which might serve to shape the child's values and interests. Similarly, as noted in a host of other studies, there was a lack of shared parent–child leisure activities. It was hypothesized that the reinforcing value of parents is enhanced by the amount of pleasurable activities shared, and hence that parental influences are thereby *reduced* in families of aggressive children.

The negative features are summarized in what might be characterized as an 'affect theory of nattering', put forward to explain the empirical finding that, in the families of aggressive children, coercive interchanges tend to be more prolonged, more likely to involve multiple family members, less likely to lead to resolution, and less likely to stop deviant behaviour than in the families of normal children (see Patterson, 1976, 1979, 1981a, 1982). It is hypothesized that the key eliciting stimulus for these coercive interchanges is *irritation* or anger, rather than some disapproved behaviour as such. In response to this feeling of irritation, the parent natters, issues commands, provides a litany of yesterday's sins and omissions, tacks on further aversive comments ('damn it, you never do what I tell you to, now get in here!'). What is communicated to the child is anger and impatience rather than a request to behave in some different way. In turn, he responds with further hostility and so the process escalates. Because these interchanges are primarily conveyors of *affective* information, and because positive and negative parental responses are used in a non-contingent fashion with respect to the key deviant behaviours, the effect is not most appropriately interpreted in reinforcement terms.

Similarly, it is suggested that although some families may lack social problem skills, that is not the main issue. In many cases the relevant skills are in their repertoire, it is just that they are not utilized effectively because of the disruptive effect of coercive interchanges.

The final crucial element in Patterson's microsocial approach to coercive family processes is the demonstration that there are consistent links between these minor moment to moment interactions and more seriously delinquent behaviour. Thus, yell, whine, non-comply, fight siblings, tease, temper, and physical attacks all form part of the same interlinked group of behaviours; as also do non-comply, lie, run around, steal and set fires. The implication that follows is that interventions which are effective in altering these maladaptive commonplace interchanges in the family will be helpful in dealing with the much less frequent serious behaviours which often take place out of sight of the parents (and hence are more difficult to influence directly).

It is too soon for there to be any adequate assessment of the validity of these ideas. So far, the empirical underpinning of the theorizing remains rather slender in terms of its reliance on a relatively small number of studies, based on selected samples of aggressive and delinquent children; moreover, some of the elements in the theory are much better substantiated than others. Nevertheless, the approach has the enormous strength of its derivation from high-quality empirical research using observational data in the real-life situation, rather than from extrapolations from a global view of human behaviour or from the findings of research using laboratory analogues with an uncertain relationship to behaviour elsewhere.

The two major contributions which are likely to stand the test of time are: (i) the demonstration that observational data can be used to translate molar concepts such as 'supervision' or 'strictness of discipline' into more meaningful sequential processes which provide a much greater leverage on the question of which qualities make the parental actions effective in attaining their desired aims; and (ii) the demonstration of the importance of the *affective* component in the parent–child interactions which are supposedly disciplinary in character. The suggestion, in common with that in other social learning theories, that 'aggression' and 'delinquency' can be usefully broken down into hierarchies of interlinked behaviours is also crucial in its provision of useful openings for therapeutic interventions.

This approach seems to be one of the most important new developments in the field of family studies of delinquent youths, and further work of this type is much needed. Large questions remain on many of the specifics in Patterson's theorizing and on how far the findings and ideas apply to the broader population of delinquents, but the approach provides a most promising new way of tackling old, but still unresolved, questions.

Psycho-analytic theories

While psycho-analytic theories have had an important influence on thinking about delinquents and delinquency, it is not possible to summarize the theoretical concepts in terms of a succinct set of propositions with clear-cut empirical implications. However, there are some basic assumptions and ideas which permeate psycho-analytic theorizing. It is supposed that children are born with unconscious primitive urges which are aggressive and destructive with the potential of being translated into delinquent behaviour. The basic task of socialization is to develop a set of internalized moral controls which are established through identification with the parents, a process that occurs in the context of warm, supportive family relationships during the pre-school period. The key postulates, then, are: (i) the importance of family relationships and upbringing during the early years; (ii) the central role of unconscious intra-psychic factors; (iii) that antisocial behaviour results from faulty personality development; (iv) that *some* cases of delinquency are a consequence of the acting out in antisocial behaviour of intra-psychic neurotic conflicts; and (v) the *unconscious* nature of the processes which determine mental activities, with the result that some delinquent acts have a symbolic meaning reflecting these intra-psychic processes (see Friedlander, 1947; Alexander and Staub, 1956; Glover, 1960; Schoenfeld, 1971).

As discussed in Chapter 6, there is a wealth of evidence linking delinquency with various family influences. The trouble here is that this postulate does not differentiate it from many other theories – especially social control and social learning approaches. There is a lack of evidence on whether the most important of these family influences operate during the pre-school years,* and a lack of empirical substantiation that the key processes are unconscious. With regard to the notions of the 'acting-out neurotic' delinquent, and the symbolic meaning of some delinquent acts, the main problem is to know just how one would tell which cases of delinquency should be included in this framework (as it is evident that these mechanisms are not intended to explain all cases of delinquency).

In recent years, much less attention has been paid to psycho-analytic theorizing regarding delinquent activities. As far as can be assessed, this declining interest has not derived from any empirical demonstration that the hypotheses are wrong (few have been subjected to rigorous test, and indeed many are expressed in a form which would make for difficulties in devising an empirical test). Rather, it is that the theories have not proved to be particularly useful either in furthering our understanding of crime or in devising effective methods of intervention.

Biological theories

There are several different varieties of biological theory for delinquent behaviour, but three may be taken as illustrative of the approaches: Quay's (1977a and b) view of psychopathy as stimulus-seeking behaviour; Eysenck's (1977; Eysenck and Eysenck, 1978) hypothesis that antisocial, criminal and psychopathic behaviour is related to genetically determined personality attributes; and Robins's (1966 and 1978) usage of the psychiatric diagnostic category of sociopathic or antisocial personality disorder.

Quay (1977a) postulates that 'those who ultimately manifest psychopathic

* One extension of psycho-analytic views was Bowlby's (1946) hypothesis that separation experiences in infancy constituted the main explanation for most cases of serious delinquency. Subsequent empirical findings have shown that the focus on physical separations *as such* was mistaken (Rutter, 1971, 1981a). However, the same research did show important associations between family discord and delinquency. It could be argued that this relationship is still in keeping with psycho-analytic views, but there is no indication of whether or not the intra-psychic mechanisms postulated by psycho-analysis are operative, nor whether these operate at the developmental phase specified in the theories.

behavior are born with a nervous system, cortical and/or autonomic, that is hyporeactive to stimulation'. As a consequence, the child

> is a stimulation seeker who experiences hedonic discomfort under circumstances that are adequately arousing for most other children ... [moreover] he does not develop adequate anticipatory responses to pain. The combination of stimulus-seeking behavior and refractoriness to the effects of both physical and social punishers obviously makes for a difficult child with whom the parents, nevertheless, must somehow cope ... Since punishment must be at a high level to produce avoidance, the child very likely receives early, excessively harsh (by most standards) punishment for much of his behavior ... [so becoming] an increasingly aversive stimulus to his parents ... Because of habituation, the child develops an increased resistance to the effects of punishment. The parents, faced with an out-of-control child, understandably retreat into hostility, rejection, and inconsistency. (pp. 379–80)

It is suggested that this process in the family serves to increase the child's deviancy in a 'seemingly endless vicious circle'.

The empirical evidence relevant to these ideas was discussed in Chapter 5. So far most of the research into autonomic responsivity has been undertaken with incarcerated adult criminals, and we do not know how far the findings can be extended to juvenile delinquents. Moreover, there have been very few studies to examine stimulus seeking *per se*. Accordingly, no conclusions can be drawn on the applicability of the theory either to delinquents as a whole, or to a smaller 'psychopathic' subgroup. However, as Quay (1977a) indicates in closing the chapter which summarizes his views, the theory does give rise to a number of quite specific predictions readily subject to experimental verification or refutation. But, perhaps, the main difficulty in doing so will be presented by the uncertainties on how to designate a 'psychopathic' subgroup.

Eysenck (Eysenck, 1977; Eysenck and Eysenck, 1978) has suggested that 'primary psychopathy' is associated with the genetically determined personality dimension of 'psychoticism' (or P), although it remains unclear *how* P is supposed to cause criminality; and that 'secondary psychopathy' is associated with genetically determined high extraversion (E) and neuroticism (N). It is postulated that conscience is the result of a long process of conditioning, and that what distinguishes the 'secondary psychopath' is his poor conditionability (associated in turn with high E and N). The supposition is that these dimensions are identifiable in childhood, that they persist into adult life, and that the concepts of 'primary' and 'secondary' psychopathy apply to much of delinquent behaviour in childhood. Eysenck is not explicit on how much, or on how one would differentiate primary from secondary psychopaths or both of these from non-psychopathic delinquents (other than through the tautology of P, E, and N dimensions).

The empirical evidence on these postulates was discussed in Chapter 5 (and is considered more fully in Farrington *et al.*, 1982; Feldman, 1977; Passingham, 1972; Powell, 1977; Trasler, 1973). In essence, it appears that antisocial behaviour in childhood is quite strongly associated with P, shows some association with N, but no consistent link with E. Psychopathy in adults is associated with impaired avoidance learning but probably not with impaired conditioning generally; whether this applies to most juvenile delinquents is not known. In short, there is evidence which is consistent with some features of Eysenck's theory, but not with others. However, quite apart from its rather limited empirical verification, there are conceptual criticisms regarding the disputed notion of any general characteristic of conditionability, of the extent to which questionnaire scores truly reflect enduring dimensions of personality, and of the independence of P from the conduct disturbances it is supposed to predict (see the references cited above). It seems likely that the theory is correct in linking recidivist delinquency with personality features, but the specific hypothesized link with conditionability seems more dubious.

Robins (1966) has argued that 'sociopathic personality' (meaning a syndrome made up of a broad variety of antisocial behaviours arising in childhood) constituted a psychiatric disease state, and not just a pseudo-explanatory term. The chief grounds for this argument were (i) that there was a common set of symptoms with a similar age of onset; (ii) that the symptoms followed a predictable course; and (iii) that it occurred in children whose fathers, siblings and offspring all had an elevated incidence of the condition. More recently, she has reiterated the arguments (Robins, 1978; Robins and Ratcliff, 1979 and 1980a) with the additional support of evidence showing: (a) that the pattern held across several very different population samples; (b) that each separate type of childhood deviant behaviour was independently correlated with the overall level of adult deviance; and (c) conversely, that each *separate type* of adult deviance was predicted by the overall level of child deviance. There can be no doubt that these findings constitute powerful supporting evidence for the coherence of the overall concept. As a consequence, it would be well worthwhile searching for possible genetic or other biological correlates of the behavioural constellation. But none of the findings necessarily indicate that the 'syndrome' has a biological origin (for example, much the same findings would be likely to apply to Roman Catholicism and its constituent 'symptoms' of the various religious observances which form part of that religion). On the other hand, the serious personal and social impairments associated with the syndrome certainly *do* suggest that it refers to far more than a variation in normal behaviour. The concept of 'disease', however, might be thought to require a further condition – namely a *qualitative*, as distinct from quantitative, departure from normality. There is no adequate evidence that might allow a decision on that issue. It warrants investigation, but regardless of the answer, the findings produced from Robins's research clearly indicate the value of looking at the constellation of behaviours in the way that she has done.

Situational perspectives

Until recently, most work in criminology (both theoretical and empirical) has been concerned with a 'historical' or 'genetic' view of causation, in which the goal has been to identify the factors which propel *persons* down criminal paths. As Gibbons (1971) observed a decade ago, situational perspectives focused on the factors which cause some *situations* to be more likely than others to elicit criminal behaviour had been correspondingly neglected. While situational perspectives can scarcely be said to constitute a theory of crime, they do constitute a real and important alternative way of viewing the issues in delinquency research (see Clarke, 1977, 1980; Sinclair and Clarke, 1982). As Hough, Clarke and Mayhew (1980) point out, the traditional dispositional bias stems from the prevailing system of criminal justice as well as from tendencies in the parent disciplines, especially psychology. Questions of who should be *punished* for their delinquent activities and who should be *treated* for the personal problems which gave rise to the criminal behaviour demand an understanding of individual differences and individual pathology. However, this had the unfortunate consequence that it forced an assumption that criminality was in some way inherent in the personality of offenders, who then *sought out* opportunities for crime. But as Hough *et al.* (1980) note, people *respond* to the situations in which they find themselves, as well as seeking out those that they desire. Situational factors, they suggest, may influence criminal opportunities through several different mechanisms, including the provision of (i) the material conditions which make crime possible; (ii) features which constitute inducements to crime; and (iii) elements which ensure that the benefits of crime can be obtained at low risk.

This approach can also be extended to include a consideration of the differential involvement of individuals in crime. Clarke (1977) explained the matter as follows:

> Some people by virtue of the *current circumstances* of their lives are exposed more frequently to criminogenic situations of particular sorts ... By no means everyone, however, who for one reason or another finds himself in a criminogenic situation will respond by behaving criminally. Whether he does or not will depend, in the first place,

on how he perceives the situation and the judgements he makes about it, i.e. on various *perceptional and cognitive processes* ... A willingness to offend can therefore more helpfully be seen as a decision reached in a particular set of circumstances; rather than as a generalized behavioural disposition. (p. 280, emphasis in original)

In psychology generally there has been a move away from simple trait theories (with the causal factors residing exclusively in the person), and from pure situational approaches (in which the stimuli are seen as the basic determinants), to a consideration of person-by-situation interactions (see Endler, 1977; Bem and Funder, 1978). While a start has been made in the direction of predicting *how* persons and situations interact, the evidence so far is fragmentary and none of it refers to delinquent behaviour.

Some of the empirical evidence on situational factors was reviewed in Chapter 6, and the application of this approach to the field of prevention is discussed more fully in Chapter 9.

Limited rationality or 'choice' theories

Both the situational perspective and concepts of deterrence (see Chapter 9) share the view that, to a significant extent, criminal acts are the outcome of immediate choices and decisions made by the offender (see Clarke, 1982; Cook, 1980). In deciding whether or not to commit a particular offence, people are likely to weigh the *chances* and *consequences* of being caught and to take advantage of a criminal opportunity only if it is in their self-interest to do so. Thus, in contrast to most other theoretical approaches, the explanation focuses on the criminal event itself (rather than past experiences); it is made specific to particular categories of crime; and both the individual's current circumstances and the immediate features of the setting are given greater weight than is usual in dispositional theories (Clarke, 1982).

These theoretical conceptions involve two key elements (Cook, 1980). Firstly, they postulate that criminal acts result from individual *choices* made on the basis of rational considerations. Observed crime rates, then, are viewed as the aggregate result of choices made by rational individuals. Secondly, essentially, the approach is an *economic* one, in which these choices are viewed in terms of a cost-benefits analysis with respect to the gains to the individual from the criminal acts, the risks taken, and the losses incurred if he is caught. Crime prevention and control are considered in terms of society's opportunities to lower crime profits and raise crime costs through improved policing, more certain apprehension of offenders, and better deterrents. This has been the basis of deterrence theories from Jeremy Bentham onwards. However, it is apparent that these traditional approaches have carried the implicit assumption that crime *opportunities* constitute a given constant. The recent impetus provided by situational perspectives emphasizes that this key item in the economic equation is not fixed. Accordingly, a third element in choice conceptions of crime concerns the availability of opportunities for crime and the ease or difficulty of the steps needed to seize those opportunities. Hence, preventive policies may be based, not on any effects on the profits and losses associated with crime, but rather on reducing the range of situations in which crime could be committed and by making criminal activities more difficult and troublesome to undertake.

The empirical evidence which provides the substantiation for these economic-choice models of crime stems from the research on the effects of deterrents and of crime prevention strategies based on environmental management and design. The findings are discussed in some detail in the next chapter, but it may be stated here that the evidence does indeed show that delinquent behaviour can be influenced, to a modest degree, by alterations in crime profits, costs and opportunities. To that extent, there is validation of the economic hypothesis. But, also, there are many objections to the use of this model as an overall explanation of juvenile delinquency.

To begin with, the empirical effects found are too weak to account for more than a small proportion of the variance. Accordingly, the theory is likely, at best, to constitute no more than a part-explanation. Nevertheless, if the effects suggest potentially effective prevention-strategies, perhaps it would be unwise to place too much weight on this objection. Secondly, it is obvious that individuals differ greatly in their response to the same crime opportunity with the same 'objective' profits and losses. Thus, people differ in their willingness to accept risks, in their 'honesty preference', in their evaluation of the profits from crime (especially when the pay-off is non-financial, as in crimes of violence or vandalism or truancy), and in their evaluation of the costs which come from apprehension and conviction (Cook, 1980). Many of these crucial individual differences must be accounted for in terms of some non-economic theoretical conception. Thirdly, it is obvious that many delinquent acts do not result from rational decisions. This may be because they are impulsive, rather than thought out, or because the acts take place in states of high emotional arousal or intoxication which impair rational decision-making. But, most fundamental of all, many studies have shown that people generally tend not to make full use of economic cost-benefits considerations in coming to decisions (see Cook, 1980). Thus there is a tendency to ignore low-probability events entirely, or to give them a wholly inappropriate excessive weight. Carroll (1978) has suggested that crime models need to be modified to take account of these findings. The potential offender '... is not viewed as the "economic person" making exhaustive and complex calculations leading to an optimal choice. Rather, it is the "psychological person", who makes a few simple and concrete examinations of his or her opportunities and makes guesses that can be far short of optimal' (p. 513). For all these reasons, the strictly economic theories have had to be abandoned and replaced by 'limited rationality' concepts. These seem to provide a potentially useful (although necessarily partial and restricted) approach to crime but, as Cook (1980) points out, the challenge now is for theorists to find predictable ways in which the 'psychological person' deviates from the 'economic person'.

Labelling perspectives on 'secondary deviance'

The term 'labelling perspective' has been applied to a rather diverse range of theoretical approaches which differ in a number of crucial respects, but especially in whether they adopt a reactive conception of deviance or, rather, propose a theory about the consequences of reactions – so-called 'secondary deviance' (see Plummer, 1979; Gibbs and Erickson, 1975). As Lemert (1972) put it: 'Secondary deviance refers to a special class of socially defined responses which people make to problems created by the societal reactions to their deviance.' There have been numerous disputes as to just what empirical predictors stem from this view (see Plummer, 1979), but at least some writers postulate that a person's view of himself is influenced by the reactions of others, that a stigmatizing label of 'delinquent' is provided by legal processing, that this labelling adversely affects the labelled person's self-image, and that, as a consequence, the labelled person then becomes more likely to engage in delinquent activities. Some of the research on the effects of legal processing was briefly reviewed in Chapter 1, where it was concluded that there was empirical evidence that, as predicted, a court appearance *did* make it more likely that a boy would maintain antisocial attitudes and increase his delinquent activities. Other research (see Bahr, 1979) points to the same effect, and it may be concluded that official processing may serve to increase the probability of future deviance. On the other hand, the same findings also indicate that the effects of labelling are not as strong, pervasive and simple as sometimes assumed; that they do not necessarily operate through changes in self-image; that the effects are most marked with first offenders and do *not* spiral as hypothesized; and that they vary by ethnic group and sex. It is also obvious that labelling accounts for only a few of the phenomena associated with delinquent activities. In particular, it is evident that labelling cannot explain the *initiation* of delinquent behaviour; it is applicable only to certain types of delinquency; it probably plays little role in the most persistent forms of recidivism; labels may deter or change deviance as well as amplify it; people vary in how they respond to labelling; and labels need not be permanent and irreversible (see Plummer, 1979; Bahr, 1979; Schrag, 1974; Wellford, 1975).

Reactive conceptions of deviance and the 'new criminology'

The 'secondary deviance' notion involves the application of labelling perspectives to a positivistic question on factors concerned with the course of an individual's delinquent activities. Many sociologists today would deny that that was an appropriate question at all. Adherents of the reactive conception of deviance argue that deviance is not an inherent property of any act or individual, but rather a property *conferred* by society. Certainly, there is power in the criticisms made of the older, traditional concepts which somehow assumed that delinquent activities could be interpreted without reference to reactions to deviance. The result of this shift in perspective has been informative analyses of the factors and consequences of the procedures involved in legal processing (briefly noted in Chapter 1). However, there are numerous conceptual and logical problems involved in definitions of deviance in terms of reactions (see the critiques by Walker, 1977, and Gibbs and Erickson, 1975). It is evident that the new definitions suffer from 'cultural and temporal relativity' just as much as the old ones did (Phillipson, 1971). As Gibbs and Erickson (1975) put it: 'Certainly the reactivist perspective now receives a great deal of attention, but it is scarcely a competing theory; and in any case it has generated far less systematic research than did sub-cultural theories. One possible reason is the failure of its advocates to specify the kind of research findings that would falsify the reactive perspective.'

Much the same applies to the 'new criminology', which has turned away completely from the issues considered in all the other theories discussed in this chapter, to a concern with the political economy of crime. Its prime interest is in the ways in which criminal laws are used to maintain social divisions in society and in the 'structured inequality in power and interest that underpin the processes whereby the laws are created and enforced' (Taylor, Walton and Young, 1974, p. 68). But so far, most writings in this mode have been concerned with political interpretations rather than the posing or answering of empirical questions. As Gibbs and Erickson (1975) argue: 'To deserve a serious hearing they must confront empirical questions such as: Is the legal proscription of particular types of crime peculiar to particular types of economic-political systems? If so, which types of crimes and which types of systems?' (p. 38). As they note: 'The point is that a theory about crime must extend beyond vague statements pertaining to power, elites, establishments, etc. It must end with potentially falsifiable assertions about (a) the distinguishing characteristics of individuals who control the enactments of criminal law, (b) the process by which criminal laws are enacted, (c) selective enforcement of criminal laws, and (d) contrasts in the criminal laws of different economic-political systems' (p. 38).

Conclusions

We are far from reaching a resolution of competing ideas and propositions in theories of crime. On the other hand, it would be wrong to suppose that no progress has been made. Empirical research over the last twenty years or so has shown that several theoretical notions were mistaken. For example, anomie and sub-cultural theories, although providing possible useful insights into certain phenomena, can now be rejected as general explanations. Others, such as psycho-analysis or concepts of conditionability related to extraversion and neuroticism, although not necessarily wrong in their main postulates, have not proved useful in shaping policy or practice. Sutherland's differential association theory, long dismissed as so poorly developed as to be untestable, now seems to have more substance to it than once supposed. While it is a non-starter as a general explanation for delinquency, recent empirical evidence suggests that there may be important peer group influences on delinquent behaviour. Social control and social learning theories have received substantial empirical support over the years, but their postulates have been at too general a level for them to be of much value as guides to policy. The recent development of microsocial approaches to coercive family processes now offers the promise of bringing greater precision to some of the concepts, precision which may have important implications for practice.

Biological theories continue to have their ups and downs. The notion that *most* juvenile delinquents are biologically distinctive from their peers can be rejected as implausible, but it seems more likely that there *may* be important biological features which characterize more extreme groups – such as those included under the rather unsatisfactory concepts of 'psychopathy' and 'antisocial personality disorder'. However, it is probable that such features differentiate recidivists by their *degree* rather than their *presence* (that is, that recidivists have *more* of some variable and not that they have some characteristic not possessed by non-delinquents). While certainly it cannot be said that we have any well-substantiated ideas on what these biological features might be, there are some leads worth following; how much they will yield cannot be assessed at present.

Situational perspectives have been most important in focusing attention on issues which were neglected hitherto. While, as yet, they have not added greatly to our understanding of mechanisms, the further development of this approach, and the 'limited rationality' concepts with which they are associated, are likely to have implications for preventive policies. Labelling perspectives and reactive conceptions of deviance have been valuable in the way in which they have drawn attention to some of the absurdities and naïveties in traditional concepts of inherently criminal individuals; and more positively in their elucidation of some of the important factors involved in the procedures of legal processing, and in the ways in which social discontent and discrimination may play a part in the genesis and shaping of delinquent activities.

The idea that there could be any one all-encompassing theoretical explanation of crime has been shown to be absurd. Delinquent activities are too varied and too widespread in society for it to be sensible to even contemplate a single explanation. One might just as well attempt to provide a single mechanism for running, for unhappiness or for poverty. But it would be wrong to suppose, therefore, that theories must be unimportant in either research or practice. On the contrary, they are essential as a means of ordering ideas and of making sense out of factual findings. The mindless collection of factual information is not the way that science proceeds. The strategies and tactics of research, as of policy and practice, need to be guided by theories and hypotheses. It is only when we have an understanding of mechanisms, and of *how* and *why* things happen in the way that they do, that we can be in a really strong position to plan effectively for the future and to improve our services.

9
Prevention and Intervention

The literature on the evaluation of different approaches to the prevention of crime and to the rehabilitation, treatment and correction of offenders is immense, although only quite a small proportion of studies have anything approaching an adequate research design (see Lipton, Martinson and Wilks, 1975; Sechrest, White and Brown, 1979; Wright and Dixon, 1977; Martinson, 1974; Ross and Gendreau, 1980; Brody, 1976, for extensive reviews of the research findings). Most reviews have ended with essentially negative conclusions – 'no delinquent prevention strategies can be definitely recommended' (Wright and Dixon, 1977); 'with few and isolated exceptions the rehabilitative efforts that have been reported so far have had no appreciable effect on recidivism' (Martinson, 1974); 'studies which have produced positive results have been isolated, inconsistent in their evidence, and open to so much methodological criticism that they must remain unconvincing' (Brody, 1976). On the other hand, in the last few years, guardedly optimistic conclusions have been claimed by a few reviewers on the basis of more recent studies – 'they provide convincing evidence that some treatment programmes, when they are applied with integrity by competent practitioners to appropriate target populations, can be effective in preventing crime or reducing recidivism' (Ross and Gendreau, 1980); 'a wide variety of treatments, from offender self-help groups to individual psychotherapy, can be made to work effectively for some subpopulations under selected conditions – at least for the short run' (Adams, 1977).

The problem that faced us, as it has faced all reviewers, was how to decide which evidence to accept and which to reject. Clearly, much of the research has been of very poor quality. As Sechrest *et al.* (1979) concluded: 'The one positive conclusion is discouraging: the research methodology that has been brought to bear on the problem of finding ways to rehabilitate criminal offenders has been generally so inadequate that only a relatively few studies warrant any unequivocal interpretations ... Although a generous reviewer of the literature might discern some glimmers of hope, these glimmers are so few, so scattered, and so inconsistent that they do not serve as a basis for any recommendation other than continued research.' Palmer (1975), on the other hand, has objected to such negative conclusions on the grounds that nearly half of the reasonably adequate studies have produced at least 'partly positive' results. Martinson (1976) countered by asserting that 'A "partly positive" result is probably akin to a partly pregnant girl friend.' As illustrated by the last quotation, this is a field in which rhetoric and invective sometimes take pride of place over the empirical evidence. Obviously, there must be some reasonable and explicit rationale for determining how to weigh the evidence; a recourse to a football score approach (6 studies show an effect, 4 do not, therefore positive results 'win') is *not* likely to be informative. This is because positive findings are much more likely to be accepted for publication than negative ones, and because any conclusion based on the numbers game will necessarily be suspect in the absence of a plausible explanation as to *why* the results have differed between projects. Accordingly, before attempting any assessment of different forms of evaluation, it is necessary to discuss some of the most important methodological issues as well as the goals of prevention and intervention.

Issues in evaluation

It is customary in reviewing evaluation studies to focus on sample size, use of control groups, adequacy of matching, availability of appropriate measures of outcome, length of follow-up, loss of subjects and appropriate statistical tests. These matters are considered below, but it is clear from an appraisal of the research that there are other equally important, but less often considered, issues (see Brody, 1976; Sechrest *et al.*, 1979; Ross and Gendreau, 1980). One of the most crucial concerns doubts on the quality of the interventions.

Has the planned intervention actually taken place?

When new therapeutic or corrective approaches are introduced on an experimental basis, there are frequently major difficulties in ensuring that the intervention actually takes place as planned. Most research reports do not give enough details of the intervention for there to be any objective assessment on this crucial point, but the few that do clearly show the difficulties. For example, the study by Kassebaum, Ward and Wilner (1971) is frequently correctly cited as a piece of research with an exemplary design (with random allocation and a 36-month follow-up). The investigation was designed to evaluate the effects of group counselling in a correctional institution, but as Quay (1977b) made clear in his appraisal of the work, the report gives ample indications that the therapy was of a generally poor quality. The counselling was not adequately conceptualized or operationalized, training meetings for the counsellors were poorly attended, most of the therapists did not believe in the value of the counselling that they were undertaking, observations of the group sessions showed a 'tendency for superficiality, a lack of emotional involvement, and evidence of insincerity', involvement in the groups was compulsory, and their composition was heterogeneous and haphazard. Not surprisingly, the outcome measures showed no benefits from this 'treatment', but because the treatment, as actually undertaken, was so very unsatisfactory, the study provides no useful evaluation of group counselling as a therapeutic method. Kassebaum *et al.*'s (1971) report of the study was unusually detailed and frank, and it is for that reason that we are able to conclude that the therapeutic interventions were too poor to provide a fair test of the treatment. Most other studies do not give enough details for this judgement, but the implication is that caution must be exercised in accepting negative findings when we cannot determine whether the intervention was actually delivered as planned.

While it is not possible to assess, from published materials, how many studies suffer from this fault, there are ample indications that the Kassebaum investigation was not an isolated example. For example, Jesness's (1975 and 1980) comparison of transactional analysis and behaviour modification programmes for delinquents constituted an even better-planned project. The training programme for both approaches was extensive, and employees had to demonstrate basic knowledge of treatment theory in order to pass their probationary period of employment. Yet, in spite of this thorough training, it was found that adequate behavioural contingency contracts could be implemented with only a small minority of the youths, and the frequency of therapeutic sessions fell short of requirements (Jesness *et al.*, 1975). In this programme a variety of measures showed that, to some extent, the treatments *had* been carried out as intended but, even so, the interventions were considerably less than optimal. Again, the California Community Treatment Project (C.T.P.) is one of the most wide-ranging and ambitious therapeutic studies so far undertaken with juvenile delinquents (Palmer, 1974). The intervention was designed as a community-based programme utilizing a variety of individually planned counselling and psychotherapeutic approaches. However, as Lerman (1975) showed, in practice, extensive use was also made of institutional placement and temporary confinement in detention centres. While it may be that this was indeed what was needed, it is essential that the inferences drawn from the research findings apply to what was *actually* done rather than the therapeutic concept in the mind of the project instigator. Of course, too, the Cambridge–Somerville study (Powers and Witmer, 1951) provides another example of a well-planned project in which the intervention failed to live up to expectations, in that the turnover of counsellors was greater and the frequency of counselling less than intended. A further problem in some studies where a high degree of co-operation is required has been a high fall-out from treatment. For example, Weathers and Liberman (1975) set out to evaluate contingency contracting with the families of delinquent adolescents. Of the 28 families referred, 16 completed the first home visit, 8 finished the baseline period, and only 6 completed the three home interventions and follow-up! Klein (1979) cites several studies of diversionary community programmes in which a third or so of the clients failed to receive the planned treatment and many received no treatment at all; Brody (1976) gives other examples of the difficulties in implementing experimental treatments.

It is important *not* to dismiss these as examples of poor work – the examples were chosen just because they represented detailed reports of systematic, carefully planned research by experienced investigators. However, there are two important lessons to be drawn. Firstly, it is no easy matter to introduce a new experimental intervention into an established service. As a result, a lack of demonstrated efficacy may mean that the treatment is of no value, but equally it may mean that practical problems in implementation have meant that it has not been given a fair trial. Secondly, no valid inference may be made unless it is known what kind and what quality of intervention has *actually* been undertaken. The fact that a few, unusually full, reports of good studies have shown that the interventions in practice have not always been equivalent to the interventions as intended should alert us to the strong probability that this also occurred in some of the weaker, less fully reported, projects. Sechrest *et al.* (1979) aptly quote Mark Twain as stating: 'Not only is the thirteenth chime of a clock in and of itself suspect, but it also casts doubt on the validity of the preceding twelve.'

What was the nature of the intervention?

A related question concerns the need to know just what form the intervention took, not just to assess its quality but because without that information it is impossible to know how to apply the results – be they positive or negative. Unfortunately, far too many studies are content to describe the intervention under some vague general term such as psychotherapy, counselling or supervision (Slaikeu, 1973). As Rezmovic (1979) comments in a most thoughtful review of methodological issues: 'Although the current concern of correctional evaluators is that "nothing works", an important question is what they would do if something did work. It is likely that they would be hard-pressed to repeat past performances if there is little accurate and coherent description of what treatment was delivered.'

There is a further very important reason for having adequate measures of the intervention process itself. Particularly in view of the considerable problems in obtaining random allocation and adequate matching of groups, there is always the problem of knowing whether any differences found were truly *caused* by the intervention, as distinct from being due to some unmeasured prior difference between the groups or some variable outside the intervention. The most powerful test of causation in these circumstances is provided by the determination of whether there is a 'dose–response' relationship (see Rutter, 1981d). In other words did the *degree* of immediate change produced by the intervention show a consistent correlation with the degree or likelihood of reduction in delinquent activities? Of course, for this to be possible there must be some clearly identifiable postulated intervening variable in the intervention strategy. Often there is not, but sometimes there is. For example, in behaviourally-oriented family therapy methods the goal may be to improve parental monitoring and supervision of the boy's activities (Patterson, 1982). If so, does the degree of change in parental supervision (within the experimental group) relate to the degree of change in the boy's delinquent activities? Or the aim may be to improve social skills and social problem-solving (for example, Sarason and Ganzer, 1973), in which case the question is whether the gains in social competence relate to reductions in delinquency. Unfortunately, this is a research strategy which has been rarely employed, although Alexander and his colleagues have made a start (Alexander and Parsons, 1973; Alexander *et al.*, 1976). While methodological limitations in their design (see below) mean that no strong conclusions on dose–response relationships are possible, they were able to show that improvements in family communication and problem-solving were associated with a reduction in recidivism rate.

Sampling and matching

In any evaluation study, the assessment has to involve some kind of systematic comparison. The comparison may be with the behaviour of the same individuals before the intervention, or it may be with that of a group treated in some other way, or it may be with an untreated group. But some form of comparison constitutes an essential component of the evaluation. In theory, the most satisfactory way of ensuring an unbiased comparison is to utilize random allocation, so that it is a matter of complete chance which 'treatment' or form of intervention each subject receives. In practice this has proved difficult to implement in intervention with delinquents, and very few studies have successfully carried out a random allocation design (Greenberg, 1977). Moreover, random allocation is no guarantee that the groups will be truly comparable in fact – indeed it is certain that occasionally chance will mean that they are not. Accordingly, even with a random allocation design it is necessary to have data on the key features known to predict outcome in order to check that comparability has been obtained.

Reference to a few well-known projects illustrates how difficult this has turned out to be. For example, in the Provo experiment (Empey and Erickson, 1972) there was a well-planned random allocation procedure designed so as not to interfere with the judicial process. All the judge had to do was decide whether ordinarily the boy would be placed on probation or sent to an institution; that decision being taken, an envelope containing randomly selected slips of paper was then opened to determine whether, within probation or institutional placement, the boy was in an experimental or control group. The procedure worked for the two probation groups, but too few cases were allocated to institutional care for the programme to be viable. Consequently the original design had to be abandoned, with all institutional cases going into the experimental group and with the selection of a separate control group from elsewhere. The effect was that the two institutional groups* were imperfectly matched. Fortunately, good background data were available to enable between-group differences to be taken into account but, without these, evaluation would have been in jeopardy. Stuart *et al.* (1976) were successful in implementing a random assignment design in their study of the use of behavioural contracts with pre-delinquent youths. There were 30 youths in the experimental group and 30 in the controls, who met with therapists for games and other activities considered essentially non-therapeutic. However, as luck would have it, the experimental group included twice as many youths from single-parent homes, 5 of the most problematic youths had to be dropped from the control group, and some of the control group youths were in fact given some of the experimental treatment in error. The results showed only small differences between the groups, with differences statistically significant in only 4 out of 13 comparisons. As the inadvertent lack of matching would seem to favour the controls, it is possible that the 'true' therapeutic effect was greater than the measurements showed, but there is no satisfactory way of telling whether this

---

* In fact the experimental group was treated in the community, but as it was matched with an institutional group it was termed the experimental institutional group.

was the case. In the California project (C.T.P.), of which mention has already been made, random assignment on a 50–50 basis was planned, but because the movement of cases through the experimental programme was slower than anticipated, a marked imbalance arose which took some years to correct; this led to some later difficulties in evaluation (Lerman, 1975). Other studies have utilized quasi-random designs. For example, Baron *et al.* (1973) made assignments to experimental and control groups according to the day of the week – a procedure which opened the way for possible bias. As no background data on the groups were published, it is not possible to determine whether bias actually occurred. Similarly, Sarason and Ganzer (1973) state that: 'Assignment of subjects to conditions was essentially random but was occasionally influenced by weekly admission rates; that is, if too few boys were admitted during a week when a new experimental group was needed, those admissions were all designated as controls.'

In most studies, there are too few data to determine whether these departures from an optimal design mattered in practice. But inevitably they raise doubts. It should be added, however, that the biases which could have occurred may have operated in either direction. The consequence is likely to have been some misleading positive and some misleading negative results – that is, the probable effect will have been to add to the confusion rather than to bend the results systematically in one direction or another.

Provided adequate background data are available, there are several research designs (see Rezmovic, 1979) which do not require random allocation – although in all cases they gain strength from a combination with randomization. The use of prediction tables, pioneered by Mannheim and Wilkins (1955), is probably the most useful. The basic principle is that systematic information is collected on all the items known to predict the course of delinquent activities (using items such as number of previous convictions, age at first court appearance, poor employment record and abnormal personality features – see Sinclair and Clarke, 1981). These are then used to derive a base expectancy rate for re-conviction. The benefits or otherwise of the intervention are then determined according to whether or not it betters the base rate (as assessed in relation to the specific characteristics of the individuals concerned in the intervention). The technique is a useful one, but its strength is heavily dependent on how good are the items included in the prediction tables. If they allow of only a weak prediction, there is always the strong possibility that other important predictive variables, not included in the table, accounted for the difference in outcome between groups.

It is because of that possibility that there must be considerable doubt about studies, especially when based on small numbers, which lack data on crucial pre-intervention features. This applies, for example, to the Massimo and Shore study (Massimo and Shore, 1963; Shore and Massimo, 1966), in which 10 boys were put into an intensive therapeutic programme involving counselling, practical help, remedial education and other features. Their outcome was assessed over a 10-year period in relation to an untreated control group, the initial assignment being random. The results were impressive in showing gains in learning, personality measures and overt behaviour 10 months later for the experimental group, with the between-group differences being maintained 10 *years* later. The therapeutic involvement was both intensive and extensive, and it could be that it was responsible for the highly persistent benefits claimed. The doubt arises from the fact that the groups were equated for age, I.Q. and socio-economic status only – variables of very little predictive value. Scepticism must also be increased by the finding that the effects were as marked at 10 years as at 10 months – a duration of effect far beyond that found in any other study.

Outcome measures

Several different problems exist with respect to outcome measures. Firstly, biases may derive from between-group differences in the duration of follow-up. For example, in an otherwise well-planned evaluative study of a 'juvenile diversion' programme (consisting of vocational and personal counselling, training and job placement, and scholastic tutoring) by Quay and Love (1977), the cases had 311 days follow-up but the controls 450 days. As Mrad (1979) pointed out, this could well have accounted for the greater arrests in the control group – they had a longer period in which to offend and to get caught.

Secondly, in that most outcome measures are based on re-conviction, it is important to ensure that biases do not result from the intervention changing the likelihood that an offence will result in conviction rather than informal action, or vice versa. There is good evidence that this did in fact occur in the California Community Treatment Project (Lerman, 1975). The experimental and control groups did not differ in terms of reported offences, but the controls had many more parole revocations initiated by the parole agent. The clear implication is that treatment had changed the ways in which the youths were processed, without having an impact on their delinquent behaviour as such. There are similar doubts about the equally well-known 'Highfields Experiment' (Weeks, 1958), in that the Highfields boys were released from the institution on probation whereas those from the comparison institution were released on parole – probation and parole differing in the degree of supervision provided (Sherwood and Walker, 1959).

The third issue concerns the lack of sensitivity of a simple presence/absence of re-convictions measure. It would be quite possible for an intervention to have a useful impact in terms of a reduction in the amount of crime or in its seriousness without that necessarily being reflected in the re-conviction rate. Indeed, it seems that that may have happened in the Provo experiment (Empey and Erickson, 1972). In all groups the majority of boys were re-convicted at least once during the follow-up period, and the differences between the experimental and control groups were quite small. On the other hand, especially with respect to the institutional control versus experimental comparison, there were substantial differences (favouring the experimental group) in terms of *degree of change*, as measured in a variety of ways. Although Martinson (1976) has criticized this type of approach on the grounds that policy-makers are not interested in *relative* improvements of this kind, that seems an unnecessarily negative viewpoint. Provided that interventions really did reduce the amount or seriousness of delinquent behaviour, that would be a most worthwhile effect, even if it did not change the proportion of offenders who had a further conviction of some sort. The real question is whether there is any evidence that this kind of effect occurs. On that point, we have very little evidence. The Provo experiment findings are useful in indicating the value of a more discriminating approach to the measurement of outcome, but it has yet to be determined whether it makes much difference in practice.

A related point concerns the need to assess aspects of social functioning other than delinquent activities. Studies of adult criminals, whose delinquent activities began in childhood, have been consistent in showing the high frequency with which they exhibit personal and social problems of varied kinds – unemployment, marital difficulties, mental disorder, and disturbed personal relationships (see Chapters 1 and 3). If intervention improved their psycho-social functioning, that too would be worthwhile even if it did not alter re-conviction rates. Relatively few studies have examined that possibility, and it is not known whether such an effect occurs and, if it does, with which sorts of treatments. On the whole, it is clear that re-conviction rates correlate reasonably well with other measures (see Sechrest *et al.*, 1979) but that may not be so with interventions primarily designed to improve personal functioning.

With these considerations in mind, we turn now to an assessment of the findings on different types of judicial and therapeutic intervention. Rather than attempt a comprehensive coverage of mostly indifferent or downright poor studies, we focus on the better-controlled investigations (whether positive or negative in outcome) and/or on those cited by others as demonstrating the supposed efficacy of one or other type of intervention. In coming to conclusions on the benefits or otherwise of different forms of intervention, we shall place weight on the studies which deal most adequately with the methodological issues just considered. When deciding how to interpret contradictory findings from apparently sound investigations, reliance will be placed on the consistency of the pattern of results (that is, do they all point in the same general direction although the differences sometimes fall short of statistical significance, and are there probable reasons for the difference in outcome – in terms of the types of offenders in the sample or in the ways in which the intervention was undertaken).

Behavioural approaches

Behavioural approaches to the modification of delinquent behaviour and to the treatment of juvenile offenders have been widely studied in recent years, and several extensive reviews of the literature are available (see, for example, Trasler and Farrington, 1979; Gross and Brigham, 1980; Davidson and Seidman, 1974; Hoefler and Bornstein, 1975; Ross and McKay, 1978; Burchard and Harig, 1976; O'Donnell, 1977; Patterson, 1980). The basic assumptions underlying these approaches are that behaviour is responsive to factors in the environment and that behaviour may be modified by its consequences (see Yule, 1977). Most use has been made of *operant* principles which, put in their simplest form, postulate that behaviour which is followed by pleasant consequences is likely to increase in frequency, whereas behaviour which culminates in unpleasant consequences will tend to decrease. However, in basing intervention on scientific knowledge regarding the learning process, operant approaches involve a variety of further assumptions about the effects of contingent consequences – for example, that *intermittent* rewarding of a behaviour will make it more difficult to eliminate than if it is rewarded every time, or that the *timing* of contingent responses will affect their impact (see Risley and Baer, 1973). But operant principles are by no means the only ones included in behavioural approaches; rather they utilize all forms of learning, such as those based on modelling (watching a skilled performance) or desensitization, as well as operants. Moreover, in all these applications an individualized problem-solving approach to intervention is central – meaning that the intervention is planned on the basis of a detailed *functional analysis* of how the individual's behaviour is affected by the environment *in actuality* (rather than on the basis of theoretical assumptions). While these general principles and assumptions apply to the broad range of behavioural interventions, there are important differences between the various ways in which they have been applied. These are most conveniently considered under the headings of interventions focused on the institution, the individual, and the family.

Institutional applications

There have been several attempts to establish a 'token economy' (Ayllon and Azrin, 1968) in institutions for delinquents. A 'token economy' means that the individual has to 'earn' all privileges through 'good' behaviour. The medium of exchange in the institution is a system of tokens (comparable to poker chips) which can be exchanged for goods or privileges. Clearly there are ethical issues involved in establishing such a total institution (see Feldman, 1977), but a sizeable number of studies have shown that a substantial degree of behavioural control can be obtained through the use of a token economy (Kazdin and Bootzin, 1972; Burchard and Harig, 1976; Ross and McKay, 1978). The use of an ABAB design (that is, the alternation of periods with and without the use of contingent tokens) has shown that the behavioural change is indeed due to the token economy and not to other factors (see, for example, Burchard, 1967; Phillips, 1968). Although the studies vary considerably in rigour and sophistication, the results show that behavioural approaches can aid institutional management in useful ways. However, there are several major problems in this method of intervention. Firstly, as many writers describe (see Burchard and Harig, 1976; Hoghughi, 1979; Jesness *et al.*, 1975), there are many practical difficulties in running a token economy – difficulties which stem both from the staff and the delinquent youths. Secondly, there is very little evidence that an institution run on token economy lines has less antisocial behaviour than one run well on other lines. The study by Jesness *et al.* (1975) comparing two institutions – one with a behavioural approach (but only a very limited token economy) and the other based on transactional analysis principles – showed negligible differences between the two. Thirdly, such limited evidence as is available shows no long-term benefits with respect to any reduction in recidivism rates.* This last problem is one common to all institutional token economies and not just to those dealing with delinquents. It arises, of course, from the

---

* Indeed, one study (Ross and McKay, 1976) showed that severely disruptive delinquent girls treated in an individualized token economy had a *worse* recidivism rate after discharge in spite of improved behaviour while in the institution. However, a peer therapist behavioural approach had persisting benefits.

very features which give strength to the behavioural approach within the institution. By tying the individual's behaviour very closely to environmental contingencies of a kind that exist within the institution, but not outside it, the method creates a circumstance in which it may be expected that any improvements will *not* generalize to conditions outside the institution. It is for this reason that these methods, when applied in isolation, have been virtually abandoned as a means of affecting a reduction in recidivism (although they may be useful still in institutional management).

As a response to this last problem, one of the most significant developments in the rehabilitation of juvenile delinquents has been the establishment of residential group homes run on behavioural lines, but closely integrated with the community (see Burchard and Harig, 1976, for a good review of the issues and findings). The most outstanding example of this approach is provided by the Achievement Place studies (Phillips *et al.*, 1971; Fixsen *et al.*, 1973; Hoefler and Bornstein, 1975). Achievement Place is usually described as a community programme because the facility is community-based, and because the boys continue to attend the same school, have the same friends, and visit their parents regularly. However, in fact, it involves residential group care for delinquents who have been placed in custody. The institution has a clear set of rules, and a token economy with fines and rewards is systematically employed to ensure that they are adhered to. But it differs from the traditional institutional token economy in (i) being run on a family-style living situation; (ii) utilizing social skills training by professional teaching-parents; (iii) emphasizing responsibility and self-control; (iv) allowing residents who behave well to go on to a merit system which avoids the token economy by allowing the individual to demonstrate satisfactory conduct in the absence of points or fines; and (v) allowing youngsters who fare well on a merit system to go home, the parents being given explicit help in knowing how to maintain the behaviours learned at Achievement Place (however, the sanction of return to the institution remains). It is a highly imaginative, well thought out programme which includes a variety of measures appropriately designed to maintain behavioural change after the youth leaves the institution.

The programme is also one which has provided detailed measurement and evaluation at all stages. The basic research design has involved various permutations on within-subject comparisons dealing with a wide variety of 'target' behaviours (many of which, however, are not directly concerned with delinquent activities as such). The results are very impressive in demonstrating functional relationships between the target behaviours and the intervention procedures. In over 90 per cent of the experiments there was a significant change in the target behaviour, and in each case the change was found to be a function of a particular intervention.

Without doubt, a great deal has been accomplished in the Achievement Place programme, but nevertheless there must be some important reservations about its value as a method of reducing delinquent behaviour in the period after the youth completes the programme. The follow-up data so far are rather weak. A random allocation study has been started, but systematic findings on recidivism are available only for a non-random control group which differed in age (see Kirigin *et al.*, 1979). It is unclear whether the outcome was better for the Achievement Place group once the age difference had been taken into account. In addition, doubts must be expressed over the relevance of some of the 'target' behaviours subjected to modification (such as making up beds neatly or maintaining a dust-free room); over the degree of aversive control needed; and over the degree of generalization of behavioural change to the natural environment (see Burchard and Harig, 1976). A somewhat diluted replication of Achievement Place by Liberman *et al.* (1975) also showed that behavioural control could be obtained. But the results differed somewhat in showing that, with some behaviours, the improvements continued even when rewards were given non-contingently (a finding which suggests that factors in the institution other than the token economy also had an impact).

The conclusion from these studies is that behavioural methods applied in the institutional setting have an undoubted effect on young people's behaviour. The community-oriented approach of Achievement Place has also shown that there may be worthwhile general improvement in social functioning. The general pattern of findings suggests that these *might* be of value in reducing delinquent activities, but so far there is no satisfactory evidence, one way or the other, as to effects on recidivism.

However, in addition to these projects designed to run whole institutions on behavioural lines, there have been studies of individually applied behavioural methods within an institutional setting. Sarason's Cascadia project (Sarason and Ganzer, 1973; Sarason, 1978) provides a good example of this approach. The prime aim was to teach social skills – such as those needed in applying for a job, in resisting peer pressures to engage in antisocial acts, in dealing with social problems, and in planning ahead. Particular emphasis was placed on the generality of the appropriate behaviours and their applicability in a wide range of interpersonal situations. Modelling, role-playing and discussion were all employed for these purposes. Assignment of subjects to conditions was essentially random, but was altered by admission rates from time to time (see above). Outcome was assessed in terms of behaviour ratings in the institution and by recidivism rates. After 33 months the recidivism rate in the experimental groups was 14–19 per cent and in the controls it was 34 per cent; at the 5-year follow-up the comparable figures for cumulative recidivism were 23 per cent versus 48 per cent. The findings are limited by lack of data on comparability between the groups in terms of pre-intervention characteristics, but the results certainly suggest the efficacy of social skills training for institutionalized delinquents.

Behavioural methods applied to individuals in the community

Methods applied to individual youths in the community have been employed both in a group setting and on a one-to-one basis. The group settings generally function on lines which are broadly comparable to those described for Achievement Place, the difference being that the young people live at home and attend only on a daily or part-time basis. The Kentfields programme, described by Davidson and Robinson (1975), is a good example of this approach. The results have consistently shown that the amount of delinquent behaviour following the programme is substantially less than that before it and that school attendance or work records are improved (see also Blakely *et al.*, 1980), with an overall recidivism rate of 36–37 per cent. However, as the youths were at an age when delinquent activities might be expected to decrease without intervention (an average age of 16 years on admission), and as there were no comparisons with a control group, no inferences on efficacy are possible. The results of other comparable programmes such as the Hunt School (see Burchard and Harig, 1976) have also shown immediate behavioural gains, but similarly lack comparative follow-up data.

Seidman *et al.* (1980) have described a community programme in which 11–17 year old delinquent youths were treated by college students for 6–8 hours per week over a 3–5 month period, using a mixture of relationship skills, behavioural contracting and child advocacy. There was quasi-random assignment – with stratification according to sex, race, etc. – to the experimental programme or a control group. Although verbal reports from the adolescent, his parents and peers showed no group differences in behavioural outcome, the experimental group had fewer and less serious police contacts during the follow-up period of 2 years. A further study separated the behavioural contracting and child advocacy components. Again, verbal reports did not differentiate the groups but, as in the first study, recidivism rates were lower in the experimental groups than in the controls, with the behavioural contracting having better results than the advocacy. As the groups were comparable in terms of frequency and seriousness of offences prior to the intervention, the outcome differences suggest that the improvement was due to the behavioural intervention.

The 'Buddy System' (Fo and O'Donnell, 1974; O'Donnell *et al.*, 1979) operates on somewhat similar lines. The adult 'buddies' were specially trained non-professional volunteers who used a combination of friendship and companionship plus behavioural contingency procedures over the course of a one-year intervention. There was random assignment to experimental and control groups. Two-year follow-up data showed that the re-arrest rate was lower for *delinquents* in the experimental group (62 per cent *v.* 81 per cent for males and 36 per cent *v.* 50 per cent for females), but the reverse pattern was found for those referred only for status offences (running away, incorrigible behaviour, etc.) or minor violations only (25 per cent *v.* 19 per cent and 18 per cent *v.* 11 per cent). The deleterious effect on pre-delinquents was attributed to the group meetings which brought them into contact with serious delinquents.

Family interventions

Behavioural approaches to family interventions have focused on several different aspects of family functioning. Alexander and Parsons (1973) placed their main emphasis on improving family communication and organization, with contingency-contracting on specific issues of dispute within the family. Families were referred from the courts for minor offences (truancy, running away or ungovernable behaviour), and there was quasi-random assignment (i.e. random, subject to programme availability) to the experimental treatment (n = 46), to family therapy with discussion but not behavioural methods (n = 30), and no-treatment controls (n = 10). The recidivism rates were 26 per cent, 57 per cent and 50 per cent respectively at a 6–18 month follow-up (said to be equivalent across groups but no details given). When criminal offences only were considered, the recidivism rates were 17 per cent, 21 per cent and 27 per cent. The results are suggestive of intervention benefits, but doubts are raised by the lack of data on comparability of the groups regarding pre-intervention characteristics and duration of follow-up, as well as by the imperfect randomization and the lack of significant differences in criminal recidivism. A further study of a similar group of minor delinquents showed that outcomes were related to therapy and therapist variables (Alexander *et al.* 1976), but unfortunately a lack of data on background characteristics limited the inferences that could be drawn.

The most extensive series of behavioural family intervention studies are those undertaken by Patterson and his colleagues at the Oregon Social Learning Center (see Patterson, 1974, 1980; Patterson *et al.*, 1973). Both aggressive children and delinquents have been treated, using a behaviourally-oriented parent training programme. Parents are helped to use positive, non-coercive methods of control; to interact more positively as a family; to monitor their children's activities better and to deal more decisively with deviant behaviour; to negotiate behavioural contracts with the children; and to develop improved social problem-solving skills. Very detailed quantified observational techniques are used to assess parental behaviour, child behaviour and parent–child interactions in the home. Within-subject designs have constituted the main evaluation strategy, but data on comparison groups have also been employed. There are no published data utilizing random assignment comparisons. The findings have shown striking reductions in deviant behaviour as a result of the intervention, and follow-up studies of aggressive children have indicated that the benefits persisted for at least 12 months. Moreover, in that the benefits have been found to extend to siblings, it seems that the parents may well have acquired generally improved child management techniques (Arnold *et al.*, 1975). Replications with larger samples (see Patterson and Fleischman, 1979) have consistently confirmed the finding of improvement in aggressive behaviour which persists for one year (although this had been disputed on the basis of earlier reports – see Kent, 1976). In contrast, a follow-up (Moore *et al.*, 1979) of 28 families of stealers who completed the parent training programme (Patterson, 1981a, 1982) showed that by one year the children had reverted to their pre-treatment modes of behaviour, although the gains immediately following treatment had been considerable (a drop from a mean rate of stealing of 0.83 per week to 0.07).

The results, then, suggest that both aggression and stealing can be reduced by this treatment approach, but that the benefits are much more short-lived with the latter group. The Oregon group have been outstanding in the rigour of their measurement techniques but, nevertheless, reservations are necessary in terms of the general utility of the treatment approach for delinquents. Firstly, so far, there are no published data with randomly assigned groups, so that it remains uncertain how the techniques compare in efficacy with other approaches. Secondly, the greatest degree of success has been with the aggressive children. While certainly they present considerable problems with their disruptive behaviour, few have been overtly delinquent. The results with delinquent children have been very encouraging in the short term, but they have been much less lasting. Thirdly, the fall-out rate from treatment is considerable. For example, Patterson (1980) reported that some of the referred families did not agree to treatment (no numbers given), but that of 114 who entered the study, 28 dropped out before completing treatment and a further 25 dropped out during the 12-month follow-up. The figures from other studies have been even higher. This high fall-out both limits the validity of the follow-up data, and also highlights the difficulty of using a treatment method demanding a high degree of cooperation with families that are notoriously uncooperative in their interactions with official agencies of all kinds. It was found that cooperation was significantly improved and dropout reduced by paying the parents for participation in the project, but even with payment it was necessary to take specific steps to motivate resistant or unengaged parents.

Overview on behavioural approaches

Behavioural interventions have been considered in some detail, as these have seemed to offer most promise of effective methods of dealing with delinquent behaviour. Research in this field has been marked by care in detailed measurements of behaviour and in the steps taken to check whether changes in behaviour are functionally related to the mode of intervention. The results leave no doubt that important changes can be brought about. Equally, however, the field has been characterized by rather short follow-ups and a paucity of randomized group comparisons. As a consequence, there is still some uncertainty on how behavioural methods compare with alternative approaches and on the degree to which benefits persist after treatment. But, so far as can be assessed, behavioural methods do appear to be more effective than most other approaches in the short term. To that extent, the claim that 'nothing works' is seriously misleading. There are methods which have at least a limited degree of success in affecting delinquent behaviour. The problem is not so much in bringing about change as in *maintaining* change. There is also the additional problem of gaining people's involvement in those modes of intervention (a problem shared with all other methods).

The two main lessons which seem to emerge from these studies are: (i) interventions need to be directed to changing the child's home environment and the patterns of parent–child interaction, and (ii) in so far as the focus is on the offender himself, it needs to be concerned with improving his social problem-solving skills and social competence generally, rather than just seeking to suppress deviant behaviour.

Counselling and psychotherapy

In the early days of criminology, there was an emphasis on using counselling with youths from high-risk families in order either to prevent or to treat delinquent behaviour. The classic study of this type was the Cambridge–Somerville study (Powers and Witmer, 1951). Boys living in a high-delinquency area were randomly assigned to an experimental or a control group. The former received counselling, sometimes remedial education, and various club and summer camp experiences. Various exigencies (including the Second World War) meant that there were more frequent changes of counsellor than planned, and also that the counselling was less intensive than hoped for – about twice a month. But treatment lasted some 2–8 years, and most counsellors and boys felt that the project had been helpful. In spite of that, systematic evaluations have consistently failed to show any benefits from the intervention and, indeed, there is some evidence that the long-term outcome for the experimental group has been slightly worse (McCord, 1978). Subsequent similar attempts to prevent delinquency through counselling have been equally unsuccessful (Tait and Hodges, 1962; Craig and Furst, 1965; Berleman *et al.*, 1972). In view of the consistently negative results from both large- and small-scale studies (most of which were well planned and several with random assignment), it is clear that this form of long-term unfocused counselling is without value as a method of preventing delinquency.*

Of the sizeable number of studies of psychotherapy with already delinquent or disruptive adolescents (see Tramontana, 1980), there are only a handful which meet acceptable standards for evaluations. The Shore and Massimo (1973) study has been mentioned already as one with random allocation but very small numbers (10 in each group). Although classed as a psychotherapeutic intervention, there was also help with job placement, remedial education, and a variety of other forms of practical assistance, so that it is not possible to determine whether the psychotherapy *per se* was beneficial. However, at the 10-year follow-up, 7 of the experimental group had remained free of arrests compared with only 2 controls.

Redfering (1972 and 1973) assessed client-centred group counselling for delinquent girls in a corrective institution; there was random assignment to the experimental and control groups (with 18 in each). The former group

---

* Although these studies are usually considered as referring to *preventive* measures, many of the subjects had already been convicted at the time they received counselling. Accordingly, the conclusion probably should be extended to the lack of efficacy of counselling as a therapeutic measure for delinquents.

were found to develop more positive attitudes (as assessed from semantic differential), and a year later more of the experimental group had been released from the institution. It is not possible from these findings to assess efficacy.

Persons (1966 and 1967) studied the effects of a combination of twice-weekly group psychotherapy and once-weekly individual therapy over a 20-week period for institutionalized delinquent boys aged 15–19. 41 pairs were matched for various background factors including number and type of offences, and then, within each pair, there was random assignment to the experimental group – the latter having just the usual institutional activities. The experimental group showed better institutional adjustment and better interpersonal relationships, and follow-up a year later showed that they had a lower recidivism rate, as measured by the number readmitted to the institution, and a better employment rate. While these results suggest benefits from treatment, it is impossible to be sure that it was the experimental group which improved rather than the controls which got worse. It is equally plausible that the controls suffered from being singled out as being *denied* treatment (there is good evidence from one drug study in an institution for delinquents that this worsening effect does indeed occur – see Molling *et al.*, 1962). Against this pair of successful outcomes from institutional psychotherapy, and the single successful outcome from psychotherapy in the community, must be placed a rather larger number of studies with negative findings (see Martinson, 1974; Brody, 1976; Lipton *et al.*, 1975). While these vary in rigour and quality of the intervention, the balance of evidence (particularly when taken in conjunction with the consistently negative results from the well-controlled so-called preventive studies – see above) suggests that counselling and psychotherapy are not particularly effective methods of intervention for most delinquents. Whether these approaches are of benefit to particular types of delinquents is considered below.

Individual differences in response to counselling/psychotherapy

One of the most important, but controversial, issues in the intervention literature is whether there are predictable individual differences in response, so that treatment may be beneficial for some kinds of people yet without effect or even harmful for others. A further development of the same idea is that the matching of therapist and client may also be important (Palmer, 1973). So far as the first possibility is concerned, the main data in support come from the California studies (see Palmer, 1975; Warren, 1977) and from the P.I.C.O. project (Adams, 1970).

The California Community Treatment Project (C.T.P.) is a complex project which is written up in a variety of overlapping reports, none of which provides a very clear account of precisely what happened with each of the groups. This makes the results difficult to evaluate, but the essence of the findings is provided in Palmer (1974), who indicates that assignment to the experimental and control groups was random. The experimental group differed not only in the treatment they received (a wide range of approaches in both community and institutional settings) and in the extent to which it was planned individually, but also in the intensity and frequency of treatment. The I-level classification (Warren, 1977; Austin, 1975) was used to categorize personality functioning. The overall results showed that recidivism during the parole period was lower in the experimental group (44 per cent *v.* 63 per cent – but see above for criticisms of this assessment), but that *after* leaving the project, the experimental group had slightly *more* convictions. In this connection, however, the key finding is that whereas the findings for 'passive-conformist' types were somewhat contradictory, and those for the 'power-oriented' youths showed that they did *worse* with the experimental treatment, the 'neurotic' group did significantly *better*. The 'neurotic' youths were characterized either by feelings of inadequacy or rejection or by symptoms of emotional disturbance. While the statistical presentation of these findings is inadequate, the published figures do suggest that the effects of treatment varied by personality type. Although Palmer (1973) has claimed that the matching of counsellor and client made a difference to outcome, the published results provide no clear demonstration of this effect.

Barkwell (1976 and 1980) has attempted to take the question further by utilizing probation officers, all of whom were trained in I-level methods. Juveniles placed on probation were randomly assigned to one of 3 groups – with 16 in each: (i) intensive treatment with worker–client matching according to I-level diagnosis; (ii) same treatment without matching; (iii) surveillance by probation officers with a much heavier case-load. The first I-level group showed a marked increase in self-concept, whereas this did not occur with either of the two other groups; the first group also showed a significantly better school or work attendance. The overall difference between groups in delinquent activities during the 3-year follow-up fell short of statistical significance, but there was a significant group × time interaction – meaning that whereas delinquent activities progressively diminished over time in the first group, this did not happen in the other two groups. Although the sample size was fairly small, the study seems well controlled and the results suggest that there may be a differential treatment effect.

The P.I.C.O. project (Adams, 1970) was concerned with the evaluation of intensive counselling and casework with 400 delinquent youths in an institution. They were allocated at random into experimental and control groups, and within each group there was a further subdivision into 'amenables' (meaning 'bright, verbal and anxious, insightful, aware of his difficulties and wanting to overcome them') and non-amenables. Both short-term and a more long-term (3-year) follow-up showed that the amenables did significantly better (in terms of reduced recidivism) with treatment whereas the non-amenables did worse.

Jesness (1965), in the 'Fricot Ranch' study, found that 'immature-neurotic' boys in the experimental institutional groups had a better outcome than controls (at least initially), whereas this was not so for other personality types. However, a later study (Jesness, 1971), in which the institutional experimental group was based on I-level matching, failed to differ from controls in outcome. In the comparison of two institutions, one run on behavioural and one on transactional analysis lines (Jesness, 1975), there was a tendency for manipulators to do better with transactional analysis and for unsocialized passives to do better in the behavioural setting, but the trend fell short of statistical significance.

There are too few data for any firm conclusion on the reality of individual differences – especially as the amenable/non-amenable and I-level classifications are not easy to translate into behavioural terms. Nevertheless, there do seem to be fairly consistent pointers that intensive counselling is likely to be of value only with rather anxious, introspective youths* who are aware of their personal problems and want help with them. Although each study is open to methodological objections, the fact that the differences go in the *same* general direction each time suggests that the differential effect may have some validity. At the very least the matter warrants further study. Martinson (1976) has criticized attempts to study this issue on the grounds that there is no point in looking for differential effects until you know that you have an effective treatment. In our view that is a completely wrong-headed approach, in that the examination of differential effects is *part* of the tests for efficacy. To assume that an intervention must work for everybody to some extent is not a sensible starting point.

---

* However, that does not necessarily mean that a psychotherapeutic approach is optimal with such individuals. Sarason and Ganzer (1973), for example, in their social skills training project, found a tendency for highly anxious subjects to do better with modelling than with discussion.

Varieties of institutional care

Success rates following institutional treatment or care have been generally poor – at least as assessed by re-conviction rates, which have usually run at about 60 to 70 per cent (see, for example, McMichael, 1974; Dunlop, 1975; Millham *et al.*, 1975 and 1978). But, of course, that could be no more than a reflection of the seriously recidivist characteristics of youths sent to institutions, just as also it could mean that most institutions are of poor quality or are inappropriately run. These issues have been studied by three principal modes of comparison: (i) custodial versus non-custodial approaches (see below); (ii) therapeutic versus correctional regimes (or a comparison of two contrasting varieties of either); and (iii) variations between institutions of ostensibly similar type (see Cornish and Clarke, 1975).

Therapeutic versus correctional regimes

Several well-planned studies in the United States have compared various forms of experimental therapeutic institutional regimes with the more traditional corrective approach. Although there have been minor differences here and there, the overall pattern has been one of a striking *lack* of difference in outcome (with respect to recidivism rates on return to the community) between institutional regimes which have differed markedly in both theory and practice. For example, Weeks (1958), in the Highfields experiment, compared a permissive regime providing group therapy with a conventional disciplinary reformatory. Black boys at Highfields had a lower re-conviction rate,* but there was evidence that they were less delinquent from the start and it is uncertain how far the predictive measures which were used were able to control for these prior differences. In the Silverlake experiment (Empey and Lubeck, 1971), recidivism rates were no different following a very liberal regime, which encouraged participation in the running of the institution as well as frequent home visits, than those after a traditional disciplinary regime (although the former may have resulted in somewhat less serious offences). In the Fricot Ranch study (Jesness, 1965), youths (especially neurotic youths) in small units of 20 boys did somewhat better in the year after discharge than youths in units of 50 – but recidivism rates after 3 years were generally similar between the two institutions. Jesness (1975 and 1980) also compared a school utilizing treatment strategies based on psychodynamic principles and group therapy methods of transactional analysis

---

* The differences fell well short of significance for white boys.

with one run on behavioural lines. There was random assignment between the two institutions. Some behaviour ratings (during the programme) favoured one institution and some the other, but re-conviction rates at all stages after discharge (from 3 to 24 months) were closely similar for the two schools.*

The results from British studies have been generally similar. Thus, Cornish and Clarke (1975) found no differences in re-conviction between a 'modified therapeutic community' and a traditional approach school regime – there being random allocation of boys to the two institutions. Bottoms and McClintock (1973) studied the effects of introducing a more individualized therapeutic approach to a Borstal. Outcomes were compared with those from earlier periods using prediction scores; no differences were found. Similarly, McMichael (1974) found no differences in the re-conviction rates of boys from an approved school run on therapeutic community lines and of boys from other schools. On the other hand, Craft *et al.* (1964) found that the outcome for adolescent psychopaths was better following an authoritarian regime than following a permissive institutional regime. A much earlier study by Mannheim and Wilkins (1955), using prediction tables to equate groups, had found better results from open Borstals; and in a more recent random allocation study, Williams (1970) found a slightly lower 2-year re-conviction rate (51 per cent) for offenders sent to a Borstal utilizing individual case-work than that (63 per cent) for institutions with a group counselling or traditional approach.

The general picture is one of remarkably similar re-conviction rates in the years immediately following discharge for institutions run on theoretically and practically different lines. It could be argued that a few studies have shown marginally better results for those run on individually therapeutic lines, but this has been so only in some studies and the general impression is one of broadly comparable outcomes.

Variations between institutions of ostensibly similar type

That finding could mean that institutions are without effect. But two other alternatives are equally plausible; perhaps the characteristics of institutions which matter are not those that are captured in the differences in orientation

---

* Jesness (1975 and 1980) has argued that the finding of various associations within institutions between staff competency and parole outcome and the slightly lower re-conviction rates in youths from both experimental institutions compared with two traditional institutions, implies that both the former were equally effective rather than that neither made a difference. This is possible, but the finding is a very weak one in the absence of either matching or random assignment.

studied, or perhaps institutions have effects on behaviour at the time but these effects do not persist for long after discharge. Both possibilities may be studied by an alternative research design – namely determining which institutions *do* differ in outcome (after controlling for intake factors), and then relating the outcome variations to the characteristics of the institutions. Several British studies have followed this strategy, and their results have been generally consistent in suggesting that institutions do have predictable effects on behaviour.

Sinclair (1971) found that the rates of absconding from probation hostels varied greatly – from under 20 per cent to over 50 per cent. Moreover, it was found that these variations were systematically associated with the wardens' styles of management. Absconding was least frequent from hostels with a strict discipline but where wardens expressed warmth to the boys and where they and their wives were agreed in their approach. However, two results suggested that the main environmental effect was an immediate, rather than an enduring, one. With one exception, the re-conviction rates of boys who did not abscond did not vary according to the hostel in which they had been placed. Also, boys who were sent to the hostel in order to achieve removal from a bad home had *lower* re-conviction rates than other boys while in the hostel, but *higher* rates on return home.

Clarke and Martin (1971, 1975) found equally great differences in absconding rates between approved schools, these differences being relatively stable (with a rank correlation of 0.65) over a 3-year period, and not explicable in terms of differences in the kinds of boys admitted to the schools. It seemed that absconding was less likely to occur when the staff expected respect and obedience from the youths (Martin, 1977). Sinclair and Clarke (1973) went on to show that schools with disproportionately high absconding rates also had the worst re-conviction rates. Broadly comparable results were obtained in Dunlop's (1975) study of approved schools. Schools which (as judged from reports from the boys) stressed mature and responsible behaviour and emphasized trade training, but were not particularly punitive, had lower rates of absconding and misbehaviour and of re-conviction. In both these studies, the school variations were most marked with respect to absconding and to other behaviours during the period while the offenders were in the school, but also there were significant differences in later rates of re-conviction. Millham *et al.* (1975), too, found marked variations between approved schools in re-conviction rates. Successful schools tended to have a harmonious atmosphere, good staff–pupil relationships, firm expectations and higher standards, and a high level of activities.

These studies of variations between institutions are entirely consistent in showing marked variations in the behaviour of youths in them. In each case, school effects have remained after controlling for differences in the intake to the schools. A causal inference seems indicated, particularly in view of the consistency of the findings on variation and on the links with the institutional characteristics. However, a random allocation study has yet to be undertaken, and in its absence conclusions have to be a little less certain.

Nevertheless, it seems possible to draw certain lessons. Firstly, it seems highly likely that institutions *do* have an important and quite substantial effect on the behaviour of young people during the course of their stay in the institution. Secondly, the features which characterize successful institutions are *not* those which differentiate so-called therapeutic and corrective institutions. The 'recipe', if there is one,* appears to be a combination of firmness, warmth, harmony, high expectations, good discipline (especially with respect to absconding), and a practical approach to training. Thirdly, because these are not the features studied in random allocation studies, it is highly desirable that such experiments should now be undertaken with schools which exhibit contrasts on what appear to be the relevant dimensions. Fourthly, pending such studies, it seems sensible to run institutional regimes along the lines suggested by research. Fifthly, the effects of institutions on recidivism after return to the community are less than on behaviour at the time; but some worthwhile enduring effects are evident.

The last point warrants more detailed study and consideration in that there is a need to determine *how* persistence of benefits (or ill-effects) occurs when it occurs, and what are the factors which limit generalization. The finding that the likelihood of re-conviction varies according to the characteristics of the environment to which the youth returns (in addition to Sinclair's study noted above, see also Buikhuisen and Hoekstra, 1974, and West, 1982, discussed in Chapter 7) suggests that the lack of persistence of institutional effects is an indication that environments *do* have effects, rather than that they do not. It is just that there tends to be very little continuity between institutional and community environments (see also the section on behavioural approaches above), and hence rather limited carry-over from one to the other. The implication is that if we wish to see the benefits of good institutional experience persist, we need to pay equal attention to the environment to which the youth returns.

The link between absconding and re-conviction (both within individuals and institutions) suggests the possible operation of another factor. It may be

---

* There is a striking parallel with the factors in the family associated with non-persistence of delinquency and protection from delinquency (see Davies and Sinclair, 1971 also Chapter 6).

that an absconder is more likely to get involved in further delinquent activities while on the run (stealing to get food or money). In this and other ways absconding itself increases the likelihood of one delinquent behaviour leading to another. In so far as that is the case, it would appear that part of the effect of institutions is in preventing behaviours, like absconding, which *increase* the likelihood of further delinquencies. In other words, it is more that some institutions make things *worse*, rather than that some make things better.

On the other hand, that does not seem to be quite the whole story. To begin with, as already noted, the factors in institutions which seem to protect against recidivism are very similar to those in families and in the natural environment which are protective (in situations where the question of absconding does not arise). But also, the findings from the studies of social skills training (see above) suggest that, to a limited extent, it is possible to help youths acquire behavioural styles and skills which may help them cope better in the community.

Custodial and non-custodial approaches

At one time there was a hope that institutional treatments would be clearly therapeutic and reformative in their effects. As the evidence mounted showing that this rarely happened, there was a growing interest in the question of whether non-custodial approaches could be as effective (or, at least, no more ineffective). The matter was first investigated by comparing reconviction rates from courts with a strong bias for or against custodial sentences (see Wilkins, 1958; Davies, 1969). The results showed no difference between courts which varied in this way. A rather better test is provided by comparing groups carefully matched on factors known to predict recidivism. Kraus (1974) used this strategy to compare 223 male juvenile offenders given probation and 223 committed to an institution in Australia. The results showed that, with the exception of 'take and use motor vehicle' offenders, recidivism was consistently greater after detention than after probation. As the groups were well matched on an exceptionally wide range of relevant variables, the findings provide convincing evidence of a differential effect – probably brought about by the *detrimental* effects of detention rather than by the benefits of probation.

The Provo experiment (Empey and Erickson, 1972) is one of the most ambitious attempts to examine the relative impact of custodial and non-custodial approaches prospectively. As discussed above, the plan to utilize a random allocation design fell through as a result of practical difficulties, and it was necessary to rely on matching. An intensive community programme was compared with a custodial institution in terms of 4-year follow-ups. The two groups were generally comparable, but the custodial group included a few more seriously delinquent individuals. The overall recidivism rate for the institutional group was worse than that for the experimental community programme group, and multiple-regression analyses which took into account background variables showed that whereas the community programme seemed to have little effect on outcome, incarceration appeared to make it *worse*.

In the absence of a fully implemented randomization design, there must be some caution in accepting the validity of the difference in outcome between custodial and non-custodial approaches in these two studies. However, taken together with other studies (see Home Office, 1969; Brody, 1976), the pattern of results is consistent in showing that non-custodial approaches do no worse than incarceration and that there is some tendency for them to have marginally better results (Wright and Dixon, 1977). No study has shown generally superior results for custodial methods, although it must also be said that many show no difference (Klein, 1979). Of course, that is not to say that some form of institutional care or treatment is never required. Obviously there are youths whose delinquent activities are so serious, or whose behaviour is so disruptive, that admission to an institution is required to protect society. Moreover, there may be subgroups of delinquents who do better with an institutional regime. This was suggested, for example, by the California project (Palmer, 1974), in which 'power-oriented' youths had a lower recidivism rate following a traditional institutional programme.

Incapacitation

It is sometimes argued that, even if incarceration does no good, at least it keeps offenders out of circulation* for a while. While, of course, that is true, it has to be remembered that institutions are very expensive to run, so the solution could prove to be quite costly. Moreover, because crimes are committed by so many youths, it is probable that even a doubling of the

---

* It is not clear how well even this is done. Tutt (1976) has noted that 'drop-outs' of children in the 1960s from the old 'approved school' system ran at 6–11 per cent, whereas in the 1970s under the current 'community homes with education' system it ran at 37–42 per cent, with a particularly high proportion (17–18 per cent) absconding. The two sets of figures are not directly comparable for a variety of reasons (for example, the 1963–6 figures were national whereas those for 1974 applied to one region), but it is obvious that the 'drop-out' rate in recent years has been unacceptably high and, almost certainly, greater than that in the 1960s.

294 Juvenile Delinquency

number incarcerated or a doubling of the duration of incarceration would bring about only a rather small reduction in the overall rate of crime (see, for example, Clarke, 1974; Pease and Wolfson, 1979; Brody and Tarling, 1980). Various attempts have been made to calculate the precise size of the potential reduction, but calculations are hugely influenced by the nature of the assumptions made about who commits unsolved or unreported crimes. Estimates of the extent to which crime would increase if *no one* was incarcerated at all range from less than 4 per cent to 20 per cent. However, in view of the problems in deciding how to determine who commits the crimes which do not lead to conviction, it is doubtful whether much is to be gained by attempts to increase the accuracy of such calculations. What is clear is that, no matter what the assumptions made, cost-benefits analyses do not suggest that increased incapacitation would be a sensible overall strategy. Furthermore, it is evident that quite substantial *reductions* in the use of custodial sentences could be achieved without any appreciable increase in crime. For example, Brody and Tarling (1980) estimated that a 40 per cent reduction in the prison population would lead to only a 1.6 per cent increase in convictions. This relative imbalance between savings (in the costs of imprisonment) and costs (in increase in crime) derives from the fact that most offenders are not sent to prison. These figures apply to adults, but it is apparent that the same effect would apply to juveniles to an even greater extent.

Although it is obvious that incapacitation does not constitute a worthwhile general strategy for the control of crime, it might be thought that it could still be useful in the case of potentially dangerous criminals, where the risks of serious physical injury to members of the general public might justify the greater costs involved in custodial solutions. However, that raises two other questions: (i) how far is violent crime restricted to a small group of violent offenders and how far is it committed on occasions by most criminals?; and (ii) how accurate are predictions of 'dangerousness'? In his study of working-class London boys, Farrington (1978) found that over a fifth of juvenile delinquent boys had committed truly violent crimes (threats, carrying weapons, jostling and snatching were *not* counted as violent). This means that nearly *7 per cent* of the general population of boys had engaged in violent crime. It is apparent that, although many offenders are never violent, a substantial proportion are violent on occasions. Not surprisingly, therefore, it has been found that predictions of dangerousness are relatively weak (see Brody and Tarling, 1980). This is both because some apparently dangerous offenders do *not* commit further violent crimes and because many hitherto non-violent offenders *do* sometimes engage in violent crime. Although aggressiveness is a reasonably persistent behavioural characteristic (see Chapter 2), and although aggressiveness is associated with violent crime (Farrington, 1978), it is a poor predictor because so many non-violent offenders are aggressive. Also, the family background characteristics associated with violent crime are very similar to those associated with non-violent crime (the only factor in the Farrington study which differentiated the two was harsh parental discipline, which was more common in violent offenders). Much the best predictor of future violent crime is repeated violent crime in the past, but even this is not a very strong predictor.*

A policy of locking up seriously dangerous offenders in order to protect the public may well be justifiable in the case of individuals committing repeated violent crimes, but 'The infrequency of really serious crimes of violence, their apparently generally random quality and the rarity of anything like a genuinely "dangerous type" offers little encouragement for a policy which aims to reduce serious assaults by selective incapacitation of those with violent records' (Brody and Tarling, 1980).

Non-custodial penal measures

Compared with the volume of studies on institutions and on specialized therapeutic programmes, there has been relatively little research into the effects of non-custodial penal measures in spite of the fact that they constitute the majority of interventions employed in practice. However, there are a few investigations which provide useful leads and ideas.

Attendance centres

The requirements of an attendance centre order are attendance at a specified place, usually for 2 hours on a Saturday afternoon at weekly or fortnightly intervals, for a period up to 24 hours (Dunlop, 1980). The aim is mainly punitive, in the deliberate deprivation of leisure time, but also there is the aim to guide youths to more constructive recreational activities. An early evalua-

---

* The major problem here is one of *base rates* (Meehl and Rosen, 1955). If one is predicting a relatively infrequent event (as one is with very severe violence), even a highly accurate predictor is bound to lead to a huge *over*-prediction. Livermore, Malmquist and Meehl (1968) make the point explicit with a hypothetical example: 'Assume that one person out of a thousand will kill. Assume also that an exceptionally accurate test is created which differentiates with 95 per cent effectiveness those who will kill from those who will not. If 100,000 people were tested, out of the 100 who would kill, 95 would be isolated. Unfortunately, out of the 99,900 who would not kill, 4,995 people would also be isolated as potential killers. In these circumstances, it is clear that we could not justify incarcerating all 5,090 people.'

tion (McClintock, 1961) suggested that attendance centres were unlikely to be effective with recidivists but that they might be helpful with young first offenders, with little or no experience of crime, and coming from a fairly normal background. A more recent appraisal (Dunlop, 1980) showed marked variations in absenteeism rates (4 per cent to 35 per cent) between centres, which could not be explained in terms of intake characteristics. The centres with low rates of absenteeism were run by officers with significantly greater experience, and success seemed to be associated with 'a style of management in which firmness of purpose and action rather than flexibility and tolerance were emphasized, particularly in relation to regularity of attendance' (Dunlop, 1980). However, the centres did *not* vary in the rates of further offending during the course of the attendance centre order. Overall, 29 per cent of boys committed at least one offence – in the great majority of cases within the first two months. McClintock (1961) found that re-offending was more likely in boys also on supervision orders, but this was not found in Dunlop's (1980) inquiry. More prolonged attendance orders were associated with a higher rate of re-offending; this was mainly a function of a longer period at risk, but not wholly so, and it seemed that there was no advantage (and possibly a slight disadvantage) in the longer orders. In that attendance centres were not compared with any other form of intervention, no conclusions on efficacy are possible. The lack of differences between centres in re-offending, in spite of differences in absenteeism, suggests that attendance centres probably have a rather marginal impact on recidivism. However, there is no evidence that the shorter attendance centre orders do any harm, and they may be helpful with some offenders.

Suspended sentences and adjournment

Shoham and Sandberg (1964) compared adult offenders given a suspended imprisonment sentence in Israel with those given other corrective measures (presumably imprisonment). First offenders given a suspended sentence had a lower re-conviction rate than those sent to prison, but the reverse applied to recidivists. Also, suspended sentences seemed more effective for property offenders and those from a middle-class background, and less effective for violent and 'professional' criminals.

It could be argued that, with first offenders, a suspended sentence could have the desired deterrent effect without either the costs of imprisonment or the possible disadvantages of prolonged contact with recidivist criminals. The Shoham and Sandberg study was concerned with adults, but the same general principles might apply in childhood. A variant of this approach was investigated by Berg and his colleagues (1978a and b) in a particularly well-designed random allocation comparison of the use of *adjournment* and of *supervision* orders for failure to attend school, in which randomization was combined with a predictive equation based on extensive information about the children. An earlier retrospective study (Berg *et al.*, 1977) had suggested that the former procedure might be more effective, and this was tested using a prospective design with a 6-month follow-up. With adjournment, the court repeatedly adjourned the case with the frequency of further court appearances being contingent on whether there had been an improvement in school attendance (i.e. fewer appearances if there had been good attendance). In addition, there could be an interim care order requiring admission to a residential assessment centre for a few weeks. In the case of a supervision order, supervision* was placed entirely in the hands of a social worker or probation officer. The results were unequivocal in showing that adjournment was more successful as assessed in terms of both improvements in school attendance and criminal offences – confirming the finding from the earlier retrospective study.

While the empirical evidence on the value of this approach is extremely limited, the findings are consistent in showing that this form of specific deterrent may be effective with first offenders. It warrants both more extended use and further study.

Cautioning

The formal police caution provides an alternative to prosecution – the aim being to provide a firm indication of disapproval of delinquent behaviour while still avoiding the stigma and possible negative side-effects of conviction. The question of whether cautioning succeeds in diverting young people from the courts was considered in Chapter 2, with the conclusion that probably it does but only at the cost of increasing the total number of people brought into the legal processing net. Here, we are concerned with the rather separate question of the efficacy of cautioning in reducing recidivism. Unfortunately, no random allocation experiments have been undertaken and no firm conclusions are possible. Gawn *et al.* (1977) found that the recidivism rate was lower for juveniles cautioned than for those taken to court, but no analyses were undertaken to determine whether or not this was a function of the differing characteristics of youths dealt with in these two ways. Better data are provided by Farrington and Bennett (1981), who compared the

---

* The published reports give very little description of what this involved.

effects of cautions and court appearances in some 900 juvenile first offenders under the age of 15 in London. It was found that, even after controlling statistically for relevant background variables, cautioned juveniles had a lower re-arrest rate. The suggestion from this study that cautioning *may* be more effective for first offenders needs to be studied further.

Probation

The evidence on the effects of probation is not much better. Straight comparisons of outcome, taking into account age and previous criminal history, have suggested that probation is not a particularly effective measure (see Home Office, 1964). Several studies (summarized in Lipton *et al.*, 1975, and Brody, 1976) have compared the effects of differences in the size of case-load; the results have been rather inconsistent and inconclusive, with some investigations showing slightly better results with small case-loads but others not. One study, however, suggested the possible importance of the qualities of the probation officers (Johnson, 1962). Empey and Erickson (1972), in the Provo experiment, used a random allocation design to compare the effects of ordinary probation with a much more intensive and extensive experimental community programme. Only marginal differences were found between the two groups in terms of various different measures of recidivism. Piercy and Lee (1976), in a very small-scale project without random allocation, compared the combination of counselling and probationary supervision with supervision alone. The groups seemed generally comparable before the intervention, and no significant differences between groups were found for official acts of misconduct during the intervention (although the former group did better when the clients of one counsellor who was with the project only a short while were excluded). Klein (1979) and his colleagues undertook a random allocation study* comparing release (i.e. nothing done), referral to a community programme, and court petition. A 27-month follow-up showed significantly lower recidivism rates for community referral than for court petition, but still lower rates with doing nothing. However, self-report data showed no differences between the three groups.

While no firm conclusions are warranted, the evidence provides no indication that probation makes any significant difference to recidivism. As Croft (1978) noted, this negative finding poses the question of whether the service should simply be abandoned or, rather, whether the energies should be

* Gibbons and Blake (1976), in a review of an earlier report on this project, note that there were violations of randomization in practice and that data were missing on many subjects. The published account of the project is too brief for any assessment of the validity of these criticisms.

directed to the invention of new methods and new approaches. Bottoms and McWilliams (1979) argue that there is still an important role for probation, but that it is necessary to respond to the research findings by accepting that it does not have an effective therapeutic function. Jones (1981) has agreed with Bottoms and McWilliams's suggestion that there is a need for community (as distinct from individual) interventions, but argued that a correctional role has a place in this approach. We return to this issue in Chapter 10, but here we note that the traditional approaches in probation and social work supervision do not seem to have succeeded in their aims in most cases.

Community programmes and diversionary policies

During the last decade or so there has been an increasing emphasis on the development of community-based interventions which might serve as alternatives to traditional forms of institutional care/treatment for some offenders. These have taken a variety of forms, and indeed reflect a range of sometimes contradictory philosophies. It is convenient to subdivide them into (i) school projects; (ii) interventions in which the prime target is the community or sections of the community rather than individuals; (iii) intensive community-based interventions in which the work is focused on individuals; and (iv) diversionary policies.

School projects

Over the years there have been several attempts to use mental health, group counselling or special educational programmes in schools to prevent problem behaviour and delinquency (for example, Gildea *et al.*, 1967; Meyer, Borgatta and Jones, 1965; Reckless and Dinitz, 1972; Kellam *et al.*, 1975), but most comparisons with control groups have shown no measurable benefits from the programmes. Apart from one small study (Bowman, 1959), in which preliminary findings suggested the possibility of benefits from placing children with disciplinary problems in special classes, the one major exception to the general picture of negative findings is Rose and Marshall's (1974) evaluation of counselling and school social work in schools in the north of England. The social workers in the experimental schools mainly utilized a case-work approach with individual children, but also it is likely that there was an impact on the school as a whole. Experimental and control schools were compared with respect to changes in delinquency rates (and other outcome measures) over twelve 3-month periods. The results showed a rather small, although consistent, gain for the experimental schools in comparison with the control schools. As the study stands in isolation at the moment it would not be justifiable to draw inferences about this mode of approach, but the strategy warrants further use and evaluation.

In addition, there is one study (Schweinhart and Weikart, 1980) which suggests the possibility that pre-school programmes may have beneficial effects on attitudes and behaviour which may lead to some reduction in delinquent activities. The initial optimism which accompanied the introduction of compensatory pre-school education for children from disadvantaged backgrounds tended to fall away with the increasing body of evidence that the initial I.Q. gains disappeared within a few years of starting regular school. More systematic long-term follow-ups of the best experimental programmes have confirmed the lack of any enduring effect on I.Q. (Darlington *et al.*, 1980). But, interestingly, the same studies have indicated probable persisting beneficial effects on other aspects of school performance. The Perry project in Michigan comprised daily pre-school education and weekly home visits over at least one year, with systematic comparisons between this experimental group and a control group, group assignment being on an essentially random basis with good matching on the crucial background variables (Schweinhart and Weikart, 1980). At 14 years the two groups did not differ in I.Q., but scholastic achievements tended to be substantially better for the experimental group youngsters, who also showed somewhat greater commitment to school as assessed from both teacher ratings and interviews with the youths themselves. Some of the measures of conduct in school favoured the experimental group, whereas others showed no differences. There was also a tendency for delinquent behaviour (as assessed from self-report) to be less frequent in the experimental group, but the statistical significance of the group difference on delinquency varied to an important extent according to the statistical techniques used (which it did not with the other outcome measures). The findings with respect to an impact on delinquency are too uncertain for much weight to be attached to them at this stage; also they need replication. Nevertheless, there are pointers to the possibility that well-planned pre-school programmes might have educational benefits with some slight spin-off effects on delinquent behaviour. While the results are not such as to recommend this approach as a preventive strategy, they do underline the interventive potential in the links between educational retardation and delinquency.

Community programmes

Street-corner worker programmes constituted one of the earlier ways of attempting to alter forces in the natural social environment. The strategy involved street-corner workers making contact with juvenile gangs or groups, gaining their confidence, and then trying to redirect their disruptive activities into more constructive channels. Several studies (see Wright and Dixon, 1977) have sought to evaluate this mode of intervention. By the nature of the strategy, it is difficult to measure effects, but the results have been generally disappointing and provide no encouragement to develop this approach further.

The Wincroft Youth Project for detached youth in a slum area of Manchester (Smith, Farrant and Marchant, 1972) represents one of the most thorough and far-reaching attempts at community intervention as a means of reducing delinquency (although its evaluation is limited by the non-random allocation design). There was extensive use of volunteers, who sought first to contact the boys on their own territory in a coffee-bar setting, and then combined group meetings with individual case-work as relationships developed. 54 boys in the programme, chosen on the basis of their delinquency and/or delinquency proneness (as assessed from scores on the Bristol Social Adjustment Guides), were compared with matched controls from a comparable socially deprived area. Both official convictions and self-report data showed less and less serious delinquency in the experimental group during the follow-up period. However, the differences were modest (37 per cent convictions $v.$ 55 per cent at the first follow-up and 50 per cent $v.$ 62 per cent a year later), there were no differences on Jesness inventory scores or employment or relationships with parents, and the benefits were most evident with the least disturbed boys. The results are mildly encouraging in suggesting that community interventions may be of some limited value, but the findings indicate only a quite limited impact which tended to fade with time.

An alternative strategy has been employed to reduce vandalism – the aim being to get people in the community to take more interest in and responsibility for the care of the public facilities available to them. The Central Policy Review Staff (1978) document gave some examples of local efforts which appeared to have had some success. For example, in one, a local community council was established and police officers who were qualified leaders took an active role in running youth clubs and sports teams. In another, police were instrumental in organizing groups of young people to clear up debris and remove graffiti, and in obtaining premises for a community centre. The British Community Development projects, designed to deal with poverty and social deprivation (see Rutter and Madge, 1976), also sought to mobilize untapped local resources and lead the community to develop their own systems of self-support. The objective of gaining constructive community involvement seems sensible and appropriate in view of the evidence on area differences in delinquency rates, but no data are available to indicate whether in fact these approaches have had any effect on delinquency rates.

Intensive community-based treatments

In Britain, intensive community-based treatments have come to be referred to as 'intermediate treatment'. As Bottoms and Sheffield (1980) indicate in their thoughtful and incisive review of the topic, the concept of intermediate treatment is both vague and wide. However, the D.H.S.S. Social Work Service Group (1977) have usefully outlined what appear to be the prime objectives of this general approach: (i) supervision by involvement of children in the centre recreational and work programme; (ii) support in relation to home stresses; (iii) the aiding of personal and emotional development; (iv) opportunities to develop satisfactory social relationships; (v) rehabilitation to enable the child to transfer learning within the programme to his wider environment; (vi) education; and (vii) social work with the family. It is clear from this list of principles that the philosophy remains a personal intervention model which may be community-based but which is not community-directed. However, it seems to combine the goals of preventing delinquency or recidivism, of preventing institutionalization, and of improving personal functioning. Moreover, it is concerned to deal with both 'high-risk', but as yet non-delinquent, groups and also convicted offenders. No adequate evaluative research has been undertaken so far, but such evidence as there is does not suggest that any lasting effect on recidivism or personal functioning is likely to occur (Bottoms and Sheffield, 1980). For example, Covington (1979), evaluating the Hammersmith Teenage Project, found that the reconviction rate in the first year was higher than that for teenagers on supervision orders (69 per cent *v.* 49 per cent); although the figures for the second year were better (41 per cent). In the absence of adequate matching, no confidence can be placed in the comparative rates of recidivism for either year. It is important in all evaluations to differentiate between the effects on delinquents and on non-delinquents, as they may not be the same. Also, it is necessary to specify what is the alternative to intermediate treatment (doing nothing, supervision order, detention centre, etc.).

While intermediate treatment as a programme has not yet been subjected to well-controlled systematic evaluation, many elements in it have been assessed. For example, Byles and Maurice (1979) assessed crisis-centred family therapy, using random allocation between the experimental group in which intervention was directed at the family as a system, and controls who were subject to the traditional Youth Bureau methods. The few differences between the groups in background characteristics were controlled statistically. A 2-year follow-up showed closely similar recidivism rates in the two groups. Baron *et al.* (1973) also evaluated a family-oriented crisis intervention service. Assignment to experimental and control groups was dependent on day of the week. A 7-month follow-up showed that 35 per cent of the experimental group and 46 per cent of controls had received further convictions; the figures for (the more serious) criminal conduct was 15 per cent and 23 per cent. Quay and Love (1977) obtained a similar degree of benefit from an experimental programme involving counselling, training and job placement, and education – but, as already noted, the group differences could have resulted from the different lengths of follow-up (Mrad, 1979). Other programmes have been reviewed by Wright and Dixon (1977), Gibbons and Blake (1976) and Reker *et al.* (1980). All comment on the rather poor quality of most of the few studies which have been undertaken. While certainly it would be premature to conclude that these intensive community-based approaches are without value, the results so far are contradictory and inconclusive. It should be added that the one study to differentiate between the effects on non-delinquents and delinquents found that, although the latter had a better outcome than their controls, the programme appeared to lead to a *worse* outcome for non-delinquents, i.e. worse than that for their controls (O'Donnell *et al.*, 1979). It may be that introducing high-risk non-delinquents into a community programme which includes recidivists serves to *increase* the likelihood of a drift into delinquent activities through the effects of peer associations, however positive the other influences. The result stands in isolation, so far, and it would not be justifiable to take it as a general finding. Equally, however, it would be unwise to assume that well-intentioned community programmes will not have adverse effects on vulnerable individuals.

Diversionary policies

This last point is relevant to a consideration of the policy of *diversion*. The term refers to the goal of attempting to replace formal institutional processing with various forms of community treatment (see Klein, 1979). Any evaluation of this policy has to be concerned not only with its efficacy in reducing recidivism in the young people subjected to informal community treatment, but also with the different question of whether it does indeed 'divert' – that is, reduce the number of people who experience formal legal processing. Klein (1979), in his critique of American programmes, highlights the many problems inherent in this policy. For the most part, the approaches have been unsystematic and inadequately implemented (and lacking evidence of efficacy in terms of reducing recidivism) – but also, rather than diverting offenders who would otherwise have been admitted to an institution, they have drawn in more and more very minor offenders who hitherto would not have been processed at all. It is partly that the concept is sufficiently ambiguous to allow expansion of the judicial net, and partly that an almost inevitable consequence of enthusiasm for a new programme which is felt to be beneficial is a desire to extend those benefits to a wide range of young people thought to be at risk. The absence of legal restraints (through determinate sentencing) means that there is nothing to restrict this expansion. Klein (1979) gives evidence that this has in fact occurred. The situation is exemplified by the Sarri and Bradley (1980) study from Australia, in which a 5-year cohort of youths processed through juvenile aid panels (a supposedly more benign and less stigmatizing mechanism) were compared with those processed through the juvenile courts during the same time period. The panels provide greater flexibility in dealing with young offenders and children in trouble, and offer support and assistance to the child and his family. Between 1972 and 1977 the number of juveniles being dealt with by panels rose from 1,961 to 3,503. In the first year this was associated with a marginal drop in the number appearing in court, but thereafter the rise in numbers dealt with by the panels was paralleled by the rise in court appearances (in population terms from 14.8 to 22.7 per 1,000 for boys appearing before panels and 21.5 to 25.7 for courts between 1972 and 1977). Moreover, the courts continued to deal with the same or increasing proportion of minor offences (18 per cent 'status, traffic and other' in 1972–3 to 19 per cent in 1976–7; and 11 per cent to 18 per cent for 'drugs, liquor and drunk and disorderly conduct'). There is the strong inference that the net had widened.

Deterrence

The last ten years or so have seen a major re-emergence of interest in the possible effects of deterrence. Zimring and Hawkins (1973), Gibbs (1975) and Cook (1980) have all provided thoughtful and thorough reviews of the complex conceptual and methodological issues of this difficult and multifaceted topic, and Beyleveld (1980) has recently published a detailed and critical appraisal of the literature together with a comprehensive annotated bibliography. Many distinctions need to be made, but perhaps the most basic is that between 'specific deterrence' (i.e., the effect of a punishment in deterring an individual offender from offending again) and 'general deterrence' (i.e., the effect of a sanction in deterring the general public from committing the offence subject to that sanction). The mechanisms of the two may or may not be similar, but here we are concerned only with the latter. The former is important, but it is difficult to disentangle the deterrent effect of a sentence from its reformatory, rehabilitative or other functions. In practice, these different effects may be combined by just looking at the effects on recidivism – as done throughout the earlier sections of this chapter.

So far as 'general deterrence' is concerned, the usual assumption is that deterrent effects will be influenced by the certainty, severity, and celerity of the sanction in question. In other words, it is argued that deterrence is most likely to take place when punishment is certain, severe and swift. But it is also supposed that deterrence may affect a person's behaviour without necessarily influencing the crime rate (for example, the individual may shift to a different form of crime or he may take better precautions against getting caught). Of course, too, some crimes and some people are more susceptible to deterrence effects than others. However, in practice, the most important conceptual and practical issue is that deterrence does not exist in isolation. Rather it is dependent on people's perceptions, attitudes and knowledge. It has often been shown that major changes in the law or in sanctions take place with a large proportion of the population being quite unaware that any kind of change has taken place at all. Similarly, it is not the *actual* certainty or severity of a sanction that matters but rather what people *think* they are.

Laboratory experiments

The question of deterrence has been studied in many different ways. The most straightforward and (relatively) easy to interpret data are provided by laboratory experiments in which the severity and certainty of sanctions are manipulated by the experimenter in order to determine their effects. The results from this body of research are consistent in showing that there *is* a deterrence effect, and that it is affected by both severity and certainty. However, the circumstances are so far removed from the real-life situation with respect to crime and punishment that they provide no adequate basis for policy inferences.

Field experiments

Something a little nearer reality can be obtained through field experiments in which some form of sanction or threat is introduced in one area but not another. For example, Buikhuisen (1974) reported a Dutch study looking at the effects of a much-publicized police campaign against driving with worn tyres. Two checks, three months apart, were made on cars parked at night in two cities to determine the 'spontaneous' renewal of worn tyres. Then, immediately before the campaign, a large number of cars were inspected; after the experiment they were relocated to determine if worn tyres had been replaced. The experiment consisted of introducing the special campaign in one city but not the other. The results showed a markedly greater renewal of worn tyres in the city in which the campaign took place. Another study (Schwartz and Orleans, 1967) examined the effects of sanctions and appeals to conscience as means of heightening compliance of federal income taxes. The results of most studies of this type are agreed in showing a deterrent effect. While they indicate that deterrence can operate in ordinary real-life circumstances, these results, too, have the considerable limitation that they refer to the *immediate* effects of a sudden *change*, in which there is a quite high likelihood of the sanction operating. In that policy issues mainly concern *enduring* effects of sanctions with a rather low likelihood of impinging on a person, the findings of field experiments provide a rather shaky basis for policy.

Time-series analyses

Time-series analyses constitute a third strategy. These are based on an analysis of trends over time as they relate to some clearly identifiable change in sanctions. Probably the best-known study of this type is the analysis of the effects of the introduction of 'breathalyzer' tests in Britain in 1967 (Ross *et al.*, 1970). The results showed that there was a significant drop in road accident casualties immediately after the breathalyzer was introduced; more detailed analyses indicated that this was indeed due to a reduction in drinking while driving. But the study also showed that this effect wore off over time – probably because people came to realize that, in fact, there was still quite a low likelihood of being caught and punished. Whether this loss of effect would still apply if there was a high objective certainty (and hence probably a high subjective certainty) – as, for example, if frequent spot checks were allowable – is not known.

However, one recent study in a closed environment – a remand centre – showed the importance of a very high probability of detection (Graham, 1981). The breaking of cell windows constituted a frequent form of vandalism in the centre, and the deterrent action comprised the introduction of a simple method of twice-daily checking which assured a very high rate of (relatively rapid) detection. The penalty for window-breaking was fixed at the low sum of £1, about that in operation before. In the 21-week period before the experimental programme there was an average weekly breakage rate of 16.4 compared with a rate of 1.7 during the 6-week experimental period and of 4.1 during the subsequent 19-week operational period during which the prison officers ran the programme. The findings suggest that, at least in a closed environment, a high likelihood of detection may markedly reduce delinquent behaviour even if the penalties remain mild.

Time-series analyses have also been utilized to look for possible deterrent effects from well-publicized 'exemplary' sentences – on the whole, few effects are measurable. Taken together, investigations using the time-series approach do not give rise to very clear-cut conclusions. Some show effects and some do not. It seems likely that much of the variation is due to differences in the extent to which people are aware of the changes in sanctions, and in the extent to which they perceive them as likely to affect themselves. But that constitutes the crux of many of the problems applying to policy issues regarding deterrence.

Cross-sectional studies

A fourth approach is afforded by cross-sectional studies of various types. The prototype of this research strategy is provided by the Gibbs and Tittle analyses, utilizing official statistics to relate homicide and felony rates in different states of the U.S.A. to the certainty and severity of punishment for those crimes in each state (see Erickson and Gibbs, 1973; Tittle and Logan, 1973). A further development of cross-sectional correlation analyses has come from the use of econometric models which rely on economic utility theory to explain the decision to commit an offence or remain law-abiding. Some of these combine the comparison of areas showing different levels of sanctions with a time-series analysis, so that some kind of cross-lagged correlational approach can be used to assess the likelihood of which way the causal relationship (if there is one) works. While the analyses are complex and necessarily rely on a number of rather questionable assumptions, the general pattern has been to find some sort of negative correlation between severity or certainty of punishment on the one hand and rates of crime on the other. There are immense problems with this approach in terms of both the assumptions which have to be made and the impossibility of adequately controlling for other factors (see Cook, 1980). Moreover, the correlations found are open to the opposite interpretation – namely, that increases in crime may overburden legal machinery and thus cause decreases in the certainty of punishment as a result (Pontell,* 1978). A further issue is that high levels of punishment may have other effects which work in the opposite direction. For example, Hart (1978) used a cross-lagged panel correlation analysis with Army units to examine the relationship between levels of non-judicial punishment and rates of less serious offences. It was found that increasingly high levels of punishment were followed by *increases* in levels of offences. Anonymous questionnaire responses showed a lack of consensus between superiors and subordinates over offence rates; leaders felt punishment was effective in improving discipline, whereas enlisted soldiers felt that punishments were being applied unnecessarily and unfairly with an associated labelling of them as insubordinate. Under these conditions, rather than conform, the enlisted soldiers responded defiantly by increasing subsequent offences, contrary to their leaders' expectations. Of course, the study applied in the rather special circumstances of the Army; moreover, there was the additional factor of black soldiers feeling that they were being discriminated against. Nevertheless, it requires little imagination to see that the same factors could well apply in areas where police–community relationships have deteriorated, where much of the policing is *felt* to be concerned with minor transgressions, and where there is a lack of consensus on norms and standards of behaviour.

The same issues have arisen in discussions on the effects of high levels of corporal punishment, or of punishment generally, in schools. Experimental data on the effects of increasing, decreasing, introducing or withdrawing corporal punishment are not available, but correlational data indicate that a simple deterrence model is not adequate to account for the findings. For example, Clarke (1966) found that for boys aged under 15 there was no significant difference in the number of days between a boy being recovered after absconding and the next boy absconding, according to whether or not the caught absconder was caned. But in older boys, caning was associated with a slight increase in delay before the next absconding. The data are consistent with a deterrence effect from caning in older boys but *not* in younger boys.

The same issues have been studied in ordinary schools. Reynolds and Murgatroyd (1977) found that attendance rates were worse in schools with a high use of corporal punishment; Heal (1978) found that misbehaviour was worse in schools with formal punishment systems; and Clegg and Megson

* The particular statistical analyses undertaken by Pontell to test this 'system capacity' model are open to important objections (especially that he examined lag-point correlations rather than lag-change relations), but the point remains that crime may influence punishment just as punishment influences crime.

(1968) noted that delinquency rates tended to be highest in schools with a great deal of corporal punishment. Rutter *et al.* (1979) found no overall significant association between levels of punishment and levels of misbehaviour (or delinquency) in secondary schools in inner London. However, the trend was for more misbehaviour and more delinquency with high levels of punishment; and this trend was significant in the case of particular forms of punishment (unofficial slapping and cuffing of children and a disciplinary style in the classroom which involved *frequent* checking and reprimanding). The overall pattern of results suggested that whereas firm discipline and the existence of sanctions were helpful in promoting good behaviour, very frequent punishments and some forms of corporal punishment were counterproductive because they tended to lead to a negative atmosphere and feelings of resentment.

Conclusions on deterrence

No clear-cut and simple conclusions on the effects of deterrence are possible. As discussed above, it is certainly evident that deterrence is a real phenomenon and it would be sensible to take deterrence effects into account when considering possible changes in the ways in which delinquents are dealt with. On the other hand, in practice, the links between delinquent acts and punishment are so indirect that it is probable that rather major changes would be required to influence deterrence. As discussed in Chapter 1, the probability that any single delinquent act will result in prosecution is very low. The evidence on deterrence is consistent in showing that both severity and certainty of punishment are relevant to deterrence. It may be that changes in severity will have little effect when certainty is at a very low level. However, there is some suggestion that a marked increase in the likelihood of detection may have important benefits even if the sanctions remain mild. The question of how far it is possible to influence certainty is discussed below. In addition, in deciding on deterrence policies it will be important to take into account the possibility that increases in the severity of punishment may make the situation worse if the increases lack public acceptance as fair and appropriate, and that certain forms of punishment may have adverse effects on the individual (as a result either of labelling – see Chapter 6 – or of the experiences entailed in the punishment). The dilemma is made particularly acute by the fact that deterrence is probably most important with first offenders, or at least with those who are not established recidivists (see findings on suspended sentences above), but so too are the effects of labelling and possibly also the resentment effects of what are felt to be unreasonable sanctions.

Policing

As an extension of the deterrence approach, it is often suggested that one element in any programme to reduce crime should be more effective policing. At first sight the assumption might seem straightforward and uncontroversial; the job of the police is to bring criminals to book, and if they can do that more effectively surely one might expect that it ought to reduce delinquent activities. In fact, as discussed in Chapter 1, the extent to which the detection of crime and apprehension of offenders is open to police control is less than sometimes thought (see Clarke and Hough, 1980). Of course, police practice *does* have an important effect in some aspects of crime control, as indicated, for example, by the sometimes spectacular increases in theft, looting and disorder when police are on strike or are otherwise unavailable. These constitute extreme cases, and here we consider some of the evidence on the consequences of more ordinary variations in police practice.

Modifications in police patrolling practice have been most studied (see Clarke and Hough, 1980). The majority of investigations have found that changes in police patrols have little or no effect on crime; however, the findings are somewhat contradictory, with some showing benefits and others unintended ill-effects in terms of a worsening in police–community relations. As Steenhuis (1980) notes, if patrolling is to be effective in reducing crime it is essential that it be accompanied by good relations between the police and the public. 'Not only do the police rely on the public to provide information essential to detection; public support is also essential if police intervention is to be kept to a minimum – arguably the hallmark of successful policing.' The issues may be illustrated by considering a few studies in detail. Schnelle *et al.* (1975) described a study of two police patrolling strategies. The first concerned the effects of introducing a special house burglary patrol in an American city. Before the experiment, two patrolmen in one car covered each zone. During the experiment there was saturation patrolling with 8–15 men in each zone; unmarked cars and plain-clothes personnel being used. Both time-series analyses and comparisons with control zones showed that the saturation patrols had no appreciable effect on the number of burglaries, although it did lead to an increase in arrests. Of course, it may well be that there is an inverse relationship between the two in relation to the effects of patrolling strategies. In that the police used unmarked cars and plain-clothes officers, it is likely that criminals were unaware of the change in practice and therefore no effect on crime could be anticipated. But perhaps it was because of their lack of awareness that the arrest rate went up. If the change had been highly publicized the reverse might have occurred.

Their second study was concerned with the introduction of walking patrols. The findings showed that the presence of policemen on the beat led to an increase in the reporting of crimes by the general public – but that this increase was confined to minor crimes.

A further investigation (Schnelle *et al.*, 1979) examined the effects of introducing a special armed robbery programme. In this system, a small transmitting device could be placed unobtrusively in a cash drawer, 'bait' money being attached to the device by a metal clip. When the money was removed, a pre-recorded robbery alarm message was transmitted to receivers in patrol cars and police headquarters. The frequency of armed robbery incidents was monitored before, during and after the intervention period. The results showed a dramatic increase in on-the-scene arrests of suspects, but no consistent changes in armed robbery arrests in *other* stores. Moreover, in the target zone as a whole and in the specific groups of target stores the programme had no effect on the rates of armed robbery – and hence no evidence of a deterrence effect or a displacement of crime to other areas. But, again, one might comment that this was scarcely likely to happen if most offenders remained unaware of the change in practice.

Other studies (see Ekblom, 1979) have evaluated the use of police patrols to pick up truants, the rationale being that truants are especially likely to engage in delinquent activities. Because of methodological limitations in the research, the evidence does not lead to clear-cut conclusions. However, it seems that truancy patrols have at most a marginal impact on rates of crime – at least in part because it is likely that the level of patrolling used means that only a minority of truants will have been picked up by the police.

The difficulties with the types of patrolling discussed so far are both that the public may be unaware of their existence and that they are concerned with crime that is geographically widespread. Studies where neither problem applies have suggested greater effects. For example, Burrows (1980) found that increased policing of underground stations (using a comparison of changes over time in crime rates in stations with and without special policing) was associated with a reduction in thefts, although not in more serious robberies. It seems likely that 'police action, while effective in deterring thefts committed largely as opportunities present themselves, often in crowds, has considerably less effect on more serious offences involving premeditation and usually taking place in situations where it is clear that the police are not present'.

These interventions have all been concerned with direct police practice, but it is necessary also to consider indirect effects stemming from police activities to publicize the steps that the *public* can take to reduce crime, or from getting the public to provide their own policing. Examples of the former strategy are provided by car security campaigns (Burrows and Heal, 1980; Riley, 1980). These have involved media publicity designed to encourage people to lock their cars. Both 'before and after' and 'experimental-control area' comparisons have generally shown that such campaigns have made little or no difference to people's behaviour in locking their cars and hence have had little effect on car theft. It is not that efficient locking is without benefits (on the contrary – see below), but rather that publicity campaigns have failed to get people to be more conscientious in locking their vehicles.

Closed circuit television (CCTV) monitoring has been used increasingly to provide more efficient surveillance in shops and on the underground. Burrows (1980) examined its effects in the latter situation by comparing changes over time in stations with and without CCTV. In the year after CCTV was introduced, recorded thefts fell to a *quarter* of their previous rate (also there may have been a lesser reduction in robberies) – providing a dramatic indication of the efficacy of this form of surveillance. However, whether this benefit *persists* is more questionable (Walsh, 1978; Burrows, 1980). From other evidence, it seems probable that it will do so only if the public can *see* that CCTV results in action.

The last policing approach to mention is that which involves getting the public to improve its own policing. Thus, Engstad and Evans (1980) give examples of how Canadian police dealt with crime in apartment buildings, and highly organized shoplifting which involved getting cash refunds from the goods stolen, by getting the management to alter their policies – apparently with good effects. Similarly, Heywood (1979) outlined the problem in a Canadian city in which a chain of rapid service restaurants was experiencing a high rate of fights and muggings. Police negotiations with the firm resulted in the employment of greater numbers of experienced staff in the late evenings and the installation of better lighting in the restaurant car park – actions which were followed by a reduction in the troubles experienced there.

Contingency contracts, too, have sometimes been found useful. Taylor (1978) has described their use in a school as a means of dealing with vandalism in the toilets. The pupils' side of the bargain was to keep the toilets free of damage and graffiti for the whole of a summer term; in return, if they succeeded in doing that, Capital Radio would provide a disco. To most people's surprise the scheme seemed to succeed. Clarke (1978) reported a similar experiment in Liverpool, where young people received financial support for a youth centre in exchange for reducing vandalism. He also gave an American example of a school which provided the student body with a set sum of money to cover window breakage, with the agreement that the student body could keep whatever was left over after window repairs were paid for. The result was a dramatic reduction in window breakage. This 'contractual' approach has very obvious limitations in terms of the difficulties of instituting negotiations with those either responsible for vandalism or able to provide effective control of the vandalized areas. Nevertheless, although reliable evidence is lacking on the efficacy of community surveillance, this appears to be an avenue well worth further exploration.

The architectural and housing estate design features discussed in Chapter 6 also provide some limited scope for improving natural surveillance. In addition, as previously noted, it has been found that apartment blocks with doormen are less vulnerable to burglary (Waller and Okihiro, 1978) and that vandalism is less on estates with resident caretakers. Similarly, the extensive use of police escorts on 'football special' trains and the planning of routes to keep apart rival groups of supporters has been followed by a marked improvement in the behaviour of football supporters on trains and railway stations (see Rutter, 1979a).

The evidence suggests that improved policing – both official and community – can have benefits in certain situations, but the nature of the circumstances in which much crime takes place means that there are quite sharp constraints on how much can be achieved by these means.

'Physical' crime prevention measures

In addition to the preventive effects of the various surveillance measures already discussed, 'physical' crime prevention strategies also need to be considered. Hough, Clarke and Mayhew (1980) have classified these in terms of target hardening, target removal, removing the means to crime, reducing the pay-off, and environmental management.

Target hardening

Perhaps the best-known example of target hardening consists of the provision of steering-column locks on cars (see Mayhew *et al.*, 1976). These locks make it more difficult for vehicles to be illegally driven away – an effect which operates in practice as well as theory. In 1969, 21 per cent of all cars illegally taken were under three years old ('new'), whereas in 1973 this was so for only 5 per cent. As all new cars have been fitted with a steering-column lock as standard equipment since 1971, it may reasonably be inferred that the existence of locks led to a drop in the theft of cars with such locks. This inference is supported by the finding that there was no drop between 1969 and 1973 in the illegal taking of 'new' commercial vehicles or motorcycles (neither of which were required to have locks), and by the fact that cars without steering-wheel locks are some ten times more at risk than those with them.

However, the same findings have also shown that this form of protection has *not* resulted in any overall reduction in car thefts in Britain. On the contrary, as fewer 'new' cars have been stolen, more old ones have been taken – with a resulting continuing rise in the theft (and illegal taking away) of motor vehicles – a rise of over 80 per cent just between 1970 and 1974. Clearly, the provision of steering-wheel locks merely served to *displace* crime to older cars. On the other hand, this did not take place in Germany where *all* cars had to be fitted with locks (and not just new ones as in the U.K.). The theft and unauthorized taking of cars in 1972 remained well below the level in 1960 (29 per cent less), in spite of a *tripling* of the number of cars registered (see Mayhew *et al.*, 1976). It is apparent that if displacement is to be avoided, it will be necessary to introduce protection across the board and not just in a piecemeal fashion. There is a further as yet unexploited potential for preventing theft of and from cars by the use of centrally activated locking mechanisms and the replacement of keys with electronically-read magnetic cards (Ekblom, 1979).

Another example of effective target hardening is provided by the Post Office's extensive strengthening programme with respect to telephone kiosk equipment. In place of the former easily broken aluminium coin boxes, the cash compartments are now constructed with heavy gauge steel, the handset is made of shatterproof plastic, and the dial is not only made of steel but is recessed to allow little opportunity for leverage. The result has been a halt in what had been a steady rise in vandalism (see Rutter, 1979a) and an even greater fall in theft from kiosks. But the data also demonstrate that the efficacy of such measures is influenced by local circumstances and the level of crime. Thus, in the country as a whole, the rate of telephone kiosk vandalism remained steady between 1972 and 1978; but in London after an initial fall it continued to rise and in the more rural south-west it fell steadily.

Target removal

The second approach consists of the removal of targets of crime from the environment. Hough *et al.* (1980) give the example of the important reduction in the robberies of takings from New York buses through the introduction of an automatic flat-fare collection. Similarly, wage snatches can be reduced if employees are paid by cheque instead of by cash. Large-scale thefts of copper from one of Britain's major ports were said to have been greatly reduced through the simple expedient of the port authority refusing to accept consignments until immediately before the date of sailing. In Italy, an attempt has been made to reduce car radio thefts by fitting radios with a small but essential and expensive component which can be removed when the car is left parked. Thefts from electricity and gas meters can be eliminated by replacing meters with a quarterly billing system. Obviously a certain amount of inconvenience is involved in these measures, and rather few of them have been systematically evaluated. However, it appears to be an approach which warrants further trial.

Removing the means to crime

A particularly striking example of removing the means to crime (although one which applies mainly to adults) is provided by the introduction, in January 1973, of screening for metal at airports to prevent the hijacking of aircraft (see Landes, 1978). There was an explosive upsurge in hijackings in 1968, and the rate remained high throughout 1968–72 in spite of a marked increase in the penalty for this offence and the use in the U.S.A. of skymarshals with power to shoot and kill hijackers. Then in 1973 the rate of hijackings plummeted and has generally remained low since. Econometric analyses showed that the screening probably reduced the level of hijackings in 1973–6 from an expected 41–67 to an actual 11. In this instance it is apparent that physical crime prevention measures were very much more effective than steps to provide increased deterrence either by more severe sanctions (which had a negligible effect) or by more certain apprehension (which had some effect). The lack of gun control in the U.S.A. has been postulated as one factor associated with the very much greater level of firearm offences in that country compared with the U.K. (a difference considerably greater than that for other crimes). While it is likely that many other factors are also involved, it would be most important to monitor the effects systematically should gun control be introduced in the U.S.A. in the future.

Comparable issues arise with respect to the effects of pricing and licensing controls in controlling alcoholism and offences associated with heavy drinking or drunkenness (see Royal College of Psychiatrists, 1979). There is a mass of evidence from data in many different countries that the price of alcohol is a major determinant of how much people drink and of levels of drunkenness. Also, there are indications that the licensing controls have a limited impact on alcohol consumption. It is uncertain whether the recent growth in the U.K. of supermarket sales of alcoholic drinks has encouraged their purchase as part of routine weekly shopping and hence increased consumption, but it may have done so. In the same way, the availability of drugs of dependence is likely to be of considerable importance in the spread, or lack of spread, of drug abuse (see De Alarcón, 1972; Wilson, 1972); and the very substantial reduction in the toxicity of domestic coal gas led to a fall in overall rate of deaths due to suicide (Hassell and Trethowan, 1972). Of course these measures do not apply to crimes, but the point of mentioning them is the relevance of evidence that if 'physical' prevention measures can have a substantial impact even on apparently 'medical' conditions, it is likely that they should have an even greater potential with delinquency.

The Home Office Standing Committee on Crime Prevention (1975) also drew attention to the possible anti-vandalism practices available to the building industry. These included perimeter fencing of the building site during the course of construction work, the securing of all sheds during non-business hours, and the storage of mechanical plant in locked compounds. Similarly, local authorities may be able to limit vandalism by ensuring that vacated buildings are firmly secured and by keeping unoccupied property to a minimum.

Most of these steps have not been subjected to systematic evaluation and the extent to which they can reduce crime has yet to be established. However, the few which have been assessed suggest that the approach has some promise of making a limited impact.

Reducing the pay-off

Hough *et al.* (1980) note that there are some measures which may reduce the pay-off from theft. For example, private individuals (as well as businesses) may mark valuable possessions with indelible codes which render the goods uniquely identifiable and thus of less value to the thief. Evaluations suggest that this measure does provide some protection from burglary, although the scheme has a number of practical difficulties. Hough *et al.* (1980) also cite the example of American 'sting' operations, in which under-cover police set themselves up as 'fences' with a view both to making a mass arrest when they have acquired a sufficiently large clientele of burglars, and also to destroying the trust between thieves and fences, so making the disposal of stolen goods more difficult.

Environmental management

We have already mentioned the example of the successful steps taken to reduce railway hooliganism on 'football specials' by keeping rival supporters apart. Some of the steps mentioned under community surveillance might also be included under the heading of environmental management. The substantial unplanned reduction in motorcycle thefts as a result of the legislation in 1973 which made it mandatory to wear crash-helmets is another example (Mayhew *et al.*, 1976).

Conclusions on 'physical' crime prevention

The samples we have given of possible 'physical' crime prevention measures indicate the scope for preventive strategies of this type. However, it is also clear that, so far, there has been very little systematic evaluation of their effects. Such evidence as is available shows that the problem of 'displacement' from a prevented crime or a protected site to some more vulnerable object for delinquent acts is not an inconsiderable one – but also, the findings suggest that steps can be taken to reduce displacement. The potential value of these preventive policies is not yet known, but the slender leads available from past research suggest that they contain the possibilities of actions which could make a worthwhile, albeit distinctly limited, impact on certain forms of delinquency.

Overall conclusions on prevention and intervention

Our review of research into prevention and intervention has emphasized the many actions which have not yet been subjected to evaluation, and the extensive conceptual and methodological problems in the research which has been undertaken. It is obvious that the empirical findings do not yet justify any firm recommendations on 'what works' in preventing delinquency or reducing recidivism. Nevertheless, it would be wrong to underestimate how much has been achieved and how much we know. Already the research findings provide some important lessons in planning future policies.

Behavioural approaches have been shown to have some power as a means of changing the behaviour of delinquent youths, but uncertainty remains on their success in affecting recidivism after the therapeutic interventions come to an end, and there are continuing problems in gaining the involvement of the most disturbed families, for whom this approach might have most to offer. The evidence clearly indicates that there are major limitations in using this approach within institutional settings, and the two main lessons are: (i) interventions need to aim to change the child's home environment; and (ii) in so far as the focus is on the offender, the intervention should seek to improve his social problem-solving skills and social competence generally rather than just suppress deviant behaviour.

Counselling and psychotherapy are of no value as means of preventing delinquency, and as a mode of treating offenders it is likely that they are useful only in a minority of cases. In that connection there are strong pointers to the existence of important individual differences in young people's response to intensive therapeutic interventions. While as yet we lack the means to make the appropriate distinctions reliably, the suggestions are that intensive counselling is probably only of value with rather anxious youths who are aware of their problems and want help with them.

Studies of different forms of therapeutic and correctional regimes in institutions have shown no consistent or marked differences in outcome according to the type of regime experienced. On the other hand, investigations of variations among institutions of an ostensibly similar type have strongly suggested that institutions *do* have an important and quite substantial impact on the behaviour of young people during the course of their stay. But the features found to characterize 'successful' institutions have not been those which differentiate so-called therapeutic and corrective regimes. Rather, the relevant features seem to involve a combination of firmness, warmth, harmony, high expectations, good discipline and a practical approach to training. The effects of institutions on recidivism after the offender's return to the community are less than on behaviour at the time, but some worthwhile enduring benefits are evident. Probably persistence and generalization depend as much on the environment to which he returns as on what happened in the institution.

Comparisons of custodial and non-custodial interventions have shown little difference between them so far as effects on recidivism are concerned – but when differences have been apparent they have usually favoured non-custodial approaches. Little is known on the relative merits of different non-custodial penal measures but there is evidence suggesting that, in some circumstances, court adjournment may be more effective than social work supervision.

In that there is evidence that delinquent behaviour is perpetuated by influences in the youth's home environment and peer group, it might be thought that interventions in which the prime target is the community (rather than individuals in it) might be effective. However, so far there have been few evaluations of such approaches, and little is known on their value.

Community-based programmes focused on individuals have also not been subjected to systematic evaluation. However, there are indications that, whatever their value for offenders, they may have unintended adverse effects on non-delinquents – presumably through their introduction into a delinquent peer group. On the whole, the evidence suggests that informal, 'diversionary' policies may have been as effective as formal interventions requiring court action. But, also it is apparent that their use has tended to widen the net of young people brought into legal processing.

While there are good grounds for supposing that deterrence effects do operate, and that they should be taken into account when considering possible changes in the ways in which delinquents are dealt with, the links between delinquent acts and punishment are so indirect that it is likely that major changes would be needed to influence deterrence.

The evidence suggests that improved policing – both official and community – can have benefits in certain situations, but the nature of the circumstances in which much crime takes place means that there are quite sharp constraints on how much can be achieved by these means.

Finally, there are indications of the potential value of 'physical' crime prevention measures, although their value remains largely unevaluated, and there are limitations in terms of the problem of displacement of delinquent activities from one site to another.

10
Implications for Research, Policy and Practice

Research and policy

Having reviewed a large body of empirical research, we now take stock of what has been achieved and, in so doing, discuss the implications for future policy and practice. In that connection we have the twin objectives of considering which avenues of research are most likely to be worth further exploration in the years to come, and of indicating what lessons can be drawn from past research in order to plan more effective policies *now*. It will be appreciated that there are many difficulties in translating research findings into policy recommendations. In part, this is because the issues at stake are as much political and moral as scientific (see Croft, 1980). Morris (1976) put the point succinctly in stating: 'If the aim of those who operate the apparatus of social control is the establishment of order then penal reformers must not avoid the question of "whose order?"' Rein and White (1977) have argued that there is an inevitable clash between science and politics; the 'game' of science being the determination of value-neutral facts, and the 'game' of politics being the design of value-expressive action. In their view, this clash is most clearly seen in evaluation studies. Because politicians rarely specify the value-derived goals of any particular programme, the researcher has himself to define what constitutes a 'good' outcome. In this way, it is suggested, the political community hands over to the researcher the problem of arriving at consensual social purposes and values. In so doing it asks the researcher to take on something outside his professional competence, and at the same time divests the policy-maker of some of his political responsibility.

Clearly there is some substance in Rein and White's arguments. Walker (1980) has eloquently outlined the issues and the dilemmas with respect to decisions on punishment in his book on the morality of criminal justice. Not only is there disagreement on just which acts should be classed as 'criminal', but also there is dispute on the basis on which such decisions should be taken. Similarly, there is debate on the relative importance of retribution, deterrence, reformation, denunciation, treatment and protection in decisions on the most appropriate forms of intervention. As the Black Committee Report

(1979) indicates, current arrangements for dealing with juvenile offenders are the result of an accommodation of differing ideologies. The 'welfare model' assumes that delinquency is a symptom of a deeper maladjustment resulting from an adverse environment. Accordingly, treatment is the intervention of choice, with the welfare of the child the paramount concern. By contrast, the 'justice model' assumes that delinquency is a matter of opportunity and choice, that society has the right to assert the norms and standards of behaviour endorsed by society. Accordingly, sanctions and controls are valid responses, with a proportionality between the seriousness of the offence and the sentence given being the paramount concern (see also Morris, Giller, Szwed and Geach, 1980). Similar debates have been taking place in the United States – as illustrated in the Twentieth Century Fund Task Force report (1978) on 'Confronting Youth Crime'. In its recommendations, the Task Force rejects the extremes of both models and instead bases its recommendations on the four principles of 'culpability, diminished responsibility resulting from immaturity, providing room to reform, and proportionality'. The Black Committee, in putting forward its proposals, argued that any strategy for dealing with juvenile offenders must take into account five key considerations:

(1) juvenile offenders have problems common to all children and like other children in need of care or assistance should have these met on their merits;

(2) most delinquency is of a minor and limited nature. Serious and persistent offences are in the minority;

(3) the impact of 'treatment' on delinquency is uncertain though it may benefit a child in other ways;

(4) prosecution and conviction can have a counter-productive labelling effect and consequently should be avoided so far as is compatible with the protection of the public and the rights of the offender; and

(5) intervention in the lives of offenders is dictated by the demand of society for protection as much as by a desire simply to afford help and support for those in need. Society expects protection from those who offend against it, including children. This is particularly so when their behaviour is either serious or persistent.

It is evident that these considerations involve a mixture of empirical evidence and value judgement. It is a fact that most delinquency is of a minor and limited nature, but it is a value that the protection of society must be given equal weight with the welfare of the child. In general we share these values, and in particular we accept the need for 'a realistic balance between welfare and justice'. Part of the current disenchantment with the welfare model stems from an ideological preference for a punitive approach to deviant behaviour, and part from a concern that rehabilitative methods do not seem to have stemmed the rising flood of crime. But also there has been a growing awareness that, at times, the therapeutic approach has become more coercive and dehumanizing than the 'just deserts' of punishment (see von Hirsch, 1976; Morris *et al.*, 1980; Zimring, 1978). The 'need for treatment' has sometimes been used as a justification for very considerable restrictions on the liberty of the child which seem out of proportion to the seriousness of the offence. Equally, however, it is evident that an exclusively 'crime control' or 'justice' approach, in which serious crimes result in strong punishment, ignores the extensive evidence that severe and persistent delinquency is often accompanied by widespread personal difficulties and disturbance which give rise to distress and social impairment for the individual, as well as 'trouble' for the community. It is apparent that therapeutic interventions generally have most impact when clients perceive a value and utility in their participation. Indeed, it has been argued that much of current practice tends to be ineffective just because the 'clients' of the juvenile justice system do not understand the rationale for intervention (Giller and Morris, 1978; Morris and Giller, 1979). On the other hand, it is also clear that sometimes those most in need of help are least likely to seek it or accept it voluntarily. The dilemma of whether and in what circumstances to enforce 'treatment' cannot be entirely avoided.

It is obvious that there can be no simple and straightforward derivation of policy from empirical research findings. Society must decide for itself what social purposes and values it considers most important. Nevertheless, research has a crucial role to play in decisions on policies (see Rutter, 1978). It would be a very foolish politician indeed who was not concerned with the factual evidence on what actions are most likely to be effective in meeting his value-determined aims. Similarly, however, only a very blinkered researcher would fail to realize that social values are inextricably tied into the business of determining the questions to be investigated. We are mindful of this uneasy relationship between research and policy, and we are sensitive to the need to be aware of the values which are necessarily implicit in all research in the social arena.

One further point regarding prevention and intervention requires emphasis. As discussed in earlier chapters, the term delinquency covers a wide range of activities engaged in by a wide range of individuals. At one end of the spectrum there is the petty vandalism and very minor theft undertaken by a high proportion of youths at one time or another as a passing phase in their development. Such youths are *not* particularly distinctive in their background or personal characteristics, the overall cost to the community is relatively slight (although the nuisance value may be greater), and in most cases the delinquent activities cease during adolescence, with the individuals growing up to become ordinary well-functioning adults. At the other extreme there is the small minority of persistent recidivists, with many personal problems apart from their delinquency, some of whom engage in serious predatory stealing or violent assaults, most of whom come from a distinctive high-risk family background, and who go on to show social impairments in adult life. In between there is a fairly sizeable intermediate group, whose delinquent activities persist over some years and may involve serious crime, who may show personal difficulties to a lesser extent than the most severe group, some of whom come from a high-risk background, but whose career of crime comes to an end in early adult life. It is not suggested that these three groups are in any way discrete – to the contrary, they shade off into one another. Nor is it argued that it is easy to tell in advance into which group any individual offender will fall. Nevertheless, it is obvious that somewhat different preventive and interventive strategies will be needed for these different forms of delinquency – even if we lack good evidence on their differential effects.

But, as our review has shown, research has given rise to a considerable body of knowledge which should be useful in indicating the likely consequences of certain policies and the need to take particular issues into account. In the section which follows we seek to utilize the empirical research findings to make some recommendations on policy and practice. These do not amount to a comprehensive programme for prevention and intervention, as the level of knowledge does not allow anything so ambitious as that. Nevertheless, the empirical findings do provide some useful guides to action. Moreover, even when satisfactory answers have yet to be obtained to fundamental research questions, the findings from past studies do provide pointers as to how the issues might be tackled more profitably in the future. Accordingly, we end our report with some recommendations on research needs and priorities.

Prevention

The topic of prevention is one which gives rise to particularly sharp divergencies of opinion. On the one hand, it is the least adequately researched and utilized aspect of applied criminology. Most reviewers have commented that, although the general idea of crime prevention seems attractive, the notion that it could be achieved is completely unrealistic – thus, Empey (1974) termed crime prevention 'the fugitive utopia'; Bittner (1970) suggested that the hope that crime could be vanquished was 'a particularly trivial kind of utopian dreaming', and Wheeler *et al.* (1967) argued that crime is 'a chronic problem which is unlikely to yield easily to preventive efforts'. On the other hand, government committees have stated that 'the surest way to prevent maladjustment from arising in children is to encourage in every possible way their healthy development, particularly on the emotional side' (Ministry of Education, 1955); and, in relation to the prevention of antisocial behaviour, bold claims have been made that 'there is now an understanding of the broad preventive measures likely to raise the general level of children's intellectual, educational, social and emotional development' (Pringle, 1974). Unfortunately, such claims are not supported by the evidence. Of course, as discussed in Chapter 6, there is a mass of evidence on the various social and family circumstances which predispose to delinquency (and to psychiatric and educational problems). There is also a reasonable measure of agreement on children's needs and on the broad principles of child-rearing. That is not the issue. The difficulty lies in knowing *how* to bring about the desired results (Rutter, 1978). There is a considerable gap between identifying a damaging factor and knowing how to eliminate it or reduce its effect. The translation of general principles into effective policies of preventive action poses many unresolved problems, and we delude ourselves if we think that we have already obtained the answers. Regrettably, we have not.

However, the conclusion that, as yet, we do not know how to intervene in a way that raises the overall level of children's psycho-social development does *not* necessarily mean that there are no actions that we can take to reduce delinquent activities. Clarke (1978) noted that, in addition to variables affecting an individual's general predisposition to offend, whether or not a criminal act is in fact committed will also depend on current crises and stresses, on whether the physical situation he is in provides opportunities for delinquency, and on cognitive and motivational factors (such as his perception of the risk of being caught and his feelings of anger or resentment) operating at the time. Similarly, Rutter (1979a) emphasized that causative influences in relation to any behaviour involved four rather separate sets of factors: individual predisposition, ecological predisposition, current circumstances, and opportunities or situation. Thus, an individual's predisposition to engage in antisocial behaviour is likely to have been affected by the kind of upbringing he has received and the stresses and traumata experienced as a child, as well as by genetic and other biological influences. The term 'ecological predisposition' refers to predisposing factors which apply to *groups* rather than to individuals. This would cover, for example, the effects of the social environment provided by schools, communities, or the peer group. Within each of these groups, individual differences will help determine *which* persons are most liable to engage in antisocial acts, but the characteristics of the social setting will influence the overall *level* of crime in the group and *how many* people will behave in a delinquent fashion. Thirdly, a person's *current* individual circumstances will affect his behaviour. Thus, as discussed in Chapter 6, quite apart from early upbringing, a boy's *immediate* family environment influences the likelihood that he will engage in delinquent activities. In this connection, it is necessary to consider both stresses and crises which increase the liability and protective factors which reduce it. Fourthly, there is the matter of the situation prevailing or the opportunities available at the time. The relevant factors here include not only the variables which determine the ease and attractiveness of delinquent activities, but also those which influence motivation and appraisal of the risks (as affected by surveillance and the chance of being seen and caught, and by knowledge of the consequences of being apprehended).

Finally, before discussing some of the possibly effective preventive strategies which could be employed, it is necessary to note that any programme of prevention must take into account the cost/benefits ratio (World Health Organization Expert Committee, 1977). As the W.H.O. Expert Committee observed:

> All preventive measures must be assessed in relation to: the importance of the area of functioning they are meant to influence; the likelihood of the measure making a real difference; the number of people who can be reached by the method of intervention; the disadvantages that come as side-effects (almost no effective intervention is free of these); political and ethical considerations (loss of personal freedom, imposition of remedies, etc.); and the cost of the preventive measure in terms of finance, resources and personnel.

Votey and Phillips (1974) also comment that the social costs of crime equal the expenditures for prevention, protection and deterrence plus the direct and indirect costs of criminal behaviour (i.e. the costs to the community of the crime itself together with the costs of apprehending, prosecuting and punishing or rehabilitating the offender). The social optimum is achieved at the point when the preventive policies are sufficiently effective for the reduction in crime costs to be greater than the expenditure on prevention. Their analysis was strictly financial, but obviously a similar equation applies to costs as measured in terms of qualities of life.

Measures affecting individual predisposition

In the field of medicine, most of the major successes in prevention have come from interventions designed to influence individual predisposition. Some of these have been community-wide public health measures (as in the immense gains to the health of children which have stemmed from improvements in sanitation and nutrition), and others have been individual interventions which also could be applied on a community-wide basis (as with immunization). There has been a temptation to apply the same philosophy to crime, with the public health equivalent being improvements in housing and the standard of living and the individual equivalent being the provision of personal counselling for high-risk youths – or, more indirectly, the introduction of compensatory pre-school education and day care. It is all too clear that these strategies have *not* been effective up to now, and the evidence suggests that they are not likely to be so in the future. So far as socio-economic disadvantage is concerned, the problem is that the links with crime appear to be indirect, and knowledge on mechanisms is lacking. Historical analyses give no hope that better housing or higher incomes would make any appreciable difference to rates of crime. This century has already seen major socio-economic improvements, but crime rates have continued to rise. Of course, efforts to raise the standards of living are extremely worthwhile in their own right and should be vigorously pursued for that reason alone, and because there *is* evidence that social improvements are likely to have benefits on the physical health of children – even if they do not reduce crime. Also, it could well be that in the past we have concentrated on the wrong social indicators. In Chapter 6 we touched on the possibility that, for example, the spread or distribution of incomes might be more important than their absolute level. Certainly the matter should be explored further but, at the moment, the empirical findings do not provide any reliable guide to effective policies of prevention.

The limiting factor in the case of personal counselling is that all the evidence suggests that such measures are likely to have no more than a trivial marginal effect (if that), so long as the child or adolescent remains in the same high-risk environment. There is no reason to suppose that improvements in counselling, however great, would make the slightest difference to the preventive efficacy. If they are to have an impact, individual measures will have to involve some worthwhile, and *lasting*, change in the environment. It is evident that, with but a few exceptions, short-term change in a chronically depriving situation will rarely have long-term benefits (see Rutter, 1979a and 1981a). Accordingly, in designing preventive measures to affect individual predisposition, it is steps which might bring about lasting improvements in the environment that we must consider. It has to be said that, at the moment, there are none known to be effective which are likely to make a major difference to rates of crime. On the other hand, there are some interventions which are worth doing for other reasons that might have some *slight* effect on levels of delinquency. As these are discussed more fully in Graham (1977), World Health Organization (1977), Department of Health and Social Security (1976) and Rutter (1979a), they are mentioned here only rather briefly.

Children whose birth was not wanted by their parents, who were born to teenage mothers, who are brought up in single-parent households or who grow up in very large families, are all subject to an increased risk of delinquency. Much could be done to reduce the disadvantages experienced by all these groups, but also it is important to reduce the number of unwanted births. Family planning, as part of a wider community service which is educational in its broadest sense, has a useful role to play in that connection.

Children who repeatedly go in and out of children's homes or foster homes, or who live with their own parents in a severely unstable and unsettled family environment, or who are reared in institutions with multiple changing caretakers, constitute another high-risk group. It seems that those from a similar background who are adopted or who receive long-term fostering in an ordinary family environment are more likely to develop normally (although there is little knowledge on the extent to which the risk of delinquency is reduced). There would appear to be two implications for preventive policies. Firstly, in the case of young children whose parents seem unlikely ever to be able to look after them adequately, an *early* decision should be taken with respect to adoption or long-term fostering. It is not in the child's interests for there to be vacillation and indecision while he shuffles to and from his parents into the care of the local authority, nor is it in his interests to remain for long periods in an institution in the forlorn hope that the parents who abandoned him and who now visit only sporadically or not at all will one day take him back. Secondly, it is important to strive to improve the quality of children's homes as environments which can meet young children's psycho-social needs. It has been possible to make institutions intellectually stimulating places, but it has proved much more difficult to ensure any kind of continuity in parenting – a feature now known to be needed. An institutional upbringing should never be a first choice, but when it constitutes the best available alternative, it is important that the experience be as positive and beneficial in its effects as we can make it.

Repeated hospital admissions, especially in young children already experiencing chronic family adversity, are associated with a somewhat increased risk of psycho-social problems (including delinquency) in later childhood and adolescence. Steps to improve hospital conditions for young children, to prepare families better for hospitalization, and to reduce the need for recurrent admissions would be worthwhile – although the likely effect on rates of delinquency would be quite minor.

It is well established that rearing by criminal parents substantially increases the chance of the children engaging in delinquent activities. Although probably part of the risk stems from genetic influences, it seems that much comes from the family difficulties, discord and disturbance associated with parental criminality. Obviously this provides an opportunity for preventive action, and it is desirable that interventions with the parents be undertaken with an eye to the possible implications for the children. However, while the preventive opportunity is inherent in the situation, it must be added that no means of intervention is known to be effective in terms of altering the risk to the children. The situation is important because of its potential and the need to develop preventive strategies, rather than because solutions are immediately to hand (or even in near prospect).

The mechanisms involved in the well-established link between educational retardation and delinquency are ill-understood (see Chapter 5), but it seems probable that to some (possibly a minor) extent it is mediated by the emotional and behavioural problems which may be increased by the experience of scholastic failure. In so far as that is the case, the effective prevention or remediation of educational difficulties (together with steps to reduce the stigma and disadvantage associated with low attainment) might have benefits. However, regrettably little is known on the prevention and remediation of educational retardation, and the effects on delinquency have not been evaluated.

It is obvious from the important associations between difficulties in parenting and delinquency (see Chapter 6) that effective steps to improve parental skills and sensitivity to children's needs would be most worthwhile. The problem lies in knowing *how* to improve parenting. Useful ideas have been put forward on 'education for parenthood', but we lack knowledge on the value of any of the steps taken or proposed.

In this section of the chapter we have drawn attention to a few possible opportunities for prevention through measures designed to affect individual predisposition. It is evident that some of the examples are *potential* opportunities only, as the means of intervening effectively are not known, in other examples the means of intervention are known but it is likely that they will affect only a tiny proportion of potential delinquents, and in all cases empirical evidence is lacking on the *actual* preventive efficacy of the interventions. The examples have been included because it is important to develop better preventive strategies and it is useful to see where the opportunities for improvement might lie. However, it is clear that, in the present state of knowledge, no measures affecting individual predisposition are likely to make much impact on delinquency.

Ecological interventions

Social ecology is concerned with social groups in terms of their features as *groups*, rather than as collections of unconnected individuals. An ecological approach, therefore, involves study of the characteristics of environmental settings and of the dynamic interplay between people and their environments (Bronfenbrenner, 1974 and 1979); hence, an ecological intervention is one designed to affect such social systems. Of course the distinction from individual interventions is far from absolute, but the difference in emphasis is useful in considering possible preventive policies (Rutter, 1979a).

The most obvious application of this approach to the prevention of delinquency concerns changes in schools. As discussed in Chapter 6, there are important differences between schools in rates of delinquency and the research findings strongly suggest that, in part, these differences reflect the effects of the school environment on pupil behaviour. While firm knowledge is lacking on just which features of the school environment most strongly affect delinquent behaviour (no experimental interventions have been undertaken), cross-school comparisons have provided important leads on the factors most likely to be influential (see Rutter, 1983). Three rather different variables seem important. Firstly, the composition of the student body is important, with delinquency rates highest in schools with a heavy preponderance of intellectually less able or socially disadvantaged pupils.* The implication is that it is desirable to take steps to ensure that all schools have a reasonably even distribution of pupils of all levels of ability. In the long run, this has implications for broader social policies, and especially for housing, but in the shorter term it means that local authorities should take steps to regulate the balance of intakes to schools. It may well not be possible to do that with parental support so long as there are major variations in the qualities of schools – hence there is a great need to improve the quality of the less adequate schools.

Secondly, it appears that pupils' behaviour is influenced by the teacher's skills in classroom management. Such skills include social group management as well as pedagogy. More attention needs to be paid to the better

---

* As discussed in Chapter 6, this is so even after controlling for individual pupil characteristics. In other words, the risk of delinquency for a less able child (or indeed a child of any given level of intelligence) is increased if he is educated in a school with a heavy preponderance of *other* less able children.

development of these skills in basic teacher training, in in-service training, and in the provision of external advisors to schools.

Thirdly, findings indicate the importance of the school's characteristics and qualities as a social organization or social institution. The suggestion is that the relevant features include actions which serve to establish school values and norms of behaviour (including those which reflect teacher expectations, the setting of appropriate academic standards, the models of behaviour provided by teachers, and the use of discriminating feedback to the pupils); the consistency of school values (as influenced by group decision-making and problem-solving, suitable supervision of teachers by senior staff, and the meeting of the needs of teachers as well as those of pupils); and pupil acceptance of school norms (as influenced by general conditions and staff attitudes to pupils, shared activities between staff and pupils, pupil positions of responsibility, and ensuring that pupils experience success and achievement).

There are reasonable grounds for supposing that suitable attention to these aspects of schooling would have important benefits with respect to pupil behaviour in school, and lesser, but still worthwhile, benefits on delinquent activities outside school. The main limitation on this preventive approach is that we have a much better (although still weak) understanding of the qualities of a successful school than we have of the organizational or other characteristics of schools which facilitate the *implementation of change* or the maintenance of quality.

While it is probable that improvements in schooling would result in only quite minor reductions in delinquency, this seems to be a worthwhile area for intervention because: (i) all children go to school and hence any benefits would affect the whole population and not just a small subgroup; (ii) the changes in schooling would be likely to have other benefits quite apart from any effects on delinquency; and (iii) the actions suggested involve minimal financial expenditure. Moreover, improvements in classroom management and in the social organization of schools are unlikely to involve any important disadvantages. The regulation of school intakes does involve a restriction on personal choice regarding schooling so long as some schools are regarded as less desirable places to send children. In the short term, a degree of regulation seems likely to be helpful as a means of improving the overall quality of schooling, and the limitation on choice seems justified in the circumstances. However, it could be acceptable as a policy only if vigorous steps are taken to raise the quality of *all* schools to an acceptable level.

In Chapter 9 we gave several examples of possibly useful interventions in terms of area and community influences. In that chapter and in Chapter 6 we also indicated the possible effects of various architectural design features and housing policies. Some of these were concerned with issues of surveillance (a topic to which we return below), but others may play some role in group predispositions to engage in delinquent activities. However, although there is good evidence that there *are* area and community influences on delinquent behaviour, we lack an understanding of the mechanisms involved which could give rise to effective policies of primary prevention. Needham (1977) and others have argued for an ecological systems approach to cities, but so far there has been little attempt to apply this approach to the question of why and how certain kinds of city life predispose to delinquency.

The mass media have a variety of different effects, but their role in prevention is most conveniently considered here. There can be little doubt that, if skilfully employed, propaganda can have substantial effects on both attitudes and behaviour. It would be reasonable, therefore, to suppose that it ought to be possible to harness the power of the mass media in the interests of social education generally and of crime prevention in particular. But, as noted in Chapter 9, the results so far have been extremely disappointing and the potential for this approach to prevention remains quite uncertain.

In contrast, the mass media do appear to have had possible effects – albeit undesired effects – in increasing violence among adolescents. As discussed in Chapter 6, it is very difficult to gauge the size of this effect, but it seems probable that it is not very great. On the other hand, television is seen for very many hours per week by most young people, so that any influence involves a high proportion of the population. The inference is that an appropriate modification of films and television programmes should have some limited, but possibly still worthwhile, benefits. The television and film companies have an obvious responsibility in this regard, and the best solution would be voluntary action on their part to make a major alteration in the violence content of programmes and then to monitor the effects. However, the evaluation would be no easy matter, both because any effects could well be swamped by the influence of other variables and because it may take quite some considerable time for a change in the media to lead to any persisting changes in attitudes regarding the acceptability of violence and in inhibitions on violent behaviour.

Current circumstances

The third potential area of prevention concerns the effects of current circumstances. Research findings show that an individual's propensity to engage in delinquent activities is quite strongly influenced by his immediate family situation, peer group and living circumstances. This observation has fundamental implications for approaches to therapeutic and corrective interventions (as we discuss below). In terms of prevention it re-emphasizes that environmental factors have a major impact *at the time*, quite apart from any effect they may have on lasting changes in personality structure. However, the dilemma remains the same – that is *how* do we improve patterns of family functioning, *how* do we make peer group influences more positive in their effects, and *how* do we create protective factors and ameliorating influences? The needs are obvious, the potential is present, and various useful leads are available (see previous chapters), but so far there is no adequate basis for preventive policies.

Situations and opportunities

The fourth avenue for prevention lies in actions designed to affect opportunities for delinquent activities. As discussed in Chapters 6 and 9, there is now a growing body of evidence on the importance of situational factors in crime. The possible modes of intervention may be summarized under the headings of access or physical crime prevention, situational features, surveillance, deterrence, and incapacitation.

There are certain circumstances in which access or physical design features can play an important part in crime prevention. In previous chapters we have discussed the introduction of steering-wheel locks on cars, the strengthening of telephone equipment in kiosks, gun control, pricing and licensing controls on alcohol, the availability of drugs of dependence, and the fencing off of building sites as examples of this type. In addition, there are a variety of building features designed to provide a protection against vandalism (see Clarke, 1978; Central Policy Review Staff, 1978; Stone and Taylor, 1977; Home Office Standing Committee on Crime Prevention, 1975). These include 'target hardening' measures such as the use of glass substitutes; of more robust finishes that are impervious to crayon, felt-tip pens and the like; of stippled paint surfaces rather than plain ones; and of moulded fibreglass instead of upholstery for the most vulnerable seats in buses (especially the rear seats on the upper deck). In addition, there are the effects of target removal, removing the means to crime and reducing the pay-off (see Chapter 9).

Opinions differ on the potential scope for this approach to prevention. Four aspects need consideration. Firstly, there is the question of how far physical crime prevention merely serves to displace crime on to other targets.

Implications for Research, Policy and Practice 333

As Hough *et al.* (1980) comment, it is difficult to determine how far, if stopped from one crime, people would turn to another. On the one hand, most offenders do *not* specialize, so that if another form of illegal activity were equally readily available they might well turn to it as an alternative. But often it is possible to reduce access to crime opportunities in ways which do *not* leave other alternatives equally available. Moreover, in so far as displacement effects occur, they might be exploited to displace crime to less serious or less important forms. Secondly, there is the problem of costs and practicality. It may well be that the scope for physical crime prevention is greater than that currently in operation, but it is clear that these measures are much more difficult or much more expensive to apply in some situations than in others. Thirdly, there is the question of acceptability. West (1982) observes that many of the as yet unexploited physical crime prevention measures involve some loss of liberty and choice, and he suggests that with any widespread extension the inconveniences would soon outstrip the benefits. Fourthly, the provision of a pleasant attractive environment is itself important in reducing propensity to commit certain sorts of crime (see Rutter, 1979a). If physical protection creates an austere, prison-like environment, it may, by virtue of the atmosphere it establishes, predispose to the very behaviours it aims to discourage. All four of these considerations provide important limitations on the scope of physical crime prevention, but it appears that, with careful planning and foresight, the disadvantages can often be overcome or minimized. The approach is suitable for certain forms of crime only, but further exploration of its use seems worthwhile.

Situational manipulations constitute the second form of intervention. These operate by creating situations in which it is less likely that people will *want* to engage in delinquent activities. For example, it is apparent that vandalism is least likely to occur in attractive, well-maintained properties in which damage is promptly repaired and graffiti quickly removed (see, for example, Pablant and Baxter, 1975; Rutter *et al.*, 1979; Central Policy Review Staff, 1978). Hough *et al.* (1980) give other examples which involve the manipulation of events such as football matches: 'Good liaison between the police, the two football clubs and supporters' clubs can reduce the opportunities and temptations for vandalism and violence; arrival and departure of supporters can be better managed so as to avoid long periods of delay; within the grounds routes of access to stands and occupation of stands can be co-ordinated so as to minimize contact between rival supporters; sale of alcohol can be controlled within, and possibly around, the grounds.' It is striking, too, that crowd violence at big sporting occasions in the United States is far less of a problem than it is in the U.K., in spite of the overall level of violent crime being much higher than in Britain. Perhaps the fact that everyone is seated, that there is extensive entertainment during intervals and in the waiting period before the match begins, and that (often) alcohol is prohibited, makes a difference. However, other factors (including the lower proportion of socially disadvantaged youths in the crowd) are also likely to be relevant. These forms of intervention are suited to a rather limited range of situations but they have few disadvantages and it seems highly desirable to seek ways of extending their scope.

As discussed in previous chapters, there are many different forms of surveillance. Probably there is rather limited scope for increases in formal police surveillance. In most instances the introduction of special patrols or of big increases in the number of police in an area has had relatively little effect on the amount of crime (although a greater effect on the number of arrests). Most crime is not readily open to police surveillance, and what is needed is an optimal level and *not* a maximal level of police control. Moreover, a very high or very intrusive police presence is likely to have counterproductive effects in reducing community cooperation with the police or in provoking resentment which may then predispose to crime (see the discussion of civil strife in Chapter 4).

In certain situations (such as underground stations, stores, or car parks), mechanical surveillance by closed circuit television (CCTV) may be effective in reducing crime (see Chapter 9). However, it is likely that for these measures to *retain* their efficacy in the long term it will be necessary for their use to lead, and to be publicly *seen* to lead, to the apprehension of offenders. Otherwise it is probable that people will become used to the presence of CCTV and take the view that mechanical surveillance has no effect on the likelihood of their getting caught.

Perhaps there is greater scope for increased surveillance by employees such as caretakers in schools or housing estates, doormen in blocks of flats, shop assistants, bus conductors, car park attendants and the like (see Chapter 9). But also there is the opportunity to increase natural surveillance by members of the community. In earlier chapters we gave examples of how the design of housing estates could both increase the opportunities for natural surveillance and also increase people's feelings of responsibility and desire to provide protection. Probably this is the aspect of prevention through restriction of opportunities which is most in need of further exploration. Our knowledge on *how* to increase natural surveillance is quite limited, and if this approach is to be extended it will be important to learn more about the factors and mechanisms involved.

As discussed in Chapter 9, there is evidence that deterrence effects do operate but equally it seems that in most circumstances there is little that can be done to increase their power. In particular, it seems probable that raising the level of punitive sanctions* would make very little difference in most instances if the chances of being apprehended for any individual criminal act are low (as they usually are). Increasing the likelihood of apprehension is a more effective approach in most cases (as shown, for example, by the effects of the introduction of the breathalyzer test and of surveillance in underground stations). However, with most forms of crime it is just not practicable to increase substantially the chances of getting caught.

Finally, there is incapacitation – the prevention of crime through keeping criminals under lock and key. This is an appropriate form of prevention in the rare instances of seriously persistent offenders committing violent crime or major predatory theft. However, even in these cases there is the problem of knowing which individuals are likely to *go on* with their career of serious crime, and hence the danger of restricting the liberty of some individuals needlessly and without justification. Moreover, as already discussed, with most crime and with most offenders incapacitation simply does not make enough difference to warrant its consideration as a useful preventive strategy.

Conclusions on prevention

Although a great deal is known on the factors which predispose to delinquency, there is a considerable gap between identifying a damaging factor and knowing how to eliminate it or reduce its effects. There are no preventive programmes available which are likely to reduce crime to a major extent; nevertheless there are some steps which might have a useful, if small, impact. Most of the major successes in preventive medicine have come from community-wide public health measures (as with improved sanitation or nutrition) or personal measures designed to influence individual predisposition (as with immunization). However, these have no known parallels

---

* It should also be appreciated that there are important disadvantages in increasing the sanctions for lesser offences (see Zimring and Hawkins, 1973). The point is that any deterrent effect is likely to be only partially effective (apparently, the hanging of pickpockets in centuries past did not stop thieves picking the pockets of the crowds around the gallows). Accordingly it is desirable to have a 'stepladder' approach which adjusts the severity of the punishment to the seriousness of the crime, in the hope that, if the potential criminal *does* decide to act, the penal code will provide an adequate further deterrent to limit the seriousness of the offence. If the bottom rungs of the 'stepladder' are set too high (i.e. there is sharp punishment for minor crimes), it may be difficult to provide sufficiently great increases in penalty for further steps – say between simple theft, theft with assault, and theft resulting in serious injury or death.

in criminology. While there are some actions which should be taken with respect to high-risk variables influencing individual predisposition, there are none likely substantially to reduce delinquency. Ecological interventions, in terms of possible changes in schools, in area or community influences, or in the mass media, warrant further exploration, although it is difficult to gauge how much could be achieved in these ways. Perhaps the most immediate possibilities for preventive action lie in those designed to affect situations and opportunities – through physical crime prevention, through environmental manipulations and through improved surveillance. The scope of actions of this type is limited, but further development of this approach should be worthwhile.

Treatment and correction of offenders

In considering possible recommendations on changes in the ways of dealing with offenders, it is as well to start with a brief review of the current situation and of trends over recent years. Perhaps there are six main observations (the evidence for which has been discussed in earlier chapters) which should constitute the backcloth to our discussion of interventions:

(i) A very high proportion of young people are now appearing before the courts. Even *excluding* those cautioned, about one in five males receive convictions by the age of 20, and in some inner city areas the proportion is a third or more.

(ii) Many offences are concerned with quite minor acts of theft or damage.

(iii) Of these youngsters who appear before the courts, about half appear just once, and even among recidivists many stop offending by early adult life.

(iv) During the last decade there has been a marked increase in the use of police cautioning – an increase which seems to have beeen accompanied by a 'widening of the net', so that legal processing has been extended to include some minor offences and some minor offenders that might not have been involved in formal actions hitherto. Moreover, the intention that the use of cautioning would *divert* young people from the courts paradoxically seems to have been associated with an *increase* in the proportion convicted.

(v) Although the Children and Young Persons Act of 1969 was intended to replace much custodial correction by rehabilitative community programmes, in practice there has been a considerable *increase* in the use of custodial measures and in the number of young people placed in 'secure' institutions. Moreover, the evidence suggests that some young people are being given residential placements on their first court appearance for non-serious offences, and that by no means all of those in secure facilities present very severe problems.

(vi) The current situation is not a particularly satisfactory one as assessed from the overall level of crime in the community, the historical evidence showing that there has been an increase in delinquency during recent decades, the high rate of re-conviction after all interventions (but especially after custodial care), and expressed dissatisfaction as shown in both official documents, such as the 1980 Government White Paper on Young Offenders, and numerous critiques.

Response to first and minor offenders

In discussing possible interventions with offenders, it is important to differentiate between the various levels of seriousness and the various stages in a delinquent career. The initial question, then, is how society should respond when it first becomes evident that a child has committed one or more delinquent acts of a relatively non-serious nature. It is known that in about half of such cases the delinquent behaviour will cease, but in others the acts may constitute the beginnings of a persistent pattern of criminal activities. There are several objectives at this point. Firstly, it is important that whatever action is taken should not interfere with the 'natural' tendency for children to 'grow out' of this troublesome phase of delinquent behaviour; secondly, if possible, steps should be taken to reduce the likelihood that delinquency will persist; thirdly, it may be desirable for society to make clear that delinquency is not an acceptable form of behaviour (in order that *other* young people should not be encouraged in that direction); and fourthly, in view of the fact that a very high proportion of young people engage in delinquent activities at some time, the actions should require the minimum of time and expense.

It is clear that it would *not* be helpful to make a court appearance the first response in most cases, because many of the delinquent acts are too trivial to warrant taking up the court's time, and most especially because of the evidence that court appearances tend to *perpetuate* delinquent activities rather than cut them short (see Chapter 6). It might seem that some court action *should* serve as a valuable deterrent procedure, but it is clear that in practice this does not occur. It is probable that there are several reasons for this lack of deterrent efficacy with minor first offenders. In that most young people engage in trivial delinquent acts at some time, there is likely to be a certain randomness (as perceived by the boys, if not in actuality) in who appears in court. Also, if court procedures are very widely used for all manner of trivia, there is likely to be a debasement of the court's currency as a means of sanction for more serious offences. Moreover, in so far as the delinquent behaviour concerns many minor acts (only one of which has resulted in apprehension) rather than one serious act which led straight to court action, the power of the court is severely curtailed. This is because sanctions are most effective when they are immediate, certain, and consistently applied. By their very nature, court appearances cannot work like that. In addition, it must be added that an impersonal legal bureaucracy has obvious limitations as a corrective force. As West (1982) comments, appearances in court are as likely to teach juveniles to be disingenuous and distrustful towards authority as to teach them a sense of personal responsibility.

If court appearances are not to be the first response to delinquent behaviour, what should replace them? Basically, three alternatives are available. There may be recourse to informal community interventions in the hope that a 'therapeutic' approach at an early stage may cut short a delinquent career. The extension of 'intermediate treatment' to youths not yet found guilty in court provides an example of this strategy. This seems an *in*appropriate strategy because: (i) it would be extremely expensive to provide such interventions for at least a fifth of all boys (the proportion shown by the delinquency figures); (ii) there is no evidence that therapeutic strategies are effective for this group of youngsters; (iii) most minor first offenders do not have personal characteristics or experiences that mark them out as different from the general population in a way which would indicate the need for treatment; (iv) if the community interventions involve the juvenile in increased interactions with a delinquent peer group, then far from reducing the risk of recidivism, the intervention may increase it; and (v) there is a danger that, if intermediate treatment is used for 'at risk' juveniles not yet delinquent, those who subsequently commit delinquent acts may be dealt with more harshly by the courts on the assumption that opportunities for community intervention have already been exhausted. As West (1982) put it: 'Where ordinary methods of discipline would have sufficed, it is a waste of money, time, resources and professional skills, and quite possibly damaging to the juvenile concerned, to deal with him as if he were a suitable case for treatment.'

The second alternative is formal police cautioning, a procedure officially regarded as an alternative to prosecution and designed to provide a firm sign of disapproval of delinquent activities, while avoiding the stigma and disadvantage of court appearance. On the whole this appears to be a sensible and economical approach which is followed by a relatively low rate of re-offending. But also it seems to have carried with it the disadvantage of increasing the number of juveniles subjected to legal processing (probably because in practice cautions have been used as an alternative to informal warnings and to no action as well as to prosecution) and of transferring the responsibility of discipline from the community to the police. While it seems most desirable to retain the use of formal police cautioning, it may well be that the reduction in the use of informal procedures has not been helpful.

Such informal procedures constitute the third alternative. The point of an informal approach would *not* be to condone, accept or ignore the delinquent behaviour. Quite the reverse. The empirical evidence (as well as common sense and experience) indicates that antisocial behaviour is likely to persist if young people are allowed to misbehave without correction, discipline or sanctions. Rather, the object of informal action would be to get the family and the community to exercise its own responsibilities in that connection. It is likely that young people will be more effectively disciplined by parents and teachers who are in daily contact with them, and whose sanctions can be immediate, understandable, flexible and appropriate, than by police action distanced in time from the behaviour in question and restricted to one formal occasion.

Response to subsequent or more serious offences

Assuming that the initial response to delinquent activities has been some form of informal action, perhaps followed by an official police caution, there is then the question of what to do next if the criminal behaviour persists or recurs. It is abundantly clear from all the evidence that we are still dealing with a very large and heterogeneous group of young people at this stage. Some are basically normal, if rather troublesome, children whose delinquent activities consist of no more than petty theft and vandalism. Some are rather more serious delinquents but, nevertheless, young people who will ultimately give up criminal activities and become well-functioning adults. A few are destined to become persistent recidivists or dangerous offenders, and a few, who managed to escape early detection, are already that. The situation raises several rather different questions.

To begin with, there is the problem of how to make the differentiation between these various groups. The evidence suggests that a number of rather different factors are relevant. Some concern the offences – the more serious the offences, the earlier the age at which serious delinquent activities began, and the greater the number, range and frequency of offences, the more likely is it that delinquent activities will persist. Some concern the offender – the greater the evidence of poor peer relationships, of abnormalities in personality functioning, of an antisocial life style, and of a pervasive pattern of disruptive or deviant behaviour outside the delinquent acts themselves, the greater the chance of recidivism. But, also, some concern the offender's family – the less satisfactory the parental supervision and discipline, the less cohesive the family, the greater the number of other delinquents in the family (parents and/or sibs), and the worse the parent–child relationship, the worse the outcome for the young person in terms of continued delinquent activities. On the basis of data such as these, it may be possible to sort out the youngsters with a very low or very high likelihood of re-offending but, even with all this information, it has to be accepted that the predictive accuracy is only moderate, at best.

Often the characteristics of the offences, the offender, and his family point to the same decision about the chances of recidivism, but not infrequently they do not. In that case there is the question of *which* should be given most weight. The proponents of the strict proportionality 'justice model' take one extreme view – that there should be a strict and inflexible tariff based solely on the seriousness of the offence, but perhaps with some limited taking into account of the number of previous offences (see Morris *et al.*, 1980). Those who advocate a 'welfare model', in contrast, argue that it is the needs of the child, rather than his offence, which should decide the action – an approach which would place most weight on the characteristics of the offender and his family rather than the offence (as reflected in the philosophy underlying the 1969 Act). Both extremes involve the deliberate throwing away or disregard of relevant information which would help in the making of decisions on how likely it is that delinquent activities will continue. Clearly it is desirable to retain some degree of tariff in order to provide a limit on the extent to which individual liberties can be curtailed. It would not be desirable for minor offences to create the justification for custodial approaches (whether therapeutic or otherwise) under the banner of the welfare needs of the child.* On the other hand, it seems to be a profoundly retrograde step to institute a purely arbitrary tariff without any regard for whether the penalties help or hinder the child. Whatever approach is taken, it is essential to evaluate the *effects* of the judicial actions (be they therapeutic, punitive or custodial) and to adjust the strategy in the light of the empirical findings on consequences. It is true that at the moment there seems to be little evidence that one form of intervention is markedly more or less effective than others, but it seems

* Of course, there *are* occasions when children need to be placed in residential care in order to protect them from severe parental abuse or neglect, but that constitutes a different type of decision which should be taken primarily on the basis of the *parent's* behaviour rather than that of the child.

unduly pessimistic to assume that that will always be the case. Moreover, it seems inherently undesirable to adopt a tariff system which assumes that there is *no need* to be concerned with the evaluation of judicial actions (on the grounds that a proportionality between the seriousness of the offence and the severity of the sentence is sufficient justification in itself).

If we assume that some kind of balance needs to be achieved between these various different considerations, and if we also assume that, even with second- or third-time offenders, informal actions may still be appropriate if the acts have been minor and there are no other indications for more formal interventions, the next question is *who* should take the decision on how to proceed? At the moment, the police have considerable discretion in whether to warn an offender, refer him on to a social agency or to pass him on to the courts. As Morris *et al.* (1980) point out, the training and traditions of the police lie in the prevention, control and detection of crime, and the normal end-product of the process is to take the apprehended individual to court. To ask the police to be the main agency for *diverting* children from the courts is liable to create a conflict in police roles. They urge the value of the new Scottish system, in which a reporter (who is independent from the police, the courts and the social agencies) acts as a *sift* between the police and the children's hearings (the Scottish equivalent of juvenile courts). The intention of the Kilbrandon Committee (Committee on Children and Young Persons, Scotland, 1964), whose recommendations led to the system, was that the role called for 'a degree of practical knowledge and understanding of children's problems' and that the person 'should preferably be an officer combining a legal qualification with a period of administrative experience relating to the child welfare and educational services'. As it turned out, such a combination is hard to find and many of the reporters now are social workers. Perhaps because of that the police have been critical of the system, arguing that in some cases a 'no action' approach has encouraged criminal activities.

No firm recommendations are possible on the desirability of the Scottish system. It has resulted in fewer referrals to the hearings than was previously the case with the juvenile courts, but once the children reached the hearings the level of intervention has been greater than that in the juvenile courts (see Morris *et al.*, 1980). However, sound evidence is lacking on whether the net result has been an increase or a reduction in recidivism or no difference either way. Nevertheless, the idea of a 'sift' system, as in Scotland, seems to have merits and the possibility warrants further exploration and evaluation.

Once the child appears in court, there is the further question of who decides whether or not the child is removed from home. The 1969 Act took away from magistrates the power to decide the placement of a child made subject to a care order, the discretion being placed instead with social service departments. As the courts still retained the power to send young people to detention centres and Borstals (and indeed have made increasing use of this power), in practice the restriction has applied to placement in community homes with education on the premises (C.H.E.s) – the old 'approved schools'. The logic of the restriction was that C.H.E.s were intended to be therapeutic rather than custodial, and hence that the decision on placement there should be in the hands of therapeutic rather than judicial agencies. However, it is doubtful whether the clients (i.e. the offenders) perceive C.H.E.s in these terms (see Morris *et al.*, 1980); the drop-out rate from C.H.E.s in the 1970s has been considerably higher than that from approved schools in the 1960s (Tutt, 1976); and magistrates have complained that their lack of power to enforce committal to C.H.E.s has forced them to make more use of detention centres and Borstals than they would have done otherwise (see House of Commons Expenditure Committee, 1975). We conclude that the present approach to C.H.E.s is not entirely satisfactory.

The Government White Paper on Young Offenders in 1980 proposed that the courts should again be given the power to make a residential care order, but with a maximum of 6 months. The logic of their proposal was the need for courts to be able to impose a custodial or residential sentence when the offender was a real danger to society, shown to be unable or unwilling to respond to non-custodial measures, and in need of care and control not possible at home. That seems reasonable in itself – clearly there must be powers to protect society. Also, the White Paper argues for a decrease in the use of custody – a desirable objective, as we discuss below. The problem is that the recommendation to increase the court's flexibility with regard to custodial sentences, in practice, is likely to lead to the *greater* use of custody unless steps are taken to control its use. This could be done, for example, by a restriction on the number of custodial places, as recommended by the Black Committee (Review Group Report, 1979), or by a linking of the costs of custodial and non-custodial provisions (see Rutherford, 1981). The latter point stems from the fact that custodial facilities are funded by central government whereas community facilities are funded by local government. As local financial resources become tighter there may be an increasing temptation to take advantage of 'no-cost' custody. This could be avoided if the costs of custodial, as well as non-custodial, provision were borne by the same group.

The issue of *how* to decide and *who* should decide on custodial restrictions is a difficult one. The basic principles seem to be: (i) the main emphasis

Implications for Research, Policy and Practice 343

should be on non-custodial rather than custodial approaches (this is scarcely a matter of controversy, as all reports and critiques have emphasized the point, but see Chapter 9 and below for a discussion of the matter); (ii) there must be power, when necessary, to restrict the liberty of serious or dangerous offenders; (iii) because this restriction stems from the offence and from the need to protect society rather than from the needs of the individual, the decision should be by the courts (rather than a social agency); and (iv) for the same reason, the sentence should be determinate, rather than indeterminate, and should be subject to remissions.

The implication is that the courts should have the power to decide on custodial and non-custodial sanctions, that the length of these sanctions should be determinate,* and that effective steps should be taken to provide firm limits on the use of custodial approaches.

The last question is *what type* of intervention should be used for this large and heterogeneous group of offenders of intermediate seriousness and chronicity. The relevant empirical findings in relation to this question are: (i) residential treatment or sanctions have been found to have no advantages over community interventions (other than incapacitation), and there has been a slight tendency for there to be greater recidivism after custodial interventions; (ii) relatively little is achieved by corrective or therapeutic approaches which focus only on the offender as an individual; (iii) if there is to be any substantial impact on delinquent behaviour, it will be necessary to influence the offender's home environment, especially in terms of the family and the peer group; (iv) in so far as individual approaches are of value, those which aim to increase practical, vocational, social problem-solving skills seem to have most to offer; and (v) in some circumstances, the deterrent or controlling function of a threat of sanctions seems to be more effective than active interventions.

In view of these considerations, it seems appropriate that the courts should make extensive use of conditional discharges or binding over, adjournment, fines and the award of compensation – as recommended by the Black Committee. The interventions all provide some form of legal sanction, are inexpensive in time and resources to operate, and are likely to carry the minimum amount of undesired side-effects from the intervention.

Where more active intervention is needed, in the first instance, this should seek to strengthen effective *community* responses to delinquent activities

---

* The question of the appropriate length of such sanctions is not one that can be decided on the basis of empirical evidence alone, and we offer no suggestions on the matter. It is noteworthy, however, that the recommendations made in official reports and in academic critiques have varied quite widely.

rather than create a reliance on official agencies. Morris et al. (1980), in discussing diversionary approaches, emphasize five needs:

1. to persuade the community, family and school to respond informally to law-breaking;
2. to emphasize positive and constructive responses to delinquency (e.g. reparation by the offender to the victim or to the community);
3. to engage, where possible, the victim directly in working out a settlement (either informally through the parents or formally through the independent sift);
4. to emphasize the responsibility of the offender (in a way which we feel formal processing often ignores);
5. to provide the offender with guidance, supervision and other assistance in coping with any difficulties *he* may feel he has. (p. 65)

These seem reasonable goals and constitute appropriate guidelines for such informal or semi-formal responses to delinquent behaviour.

In other cases, greater control, punitive sanctions or treatment will be called for. Increased effective control in the community can come only from those people in day-to-day contact with the offender – particularly parents and teachers. Accordingly, probation and supervision need to be concerned with aiding parents (and teachers) at least as much as providing a degree of control over the individual himself. There has been no systematic evaluation of the efficacy of attendance centre orders as compared with other interventions, but the limited available evidence on their use suggests that probably they have a useful place in the range of options open to the court.

Many critics of the judicial system have argued that there is no evidence of the value of any form of treatment for delinquents and, hence, that therapeutic approaches have no place. The empirical findings do not support such an extremely negative view. In the first place, as reviewed in Chapter 9, the evaluations of treatment have *not* all been negative. Therapeutic interventions which succeed in changing the home environment, or which provide increased social and vocational skills, or which open up more constructive social activities with a different peer group, have had a modest success when the interventions have been systematic, well thought out and skilfully applied. There are real difficulties in bringing about a change in delinquent behaviour, but much the greater problem has lain in the *maintenance* of change in the face of an unchanging environment. In the second place, the assumption that all offenders can be dealt with as individuals whose only problem is the commission of some delinquent act and who can be regarded as entirely responsible for their own actions and futures (see Morris *et al.*, 1980) is inconsistent with the empirical findings on the widespread and persistent psycho-social impairments shown by the most seriously recidivist offenders. Of course they constitute a minority of offenders, but still their needs should be met. The therapeutic approach to delinquency was hopelessly oversold by the enthusiastic pioneers, but it would be quite out of keeping with the evidence to reject it completely.

The questions, then, are *who* should receive therapeutic interventions, what form should therapy take, and should treatment be compulsorily imposed? No clear-cut criteria can be provided for an answer to the first question – as the research on individual differences in therapeutic response is at a rather early stage of development. However, it would seem that, perhaps, intensive efforts should mainly be concentrated on two groups.* Firstly, there are what might be termed the 'neurotic', 'amenable' offenders – the rather anxious introspective youths with emotional difficulties, who are aware of their personal problems and who want help with them. The pointers suggest that this is the group where individual counselling is likely to be of most value. Most of these youths are likely to accept help if offered, and there is neither need nor justification for any compulsion. Secondly, there are the youths in whom delinquent activities are associated with an antisocial life style, widespread disruptive behaviour and disordered interpersonal relationships. In many cases their parents are lax and careless in their supervision of the youths' activities, fail to provide appropriate training in the ordinary social skills, allow behaviour to get out of hand and then over-react with ineffectual harshness as part of a generally coercive and abrasive style of family interaction. It is this group where intensive therapeutic endeavours, oriented on the family rather than the individual, and which utilize behavioural techniques, may be of value. However, it is also this group of families who are least likely to cooperate with any form of intervention, their lack of involvement being part of a generally chaotic life style which lacks foresight and planning. Even so, the task of *gaining* the family's participation should be regarded as *part* of the intervention; it is clear that all forms of treatment are much more likely to be successful if it is voluntarily sought or accepted rather than officially imposed. Nevertheless, it would seem reasonable, as at present, for supervision or care orders to be employed as a means of securing participation if it can be justified on the grounds of the child's needs rather than his offence, and if it cannot be obtained in other ways (see the Black Committee Report). With this severely antisocial group, persistently and sometimes seriously delinquent behaviour may otherwise

* The description of both groups is stereotypical. It is based on the research evidence discussed in Chapter 9, but there is no indication that the groups are in any way discrete or homogeneous – the descriptions do no more than serve as a rather general pointer to the circumstances in which a therapeutic approach might be considered.

force some form of custodial action, and it seems a disservice to choose punitive incarceration rather than compulsory community treatment under the banner of respecting the liberty of the subject! However, it is important that compulsion should be utilized as a last resort rather than a first response, that it should be warranted on the basis of the seriousness of the youth's delinquent activities, and that the compulsion should be for a determinate period, with all appropriate legal safeguards.

The question of so-called 'intermediate treatment' (I.T.) needs also to be considered here. As indicated in Chapter 9, the term is a rather general one which covers a rather heterogeneous range of community-based, but mainly individual-oriented, interventions. In some quarters, high hopes have been placed on the utility of this approach. So far it lacks evaluation, and any conclusions on its likely efficacy must necessarily be tentative and provisional. Nevertheless, two points may be made about the approach. On the positive side, actions such as supervision by involvement of the children in a recreational and work programme at a day centre, the provision of opportunities to develop satisfactory social relationships, and rehabilitative and educational interventions all seem likely to be generally positive and helpful. On the negative side, however, in so far as the intervention does not attempt to alter the quality of the relationship between the child and his parents, the nature of parental supervision or the influence of peers, there is no reason to suppose that it will be any more effective than the treatments previously provided on a residential basis (Sinclair and Clarke, 1981). The implication is that the ultimate utility of I.T. may well be dependent on the extent to which it can succeed in involving *families*, rather than just individual offenders – but that proposition has not yet been put to the empirical test.

In Chapter 9 we also discussed the possible value of community interventions, such as the Wincroft Youth Project, in which there is an attempt to work directly with community peer groups. At present, there is too little evidence for any conclusion on the efficacy of this approach. If such interventions can succeed in influencing peer group attitudes and behaviour, or can direct youths into less crime-oriented social activities, they could well be of value. The real question is how far it is possible to affect community life in this way. The approach warrants further exploration on an experimental basis but cannot be recommended as a general strategy at the moment.

In suggesting the *occasional* value of therapeutic interventions, we are *not* advocating them as a general strategy for most delinquency. In the first place, the number of children who behave in a delinquent way is so great that no treatment programme could possibly reach all those likely to become confirmed offenders. But, secondly, the track record of therapeutic interventions provides no indication that this would constitute an effective or sensible approach even if resources were unlimited (which manifestly they are not). Thirdly, there is evidence that, sometimes, well-intentioned interventions may actually be *worse* than a policy of simple sanctions (see, for example, Berg *et al.*, 1978a and b). The natural inclination to feel that social service departments ought to 'do something' with all delinquents and that, even if not very effective, it is better to do something than nothing, may well be misplaced. For the reasons we have given, there is value in continuing attempts to develop better methods of treatment (mainly focused on the family rather than the individual) for use with selected individuals, but it would be futile to adopt this as any kind of general strategy – as well as possibly damaging in diverting resources from other areas where they may be of greater value (Sinclair and Clarke, 1981).

Removal from home and institutional placements

The next questions are when removal from home or an institutional placement should be considered and what can be achieved by these approaches. As already noted, during recent years there has been a tendency to make an increasing use of compulsory detention in one form or another. Also, this increasing use has been accompanied by a feeling among many magistrates (see House of Commons Expenditure Committee, 1975) that they need *greater* powers to enforce the placement of juveniles in secure accommodation. This view is an understandable reflection of an entirely appropriate concern that we have not yet developed a satisfactory means of dealing with the most troublesome and difficult group of serious and persistent delinquents. Nevertheless, all the research findings indicate that a policy of more and more incarceration is not likely to be effective and could well make things worse. On the other hand, even if often over-used, there are occasions when removal from home, or placement in an institution, are appropriate.

Before discussing those circumstances, it is appropriate to pause for a moment to consider a few of the concepts and findings on institutional approaches. As Sinclair and Clarke (1982) emphasize, the evidence suggests that institutions *do* have an impact on young people's behaviour while they are in the institutions; the problem is that the benefits do not last. They argue that institutional treatments were developed on the basis of an inappropriate 'medical' model which assumed that it was the child himself who needed changing, and that if the 'treatment' was successful, the child could then cope

348 *Juvenile Delinquency*

satisfactorily on return to his original environment. As they point out, the research evidence indicates that usually this does not happen. Accordingly the implication is that it is necessary to modify the damaging features of the environment. However, it would be seriously misleading to suppose that *all* that is needed is a non-noxious environment. Not only are there important *individual* differences in how young people respond to stress and adversity (see Chapter 5), but also there is substantial evidence of considerable *persistence* of antisocial behaviour over time and across environments (see Chapter 2). Offenders are indeed responsive to environmental change, but it would be futile to hope that the mere placement of delinquents in a benign environment would bring to an end a well-entrenched pattern of antisocial behaviour. Even in very good environmental circumstances, many recidivist delinquents continue to behave in exceedingly troublesome and disruptive ways.

The removal of a delinquent from his home needs to be considered in two main circumstances: (i) when the family influence is so damaging and so irremediable that the youth needs to be removed from it; and (ii) when the youth's criminal behaviour is so serious and persistent that removal from the community is required in order to protect society. It is tempting to suppose that if some forms of serious delinquent behaviour develop in part because of seriously inappropriate, deficient or damaging parenting, then removal from home is the most sensible way of dealing with the situation. Clearly, there are circumstances when that seems the most appropriate action to take – by means of care proceedings or some other action. Of course, there are (and should be) strict constraints through the need to justify such action in terms of *both* the damaging effect of the family environment *and* the failure of attempts to help the family modify its style of functioning. But, even when shown to be justifiable, additional constraints on the efficacy of this move are imposed by the severe difficulties in practice in arranging the provision of a better alternative environment. Boarding schools of one sort or other (although not systematically evaluated) are unlikely to have a major lasting impact if the youth returns to the same damaging environment each holiday. Institutions, where the youth remains as if it were his home, constitute a rather inadequate substitute for a family upbringing. There have been recent attempts (see Hazel, 1977 and 1978) to develop time-limited family fostering as an alternative to residential placement for delinquent boys and girls. Foster parents are provided with a salary (rather than the usual nominal fee) and there is extensive support through group meetings. The idea seems worth further exploration but, so far, there has not been a systematic evaluation of the efficacy of this approach. With all these forms of residential care, the benefits are likely to be short-lived if the offender returns to the same environment, without there having been successful efforts to change its characteristics or impact.

The recognition that institutional care needs to be accompanied by an equal investment in improving the environment led to the development of community-linked facilities such as 'Achievement Place' (see Chapter 9), in which the institution staff worked with the family as well as with the youth himself. The results so far do not suggest that it has been easy to make this bridge, but the aim to do so seems appropriate.

The same issues arise when institutional placement is required because of the serious nature of the youth's antisocial behaviour. In both cases, there is the additional question of the form that the institutional regime should take. The research reviewed in the preceding chapter suggests that the qualities of the institution *do* matter, but that the crucial features concern social structure and interpersonal relationships rather than the theoretical orientation of the establishment. Cawson (1978), in the report of her study of residential staff in community homes, provided a useful discussion of the issues and of the ways in which some of the difficulties in running a successful institution stem from the organizational structure of the Homes and from the traditions of staff behaviour. Sinclair and Clarke (1982) suggest that it is the combination of firmness, consistency, kindness and a thorough-going attempt to forestall absconding – possibly combined with vocational training – that is most likely to be successful. The finding that institutional placements have a very limited impact on long-term recidivism should not in any way detract from the need to make the institution as harmonious and beneficial an environment as it can be in the short term. As indicated, research findings provide useful guidelines on the approaches to follow.

The need for secure units raises other issues. On the one hand, many of the boys currently in secure units do pose quite substantial problems. Millham *et al.* (1978) found that three-quarters were persistent delinquents with a history of recurrent breakdowns of residential placements as a result of persistent absconding and socially provocative behaviour; 16 per cent were grave offenders guilty of offences such as rape, violent robbery or arson; and 8 per cent had severe and often bizarre behaviour problems, with spasmodic violence to staff and attempts at suicide. It might be thought that increasing use of secure provision for younger and younger boys was a necessary and inevitable response to a worsening situation. On the other hand, there are several reasons for not accepting that argument. Firstly, the same evidence showed that there were similarly difficult youths being successfully contained in non-secure establishments. Secondly, it was found that some residential

350   *Juvenile Delinquency*

facilities sent more boys on to secure units than did others. High rates of absconding, of transfer, and of failure tend to go together, and it appears that, to some degree, the extent of the need for secure units will be influenced by the quality of other placements. The clear implication is that the first response to difficult behaviour needs to be to improve the functioning of the non-secure institutions rather than to pass the youth on to more and more secure environments. Substantial degrees of security may be obtained by generous staffing ratios, by appropriate structure and discipline, and by close relationships between staff and boys as well as by locks and bolts. Moreover, the need for security may be reduced by appropriate training in social skills and by other steps to help the boys develop more effective coping strategies for dealing with their problems.

Thirdly, the results of secure provisions are quite discouraging. Millham *et al.* (1978) found that a quarter of the boys go on to other custodial settings, and of the remainder less than a quarter commit no further offences during the next two years. Obviously, there is a need for some secure units and it is important that they be provided. But it may well be that in many cases only relatively short spells of security are required because the crisis of control wanes and, as it does so, other methods of response become possible (Millham *et al.*, 1978). The point is that the behaviour of adolescents is influenced by the environment in which they live and long periods of physically enforced security may not be the best means of providing rehabilitation. Probably, it is wisest to see secure provision as one shorter-term element that is available when needed as part of a broader programme, rather than as the main form of intervention even with the more difficult and intransigent delinquents.

Conclusions on treatment and correction

In the last two sections of this chapter we have discussed therapeutic interventions and residential facilities at some length because they constitute topics of controversy with respect to the response to the most serious and persistent offenders. However, in order to right the perspective it is necessary to conclude our consideration of interventions with delinquents with a restatement of the overall approaches suggested by empirical research findings. The first point is that delinquent behaviour is very pervasive among children and adolescents, most delinquency is minor, most youths who commit minor delinquent acts are not particularly distinctive in their personal characteristics or family background, and in most cases the delinquency constitutes a passing phase that will come to an end without the need for rigorous intervention. As a consequence, a policy of minimal intervention is most appropriate with first and minor offenders. Disapproval of the delinquent behaviour should be firm and unequivocal, but such discipline is more effectively applied by parents and teachers than by the police or the courts. Informal community interventions of various kinds designed to increase the responsibility of the offender and of his family should be the first resort (and often the second or subsequent resort for minor offences), because there is no indication that formal processing is more successful and because of the evidence that a court appearance may make things worse.

In cases where these actions do not prove successful, the next steps should be formal cautions or judicial responses (such as adjournment, conditional discharge, binding over, fines, or compensation to the victim) which provide sanctions and deterrence but require a minimum of active intervention. In more serious cases an attendance centre order may serve the same purpose.

When a more intensive intervention is required, community programmes are generally to be preferred to custodial sentences. In such community approaches the main emphasis should be on working to improve the family environment, to make the peer group influence less crime-directed, and to give the offender better social problem-solving and vocational skills.

Therapeutic interventions have a quite limited, but still important, role. They do *not* constitute a suitable strategy for dealing with the broad run of delinquents, but they *may* be of value for offenders with emotional problems for which they desire help or for the more pervasively antisocial youths whose delinquency is part of a broader pattern of social difficulties.

Residential placements will be needed in some instances because of the severely damaging quality of the family environment or because of the seriousness or dangerousness of the offender's antisocial activities. It is not likely that residential interventions will have much lasting impact on recidivism, unless they are combined with efforts to improve the home environment, but attention to the qualities of the institution is important in ensuring that the short-term impact is beneficial. There is a need for some secure facilities, but it is not desirable to escalate the amount of secure provision. Physical security is most appropriately seen as something that usually is needed as a short-term response to crisis (as part of a broader intervention strategy), and the needs for which can be kept to a minimum by maintaining a high quality of care in non-secure institutions.

Research needs

Throughout this book we have made various suggestions regarding possibly fruitful avenues for further research. In this final section we summarize some of the main topics and strategies that warrant priority, either because there are crucial gaps in knowledge which need filling or because past research has shown that further studies are likely to be rewarding. Our list of research areas should not be seen as definitive or comprehensive. We know that there are important topics not included (indeed, some are mentioned elsewhere in our review). Moreover, new findings or new research strategies or new measures can rapidly transform an area so that topics which have proved unrewarding hitherto become fruitful and need to be given a much higher priority. Of course, too, it is inevitable that to some extent priorities are influenced by personal interests and preferences, and ours are no exception to that tendency. Nevertheless, we have tried to utilize our review of past research to identify areas which seem either particularly promising or particularly in need of development.

Historical trends

In Chapter 3 we noted the considerable difficulties involved in any assessment of whether crime is increasing, decreasing or changing in character. It was apparent that official statistics provided a rather fallible guide in view of the many factors (other than number of crimes and number of offenders) that can and do influence them. There are a variety of changes (none of which are free from difficulties) which could facilitate the use of crime statistics as a guide to historical trends. For example, it would be helpful, with respect to juveniles as well as adults, for there to be a more detailed breakdown of offences in ways that would allow an assessment of whether an apparent rise in crime is due to more minor crimes being drawn into the statistics, or whether there is still a rise when like is being compared with like. Thus, inflation has meant that more cases of damage are coming above the £20 cut-off point, thereby creating a misleading impression of an increase in cases of damage. Similarly, 'violent' offences cover a very wide range, extending from those involving no actual injury to those resulting in permanent crippling. It would be helpful if there could be some systematic recording of a measure of 'seriousness'. However, it may be that it would be more realistic to consider gathering such information in a series of special surveys – say every five years – rather than as a routine (both because of the time and expense involved and because of the probable unreliability of such informa-

Implications for Research, Policy and Practice 353

tion when gathered as part of ordinary practice). If such surveys were undertaken, they would provide a much improved guide to historical trends. It would be possible, too, as part of these special inquiries, to obtain more detailed information on items such as number of previous offences, family background, place of residence, and place of offence, which would be valuable in allowing a more accurate pin-pointing of the particular nature of any increase or decrease in crime that takes place.

In addition, it is highly desirable to use other means to assess possible changes over time. Victimization data provide one useful approach. Although they are by no means free of measurement problems, they can give rise to reasonable estimates of many sorts of crime if proper attention is paid to the necessary safeguards. The inclusion of questions on victimization in the 1972, 1973 and 1979 Household Surveys has shown the practicality of this approach, and it is highly desirable that directly comparable questions be included in future surveys. Up to now the victimization questions have been limited in scope, and it would be helpful if additional questions could be added in order to cover a wider range of crimes.

A variety of special observational and reporting methods for measuring crime have been noted in the text of earlier chapters when discussing vandalism, crime in underground stations, shoplifting and the like. Again, it would be useful to undertake directly comparable special studies of this kind every five years or so in order to monitor possible changes in crime rates. Self-report data might also be informative but delinquent acts would require very careful definition if the information was to be valid for making comparisons over time.

Intervention and prevention

All reviews of interventions with offenders have commented on the paucity of good evaluative studies, and our appraisal of the evidence has been similarly hampered. As the American Panel on Research on Rehabilitative Techniques (Sechrest *et al.*, 1979) concluded: 'Insistence on careful, and even stringent, evaluation of rehabilitative programs is grounded in the legitimate concerns of several constituencies of the criminal justice system.' They went on to argue that: 'it does not seem likely that much reliance can be placed on methods of gaining knowledge other than experimentation. Case studies, demonstration projects, systems analyses, surveys and the like are simply untrustworthy as a basis on which to make policy and invest in programs ... Experiments must be favored because of the higher degree of certainty their results provide and because they provide that certainty in a shorter period of time and at lower total cost than is usually possible with other evaluative methods.' We agree. A wide range of corrective, punitive, therapeutic, and supervisory interventions are being employed with young offenders, but in most cases information is lacking on whether one approach is better than another. Clearly that is unsatisfactory.

Sometimes objections are raised to an experimental approach on the grounds that it is wrong that decisions on issues as important as criminal justice should be decided on the spin of a coin – as would be involved in random allocation to different forms of intervention. At first sight that sounds a weighty objection, until it is appreciated that in the absence of evidence on efficacy *all* interventions are experimental. The implication is that it is ethical to experiment with all offenders but not with only half of them! Not only are experimental evaluations of interventions entirely ethical, but also they are *essential* whenever there is real doubt as to whether one intervention is to be preferred to another. It is obvious that there is indeed real doubt with most current interventions, in that there are such wide variations in usage between different magistrates and different parts of the country. It is precisely in these circumstances that random allocation studies are warranted and needed. The procedure is practicable in the British juvenile justice system, as shown by the randomization comparison of adjournment and social work supervision in the study undertaken by Berg and his colleagues (1978a and b). Of course, magistrates must remain free to decide on the range of sanctions appropriate in any individual case, but within that range it is usual for there to be several alternatives that could be employed. For example, it would be most informative to compare simple sanctions such as adjournment, conditional discharge, binding over, fines or compensation to the victim with social work supervision or probation in the case of minor offences. Or, perhaps, intermediate treatment might be compared with attendance centre orders. Or, again, there might be random allocation to institutions known to vary on the organizational variables shown to be important in non-experimental cross-institution comparisons (see Sinclair and Clarke, 1981). Or intensive family-oriented community interventions might be contrasted with residential placements.

When undertaking experimental evaluations of interventions, it will be important to take account of the lessons of previous research in this area. The key needs include: (i) the use of predictive measures (based on characteristics of the offences, the offender and his family) as well as random allocation; (ii) assessment of the quality and characteristics of the intervention process itself; (iii) the use of within-group comparisons to relate the degree of success to the degree of change in the postulated intervening mechanism in the intervention (see Chapter 9); (iv) the study of possible individual differences in response;* (v) evaluation in terms of a broader range of outcome variables than simple re-conviction (these should include measures of social functioning as well as the frequency and seriousness of offences); (vi) study of immediate and short-term effects as well as long-term outcome; and (vii) careful monitoring, with quality controls, of the intervention itself.

The last point raises the issue that evaluation of intensive active interventions involves two rather separate questions: firstly, which methods are truly effective given optimal conditions; and, secondly, given that it is known that a method *is* effective in these conditions, can it be applied successfully on a community-wide basis (see Rutter, 1979a). The former requires intensive small-scale studies with a tight control over what is done, whereas the latter involves large-scale research with the necessarily looser control of a real-life application across a range of different community settings. If both are combined in one overall research design there is a danger that no unequivocal answer will be obtained to either question. Both research strategies are needed, but the first should precede the second.

Closely comparable needs and issues arise with respect to the evaluation of preventive measures. Earlier in this chapter we outlined various possible preventive strategies and tactics which seemed to hold promise, but very few have been subjected to systematic evaluation as yet. It is important that they should be.

Policing and processing

One of the dilemmas currently faced by the police is how to deal with socioculturally or ethnically distinctive inner city areas thought to have high rates of crime, and how to deal with situations involving the accumulation of large crowds of people in circumstances which involve the risk of confrontation, tension and disturbance (as in many demonstrations, festivals, and some sporting occasions). If they fail to provide extra policing and trouble breaks out, they tend to be blamed for not taking the necessary precautions. On the other hand, if extra policing is provided, they may be blamed equally for precipitating trouble through the 'provocation' of an excessive police presence or intrusive police controls. Over the years the police have gained

---

* This requires improvements in the measurement and categorization of the relevant offender characteristics. Concepts of 'amenability' and I-level 'maturity of personality' provide pointers as to what kinds of variables might be important, but the particular measures used in the past leave a lot to be desired.

considerable experience and expertise in the management of these potentially difficult crowd or community occasions. Nevertheless there are times when the situation gets out of hand, and in a few instances there has been rioting with unpleasant and dangerous violent confrontations both within the community and between the community and the police. These circumstances underline the importance of good police–community relations, as effective policing and crime control are heavily dependent on the cooperation of the general public. We lack adequate understanding of the factors which influence police–community relations, of the optimal policing policies, and of the variables which determine crowd behaviour. These issues warrant further study.

As outlined in Chapter 1, it is clear that there are important variations in the process by which crimes and suspected offenders are dealt with. Also, there have been many accusations that these variations reflect bias and prejudice. The empirical findings are much more equivocal with respect to bias than they are on variations. It is *not* self-evident that processing procedures should be rigid and inflexible, paying no regard to the seriousness of the offence or the number and type of previous offences, or the characteristics of the offender, or the nature of family circumstances. Equally, however, it is not acceptable that discretion should be operated on the basis of personal prejudice or discriminatory practice. It would be worthwhile to undertake further systematic studies of processing procedures and their consequences.

Individual differences

Although it has become unfashionable to talk about the importance of individual differences, the evidence clearly points to their pertinence and influence. There is a world of difference between the basically normal youngster who gets into trouble with the police for a transient phase of mildly delinquent behaviour, but who does not offend again and who grows up to become a socially successful and law-abiding adult, and the persistent recidivist who has a host of interpersonal and social problems apart from his delinquency, which is itself part of an antisocial life style, and who continues with his criminal career well into adult life with all manner of accompanying psycho-social difficulties and impairments. No one doubts this degree of variation, but there is a lack of agreement on *how* delinquents should be categorized or subdivided. There are useful pointers to the possible relevance of personality variables, of attentional deficits, and of the autonomic, stimulus-seeking and avoidance-learning features associated with the con-

Implications for Research, Policy and Practice 357

cept of psychopathy, to mention but three examples. But good data to validate these approaches are lacking, and they are especially lacking in the case of juveniles. The very limited evidence on the individual characteristics which *might* be important was reviewed in Chapters 1 and 5. What is needed now is a more systematic follow-through on the investigation of these leads.

In essence, the strategy required is the application of appropriate measures to representative groups of delinquents in order to determine how far dimensional 'scores' or categorical distinctions based on the measures relate to other variables (such as the type of delinquency, family background, recidivism, associated behavioural or social impairments, or response to particular forms of intervention).

There are two specific aspects of individual differences which warrant separate mention. Firstly, the link between educational retardation and delinquency is one of the most consistent of all associations in the literature. Yet we have a very limited understanding of the possible mechanisms involved in the association. They require further study – by longitudinal analyses to determine the possibly changing patterns of the association over time; by cross-sectional studies comparing delinquents with and delinquents without educational retardation (both groups also being compared with nondelinquent children with educational retardation and children with neither delinquency nor educational problems); by intervention studies to determine the effects on delinquent behaviour of the successful remediation of educational difficulties; and by studies to compare the behavioural effects of different school policies in dealing with educational difficulties.

Secondly, there is the even better-established association between gender and delinquency. Little is known on the reasons why girls are so much less prone to engage in delinquent behaviour, and even less is known on why the sex ratio for delinquency has been changing over recent years (with a reduction in the male preponderance). Both questions require further study. There are a number of possible mechanisms which have been proposed (see Chapter 4), but none has yet been adequately studied and it is likely that further investigation of the nature and meaning of these sex differences would be informative. As a corollary, it is noteworthy how few investigations have been undertaken into delinquency in girls, and there are none based on the kinds of longitudinal studies of general population samples that have proved so useful in the investigation of male delinquency. Studies of representative samples of delinquent girls are indicated.

Environmental influences

We have a considerable knowledge of the environmental indices associated with an increased risk of delinquency. These include variables such as parental criminality; poor parental supervision; family discord, disruption and disharmony; large family size; and a delinquent peer group. Little is to be gained by further large-scale surveys to demonstrate the associations yet again. The reality and consistency of the findings across varying social groups is well established. However, the *meaning* of the associations and the causal *mechanisms* they represent are not well understood, and it is these issues that should constitute the focus of further research in this area.

One of the problems in disentangling mechanisms is the considerable overlap between different family adversities, a problem which is compounded by the over-general conceptualization of the variables – in terms such as 'supervision' or 'discord'. Detailed observational studies of sequences of family interaction carry some promise of cutting through this Gordian knot by virtue of their better delineation of the processes involved in discipline or in coercive family interactions. This research approach, however, is much strengthened by linking such observations to changes in young people's behaviour over time or across situations, and even more so by using intervention studies to determine whether there is any systematic association between, for example, *changes* in the quality of parental supervision or an increase in family harmony or improvements in family social problem-solving on the one hand, and on the other, changes in the frequency or seriousness of the child's delinquent behaviour.

In Chapter 7 we outlined a few of the available research leads on the general topic of possible protective factors. All research has shown the considerable variation in how young people respond to apparently similar environmental adversities. Some become delinquent, others develop emotional disturbances or social impairment, but also many appear to develop normally without any substantial signs of damage from their experiences. Some of this variation in response is a consequence of differences in the seriousness or chronicity of the environmental hazards, and some is due to temperamental or other factors in the child. But, also, it seems that some is a result of the counter-balancing effect of *positive* experiences or ameliorating circumstances. Possible examples of this kind are provided by the apparently protective effect of a move to a less delinquent environment, of one good relationship in the context of family discord, of good schooling, and of scholastic (and possibly other) success. However, all of these examples derive from a very small number of studies and it is all too apparent that a preoccupation with the harmful effects of negative features of the environment has led to a neglect of the possible beneficial effect of positive features – even when these are present against a background of deprivation and disadvantage. There is a great need to explore the role of protective factors much more systematically than has been done up to now. The basic research strategy simply consists of comparing young people with 'good' and 'bad' outcomes within a group *all* of whom suffer serious adversity, but with the measurement of *positive*, as well as negative, features of the environment.

As indicated in Chapter 6, there are a few sound studies showing an association between the characteristics of schools and rates of delinquent behaviour in the pupils. The inference is that schools exert some *influence* on the behaviour of their students. However, further investigations are required to confirm (or refute) these findings. Such investigations will require some kind of longitudinal strategy in order to control for the intake characteristics of the pupils, and to study *changes* in pupil behaviour in response to changes in the school environment (as a result of the pupil moving to a different school or of the school altering as a consequence of a change in policy, or the appointment of a new head teacher, or because of a planned experiment).

The school studies, as also the various studies reviewed in Chapter 7, all point to the importance of the peer group. However, although peer group influences have been a topic of interest ever since Sutherland (1939) first put forward his theory of differential association, they have been the subject of remarkably little systematic research. Further studies are needed to delineate both how peer groups operate and also how they influence delinquent behaviour.

Area influences constitute another topic which needs a fresh look. As reviewed in Chapter 6, there is an abundance of studies showing large and striking differences between areas in their rates of delinquency. Further large-scale studies based on census type data are most unlikely to add appreciably to what we know already. What are lacking are detailed studies of the characteristics of the *areas themselves*. We need to determine just what it is that makes some areas predispose to and others protect from crime. *Which* factors are influential and *how* do they operate?

A more ambitious extension of the same basic strategy is provided by cross-national studies. On the whole, historical trends in crime rates have been remarkably similar in all industrialized countries. But there are a few striking exceptions with respect both to the level of crime and to changes in level over time. In Chapter 3, we noted the example of Japan as one that applied to levels and change. But knowledge on the reasons for these cross-national differences is lacking. The matter is worth further exploration.

A somewhat related issue concerns the effects of social change. Earlier in this report we commented on the sometimes striking disparity between cross-sectional studies and studies of historical change. At any one point in time, for example, poverty and unemployment are associated with an increased risk of delinquency, but historical analyses have generally failed to show any effect on delinquency of increases in affluence or of rises or falls in unemployment. The analysis of the effects of social change involves many difficulties, but the topic is important and much neglected. The development of improved strategies for studying social change should be a research priority.

In recent years there has been an increasing interest in situational effects. Several studies (reviewed in Chapters 6 and 9) have shown that young people are more likely to behave in delinquent ways in some situations than in others. Such research carried the potential for an increased understanding of the forces which result in delinquent behaviour and for the development of possible preventive strategies. However, if this area of work is to develop its potential, it will be important to investigate the specific characteristics of situations which influence delinquent behaviour either positively or negatively, and by this means to identify the possible mechanisms involved. Other research also suggests that individuals differ in their reactions to the same situational stimuli. Although it is undoubtedly true that behaviour is more situation-specific than trait theory acknowledges, it is also the case that situations are more person-specific than situationism theory has allowed (Rutter, 1980b). Future research will need to investigate and take account of the *interactions* between persons and situations.

Finally, with respect to environmental influences, there is a need to investigate the effects of massive and comprehensive changes in the environment. Although such changes are infrequent occurrences, assessment of their effects is important to an understanding of the operation of environmental influences. There are various possibilities for studying the consequences of environmental transformation, but perhaps adoption (or long-term fostering) of the children of criminal parents provides the most striking example. Cross-fostering or adoption research designs have been used extensively to assess the heritability of particular behaviours or psychopathological syndromes. Further research of that kind is needed to provide a better delineation of the operation of genetic factors in delinquency (see Chapter 5), but in addition they may be used with profit (but rarely have been) to discover how far massive changes in the environment – in infancy and at various stages of childhood – alter the risk for delinquency. There is surprisingly little good information on this crucial point, and studies to investigate the matter further would be most worthwhile.

Continuities between childhood and adult life

The last research need to be mentioned is the study of continuities and discontinuities between childhood and adult life. We know that most juvenile delinquents cease their criminal activities before or soon after reaching adulthood; we know also that most adult criminals were already delinquent in childhood. However, there are huge and important areas of ignorance on this general topic. For example, we know little about the social outcome in middle adult life of juvenile recidivists who give up crime in late adolescence. To what extent do they show interpersonal or parenting difficulties? What is the delinquency risk for their children? Similarly, we lack an understanding of the effects of marriage on a delinquent career. Very early marriage or marriage to another delinquent does not seem to be helpful, but does this apply similarly to marriage in the early or mid-twenties to a non-delinquent partner? Conversely, how do adults who begin their criminal activities during their twenties or later differ from those with a childhood onset? Were there precursors in childhood of a non-delinquent type, or was the adult onset of criminality quite unrelated to childhood behaviour or experiences? In order to answer these and other similar questions, it would be necessary to utilize longitudinal studies which already extend into early adult life (such as the National Survey or the Cambridge Study of Delinquent Development). However, in addition, it would be important to compare adult criminals according to whether or not there was a childhood onset of delinquent activities.

Conclusions on research needs

Not surprisingly, this review of research into juvenile delinquency ends with the conclusion that much has still to be learned about the subject. But we do *not* conclude that more research of the same kind is needed. Rather, we have attempted to highlight some key areas where *new* developments or changes of emphasis are required. These include the use of special surveys every five years, together with victimization data to study historical changes in rates of crime; the experimental comparison of different forms of intervention and prevention; investigations into policing and into the processing of delinquents; the study of individual differences with particular reference to personality variables, to attentional deficits, to the autonomic, avoidance-learning, and stimulus-seeking variables associated with the concept of psychopathy, to educational retardation and to sex; the delineation of environmental influences with a special attention to observational studies of family interaction at home, the identification of protective factors, the investigation of school influences, the study of peer group effects, detailed comparative studies of the area characteristics associated with high and low delinquency rates, cross-national studies, the historical analysis of the effects of social change, the investigation of situational effects and of person–situation interactions, and the effects of adoption; together with a better delineation of the continuities and discontinuities between childhood and adult life.

References

ACHENBACH, T. M., and EDELBROCK, C. S. (1978): 'The classification of child psychopathology: a review and analysis of empirical efforts'. *Psychol. Bull.*, **85**, 1275–1301.

ADAMS, S. (1970): 'The PICO Project'. In Johnston, N., Savitz, L., and Wolfgang, M. E. (eds.), *The Sociology of Punishment and Correction*. New York: Wiley.

ADAMS, S. (1977): 'Evaluating correctional treatments: toward a new perspective'. *Criminal Justice & Behav.*, **4**, 323–38.

ADELSTEIN, A., and MARDON, C. (1975): 'Suicides 1961–74'. *Population Trends*, **2**, 13–18.

ADLER, F. (1977): 'The interaction between women's emancipation and female criminality: A cross-cultural perspective'. *Internat. J. Criminol. Penol.*, **5**, 101–12.

AGETON, S., and ELLIOTT, D. (1974): 'The effects of legal processing on delinquent orientations'. *Social Problems*, **22**, 87–100.

ALEXANDER, F., and STAUB, H. (1956): *The Criminal, the Judge and the Public: A psychological analysis*. Glencoe, Ill.: Free Press.

ALEXANDER, J. F., BARTON, C., SCHIAVO, R. S., and PARSONS, B. V. (1976): 'Systems-behavioral intervention with families of delinquents: therapist characteristics, family behavior and outcome'. *J. Consult. Clin. Psychol.*, **44**, 656–64.

ALEXANDER, J. F., and PARSONS, B. V. (1973): 'Short-term behavioral intervention with delinquent families: impact on family process and recidivism'. *J. Abnorm. Psychol.*, **81**, 219–25.

ALLSOP, J., and FELDMAN, M. (1976): 'Personality and anti-social behaviour'. *Brit. J. Criminol.*, **16**, 337–51.

AMERICAN PSYCHIATRIC ASSOCIATION (1980): *Diagnostic and Statistical Manual of Mental Disorders (Third Edition) – DSM-III*. Washington, D.C.: American Psychiatric Association.

ANNESLEY, P. T. (1961): 'Psychiatric illness in adolescence: presentation and prognosis'. *J. Ment. Sci.*, **107**, 268–78.

ANTONOVSKY, A. (1979): *Health, Stress and Coping*. San Francisco: Jossey-Bass.

APPEL, M. H. (1942): 'Aggressive behaviour of nursery school children and adult procedures in dealing with such behaviour'. *J. Experiment. Educ.*, **11**, 185–99.

ARCHER, D., and GARTNER, R. (1976): 'Violent acts and violent times: A comparative approach to postwar homicide rates'. *Amer. Sociol. Rev.*, **41**, 937–63.

ARMSTRONG, D., and WILSON, M. (1973): 'City politics and deviancy amplification'. In Taylor, I., and Taylor, L. (eds.), *Politics and Deviance*. Harmondsworth: Penguin.

ARNOLD, J. E., LEVINE, A. G., and PATTERSON, G. R. (1975): 'Changes in sibling behavior following family intervention'. *J. Consult. Clin. Psychol.*, **43**, 683–8.

AROMAA, K. (1974): 'Our Violence: Registered crimes of violence in Finland 1960–1971'. *Scand. Studies in Criminol.*, **5**, 35–46.

AUSTIN, R. L. (1975): 'Construct validity of I-level classification'. *Criminal Justice and Behavior*, **2**, 113–29.

AUSTIN, R. L. (1981): 'Liberation and female criminality in England and Wales'. *Brit. J. Criminol.*, **21**, 371–4.

AYLLON, T., and AZRIN, N. (1968): *The Token Economy*. New York: Appleton-Century.

AYLLON, T., and ROBERTS, M. D. (1974): 'Eliminating discipline problems by strengthening academic performance'. *J. Appl. Behav. Anal.*, **7**, 71–6.

BACHMAN, J. G., O'MALLEY, P. M., and JOHNSTON, J. (1978): *Adolescence to Adulthood – Change and Stability in the Lives of Young Men. Youth in Transition, Vol. VI.* Ann Arbor, Mich.: Institute for Social Research, University of Michigan.

BAGLEY, C. (1965): 'Juvenile delinquency in Exeter'. *Urban Studies*, **2**, 35–9.

BAGLEY, C. (1972): 'Deviant behaviour in English and West Indian schoolchildren'. *Research in Educ.*, **8**, 47–55.

BAHR, S. J. (1979): 'Family determinants and effects of deviance'. In Burr, W. R., Hill, R., Nye, F. I., and Reiss, I. L. (eds.), *Contemporary Theories about the Family: Research-Based Theories, Vol. 1.* New York: Free Press; London: Collier-Macmillan.

BALDWIN, J. (1975): 'British areal studies of crime: an assessment'. *Brit. J. Criminol.*, **15**, 211–27.

BALDWIN, J. (1979): 'Ecological and areal studies in Great Britain and the United States'. In Morris, N., and Tonry, M. (eds.), *Crime and Justice: An annual review of research, Vol. I*, 29–66. Chicago and London: University of Chicago Press.

BALDWIN, J., and BOTTOMS, A. E. (1976): *The Urban Criminal: A study in Sheffield*. London: Tavistock Publications.

BANDURA, A. (1969): 'Social-learning theory of identificatory processes'. In Goslin, D. A. (ed.), *Handbook of Socialization Theory and Research*. New York: Rand McNally.

BANTON, M. (1955): *The Coloured Quarter*. London: Cape.

BANTON, M. (1973): *Police–Community Relations*. London: Collins.

BARKWELL, L. J. (1976): 'Differential treatment of juveniles on probation: an evaluative study'. *Canad. J. Criminology and Corrections*, **18**, 363–78.

BARKWELL, L. J. (1980): 'Differential probation treatment of delinquency'. In Ross, R. R., and Gendreau, P. (eds.), *Effective Correctional Treatment*, 281–97. Toronto: Butterworths.

BARNES, J. (1975): *Educational Priority, Vol. 3*. London: H.M.S.O.

BARON, R., FEENEY, F., and THORNTON, W. (1973): 'Preventing delinquency through diversion: the Sacramento 601 diversion project'. *Federal Probation*, **37**, 13–18.

BARON, R. M., and NEEDEL, S. P. (1980): 'Toward an understanding of the differences in the responses of humans and other animals to density'. *Psychol. Rev.*, **87**, 320–26.
BARRACLOUGH, B., SHEPHARD, D., and JENNINGS, C. (1977): 'Do newspaper reports of coroners' inquests incite people to commit suicide?' *Brit. J. Psychiat.*, **131**, 528–32.
BASHAM, R. (1978): *Urban Anthropology: the cross-cultural study of complex societies.* Palo Alto, Calif.: Mayfield.
BATTA, I. D., MCCULLOCH, J. W., and SMITH, N. J. (1975): 'A study of juvenile delinquency among Asians and half-Asians'. *Brit. J. Criminol.*, **15**, 32–42.
BAUM, A., and DAVIS, G. E. (1980): 'Reducing the stress of high-density living: an architectural intervention'. *J. Pers. Soc. Psychol.*, **38**, 471–81.
BAUMRIND, D. (1981): 'Gender-differences and sex-related socialization effects'. (Submitted for publication.)
BEASLEY, R. W., and ANTUNES, G. (1974): 'The etiology of urban crime: an ecological analysis'. *Criminology*, **11**, 439–60.
BECKER, H. S. (1963): *Outsiders: Studies in the Sociology of Deviance.* New York: Free Press.
BEHAR, L., and STRINGFIELD, S. (1974): 'A behavior rating scale for the preschool child'. *Develop. Psychol.*, **10**, 601–10.
BELL, R. R. (1971): *Marriage and Family Intervention (3rd edition).* Homewood, Ill.: Dorsey Press.
BELL, R. W., and HARPER, L. V. (1977): *Child Effects on Adults.* Hillsdale, N.J.: Erlbaum.
BELSON, W. A. (1968): 'The extent of stealing by London boys'. *Advancement of Science*, **25**, 171–84.
BELSON, W. A. (1975): *Juvenile Theft: The Causal Factors.* London: Harper & Row.
BELSON, W. A. (1978): *Television Violence and the Adolescent Boy.* Farnborough: Saxon House.
BEM, D. J., and FUNDER, D. C. (1978): 'Predicting more of the people more of the time: assessing the personality of situations'. *Psychol. Rev.*, **85**, 485–501.
BENNETT, T. (1979): 'The social distribution of criminal labels: police "proaction" or "reaction"?' *Brit. J. Criminol.*, **19**, 134–45.
BENTOVIM, A. (1973): 'Disturbed and under five'. *Special Educ.*, **62**, 31–5.
BERG, I. (1980a): 'Absence from school and the law'. In Hersov, L., and Berg, I. (eds.), *Out of School: Modern Perspective in Truancy and School Refusal*, 137–47. Chichester: Wiley.
BERG, I. (1980b): 'School refusal in early adolescence'. In Hersov, L., and Berg, I. (eds.), *Out of School: Modern Perspectives in Truancy and School Refusal*, 231–49. Chichester: Wiley.
BERG, I., CONSTERDINE, M., HULLIN, R., MCGUIRE, R., and TYRER, S. (1978a): 'The effect of two randomly allocated court procedures on truancy'. *Brit. J. Criminol.*, **18**, 323–44.
BERG, I., HULLIN, R., and MCGUIRE, R. (1978b): 'A randomly controlled trial of two

court procedures in truancy'. In Hawkins, K., and Lloyd-Bostock, S. (eds.), *Psychology, Law and Legal Processes*, 143–51. London: Macmillan.

BERG, I., HULLIN, R., MCGUIRE, R., and TYRER, S. (1977): 'Truancy and the courts: research note'. *J. Child Psychol., Psychiat.*, **18**, 359–65.

BERGER, A. S., and SIMON, W. (1974): 'Black families and the Moynihan report: a research evaluation'. *Social Problems*, **22**, 145–61.

BERGER, M., YULE, W., and RUTTER, M. (1975): 'Attainment and adjustment in two geographical areas. II. The prevalence of specific reading retardation'. *Brit. J. Psychiat.*, **126**, 510–19.

BERKOWITZ, L. (1973): 'Control of aggression'. In Caldwell, B. M., and Ricciuti, H. N. (eds.), *Review of Child Development Research, Vol. 3*, 95–140. Chicago and London: University of Chicago Press.

BERKOWITZ, L., PARKE, R. D., LEYENS, J. P., WEST, S., and SEBASTIAN, J. (1978): 'Experiments on the reactions of juvenile delinquents to filmed violence'. In Hersov, L. A., Berger, M., and Shaffer, D. (eds.), *Aggression and Antisocial Behaviour in Childhood and Adolescence*, 59–71. Oxford: Pergamon.

BERLEMAN, W. C., SEABERG, J. R., and STEINBURN, T. W. (1972): 'The delinquency prevention experiment of the Seattle Atlantic Street Center: a final evaluation'. *Social Service Rev.*, **46**, 323–46.

BERLINS, M., and WANSALL, G. (1974): *Caught in the Act*. Harmondsworth: Penguin.

BEWLEY, T. H. (1975): 'An introduction to drug dependence'. In Silverstone, T., and Barraclough, B. (eds.): *Contemporary Psychiatry*. London: Royal College of Psychiatrists.

BEYLEVELD, D. (1980): *A Bibliography on General Deterrence*. Farnborough: Saxon House.

BIDERMAN, A. D., and REISS, A. J. (1967): 'On Exploring the "Dark Figure" of Crime'. *The Annals*, **374**, 1–15.

BILLER, H. B. (1974): *Paternal Deprivation: Family, School, Sexuality and Society*. London: D. C. Heath.

BITTNER, E. (1970): *The Functions of the Police in Modern Society*. Publication No. 2059. Washington D.C.: U.S. Government Printing Office. (Cited by Empey, 1974.)

BLACK, D. J. (1970): 'Production of crime rates'. *Amer. Sociol. Rev.*, **35**, 733–48.

BLACK, D. J., and REISS, A. J. (1970): 'Police control of juveniles'. *Amer. Sociol. Rev.*, **35**, 63–77.

BLACK REPORT (THE): See CHILDREN AND YOUNG PERSONS REVIEW GROUP.

BLAKELY, C. H., DAVIDSON, W. S., SAYLOR, C. A., and ROBINSON, M. J. (1980): 'Kentfields rehabilitation program: ten years later'. In Ross, R. R., and Gendreau, P. (eds.), *Effective Correctional Treatment*, 321–6. Toronto: Butterworths.

BLASI, A. (1980): 'Bridging moral cognition and moral action: a critical review of the literature'. *Psychol. Bull.*, **88**, 1–45.

BLOCK, J. H., BLOCK, J., and MORRISON, A. (1981): 'Parental agreement–disagreement on childrearing orientations and gender-related personality correlates in children'. *Child Develop.*, **52**, 965–74.

BLOOM, L. (1969): *Study of Butetown, Cardiff*. Unpublished survey material reported in Rose, E. J. B., *et al*. (1969), *Colour and Citizenship*. Oxford: Oxford University Press/Institute of Race Relations.

BOGAARD, C. (1976): *Relationship between aggressive behavior in children and parent perception of child behavior*. Unpublished dissertation. University of Oregon.

BOHMAN, M. (1970): *Adopted Children and Their Families*. Stockholm: Proprius.

BOHMAN, M. (1978): 'Some genetic aspects of alcoholism and criminality'. *Arch. Gen. Psychiat*., **35**, 269–76.

BOHMAN, M., CLONINGER, C. R., SIGVARDSSON, S., and VAN KNORRING, A.-L. (1983): 'Gene-environment interaction in the psychopathology of adoptees: some recent studies of the origin of alcoholism and criminality'. In Magnusson, D., and Allen, V. (eds.), *Human Development: An interactional perspective*. New York and London: Academic Press (in press).

BOHMAN, M., and SIGVARDSSON, S. (1978): 'An 18-year prospective, longitudinal study of adopted boys'. In Anthony, E. J., and Koupernik, C. (eds.), *The Child in His Family: Vulnerable Children*. London: Wiley.

BOHMAN, M., and SIGVARDSSON, S. (1980): 'A prospective, longitudinal study of children registered for adoption: a 15 year follow-up'. *Acta Psychiat. Scand*., **61**, 339–55.

BOLAND, B., and WILSON, J. Q. (1978): 'Age, crime and punishment'. *Public Interest*, **51**, 22–34.

BORKOVEC, T. D. (1970): 'Autonomic reactivity to sensory stimulation in psychopathic, neurotic and normal juvenile delinquents'. *J. Consult. Clin. Psychol*., **35**, 217–22.

BOSHIER, R., and JOHNSON, D. (1974): 'Does conviction affect employment opportunities?' *Brit. J. Criminol*., **14**, 264–8.

BOTTOMLEY, A. K. (1973): *Discussions in the Penal Process*. London: Martin Robertson.

BOTTOMLEY, A. K., and COLEMAN, C. A. (1976): 'Criminal statistics: the police role in the discovery and detection of crime'. *Int. J. Criminol. Penol*., **4**, 33–58.

BOTTOMLEY, A. K., and COLEMAN, C. A. (1980): 'Police effectiveness and the public: the limitations of official crime rates'. In Clarke, R. V. G., and Hough, J. M. (eds.), *The Effectiveness of Policing*. Farnborough: Gower.

BOTTOMS, A. (1967): 'Delinquency amongst immigrants'. *Race*, **8**, 357–83.

BOTTOMS, A. E. (1973): 'Crime and delinquency in immigrant and minority groups'. In Watson, P. (ed.), *Psychology and Race*. Harmondsworth: Penguin.

BOTTOMS, A. E. (1974): 'Review of "Defensible Space"'. *Brit. J. Criminol*., **14**, 203–6.

BOTTOMS, A. E., and MCCLINTOCK, F. H. (1973): *Criminals Coming of Age*. London: Heinemann Educational.

BOTTOMS, A. E., and MCWILLIAMS, W. (1979): 'A non-treatment paradigm for probation practice'. *Brit. J. Social Work*, **9**, 159–202.

BOTTOMS, A. E., and SHEFFIELD, C. (1980): *Report on Feasibility of Research into Intermediate Treatment*. Report to the Department of Health and Social Security, London.

BOTTOMS, A. E., and WILES, P. (1975): 'Race, crime and violence'. In Ebling, F. J. (ed.), *Racial Variation in Man*. London: Institute of Biology.
BOWLBY, J. (1946): *Forty-four Juvenile Thieves: their characters and home-life*. London: Baillière Tindall & Cox.
BOWLBY, J. (1969): *Attachment and Loss: I. Attachment*. London: Hogarth Press.
BOWMAN, P. H. (1959): 'Effects of a revised school programme on potential delinquencies'. *Ann. Amer. Acad. Polit. Soc. Sci.*, **322**, 53–61.
BOX, S. (1971): *Deviance, Reality and Society*. London: Holt, Rinehart & Winston.
BRAITHWAITE, J. (1979): *Inequality, Crime and Social Policy*. London and Boston: Routledge & Kegan Paul.
BRAITHWAITE, J. (1981): 'The myth of social class and criminality reconsidered'. *Amer. Sociol. Rev.*, **46**, 36–57.
BRAKE, M. (1980): *The Sociology of Youth Cultures and Youth Subcultures*. London: Routledge & Kegan Paul.
BRANTINGHAM, P. J., and BRANTINGHAM, P. L. (1975a): 'The spatial patterning of burglary'. *Howard J. Penol. Crime Prevention*, **14**, 11–23.
BRANTINGHAM, P. J., and BRANTINGHAM, P. L. (1975b): 'Residential burglary and urban form'. *Urban Studies*, **12**, 273–84.
BRICKER, W. A., and BRICKER, D. D. (1974): 'An early language training strategy'. In Schiefelbusch, R. L., and Lloyds, L. L. (eds.), *Language Perspectives – Acquisition, Retardation, and Intervention*, 615–46. London: Macmillan.
BRODY, S. R. (1976): *The Effectiveness of Sentencing – a review of the literature*. Home Office Research Study No. 35. London: H.M.S.O.
BRODY, S. (1977): *Screen Violence and Film Censorship – a review of research*. Home Office Research Study No. 40. London: H.M.S.O.
BRODY, S., and TARLING, R. (1980): *Taking Offenders out of Circulation*. Home Office Research Study No. 64. London: H.M.S.O.
BRONFENBRENNER, U. (1974): *Is Early Intervention Effective? A report on the longitudinal evaluations of pre-school programmes*. Bethesda, Maryland: Office of Child Development, U.S. Department of Health, Education and Welfare.
BRONFENBRENNER, U. (1976): 'Who cares for America's children'. In Vaughan, V. C., and Brazelton, T. B. (eds.), *The Family – Can it be Saved?* 3–32. Chicago: Year Book Medical Publ. Inc.
BRONFENBRENNER, U. (1979): *The Ecology of Human Development: experiments by nature and design*. Cambridge, Mass.: Harvard University Press.
BRONSON, W. C. (1967): 'Adult derivatives of emotional expressiveness and reactivity-control: developmental continuities from childhood to adulthood'. *Child Develop.*, **38**, 801–17.
BROWN, G. W., and HARRIS, T. (1978a): *Social Origins of Depression*. London: Tavistock.
BROWN, G. W., and HARRIS, T. (1978b): 'Social origins of depression: a reply'. *Psychol. Med.*, **8**, 577–88.
BRYAN, J. H., and LONDON, P. (1970): 'Altruistic behavior by children'. *Psychol. Bull.*, **73**, 200–211.

BRYCE-SMITH, D., and WALDRON, H. A. (1974): 'Lead behavior and criminality'. *Ecologist*, **4**, 367–77.
BUIKHUISEN, W. (1974): 'General deterrence: research and theory'. *Abstracts on Criminology and Penology*, **14**, 285–98.
BUIKHUISEN, W., and DIJKTERHUIS, F. P. H. (1971): 'Delinquency and stigmatization'. *Brit. J. Criminol.*, **11**, 185–7.
BUIKHUISEN, W., and HOEKSTRA, H. A. (1974): 'Factors related to recidivism'. *Brit. J. Criminol.*, **14**, 63–9.
BURCHARD, J. D. (1967): 'Systematic socialization: a programmed environment for the habilitation of antisocial retardates'. *Psychol. Record*, **17**, 461–76.
BURCHARD, J. D., and HARIG, P. T. (1976): 'Behavior modification and juvenile delinquency'. In Leiternberg, H. (ed.), *Handbook of Behavior Modification and Behavior Therapy*, 405–52. Englewood Cliffs, N.J.: Prentice-Hall.
BURROWS, J. (1980): 'Closed circuit television and crime on the London Underground'. In Clarke, R. V. G., and Mayhew, P. (eds.), *Designing Out Crime*, 75–83. London: H.M.S.O.
BURROWS, J., EKBLOM, P., and HEAL, K. (1979): *Crime Prevention and the Police*. Home Office Research Study No. 55. London: H.M.S.O.
BURROWS, J., and HEAL, K. (1980): 'Police car security campaign'. In Clarke, R. V. G., and Hough, J. M. (eds.), *The Effectiveness of Policing*, 99–111. Farnborough: Gower.
BYLES, J. A., and MAURICE, A. (1979): 'The Juvenile Services Project: an experiment in delinquency control'. *Canad. J. Criminol.*, **21**, 155–65.
CADORET, R. J., and CAIN, C. (1980): 'Sex differences in predictors of antisocial behavior in adoptees'. *Arch. Gen. Psychiat.*, **37**, 1171–5.
CADORET, R. J., CUNNINGHAM, L., LOFTUS, R., and EDWARDS, J. (1975): 'Studies of adoptees from psychiatrically disturbed biological parents. II. Temperament, hyperactive, antisocial and developmental variables'. *J. Pediat.*, **87**, 301–6.
CAIN, M. (1973): *Society and the Policeman's Role*. London: Routledge & Kegan Paul.
CAIRNS, R. B. (ed.) (1979): *The Analysis of Social Interactions: Methods, Issues and Illustrations*. Hillsdale, N.J.: Erlbaum.
CAMERON, M. O. (1964): *The Booster and the Snitch*. New York: Free Press.
CAMPBELL, A. (1981): *Girl Delinquents*. Oxford: Basil Blackwell.
CAMPBELL, A., and CONVERSE, P. (eds.) (1972): *The Human Meaning of Social Change*. New York: Russell Sage Foundation.
CANADA: DEPARTMENT OF JUSTICE (1975): *Crime Statistics, 1974*. Ottawa: Department of Justice.
CANTWELL, D. (1974): 'Genetic Studies of hyperactive children: Psychiatric illness in biologic and adopting parents'. In Fieve, R., Rosenthal, D., and Brill, H. (eds.), *Genetic Research in Psychiatry*. Baltimore: Johns Hopkins University Press.
CANTWELL, D. (1980): 'Hyperactivity and antisocial behavior revisited: A critical review of the literature'. In Lewis, D. (ed.), *Biopsychosocial Vulnerabilities to Delinquency*. New York: Spectrum.

CAPLAN, P. J., AWAD, G. A., WILKS, C., and WHITE, G. (1980): 'Sex differences in a delinquent clinic population'. *Brit. J. Criminol.*, **20**, 311–28.

CARROLL, J. S. (1978): 'A psychological approach to deterrence; the evaluation of crime opportunities'. *J. Personality Soc. Psychol.*, **36**, 1512–20.

CARTWRIGHT, A. (1976): *How Many Children?* London: Routledge & Kegan Paul.

CASTLE, I. M., and GITTUS, E. (1957): 'The distribution of social defects in Liverpool'. *Social. Rev.*, **5**, 43–64.

CAWSON, P. (1978): *Community Homes: A Study of Residential Staff.* Department of Health and Social Security Research Report No. 2. London: H.M.S.O.

CAWSON, P., and MARTELL, M. (1979): *Children Referred to Closed Units.* Department of Health and Social Security Research Report No. 5. London: H.M.S.O.

CENTRAL POLICY REVIEW STAFF (1978): *Vandalism.* London: H.M.S.O.

CENTRAL STATISTICAL OFFICE (1972): *Social Trends, No. 3.* London: H.M.S.O.

CENTRAL STATISTICAL OFFICE (1977): *Social Trends, No. 8.* London: H.M.S.O.

CENTRAL STATISTICAL OFFICE (1978): *Social Trends, No. 9.* London: H.M.S.O.

CENTRAL STATISTICAL OFFICE (1980): *Social Trends, No. 11.* London: H.M.S.O.

CERNKOVICH, S. A., and GIORDANO, P. C. (1979): 'A comparative analysis of male and female delinquency'. *Sociolog. Quart.*, **20**, 131–45.

CHALLINGER, D. (1977): *Young Offenders.* Victoria, Aus.: Victorian Association for the Care and Resettlement of Offenders.

CHAMBLISS, W., and NAGASAWA, R. (1969): 'On the validity of official statistics: a comparative study of white, black and Japanese high school boys'. *J. Res. Crime and Delinq.*, **6**, 71–7.

CHESNEY-LIND, M. (1979a): 'Young Women in the Arms of the Law'. In Bowker, L. (ed.), *Women, Crime and the Criminal Justice System.* Lexington: Lexington Books.

CHESNEY-LIND, M. (1979b): 'Chivalry re-examined: Women and the Criminal Justice System'. In Bowker, L. (ed.), *Women, Crime and the Criminal Justice System.* Lexington: Lexington Books.

CHESTER, R. (1972): 'Current incidence and trends in marital breakdown'. *Postgrad. Med. J.*, **48**, 529–41.

CHILDREN AND YOUNG PERSONS REVIEW GROUP (1979): Report (The Black Report). Belfast: H.M.S.O.

CHOLDIN, H. M. (1978): 'Urban density and pathology'. *Ann. Rev. Sociol.*, **4**, 91–113.

CHRISTENSEN, K. R., and NIELSEN, J. M. (1974): 'Incidence of chromosome aberrations in a child psychiatric hospital'. *Clin. Genet.*, **5**, 205–10.

CHRISTIANSEN, K. O. (1960): 'Industrialization and urbanization in relation to crime and juvenile delinquency'. *Int. Rev. Criminal Policy*, **16**, 3–8.

CHRISTIANSEN, K. O. (1977a): 'A review of studies of criminality among twins'. In Mednick, S., and Christiansen, K. O. (eds.), *Biosocial Bases of Criminal Behavior*, 45–88. New York: Gardner Press.

CHRISTIANSEN, K. O. (1977b): 'A preliminary study of criminality among twins'. In Mednick, S., and Christiansen, K. O. (eds.), *Biosocial Bases of Criminal Behavior*, 89–108. New York: Gardner Press.

CHRISTIANSEN, K. O., and JENSEN, S. G. (1972): 'Crime in Denmark – a statistical history'. *J. Crim. Law, Criminol. & Police Science*, **63**, 82–92.
CHRISTIE, N., ANDENAES, J., and SKIRBEKK, S. (1965): 'A study of self-reported crime'. *Scand. Studies in Criminol.*, **1**, 86–116.
CICOUREL, A. V. (1968): *The Social Organisation of Juvenile Justice*. London: Wiley. (Re-issued with a new introduction, 1976. London: Heinemann Books.)
CICOUREL, A. (1976): *The Social Organization of Juvenile Justice*. London: Heinemann.
CLAEYS, W., and DE BOEK, P. (1976): 'The influence of some parental characteristics on children's primary abilities and field independence: a study of adopted children'. *Child Develop.*, **47**, 842–5.
CLARK, J. P., and TIFFT, L. L. (1966): 'Polygraph and interview validation of self-reported deviant behavior'. *Amer. Sociol. Rev.*, **31**, 516–23.
CLARK, J. P., and WENNINGER, E. P. (1962): 'Socio-economic class and area as correlates of illegal behavior among juveniles'. *Amer. Sociol. Rev.*, **27**, 826–34.
CLARK, M. M. (1970): *Reading Difficulties in School*. Harmondsworth: Penguin.
CLARKE, A., and CLARKE, A. (eds.) (1976): *Early Experience: Myth and Evidence*. London: Open Books.
CLARKE, J. (1976): 'The skinheads and the magical recovery of community'. In Hall, S., and Jefferson, T. (eds.), *Resistance Through Rituals*. London: Hutchinson.
CLARKE, J., and JEFFERSON, T. (1976): 'Working class youth cultures'. In Mungham, G., and Pearson, G. (eds.), *Working Class Youth Culture*. London: Routledge & Kegan Paul.
CLARKE, R. V. G. (1966): 'Approved school boy absconders and corporal punishment'. *Brit. J. Criminol.*, **6**, 364–75.
CLARKE, R. V. G. (1977): 'Psychology and crime'. *Bull. Brit. Psychol. Soc.*, **30**, 280–83.
CLARKE, R. V. G. (ed.) (1978): *Tackling Vandalism*. Home Office Research Study No. 47. London: H.M.S.O.
CLARKE, R. V. G. (1980): '"Situational" crime prevention: theory and practice'. *Brit. J. Criminol.*, **20**, 136–47.
CLARKE, R. V. G. (1982): 'Crime prevention through environmental management and design'. In Gunn, J., and Farrington, D. P. (eds.), *Abnormal Offenders: Delinquency and the Criminal Justice System*, 213–30. Chichester: Wiley.
CLARKE, R. V. G., and CORNISH, D. B. (1978): 'The effectiveness of residential treatment'. In Hersov, L. A., Berger, M., and Shaffer, D. (eds.), *Aggression and Antisocial Behaviour in Childhood and Adolescence*, 143–59. Oxford: Pergamon.
CLARKE, R. V. G., and HOUGH, J. M. (eds.) (1980): *The Effectiveness of Policing*. Farnborough: Gower.
CLARKE, R. V. G., and MARTIN, D. N. (1971): *Absconding from Approved Schools*. Home Office Research Study No. 12. London: H.M.S.O.
CLARKE, R. V. G., and MARTIN, D. N. (1975): 'A study of absconding and its implications for the residential treatment of delinquents'. In Tizard, J., Sinclair, I. A. C., and Clarke, R. V. G. (eds.), *Varieties of Residential Experience*, 249–74. London: Routledge & Kegan Paul.

CLARKE, R. V. G., and MAYHEW, P. (eds.) (1980): *Designing Out Crime*. London: H.M.S.O.

CLARKE, S. H. (1974): 'Getting 'em out of circulation: does incarceration of juvenile offenders reduce crime?' *J. Crim. Law & Criminol.*, **65**, 528–35.

CLEGG, A., and MEGSON, B. (1968): *Children in Distress*. Harmondsworth: Penguin Education Special.

CLIFFORD, W. (1976): *Crime Control in Japan*. Toronto and London: Lexington Books.

CLINARD, M. B. (1968): *Sociology of Deviant Behavior (3rd edition)*. New York: Holt, Rinehart & Winston.

CLINARD, M. B., and ABBOTT, D. J. (1973): *Crime in Developing Countries: A comparative perspective*. New York: Wiley.

CLINE, H. F. (1980): 'Criminal behavior over the life span'. In Brim, O. G., and Kagan, J. (eds.), *Constancy and Change in Human Development*. Cambridge, Mass.: Harvard University Press.

CLONINGER, C. R., CHRISTIANSEN, K. O., REICH, T., and GOTTESTMAN, I. I. (1978): 'Implications of sex differences in the prevalences of antisocial personality, alcoholism, and criminality for familial transmission'. *Arch. Gen. Psychiat.*, **35**, 941–51.

CLOWARD, R. A., and OHLIN, L. E. (1960): *Delinquency and Opportunity*. Chicago: Free Press.

COCKBURN, J. J., and MACLAY, I. (1965): 'Sex differences in juvenile delinquency'. *Brit. J. Criminol.*, **5**, 289–308.

COELHO, G. V., HAMBURG, D. A., and ADAMS, J. E. (eds.) (1974): *Coping and Adaptation*. New York: Basic Books.

COHEN, A. K. (1956): *Delinquent Boys: The Culture of the Gang*. London: Routledge & Kegan Paul.

COHEN, F., and LAZARUS, R. S. (1979): 'Coping with the stress of illness'. In Stone, G. C., Cohen, F., Adler, N. E., and Associates (eds.), *Health Psychology: A Handbook*. San Francisco: Jossey-Bass.

COHEN, L. E., and FELSON, M. (1979a): 'Estimating the social costs of national economic policy: a critical examination of the Brenner study'. *Soc. Indicators Res.*, **6**, 251–9.

COHEN, L. E., and FELSON, M. (1979b): 'Social change and crime rate trends: a routine activity approach'. *Amer. Sociol. Rev.*, **44**, 588–608.

COHEN, P. (1972): *Subcultural Conflict and Working Class Community*. Working Papers in Cultural Studies No. 2. Birmingham: Centre for Contemporary Cultural Studies.

COLEMAN, C. A., and BOTTOMLEY, A. K. (1976): 'Police conceptions of "Crime" and "No Crime"'. *Crim. Law Rev.* (June), 344–60.

COLLINS, S. (1957): *Coloured Minorities in Britain*. London: Lutterworth Press.

COMMISSION FOR RACIAL EQUALITY (1978): *Looking for Work – black and white school leavers in Lewisham*. London: Commission for Racial Equality.

COMMITTEE ON CHILDREN AND YOUNG PERSONS (SCOTLAND) (1964): *Report*. Cmnd 2306. Edinburgh: H.M.S.O.

COMMUNITY RELATIONS COMMISSION (1974): *Unemployment and Homelessness: a report*. London: H.M.S.O.
CONGER, J. J., and MILLER, W. C. (1966): *Personality, Social Class and Delinquency*. New York: Wiley.
CONKLIN, J. E. (1971): 'Criminal environment and support for the law'. *Law and Society Review*, **6**, 247–59.
CONNELL, P. H. (1977): 'Clinical aspects of drug misuse'. In Rutter, M., and Hersov, L. (eds.), *Child Psychiatry: Modern Approaches*. Oxford: Blackwell Scientific.
CONWAY, E. S. (1957): *The Institutional Care of Children: a case history*. Unpublished Ph.D. thesis, University of London.
COOK, P. J. (1980): 'Research in criminal deterrence: laying the ground work for the second decade'. In Morris, N., and Tonry, M. (eds.), *Crime and Justice: An Annual Review of Research*, 211–68. Chicago: University of Chicago Press.
COPPERMAN, P. (1978): *The Literacy Hoax*. New York: Wm. Morrow.
CORNISH, D. B., and CLARKE, R. V. G. (1975): *Residential Treatment and Its Effects on Delinquency*. Home Office Research Study No. 32. London: H.M.S.O.
CORRIGAN, P. (1979): *Schooling the Smash Street Kids*. London: Macmillan.
COURT, S. D. M. (1976): See DEPARTMENT OF HEALTH AND SOCIAL SECURITY (1976).
COVINGTON, C. (1979): *Evaluation of the Hammersmith Teenage Project – Summary of Research*. London: N.A.C.R.O.
COWIE, J., COWIE, V., and SLATER, E. (1968): *Delinquency in Girls*. London: Heinemann.
COX, A., RUTTER, M., YULE, B., and QUINTON, D. (1977): 'Bias resulting from missing information: Some epidemiological findings'. *Brit. J. Prev. Soc. Med.*, **31**, 131–6.
CRAFT, M. J. (ed.) (1966): *Psychopathic Disorders and Their Assessment*. Oxford: Pergamon.
CRAFT, M., STEPHENSON, G., and GRANGER, C. (1964): 'A controlled trial of authoritarian and self-governing regimes with adolescent psychopaths'. *Amer. J. Orthopsychiat.*, **34**, 543–54.
CRAIG, M. M., and FURST, P. W. (1965): 'What happens after treatment?' *Soc. Service Rev.*, **39**, 165–71.
CRAIG, M. M., and GLICK, S. J. (1963): 'Ten years experience with the Glueck Social Prediction Table'. *Crime and Delinquency*, **9**, 249–61.
CRAIG, M. M., and GLICK, S. J. (1965): *A Manual of Procedures for Application of the Glueck Prediction Table*. London: University of London Press.
CRELLIN, E., PRINGLE, M. L. K., and WEST, P. (1971): *Born Illegitimate: social and educational implications*. Slough: N.F.E.R.
CRESSEY, D. R. (1964): *Delinquency, Crime and Differential Assocations*. The Hague: Martinus Nijhoff.
CROFT, J. (1978): *Research in Criminal Justice*. Home Office Research Study No. 44. London: H.M.S.O.
CROFT, J. (1980): *Research and Criminal Policy*. Home Office Research Study No. 59. London: H.M.S.O.

CROWE, R. R. (1974): 'An adoption study of antisocial personality'. *Arch. Gen. Psychiat.*, **31**, 785–91.

CROWE, R. R. (1978): 'Genetic studies of antisocial personality and related disorders'. In Spitzer, R. L., and Klein, D. F. (eds.), *Critical Issues in Psychiatric Diagnosis*. New York: Raven Press.

DAITZMAN, R., and ZUCKERMAN, M. (1980): 'Disinhibitory sensation seeking, personality and gonadal hormones'. *Person. Ind. Diff.*, **1**, 103–10.

DALGAARD, O. C., and KRINGLEN, E. (1976): 'A Norwegian twin study of criminality'. *Brit. J. Criminol.*, **16**, 213–32.

DANIEL, W. W. (1968): *Racial Discrimination in England*. Harmondsworth: Penguin.

DANZIGER, S., and WHEELER, D. (1975): 'The economics of crime: punishment or income distribution'. *Review of Social Economy*, **33**, 113–31.

DARLINGTON, R. B., ROYCE, J. M., SNIPPER, A. S., MURRAY, H. W., and LAZAR, I. (1980): 'Pre-school programs and later school competence of children from low-income families'. *Science*, **208**, 202–4.

DAVIDSON, W. S., and ROBINSON, M. J. (1975): 'Community psychology and behavior modification: A community based program for the prevention of delinquency'. *Corrective & Soc. Psychiat.*, **21**, 1–12.

DAVIDSON, W. S., and SEIDMAN, E. (1974): 'Studies of behavior modification and juvenile delinquency'. *Psychol. Bull.*, **81**, 998–1011.

DAVIES, J. (1976): 'Girls appearing before a Juvenile Court'. In *Further Studies of Female Offenders*. Home Office Research Studies No. 33. London: H.M.S.O.

DAVIES, J. G. V., and MALIPHANT, R. (1971a): 'Refractory behaviour at school in normal adolescent males in relation to psychopathy and early experience'. *J. Child Psychol. Psychiat.*, **12**, 35–42.

DAVIES, J. G. V., and MALIPHANT, R. (1971b): 'Autonom responses of male adolescents exhibiting refractory behaviour in school'. *J. Child Psychol. Psychiat.*, **12**, 115–28.

DAVIES, J. G. V., and MALIPHANT, R. (1974): 'Refractory behaviour in school and avoidance learning'. *J. Child Psychol. Psychiat.*, **15**, 23–32.

DAVIES, M. (1969): *Probationers in their Social Environment. A study of male probationers aged 17–20, together with an analysis of those reconvicted within twelve months*. Home Office Research Study No. 2. London: H.M.S.O.

DAVIES, M., and SINCLAIR, I. A. C. (1971): 'Families, hostels and delinquents: an attempt to assess cause and effect'. *Brit. J. Criminol.*, **11**, 213–29.

DAVIS, K. (ed.) (1973): *Cities: Their Origin, Growth and Human Impact*. Readings from *Scientific American*. San Francisco: W. H. Freeman.

DAWE, H. C. (1934): 'An analysis of two hundred quarrels of preschool children'. *Child Develop.*, **5**, 139–57.

DE ALARCÓN, R. (1972): 'An epidemiological evaluation of a public health measure aimed at reducing the availability of methylamphetamine'. *Psychol. Med.*, **2**, 293–300.

DELFINI, L. F., BERNAL, M. E., and ROSEN, P. M. (1976): 'Comparison of deviant and normal boys in home settings'. In Mash, E. J., Hamerlynck, L. A., and

Handy, L. C. (eds.), *Behavior Modification and Families*. New York: Brunner/Mazel.
DeMYER-GAPIN, S., and SCOTT, T. J. (1977): 'Effect of stimulus novelty on stimulation seeking in antisocial and neurotic children'. *J. Abnorm. Psychol.*, **86**, 96–8.
DENTLER, R. A., and MONROE, L. J. (1961): 'Social correlates of early adolescent theft'. *Amer. Sociol. Rev.*, **26**, 733–43.
DEPARTMENT OF THE ENVIRONMENT (1977): *Housing Management and Design (Lambeth Inner Area Study)*. *IAS/IA/18*. London: Department of the Environment.
DEPARTMENT OF HEALTH AND SOCIAL SECURITY (1972): *Children and Young Persons Act – Memorandum of a survey by the Social Work Service*. Unpublished mimeograph. London: Department of Health and Social Security.
DEPARTMENT OF HEALTH AND SOCIAL SECURITY (1974): *One-Parent Families*. Report of the Committee. Chairman: Hon. Sir Morris Finer, Cmnd. 5629. London: H.M.S.O.
DEPARTMENT OF HEALTH AND SOCIAL SECURITY SOCIAL WORK SERVICE GROUP (1977): *Intermediate Treatment – Planning for Action: Report of Two Study Groups*. London: Department of Health and Social Security.
DEPARTMENT OF HEALTH AND SOCIAL SECURITY (1976): *Fit for the Future*. Report of the Committee on Child Health Services. Chairman: Professor S. D. M. Court. London: H.M.S.O.
DEPARTMENT OF HEALTH AND SOCIAL SECURITY (1980): *Lead and Health*. The Report of a D.H.S.S. Working Party on Lead in the Environment. Chairman: Professor P. J. Lawther. London: H.M.S.O.
DESCHAMPS, J. P., and VALANTIN, G. (1978): 'Pregnancy in adolescence: Incidence and outcome in European countries'. In Parkes, A. S., Short, R. V., Potts, M., and Herbertson, M. A. (eds.), *Fertility in Adolescence. J. Biosoc. Sci.*, Suppl. 5, 101–16. Cambridge: Galton Foundation.
DIAMOND, LORD (1978): See ROYAL COMMISSION ON THE DISTRIBUTION OF INCOME AND WEALTH (1978).
DITCHFIELD, J. A. (1976): *Police Cautioning in England and Wales*. Home Office Research Study No. 37. London: H.M.S.O.
DODD, D. (1978): 'Police and thieves on the streets of Brixton'. *New Society*, 16 March 1978.
DOLESCHAL, E., and KLAPMUTS, N. (1973): 'Towards a new criminology'. *Crime & Delinq. Literature*, **5**, 607–26.
DONNAN, S., and HASKEY, J. (1977): 'Alcoholism and cirrhosis of the liver'. *Population Trends*, **7**, 18–24.
DOOLEY, D., and CATALANO, R. (1980): 'Economic change as a cause of behavioral disorder'. *Psychol. Bull.*, **87**, 450–68.
DOUGLAS, J. W. B. (1975): 'Early hospital admissions and later disturbances of behaviour and learning'. *Devel. Med. Child Neurol.*, **17**, 456–80.
DOUGLAS, J. W. B., and MANN, S. (1979): personal communication.
DOUGLAS, J. W. B., ROSS, J. M., HAMMOND, W. A., and MULLIGAN, D. G. (1966): 'Delinquency and social class'. *Brit. J. Criminol.*, **6**, 294–302.

DOUGLAS, J. W. B., ROSS, J. M., and SIMPSON, H. R. (1968): *All Our Future: A longitudinal study of secondary education.* London: Peter Davies.

DOUGLAS, V. I., and PETERS, K. G. (1979): 'Toward a clearer definition of the attentional deficit of hyperactive children'. In Hale, G. A., and Lewis, M. (eds.), *Attention and Cognitive Development*, 173–247. New York: Plenum.

DOWNES, D. (1966): *The Delinquent Solution: A study of subcultural theory.* London: Routledge & Kegan Paul.

DRILLIEN, C. M. (1964): *Growth and Development of the Prematurely Born Infant.* Edinburgh: Livingstone.

DRYFOOS, J. G. (1978): 'The incidence and outcome of adolescent pregnancy in the United States'. In Parkes, A. S., Short, R. V., Potts, M., and Herbertson, M. A. (eds.), *Fertility in Adolescence. J. Biosoc. Sci.*, Suppl. 5, 85–99. Cambridge: Galton Foundation.

DUDDLE, M. (1973): 'An increase of anorexia nervosa in a University population'. *Brit. J. Psychiat.*, **123**, 711–12.

DUNLOP, A. B. (1975): *The Approved School Experience.* Home Office Research Study No. 25. London: H.M.S.O.

DUNLOP, A. B. (1980): *Junior Attendance Centres.* Home Office Research Study No. 60. London: H.M.S.O.

EARLS, F. (1980): 'Prevalence of behavior problems in 3 year old children: a cross-national replication'. *Arch. Gen. Psychiat.*, **37**, 1153–7.

EAST, W. N., STOCKS, P., and YOUNG, H. Y. P. (1942): *The Adolescent Criminal.* London: Churchill.

ECK, J. E., and RICCIO, L. J. (1979): 'Relationship between reported crime rates and victimization survey results: an empirical and analytical study'. *J. Criminal Justice*, **7**, 293–308.

EDWARDS, A. (1973): 'Sex and area variations in delinquency rates in an English city'. *Brit. J. Criminol.*, **13**, 121–37.

EKBLOM, P. (1979): 'Police truancy patrols'. In Burrows, J., Ekblom, P., and Heal, K. (eds.), *Crime Prevention and the Police*, 18–33. Home Office Research Study No. 55. London: H.M.S.O.

ELLIOTT, D. S., and AGETON, S. S. (1980): 'Reconciling race and class differences in self-reported and official estimates of delinquency'. *Amer. Sociol. Rev.*, **45**, 95–110.

ELLIOTT, D. S., AGETON, S. S., and CANTER, R. J. (1979): 'An integrated theoretical perspective on delinquent behavior'. *J. Res. Crime & Delinquency*, **16**, 3–27.

ELLIOTT, D. S., and VOSS, H. L. (1974): *Delinquency and Dropout.* Toronto and London: Lexington Books.

EME, R. F. (1979): 'Sex differences in childhood psychopathology: a review'. *Psychol. Bull.*, **86**, 574–95.

EMERY, R. E., and O'LEARY, K. D. (1982): 'Children's perceptions of marital discord and behavior problems of boys and girls'. *J. Abnorm. Child Psychol.*, **10**, 11–24.

EMMERICH, W. (1964): 'Continuity and stability in early social development'. *Child Develop.*, **35**, 311–32.

EMMERICH, W. (1968): 'Personality development and concepts of structure'. *Child Develop.*, **39**, 671–90.

EMPEY, L. T. (1974): 'Crime prevention: the fugitive utopia'. In Glaser, D. (ed.), *Handbook of Criminology*, 1095–1123. Chicago: Rand McNally.

EMPEY, L. T. (1978): *American Delinquency*. Homewood, Ill.: Dorsey.

EMPEY, L. T., and ERICKSON, M. L. (1972): *The Provo Experiment: Evaluating Community Control of Delinquency*. Lexington, Mass.: D. C. Heath.

EMPEY, L. T., and LUBECK, S. G. (1971): *The Silverlake Experiment: Testing Delinquency Theory and Community Intervention*. Chicago: Aldine Publ. Co.

ENDLER, N. S. (1977): 'The role of person-by-situation interactions in personality theory'. In Uzgiris, I. C., and Weizmann, F. (eds.), *The Structuring of Experience*, 343–70. New York: Plenum.

ENGSTAD, P., and EVANS, J.L. (1980): 'Responsibility, competence and police effectiveness in crime control'. In Clarke, R. V. G., and Hough, J. M. (eds.), *The Effectiveness of Policing*, 139–62. Farnborough: Gower.

ENNIS, P. (1967): *Criminal Victimization in the United States: A report of a national survey*. Washington, D.C.: U.S. Government Printing Office.

EPPS, P., and PARNELL, R. W. (1952): 'Physique and temperament of women delinquents compared with women undergraduates'. *Brit. J. Med. Psychol.*, **25**, 249–55.

EPSTEIN, S. (1979): 'The stability of behavior: I. On predicting most of the people much of the time'. *J. Pers. Soc. Psychol.*, **37**, 1097–1126.

ERIKSON, K. T. (1962): 'Notes on the sociology of deviance'. *Social Problems*, **9**, 307–14.

ERIKSON, K. T. (1966): *Wayward Puritans: a study in the sociology of deviance*. New York: Wiley.

ERICKSON, M. L. (1972): 'The changing relationship between official and self-reported measures of delinquency: an exploratory-predictive study'. *J. Crim. Law, Criminol. & Police Science*, **63**, 388–95.

ERICKSON, M. L., and EMPEY, L. T. (1963): 'Court records, undetected delinquency and decision-making'. *J. Crim. Law, Criminol. & Police Science*, **54**, 456–69.

ERICKSON, M. L., and GIBBS, J. P. (1973): 'The deterrence question: some alternative methods of analysis'. *Social Science Quarterly*, **54**, 534–51.

ESSEN, J., and WEDGE, P. (1980): *Social disadvantage between 11 and 16 years of age: a national longitudinal study*. Report to the D.H.S.S./S.S.R.C. Working Party on Transmitted Deprivation. London: Social Science Research Council.

EUROPEAN COMMITTEE ON CRIME PROBLEMS (1979): *Social Change and Juvenile Delinquency*. Strasbourg: Council of Europe.

EVERITT, B. S., and SMITH, A. M. R. (1979): 'Interactions in contingency tables: a brief discussion of alternative definitions'. *Psychol. Med.*, **9**, 581–4.

EYSENCK, H. J. (1967): *The Biological Basis of Personality*. Springfield, Ill.: Chas. C. Thomas.

EYSENCK, H. J. (1977): *Crime and Personality*. London: Paladin.

EYSENCK, H. J., and EYSENCK, S. B. G. (1978): 'Psychopathy, personality and genetics'. In Hare, R., and Schalling. D. (eds.), *Psychopathic Behavior: Approaches to Research*, 197–223. New York: Wiley.

EYSENCK, H. J., and NIAS, D. K. B. (1980): *Sex, Violence and the Media*. London: Granada.

EYSENCK, M. W., and EYSENCK, H. J. (1980): 'Mischel and the concept of personality'. *Brit. J. Psychol.*, **71**, 191–204.

EYSENCK, S. B. G., and EYSENCK, H. J. (1973): 'Test re-test reliabilities of a new personality questionnaire for children'. *Brit. J. Educ. Psychol.*, **43**, 126–30.

FARRELL, C., and KELLAHER, L. (1978): *My Mother Said: The Way Young People Learn About Sex and Birth Control*. London: Routledge & Kegan Paul.

FARRINGTON, D. P. (1972): 'Delinquency begins at home'. *New Society*, **21**, 495–7.

FARRINGTON, D. P. (1973): 'Self-Reports of Deviant Behaviour: Productive and Stable?' *J. Criminal Law & Criminol.*, **64**, 99–110.

FARRINGTON, D. P. (1977): 'The effects of public labelling'. *Brit. J. Criminol.*, **17**, 112–25.

FARRINGTON, D. P. (1978): 'The family backgrounds of aggressive youths'. In Hersov, L. A., Berger, M., and Shaffer, D. (eds.), *Aggression and Antisocial Behaviour in Childhood and Adolescence*, 73–93. Oxford: Pergamon.

FARRINGTON, D. P. (1979): 'Longitudinal research on crime and delinquency'. In Morris, N., and Tonry, M. (eds.), *Criminal Justice: An annual review of research*, Vol. *1*, 289–348. Chicago & London: University of Chicago Press.

FARRINGTON, D. P. (1981a): 'The prevalence of convictions'. *Brit. J. Criminol.*, **21**, 173–5.

FARRINGTON, D. P. (1981b): 'Delinquency from 10 to 25'. Paper given at the Society for Life History Research meeting on 'Antecedents of Aggression and Antisocial Behavior', Monterey, California: November 1981.

FARRINGTON, D. P., and BENNETT, T. (1981): 'Police cautioning of juveniles in London'. *Brit. J. Criminol.*, **21**, 123–35.

FARRINGTON, D. P., BIRON, L., and LEBLANC, M. (1982): 'Personality and delinquency in London and Montreal'. In Gunn, J., and Farrington, D. P. (eds.), *Abnormal Offenders: Delinquency and the Criminal Justice System*. Chichester: Wiley.

FARRINGTON, D. P., GUNDRY, G., and WEST, D. J. (1975): 'The familial transmission of criminality'. *Medicine, Science & the Law*, **15**, 177–86.

FARRINGTON, D. P., OSBORN, S., and WEST, D. J. (1978): 'The persistence of labelling effects'. *Brit. J. Criminol.*, **18**, 277–84.

FELDMAN, M. P. (1977): *Criminal Behaviour: A Psychological Analysis*. London: Wiley.

FENIGSTEIN, A. (1979): 'Does aggression cause a preference for viewing media violence?' *J. Pers. Soc. Psychol.*, **37**, 2307–17.

FERGUSON, H. B., and RAPOPORT, J. (1983): 'Outstanding issues on nosology'. In Rutter, M. (ed.), *Developmental Neuropsychiatry*. New York: Guilford Press (in press).

FERRI, E. (1976): *Growing Up in a One-Parent Family*. Slough: N.F.E.R.

FESHBACH, S., and SINGER, J. L. (1971): *Television and Aggression*. San Francisco: Jossey-Bass.
FIELD, E. (1967): *A Validation of Hewitt and Jenkins' Hypothesis*. Home Office Research Study in the Causes of Delinquency and the Treatment of Offenders No. 10. London: H.M.S.O.
FINER, M. (1974): See DEPARTMENT OF HEALTH AND SOCIAL SECURITY (1974).
FINLAYSON, D. S., and LOUGHRAN, J. L. (1976): 'Pupils' perceptions in high and low delinquency schools'. *Educ. Res.*, **18**, 138–45.
FISHER, S. (1972): 'Stigma and deviant careers in school'. *Social Problems*, **20**, 78–83.
FITZHERBERT, K. (1967): *West Indian Children in London*. Occasional papers on Social Administration No. 19. London: H.M.S.O.
FIXSEN, D. L., PHILLIPS, E. L., and WOLF, M. M. (1973): 'Achievement Place: experiments in self government with predelinquents'. *J. Appl. Behav. Anal.*, **6**, 31–49.
FLEISHER, B. M. (1966): *The Economics of Delinquency*. Chicago: Quadrangle.
FO, W. S. O., and O'DONNELL, C. R. (1974): 'The Buddy System: relationship and contingency conditions in a community intervention program for youth with non-professionals as behavior change agents'. *J. Consult. Clin. Psychol.*, **42**, 163–9.
FOREHAND, R., KING, H., PEED, S., and YODER, P. (1975): 'Mother-child interaction: Comparison of a non-compliant clinic group and a non-clinic group'. *Behav. Res. & Therapy*, **13**, 79–84.
FORREST, R. (1977): 'Personality and delinquency: a multivariate examination of Eysenck's theory with Scottish delinquent and non-delinquent boys'. *Soc. Behav. Personality*, **5**, 157–67.
FORSLUND, M. A. (1970): 'A comparison of negro and white crime rates'. *J. Crim. Law, Criminol. & Police Science*, **61**, 214–18.
FOSTER, J., DINITZ, S., and RECKLESS, W. (1972): 'Perceptions of stigma following public intervention for delinquent behaviour'. *Social Problems*, **20**, 202–9.
FREEDMAN, J. L. (1979): 'Reconciling apparent differences between the responses of humans and other animals to crowding'. *Psychol. Review*, **86**, 80–85.
FRIDAY, P. (1980): 'International review of youth crime and delinquency'. In Newman, G. (ed.), *Deviance and Crime: International Perspectives*. London: Sage.
FRIEDLANDER, K. (1947): *The Psychoanalytic Approach to Juvenile Delinquency*. London: Routledge & Kegan Paul.
FRIEDRICH, L. K., and STEIN, A. H. (1973): 'Aggressive and prosocial television programs and the natural behavior of preschool children'. *Monogr. Soc. Res. Child Develop.*, **38**, Serial No. 151.
FRITH, S. (1978): *Sociology of Rock*. London: Constable.
GANS, H. J. (1962): *The Urban Villagers: Group and Class in the Life of Italian-Americans*. New York: Free Press.
GANZER, V. J., and SARASON, I. G. (1973): 'Variables associated with recidivism among juvenile delinquents'. *J. Consult. Clin. Psychol.*, **40**, 1–5.
GATES, A. I., and BOND, G. L. (1936): 'Failure in reading and social maladjustment'. *National Education Assoc. J.*, **25**, 205–6.
GATH, D., COOPER, B., GATTONI, F., and ROCKETT, D. (1977): *Child Guidance and*

Delinquency in a London Borough. Institute of Psychiatry Maudsley Monographs No. 24. London: Oxford University Press.

GAWN, J., MOTT, J., and TARLING, R. (1977): 'Dealing with juvenile offenders in a new town, 1966/77 and 1973'. *Justice of the Peace*, **141**, 279–80.

GERSTEN, J. C., LANGNER, T. S., EISENBERG, J. G., SIMCHA-FAGAN, O., and MCCARTH, E. D. (1976): 'Stability and change in types of behavioral disturbance of children and adolescents'. *J. Abnorm. Child Psychol.*, **4**, 111–28.

GIBBENS, T. C. N. (1963): *Psychiatric Studies of Borstal Lads*. London: Oxford University Press.

GIBBENS, T. C. N., and PRINCE, J. (1962): *Shoplifting*. London: Institute for the Study and Treatment of Delinquency.

GIBBENS, T. C. N., and PRINCE, J. (1965): *The Results of Borstal Training. Sociol. Rev. Monogr.* No. 9. University of Keele.

GIBBONS, D. C. (1971): 'Observations on the study of crime causation'. *Amer. J. Sociol.*, **77**, 262–78.

GIBBONS, D. C., and BLAKE, G. F. (1976): 'Evaluating the impact of juvenile diversion programs'. *Crime & Delinq.*, **22**, 411–20.

GIBBS, J. P. (1975): *Crime, Punishment and Deterrence*. Amsterdam: Elsevier.

GIBBS, J. P., and ERICKSON, M. L. (1975): 'Major developments in the sociological study of deviance'. *Ann. Rev. Sociol.*, **1**, 21–42.

GIBBS, L. (1974): 'The effects of juvenile legal procedures on juvenile offenders' self-attitudes'. *J. Res. Crime Delinq.*, **11**, 51–5.

GIBSON, H. B. (1969): 'Early delinquency in relation to broken homes'. *J. Child Psychol. Psychiat.*, **10**, 195–204.

GIFFEN, P. J. (1976): 'Official Rates of Crime and Delinquency'. In McGrath, W. (ed.), *Crime and its Treatment in Canada*. Toronto: Macmillan.

GILDEA, M. C.-L., GLIDEWELL, J. C., and KANTOR, M. B. (1967): 'The St. Louis school mental health project: History and evaluation'. In Cowen, E. L., Gardner, E. A., and Zax, M. (eds.), *Emergent Approaches to Mental Health Problems*. New York: Meredith Publ. Co.

GILL, O. (1977): *Luke Street: Housing Policy, Conflict and the Creation of the Delinquency Area*. London: Macmillan.

GILLER, H., and MORRIS, A. (1976): 'Children who offend: care, control or confusion?' *Criminal Law Rev.*, 656–65.

GILLER, H., and MORRIS, A. (1978): 'Supervision orders: the routinization of treatment'. *Howard J.*, **17**, 149–59.

GILLER, H., and MORRIS, A. (1981): *Care and Discretion*. London: Burnett Books.

GIORDANO, P. C. (1978): 'Girls, guys and gangs: The changing social context of female delinquency'. *J. Criminal Law & Criminol.*, **69**, 126–32.

GLADSTONE, F. J. (1978): 'Vandalism among Adolescent Schoolboys'. In Clarke, R. V. G. (ed.), *Tackling Vandalism*. Home Office Research Study No. 47. London: H.M.S.O.

GLADSTONE, F. J. (1980): *Co-ordinating Crime Prevention Efforts*. Home Office Research Study No. 62. London: H.M.S.O.

GLASER, D. (1979): 'A review of crime-causation theory and its application'. In Morris, N., and Tonry, M. (eds.), *Crime and Justice: An Annual Review of Research, Vol. 1*, 203–37. Chicago and London: University of Chicago Press.
GLASER, D., and RICE, K. (1959): 'Crime, age and employment'. *Amer. Sociol. Rev.*, **24**, 679–86.
GLOVER, E. (1960): *The Roots of Crime: Selected Papers on Psychoanalysis Vol. II*. London: Imago.
GLUECK, S., and GLUECK, E. (1940): *Juvenile Delinquents Grown Up*. New York: The Commonwealth Fund.
GLUECK, S., and GLUECK, E. (1950): *Unravelling Juvenile Delinquency*. Cambridge, Mass.: Harvard University Press.
GLUECK, S., and GLUECK, E. (1956): *Physique and Delinquency*. New York: Harper & Row.
GLUECK, S., and GLUECK, E. (1964): 'Potential juvenile delinquents can be identified: what next?' *Brit. J. Criminol.*, **4**, 215–26.
GOLD, M. (1963): *Status Forces in Delinquent Boys*. Ann Arbor: Institute for Social Research.
GOLD, M. (1966): 'Undetected delinquent activity'. *J. Res. Crime Delinq.*, **3**, 27–46.
GOLD, M. (1970): *Delinquent Behavior in an American City*. Belmont, Calif.: Brooks/Cole.
GOLD, M., and REIMER, D. J. (1975): 'Changing patterns of delinquent behavior among Americans 13 through 16 years old: 1967–72'. *Crime and Delinquency Literature*, **7**, 483–517.
GOLD, M., and WILLIAMS, J. R. (1969): 'National study of the aftermath of apprehension'. *Prospectus*, **3**, 3–12.
GOLDMAN, N. (1961): 'A socio-psychological study of school vandalism'. *Crime & Delinq.*, **7**, 221–30.
GOODENOUGH, F. L. (1931): *Anger in Young Children*. Minneapolis: University of Minnesota Press.
GOODMAN, N., MALONEY, E., and DAVIS, J. (1976): 'Borstal girls eight years after release'. In *Further Studies of Female Offenders*, 3–20. Home Office Research Study No. 33. London: H.M.S.O.
GOVE, W. R., HUGHES, M., and GALE, O. R. (1979): 'Overcrowding in the home: An empirical investigation of its possible pathological consequences'. *Amer. Sociol. Rev.*, **44**, 59–80.
GOVERNMENT WHITE PAPER (1980): *Young Offenders*. Cmnd 8045. London: H.M.S.O.
GRAHAM, F. (1981): 'Probability of detection and institutional vandalism'. *Brit. J. Criminol.*, **21**, 361–5.
GRAHAM, P. J. (1977): 'Possibilities for prevention'. In Graham, P. J. (ed.), *Epidemiological Approaches in Child Psychiatry*, 377–97. London: Academic Press.
GRAHAM, P. (1980): 'Moral development'. In Rutter, M. (ed.), *Scientific Foundations of Developmental Psychiatry*, 339–53. London: Heinemann Medical.
GRAHAM, P. J., and MEADOWS, C. E. (1967): 'Psychiatric disorder in the children of West Indian immigrants'. *J. Child Psychol. Psychiat.*, **8**, 105–16.

GRAHAM, P., and RUTTER, M. (1973): 'Psychiatric disorder in the young adolescent: A follow-up study'. *Proc. Roy. Soc. Med.*, **66**, 1226–9.

GRAY, G. (1981): Unpublished data.

GRAY, G., SMITH, A., and RUTTER, M. (1980): 'School attendance and the first year of employment'. In Hersov, L., and Berg, I. (eds.), *Out of School: Modern Perspectives in Truancy and School Refusal*, 343–70. Chichester: Wiley.

GREEN, E. (1970): 'Race, social status, and criminal arrest'. *Amer. Sociol. Rev.*, **35**, 476–90.

GREENBERG, P. F. (1977): 'The correctional effects of corrections: a survey of evaluations'. In Greenberg, D. F. (ed.), *Corrections and Punishment*, 111–48. Beverly Hills, Calif.: Sage.

GREENWOOD, P. W., CHAIEKN, J. M., and PETERSILIA, J. (1977): *The Criminal Investigation Process*. Lexington, Mass.: D. C. Heath.

GREGORY, I. (1965): 'Anterospective data following childhood loss of a parent'. *Arch. Gen. Psychiat.*, **13**, 110–20.

GROSS, A. M., and BRIGHAM, T. A. (1980): 'Behavior modification and the treatment of juvenile delinquency: a review and a proposal for future research'. *Corrective & Soc. Psychiat.*, **26**, 98–108.

GRÜNHUT, M. (1956): *Juvenile Offenders Before the Courts*. Oxford: Oxford University Press.

GUNNAR-VONGNECHTEN, M. R. (1978): 'Changing a frightening toy into a pleasant toy by allowing the infant to control its actions'. *Develop. Psychol.*, **14**, 157–162.

GURR, T. (1979): 'Crime trends in modern democracies since 1945'. In Brown, J. (ed.), *The Cranfield Papers*, 56–93. London: Peel Press.

GURR, T., GRABOSKY, P., and HULA, R. (1977): *The Politics of Crime and Conflict: A comparative history of four cities*. London: Sage.

HALL, S., CRITCHER, C., JEFFERSON, T., CLARKE, J., and ROBERTS, B. (1978): *Policing the Crisis*. London: Macmillan.

HAMPARIAN, D. M., SCHUSTER, R., DINITZ, S., and CONRAD, J. P. (1978): *The Violent Few: A Study of Dangerous Juvenile Offenders*. Lexington, Mass.: D. C. Heath (Lexington Books).

HANEY, W. G., and KNOWLES, E. S. (1978): 'Perception of neighborhoods by city and suburban residents'. *Human Ecolog.*, **6**, 201–14.

HARDT, R. H., and BODINE, G. E. (1965): *Development of Self-Report Instruments in Delinquency Research*. Syracuse University: Youth Development Center. Cited by Hirschi (1969).

HARE, R. (1970): *Psychopathy, Theory and Research*. New York: Wiley.

HARE, R. D., and SCHALLING, D. (eds.) (1978): *Psychopathic Behavior: Approaches to Research*. New York: Wiley.

HARGREAVES, D. (1967): *Social Relations in a Secondary School*. London: Routledge & Kegan Paul.

HART, R. J. (1978): 'Crime and punishment in the Army'. *J. Pers. Soc. Psychol.*, **36**, 1456–71.

HASSELL, C., and TRETHOWAN, W. H. (1972): 'Suicide in Birmingham'. *Brit. Med. J.*, **1**, 717–18.
HASTINGS, J. E., and BARKLEY, R. A. (1978): 'A review of psychophysiological research with hyperkinetic children'. *J. Abnorm. Child Psychol.*, **6**, 413–48.
HATHAWAY, S. R., and MONACHESI, E. D. (1963): *Adolescent Personality and Behavior*. Minneapolis: University of Minnesota Press.
HAVIGHURST, R. J., BOWMAN, P. H., LIDDLE, G. P., MATTHEWS, C. V., and PIERCE, J. V. (1962): *Growing Up in River City*. New York and London: Wiley.
HAYASHI, S. (1967): 'A study of juvenile delinquency in twins'. In Mitsuda, H. (ed.), *Clinical Genetics in Psychiatry*. Tokyo: Igaku Shoin.
HAZEL, N. (1977): 'How family placements can combat delinquency'. *Social Work Today*, **8**, 6–7.
HAZEL, N. (1978): 'Teaching family placement'. *Adoption and Fostering*, **94**, 31–5.
HEAL, K. H. (1978): 'Misbehaviour among school children: the role of the school in strategies for prevention'. *Policy & Politics*, **6**, 321–2.
HEBDIGE, D. (1976): 'Reggae, rastas and rudies'. In Hall, S., and Jefferson, T. (eds.), *Resistance through Rituals*. London: Hutchinson.
HEIDENSOHN, F. (1968): 'The deviance of women: a critique and an enquiry'. *Brit. J. Sociol.*, **19**, 160–75.
HELLON, C. P., and SOLOMON, M. I. (1980): 'Suicide and age in Alberta, Canada, 1951 to 1977: the changing profile'. *Arch. Gen. Psychiat.*, **37**, 505–13.
HENN, F. A., BARDWELL, R., and JENKINS, R. L. (1980): 'Juvenile delinquents revisited: Adult criminal activity'. *Arch. Gen. Psychiat.*, **37**, 1160–63.
HEPBURN, J. K. (1978): 'Race and the decision to arrest'. *J. Res. Crime Delinq.*, **15**, 54–73.
HERSOV, L., and BERG, I. (eds.) (1980): *Out of School: Modern Perspectives in Truancy and School Refusal*. Chichester: Wiley.
HESS, R. D., and CAMERA, K. A. (1979): 'Post-divorce family relationships as mediating factors in the consequences of divorce for children'. *J. Social Issues*, **35**, 79–96.
HETHERINGTON, E. M. (1981): 'Children and divorce'. In Henderson, R. (ed.), *Parent-Child Interaction: Theory, Research and Prospect*. New York: Academic Press.
HETHERINGTON, E. M., COX, M., and COX, R. (1978): 'The aftermath of divorce'. In Stevens, J. H., and Matthews, M. (eds.), *Mother-Child Father-Child Relations*. Washington, D.C.: National Association for the Education of Young Children.
HETHERINGTON, E. M., COX, M., and COX, R. (1979a): 'Play and social interaction in children following divorce'. *J. Soc. Issues*, **35**, 26–49.
HETHERINGTON, E. M., COX, M., and COX, R. (1979b): 'Family interaction and the social, emotional and cognitive development of children following divorce'. In Vaughan, V., and Brazelton, T. (eds.), *The Family: Setting Priorities*. New York: Science and Medicine.
HETHERINGTON, E. M., and MARTIN, B. (1979): 'Family interaction'. In Quay, H. C., and Werry, J. S. (eds.), *Psychopathological Disorders of Childhood*, 2nd edition, 247–302. New York: Wiley.

HETHERINGTON, E. M., STOUWIE, R., and RIDBERG, E. H. (1971): 'Patterns of family interaction and child rearing attitudes related to three dimensions of juvenile delinquency'. *J. Abnorm. Psychol.*, **77**, 160–76.

HEWITT, L. E., and JENKINS, R. L. (1946): *Fundamental Patterns of Maladjustment*. Illinois: Michigan Child Guidance Institute.

HEYWOOD, R. (1979): 'Traditional and innovative policing'. In Engstad, R., and Lioy, M. (eds.), *Proceedings: Workshop on Police Productivity and Performance*. Ottawa: Solicitor General of Canada. Cited by Hough, J. M., and Clarke, R. V. G. (1980).

HILL, R., and ALDOUS, J. (1969): 'Socialization for marriage and parenthood'. In Goslin, D. A. (ed.), *Handbook of Socialization Theory and Research*, 885–950. Chicago: Rand McNally.

HILLIER, W. (1973): 'In defence of space'. *J. Roy. Inst. Brit. Architects*, **80**, 539–544.

HIMMELWEIT, H. T., OPPENHEIM, A. N., and VINCE, P. (1958): *Television and the Child*. London: Oxford University Press.

HINDE, R. A. (1980): 'Family influences'. In Rutter, M. (ed.), *Scientific Foundations of Developmental Psychiatry*. London: Heinemann Medical.

HINDELANG, D. (1971): 'Extroversion, neuroticism, and self-reported delinquent involvement'. *J. Res. Crime & Delinq.*, **8**, 23–31.

HINDELANG, M. (1973): 'Causes of delinquency: a partial replication and extension'. *Social Problems*, **20**, 471–87.

HINDELANG, M. J. (1976): *Criminal Victimization in Eight American Cities*. Cambridge, Mass.: Ballinger.

HINDELANG, M. (1978): 'Race and involvement in common law personal crimes'. *Amer. Sociol. Rev.*, **43**, 93–109.

HINDELANG, M. J., HIRSCHI, T., and WEIS, J. G. (1979): 'Correlates of delinquency: the illusion of discrepancy between self-report and official measures'. *Amer. Sociol. Rev.*, **44**, 995–1014.

HINE, J., and MCWILLIAMS, B. (1981): 'Social inquiry practice'. *Probation Journal*, **28**, 93–7.

HIRSCHI, T. (1969): *Causes of Delinquency*. Berkeley and Los Angeles: University of California Press.

HIRSCHI, T., and HINDELANG, M. J. (1977): 'Intelligence and delinquency: a revisionist review'. *Amer. Sociol. Rev.*, **42**, 571–87.

HIRSCHI, T., and SELVIN, H. (1967): *Delinquency Research: An Appraisal of Analytic Methods*. New York: Free Press.

HODGINS, S. (1979): ' "Psychopathy": An examination of the psychophysiological findings'. Paper presented to the American Society of Criminology, Philadelphia, November, 1979.

HOEFLER, S. A., and BORNSTEIN, P. H. (1975): 'Achievement Place: an evaluative review'. *Criminal Justice & Behavior*, **2**, 146–68.

HOFFMAN, M. L. (1977): 'Sex differences in empathy and related behaviors'. *Psychol. Bull.*, **84**, 712–22.

HOGARTH, J. (1971): *Sentencing as a Human Process*. Toronto: University of Toronto Press.
HOGHUGHI, M. (1979): 'The Aycliffe token economy'. *Brit. J. Criminol.*, **19**, 384–99.
HOKANSON, J. E., BURGESS, M., and COHEN, M. F. (1963): 'Effects of displaced aggression on systolic blood pressure'. *J. Abnorm. Soc. Psychol.*, **67**, 214–18.
HOLE, W. V., and POUNTNEY, M. T. (1971): *Trends in Population, Housing and Occupancy Rates, 1861–1961*. London: H.M.S.O.
HOLMAN, R. (1973): *Trading in Children: a study of private fostering*. London: Routledge & Kegan Paul.
HOME OFFICE (1964): *Criminal Statistics England and Wales, 1963*. London: H.M.S.O.
HOME OFFICE (1965): *The Child, the Family and the Young Offender*. Cmnd 2742. London: H.M.S.O.
HOME OFFICE (1968): *Children in Trouble*. Cmnd 3601. London: H.M.S.O.
HOME OFFICE (1969): *Sentence of the Court*. London: H.M.S.O.
HOME OFFICE (1977): *Criminal Statistics England and Wales, 1976*. London: H.M.S.O.
HOME OFFICE (1978): *Criminal Statistics England and Wales, 1977*. London: H.M.S.O.
HOME OFFICE (1979): *Criminal Statistics England and Wales, 1978*. London: H.M.S.O.
HOME OFFICE (1980): *Criminal Statistics England and Wales, 1979*. London: H.M.S.O.
HOME OFFICE (1981a): *Criminal Statistics England and Wales, 1980*. London: H.M.S.O.
HOME OFFICE (1981b): *The Brixton Disorders 10–12 April 1981*. Report of an inquiry by the Rt Hon. The Lord Scarman, O.B.E. London: H.M.S.O.
HOME OFFICE STANDING COMMITTEE ON CRIME PREVENTION (1975): *Protection Against Vandalism*. London: H.M.S.O.
HOOD, C., OPPÉ, T. E., PLESS, I. B., and APTE, E. (1970): *Children of West Indian Immigrants: A study of one-year-olds in Paddington*. London: Institute of Race Relations.
HOOD, R. (1972): *Sentencing the Motoring Offender*. London: Heinemann.
HOOD, R., and SPARKS, R. (1970): *Key Issues in Criminology*. London: World University Library.
HOUGH, J. M., and CLARKE, R. V. G. (1980): 'Introduction'. In Clarke, R. V. G., and Hough, J. M. (eds.), *The Effectiveness of Policing*, 1–16. Farnborough: Gower.
HOUGH, J. M., CLARKE, R. V. G., and MAYHEW, P. (1980): 'Introduction'. In Clarke, R. V. G., and Mayhew, P. (eds.), *Designing Out Crime*, 1–18. London: H.M.S.O.
HOUSE OF COMMONS EXPENDITURE COMMITTEE (1975): *Eleventh Report: The Children and Young Persons Act, 1969*. Order no. HC534-1. London: H.M.S.O.
HUMPHREY, D. (1972): *Police Power and Black People*. London: Panther.
HURWITZ, S. (1952): *Criminology*. London: Allen & Unwin.
HUTCHINGS, B., and MEDNICK, S. A. (1974): 'Registered criminality in the adoptive

and biological parents of registered male adoptees'. In Mednick, S. A., Schulsinger, F., Higgins, J., and Bell, B. (eds.), *Genetics, Environment and Psychopathology*, 215–27. Amsterdam: North-Holland.

INSTITUTE OF RACE RELATIONS (1979): *Police Against Black People*. Evidence submitted to the Ray Commission on Criminal Procedure. London: Institute of Race Relations.

JAMES, A. G. (1974): *Sikh Children in Britain*. London: Institute of Race Relations, Oxford University Press.

JAPAN MINISTRY OF JUSTICE (1980): *Outline of the White Paper on Crime*. Tokyo: Foreign Press Centre.

JEFFERSON, T. (1976): 'The Teds – a political resurrection'. In Hall, S., and Jefferson, T. (eds.), *Resistance Through Rituals*. London: Hutchinson.

JENCKS, C., SMITH, M., ACLAND, H., BANE, M. J., COHEN, D., GINTIS, H., HEYNS, B., and MICHELSON, S. (1972): *Inequality: A reassessment of the effects of family and schooling in America*. New York: Basic Books.

JENKINS, R. L. (1973): *Behavior Disorders of Childhood and Adolescence*. Springfield, Ill.: Chas C. Thomas.

JENKINS, R. L., and BOYER, A. (1967): 'Types of delinquent behavior and background factors'. *Internat. J. Soc. Psychiat.*, **14**, 65–76.

JENNINGS, C., BARRACLOUGH, B. M., and MOSS, J. R. (1978): 'Have the Samaritans lowered the suicide rate'. *Psychol. Med.*, **8**, 413–22.

JENNINGS, M., and NIEMI, R. (1975): 'Continuity and change in political orientations: A longitudinal study of two generations'. *Amer. Polit. Sci. Rev.*, **69**, 1316–75.

JENSEN, G. F. (1972): 'Parents, peers and delinquent action: a test of the differential association perspective'. *Amer. J. Sociol.*, **78**, 562–75.

JENSEN, G. J., and EVE, R. (1976): 'Sex differences in delinquency: An examination of popular sociological explanations'. *Criminology*, **13**, 427–48.

JENSON, G. (1972): 'Delinquency and adolescent self-conceptions: A study of the personal relevance of infraction'. *Social Problems*, **20**, 84–103.

JEPHCOTT, A. P., and CARTER, M. P. (1954): *The Social Background of Delinquency*. Nottingham: University Press.

JESNESS, C. F. (1965): *The Fricot Ranch Study*. Report No. 47, Department of the Youth Authority, California. Abstract in Lipton *et al.* (1975).

JESNESS, C. F. (1971): 'The Preston Typology study: an experiment with differential treatment in an institution'. *J. Res. Crime & Delinq.*, **8**, 38–52.

JESNESS, C. F. (1975): 'Comparative effectiveness of behavior modification and transactional analysis programs for delinquents'. *J. Consult. Clin. Psychol.*, **43**, 758–79.

JESNESS, C. F. (1979): 'The Youth Center Project: transactional analysis and behavior modification programs for delinquents'. In Stumphauzer, J. S. (ed.), *Progress in Behavior Therapy with Delinquents*. Springfield, Ill.: Chas C. Thomas.

JESNESS, C. F. (1980): 'Was the Close-Holton project a "bummer"?' In Ross, R. R., and Gendreau, P. (eds.), *Effective Correctional Treatment*, 359–66. Toronto: Butterworths.

JESNESS, C. F., ALLISON, T., MCCORMICK, P., WEDGE, P., and YOUNG, M. (1975):

Cooperative Behavior Demonstration Project. Sacramento, Calif.: California Youth Authority.
JESSOR, R., and JESSOR, S. L. (1977): *Problem Behavior and Psychosocial Development: a longitudinal study of youth.* New York: Academic Press.
JOHNSON, B. M. (1962): *An Analysis of Parole Performance and of Judgements of Supervision in the Parole Research Project.* Research Report No. 32. Sacramento, Calif.: California Youth and Adult Corrections Agency. Cited in Brody, S. (1976).
JOHNSON, R. E. (1979): *Juvenile Delinquency and its Origins.* Cambridge: Cambridge University Press.
JOHNSON, S. M., WAHL, G., MARTIN, S., and JOHANSSEN, S. (1974): 'How deviant is the normal child: a behavioral analysis of the preschool child and his family'. In Rubin, D. R., Brady, J. P., and Henderson, J. D. (eds.), *Advances in Behavior Therapy, Vol. 4.* New York: Academic Press.
JONES, H. (1958): 'Approaches to an ecological study'. *Brit. J. Delinq.*, **8**, 277–93.
JONES, H. (1981): 'A case for correction'. *Brit. J. Social Work*, **11**, 1–17.
JONSSON, G. (1967): *Delinquent Boys, Their Parents and Grandparents.* Copenhagen: Munksgaard.
JURKOVIC, G. J. (1980): 'The juvenile delinquent as a moral philospher: a structural-developmental perspective'. *Psychol. Bull*, **88**, 709–27.
KAGAN, J. (1981): *The Second Year: The Emergence of Self-Awareness.* Cambridge, Mass.: Harvard University Press.
KAGAN, J., and MOSS, M. A. (1962): *Birth to Maturity.* New York: Wiley.
KAHN, J., CARTER, W. I., DERNLEY, N., and SLATER, E. T. O. (1969): 'Chromosome studies in remand home and prison populations'. In West, D. J. (ed.), *Criminological Implications of Chromosome Abnormalities*, 44–8. Cambridge: Institute of Criminology.
KAHN, M. (1966): 'The physiology of catharsis'. *J. Pers. Soc. Psychol.*, **3**, 278–86.
KASARDA, J. D., and JANOWITZ, M. (1974): 'Community attachment in mass society'. *Amer. Sociol. Rev.*, **39**, 328–39.
KASSEBAUM, G., WARD, D., and WILNER, D. (1971): *Prison Treatment and Parole Survival: an empirical assessment.* New York: Wiley.
KASTRUP, M. (1977): 'Urban-rural differences in 6 year olds'. In Graham, P. J. (ed.), *Epidemiological Approaches in Child Psychiatry*, 181–94. London: Academic Press.
KAZDIN, A. E., and BOOTZIN, R. R. (1972): 'The token economy: An evaluative review'. *J. Appl. Behav. Anal.*, **5**, 343–72.
KELLAM, S. G., BRANCH, J. D., AGRAWAL, K. C., and ENSMINGER, M. E. (1975): *Mental Health and Going to School: The Woodlawn Program of Assessment, Early Intervention and Evaluation.* Chicago: University of Chicago Press.
KELLEY, C. M. (1974): *Uniform Crime Reports from the United States – 1973.* Washington, D.C.: U.S. Government Printing Office.
KELLEY, C. (1977): *Crime in the United States.* Washington, D.C.: U.S. Government Printing Office.
KELLING, G., PATE, T., DIECKMAN, D., and BROWN, C. (1974): *The Kansas City Preventive Patrol Experiment.* Washington, D.C.: Police Foundation.

References

KENDELL, R. E., HALL, D. J., HAILEY, A., and BABIGIAN, H. M. (1973): 'The epidemiology of anorexia nervosa'. *Psychol. Med.*, **3**, 200–203.

KENNY, D. A. (1975): 'Cross-lagged panel correlation: A test for spuriousness'. *Psychol. Bull.*, **82**, 887–903.

KENT, R. (1976): 'A methodological critique of interviewing for boys with conduct problems'. *J. Consult. Clin. Psychol.*, **44**, 297–9.

KERNER, O. (1968): *Report of the National Advisory Commission on Civil Liberties*. New York: Bantam Books.

KHLEIF, B. B. (1964): 'Teachers as predictors of juvenile delinquency and psychiatric disturbance'. *Social Problems*, **11**, 270–82.

KIRIGIN, K. A., WOLF, M. M., BRAUKMAN, C. J., FIXSEN, D. L., and PHILLIPS, E. L. (1979): 'Achievement Place: A preliminary outcome evaluation'. In Stumphauzer, J. S. (ed.), *Progress in Behavior Therapy with Delinquents*, 118–45. Springfield, Ill.: Chas C. Thomas.

KITSUSE, J., and CICOUREL, A. (1963): 'A note on the use of official statistics'. *Social Problems*, **11**, 131–9.

KLEIN, M. W. (1974): 'Labelling, deterrence, and recidivism: A study of police disposition of juvenile offenders'. *Social Problems*, **22**, 292–303.

KLEIN, M. W. (1979): 'Deinstitutionalization and diversion of juvenile offenders: a litany of impediments'. In Morris, N., and Tonry, M. (eds.), *Crime and Justice: An Annual Review of Research*, *Vol. 1*, 145–201. Chicago and London: University of Chicago Press.

KNIGHT, B. J., OSBORN, S. G., and WEST, D. J. (1977): 'Early marriage and criminal tendency in males'. *Brit. J. Criminol.*, **17**, 348–60.

KNIGHT, B. J., and WEST, D. J. (1975): 'Temporary and continuing delinquency'. *Brit. J. Criminol.*, **15**, 43–50.

KNIGHT, B. J., and WEST, D. J. (1977): 'Criminality and welfare dependency in two generations'. *Medicine, Science and the Law*, **17**, 64–7.

KOBAYASHI, S., MIZUZHIMA, K., and SHINOHARA, M. (1967): 'Clinical groupings of problem children based on symptoms and behavior'. *Internat. J. Soc. Psychiat.*, **13**, 206–15.

KOHLBERG, L. (1976): 'Moral stages and moralization'. In Lickona, T. (ed.), *Moral Development and Behavior: Theory, research and social issues*. New York: Holt, Rinehart & Winston.

KOHN, M. (1977): *Social Competence, Symptoms and Underachievement in Childhood: a longitudinal perspective*. London: Wiley.

KORNHAUSER, R. R. (1978): *Social Sources of Delinquency: An appraisal of analytic models*. Chicago and London: University of Chicago Press.

KRATCOSKI, P. C. (1974): 'Differential treatment of delinquent boys and girls in Juvenile Court'. *Child Welfare*, **53**, 16–21.

KRATCOSKI, P. C., and KRATCOSKI, J. E. (1975): 'Changing patterns in the delinquent activities of boys and girls: a self-reported delinquency analysis'. *Adolescence*, **37**, 83–91.

KRATCOSKI, P. C., and KRATCOSKI, J. E. (1977): 'The balance of social status groupings within schools as an influencing variable on the frequency and character of delinquent behavior'. In Friday, P. C., and Stewart, V. L. (eds.), *Juvenile Justice: International Perspectives*, 160–71. New York: Praeger.

KRAUS, J. (1974): 'A comparison of corrective effects of probation and detention on male juvenile offenders'. *Brit. J. Criminol.*, **14**, 49–62.

KRAUS, J. (1977): 'Trends in juvenile delinquency'. In Chappell, D., and Wilson, P. (eds.), *The Australian Criminal Justice System*. Sydney: Butterworths.

KREITMAN, N. (ed.) (1977): *Parasuicide*. London: Wiley.

KROHN, M. D. (1976): 'Inequality, unemployment and crime: a cross-national analysis'. *The Sociological Quarterly*, **17**, 303–13.

KULIK, J. A., STEIN, K. B., and SARBIN, T. R. (1968): 'Disclosure of delinquent behaviour under conditions of anonymity and nonanonymity'. *J. Consult. Clin. Psychol.*, **32**, 506–9.

KUPFERSMID, J. H., and WONDERLY, D. M. (1980): 'Moral maturity: failure to find a link'. *J. Youth and Adolescence*, **9**, 249–61.

KVARACEUS, W. C. (1960): *Anxious Youth: Dynamics of Delinquency*. Columbus, Ohio: C. E. Merrill.

LAMB, M. E. (ed.) (1976): *The Role of the Father in Child Development*. New York: Wiley.

LAMBERT, J. (1970): *Crime, Police and Race Relations*. London: Oxford University Press.

LAMBERT, L., ESSEN, J., and HEAD, J. (1977): 'Variations in behaviour ratings of children who have been in care'. *J. Child Psychol. Psychiat.*, **18**, 335–46.

LANDAU, S. F. (1981): 'Juveniles and the Police'. *Brit. J. Criminol.*, **21**, 27–46.

LANDER, B. (1954): *Towards an Understanding of Juvenile Delinquency*. New York: Columbia University Press.

LANDES, W. M. (1978): 'An economic study of U.S. aircraft hijacking 1961–1976'. *J. Law & Economics*, **21**, 1–31.

LAVIK, N. J. (1977): 'Urban-rural differences in rates of disorder. A comparative psychiatric population study of Norwegian adolescents'. In Graham, P. J. (ed.), *Epidemiological Approaches in Child Psychiatry*, 223–51. London: Academic Press.

LAZARUS, R. S., COHEN, J. B., FOLKMAN, S., KANNER, A., and SCHAEFER, C. (1980): 'Psychological stress and adaptation: some unresolved issues'. In Selye, H. (ed.), *Guide to Stress Research*. New York: Van Nostrand Reinhold.

LAZARUS, R. S., and LAUNIER, R. (1978): 'Stress-related transactions between person and environment'. In Pervin, L. A., and Lewis, M. (eds.), *Perspectives in Interactional Psychology*, 287–327. New York: Plenum.

LEE, T. (1968): 'Urban neighborhood as a socio-spatial scheme'. *Human Relations*, **21**, 241–68.

LEE, T. (1973): 'Psychology and living space'. In Downes, R. M., and Strea, D. (eds.), *Image and Environment: Cognitive Mapping and Spatial Behavior*, 11–36. Chicago: Aldine.

LEETE, R. (1976): 'Marriage and divorce'. *Population Trends*, **3**, 3–8.

LEETE, R. (1978a): 'One parent families: numbers and characteristics'. *Population Trends*, 13, 4–9.

LEETE, R. (1978b): 'Adoption trends and illegitimate births 1951–1977'. *Population Trends*, 14, 9–16.

LEETE, R. (1979): 'New directions in family life'. *Population Trends*, 15, 4–9.

LEFKOWITZ, M. M., ERON, L. D., WALDER, L. O., and HUESMANN, L. R. (1977): *Growing Up to be Violent: A longitudinal study of aggression*. Oxford: Pergamon.

LEMERT, E. M. (1972): *Human Deviance, Social Problems and Social Control*, (2nd edition). Englewood Cliffs, N.J.: Prentice-Hall.

LERMAN, P. (1975): *Community Treatment and Social Control: A critical analysis of juvenile correctional policy*. Chicago and London: University of Chicago Press.

LESLIE, S. A. (1974): 'Psychiatric disorder in the young adolescents of an industrial town'. *Brit. J. Psychiat.*, 125, 113–24.

LEVINE, J. P. (1976): 'The potential for crime overreporting in criminal victimization surveys'. *Criminology*, 14, 307–27.

LEVINE, J. P. (1978): 'Reply to Singer'. *Criminology*, 16, 103–7.

LEVY, D. M., and TULCHIN, S. H. (1923): 'The resistance of infants and children during mental tests'. *J. Experimental Psychol.*, 6, 304–22.

LEVY, D. M., and TULCHIN, S. H. (1925): 'The response behaviour of infants and children. II'. *J. Experimental Psychol.*, 8, 209–24.

LEVY, L., and ROWITZ, L. (1970): 'The spatial distribution of treated mental disorders in Chicago'. *Social Psychiat.*, 5, 1–11.

LEVY, L., and ROWITZ, L. (1971): 'Ecological attributes of high and low rate mental hospital utilization areas in Chicago'. *Social Psychiat.*, 6, 20–28.

LEWIS, A. (1974): 'Psychopathic personality: a most elusive category'. *Psychol. Med.*, 4, 133–40.

LEWIS, D. O., and SHANOK, S. S. (1977): 'Medical histories of delinquent and non-delinquent children: an epidemiological study'. *Amer. J. Psychiat.*, 134, 1020–25.

LEWIS, D. O., SHANOK, S. S., and BALLA, D. A. (1979a): 'Parental criminality and medical histories of delinquent children'. *Amer. J. Psychiat.*, 136, 288–92.

LEWIS, D. O., SHANOK, S. S., and BALLA, D. A. (1979b): 'Perinatal difficulties, head and face trauma, and child abuse in the medical histories of seriously delinquent children'. *Amer. J. Psychiat.*, 136, 419–23.

LEWIS, H. (1954): *Deprived Children*. London: Oxford University Press.

LEYENS, J. P., CAMINO, L., PARKE, R. D., and BERKOWITZ, L. (1975): 'The effects of movie violence on aggression in a field setting as a function of group dominance and cohesion'. *J. Pers. Soc. Psychol.*, 32, 346–60.

LIBERMAN, R. P., FERRIS, C., SALGADO, P., and SALGADO, J. (1975): 'Replication of the Achievement Place model in California'. *J. Appl. Behav. Anal.*, 8, 287–99.

LICKONA, T. (ed.) (1976): *Moral Development and Behavior: Theory, research and social issues*. New York: Holt, Rinehart & Winston.

LIPTON, D., MARTINSON, R., and WILKS, J. (1975): *The Effectiveness of Correctional*

Treatment: A survey of treatment evaluation studies. New York and London: Praeger.

LISKA, A. E. (1969): 'Interpreting the causal structure of differential association theory'. *Social Problems*, 16, 485–92.

LISKA, A. E., and TAUSIG, M. (1979): 'Theoretical interpretations of social class and race differentials in legal decision-making for juveniles'. *Sociological Quart.*, 20, 197–207.

LITTLE, A. N. (1978): *Educational Policies for Multi-Racial Areas.* London: University of London, Goldsmiths' College.

LITTLE, K. (1947): *Negroes in Britain.* London: Kegal Paul.

LITTLE, W. R., and NTSEKHE, V. R. (1959): 'Social class background of young offenders from London'. *Brit. J. Criminol.*, 10, 130–35.

LIVERMORE, J., MALMQUIST, C., and MEEHL, P. (1968): 'On the justification for civil commitment'. University of Pennsylvania Law Review, 117, 75–96.

LOBITZ, G. K., and JOHNSON, S. M. (1975a): 'Parental manipulation of the behavior of normal and deviant children'. *Child Develop.*, 46, 719–26.

LOBITZ, G. K., and JOHNSON, S. M. (1975b): 'Normal versus deviant children: A multimethod comparison'. *J. Abnorm. Child Psychol.*, 3, 353–74.

LONEY, J. (1980): 'Hyperkinesis come of age: what do we know and where should we go?'. *Amer. J. Orthopsychiat.*, 50, 28–42.

LYKKEN, D. (1957): 'A study of anxiety in the sociopathic personality'. *J. Abnorm. Soc. Psychol.*, 55, 6–10.

LYKKEN, D. (1981): *A Tremor in the Blood: Uses and abuses of the lie detector.* New York: McGraw-Hill.

MCCABE, S., and SUTCLIFFE, F. (1978): *Defining Crime: A Study of Police Decisions.* Oxford: Blackwell.

MCCARTHY, D., and SAEGERT, S. (1978): 'Residential density, social overload, and social withdrawal'. *Human Ecolog.*, 6, 253–72.

MCCLINTOCK, F. H. (1961): *Attendance Centres.* London: Macmillan.

MCCLINTOCK, F. H. (1963): *Crimes of Violence.* London: Macmillan.

MCCLINTOCK, F. H., and AVISON, N. H. (1968): *Crime in England and Wales.* London: Heinemann Educational.

MACCOBY, E. E. (1951): 'Television: its impact on school children'. *Public Opinion Quarterly*, 15, 421–44.

MACCOBY, E. E. (ed.) (1966): *The Development of Sex Difference.* Stanford, Calif.: Stanford University Press.

MACCOBY, E. E., and JACKLIN, C. N. (1974): *Psychology of Sex Differences.* Stanford, Calif.: Stanford University Press.

MACCOBY, E. E., and JACKLIN, C. N. (1980a): 'Psychological sex differences'. In Rutter, M. (ed.), *Scientific Foundations of Developmental Psychiatry*, 92–100. London: Heinemann Medical.

MACCOBY, E. E., and JACKLIN, C. N. (1980b): 'Sex differences in aggression: a rejoinder and reprise'. *Child Develop.*, 51, 964–80.

MACCOBY, E. E., JOHNSON, J. P., and CHURCH, R. M. (1968): 'Community integration and the social control of juvenile delinquency'. In Stratton, J. R., and Terry, R. M. (eds.), *Prevention of Delinquency: Problems and Programs*, 300–313. New York: Macmillan.

MCCORD, J. (1978): 'A thirty year follow-up of treatment effects'. *Amer. Psychol.*, **33**, 284–9.

MCCORD, J. (1979): 'Some child-rearing antecedents of criminal behavior in adult men'. *J. Pers. Soc. Psychol.*, **37**, 1477–86.

MCCORD, J. (1980): 'Antecedents and correlates of vulnerability and resistance to psychopathology'. In Zucker, R., and Rabin, A. (eds.), *Further Explorations in Personality*. New York: Wiley.

MCCORD, W., and MCCORD, J. (1959): *Origins of Crime: a new evaluation of the Cambridge-Somerville study*. New York: Columbia University Press.

MCDONALD, L. (1969): *Social Class and Delinquency*. London: Faber & Faber.

MCDONALD, L. (1976): *The Sociology of Law and Order*. London: Faber & Faber.

MACFARLANE, J. W., ALLEN, L., and HONZIK, M. P. (1954): *A Developmental Study of the Behavior Problems of Normal Children between 21 months and 14 years*. Berkeley, Calif.: University of California Press.

MCGREGOR, O. R. (1967): 'Towards divorce law reform'. *Brit. J. Sociol.*, **18**, 91–9.

MCINTOSH, N., and SMITH, D. J. (1974): *The Extent of Racial Discrimination*. Broadsheet No. 547. London: P.E.P.

MCKISSACK, I. J. (1973): 'Property offending and the school leaving age'. *Int. J. Criminol. Penol.*, **1**, 353–62.

MCMICHAEL, P. (1974): 'After-care, family relationships and re-conviction in a Scottish approved school'. *Brit. J. Criminol.*, **14**, 236–47.

MCMICHAEL, P. (1979): 'The hen or the egg? Which comes first – antisocial emotional disorders or reading disability'. *Brit. J. Educ. Psychol.*, **49**, 226–38.

MADGE, C. (1980): 'Poverty in the United Kingdom: a review'. In Brown, M., and Baldwin, S. (eds.), *The Year Book of Social Policy in Britain 1979*. London: Routledge & Kegan Paul.

MALLICK, S. K., and MCCANDLESS, B. R. (1966): 'A study of catharsis of aggression'. *J. Person. Soc. Psychol.*, **4**, 591–6.

MANGUS, A. R. (1950): 'Effect of mental and educational retardation on personality development of children'. *Amer. J. Ment. Defic.*, **55**, 208–12.

MANNHEIM, H., SPENCER, J., and LYNCH, G. (1957): 'Magisterial policy in the London juvenile courts'. *Brit. J. Delinq.*, **18**, 13–33 and 119–38.

MANNHEIM, M., and WILKINS, L. T. (1955): *Prediction Methods in Relation to Borstal Training*. London: H.M.S.O.

MARSH, P., ROSSER, E., and HARRÉ, R. (1978): *The Rules of Disorder*. London: Routledge & Kegan Paul.

MARTIN, D. N. (1977): 'Disruptive behaviour and staff attitudes at the St. Charles Treatment Centre'. *J. Child Psychol. Psychiat.*, **18**, 221–8.

MARTIN, J. A., MACCOBY, E. E., and JACKLIN, C. N. (1981): 'Mothers' responsiveness to interactive bidding and non-bidding in boys and girls'. *Child Develop.*, **52**, 1064–7.

MARTIN, J. P., and WEBSTER, D. (1971): *Social Consequences of Conviction*. London: Heinemann.
MARTINSON, R. (1974): 'What works? – questions and answers about prison reform'. *Public Interest*, **10**, 22–54.
MARTINSON, R. (1976): 'California research at the crossroads'. *Crime and Delinquency*, **22**, 180–91.
MASSIMO, J. L., and SHORE, M. F. (1963): 'The effectiveness of a comprehensive vocationally oriented psychotherapeutic program for adolescent delinquent boys'. *Amer. J. Orthopsychiat.*, **33**, 634–42.
MASTERSON, J. F. (1958): 'Prognosis in adolescent disorders'. *Amer. J. Psychiat.*, **114**, 1097–1103.
MASTERSON, J. F. (1967): *The Psychiatric Dilemma of Adolescence*. London: Churchill.
MATZA, D. (1964): *Delinquency and Drift*. New York and London: Wiley.
MAWBY, R. I. (1977a): 'Kiosk Vandalism: A Sheffield study'. *Brit. J. Criminol.*, **17**, 30–46.
MAWBY, R. I. (1977b): 'Defensible space: A theoretical and empirical appraisal'. *Urban Studies*, **14**, 169–79.
MAWBY, R. I. (1979): *Policing the City*. Farnborough: Saxon House.
MAWBY, R. I., MCCULLOCH, J. W., and BATTA, I. D. (1979): 'Crime among Asian juveniles in Bradford'. *Int. J. Sociology of Law*, **7**, 297–306.
MAY, D. (1975): *Juvenile Offenders and the Organisation of Juvenile Justice: An examination of juvenile delinquency in Aberdeen, 1959–67*. Unpublished Ph.D. Thesis, University of Aberdeen.
MAY, D. (1977): 'Delinquent girls before the courts'. *Medicine, Science and the Law*, **17**, 203–12.
MAYHEW, P. (1979): 'Defensible space: the current status of a crime prevention theory'. *Howard J.*, **18**, 150–59.
MAYHEW, P., CLARKE, R. V. G., BURROWS, J. N., HOUGH, J. M., and WINCHESTER, S. W. C. (1979): *Crime in Public View*. Home Office Research Study No. 49. London: H.M.S.O.
MAYHEW, P., CLARKE, R. V. G., HOUGH, J. M., and WINCHESTER, S. W. C. (1980): 'Natural surveillance and vandalism to telephone kiosks'. In Clarke, R. V. G., and Mayhew, P. (eds.), *Designing Out Crime*. London: H.M.S.O.
MAYHEW, P., CLARKE, R. V. G., STURMAN, A., and HOUGH, J. M. (1976): *Crime as Opportunity*. Home Office Research Study No. 34. London: H.M.S.O.
MAYS, J. B. (1954): *Growing Up in the City*. Liverpool: University Press.
MAYS, J. B. (ed.) (1972): *Juvenile Delinquency: The Family and The Social Group; A Reader*. London: Longmans.
MEDNICK, S. A., MOFFIT, T., POLLOCK, V., TALOVIC, S., and GABRIELLI, W. (1983): 'The inheritance of human deviance'. In Magnusson, D., and Allen, V. (eds.), *Human Development: An interactional perspective*. New York and London: Academic Press (in press).
MEEHL, P. E., and ROSEN, A. (1955): 'Antecedent probability and the efficiency of psychiatric signs, patterns or cutting scores'. *Psychol. Bull.*, **52**, 194–216.

MELLSOP, G. W. (1972): 'Psychiatric patients seen as children and adults: childhood predictors of adult illness'. *J. Child Psychol. Psychiat.*, **13**, 91–101.
MERTON, R. K. (1938): 'Social structure and anomie'. *Amer. Sociol. Rev.*, **3**, 672–82.
MERTON, R. K. (1957): *Social Theory and Social Structure*. New York: Free Press.
MEYER, H. J., BORGATTA, E. F., and JONES, W. C. (1965): *Girls at Vocational High*. New York: Russell Sage.
MICHAEL, C. M. (1957): 'Relative incidence of criminal behavior in long term follow-up studies of shy children'. *Dallas Medical Journal*, January 1957.
MICHAEL, C. M., MORRIS, D. P., and SOROKER, E. (1957): 'Follow-up studies of shy, withdrawn children. II. Relative incidence of schizophrenia'. *Amer. J. Orthopsychiat.*, **27**, 331–7.
MILGRAM, S., and SHOTLAND, R. L. (1973): *Television and Antisocial Behavior: field experiments*. New York: Academic Press.
MILLHAM, S., BULLOCK, R., and CHERRETT, P. (1975): *After Grace – Teeth: A comparative study of the residential experiences of boys in approved schools*. London: Human Context Books.
MILLHAM, S., BULLOCK, R., and HOSIE, K. (1978): *Locking Up Children: Secure Provision Within the Child-Care System*. Farnborough: Saxon House.
MINDE, K., and MINDE, R. (1977): 'Behavioural screening of pre-school children – A new approach to mental health?' In Graham, P. J. (ed.), *Epidemiological Approaches in Child Psychiatry*, 139–64. London: Academic Press.
MINISTRY OF EDUCATION (1955): *Report of the Committee on Maladjusted Children*. London: H.M.S.O.
MISCHEL, W. (1979): 'On the interface of cognition and personality: beyond the person-situation debate'. *Amer. Psychol.*, **34**, 740–54.
MOLLING, P., LOCKNER, A., SAULS, R. J., and EISENBERG, L. (1962): 'Committed delinquent boys. The impact of perphenazine and of placebo'. *Arch. Gen. Psychiat.*, **7**, 70–76.
MOORE, D. R., CHAMBERLAIN, P., and MUKAI, L. H. (1979): 'Children at risk for delinquency: a follow-up comparison of aggressive children and children who steal'. *J. Abnorm. Child Psychol.*, **7**, 345–55.
MOORE, R. (1975): *Racism and Black Resistance*. London: Plato.
MORRIS, A. (1976): 'Juvenile Justice – where next?' *Howard J.*, **15**, 26–37.
MORRIS, A., and GILLER, H. (1979): 'Juvenile justice and social work in Britain'. In Parker, H. (ed.), *Social Work and the Courts*. London: Edward Arnold.
MORRIS, A., GILLER, H., SZWED, E., and GEACH, H. (1980): *Justice for Children*. London: Macmillan.
MORRIS, H. H. JR., ESCOLL, P. J., and WEXLER, R. (1956): 'Aggressive behavior disorders of childhood: A follow-up study'. *Amer. J. Psychiat.*, **112**, 991–7.
MORRIS, N., and TONRY, M. (eds.) (1979): *Crime and Justice: An Annual Review of Research, Vol. 1*. Chicago: University of Chicago Press.
MORRIS, P., and HEAL, K. (1981): *Crime Control and the Police: a review of research*. Home Office Research Study No. 67. London: H.M.S.O.
MORRIS, T. (1957): *The Criminal Area*. London: Routledge & Kegan Paul.

MORRIS, T. (1976): *Deviance and Control: the secular heresy*. London: Hutchinson.
MORRISON, J., and STEWART, M. (1973): 'The psychiatric status of the legal families of adopted hyperactive children'. *Arch. Gen. Psychiat.*, **28**, 888–91.
MORTIMORE, P. (1978): *Schools as Institutions: A Comparative Study of Secondary Schools*. Ph.D. thesis, University of London.
MOTT, J. (1969): *The Jesness Inventory: Application to Approved School Boys*. London: H.M.S.O.
MOTT, J. (1973): 'London juvenile drug offenders'. *Brit. J. Criminol.*, **13**, 209–17.
MOTT, J. (1977): 'Decision making and social inquiry reports in one juvenile court'. *Brit. J. Social Work*, **7**, 431–2.
MRAD, D. (1979): 'The effect of differential follow-up on rearrests: a critique of Quay and Love'. *Criminal Justice & Behavior*, **6**, 23–9.
MULLIGAN, G., DOUGLAS, J. W. B., HAMMOND, W. A., and TIZARD, J. (1963): 'Delinquency and symptoms of maladjustment'. *Proc. Roy. Soc. Med.*, **56**, 1083–6.
MURCHISON, N. (1974): 'Illustrations of the difficulties of some children in one-parent families'. In Finer, M. (1974), Vol. 2, 364–87.
MURDOCH, G., and MCCRON, R. (1976): 'Youth and class'. In Mungham, G., and Pearson, G. (eds.), *Working Class Youth Cultures*. London: Routledge & Kegan Paul.
MURPHY, G. E., and WETZEL R. D. (1980): 'Suicide risk by birth cohort in the United States, 1949 to 1974'. *Arch. Gen. Psychiat.*, **37**, 519–23.
MURPHY, L. B., and MORIARTY, A. E. (1976): *Vulnerability, Coping, and Growth*. New Haven, Conn.: Yale University Press.
N.A.C.R.O. (1978): *Vandalism: An Approach through Consultation; a pilot project*. London: Barry Rose.
NATIONAL COMMISSION ON MARIJUANA AND DRUG ABUSE (1973): *Drug Use in America: problems of perspective*. Second Report of the Commission. Washington, D.C.: U.S. Government Printing Office.
NATIONAL INSTITUTE OF MENTAL HEALTH (1982): *Television and Behavior: Ten Years of Scientific Progress and Implications for the Eighties. Vol. 1: Summary Report*. D.H.H.S. Publication No. (ADM) 82-1195. Bethesda, Md: U.S. Department of Health and Human Sciences.
NEEDHAM, B. (1977): *How Cities Work: An Introduction*. Oxford: Pergamon.
NEWCOMB, T., KOENIG, K. E., FLACKS, R., and WARWICK, D. P. (1967): *Persistence and Change: Bennington College and Its Students after Twenty-five Years*. New York: Wiley.
NEWMAN, O. (1973a): *Defensible Space*. London: Architectural Press.
NEWMAN, O. (1973b): *Architectural Design for Crime Prevention*. Washington, D.C.: U.S. Government Printing Office.
NEWMAN, O. (1975): 'Reactions to the "Defensible Space" study and some further findings'. *Int. J. Mental Health*, **4**, 48–70.
NEWMAN, O. (1976): *Design Guidelines for Creating Defensible Space*. Washington, D.C.: U.S. Government Printing Office.

NICOL, A. R. (1971): 'Psychiatric disorder in the children of Caribbean immigrants'. *J. Child Psychol. Psychiat.*, **12**, 233–81.

NIELSEN, J., and NORDLAND, E. (1975): 'Length of Y chromosome and activity in boys'. *Clin. Genet.*, **8**, 291–6.

NOBLIT, G. (1976): 'The adolescent experience and delinquency'. *Youth and Society*, **8**, 27–44.

NORMANDEAU, A. (1970): 'Canadian Criminal Statistics – Not Again!' *Canad. J. Corrections*, **12**, 198–206.

NYE, F. I. (1958): *Family Relationships and Delinquent Behavior*. New York: Wiley.

NYLANDER, I. (1960): 'Children of alcoholic fathers'. *Acta Paediat. Scand.*, Suppl. 121.

NYLANDER, I. (1979): 'A 20-year prospective follow-up study of 2164 cases at the child guidance clinics in Stockholm'. *Acta Paediat. Scand.*, Suppl. 276.

O'DONNELL, C. R. (1977): 'Behavior modification in community settings'. In Hersen, M., Eisler, R. M., and Miller, P. M. (eds.), *Progress in Behavior Modification, Vol. 4*, 69–117. New York: Academic Press.

O'DONNELL, C. R., LYDGATE, T., and FO, W. S. O. (1979): 'The Buddy System: review and follow-up'. *Child Behavior Therapy*, **1**, 161–9.

OFFICE OF POPULATION CENSUSES AND SURVEYS (1978): *Trends in Mortality 1951–75*. London: H.M.S.O.

OFFICE OF POPULATION CENSUSES AND SURVEYS (1979): *Population Trends, 15*. London: H.M.S.O.

OFFICE OF POPULATION CENSUSES AND SURVEYS, SOCIAL SURVEY DIVISION (1981): General Household Survey, No. 9, 1979. London: H.M.S.O.

OFFORD, D. R. (1982): 'Family backgrounds of male and female delinquents'. In Gunn, J., and Farrington, D. P. (eds.), *Abnormal Offenders: Delinquency and the Criminal Justice System*, 129–51. Chichester: Wiley.

OFFORD, D. R., POUSHINSKY, M. F., and SULLIVAN, K. (1978): 'School performance, IQ and delinquency'. *Brit. J. Criminol.*, **18**, 110–27.

OFFORD, D. R., SULLIVAN, K., ALLEN, N., and ABRAMS, N. (1979): 'Delinquency and hyperactivity'. *J. Nerv. Ment. Dis.*, **167**, 734–41.

OLIVER, I. T. (1973): 'The Metropolitan Police juvenile bureau scheme'. *Criminal Law Rev.*, 499–506.

OLIVER, I. T. (1978): *The Metropolitan Police Approach to the Prosecution of Juvenile Offenders*. London: Peel Press.

OLWEUS, D. (1979): 'Stability of aggressive reaction patterns in males: a review'. *Psychol. Bull.*, **86**, 852–75.

OLWEUS, D. (1980a): 'The consistency issue in personality psychology revisited – with special reference to aggression'. *Brit. J. Soc. Clin. Psychol.*, **19**, 377–90.

OLWEUS, D. (1980b): 'Familial and temperamental determinants of aggressive behavior in adolescent boys: a causal analysis'. *Develop. Psychol.*, **16**, 644–660.

OLWEUS, D., MATTSON, A., SCHALLING, D., and LÖW, H. (1980): 'Testosterone, aggression, physical and personality dimensions in normal adolescent males'. *Psychosom. Med.*, **42**, 253–69.

ORRIS, J. B. (1969): 'Visual monitoring performance in three subgroups of male delinquents'. *J. Abnorm. Psychol.*, **74**, 227–9.

OSBORN, S. G. (1980): 'Moving home, leaving London and delinquent trends'. *Brit. J. Criminol.*, **20**, 54–61.

OSBORN, S. G., and WEST, D. J. (1978): 'The effectiveness of various predictors of criminal careers'. *J. Adolescence*, **1**, 101–17.

OSBORN, S. G., and WEST, D. J. (1979): 'Conviction records of fathers and sons compared'. *Brit. J. Criminol.*, **19**, 120–33.

OSBORN, S. G., and WEST, D. J. (1980): 'Do young delinquents really reform?' *J. Adolescence*, **3**, 99–114.

OUSTON, J. (1983): 'Delinquency, family background and educational attainment'. *Brit. J. Criminol.* (accepted for publication.)

PABLANT, P., and BAXTER, J. C. (1975): 'Environmental correlates of school vandalism'. *Amer. Institute of Planners J.*, **241**, 270–79.

PAHL, R. E. (1970a): *Patterns of Urban Life*. London: Longmans.

PAHL, R. E. (1970b): *Whose City?* London: Longmans.

PALMAI, G., STOREY, P. B., and BRISCOE, O. (1967): 'Social class and the young offender'. *Brit. J. Psychiat.*, **113**, 1073–82.

PALMER, T. B. (1973): 'Matching worker and client in corrections'. *Social Work*, **18**, 95–103.

PALMER, T. B. (1974): 'The Youth Authority's Community Treatment Project'. *Federal Probation*, **38**, 3–14.

PALMER, T. (1975): 'Martinson revisited'. *J. Res. Crime & Delinq.*, **12**, 133–52.

PARKE, R. D., BERKOWITZ, L., LEYENS, J. P., WEST, S., and SEBASTIAN, R. J. (1977): 'Film violence and aggression: a field experimental analysis'. In Berkowitz, L. (ed.), *Advances in Experimental Social Psychology, Vol. 10*. New York: Academic Press.

PARKER, H. (1974): *View from the Boys*. Newton Abbot: David & Charles.

PARKER, H., CASBURN, M., and TURNBULL, D. (1981): *Receiving Juvenile Justice*. Oxford: Basil Blackwell.

PARSLOE, P. (1978): *Juvenile Justice in Britain and the United States*. London: Routledge & Kegan Paul.

PASAMANICK, B., and KNOBLOCH, H. (1966): 'Retrospective studies on the epidemiology of reproductive casualty: old and new'. *Merrill-Palmer Quart.*, **12**, 7–26.

PASSINGHAM, R. E. (1972): 'Crime and personality: a review of Eysenck's theory'. In Nebylitsyn, V. D., and Gray, J. S. (eds.), *Biological Bases of Individual Behaviour*, 342–71. London: Academic Press.

PATTERSON, G. R. (1974): 'Interventions for boys with conduct problems: multiple settings, treatments and criteria'. *J. Consult. Clin. Psychol.*, **43**, 471–81.

PATTERSON, G. R. (1976): 'The aggressive child: victim and architect of a coercive system'. In Hamerlynck, L. A., Handy, L. C., and Mash, E. J. (eds.), *Behavior Modification and Families. I. Theory and Research*, 367–76. New York: Brunner/Mazel.

PATTERSON, G. R. (1977): 'Accelerating stimuli for two classes of coercive behaviors'. *J. Abnorm. Child Psychol.*, **5**, 335–50.

PATTERSON, G. R. (1979): 'A performance theory for coercive family interaction'. In Cairns, R. B. (ed.), *The Analysis of Social Interactions: Methods, Issues and Illustrations*, 119–62. Hillsdale, N.J.: Erlbaum.

PATTERSON, G. R. (1980): 'Treatment for children with conduct problems: a review of outcome studies'. In Feshbach, S., and Fraczek, A. (eds.), *Aggression and Behavior Change: Biological and Social Processes*, 83–132. New York: Praeger.

PATTERSON, G. R. (1981a): 'Some speculations and data relating to children who steal'. In Hirschi, T., and Gottfredson, M. (eds.), *Theory and Fact in Contemporary Criminology*. Beverly Hills, Calif.: Sage Publ.

PATTERSON, G. R. (1981b): 'Mothers: The Unacknowledged Victims'. *Monogr. Soc. Res. Child Develop.*, **46**, No. 5, 1–63.

PATTERSON, G. R. (1982): *Coercive Family Processes*. Eugene, Oregon: Castalia Publ. Co.

PATTERSON, G. R., COBB, J. A., and RAY, R. S. (1973): 'A social engineering technology for retraining the families of aggressive boys'. In Adams, H. E., and Unikel, I. P. (eds.), *Issues and Trends in Behavior Therapy*, 139–224. Springfield, Ill.: Chas C. Thomas.

PATTERSON, G. R., and FLEISCHMAN, M. J. (1979): 'Maintenance of treatment effects: some considerations concerning family systems and follow-up data'. *Behav. Therapy*, **10**, 168–85.

PEARCE, D., and FARID, S. (1977): 'Illegitimate births: changing patterns'. *Population Trends*, **9**, 20–23.

PEARCE, K. (1974): 'West Indian boys in community home schools'. *Community Schools Gazette*, **68**, 317–39 and 376–407.

PEARSON, G. (1975): *The Deviant Imagination*. London: Macmillan.

PEASE, K., and WOLFSON, J. (1979): 'Incapacitation studies: a review and commentary'. *Howard J.*, **18**, 160–67.

PERSONS, R. W. (1966): 'Psychological and behavioral change in delinquents following psychotherapy'. *J. Clin. Psychol.*, **22**, 337–40.

PERSONS, R. W. (1967): 'Relationship between psychotherapy with institutionalized boys and subsequent community adjustment'. *J. Consult. Psychol.*, **31**, 137–41.

PHILLIPS, E. L. (1968): '"Achievement Place": Token reinforcement procedures in a home-style rehabilitation setting for "pre-delinquent" boys'. *J. Appl. Behav. Anal.*, **1**, 213–23.

PHILLIPS, E. L., PHILLIPS, E. A., FIXSEN, D. L., and WOLF, M. M. (1971): 'Achievement Place: modification of the behaviors of pre-delinquent boys within a token economy'. *J. Appl. Behav. Anal.*, **4**, 45–59.

PHILLIPS, J. C., and KELLY, D. H. (1979): 'School failure and delinquency: What causes which?' *Criminology*, **17**, 194–207.

PHILLIPS, L., VOTEY, H. L., and MAXWELL, D. (1972): 'Crime, youth and the labour market'. *J. Political Economy*, **80**, 491–504.

PHILLIPSON, M. (1971): *Sociological Aspects of Crime and Delinquency*. London: Routledge & Kegan Paul.

PIERCY, F., and LEE, R. (1976): 'Effects of a dual treatment approach on the rehabilitation of habitual juvenile delinquents'. *Rehabilitation Counselling Bull.*, **19**, 482–91.

PILIAVIN, I., and BRIAR, S. (1964): 'Police encounters with juveniles'. *Amer. J. Sociol.*, **70**, 206–14.

PILLING, D., and PRINGLE, M. K. (1978): *Controversial Issues in Child Development.* London: Paul Elek.

PLUMMER, K. (1979): 'Misunderstanding Labelling Perspectives'. In Downes, D., and Rock, P. (eds.), *Deviant Interpretations.* London: Martin Robertson.

POLLAK, M. (1972): *Today's Three Year Olds in London.* London: Heinemann/S.I.M.P.

PONTELL, H. N. (1978): 'Deterrence: theory versus practice'. *Criminology*, **16**, 3–46.

PORTER, B., and O'LEARY, K. D. (1980): 'Marital discord and childhood behavior problems'. *J. Abnorm. Child Psychol.*, **8**, 287–96.

POST OFFICE TELECOMMUNICATIONS (1979): personal communication.

POWELL, G. E. (1977): 'Psychoticism and social deviancy in children'. *Adv. Behav. Res. & Therapy*, **1**, 27–56.

POWER, M. J., ALDERSON, M. R., PHILLIPSON, C. M., SCHOENBERG, E., and MORRIS, J. N. (1967): 'Delinquent schools?' *New Society*, **10**, 542–3.

POWER, M. J., ASH, P. M., SCHOENBERG, E., and SOREY, E. C. (1974): 'Delinquency and the family'. *Brit. J. Social Work*, **4**, 13–38.

POWER, M. J., BENN, R. T., and MORRIS, J. N. (1972): 'Neighbourhood, school and juveniles before the courts'. *Brit. J. Criminol.*, **12**, 111–32.

POWERS, E., and WITMER, H. (1951): *An Experiment in the Prevention of Delinquency: The Cambridge-Somerville Youth Study.* New York: Columbia University Press.

PRESIDENT'S COMMISSION ON LAW ENFORCEMENT AND ADMINISTRATION OF JUSTICE (1967): *The Challenge of Crime in a Free Society.* Washington, D.C.: U.S. Government Printing Office.

PRIESTLEY, P., FEARS, D., and FULLER, R. (1977): *Justice for Juveniles.* London: Routledge & Kegan Paul.

PRINGLE, M. L. K. (1974): *The Needs of Children.* London: Hutchinson.

PRINGLE, M. L. K., and BOSSIO, V. (1960): 'Early prolonged separations and emotional adjustment'. *J. Child Psychol. Psychiat.*, **1**, 37–48.

PRINGLE, M. L. K., and CLIFFORD, L. (1964): 'Conditions associated with emotional maladjustment among children in care'. *Educ. Rev.*, **14**, 112–23.

PRYCE, K. (1979): *Endless Pressure.* Harmondsworth: Penguin.

QUADAGNO, D. M., BRISCOE, R., and QUADAGNO, J. S. (1977): 'Effect of perinatal gonadal hormones on selected nonsexual behavior patterns: a critical assessment of the nonhuman and human literature'. *Psychol. Bull.*, **84**, 62–80.

QUAY, H. C. (1965): 'Psychopathic personality as pathological stimulation-seeking'. *Amer. J. Psychiat.*, **122**, 180–83.

QUAY, H. C. (1977a): 'Psychopathic behavior: reflections on its nature, origins and treatment'. In Uzgiris, I. C., and Weizmann, F. (eds.), *The Structuring of Experience*, 371–83. New York: Plenum.

QUAY, H. C. (1977b): 'The three faces of evaluation: what can be expected to work'. *Criminal Justice & Behavior*, **4**, 341–54.

QUAY, H. C. (1979): 'Classification'. In Quay, H. C., and Werry, J. S. (eds.), *Psychopathological Disorders of Childhood*, 2nd edition, 1–42. New York: Wiley.

QUAY, H. C., and LOVE, C. T. (1977): 'The effect of a juvenile diversion program on rearrests'. *Criminal Justice & Behavior*, **4**, 377–96.

QUINNEY, R. (1970): *Explaining Crime*. Boston: Little Brown.

QUINTON, D. (1980): 'Family life in the inner city: Myth and reality'. In Marland, M. (ed.), *Education for the Inner City*. London: Heinemann Educational.

QUINTON, D., and RUTTER, M. (1976): 'Early hospital admissions and later disturbances of behaviour: An attempted replication of Douglas's findings'. *Develop. Med. Child Neurol.*, **18**, 447–59.

QUINTON, D., and RUTTER, M. (1983a): 'Parents with children in care. I. Current circumstances and parenting skills'. *J. Child Psychol. Psychiat.* (in press).

QUINTON, D., and RUTTER, M. (1983b): 'Parents with children in care. II. Intergenerational continuities'. *J. Child Psychol. Psychiat.* (in press).

QUINTON, D., RUTTER, M., and ROWLANDS, O. (1976): 'An evaluation of an interview assessment of marriage'. *Psychol. Med.*, **6**, 577–86.

RADZINOWICZ, L., and KING, J. (1977): *The Growth of Crime*. London: Hamish Hamilton.

RAYNOR, L. (1980): *The Adopted Child Comes of Age*. London: Allen & Unwin.

RECKLESS, W. C., and DINITZ, S. (1967): 'Pioneering with self-concept as a vulnerability factor in delinquency'. *J. Crim. Law, Criminol. & Police Science*, **58**, 515–23.

RECKLESS, W., and DINITZ, S. (1972): *The Prevention of Juvenile Delinquency*. Columbus: Ohio State University Press.

REDFERING, D. L. (1972): 'Group counseling with institutionalized delinquent females'. *Amer. Corrective Therapy J.*, **26**, 160–63.

REDFERING, D. L. (1973): 'Durability of effects of group counseling with institutionalized delinquent females'. *J. Abnorm. Psychol.*, **82**, 85–6.

REES, L. (1973): 'Constitutional factors and abnormal behaviour'. In Eysenck, H. J. (ed.), *Handbook of Abnormal Psychology*, 2nd edition, 487–539. London: Pitman Medical.

REID, J. B., and PATTERSON, G. R. (1976): 'Follow-up analyses of behavioral treatment program for boys with conduct problems: a reply to Kent'. *J. Consult. Clin. Psychol.*, **44**, 299–302.

REIN, M., and WHITE, S. H. (1977): 'Policy research: belief and doubt'. *Policy Analysis*, **3**, 239–71.

REINISCH, J. M., and KAROW, W. G. (1977): 'Prenatal exposure to synthetic progestins and estrogens: effects on human development'. *Arch. Sex. Behav.*, **6**, 257–88.

REISS, A. J. (1971): *The Police and the Public*. New Haven: Yale University Press.

REISS, A., and RHODES, A. (1961): 'The distribution of juvenile delinquency in the social class structure'. *Amer. Sociol. Rev.*, **26**, 730–32.

REISS, A. J., and RHODES, A. L. (1964): 'An empirical test of differential association theory'. *J. Res. Crime & Delinq.*, **1**, 5–18.

REISS, I. L. (1976): *Family Systems in America*, 2nd edition. Hinsdale, Ill.: The Dorsey Press.
REKER, G. T., CÔTÉ, J. E., and PEACOCK, E. J. (1980): 'Juvenile diversion; conceptual issues and program effectiveness'. *Canad. J. Criminol.*, **22**, 36–50.
REMSCHMIDT, H., HOHNER, G., and MERSCHMANN, W. (1977): 'Epidemiology of delinquent behaviour in children'. In Graham, P. J. (ed.), *Epidemiological Approaches in Child Psychiatry*, 253–74. London: Academic Press.
REPPETTO, T. A. (1974): *Residential Crime*. Cambridge, Mass.: Ballinger.
REX, J., and MOORE, R. (1967): *Race, Community and Conflict*. London: Oxford University Press for the Institute of Race Relations.
REYNOLDS, D., JONES, D., and ST LEGER, S. (1976): 'Schools do make a difference'. *New Society*, **37**, 321.
REYNOLDS, D., JONES, D., ST LEGER, S., and MURGATROYD, S. (1980): 'School factors and truancy'. In Hersov, L., and Berg, I. (eds.), *Out of School: Modern Perspectives in Truancy and School Refusal*, 85–110. Chichester: Wiley.
REYNOLDS, D., and MURGATROYD, S. (1977): 'The sociology of schooling and the absent pupil: the school as a factor in the generation of truancy'. In Carroll, H. C. M. (ed.), *Absenteeism in South Wales: Studies of Pupils, Their Homes and Their Secondary Schools*. Swansea: Faculty of Education, University of Swansea.
REZMOVIC, E. L. (1979): 'Methodological considerations in evaluating correctional effectiveness: issues and chronic problems'. In Sechrest, L., White, S. O., and Brown, E. D. (eds.), *The Rehabilitation of Criminal Offenders: Problems and Prospects*. National Research Council Report. Washington, D.C.: National Academy of Sciences.
RICH, J. (1956): 'Types of stealing'. *Lancet*, **1**, 496–8.
RICHMAN, N. (1977): 'Disorders in pre-school children'. In Rutter, M., and Hersov, L. (eds.), *Child Psychiatry: Modern Approaches*. Oxford: Blackwell Scientific.
RICHMAN, N., STEVENSON, J., and GRAHAM, P. J. (1982): *Pre-school to School: A behavioural study*. London: Academic Press.
RICHMOND, A. H. (1954): *Colour Prejudice in Britain: A study of West Indian workers in Liverpool, 1942–1951*. London: Routledge & Kegan Paul.
RICHMOND, A. H. (1973): *Migration and Race Relations in an English City: A study in Bristol*. London: Oxford University Press/Institute of Race Relations.
RIE, H. E., and RIE, E. D. (eds.) (1980): *Handbook of Minimal Brain Dysfunction: A critical view*. New York: Wiley.
RILEY, D. (1980): 'An evaluation of a campaign to reduce car thefts'. In Clarke, R. V. G., and Hough, J. M. (eds.), *The Effectiveness of Policing*, 113–25. Farnborough: Gower.
RISLEY, T. R., and BAER, D. M. (1973): 'Operant behavior modification: the deliberate development of behavior'. In Caldwell, B. M., and Ricciuti, H. N. (eds.), *Review of Child Development Research Vol. 3, Child Development and Social Policy*. Chicago: University of Chicago Press.
ROBIN, G. D. (1970): 'The corporate and judicial dispositions of employee thieves'. In

Smigel, E. O., and Ross, H. L. (eds.), *Crimes Against Bureaucracy*, 124–46. New York: Van Nostrand Reinhold.

ROBINS, L. (1966): *Deviant Children Grown Up*. Baltimore: Williams & Wilkins.

ROBINS, L. (1978): 'Sturdy childhood predictors of adult antisocial behaviour: replications from longitudinal studies'. *Psychol. Med.*, **8**, 611–22.

ROBINS, L. (1979): 'Longitudinal methods in the study of normal and pathological development'. In Kisker, K. P., Meyer, J.-E., Müller, C., and Stromgren, E. (eds.), *Psychiatrie der Gegenwart, Band 1. 'Grundlagen und Methoden der Psychiatrie'*, 2 Auflage. Heidelberg: Springer-Verlag.

ROBINS, L. N., DAVIS, D. H., and WISH, E. (1977): 'Detecting predictors of rare events: demographic, family and personal deviance as predictors of stages in the progression toward narcotic addiction'. In Strauss, J. S., Babigian, H. M., and Roff, M. (eds.), *The Origins and Course of Psychopathology*, 379–406. New York and London: Plenum.

ROBINS, L. N., GYMAN, H., and O'NEAL, P. (1962): 'The interaction of social class and deviant behavior'. *Amer. Sociol. Rev.*, **27**, 480–92.

ROBINS, L., and HILL, S. Y. (1966): 'Assessing the contributions of family structure, class and peer groups to juvenile delinquency'. *J. Crim. Law, Criminol. & Police Science.*, **57**, 325–34.

ROBINS, L. N., and LEWIS, R. G. (1966): 'The role of the antisocial family in school completion and delinquency: a three-generation study'. *Sociol. Quart*, **7**, 500–514.

ROBINS, L. N., and RATCLIFF, K. S. (1979): 'Risk factors in the continuation of childhood antisocial behaviors into adulthood'. *Int. J. Ment. Health*, **1**, 96–116.

ROBINS, L. N., and RATCLIFF, K. S. (1980a): 'Childhood conduct disorders and later arrest'. In Robins, L. N., Clayton, P., and Wing, J. (eds.), *Social Consequences of Psychiatric Illness*, 248–63. New York: Brunner/Mazel.

ROBINS, L. N., and RATCLIFF, K. S. (1980b): 'The long-term outcome of truancy'. In Hersov, L., and Berg, I. (eds.), *Out of School: Modern Perspectives in Truancy and School Refusal*, 65–83. Chichester: Wiley.

ROBINS, L. N., RATCLIFF, K. S., and WEST, P. A. (1979): 'School achievement in two generations: A study of 88 urban black families'. In Shamsie, S. J. (ed.), *New Directions in Children's Mental Health*, 105–29. New York: S.P. Medical and Scientific Books.

ROBINS, L. N., and TARBLESON, M. H. (1972): 'An actuarial method for assessing the direction of influence between two datable life events'. *Sociological Methods and Research*, **1**, 243–70.

ROBINS, L., WEST, P. A., and HERJANIC, B. L. (1975): 'Arrests and delinquency in two generations: a study of black urban families and their children'. *J. Child Psychol. Psychiat.*, **16**, 125–40.

ROBINS, L. N., and WISH, E. (1977): 'Childhood deviance as a developmental process: a study of 223 urban black men from birth to 18'. *Social Forces*, **56**, 4468–73.

ROBINSON, W. S. (1950): 'Ecological correlations and the behavior of individuals'. *Amer. Sociol. Rev.*, **15**, 351–7.

ROFF, M., SELLS, S. B., and GOLDEN, M. M. (1972): *Social Adjustment and Personality Development in Children*. Minneapolis: University of Minnesota Press.

ROHNER, R. P. (1975): *They Love Me, They Love Me Not: A world-wide study of the effects of parental acceptance and rejection*. New Haven, Conn.: H.R.A.F. Press.

ROSANOFF, A. J., HANDY, L. M., and PLESSEY, I. R. (1941): 'The etiology of child behavior difficulties, juvenile delinquency and adult criminality with special reference to their occurrence in twins'. *Psychiat. Monogr. (California)*, No. 1. Sacramento: Department of Institutions.

ROSE, G. (1967): 'Early identification of delinquents'. *Brit. J. Criminol.*, 7, 6–35.

ROSE, G. N. G. (1968): 'The artificial delinquent generation'. *J. Crim. Law, Criminol. & Police Science*, 59, 370–85.

ROSE, G., and MARSHALL, T. F. (1974): *Counselling and School Social Work: An experimental study*. London: Wiley.

ROSENTHAL, D., WENDER, P. H., KETY, S. S., SCHULSINGER, F., WELNER, J., and RIEDER, R. O. (1975): 'Parent-child relationships and psychopathological disorder in the child'. *Arch. Gen. Psychiat.*, 32, 466–76.

ROSS, D. M., and ROSS, S. A. (1976): *Hyperactivity: Research, Theory and Action*. New York: Wiley.

ROSS, H. (1937): 'Crime and the native born sons of European immigrants'. *J. Crimin. Law, Criminol. & Police Science*, 28, 202–9.

ROSS, H. L., CAMPBELL, D. T., and GLASS, G. V. (1970): 'Determining the social effects of a legal reform: the British "breathalyser" crackdown of 1967'. *Amer. Behav. Sci.*, 13, 493–509.

ROSS, R. R., and GENDREAU, P. (eds.) (1980): *Effective Correctional Treatment*. Toronto: Butterworths.

ROSS, R. R., and MCKAY, H. B. (1976): 'A study of institutional treatment programs'. *Int. J. Offender Therapy & Comparative Criminol.*, 20, 167–73.

ROSS, R. R., and MCKAY, B. (1978): 'Behavioral approaches to treatments and corrections: requiem for a panacea'. *Canad. J. Criminol.*, 20, 279–95.

ROSSI, P. H., WAITE, E., BOSE, C. E., and BERK, R. E. (1974): 'The seriousness of crimes, normative structure and individual differences'. *Amer. Sociol. Rev.*, 39, 224–37.

ROYAL COLLEGE OF PSYCHIATRISTS (1979): *Alcohol and Alcoholism*. London: Tavistock.

ROYAL COMMISSION ON THE DISTRIBUTION OF INCOME AND WEALTH (1978): *Report No. 6, Lower Incomes*. Chairman: Lord Diamond. London: H.M.S.O.

RUMBAUT, R. G., and BITTNER, E. (1979): 'Changing conception of the police role: a sociological review'. In Morris, N., and Tonry, M. (eds.), *Criminal Justice: An annual review of research*, Vol. 1, 239–88. Chicago and London: University of Chicago Press.

RUTHERFORD, A. (1981): 'Young offenders: comments on the White Paper on Young Adult and Juvenile Offenders'. *Brit. J. Criminol.*, 21, 74–8.

RUTTER, M. (1970): 'Sex differences in children's response to family stress'. In Anthony, E. J., and Koupernik, C. (eds.), *The Child in His Family*, 165–96. New York: Wiley.

RUTTER, M. (1971): 'Parent-child separation: psychological effects on the children'. *J. Child Psychol. Psychiat.*, **12**, 233–60.

RUTTER, M. (1977a): 'Separation, loss and family influences'. In Rutter, M., and Hersov, L. (eds.), *Child Psychiatry: Modern Approaches*, 47–73. Oxford: Blackwell Scientific.

RUTTER, M. (1977b): 'Other family influences'. In Rutter, M., and Hersov, L. (eds.), *Child Psychiatry: Modern Approaches*, 74–108. Oxford: Blackwell Scientific.

RUTTER, M. (1977c): 'Prospective studies to investigate behavioral change'. In Strauss, J. S., Babigian, H. M., and Roff, M. (eds.), *The Origins and Course of Psychopathology*. New York: Plenum.

RUTTER, M. (1978): 'Research and prevention of psychosocial disorders in childhood'. In Barnes, J., and Connolly, N. (eds.), *Social Care Research*. London: Bedford Square Press.

RUTTER, M. (1979a): *Changing Youth in a Changing Society*. London: Nuffield Provincial Hospitals Trust (1980, Cambridge, Mass.: Harvard University Press).

RUTTER, M. (1979b): 'Protective factors in children's responses to stress and disadvantage'. In Kent, M. W., and Rolf, J. E. (eds.), *Primary Prevention of Psychopathology: Vol. 3: Social Competence in Children*. Hanover, N. H.: University Press of New England.

RUTTER, M. (1980a): 'Raised lead levels and impaired cognitive/behavioural functioning: A review of the evidence'. Supplement No. 42 to *Develop. Med. Child Neurol.*, **22**, No. 1.

RUTTER, M. (1980b): 'Introduction'. In Rutter, M. (ed.), *Scientific Foundations of Developmental Psychiatry*, 1–8. London: Heinemann Medical.

RUTTER, M. (1981a): *Maternal Deprivation Reassessed* (2nd edition). Harmondsworth: Penguin.

RUTTER, M. (1981b): 'Social/emotional consequences of day care for pre-school children'. *Amer. J. Orthopsychiat.*, **51**, 4–28.

RUTTER, M. (1981c): 'The city and the child'. *Amer. J. Orthopsychiat.*, **51**, 610–25.

RUTTER, M. (1981d): 'Epidemiological/longitudinal strategies and causal research in child psychiatry'. *J. Amer. Acad. Child Psychiat.*, **20**, 513–44.

RUTTER, M. (1981e): 'Stress, coping and development: some issues and some questions'. *J. Child Psychol. Psychiat.*, **22**, 323–56.

RUTTER, M. (1981f): 'Psychological sequelae of brain damage in childhood'. *Amer. J. Psychiat.*, **138**, 1533–44.

RUTTER, M. (1982a): 'Syndromes attributed to "Minimal brain dysfunction" in children'. *Amer. J. Psychiat.*, **139**, 21–33.

RUTTER, M. (1982b): 'Epidemiological-longitudinal approaches to the study of development'. In Collins, W. A. (ed.), *The Concept of Development: Minnesota Symposia on Child Psychology, Vol. 15*. Hillsdale, N.J.: Erlbaum.

RUTTER, M. (1983): 'School effects on pupil progress: Research findings and policy implications'. *Child Dev.* (in press).

RUTTER, M., COX, A., TUPLING, C., BERGER, M., and YULE, W. (1975a): 'Attainment and adjustment in two geographical areas. I. The prevalence of psychiatric disorder'. *Brit. J. Psychiat.*, **126**, 493–509.

RUTTER, M., GRAHAM, P., CHADWICK, O., and YULE, W. (1976a): 'Adolescent turmoil: fact or fiction?' *J. Child Psychol. Psychiat.*, **17**, 35–56.

RUTTER, M., and MADGE, N. (1976): *Cycles of Disadvantage: A review of research.* London: Heinemann Educational.

RUTTER, M., MAUGHAN, B., MORTIMORE, P., OUSTON, J., with SMITH, A. (1979): *Fifteen Thousand Hours: Secondary schools and their effects on children.* London: Open Books; Cambridge, Mass: Harvard University Press.

RUTTER, M., and QUINTON, D. (1977): 'Psychiatric disorder – ecological factors and concepts of causation'. In McGurk, H. (ed.), *Ecological Factors in Human Development.* Amsterdam: North-Holland.

RUTTER, M., QUINTON, D., and LIDDLE, C. (1983): 'Parenting in two generations: Looking backwards and looking forwards'. In Madge, N. (ed.), *Families at Risk.* London: Heinemann Educational (in press).

RUTTER, M., and RUSSELL JONES, R. (eds.) (1983): *Lead Versus Health: Sources and effects of low level lead exposure.* Chichester: Wiley (in press).

RUTTER, M., SHAFFER, D., and SHEPHERD, M. (1975): *A Multi-axial Classification of Child Psychiatric Disorders.* Geneva: World Health Organization.

RUTTER, M., TIZARD, J., and WHITMORE, K. (eds.) (1970): *Education, Health and Behaviour.* London: Longmans.

RUTTER, M., TIZARD, J., YULE, W., GRAHAM, P., and WHITMORE, K. (1976b): 'Research Report: Isle of Wight Studies 1964–74'. *Psychol. Med.*, **6**, 313–32.

RUTTER, M., YULE, B., MORTON, J., and BAGLEY, C. (1975b): 'Children of West Indian immigrants: III. Home circumstances and family patterns'. *J. Child Psychol. Psychiat.*, **16**, 105–23.

RUTTER, M., YULE, B., QUINTON, D., ROWLANDS, O., YULE, W., and BERGER, M. (1975c): 'Attainment and adjustment in two geographical areas. III. Some factors accounting for area differences'. *Brit. J. Psychiat.*, **126**, 520–33.

RUTTER, M., and YULE, W. (1981): Unpublished data.

RUTTER, M., YULE, W., BERGER, M., YULE, B., MORTON, J., and BAGLEY, C. (1974): 'Children of West Indian immigrants. I. Rates of behavioural deviance and of psychiatric disorder'. *J. Child Psychol. Psychiat.*, **15**, 241–62.

RYDELIUS, P.-A. (1981): 'Children of alcoholic fathers: their social adjustment and their health status over 20 years'. *Acta Paediat. Scand.*, Suppl. 286.

SAINSBURY, P. (1955): *Suicide in London.* London: Chapman & Hall.

SAMEROFF, A. J., and CHANDLER, M. J. (1975): 'Reproductive risk and the continuum of caretaking casualty'. In Horowitz, F. D. (ed.), *Review of Child Development Research, Vol. 4.* Chicago: University of Chicago Press.

SANDBERG, S. T., RUTTER, M., and TAYLOR, E. (1978): 'Hyperkinetic disorder in psychiatric clinic attenders'. *Develop. Med. Child Neurol.*, **20**, 279–99.

SANDBERG, S. T., WIESELBERG, M., and SHAFFER, D. (1980): 'Hyperkinetic and conduct problem children in a primary school population: some epidemiological considerations'. *J. Child Psychol. Psychiat.*, **21**, 293–311.

SARASON, I. G. (1978): 'A cognitive social learning approach to juvenile delinquency'. In Hare, R., and Schalling, D. (eds.), *Psychopathic Behavior: Approaches to Research*, 299–317. New York: Wiley.

SARASON, I. G., and GANZER, V. J. (1973): 'Modeling and group discussion in the rehabilitation of juvenile delinquents'. *J. Counsel. Psychol.*, **20**, 442–9.

SARRI, R., and BRADLEY, P. W. (1980): 'Juvenile aid panels: an alternative to juvenile court processing in South Australia'. *Crime and Delinquency*, **26**, 42–62.

SCARMAN, LORD (1981): See HOME OFFICE (1981).

SCHMAUK, F. J. (1970): 'Punishment, arousal and avoidance learning in sociopaths'. *J. Abnorm. Psychol.*, **76**, 326–35.

SCHMIDT, D. E., and KEATING, J. P. (1979): 'Human crowding and personal control: an integration of the research'. *Psychol. Bull.*, **86**, 680–700.

SCHNELLE, J. F., KIRCHNER, R. E., GALBAUGH, F., DOMASH, M., CARR, A., and LARSON, L. (1979): 'Program evaluation research: an experimental cost-effectiveness analysis of an armed robbery intervention program'. *J. Appl. Behav. Anal.*, **12**, 615–23.

SCHNELLE, J. F., KIRCHNER, R. E., MCNEES, M. P., and LAWLER, J. M. (1975): 'Social evaluation research: the evaluation of two police patrolling strategies'. *J. Appl. Behav. Anal.*, **8**, 353–65.

SCHOENFELD, C. G. (1971): 'A psychoanalytic theory of juvenile delinquency'. *Crime & Delinq.*, **17**, 479–80.

SCHOFIELD, M. (1965): *The Sexual Behaviour of Young People*. London: Longmans.

SCHOFIELD, M. (1973): *The Sexual Behaviour of Young Adults*. London: Allen Lane.

SCHONELL, F. J. (1961): *The Psychology and Teaching of Reading*. Edinburgh: Oliver & Boyd.

SCHOOLS COUNCIL (1970): *Teaching English to West Indian Children*. Working Paper No. 29. London: Evans/Methuen Education.

SCHRAG, C. (1974): 'Theoretical foundations for a social science of corrections'. In Glaser, D. (ed.), *Handbook of Criminology*, 705–43. Chicago: Rand McNally.

SCHRAMM, W., LYLE, J., and PARKER, E. B. (1961): *Television in the Lives of Our Children*. Stanford, Calif.: Stanford University Press.

SCHUESSLER, K. F., and CRESSEY, D. B. (1950): 'Personality characteristics of criminals'. *Amer. J. Soc.*, **55**, 476–84.

SCHULSINGER, F. (1972): 'Psychopathy: Heredity and environment'. *Internat. J. Ment. Health*, **1**, 190–206.

SCHWARTZ, R. D., and ORLEANS, S. (1967): 'On legal sanctions'. *Univ. Chicago Law Review*, **34**, 274–300.

SCHWARTZ, R. D., and SKOLNICK, J. H. (1962): 'Two studies of legal stigma'. *Social Problems*, **10**, 133–42.

SCHWEINHART, L. J., and WEIKART, D. P. (1980): *Young Children Grow Up: The effects of the preschool program on youths through age 15*. Monogr. High/Scope Educ. Res. Found. No. 7. Ypsilanti, Michigan: The High/Scope Press.

SCOTT, P. D. (1965): 'Delinquency'. In Howells, J. G. (ed.), *Modern Perspectives in Child Psychiatry*. Edinburgh and London: Oliver & Boyd.

References 407

SECHREST, L., WHITE, S. O., and BROWN, E. D. (eds.) (1979): *The Rehabilitation of Criminal Offenders: Problems and Prospects.* National Research Council Report. Washington, D.C.: National Academy of Sciences.

SEGLOW, J., PRINGLE, M. K., and WEDGE, P. (1972): *Growing Up Adopted.* Slough: N.F.E.R.

SEIDMAN, E., RAPPAPORT, J., and DAVIDSON, W. S. (1980): 'Adolescents in legal jeopardy: initial success and replication of an alternative to the criminal justice system'. In Ross, R. R., and Gendreau, P. (eds.), *Effective Correctional Treatment,* 101–23. Toronto: Butterworths.

SELECT COMMITTEE ON RACE RELATIONS AND IMMIGRATION (1976–7): *The West Indian Community.* H.C. 180. London: H.M.S.O.

SELLIN, T. (1958): 'Recidivism and maturation'. *Nat. Probation and Parole Assoc. J.,* **4,** 241–50.

SELLIN, T., and WOLFGANG, M. (1964): *The Measurement of Delinquency.* New York: Wiley.

SHAFFER, D., MEYER-BAHLBURG, H. F. L., and STOCKMAN, C. L. J. (1980): 'The development of aggression'. In Rutter, M. (ed.), *Scientific Foundations of Developmental Psychiatry,* 353–68. London: Heinemann Medical.

SHAFFER, D., PETTIGREW, A., WOLKIND, S., and ZAJICEK, E. (1978): 'Psychiatric aspects of pregnancy in schoolgirls: a review'. *Psychol. Med.,* **8,** 119–30.

SHAPLAND, J. M. (1978): 'Self-reported delinquency in boys aged 11 to 14'. *Brit. J. Criminol.,* **18,** 255–66.

SHAW, C. R. (1929): *Delinquency Areas.* Chicago: University of Chicago Press.

SHAW, C. R., and MACKAY, H. D. (1942): *Juvenile Delinquency and Urban Areas.* Chicago: University of Chicago Press.

SHELDON, W. H., STEVENS, S., and TUCKER, W. B. (1940): *The Varieties of Human Physique.* New York: Harper.

SHEPHERD, M., OPPENHEIM, B., and MITCHELL, S. (eds.) (1971): *Childhood Behaviour and Mental Health.* London: University of London Press.

SHERWOOD, C. C., and WALKER, W. C. (1959): 'Some unanswered questions about Highfields'. *Amer. J. Correction.,* **21,** 8–27.

SHIELDS, J. (1977): 'Polygenic influences'. In Rutter, M., and Hersov, L. (eds.), *Child Psychiatry: Modern Approaches,* 22–46. Oxford: Blackwell Scientific.

SHOHAM, S., and SANDBERG, M. (1964): 'Suspended sentences in Israel: an evaluation of the preventive efficacy of prospective imprisonment'. *Crime & Delinq.,* **10,** 74–83.

SHOHAM, S., SHOHAM, N., and ABD-EL-RAZEK, A. (1966): 'Immigration, ethnicity and ecology as related to juvenile delinquency in Israel'. *Brit. J. Criminol.,* **6,** 391–409.

SHORE, M. F., and MASSIMO, J. L. (1966): 'Comprehensive vocationally oriented psychotherapy for adolescent delinquent boys: a follow-up study'. *Amer. J. Orthopsychiat.,* **36,** 609–15.

SHORE, M. F., and MASSIMO, J. L. (1973): 'After ten years: a follow-up study of comprehensive vocationally oriented psychotherapy'. *Amer. J. Orthopsychiat.,* **43,** 128–32.

SHORT, J. F. (1964): 'Gang delinquency and anomie'. In Clinard, M. B. (ed.), *Anomie and Deviant Behavior*. New York: Free Press.

SHURE, M., and SPIVACK, G. (1978): *Problem solving techniques in child rearing*. San Francisco: Jossey-Bass.

SIDDLE, D. A. T., MEDNICK, S. A., NICOL, A. R., and FOGGITT, R. H. (1976): 'Skin conductance recovery in anti-social adolescents'. *Brit. J. Soc. Clin. Psychol.*, **15**, 425–8.

SIDDLE, D. A. T., NICOL, A. R., and FOGGITT, R. H. (1973): 'Habituation and over-extinction of the GSR component of the orienting response in anti-social adolescents'. *Brit. J. Soc. Clin. Psychol.*, **12**, 303–8.

SIMON, F. H. (1971): *Prediction Methods in Criminology*. Home Office Research Study No. 7. London: H.M.S.O.

SIMONS, R. L., MILLER, M. G., and AIGNER, S. M. (1980): 'Contemporary theories of deviance and female delinquency: An empirical test'. *J. Res. Crime & Delinq.*, **17**, 42–56.

SINCLAIR, I. A. C. (1971): *Hostels for Probationers*. Home Office Research Study No. 6. London: H.M.S.O.

SINCLAIR, I. A. C., and CLARKE, R. V. G. (1973): 'Acting out behaviour and its significance for the residential treatment of delinquents'. *J. Child Psychol. Psychiat.*, **14**, 283–91.

SINCLAIR, I. A. C., and CLARKE, R. V. G. (1982): 'Predicting, treating and explaining delinquency: the lessons from research on institutions'. In Feldman, M. P. (ed.), *The Prevention and Control of Offending*. Chichester and New York: Wiley.

SINGER, S. I. (1978): 'A comment on alleged overreporting'. *Criminology*, **16**, 99–102.

SKOGAN, W. G. (1977): 'Dimensions of the dark figure of unreported crime'. *Crime & Delinq.*, **23**, 41–50.

SKOLNICK, J. H. (1966): *Justice without Trial: Law Enforcement in Democratic Society*. New York: Wiley.

SLAIKEU, K. A. (1973): 'Evaluation studies on group treatment of juvenile and adult offenders in correctional institutions: a review of the literature'. *J. Res. Crime & Delinq.*, **10**, 87–100.

SMART, C. (1977): *Women, Crime and Criminology: A feminist critique*. London: Routledge & Kegan Paul.

SMART, C. (1979): 'The new female criminal: reality or myth?' *Brit. J. Criminol.*, **19**, 50–59.

SMITH, C. S., FARRANT, M. R., and MARCHANT, H. J. (1972): *The Wincroft Youth Project: a social work programme in a slum area*. London: Tavistock.

SNYDER, J. J. (1977): 'A reinforcement analysis of interaction in problem and non-problem children'. *J. Abnorm. Psychol.*, **86**, 528–35.

SOCIAL SCIENCE RESEARCH COUNCIL AND SPORTS COUNCIL (1978): *A Joint Report, Public Disorder and Sporting Events*. London: The Sports Council/S.S.R.C.

SOOTHILL, K. L., and POPE, P. J. (1973): 'Arson: A Twenty-Year Cohort Study'. *Medicine, Science & the Law*, **13**, 127–38.

SORENSON, R. C. (1973): *Adolescent Sexuality in Contemporary America: personal*

values and sexual behaviour ages thirteen to nineteen. New York: World Publishing.
SPARKS, R. F., GENN, H. G., and DODD, D. J. (1977): *Surveying Victims*. Chichester: Wiley.
SPIVACK, G., PLATT, J., and SHURE, M. (1976): *The Problem Solving Approach to Adjustment*. San Francisco: Jossey-Bass.
SPRINGHALL, J. (1977): *Youth, Empire and Society*. London: Croom Helm.
STANFIELD, R. E. (1966): 'The interaction of family and gang variables in the aetiology of delinquency'. *Social Problems*, 13, 411–17.
START, K. B., and WELLS, B. K. (1972): *The Trend of Reading Standards*. Slough: N.F.E.R.
STEENHUIS, D. W. (1980): 'Experiments on police effectiveness: the Dutch experience'. In Clarke, R. V. G., and Hough, J. M. (eds.), *The Effectiveness of Policing*, 124–38. Farnborough: Gower.
STEFFENSMEIER, D. J. (1978): 'Crime and the contemporary woman: an analysis of changing levels of female property crime, 1960–75'. *Social Forces*, 57, 566–84.
STEFFENSMEIER, D. (1980): 'Sex differences in patterns of adult crime: a review and assessment'. *Social Forces*, 58, 1080–1108.
STEIN, A. H., and FRIEDRICH, L. K. (1975): 'Impact of television on children and youth'. In Hetherington, E. M. (ed.), *Review of Child Development Research, Vol. 5*, 183–256. Chicago and London: University of Chicago Press.
STEVENS, P., and WILLIS, C. F. (1979): *Race, Crime and Arrests*. Home Office Research Study No. 58. London: H.M.S.O.
STEWART, M. A., ADAMS, C. C., and MEARDON, J. K. (1978): 'Unsocialized aggressive boys: a follow-up study'. *J. Clin. Psychiat.*, 39, 797–9.
STEWART, M. A., DE BLOIS, C. S., and CUMMINGS, C. (1980): 'Psychiatric disorder in the parents of hyperactive boys and those with conduct disorder'. *J. Child Psychol. Psychiat.*, 21, 283–92.
STEWART, M. A., CUMMINGS, C., SINGER, S., and DE BLOIS, C. S. (1981): 'The overlap between hyperactive and unsocialized aggressive children'. *J. Child Psychol. Psychiat.*, 22, 35–46.
STONE, J., and TAYLOR, F. (1977): *Vandalism in Schools*. London: Save the Children Fund.
STOTT, D. H. (1960): 'The prediction of delinquency from non-delinquent behaviour'. *Brit. J. Delinq.*, 10, 195–210.
STOTT, D. H. (1966): *Studies of Troublesome Children*. London: Tavistock.
STOTT, D. H., and WILSON, D. M. (1977): 'The adult criminal as juvenile'. *Brit. J. Criminol.*, 17, 47–57.
STUART, R. B., JAYARATNE, S., and TRIPODI, T. (1976): 'Changing adolescent behavior through reprogramming the behavior of parents and teachers: an experimental evaluation'. *Canad. J. Behav. Sci.*, 8, 132–44.
STURGE, C. (1982): 'Reading retardation and antisocial behaviour'. *J. Child Psychol. Psychiat.*, 23, 21–31.
STURMAN, A. (1978): 'Measuring vandalism in a city suburb'. In Clarke, R. V. G. (ed.), *Tackling Vandalism*. Home Office Research Study No. 47. London: H.M.S.O.

SUGARMAN, B. (1967): 'Involvement in youth culture, academic achievement and conformity in school: an empirical study of London school boys'. *Brit. J. Sociol.*, **18**, 151–64.

SULLIVAN, C., GRANT, M. Q., and GRANT, J. D. (1957): 'The development of interpersonal maturity: applications to delinquency'. *Psychiatry*, **20**, 373–85.

SULLIVAN, D., and SEIGEL, L. (1972): 'How police use information to make decisions'. *Crime & Delinq.*, **18**, 253–62.

SUNDBY, H. S., and KREYBERG, P. C. (1968): *Prognosis in Child Psychiatry*. Baltimore: Williams & Wilkins.

SUSSENWEIN, F. (1977): 'Psychiatric social work'. In Rutter, M., and Hersov, L. (eds.), *Child Psychiatry: Modern Approaches*. Oxford: Blackwell Scientific.

SUTER, L. E., and MILLER, H. P. (1973): 'Income differences between men and career women'. In Huber, J. (ed.), *Changing Women in a Changing Society*. Chicago: University of Chicago Press.

SUTHERLAND, E. H. (1939): *Principles of Criminology*. Philadelphia: Lippincott.

SUTHERLAND, E., and CRESSEY, D. (1970): *Principles of Criminology*. Philadelphia: Lippincott.

TAIT, C. D., and HODGES, E. F. (1962): *Delinquents, Their Families and the Community*. Springfield, Ill.: Chas C. Thomas.

TANNER, J. M. (1970): 'Physical growth'. In Mussen, P. H. (ed.), *Carmichael's Manual of Child Psychology*, 3rd edition, Vol. 1, 77–155. New York: Wiley.

TARLING, R. (1979): *Sentencing Practice in Magistrates' Courts*. Home Office Research Study No. 56. London: H.M.S.O.

TAYLOR, F. (1978): 'How the graffiti disappeared from the ladies' loos'. *Education*, 27 September.

TAYLOR, I., and WALL, D. (1976): 'Beyond the Skinheads'. In Mungham, G., and Pearson, G. (eds.), *Working Class Youth Cultures*. London: Routledge & Kegan Paul.

TAYLOR, I., WALTON, P., and YOUNG, J. (1974): *The New Criminology*. New York: Harper & Row.

TAYLOR, J. H. (1976): *The Half-Way Generation: A Study of Asian youths in Newcastle upon Tyne*. Slough: N.F.E.R.

TAYLOR, M. (1971): *Study of the Juvenile Liaison Scheme in West Ham 1961–1965*. Home Office Research Study No. 8. London: H.M.S.O.

TENNENBAUM, D. J. (1977): 'Personality and criminality: a summary and implications of the literature'. *J. Crim. Justice*, **5**, 225–35.

TERRY, R. (1965): 'Discrimination in the handling of juvenile offenders by social control agencies'. In Garabedian, P., and Gibbons, D. (eds.), *Becoming Delinquent*. New York: Aldine Press.

THEANDER, S. (1970): 'Anorexia nervosa. A psychiatric investigation of 94 female patients'. *Acta Psychiat. Scand.*, Suppl. 214.

THOMPSON, J. (1976): 'Fertility and abortion inside and outside marriage'. *Population Trends*, No. 5, 3–8.

THORNBERRY, T. P. (1979): 'Sentencing disparities in the juvenile justice system'. *J. Criminal Law and Criminology*, **70**, 164–71.

THORNBERRY, T., and FIGLIO, R. M. (1978): 'Juvenile and Adult Offense Careers in the Philadelphia Birth Cohort of 1945'. Paper presented at the 1978 Annual Meeting of the American Society of Criminology.

THORNES, B., and COLLARD, J. (1979): *Who Divorces?* London: Routledge & Kegan Paul.

THORPE, D. (1977): *Services to Juvenile Offenders.* Unpublished paper, University of Lancaster.

THORPE, D., SMITH, D., GREEN, C., and PALEY, J. (1980): *Out of Care: The Community Support of Juvenile Offenders.* London: Allen & Unwin.

THORPE, J. (1979): *Social Inquiry Reports: A survey.* Home Office Research Study No. 48. London: H.M.S.O.

TIEGER, T. (1980): 'On the biological basis of sex differences in aggression'. *Child Develop.*, **51**, 943–63.

TITTLE, C. R., and LOGAN, C. H. (1973): 'Sanctions and deviance: evidence and remaining questions'. *Law and Society Review*, **7**, 371–92.

TITTLE, C. R., VILLEMEZ, W. J., and SMITH, D. A. (1978): 'The myth of social class and criminality: an empirical assessment of the empirical evidence'. *Amer. Sociol. Rev.*, **43**, 643–56.

TIZARD, B. (1977): *Adoption: a second chance.* London: Open Books.

TONGE, W. L., LUNN, J. E., GREATHEAD, M., MCLAREN, S., and BOSANKO, C. (1980): *Generations of Problem Families in Sheffield.* Report to the D.H.S.S./S.S.R.C. Working Party on Transmitted Deprivation. London: Social Science Research Council.

TOWNSEND, H. E. R., and BRITTAN, E. M. (1972): *Organization in Multiracial Schools.* Slough: N.F.E.R.

TOWNSEND, P. (1979): *Poverty in the United Kingdom: a survey of household resources and standards of living.* Harmondsworth: Penguin.

TRAMONTANA, M. G. (1980): 'Critical review of research on psychotherapy outcome with adolescents: 1967–1977'. *Psychol. Bull.*, **88**, 429–50.

TRASLER, G. B. (1973): 'Criminal Behaviour'. In Eysenck, H. J. (ed.), *Handbook of Abnormal Psychology*, 2nd edition. London: Pitman Medical.

TRASLER, G. B., and FARRINGTON, D. P. (eds.) (1979): *Behaviour Modification with Offenders: A Criminological Symposium.* Cambridge: Cambridge University Institute of Criminology.

TRISELIOTIS, J. (1978): 'Growing up fostered'. *Adoption and Fostering*, **94**, 11–23.

TRISELIOTIS, J. (1980): *A Retrospective Study of Adoption, Long-Term Foster Care and Residential Care of Children Identified as Having Special Needs.* Report to the D.H.S.S./S.S.R.C. London: Social Science Research Council.

TRIVIZAS, E. (1980): 'Offences and offenders in football crowd disorders'. *Brit. J. Criminol.*, **20**, 276–88.

TUTT, N. (1976): 'Recommittals of juvenile delinquents'. *Brit. J. Criminol.*, **16**, 385–8.

TWENTIETH CENTURY FUND TASK FORCE ON SENTENCING POLICY TOWARD YOUNG OFFENDERS (1978): *Confronting Youth Crime.* New York: Holmes & Meier.

UNITED NATIONS (1977): *Crime Prevention and Control.* New York: United Nations General Assembly.

U.S. BUREAU OF THE CENSUS (1977): *Statistical Abstract of the United States.* Washington, D.C.: U.S. Government Printing Office.

U.S. DEPARTMENT OF JUSTICE, FEDERAL BUREAU OF INVESTIGATION 1980): *Uniform Crime Reports.* Washington, D.C.: U.S. Government Printing Office.

UNITED STATES NATIONAL COMMISSION ON MARIJUANA AND DRUG ABUSE (1973): See NATIONAL COMMISSION ON MARIJUANA AND DRUG ABUSE.

URBAIN, E. S., and KENDALL, P. C. (1980): 'Review of social-cognitive problem-solving interventions with children'. *Psychol. Bull.*, **88**, 109–43.

VARLAAM, A. (1974): 'Educational attainment and behaviour at school'. *Greater London Intelligence Quarterly*, No. 29, 29–37.

VON HIRSCH, A. (1976): *Doing Justice: Committee for the Study of Incarceration.* New York: Hill & Wang.

VOSS, H. L. (1963): 'The predictive efficiency of the Glueck Social Prediction Scale'. *J. Crim. Law, Criminol. & Police Science*, **54**, 421–30.

VOTEY, H. L., and PHILLIPS, L. (1974): 'The control of criminal activity'. In Glaser, D. (ed.), *Handbook of Criminology*, 1055–93. Chicago: Rand McNally.

WADSWORTH, M. E. J. (1976): 'Delinquency, pulse rates and early emotional deprivation'. *Brit. J. Criminol.*, **16**, 245–56.

WADSWORTH, M. (1979): *Roots of Delinquency: infancy, adolescence and crime.* Oxford: Martin Robertson.

WALDO, G. P., and DINITZ, S. (1967): 'Personality attributes of the criminal: An analysis of research studies, 1950–1965'. *J. Res. Crime & Delinq.*, **4**, 185–202.

WALKER, M. A. (1978): 'Measuring the seriousness of crimes'. *Brit. J. Criminol.*, **18**, 348–54.

WALKER, N. (1971): *Crimes, Courts and Figures: An introduction to criminal statistics.* Harmondsworth: Penguin.

WALKER, N. (1977): *Behaviour and Misbehaviour: Explanations and non-explanations.* Oxford: Basil Blackwell.

WALKER, N. (1980). *Punishment, Danger and Stigma: The morality of criminal justice.* Oxford: Basil Blackwell.

WALLER, I., and OKIHIRO, N. (1978): *Burglary: The Victim and the Public.* Toronto: University of Toronto Press.

WALLERSTEIN, J. S., and KELLY, J. B. (1980): *Surviving the Break Up: How children and parents cope with divorce.* New York: Basic Books; London: Grant McIntyre.

WALLIS, C. P., and MALIPHANT, R. (1967): 'Delinquent areas in the county of London: ecological factors'. *Brit. J. Criminol.*, **7**, 250–84.

WALSH, D. P. (1978): *Shoplifting: Controlling a Major Crime.* London: Macmillan.

WALTERS, A. A. (1963): 'Delinquent generations?' *Brit. J. Criminol.*, **3**, 391–5.

WALTERS, G. C., and GRUSEC, J. E. (1977): *Punishment.* San Francisco: Freeman.

WARREN, M. (1977): 'Correctional treatment and coercion: the differential effectiveness perspective'. *Crim. Justice & Behav.*, **4**, 355–76.

WARREN, W. (1965): 'A study of adolescent psychiatric inpatients and the outcome six or more years later. II. The follow-up study'. *J. Child Psychol. Psychiat.*, **6**, 141–60.
WEATHERS, L., and LIBERMAN, R. P. (1975): 'Contingency contracting with families of delinquent adolescents'. *Behav. Therapy*, **6**, 356–66.
WEDGE, P., and PROSSER, N. (1973): *Born to Fail?* London: Arrow Books.
WEEKS, H. A. (1958): *Youthful Offenders at Highfields*. Ann Arbor, Michigan: University of Michigan Press.
WEISS, G. (1983): 'Long-Term Outcome: Findings, concepts and practical implications'. In Rutter, M. (ed.), *Developmental Neuropsychiatry* New York: Guilford Press (in press).
WEISSMAN, M. M., and KLERMAN, G. L. (1977): 'Sex differences and the epidemiology of depression'. *Arch. Gen. Psychiat.*, **34**, 98–111.
WELLFORD, C. (1975): 'Labelling theory and criminology: an assessment'. *Social Problems*, **22**, 332–45.
WERNER, E. E. (1979): *Cross-cultural Child Development: A view from the Planet Earth.* Monterey, Calif.: Brooks/Cole.
WERNER, E. E., BIERMAN, J. M., and FRENCH, F. E. (1971): *The Children of Kauai: A longitudinal study from the prenatal period to age 10.* Honolulu: University Press of Hawaii.
WERNER, E. E., and SMITH, R. S. (1977): *Kauai's Children Come of Age.* Honolulu: University Press of Hawaii.
WERNER, E. E., and SMITH, R. S. (1981): *Vulnerable but Invincible: a longitudinal study of resilient children and youth.* New York: McGraw Hill.
WERRY, J. S., and QUAY, H. C. (1971): 'The prevalence of behavior symptoms in younger elementary schoolchildren'. *Amer. J. Orthopsychiat.*, **41**, 136–43.
WEST, D. J. (1967): *The Young Offender.* Harmondsworth: Penguin.
WEST, D. J. (1982): *Delinquency: Its roots, careers and prospects.* London: Heinemann.
WEST, D. J., and FARRINGTON, D. P. (1973): *Who Becomes Delinquent?* London: Heinemann Educational.
WEST, D. J., and FARRINGTON, D. P. (1977): *The Delinquent Way of Life.* London: Heinemann Educational.
WHEELER, S. (1967): 'Criminal statistics: a reformulation of the problem'. *J. Crim. Law, Criminol. & Police Science*, **58**, 317–24.
WHEELER, S., COTTRELL, L. S., and ROMASCO, A. (1967): 'Juvenile delinquency: its prevention and control'. In President's Commission on Law Enforcement and Administration of Justice, Task Force Report, *Juvenile Delinquency and Youth Crime.* Washington, D.C.: U.S. Government Printing Office.
WHITEHEAD, L. (1979): 'Sex differences in children's responses to family stress: a re-evaluation'. *J. Child Psychol. Psychiat.*, **20**, 247–54.
WHITEHILL, M., DeMYER-GAPIN, S., and SCOTT, T. J. (1976): 'Stimulation seeking in antisocial preadolescent children'. *J. Abnorm. Psychol.*, **85**, 101–4.
WHITING, B. B., and WHITING, J. W. M. (1975): *Children of Six Cultures: A Psycho-Cultural Analysis.* Cambridge, Mass.: Harvard University Press.

WILKINS, D. (1964): *Social Deviance: Social Policy, Action and Research*. London: Tavistock.

WILKINS, L. (1960): *Delinquent Generations*. London: H.M.S.O.

WILKINS, L. T. (1958): 'A small comparative study of the effects of probation'. *Brit. J. Delinq.*, **3**, 201.

WILLCOCK, H. D. (1974): *Deterrents and Incentives to Crime among Boys and Young Men aged 15–21*. O.P.C.S. Social Survey Division (SS 352). London: H.M.S.O.

WILLIAMS, G. (1975): 'The definition of crime'. In Smith, J. and Hogan, B. (eds.), *Criminal Law* (2nd edition). London: Butterworths.

WILLIAMS, M. (1970): *A Study of Some Aspects of Bristol Allocation*. Report No. 33, Office of the Chief Psychologist, Prison Department, Home Office. Cited in Brody (1976).

WILLMOTT, P. (1966): *Adolescent Boys of East London*. London: Routledge & Kegan Paul.

WILSON, C. W. M. (1972): 'Amphetamine abuse and government legislation'. *Brit. J. Addict.*, **67**, 107–12.

WILSON, H. (1974): 'Parenting in poverty'. *Brit. J. Social Work*, **4**, 241–54.

WILSON, H. (1980): 'Parental supervision: a neglected aspect of delinquency'. *Brit. J. Criminol.*, **20**, 203–35.

WILSON, H., and HERBERT, G. W. (1978): *Parents and Children in the Inner City*. London: Routledge & Kegan Paul.

WILSON, J. Q. (1968a): *Varieties of Police Behavior: The management of law and order in eight communities*. Cambridge, Mass.: Harvard University Press.

WILSON, J. Q. (1968b): 'The police and the delinquent in two cities'. In Wheeler, S. (ed.), *Controlling Delinquents*. New York: Wiley.

WILSON, J. Q. (1975): *Thinking About Crime*. New York: Basic Books.

WILSON, R. (1963): *Difficult Housing Estates*. London: Tavistock.

WILSON, S. (1978): 'Vandalism and "defensible space" on London housing estates'. In Clarke, R. (ed.) *Tackling Vandalism*. Home Office Research Study No. 47. London: H.M.S.O.

WITKIN, H. A., MEDNICK, S. A., SCHULSINGER, F., et al. (1976): 'Criminality in XYY and XXY men'. *Science*, **193**, 547–55.

WOLFF, S. (1961): 'Symptomatology and outcome of pre-school children with behaviour disorders attending a child guidance clinic'. *J. Child Psychol. Psychiat.*, **2**, 269–76.

WOLFF, S. (1971): 'Dimensions and clusters of symptoms in disturbed children'. *Brit. J. Psychiat.*, **118**, 421–7.

WOLFGANG, M. E., FIGLIO, R. M., and SELLIN, T. (1972): *Delinquency in a Birth Cohort*. Chicago: University of Chicago Press.

WOLKIND, S. (1971): *Children in Care: A psychiatric study*. Unpublished M.D. thesis, University of London.

WOLKIND, S. N., and EVERITT, B. (1974): 'A cluster analysis of the behavioural items in the preschool child'. *Psychol. Med.*, **4**, 422–7.

WOLKIND, S., and RUTTER, M. (1973): 'Children who have been "In care" – an epidemiological study'. *J. Child Psychol. Psychiat.*, **14**, 97–105.

WOODS, P. (1977): *Youth, Generations and Social Class*. Milton Keynes: Open University Press.

WOOTTON, B. (1959): *Social Science and Social Pathology*. London: Allen & Unwin.

WORLD HEALTH ORGANIZATION EXPERT COMMITTEE (1977): *Child Mental Health and Psychosocial Development*. Technical Report Series 613. Geneva: W.H.O.

WRIGHT, W. E., and DIXON, M. C. (1977): 'Community prevention and treatment of juvenile delinquency: a review of evaluation studies'. *J. Res. Crime & Delinq.*, **14**, 35–67.

YANKELOVICH, D. (1974): *The New Morality: a profile of American youth in the 70s*. New York: McGraw Hill.

YUDKIN, S. (1967): *0–5: A report on the care of pre-school children*. London: National Society of Children's Nurseries.

YULE, W. (1977): 'Behavioural approaches'. In Rutter, M., and Hersov, L. (eds.), *Child Psychiatry: Modern Approaches*, 923–48. Oxford: Blackwell Scientific.

YULE, W., BERGER, M., RUTTER, M., and YULE, B. (1975): 'Children of West Indian Immigrants: II. Intellectual performance and reading attainment'. *J. Child Psychol. Psychiat.*, **16**, 1–17.

ZELLWEGER, H., and SIMPSON, J. (1977): *Chromosomes of Man*. Clinics in Developmental Medicine Nos. 65/66. London: Heinemann/S.I.M.P.

ZIMRING, F. E. (1978): 'Background Paper'. In *Confronting Youth Crime: Report of the Twentieth Century Fund Task Force on Sentencing Policy Toward Young Offenders*, 27–120. New York and London: Holmes & Meier.

ZIMRING, F. E. (1979): 'American youth violence: issues and trends'. In Morris, N., and Tonry, M. (eds.), *Criminal Justice: An annual review of research*, Vol. 1, 67–107. Chicago and London: University of Chicago Press.

ZIMRING, F. E. and HAWKINS, G. J. (1973): *Deterrence: The Legal Threat in Crime Control*. Chicago and London: University of Chicago Press.

Author Index

Abbot, D. J., 96, 97, 113, 208, 216
Achenbach, T. M., 40, 174
Adams, S., 267, 285, 287
Adelstein, A., 100, 214
Adler, F., 111, 124
Ageton, S., 26, 31, 135, 136, 137, 154, 198, 242, 251
Aldous, J., 99
Alexander, F., 257
Alexander, J. F., 271, 281
Allsop, J., 175
American Psychiatric Association, 174
Annesley, P. T., 59
Antovsky, A., 239
Antunes, G., 206
Appel, M. H., 49
Archer, D., 215
Armstrong, D., 25, 209
Arnold, J. E., 282
Aromaa, K., 203
Austin, R. L., 44, 111, 124, 286
Avison, N. H., 66, 77, 78, 87, 102, 120, 202, 217
Ayllon, T., 166, 277
Azrin, N., 277

Bachman, J. G., 164, 228, 229, 232, 233
Baer, D. M., 276
Bagley, C., 156, 206, 207
Bahr, S. J., 180, 242, 245, 249, 251, 263, 264
Baldwin, J., 202, 204, 205, 206, 207, 209, 210
Bandura, A., 191, 192
Banton, M., 155, 158
Barkley, R. A., 172
Barkwell, L. J., 286
Barnes, J., 151
Baron, R., 273
Baron, R. M., 206
Barraclough, B., 194

Basham, R., 113, 216
Batta, I. D., 159
Baum, A., 207
Baumrind, D., 129
Baxter, J. C., 199, 213, 333
Beasley, R. W., 206
Becker, H. S., 196
Behar, L., 47
Bell, R. R., 99, 110
Bell, R. W., 190
Belson, W. A., 27, 55, 133, 134, 135, 140, 156, 192
Bem, D. J., 261
Bennett, T., 21, 74, 77, 79, 80, 135, 297
Bentovim, A., 47
Berg, I., 18, 197, 297, 347, 354
Berger, A. S., 123, 154
Berger, M., 203
Berkowitz, L., 193, 195
Berleman, W. C., 284
Berlins, M., 83
Bewley, T. H., 101
Beyleveld, D., 304
Biderman, A. D., 15
Biller, H. B., 108
Bittner, E., 16, 323
Black, D. J., 19, 20, 155
Black Report, 321, 342
Blake, G., 298, 303
Blakely, C. W., 280
Blasi, A., 54
Block, J. H., 127, 128
Bloom, L., 155
Bodine, G. E., 135
Bogaard, C., 181
Bohman, M., 177, 178, 236
Boland, B., 52
Bond, G. L., 166
Bootzin, R. R., 277

418 Index

Borgatta, E. F., 299
Borkovec, T. D., 171
Bornstein, P. H., 276, 278
Boshier, R., 197
Bossio, V., 237
Bottomley, A. K., 15, 18, 19
Bottoms, A. E., 33, 106, 153, 156, 202, 204, 205, 206, 207, 209, 211, 289, 299, 302
Bowlby, J., 191, 257
Bowman, P. H., 299
Box, S., 16
Boyer, A., 40
Bradley, P. W., 304
Braithwaite, J., 115, 132
Brake, M., 158
Brantingham, P. J., 211, 212
Brantingham, P. L., 211, 212
Bricker, D. D., 253
Bricker, W. A., 253
Brigham, T. A., 276
Brody, S. R., 192, 195, 196, 267, 268, 270, 285, 293, 294, 295, 298
Bronfenbrenner, U., 68, 107, 108, 110, 111, 112
Bronson, W. C., 176
Brown, E. D., 267
Brown, G. W., 109, 232, 240
Bryan, J. H., 54
Bryce-Smith, D., 113
Buikhuisen, W., 197, 229, 291, 306
Burchard, J. D., 276, 277, 278, 279, 280
Burrows, J., 214, 311, 312
Byles, J., 302

Cadoret, R. J., 127, 177, 178, 189
Cain, C., 127, 178, 189
Cain, M., 158
Cairns, R. B., 252, 253
Camera, A. K. A., 190, 191
Cameron, M. O., 18
Campbell, A., 215
Campbell, A., 121
Canter, R. J., 242, 251
Cantwell, D., 174
Caplan, P. J., 121, 122, 130
Carroll, J. S., 262
Carter, M. P., 141, 204
Cartwright, A., 110
Castle, I. M., 204
Catalano, R., 216

Cawson, P., 82, 83, 349
Central Policy Review Staff, 90, 301, 332, 333
Central Statistical Office, 80, 102, 105, 108, 109, 110, 111, 112, 115, 218
Cernkovich, S. A., 121, 123
Challinger, D., 96
Chambliss, W., 155
Chandler, M. J., 240
Chesney-Lind, M., 121
Chester, R., 107
Choldin, H. M., 206
Christensen, K. R., 177
Christiansen, K. O., 102, 113, 120, 176
Christie, N., 203
Cicourel, A. V., 16, 25, 140, 155
Claeys, W., 129
Clark, J. P., 26, 203, 205
Clark, M. M., 165
Clarke, A., 236
Clarke, J., 141, 142, 144, 207
Clarke, R. V. G., 16, 52, 62, 90, 147, 210, 214, 260, 261, 273, 288, 289, 290, 308, 310, 313, 324, 332, 346, 347, 349
Clarke, S. H., 294
Clegg, A., 308
Clifford, L., 217
Clifford, W., 96, 97, 124, 216
Clinard, M. N., 96, 97, 113, 202, 208, 216
Cline, H. F., 50, 51, 58
Cloninger, C. R., 129, 130, 177
Cloward, R. A., 246
Cockburn, J. J., 121
Coelho, G. V., 239
Cohen, A. K., 166, 245, 246
Cohen, F., 239
Cohen, L., 217
Cohen, P., 25, 141, 142
Coleman, C. A., 18, 19
Collard, J., 107
Collins, S., 155
Commission for Racial Equality, 158
Community Relations Commission, 158
Conklin, J. E., 84
Conger, J. J., 35, 40, 57, 140, 248
Connell, P. H., 104
Converse, P., 215
Conway, E. S., 237
Cook, P. J., 261, 262, 263, 304, 307
Copperman, P., 98

Cornish, D. B., 62, 288, 289
Corrigan, P., 141
Court, S. D. M., 99, 100, 109, 114
Covington, C., 302
Cowie, J., 121, 130
Cox, A., 31
Craft, M. J., 44, 289
Craig, M. M., 190, 221, 284
Crellin, E., 110, 236
Cressley, D. R., 175, 248
Croft, J., 298, 320
Crowe, R. R., 176, 178, 189

Daitzman, R., 126
Dalgaard, O. C., 177
Daniel, W. W., 150
Danzigers, S., 116
Darlington, R. B., 300
Davidson, W. S., 276, 280
Davies, J., 121, 130
Davies, J. G., 171, 172
Davies, M., 53, 231, 291, 292
Davis, G., 207
Davis, K., 113, 216
Dawe, H. C., 49
De Alarcón, R., 214, 316
DeBoek, P., 129
Delfini, L. F., 181
DeMyer-Gapin, S., 173
Dentler, R. A., 121
Department of the Environment, 103
Department of Health and Social Security, 83, 114, 302, 327
Deschamps, J. P., 110
Diamond, Lord, 106, 115, 217, 218
Dijkterhuis, F. P. H., 197
Dinitz, J., 35, 175, 299
Ditchfield, J. A., 74
Dixon, M. C., 267, 293, 301, 303
Dodd, D., 158
Doleschal, E., 165
Donnan, S., 65
Dooley, D., 216
Douglas, J. W. B., 107, 108, 112, 120, 170, 176, 190
Douglas, V. I., 174
Downes, D., 139, 246, 247
Drillien, C. M., 240
Dryfoos, J. G., 110

Duddle, M., 100
Dunlop, A. B., 288, 290, 295, 296

Earls, F., 47
East, W. N., 106
Eck, J. E., 85, 94
Edelbrock, C. S., 40, 174
Edwards, A., 204
Ekblom, P., 311, 314
Elliot, D. S., 26, 31, 121, 135, 136, 137, 154, 166, 198, 228, 231, 242, 245, 246, 251
Eme, R. P., 125, 128
Emery, R. E., 127, 129
Emmerich, W., 61
Empey, L. T., 28, 29, 32, 38, 248, 274, 275, 288, 292, 298, 323
Endler, N. S., 261
Engstad, P., 312
Ennis, P., 86, 203
Epps, P., 169
Epstein, S., 57, 62
Erikson, K. T., 16
Erickson, M. L., 25, 26, 28, 29, 38, 242, 263, 264, 272, 275, 292, 298
Essen, J., 240
Evans, J. L., 312
Eve, R., 111, 121
Everitt, B. S., 47, 240
Eysenck, H. J., 62, 175, 192, 252, 257, 258
Eysenck, M. W., 62
Eysenck, S. B. G., 175, 257, 258

Farid, S., 99, 110
Farrant, M. R., 301
Farrell, C., 99, 110
Farrington, D. P., 21, 26, 27, 28, 29, 30, 34, 37, 38, 40, 41, 51, 52, 55, 57, 58, 59, 60, 74, 77, 78, 79, 80, 89, 104, 108, 120, 133, 134, 135, 136, 138, 140, 141, 163, 164, 165, 167, 168, 169, 170, 171, 175, 176, 180, 182, 183, 185, 186, 187, 188, 189, 191, 196, 197, 198, 199, 217, 221, 222, 223, 224, 226, 227, 228, 231, 248, 249, 259, 276, 294, 295, 297
Feldman, M. P., 15, 16, 175, 242, 245, 252, 259, 277
Felson, M., 217
Fenigstein, A., 194
Ferguson, H. B., 174
Ferri, E., 107

Feshbach, S., 193, 195
Field, E., 39
Figlio, R. M., 38
Finer, M., 107
Finlayson, D. S., 200
Fisher, S., 198
Fitzherbert, K., 151
Fixsen, D. L., 278
Fleischman, M. J., 282
Fleisher, B. M., 217
Fo, W. S. O., 281
Forehand, R., 181
Forrest, R., 176
Forslund, M. A., 123
Foster, J., 198
Freedman, J. L., 206
Friday, P., 161, 181
Friedlander, K., 257
Friedrich, L. K., 192, 193, 194, 195
Frith, S., 158
Funder, D. C., 261
Furst, P. W., 284

Gans, H. J., 208
Ganzer, V. J., 121, 271, 273, 279, 287
Gartner, R., 104, 215
Gates, A. I., 166
Gath, D., 199, 204, 205, 206
Gawn, J., 79, 297
Geach, H., 321
Gendreau, P., 267, 268
Gersten, J. C., 50, 59
Gibbens, T. C. N., 103, 131, 169
Gibbons, D. C., 260, 298, 303
Gibbs, L., 65, 198
Gibbs, J. P., 25, 243, 263, 264, 304, 307
Gibson, H. B., 107, 190
Giffen, P. J., 96
Gildea, M. C. L., 299
Gill, O., 24, 209
Giller, H. J., 23, 83, 321, 322
Giordano, P. C., 111, 121, 123
Gittus, E., 204
Gladstone, F. J., 27, 28, 92, 228
Glaser, D., 106, 245
Glick, S. J., 190, 221
Glover, E., 257
Glueck, E., 169, 221, 249
Glueck, S., 40, 169, 221, 249

Gold, M., 26, 55, 93, 99, 121, 183, 197
Goldman, N., 199
Goodenough, F. L., 48, 49
Goodman, N., 130, 131
Gove, W. R., 206
Graham, F., 306
Graham, P., 43, 53, 59, 60, 122, 134, 157, 327
Grant, M., 44
Gray, G., 152, 158
Green, E., 123
Greenberg, P. F., 272
Greenwood, P. W., 19
Gregory, I., 107, 190
Gross, A. M., 276
Grunhut, M., 22
Gunnar-Vongnechten, M. R., 128
Gurr, T., 65, 68, 96, 97, 116, 117, 118, 147

Hall, S., 141, 142, 143, 146, 157
Hamparian, D. M., 52
Haney, W. G., 207
Hardt, R. H., 135
Hare, R., 43, 172
Hargreaves, D., 144, 201
Harig, P., 276, 277, 278, 279, 280
Harper, L., 190
Harris, T., 109, 232, 240
Hart, R. J., 197, 308
Haskey, J., 65, 100
Hassell, C., 316
Hastings, J. E., 172
Hathaway, S. R., 35
Havighurst, R. J., 55, 57
Hawkins, G., 304, 335
Hayashi, S., 177
Hazel, N., 348
Heal, K. H., 147, 199, 308, 312
Hebdige, D., 142
Heidensohn, F., 111
Hellon, C. P., 100
Henn, F. A., 40
Hepburn, J. K., 20
Herbert, G. W., 185
Hersov, L., 18
Hess, R. D., 190, 191
Hetherington, E. M., 39, 108, 127, 128, 180, 188, 189, 190, 191, 235, 237
Hewitt, L. E., 39
Heywood, R., 312

Hill, R., 99
Hill, S., 167, 221, 249
Hillier, W., 211
Himmelweit, H. T., 194
Hinde, R. A., 180
Hindeland, M., 17, 26, 32, 33, 55, 121, 135, 153, 154, 155, 163, 164, 165, 251
Hine, J., 23
Hirschi, T., 31, 55, 132, 133, 136, 153, 154, 163, 164, 165, 183, 242, 245, 246, 247, 250, 251
Hodges, E. F., 190, 221, 284
Hodgins, S., 43, 44, 172
Hoefler, S. A., 276, 278
Hoekstra, H. A., 229, 291
Hoffman, M. L., 126
Hogarth, J., 23
Hoghughi, M., 277
Hokanson, J. E., 195
Hole, W. V., 115
Holman, R., 150
Home Office, 19, 21, 66, 67, 68, 72, 78, 79, 82, 84, 86, 87, 88, 90, 94, 102, 120, 121, 122, 124, 217, 293, 298, 316, 332
Hood, C., 151
Hood, R., 23, 26
Hough, J. M., 16, 147, 214, 260, 310, 313, 315, 316, 333
House of Commons Expenditure Committee, 83, 347
Humphrey, D., 158
Hurwitz, S., 233
Hutchings, B., 178, 189

Institute of Race Relations, 158

Jacklin, C. N., 125, 129
James, A. G., 150
Janowitz, M., 207
Japan Ministry of Justice, 96
Jefferson, T., 141, 142
Jencks, C., 200
Jenkins, R. L., 39, 40
Jennings, M., 99
Jensen, G., 111, 120, 121, 249
Jenson, G., 198
Jephcott, A. P., 141, 204
Jesness, C. F., 269, 277, 287, 288, 289
Jessor, R., 35

Johnson, B. M., 298
Johnson, D., 197
Johnson, R. E., 242, 249
Johnson, S., 181
Jones, H., 207, 299
Jones, W., 299
Jonsson, G., 120, 182
Jurkovic, G., 54

Kagan, J., 53, 56, 61
Kahn, J., 177
Kahn, M., 195
Karow, W. G., 122
Kasarda, S. D., 207
Kassebaum, G., 268, 269
Kastrup, M., 122
Kazdin, A. E., 277
Keating, J. P., 206
Kellaher, L., 99, 110
Kellam, S. G., 299
Kelley, C., 101, 153
Kelling, G., 214
Kelly, D., 166
Kelly, J., 108, 189, 190, 191, 235
Kendall, P. C., 239
Kendell, R., 100
Kenny, D. A., 193
Kent, R., 282
Kerner, O., 145, 146
Khleif, B. B., 35
King, J., 66
Kirigin, K. A., 279
Kitsuse, J., 16
Klapmuts, N., 165
Klein, M., 197, 203, 270, 298, 303, 304
Klerman, G. L., 122
Knight, B. J., 52, 58, 182, 232, 233, 234
Knobloch, H., 170
Knowles, E., 207
Kobayashi, S., 40
Kohlberg, L., 54
Kohn, M., 47, 50, 56
Kornhauser, R. R., 245, 248
Kratcoski, J., 121, 201
Kratcoski, P., 121, 201
Kraus, J., 96, 292
Kreitman, N., 100, 205
Kreyberg, P. C., 41
Krohn, M. D., 116

Kringlen, E., 177
Kvaraceus, W. C., 35
Kulik, J. A., 26
Kupfersmid, J. H., 54, 126

Lamb, M. E., 128
Lambert, J., 19, 105, 156, 157
Lambert, L., 190
Landau, S., 21
Lander, B., 206
Landes, W. M., 315
Launier, R., 239
Lavik, N. J., 122, 203
Lazarus, R. S., 237, 239
Lee, R., 298
Lee, T., 207
Leete, R., 96, 106, 107, 109, 110
Lefkowitz, M. M., 192
Lemert, E. M., 263
Lerman, P., 269, 273, 274
Leslie, S. A., 122
Levine, J., 33
Levy, D., 48
Levy, L., 203
Lewis, A., 43
Lewis, D., 170
Lewis, H., 39
Lewis, R., 182
Leyens, J., 193
Liberman, R. P., 270, 279
Lickona, T., 54
Liddle, C., 138, 184, 191, 234, 237
Lipton, D., 267, 285, 298
Liska, A. E., 20, 249
Little, A. N., 104, 124, 149, 150, 151
Little, K., 155
Little, W. R., 134
Livermore, J., 295
Lobitz, G. K., 181
Logan, C. H., 307
Loney, I., 174
London, P., 54
Love, C. T., 274, 303
Lubeck, S. G., 288
Lykken, D., 26, 44, 172
Lyle, J., 193

McCabe, S., 18, 19
McCandless, B. R., 195
McCarthy, D., 207
McClintock, F. H., 38, 66, 77, 78, 79, 81, 87, 102, 106, 120, 156, 202, 217, 289, 296
McCord, J., 50, 108, 140, 180, 183, 188, 190, 284
McCord, W., 50, 108, 180, 183, 190
McCron, R., 142
McDonald, L., 117, 118, 133, 134, 147, 205
McFarlane, J., 48–9
McGregor, L., 107
McInsogh, N., 150
MacKay, B., 202
McKay, H. B., 276, 277
McKissak, I. J., 229
McMichael, P., 167, 288, 189
McWilliams, W., 23, 299
Maccoby, E. E., 112, 125, 126, 129, 207, 208
Maclay, I., 121
Madge, C., 115
Madge, N., 107, 111, 115, 137, 150, 151, 157, 185, 217, 218, 219, 231, 244, 301
Maliphant, R., 171, 172, 204, 206
Mallick, S. L., 195
Malmquist, C., 295
Martell, M., 82
Mann, S., 176
Mangus, A. R., 166
Mannheim, H., 53, 134, 289
Marchant, H., 301
Mardon, C., 100, 214
Marsh, P., 143, 144
Marshall, T., 299
Martin, B., 180
Martin, D. N., 290
Martin, J. A., 129
Martin, J. P., 233
Martinson, R., 267, 268, 275, 285, 287
Massimo, L. L., 274, 284
Masterson, J. F., 59
Matza, D., 242, 247
Maurice, A., 302
Mawby, R. K., 33, 159, 209, 211, 213
May, D., 21, 35, 38, 121, 130, 131, 133, 136, 164
Mays, J. B., 40, 139, 247
Mayhew, P., 33, 102, 209, 210, 211, 212, 213, 214, 260, 313, 314, 316
Mednick, S. A., 138, 178, 189
Meehl, P. E., 295

Meadows, C., 157
Megson, B., 308
Mellsop, G. W., 59
Merton, R. K., 245
Meyer, H. J., 299
Michael, C. M., 59
Milgram, S., 126, 194
Miller, H., 111
Miller, W., 35, 40, 57, 140, 248
Millham, S., 82, 288, 290, 349, 350
Mind, K., 55
Minde, R., 55
Ministry of Education, 324
Mischel, W., 62
Molling, P., 285
Monachesi, E., 35
Monroe, L. J., 121
Moore, D. R., 41, 282
Moore, R., 158, 207
Moriarty, A., 239
Morris, A. M., 23, 83, 321, 322, 340, 341, 342, 344
Morris, H., 59
Morris, P., 147
Morris, T., 134, 204, 206, 320
Morrison, J., 174
Mortimore, P., 50
Moss, M. A., 56, 61
Mott, J., 22, 23, 38, 79
Mrad, D., 274, 303
Mulligan, G., 35
Murchison, N., 108
Murdoch, G., 141, 142
Murgatroyd, S., 199, 308
Murphy, G. E., 100
Murphy, L., 239

N.A.C.R.O., 214
Nagasawa, R., 155
National Institute of Mental Health, 192
Needel, S. P., 206
Needham, B., 331
Newcomb, T., 233
Newman, O., 210, 211, 214
Nias, D., 192
Nicol, A. R., 123, 157
Nielsen, J., 177
Niemi, L., 99
Noblit, G., 168

Nordland, E., 177
Ntsekhe, V. R., 134
Nye, F. I., 250
Nylander, I., 236

O'Donnell, C. R., 62, 197, 276, 281, 303
Office of Population Consensus and Surveys, 86, 94, 107, 109, 110
Offord, D. R., 131, 167, 168, 174, 186
Ohlin, L., 246
Okihiro, N., 103, 212, 214, 313
O'Leary, K. D., 127, 129, 190
Oliver, I. T., 72
Olweus, D., 56, 57, 126, 174
Orleans, S., 306
Orris, J. B., 173
Osborn, S. G., 26, 34, 52–3, 58–9, 179, 182, 189, 203, 218, 226
Ouston, J., 35, 38, 55, 57, 58, 123, 131, 133, 160

Pablant, P., 199, 213, 333
Palmi, G., 134
Palmer, T., 44, 267, 269, 285, 286, 293
Parke, R. D., 193
Parker, E., 193
Parker, H., 22, 25
Parnell, E., 169
Parsloe, P., 22
Parsons, B., 271, 281
Pasamanick, B., 170
Passingham, R. E., 259
Patterson, G. R., 42, 181, 183, 184, 190, 191, 253, 254, 255, 271, 276, 282
Pearce, D., 99, 110
Pearce, K., 157
Pearson, G., 65
Pease, K., 294
Persons, R. W., 285
Peters, K., 174
Phillips, E., 277, 278
Phillips, J., 166
Phillips, L., 217, 325
Phillipson, M., 264
Piercy, F., 21, 22, 298
Piliavin, I., 20, 155
Pilling, D., 108
Plummer, K., 25, 263, 264
Pollak, M., 151

Index

Pontell, H. N., 308
Pope, P. J., 38
Porter, B., 127, 190
Poutney, M., 115
Powell, G. E., 127, 175, 176, 190, 259
Power, M., 49, 108, 109, 190, 199
Pringle, M. L. K., 108, 237, 324
Prosser, N., 219
Pryce, K., 158

Quadagno, D. M., 128
Quay, H. C., 39, 40, 122, 173, 174, 257, 268, 274, 303
Quinney, R., 153
Quinton, D., 111, 112, 138, 184, 191, 203, 204, 208, 234, 237, 240

Radzinowicz, L., 66
Rapoport, J., 174
Raynor, L., 236
Reckless, W., 35, 299
Redfering, D. L., 284
Rees, L., 169
Reid, J. B., 181
Reimer, D. J., 93, 99
Rein, M., 320
Reinisch, J. M., 128
Reiss, A., 206, 249
Reiss, A. J., 15, 18, 20, 155
Reiss, I. L., 99, 110
Reker, G. T., 303
Remschmidt, T. H., 122
Reppetto, T. A., 103, 214
Rex, T., 207
Reynolds, D., 199, 308
Rezmovic, E. L., 270, 273
Rhodes, A., 206, 249
Riccio, L. J., 85, 94
Rice, K., 106
Rich, J., 45
Richman, N., 47, 50, 55, 123, 127, 165, 167, 168, 187
Richmond, A. H., 151, 155
Rie, E., 174
Rie, H., 174
Riley, D., 312

Risley, T. R., 276
Roberts, M., 166
Robin, G. D., 18
Robins, L., 37, 40, 41, 51, 52, 57, 58, 59, 60, 89, 138, 141, 167, 182, 186, 188, 189, 228, 230, 237, 245, 248, 249, 257, 259
Robinson, M. J., 280
Robinson, W. S., 206
Roff, M., 41, 141, 248
Rohner, R. P., 181
Rosanoff, A. J., 171
Rose, G. N., 104, 221, 299
Rosen, A., 295
Rosenthal, D., 189
Ross, D., 173
Ross, H., 152, 306
Ross, R., 267, 268, 276, 277
Ross, S., 173
Rossi, P. H., 38
Rowitz, L., 203
Royal College of Psychiatrists, 24, 316
Rumbaut, R. G., 16
Russell Jones, R., 113
Rutherford, A., 342
Rutter, M., 36, 40, 42, 43, 49, 50, 51, 55, 58, 59, 60, 62, 89, 91, 93, 98, 99, 101, 107, 108, 111, 112, 113, 115, 122, 123, 124, 127, 128, 131, 133, 134, 137, 138, 149, 150, 151, 152, 156, 157, 165, 166, 170, 174, 180, 183, 184, 185, 187, 188, 189, 190, 191, 199, 200, 201, 203, 204, 214, 217, 218, 219, 222, 231, 234, 235, 236, 237, 238, 239, 240, 241, 243, 244, 257, 271, 301, 309, 313, 314, 322, 324, 326, 327, 329, 333, 355
Rydelius, P. A., 236

Saegert, S., 207
Sainsbury, P., 204
Sameroff, A. J., 240
Sandberg, S. T., 36, 174, 296
Sarason, I. G., 121, 271, 273, 279, 287
Sarri, R., 304
Scarman, Lord, 145, 146
Schmauk, F. J., 172
Schmidt, D. E., 206
Schnelle, J. F., 18, 310, 311
Schoenfeld, C. G., 257
Schofield, M., 99
Schonell, F., 166

Index 425

Schools Council, 156
Schrag, C., 264
Schramm, W., 193, 194
Schuessler, K. K., 174
Schulsinger, F., 178
Schwartz, R. D., 197, 306
Schweinhart, L. J., 300
Scott, P. D., 44
Scott, T. J., 173
Sechrest, L., 267, 268, 270, 275, 353
Seglow, J., 236
Seidman, E., 276, 280
Seigel, L., 20, 155
Select Committee on Race Relations and Immigration, 150
Sellin, T., 38, 52
Selvin, H., 31, 242
Shaffer, D., 109, 122, 176
Shanok, S. S., 170
Shapland, J., 26, 28, 31, 51, 54
Shaw, C. R., 202
Sheffield, C., 302
Sheldon, W. H., 168
Shepherd, M., 48, 49, 55, 122, 134
Sherwood, C. C., 275
Shields, J., 177
Shoham, S., 152, 296
Shore, M. F., 274, 284
Short, J. F., 245
Shotland, R. L., 126, 194
Shure, M., 239
Siddle, D. A. T., 171
Sigvardsson, S., 177, 236
Simon, F. H., 53, 123, 154
Simons, R. L., 130
Simpson, J., 177
Sinclair, I., 52, 160, 273, 290, 291, 346, 347, 349
Singer, J. L., 193, 195, 196
Singer, S. I., 33
Skogan, W. G., 17
Skolnick, J. H., 19, 197
Slaikev, K. A., 270
Smart, C., 111, 122, 124
Smith, A., 240
Smith, C. S., 301
Smith, D. J., 150
Smith, R., 237, 241
Snyder, J. J., 181

Soothill, K. L., 38
Solomon, M. I., 100
Sorenson, C., 99, 110
Sparks, R. F., 17, 19, 26, 32, 33, 38, 160
Spivack, G., 239
Sports Council, 143
Springhall, J., 65
Stanfield, R. E., 249
Start, K. B., 98
Staub, H., 257
Steenhuis, D. W., 310
Steffensmeier, D., 70, 111, 124
Stein, A. H., 192, 193, 194
Stevens, P., 32, 104, 150, 159, 160
Stewart, M. A., 36, 174, 235
Stone, J., 90, 92, 93, 332
Stott, D. H., 35, 40, 140, 169, 170, 248
Stringfield, S., 47
Stuart, R. B., 272
Sturge, C., 165, 166
Sturman, A., 17, 33
Sugarman, B., 141
Sullivan, C., 20
Sullivan, D., 155
Sundby, H. S., 41
Sutcliffe, F., 18, 19
Suter, L. E., 111
Sutherland, E. H., 246
Szwed, E., 321

Tait, C. D., 190, 221, 284
Tanner, J. M., 114
Tarbleson, M. H., 230
Tarling, R., 22, 23, 79, 294, 295
Tausig, M., 20
Taylor, F., 90, 92, 93, 312, 332
Taylor, I., 142, 143, 153, 264
Taylor, J., 150, 151
Taylor, M., 77
Terry, R., 155
Tennenbaum, D. J., 175
Theander, S., 100
Thompson, J., 109
Thornberry, T. P., 20, 38
Thornes, B., 107
Thorpe, D., 23, 24, 83
Thorpe, J., 23
Tieger, T., 125
Tifft, L., 26

Index

Tittle, C. R., 132, 133, 307
Tizard, B., 36, 42, 43, 122, 123, 124, 165, 236
Tonge, W. L., 236, 239
Townsend, H. E. R., 152
Townsend, P., 115
Tramontana, M. G., 284
Trasler, G. B., 172, 245, 259, 276
Trethowan, W. H., 316
Triseliotis, J., 236
Trivizas, E., 143, 145
Tulchin, S., 48
Tutt, N. S., 293, 342
Twentieth Century Fund Task Force, 321

United Nations, 96
U.S. Department of Justice, 95
United States National Commission on Marijuana and Drug Abuse, 101
Urbain, E. S., 239

Valatin, G., 110
Varlaam, A., 165, 166
Von Hirsch, A., 322
Voss, H. L., 121, 166, 221, 228, 231, 245, 246, 249
Votey, H. L., 325

Wadsworth, M., 38, 41, 108, 120, 121, 130, 131, 133, 135, 169, 170, 171, 180, 185, 221
Waldo, G. P., 175
Waldron, H. A., 113
Walker, M. A., 38
Walker, N., 15, 16, 78, 80, 197, 242, 243, 264, 320
Walker, W. C., 275
Wall, D., 142
Waller, I., 103, 212, 214, 313
Wallerstein, J. S., 108, 189, 190, 191, 235
Wallis, C. P., 204, 206
Walsh, D. P., 102, 214, 312
Walters, A. A., 104
Walton, P., 264
Wansall, G., 83
Ward, D., 268
Warren, M., 285, 286
Warren, W., 44
Weathers, L., 270
Webster, D., 233
Wedge, P., 219, 240

Weeks, H. A., 274, 288
Weikart, D. P., 300
Weis, J., 55
Weiss, G., 174
Weissman, M. M., 122
Wellford, C., 264
Wells, B. K., 98
Wenninger, E. P., 203, 204
Werner, E. E., 180, 237, 241
Werry, J. S., 122
West, D. J., 13, 26, 27, 28, 29, 34, 35, 37, 38, 40, 41, 50, 52, 53, 55, 57, 58, 59, 60, 65, 89, 104, 106, 108, 133, 135, 136, 138, 140, 141, 163, 164, 165, 167, 168, 169, 170, 171, 179, 180, 182, 182, 185, 188, 189, 191, 217, 221, 222, 223, 224, 225, 226, 227, 228, 229, 231, 236, 239, 242, 248, 249, 291, 333, 338
Wetzel, R. D., 100
Wheeler, D., 116
Wheeler, S., 15, 324
White, S., 267
White, S. H., 320
Whitehead, L., 127, 128
Whitehill, M., 173
Whiting, B. B., 111
Whiting, J., 111
Whitmore, K., 36, 42, 43, 122, 123, 134, 165
Wiles, P., 33, 153
Wilkins, L., 53, 104, 242, 289, 292
Wilks, J., 267
Willcock, H. D., 27
Williams, G., 15
Williams, J., 197
Williams, M., 289
Willis, C. F., 32, 105, 150, 159, 160
Willmott, P., 40, 139, 247
Wilner, D., 268
Wilson, C. W. M., 316
Wilson, H., 180, 184, 185, 188, 191, 228
Wilson, J., 16, 18, 20, 21, 52
Wilson, M., 25, 209
Wilson, R., 209
Wilson, S., 103, 209, 211
Wish, E., 230
Witkin, H. A., 176
Witmer, H., 270, 284
Wolff, S., 42, 47
Wolfgang, M. E., 38, 41, 50, 55, 57, 153
Wolfson, J., 294

Wolkind, S. N., 47, 127, 237
Wonderly, D. M., 54, 126
Woods, P., 142
Wootton, B., 13, 106, 120, 140, 161, 202, 231
World Health Organization, 325, 327
Wright, W. E., 267, 293, 301, 303

Yankelovich, D., 99, 110

Young, J., 264
Yudkins, G., 151
Yule, W., 49, 50, 151, 157, 276

Zellweger, H., 177
Zimring, F. E., 52, 68, 90, 95, 121, 304, 322, 335
Zuckerman, M., 126

Subject Index

Adoption
  delinquency and, 178, 189, 236
Age trends
  conduct disorders and, 47–53
  delinquency and, 58, 70
  cautioning and, 74–8
Aggression (*see also* Violence)
  delinquency and, 37, 39, 254, 295
  sex differences, 125–7
  stealing and, 41–2, 253, 254–6, 282
Alcohol abuse, 35, 37, 100–101
Antisocial character, *see* Behavioural characteristics
Area differences, *see* Regional differences
Asians, *see* Race differences
Attendance centres, *see* Interventions

Behavioural characteristics (*see also* Conduct disorders)
  continuity of disorders, 54–61
  offenders, 33–7, 165–8
Brain damage, *see* Physical health
Body build
  delinquency and, 168–9
Burglary, 21, 27, 33, 103, 211–12, 217, 313

Cautioning, 21, 31, 72–9, 135, 297–8, 336, 338–9
Childrearing, *see* Parenting
Children and Young Persons Act, 72, 81–4, 336
Chromosomal abnormalities, *see* Genetics
Conduct disorders
  age trends and, 47–53, 59–61
  area influences on, 203–4
  classification of, 37–45
  family discord and, 190–91, 235–6
  intelligence and, 163–5
  interactive effects of, 240

  sex differences, 122
  social class differences, 134
Crime rates
  England and Wales, 65–89
  inter-generational comparisons, 89–90
  international comparisons, 95–7, 359
    Australia, 96
    Canada, 95–6
    Europe, 96, 97
    Japan, 96–7
    United States, 68, 95, 97, 123–4
  race differences, 153–62
  sex differences, 120–25

'Defensible space', 210–14
Deterrence, *see* Interventions
Differential association, *see* Theories of Crime
Divorce (*see also* Marital breakdown), 106–8
Drug abuse, 35, 101

Economic status, *see* Poverty
Educational performance (*see also* Schools)
  crime prevention and, 328
  drop-out and, 228
  intelligence and, 163–8
  racial differences and, 151–2, 156–7
  secular trends in, 98–9
Emotional disturbance
  conduct disorder and, 42–3, 59–60
  area influences on, 203–4
Employment, *see* Unemployment
Ethnic minorities, *see* Race differences

Family size
  delinquency and, 35, 109–10, 185–6
  secular trends in, 109
  race differences in, 151
Football hooliganism, 142–5, 141, 313, 317
Fostering, *see* Interventions

Genetics
  chromosomal abnormalities and polygenic influences, 176–9
  environmental interactions, 189
  sex differences, 129–30

Housing
  delinquent areas, 205–10, 217–18, 249
  vandalism and, 103, 209–11, 213–15
  victimization and, 33, 248
Hyperactivity
  delinquency and, 173–5
Heredity, *see* Genetics

Inheritance, *see* Genetics
Intelligence
  conduct disorders and, 163–5
  delinquency and, 163–8
  educational performance and, 163–8
Interventions
  deterrence, 296–7, 304–10, 311, 334–5, 337
  evaluations of, 267–76, 353–5
  non-custodial penal measures
    adjournment, 297
    attendance centres, 295–6, 344
    supervision orders/probation, 297, 298–9, 344
    suspended sentences, 296
  prevention programmes, 323–36
    cautioning, 297–8
    community-based, 300–302, 346
    diversion, 303–4, 338, 346
    intermediate treatment, 302–3, 338, 346
    physical measures, 313–17
    school-based, 299–300
  treatment programmes
    behavioural approaches, 276–83
    community-based, 280–81
    counselling and psychotherapy, 284–5, 289, 303
    family-based, 281–3, 302–3
    foster care, 348
    incapacitation, 292–5, 335
    residential, 62, 277–80, 228–93, 342–3, 344, 347–50
    secure units, 336–7, 349–50

'Justice model', 321, 340
Juvenile crime
  rates of, 65–89, 95–7

relationship with adult offending, 52, 54–61
Labelling perspective, *see* Theories
Lead levels
  delinquency and, 113–14

Marital breakdown
  delinquency and, 107–8, 183, 190–91
  effects on children, 127–9, 235–6
  secular trends, 106–7
Marriage
  delinquency and, 232–5
Moral development
  delinquency and, 53–4
Moving away, 229–30

'New criminology', *see* Theories

Offences (*see also* Crime rates)
  legal definition of, 16–17
  measurement of seriousness, 38–9, 352
  recording of, 18–19
Opportunity for crime, 101–4, 210–15, 261–3, 324–5, 332–5

Parental criminality, 28, 35, 182–3, 186–8, 249, 250–51, 328
Parenting
  effects on convictions, 186–8
  discord, 127–9, 183–5, 190–91, 236–7, 358
  generation gap, 99
  kinship and, 111–12
  race differences, 150–51
  social class and, 138
  supervision, 28, 35, 228, 249, 250, 328, 358
Peers
  delinquents' relationship with, 28, 225–30, 238, 246, 250, 359
  ratings of, 57, 141
Personality dimensions
  continuity of, 61–2
  delinquents, 43–4, 175–6, 252–3
  psychopathy, 43–4, 171–3, 257–9
  sociopathic personality, 259–60
Physical health, 112–13, 114–15, 169–71, 327–8
Police
  attitudes to, 198, 209–10
  cautioning, 72–9
  clear-up rate, 19–20, 84, 147
  community policing, 147–8, 214
  discretion, 20–21, 24–5

Police – *cont.*
  policing, 310–13, 334, 341, 355–6
  race relations, 146–7, 158–60
  recording of offences, 18–19, 32, 67–8, 80–84, 86
  reporting of offences, 17–18, 84–8
Poverty (*see also* Social disadvantage)
  crime and, 115, 185, 218–19
Prediction of delinquency, 221–2, 340
Prevention, *see* Interventions
Probation, *see* Interventions
Psychiatric disorder (*see also* Conduct disorders *and* Emotional disturbance)
  trends over time, 100–101
Public order, 21, 116–18, 145

Race differences in
  arrests, 21
  crime in England and Wales, 155–61
  crime in United States, 153
  immigrants and crime, 104–5, 148–53, 155
  school performance, 156–7
  sex ratio in offending, 123, 124
  victimization, 32
Recidivists
  behavioural characteristics of, 34–7, 57–61, 224, 259, 323
  crime rates of, 78–9, 88–9
  genetic factors, 178–9, 189
  interviews with, 339–51
  minor delinquents and, 29, 31
  temporary, 52–3
Regional differences
  Cities and crime, 21, 68, 113, 216
  crime rates, 67–8
  high delinquency areas, 40, 204–10, 249, 359
  urban-rural differences, 202–4

Schools (*see also* Educational performance)
  behavioural problems and, 50, 156–7, 308–9
  delinquency and, 166–8, 199, 227, 238, 249, 308–9, 329–30, 357, 359
Self-report studies, 16, 26–31, 51, 54–5, 93–4, 121, 133–5, 153, 196, 353
Sentencing
  juvenile offenders, 22–4, 82–4, 336–7
  sex bias in, 130
  reform of, 337–50

Sex differences
  aggression, 125–7
  delinquency, 58, 70–71, 97–8, 120–25, 222, 357
  family discord, response to, 127–9
Sexual attitudes
  secular trends, 99–100
  women's changing role, 110–11
Situational perspectives on crime, *see* Theories
Social class
  delinquency and, 132–45, 245, 246
  dispositions and, 21
  family stress and, 188–9
Social control, *see* Theories
Social disadvantage (*see also* Poverty), 30, 185–6, 326, 329
Social learning, *see* Theories
Sub-cultures (*see also* Theories)
  'normal' behaviour, 36, 139–45, 247
  race differences in, 158
Suicide, 97, 100–101

Teacher ratings, 57–8
Television, 112, 191–6, 331
Theories of crime
  anomie/strain, 245–7
  biological, 257–60
  choice, 261–3
  differential association, 248–50
  family processes, 253–6
  labelling perspective, 25, 196–8, 263–4
  multifactorial explanations, 242–5
  'new criminology', 25, 264–5
  psycho-analytic, 256–7
  situational perspective, 260–61
  social control, 250–61
  social learning, 251–2
  sub-cultural approaches, 247–8
Truancy
  age trends in, 51
  delinquency and, 18, 297, 308–9, 311

Unemployment
  crime and, 106, 217, 231–2
  secular trends, 105–6

Vandalism
  prevalence of, 17, 27, 28, 33, 51, 90–93, 103, 209

Vandalism – *cont.*
  prevention of, 210–11, 213–15, 228, 301, 307, 312–13, 314, 316, 333
Victim studies, 16, 17, 31–3, 85–6, 94–5, 160–61, 353
Violence
  age trends, 50–51
  aggression and, 41–2, 295
  crimes of, 21, 67, 68, 71–2, 87–9, 294
  films, television and, 112, 191–6, 331
  race differences and, 32–3, 154, 156, 160–61

War
  crime rates since, 66–8
  effects on crime, 104, 215–16
Welfare model, 321–2, 340
Working mothers
  delinquency and, 108–9
  secular trends, 108, 151